AF291272

HOKUSAI'S FUJI

HOKUSAI'S FUJI

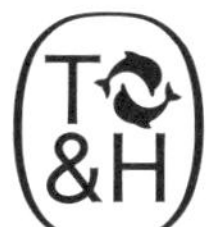

Translated from the Japanese by Lis-Britt Dalkarl

First published in the United Kingdom in 2023 by
Thames & Hudson Ltd, 181A High Holborn, London WC1V 7QX

First published in the United States of America in 2023 by
Thames & Hudson Inc., 500 Fifth Avenue, New York, New York 10110

Original edition © 2023 Goliga Books, Tokyo
This edition © 2023 Thames & Hudson Ltd, London

British Library Cataloguing-in-Publication Data
A catalogue record for this book is available
from the British Library

Library of Congress Control Number 2023935658

ISBN 978-0-500-02655-7

Printed in Singapore

Be the first to know about our new releases,
exclusive content and author events by visiting
thamesandhudson.com
thamesandhudsonusa.com
thamesandhudson.com.au

'Ever since I was six, I have been obsessed with drawing the shapes of things. By the time I was fifty, I had published countless drawings, but nothing I produced before the age of seventy is worthy of note. As I turned seventy-three, I partially succeeded in capturing the physique of all living things and the vitality of plants. For that reason, from the age of eighty-six, I shall make great progress while at the age of ninety I will do so even more. It is my greatest wish to reach one hundred, when my work would become truly marvellous. If I live to be one hundred and ten, every dot and every line would be as if coming to life. I would ask any wise person who lives as long as I do to see if I am true to my word.'

Katsushika Hokusai

One Hundred Views of Mount Fuji
Afterword to first and second editions

Notes for the reader

- The plates are arranged in chronological order of production. However, when the year of production is unclear, or if a work can only be attributed to a wider period or era, the chronology may not be exact. For the reader's convenience, Chapter 1 groups images by genre, motif, or elements other than the year of production.

- The numbering of plates reflects the number of times Mount Fuji appears in each image. So if one plate contains multiple depictions of Mount Fuji, the plate number will increase by that number.

- Numbers in square brackets [ ] in the text refer to page numbers.

- Japanese artistic terms are explained in the glossary on page 413.

Contents

Introduction

How many images of Mount Fuji did Hokusai draw in his lifetime? Well, to begin with, the famous series *Thirty-Six Views of Mount Fuji* actually includes forty-six prints. This is because the initial thirty-six prints proved so popular that another ten prints, entitled 'Fuji from the Rear', were added, making a total of forty-six. Hokusai's next work, the illustrated book *One Hundred Views of Mount Fuji*, actually contains 102 views, despite its title. This makes a total of 148 prints. This number alone represents quite a few images of Mount Fuji, but if we look into the matter further, there are many works pre-dating these two major series in which Hokusai skilfully incorporated images of Mount Fuji. The motifs, styles and techniques of these images are wide-ranging. They include pictures of famous places (*meisho-e*), pictures focusing on the beauty, manners and customs of women (*bijinga*), parody and pun pictures (*mitate-e*), and prints that incorporated Western influences. There are also some superb brush paintings (*nikuhitsu-ga*) from Hokusai's later years.

So what motivated Hokusai to draw Mount Fuji so frequently? There was one simple reason: a growing public demand for images of Fuji. In the mid-Edo period, the belief that Fuji was the home of spirits was widespread among ordinary people. At the time, it was said that there were Fujikō devotees in every district of Edo, and that they numbered as high as 80,000. This accounts for the popularity of pictures of Mount Fuji.

During the Genroku era (1688–1704), a peaceful period with few conflicts, ordinary people with money to spare started to pay visits to Ise Shrine and other temples and shrines. They used the roads and inns that had been built for feudal lords travelling to and from Edo due to the *sankin-kōtai* or 'alternate residence' system, which obliged them to spend half their time in their own lands and half in the capital. In the Bunka (1804–18) and Bunsei (1818–30) eras, an element of pleasure was added to these journeys, with travellers stopping to see famous sites or visiting theatres to enjoy plays. Even so, for ordinary people, travel was still an extravagance and a source of envy. Therefore, *ukiyo*-e artists, who were sensitive to changing fashions and public tastes, found Mount Fuji to be a popular motif. It is hardly surprising that many *ukiyo*-e artists, including Hokusai, chose to depict the mountain.

However, what sets Hokusai apart from other artists is his wit and his convincing, detailed compositions. Many of the scenes he drew were entirely plausible, though it would be difficult to claim that he drew from life. Mount Fuji as depicted by Hokusai was somehow 'painterly'.

Perhaps it was Hokusai's tremendous drive and desire to improve pictorial representation that drove him to use Mount Fuji as a motif in order to refine the art of painting – much as Cézanne, often called the father of modern painting, did when he painted apples again and again. The series *Thirty-Six Views of Mount Fuji* was a culmination of Hokusai's experiments, which then continued in the book *One Hundred Views of Mount Fuji*.

Chapter 1 of this book, entitled *Early Faces of Fuji*, includes Hokusai's images of Fuji from the Kansei era (1789–1801) up to the time he created the images for *Thirty-Six Views of Mount Fuji*

(1840s). There are examples of compositions and themes directly linked to both *Thirty-Six Views of Mount Fuji* and *One Hundred Views of Mount Fuji*. In short, the section is an overview of the long path that led Hokusai to his later masterpieces. Chapter 2, *Thirty-Six Views of Mount Fuji*, and Chapter 3, *One Hundred Views of Mount Fuji*, include all the prints from both series. Finally, the pictures of Mount Fuji that Hokusai painted towards the end of his life are collected in Chapter 4, named *Fuji Forever*, after the mountain that can never be fully captured in a single image.

Like Picasso, who changed the style and content of his work many times over the course of his career, Hokusai did not follow one specific style or school. He was driven by a desire to create and an insatiable curiosity about drawing, avidly working in a variety of styles and techniques at a time when artists of the Edo period were limited to specific schools and prohibited from freely incorporating the techniques of other schools. This may be one reason why Hokusai created such a huge variety of work on the single theme of Mount Fuji.

This book traces Hokusai through each period of his career, looking at the subjects and techniques that interested him, and how he experimented and put ideas into practice. It is also a visual biography that traces the shifts in Hokusai's long artistic career through his depictions of Fuji. Another feature of this book is that all pictures included here, with the exception of one of the brush paintings, are held in collections outside of Japan. In the late Edo period and early Meiji era (c. 1860–1880), many *ukiyo-e* prints were taken overseas. According to estimates, approximately 300,000 *ukiyo-e* prints still remain in Japan, while up to 500,000 were exported overseas. How many people have looked at, desired, enjoyed, been influenced by, and treasured these prints on their way across the oceans? The overseas collections included in this book reflect the European artistic craze of the late 19th century known as Japonisme. These prints caused a sensation in Western art, particularly among the Impressionists.

Frank Feltens, curator of Japanese art at the Smithsonian's National Museum of Asian Art, which holds the world's largest collection of brush paintings by Hokusai, contributes an essay on how the rest of the world sees Hokusai's Fuji. In his concluding essay, Fuse Hideto, whose field as an art critic ranges from cave paintings to contemporary art, decodes Hokusai's Fuji from the point of view of universal art.

In his afterword to *One Hundred Views of Mount Fuji*, Hokusai, who was nearly seventy-five at the time, wrote about his determination to take drawing to new heights. For Hokusai, Mount Fuji must have represented the artistic sovereignty he wanted to reach: high enough to pierce the sky, a tall figure with no equal. It is almost as if Hokusai was projecting onto Fuji the ego of an artist who was reaching high, higher still and even further beyond, to new heights.

Wada Kyoko, editor

Hokusai's Fuji:
A Global Perspective

Frank Feltens

Pre-Hokusai Fuji

Mount Fuji was not always a symbol of Japan in the way that it is now. Over the centuries leading up to Hokusai's own time – the Edo period – the mountain served as a metaphor for the eastern regions of Japan, an area that was as untamed as it was fascinating to the people in faraway Kyoto. The long (and complicated) history of Mount Fuji in Japanese culture laid the groundwork for its global role today. In order to understand Hokusai's part in this, it is important to travel far back in time and summarize the evolution of Mount Fuji from a faraway peak to an international celebrity.

From the Heian to the Momoyama periods, courtiers and others in the ancient capital viewed the Kantō region as a territory so far removed that it was almost thought of as a different realm, nearly as exotic and alluring as the lands across the sea. When the warriors of the Minamoto clan arrived from eastern Japan to seize Kyoto in the Genpei war, handscrolls for centuries after portrayed them as bearded brutes with morals far removed from the etiquette of the court. The painters and patrons of those handscrolls try to tell us that these eastern fighters from the foot of Mount Fuji were so unimpressed by the aristocracy's clout that they would not hesitate to set the palace ablaze and cut the throats of its refined inhabitants. The east, so we are told, had marred the very marrow of Japanese culture and polity.

But despite this horror, the eastern regions and, with them Mount Fuji, held a perpetual allure to the people of the capital. The oldest surviving depiction of the mountain dates to the mid-11th century and shows Shōtoku Taishi flying past Mount Fuji on his horse, an iconic moment in the mythology of Japanese Buddhism that captures in one picture the millennia-old role of the volcano as a sacred site. The image also reminds us how Hokusai and other artists eventually altered the pictorial representation of

Hata no Chitei, *Illustrated Biography of Prince Regent Shōtoku* (detail), 1069, colour on figured silk, Tokyo National Museum

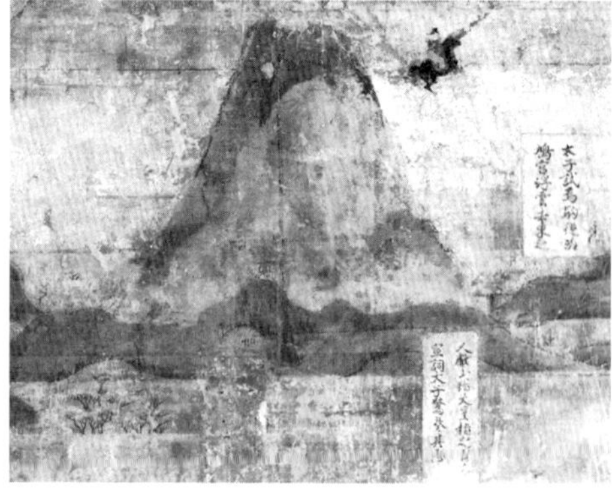

Mount Fuji. The pudding shape in the Shōtoku Taishi painting was common in depictions of the Heian and Kamakura periods, and can be found again in the Izumi City Kuboso Memorial Museum's famous handscroll of the *Tales of Ise*, in which the protagonist is struck by awe as he passes by Mount Fuji.

> *A peak that ignores*
> *all seasons: that is Fuji*
> *What month is it, then,*
> *that fawn-dappled flecks of white*
> *should betray a fall of snow?*

from *The Ise Stories*, trans. Joshua S. Mostow &
Royall Tyler, Honolulu: University of Hawaii Press, 2010

This poem from the ninth chapter of the *Tales of Ise* encapsulates how Mount Fuji did not fit neatly into the seasonality of Japanese traditional poetry and in many ways represented timelessness. The *Tales of Ise* all but secured Mount Fuji's place in Japanese poetry and visual culture. This position in the arts helped add a new layer to religious significance of the mountain, effectively turning Mount Fuji into a religio-aesthetic emblem. Few people ever travelled far enough to see Mount Fuji in person. Thus, through its repeated appearance as an artistic trope from the Heian through the Momoyama periods, the mountain was detached from its physical site and turned into a symbol. This process was continued in the Muromachi period when the famous artist Sesshū gave Mount

Fuji its iconic three-peaked appearance that effectively translated earlier colour images of the mountain into the ink medium. The symbolic identity of Fuji as a visual and literary trope continued into the Edo period, when other Kyoto-based artists like Tawaraya Sōtatsu and painters from courtly ateliers like the Tosa, none of whom ever saw the mountain, imagined it in pictures. Way into the first half of the Edo period, Mount Fuji retained its ethereal aura as an emblem for the Kantō region and the journey there from the capital, a phenomenon embodied by the term *azuma kudari* or 'journey to the east' – a phrase that sums up the centuries-old fear and fascination with Japan's eastern region in art, literature, religion and culture.

Hokusai's Fuji

The allusive existence of Mount Fuji changed with Edo-based artists embracing it as central element of their local pride and artistic inspiration. By depicting the subject again and again, artists in Edo made Mount Fuji a firm component of the city's early modern skyline and through their sheer quantity, their images laid the foundations for the mountain's international fame. More than any other artist, Hokusai played a part in the sacred mountain taking on the role of a global icon that represents Japan as a nation and as a culture. As this book shows, Hokusai created a staggering number of depictions of Mount Fuji – arguably more than any other artist. Ranging from famous print series like *Thirty-Six Views of Mount Fuji* [116–207] to paintings such as *Boy Viewing Mount*

Fuji [396–397], it is clear that he absorbed the mountain as a core part of his artistic identity. Even his most personal manifesto, *One Hundred Views of Mount Fuji* [215–380], is devoted to the mountain. Published in 1834 when he was seventy-five, Hokusai lays bare his own ambitions as a man and as an artist at the end of this book [5]. It is here that he declares: 'As I turned seventy-three, I partially succeeded in capturing the physique of all living things and the vitality of plants. For that reason, from the age of eighty-six, I shall make great progress while at the age of ninety I will do so even

BELOW LEFT
Tawaraya Sōtatsu, *Narihira's Journey to the East* (*The Tales of Ise*, detail of Mount Fuji), Edo period, colour on paper, 23.9 × 20.4 cm, The Gotō Museum

BELOW RIGHT
The Tales of Ise, Chapter 7 (detail), Kamakura period, colour on paper, 26.8 × 412 cm, Kuboso Memorial Museum of Arts, Izumi

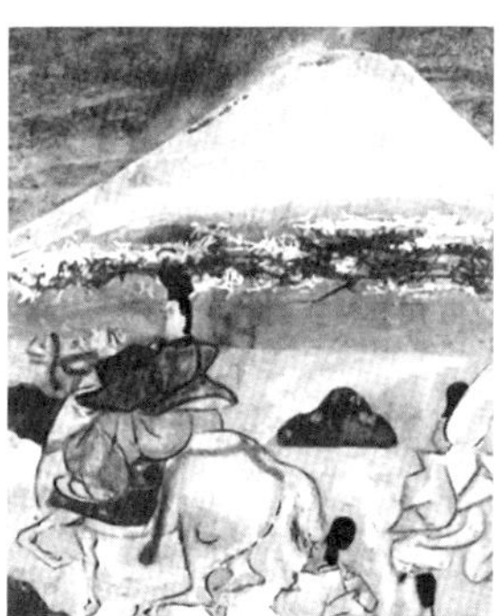

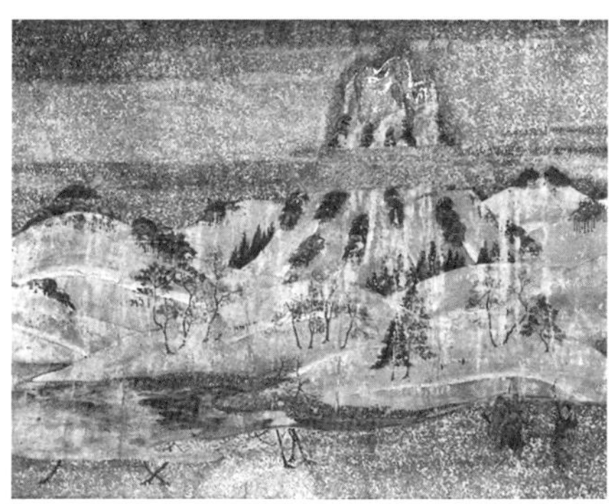

more. It is my greatest wish to reach one hundred, when my work would become truly marvellous. If I live to be one hundred and ten, every dot and every line would be as if coming to life.' Preceding this text, every image in the three-volume set – published at different intervals of his life – features the mountain, sometimes as a towering summit and at other times as a quiet observer to the daily hustle and bustle below.

Hokusai's Devotion

Hokusai's Mount Fuji did not escape collectors and connoisseurs abroad. Overseas, too, the history of Fuji has many facets. For example, Louis Gonse in his 1883 treatise *L'art japonais* offers a reflection of the tastes and viewpoints of Japanese art among European audiences at the time. Hokusai occupies a significant portion in Gonse's discussion of Japanese painting and heralds him as one of the greatest Japanese artists. Yet, curiously, Gonse does not refer to Hokusai's depictions of Mount Fuji at all, except for citing Hokusai's manifesto as published in *One Hundred Views of Mount Fuji*. In fact, the only image of Fuji found in that section of *L'art japonais* is by Hokusai's rival, Hiroshige. In the section on prints, however, Gonse hails Hokusai's works as reflections of the lives and day-to-day activities of the people of Edo. Indeed, he lavishes particular praise on *One Hundred Views*, whose first two volumes he extols as being of 'great rarity' in quality and design. By extension, Mount Fuji – a recurring feature in many of Hokusai's landscapes – was an integral part of everyday life in Edo. The mountain, in essence, was not an elite symbol, but an emblem of the townspeople of Edo to whom Hokusai himself belonged. In this way, by explicitly associating Hokusai and his oeuvre with the arts of the people – as opposed to elite art production – Gonse implicitly connects Fuji with the ordinary people living in the imperial seat of power. As part of the city's landscape, Fuji was a democratic landmark that belonged to everyone.

A couple of decades later, Ernest Fenollosa continued this association of Mount Fuji with the arts of the people, of which Hokusai was a major representative. In a chapter of his book *Epochs of Chinese and Japanese Art* (1912) entitled 'Modern Plebeian Art in Kioto' (*sic*), Fenollosa cites four landscapes that feature Fuji from the collection of the Museum of Fine Arts, Boston. In the chapter that follows, 'Modern Plebeian Art in Yedo', Fenollosa connects Hokusai to the Fuji theme by citing his late use of a Fuji-shaped seal, and reproduces the now world-famous print *Under the Wave off Kanagawa*, simply entitling it 'The Wave'. The print is shown

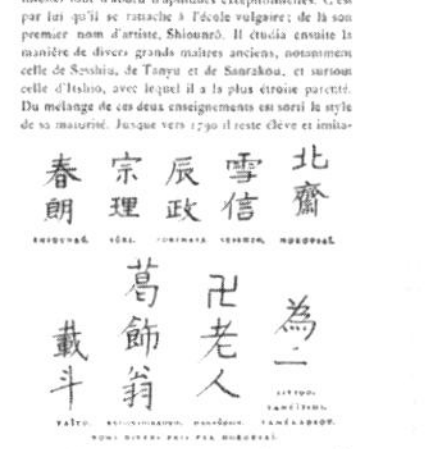

Louis Gonse dedicated a double page in *L'art japonais* (1883) to Hokusai and his work.

together with the similarly renowned *A Mild Breeze on a Fine Day*, also known as *Red Fuji*. In fact, Hokusai is the artist that Fenollosa most closely associates with Fuji. Most featured images by other artists, such as Hiroshige, do not include the mountain.

It is tempting to speculate that it was Fenollosa's choice of images that both reflected and spawned a growing association of Hokusai with Japan's most famous peak among Western collectors and connoisseurs. The two prints reproduced in Fenollosa's book are now the two most recognizable images by Hokusai and, indeed, in all of Japanese art. The Japanese government has recognized the international fame of Hokusai by effectively turning these two Fuji pictures into symbols of Japan as a nation and a culture, both within and beyond the country. In 2024, the Bank of Japan plans to issue a redesigned set of banknotes, with the most widely circulated 1,000 yen bill bearing Hokusai's *Great Wave* on its front. The Japanese passport already includes an image from the series *Thirty-Six Views of Mount Fuji* – including the *Great Wave* and *Red Fuji* – on every page. Hokusai's influence is also apparent to anyone entering Japan as a foreign tourist: the entry stamp features Hokusai's *Red Fuji*. The national and international role and marketability of Fuji reached another peak when the mountain was declared a UNESCO World Heritage site in 2013. What's more, the emoji for 'wave' on many smartphones worldwide is a pixelated rendering of Hokusai's *Great Wave*. And the list goes on.

More recently, the Museum of Fine Arts, Boston, and fashion brand Uniqlo collaborated on a range of t-shirts that allow people around the world to wear images from Hokusai's *Thirty-Six Views of Mount Fuji* on their chests. Hokusai and Mount Fuji, it seems, are inextricably entwined and are woven into the very fabric of Japan's identity. Although Fuji and Japan have a long and layered history, Hokusai's life-long infatuation with Mount Fuji in prints and paintings set the stage for Mount Fuji's global fame. In many ways, Hokusai regularized Japan's relationship with one of its remaining active volcanoes, its dangerous beauty looming just on the edge of Tokyo, the world's biggest city.

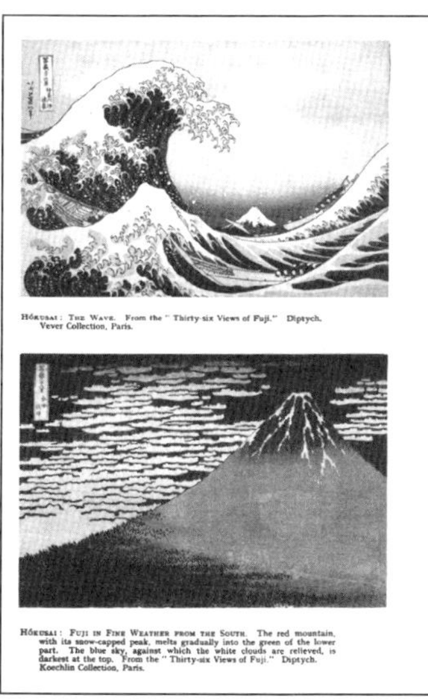

HÓKUSAI : THE WAVE. From the " Thirty-six Views of Fuji." Diptych. Vever Collection, Paris.

HÓKUSAI : FUJI IN FINE WEATHER FROM THE SOUTH. The red mountain, with its snow-capped peak, melts gradually into the green of the lower part. The blue sky, against which the white clouds are relieved, is darkest at the top. From the " Thirty-six Views of Fuji." Diptych. Koechlin Collection, Paris.

Two of Hokusai's images of Mount Fuji, published in Ernest Fenollosa's *Epochs of Chinese and Japanese Art* (1912).

Early Faces of Fuji

Hokusai was born in 1760 in Honjo-Warigesui in the city of Edo. He was around six years old when he first developed an interest in drawing. At the age of twelve or thirteen, he taught himself to draw by studying the illustrations in woodblock-printed books while working as an apprentice at a book rental library. At the age of fourteen, he was apprenticed to a block cutter. This brief summary suggests that Hokusai was familiar with illustrated books and prints from childhood, and that he had been taught the basic skills of an artist. In addition, Edo, where Hokusai was born and raised and where he spent his career, soon became a flourishing city that nourished extraordinary artists. The mid-18th century was also the time when the cultural centre of Japan moved from Kyoto and its environs to Edo, and the time when the techniques for producing full-colour woodblock prints were developed. The signs of the golden age of *ukiyo*-e in Edo were all there by the time Hokusai was a young man.

When Hokusai was nineteen, he decided to become an artist and entered the studio of Katsukawa Shunshō, whose portraits of stage actors were very popular. As early as the following year, Hokusai made his debut under the name Katsukawa Shunrō and distinguished himself with a series of pictures of actors. When Shunshō died, Hokusai left the Katsukawa studio. He then took the name Tawaraya Sōri, drawing his inspiration from the Rinpa movement, which traces its origins to Tawaraya Sōtatsu. By this time, Hokusai was in his mid-thirties. The works included in this chapter introduce images of Fuji from a period of roughly forty years, starting with works from the time when he was developing the Sōri style, which is characterized by a graceful elegance, and continuing through many twists and turns that led to the great achievement of the *Thirty-Six Views of Mount Fuji*.

In his Sōri period, Hokusai earned a reputation for *surimono* prints and illustrations for printed books of comic verses (*kyōka ehon*). Unlike *ukiyo*-e prints, which publishers produced to sell in quantity, *surimono* were commissioned by wealthy connoisseurs from popular artists. Many *surimono* are elaborate, luxurious, and finely worked using expensive techniques such as *karazuri* embossing. For an illustrated calendar, Hokusai drew scenes associated with the time of year. In one scene, Mount Fuji appears in the first dreams of the new year of a man and a woman dozing around a *kotatsu* table [33], and also features in a scene depicting the Boys' Day celebrations in May [60–61]. In fact, Hokusai showed off his talent by depicting a variety of motifs. The classical tall and willowy, slim-waisted *bijinga* beauty with her oval face and widow's peak [40–41] is an example of a *surimono* print commissioned by a writer of humorous verses. Other examples are advertisements for merchandise or entertainments. *The Tales of Ise*, which tells the story of Ariwara no Narihira and his journey to the east [80–83], is an example of a motif from this period.

Many *surimono* prints are roughly square in shape, but in the Kansei era (1789–1801), thick *hōsho* paper was produced in a long, horizontal format that was folded in half lengthwise. Hokusai made effective use of this panoramic form by placing human figures or other subjects in the foreground on the right, and creating a sense of depth by depicting endlessly flowing scenery on the left [44–47, 60–61, 74–75]. He also exercised his wits by including Mount Fuji within paintings that were shown as part of the interior decoration of rooms [60–61].

Similarly to *surimono* prints, many picture books of humorous verse (*kyōka ehon*) are beautifully finished. In the Tenmei era (1781–1789), comic verses were extremely popular in Edo, and expensive books with illustrations by Kitagawa Utamaro and other artists were published. Hokusai also produced many illustrations for picture books. There are some remarkable examples of his work dating to the late Kansei era (1789–1801). For example, the composition *Spring at Enoshima*, from the *Yanagi no Ito* or *Willow-Silk* album [34–35], contrasts a detailed depiction of waves breaking on the shore and the gestures of a group of travellers, caught deep in conversation, with the solemn stillness of Fuji. Similar compositions can be seen in *Enoshima* [36–37] and *Gathering Shellfish* [46–47]. Elsewhere, he depicts a pastoral tea house in *The Mist of Sandara* [40–41], the beauty of elegant women in *Mountains upon Mountains* [50–51], and the lively streets of Edo in *Panoramic Views along the Banks of the Sumida River* [52–53].

In this period, Hokusai refined not only the graceful elegance of his Sōri style, but also his sense of spatial organization and composition. In *Panoramic Views along the Banks of the Sumida River*, the composition is not based on double-page spreads, but is carefully arranged in such a way that the scenery continues as the pages are turned. All the pages connect to form one continuous landscape, just like a picture scroll. It is a work based on the limitations and characteristics of the book medium. Since *surimono* prints and *kyōka ehon* were produced on a generous budget, it must have been a valuable experience for Hokusai to be able to focus fully on woodblock prints in privileged circumstances, working with highly skilled craftsmen who handled both carving and printing, using expensive paper and pigments. The compositional skills and interpretations of motifs that Hokusai learned in this period reappear in a more refined format in *Thirty-Six Views of Mount Fuji*.

In around 1798, when he was thirty-nine, Hokusai passed the Sōri name to a student and took the name Hokusai Tokimasa.

In addition to *kyōka ehon* and *surimono* prints, he expanded his activities to include illustrations for *yomihon*, novels printed from woodblocks, in a tremendously productive period. He returned to *ukiyo-e*, which he had avoided during the Sōri period, to produce large full-colour woodblock prints. *The Storehouse of Loyal Retainers, a Primer* [84–87] is an example of a series of prints published under a shared title, a *soroimono*. This early 18th-century tale of the Forty-Seven Rōnin and their quest for revenge was the subject of popular *jōruri* recitals and kabuki plays. Kitagawa Utamaro was the first to depict the story in *ukiyo*-e form, but the tale was still being illustrated in the mid-19th century by artists of the Utagawa school. To represent the first act of the eleven-act play, Hokusai depicted the seaside at Kamakura with a view of Mount Fuji, setting the action against a landscape with a sense of depth.

During the same period, Hokusai also included Fuji in around seven different series based on *Fifty-Three Stations on the Tōkaidō Road* [64–79]. In the Edo period, roads and inns were built for the feudal lords who regularly travelled to and from Edo, and, by the early 18th century, travel had also become popular with ordinary people. The popularity of the comic novel *Tōkaidōchū hizakurige* (*Travels on the Eastern Seaboard*) by Jippensha Ikku, published in 1802, sparked a similar widespread fascination with travel that led to a boom in the publication of images of famous places.

The series *Fifty-Three Stations on the Tōkaidō Road* [70–75], published in early 1804, is an outstanding *soroimono* consisting of a total of fifty-nine prints. Mount Fuji appears in the images of Nihonbashi, Shinagawa and Hara. The series was initially produced as *kyōka surimono* prints, which incorporated comic verses, but these were later removed and the prints were sold to a wider audience. Many pictures of famous places focused on the scenery by the roads or the inns, but in addition to well-known sights and the figures of travellers, Hokusai also produced variations that included local specialities, and the customs of the people living in different areas. This trait is also found in Hokusai's other versions of *Fifty-Three Stations on the Tōkaidō Road*, as well in *Thirty-Six Views of Mount Fuji* and *One Hundred Views of Mount Fuji*.

While he continued to work intensively in a variety of genres and consolidated his reputation, this was a period when Hokusai was still eagerly experimenting and assimilating new techniques, never growing complacent. Not only did he study the techniques of other schools, but he looked everywhere, East and West. It must have been particularly exciting for Hokusai to encounter foreign artistic styles he had never seen before as he developed his own techniques. One of these styles was the Nanpin School, which had been brought to Nagasaki from China in the first half of the 18th century and then circulated among artists in Edo. Hokusai was inspired by this style of painting's delicate lines and realistic reproductions of its subject matter, which he adapted into his own style. Its influence can be seen in his *yomihon* illustrations depicting true-to-life situations in the Bunka era (1804–1818), and in the textures of the tree bark he rendered so carefully in his *surimono* prints.

Hokusai also had the confidence to tackle Western painting techniques. Undeniably, he had not yet fully assimilated the techniques because the works from this period that incorporate perspective or shading are still awkward. *Eight Views of Edo*, an album of Western-style prints, is an ambitious work in which he imitates copperplate engravings [92–95]. In comparison with the typical *ukiyo*-e of the time, it is obvious from the dark shading that he was aware of copperplate prints. In contrast to *ukiyo*-e where the contours and colour surfaces have no shading, he has incorporated crosshatching as a way to convey light and shade through line density. It is possible that he referenced hatching to draw a clear distinction between intense light and shadows in his book illustrations. Looking at *Surugachō*, from the series *The Dutch Picture Lens: Eight Views of Edo,* whic features a road that runs straight towards Mount Fuji, it is clear that he has incorporated perspective into the composition. In this period, Hokusai's inquiring mind was exploring techniques that were new to him. His experimental approach and ambitious discipline made him a pioneer of one new technique after another, which would bear fruit in important ways at a later stage. For example, he improved the accuracy of the composition for *Mount Fuji Under High Bridge* [88–89] and used it for *Beneath Mannen Bridge in Fukagawa* [142–143] from *Thirty-Six Views of Mount Fuji.*

In 1810, Hokusai took the name Taito. This was the year when he published his first *edehon, Foolish Ono's Nonsense Picture Dictionary.* An *edehon* is a drawing manual, a genre that Hokusai enthusiastically explored during the Bunka and Bunsei eras (1804–1830). Rather than a serious teaching aid, *Foolish Ono's Nonsense Picture Dictionary* is a playful guide to drawing *moji*-e, a type of visual pun in which Japanese and Chinese characters are arranged to form the outlines of the images, including people and animals. He also produced many other ingenious drawing manuals including *Quick Lessons in Simplified Drawing Part 1*, which included verses to recite while drawing pictures and the use of compass and ruler to capture the structure of figures based on geometric shapes. To provide some context, these drawing manuals were published because Hokusai had become a highly respected figure and role model in the art world.

In 1814, *Hokusai Manga* was published. This manual was an unprecedented success. Although it was initially planned as a one-off project, a long series of sequel volumes followed. Eventually, the series concluded with a fifteenth volume, published posthumously in 1878. The manual was a bestseller and enjoyed long-term steady sales. *Hokusai Manga* contains three images of Fuji, including *Mishima Pass in Kai Province* [106–107].

Manuals could also offer a collection of designs for craftsmen to emulate. *Popular Designs for Combs and Tobacco Pipes*, aimed at comb and pipe makers, contains eight sketches for ornamental combs adorned with an image of Fuji in a range of different moods, according to the season, time of day, and weather [108–109]. An advertisement at the back of the book announces 'Eight Views of Mount Fuji' as a forthcoming publication. While that particular book was never published, the idea foreshadowed *Thirty-Six Views of Mount Fuji*, which is discussed in the next chapter.

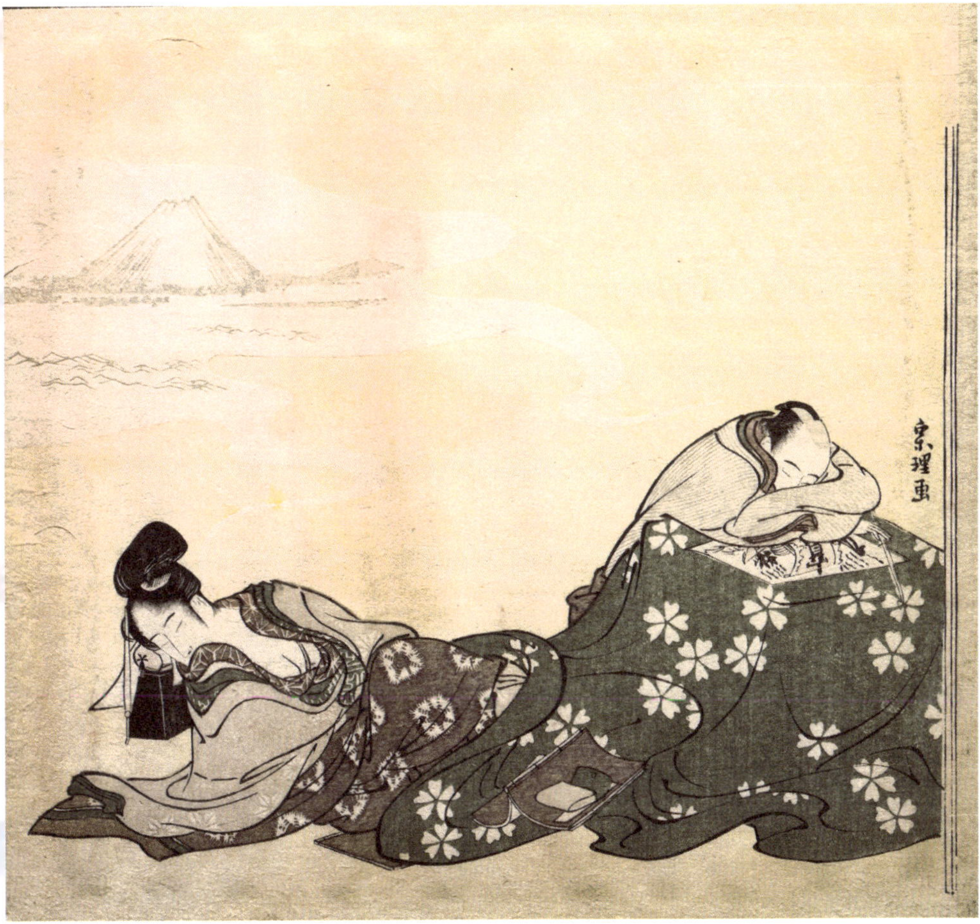

Man and Woman Asleep Beside a Kotatsu Table
surimono, signed Sōri ga

c. 1795–1798. Size unspecified. Charles Stewart Smith collection of Japanese prints,
The New York Public Library, 57378864

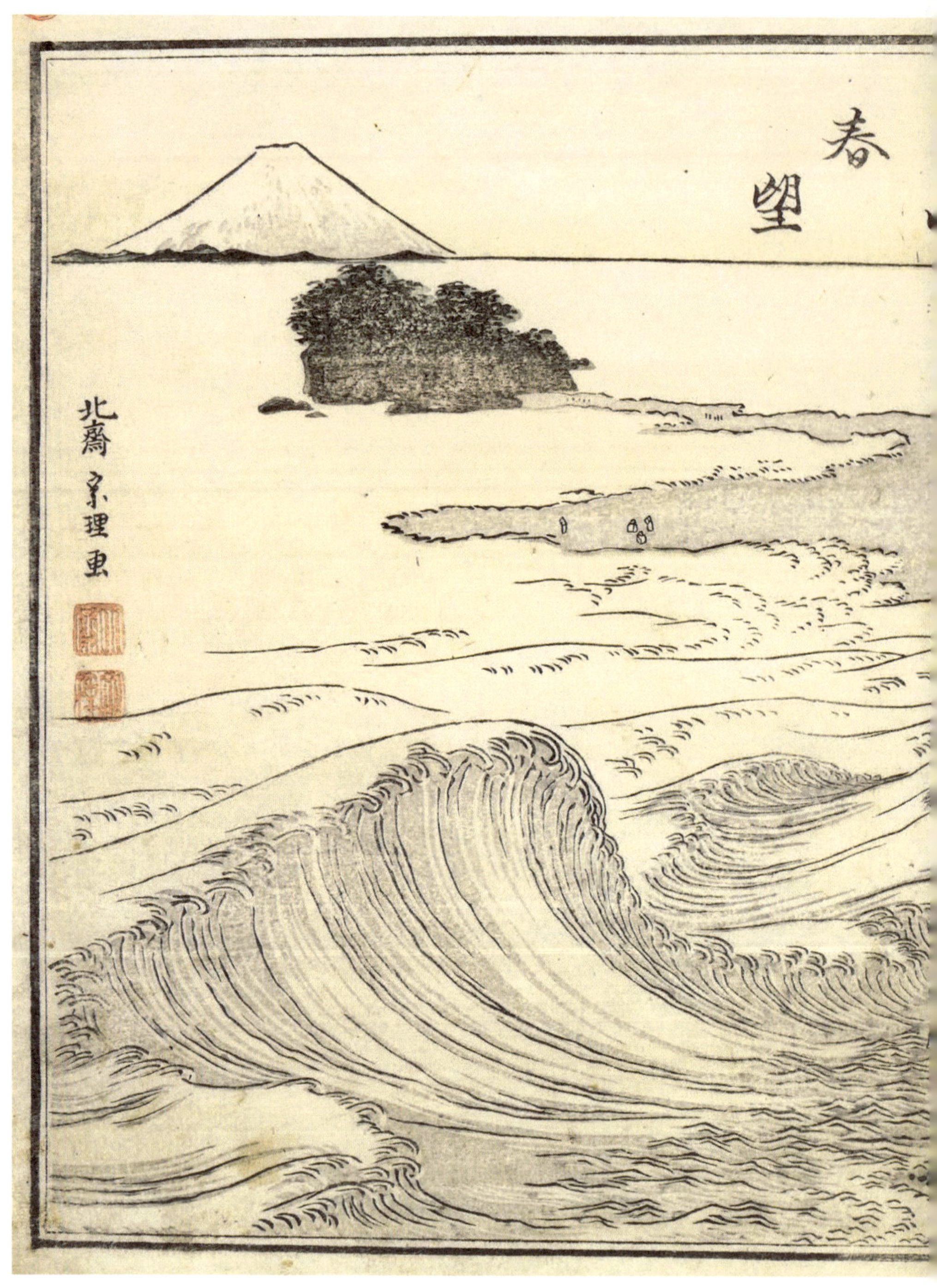

2 *Spring at Enoshima*, from the *Willow-Silk* album
kyōka ehon, signed Hokusai Sōri ga

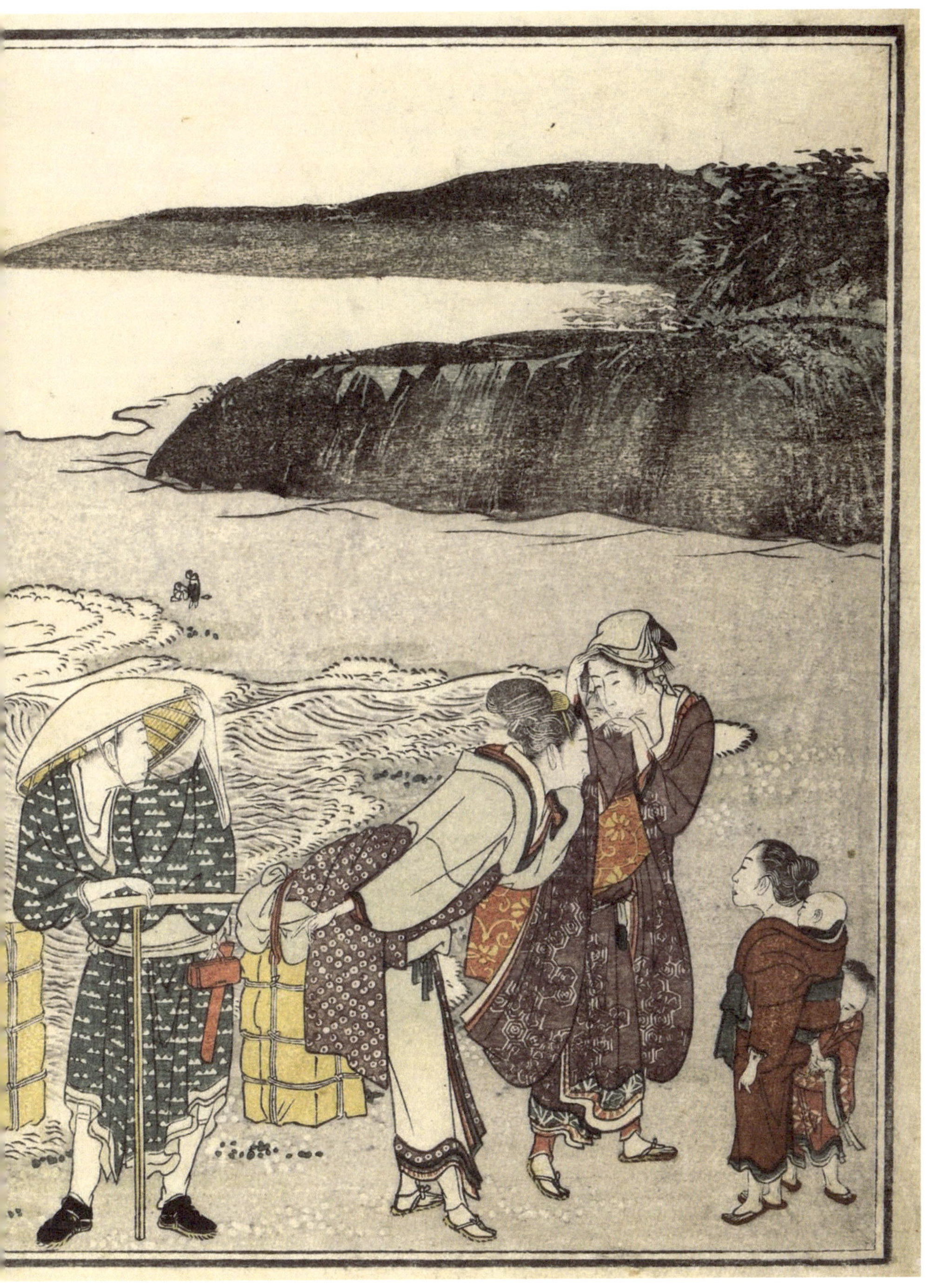

1797. 24.9 × 38 cm. © The Trustees of the British Museum, 1937,0710,0.206

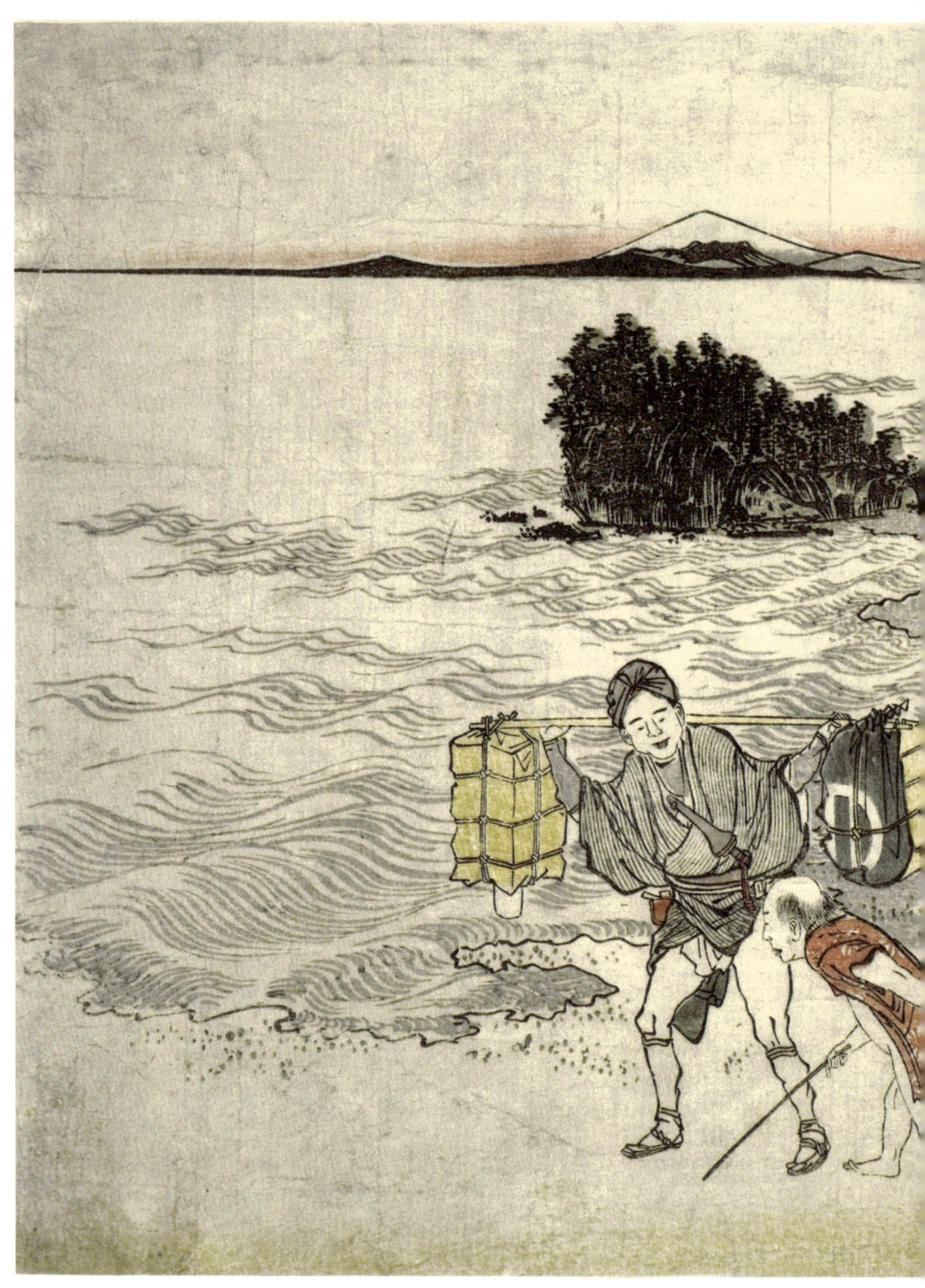

3 *Enoshima*
ōban nishiki-e, unsigned

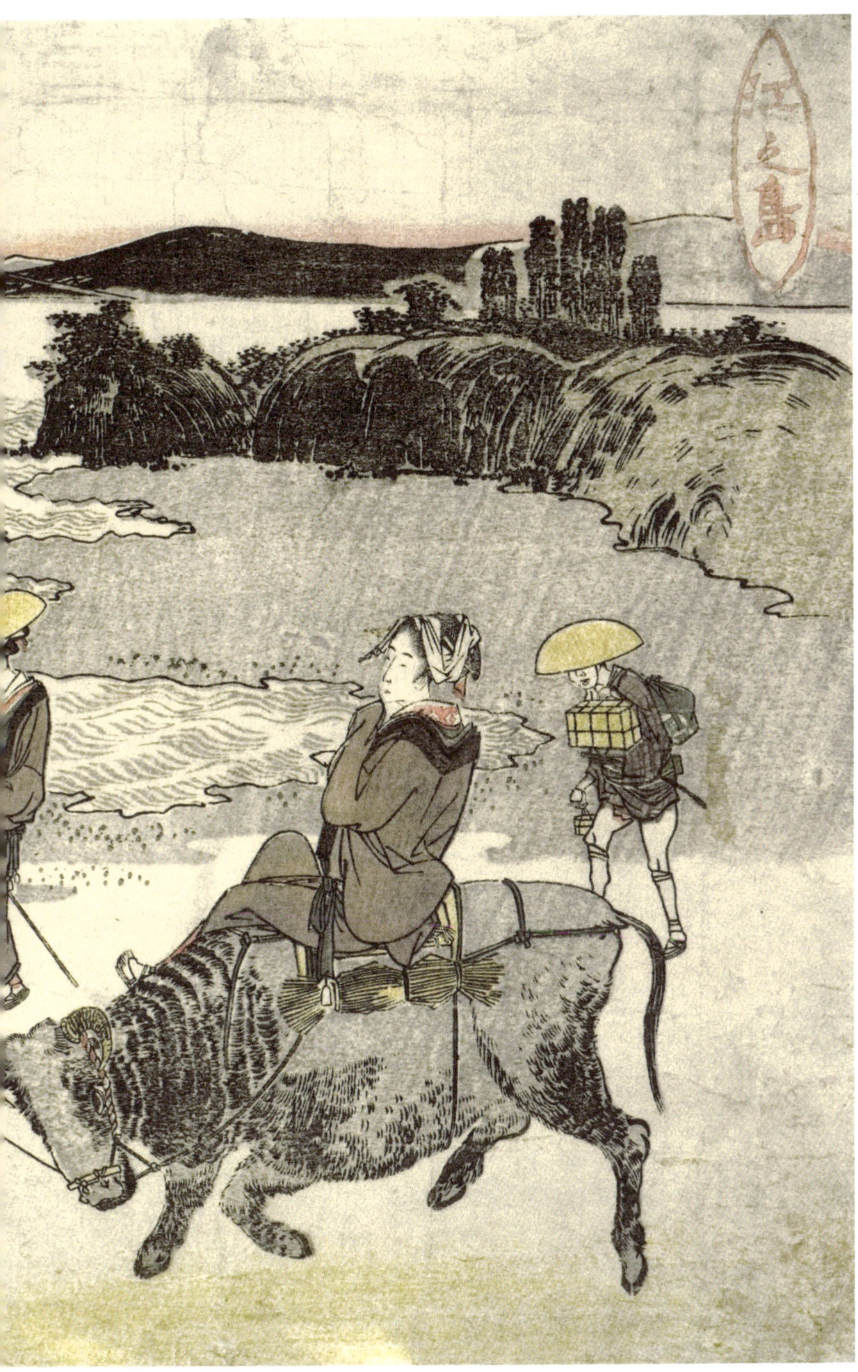

Date unknown. 24.2 × 36.4 cm. Frederick W. Gookin Collection, The Art Institute of Chicago, 1939.1125

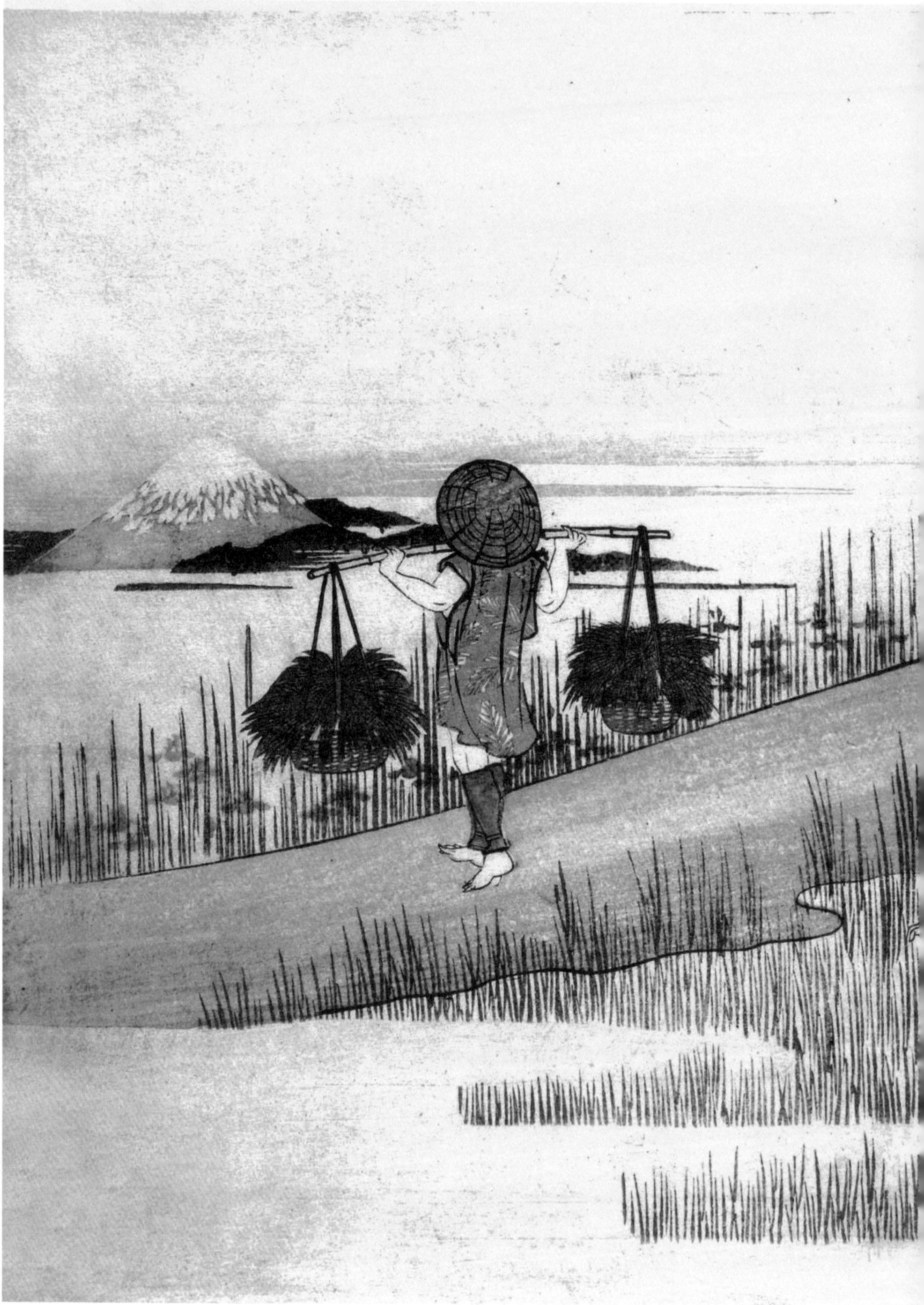

Untitled
ōban nishiki-e, unsigned

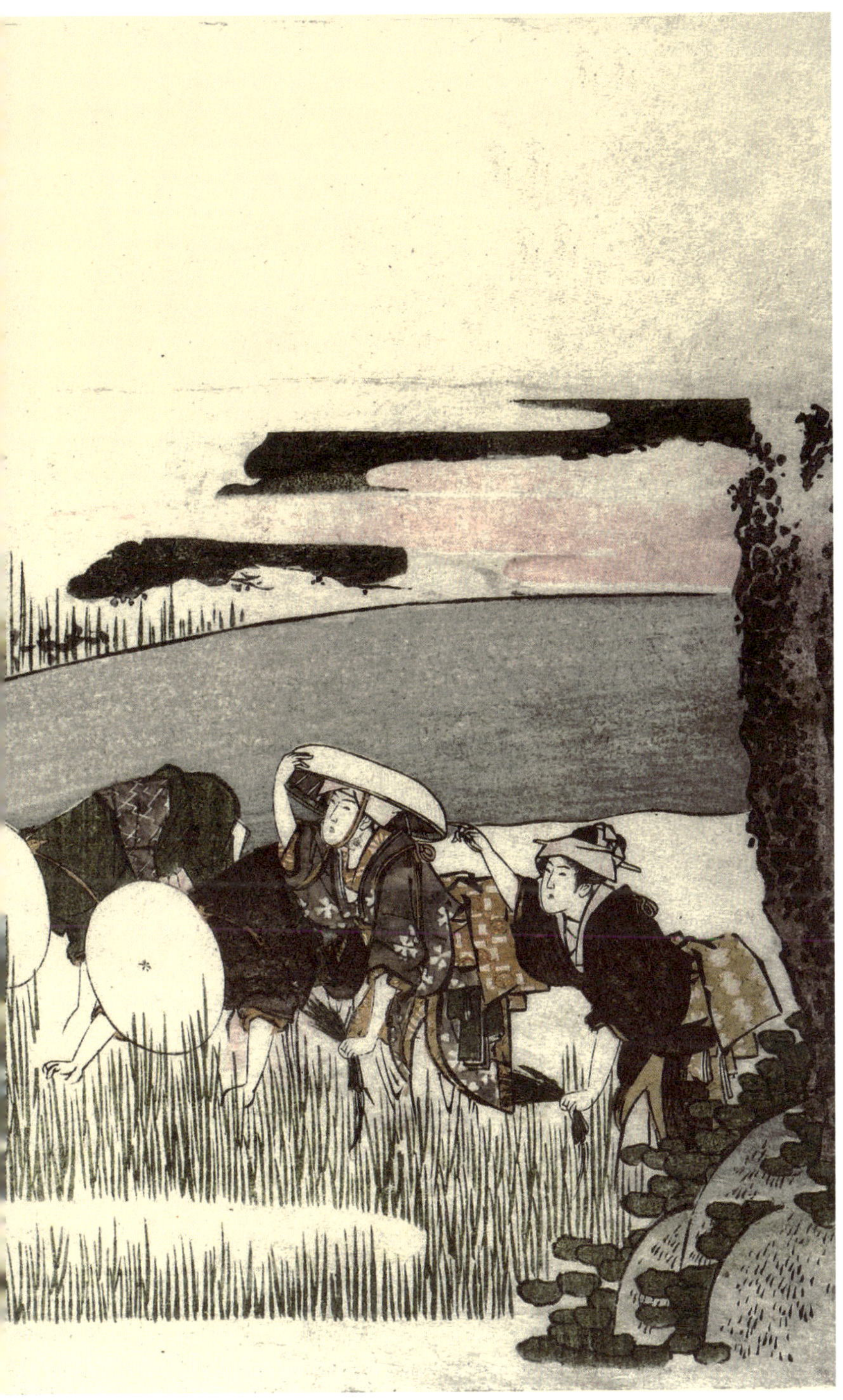

c. 1790–1810. Size unspecified. © The Trustees of the British Museum, 1945,1101,0.50

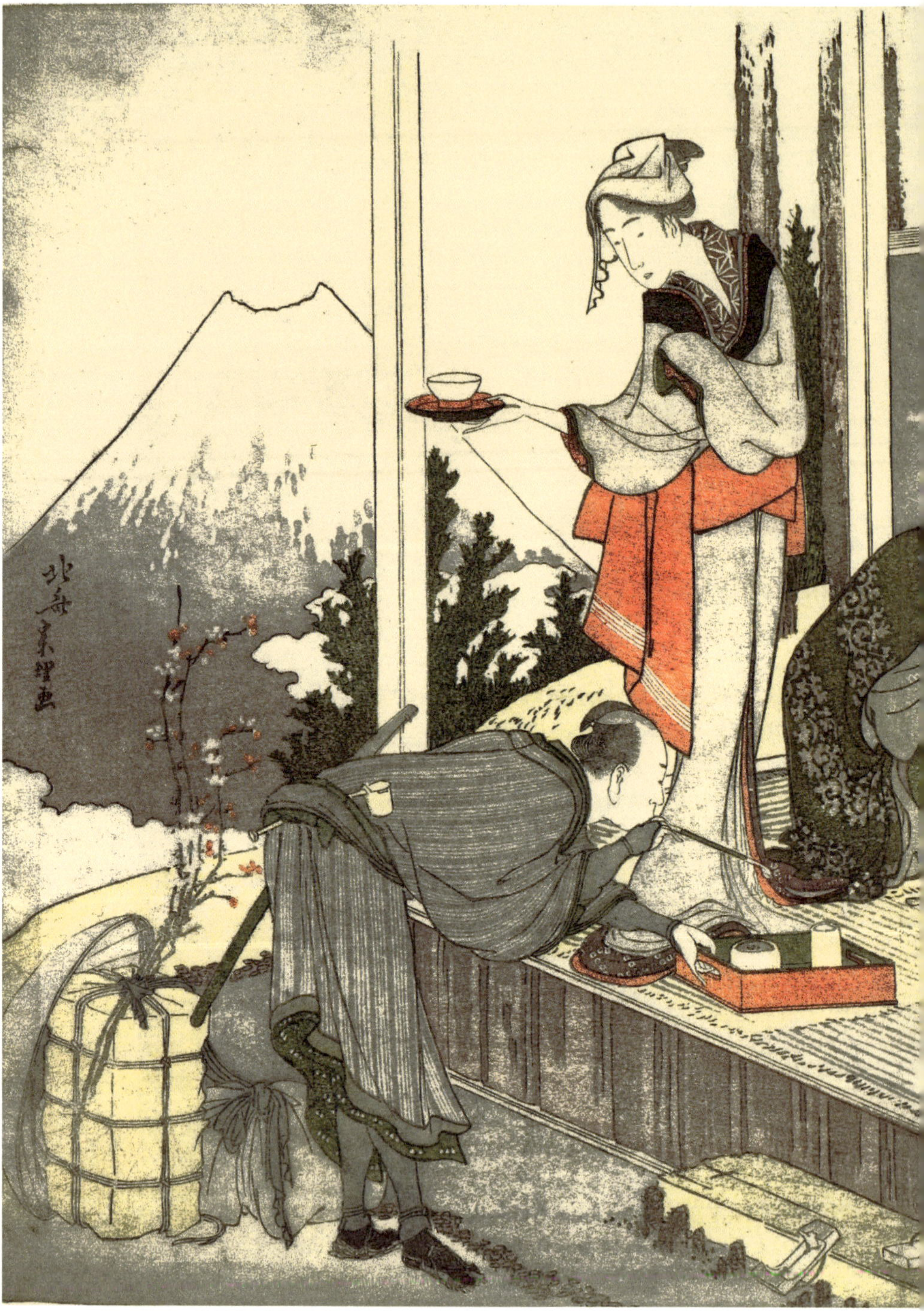

An Artisan's Shop, from the album *The Mist of Sandara*
kyōka ehon, signed Hokusai Sōri ga

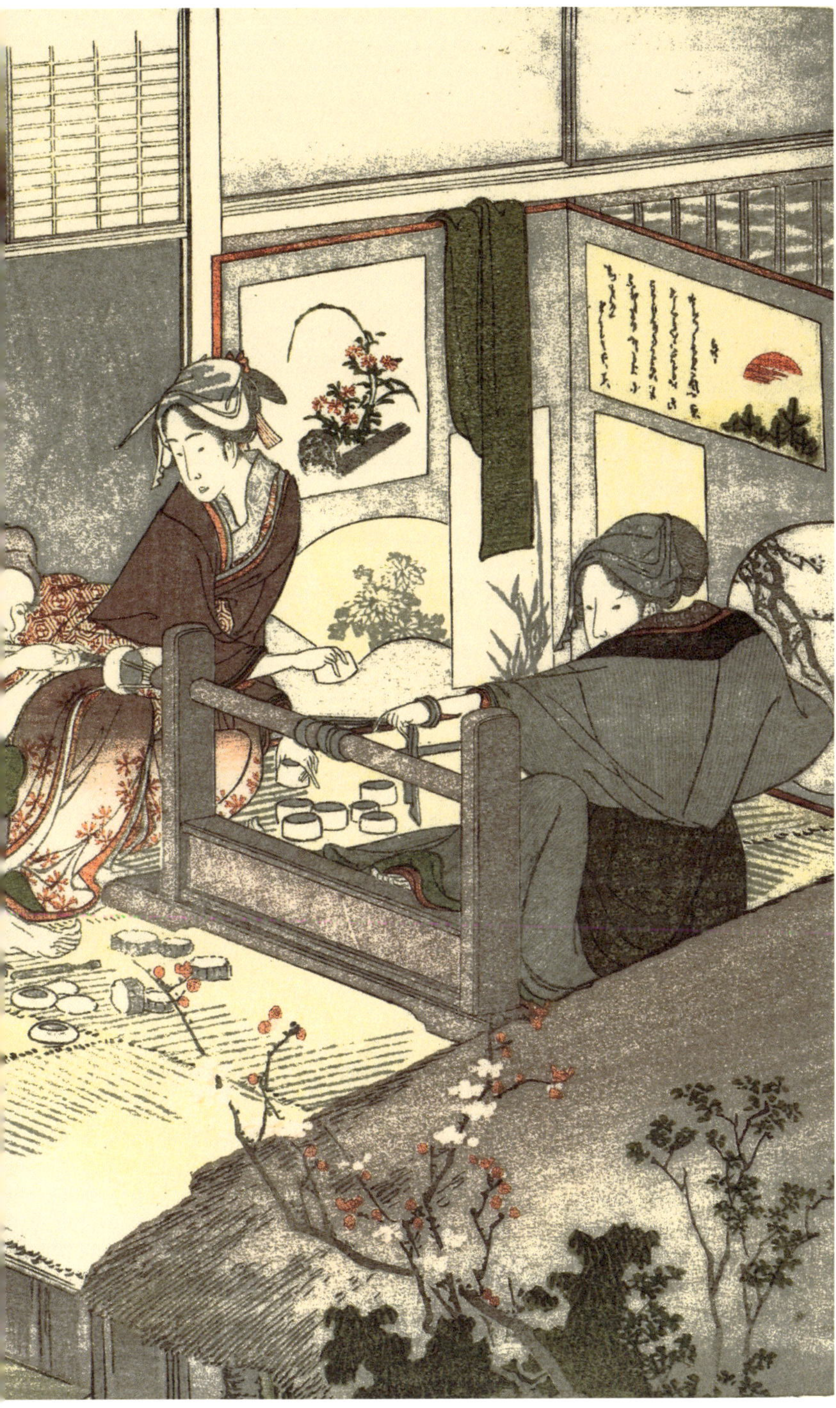

1797. 22 × 31.6 cm. Clarence Buckingham Collection, The Art Institute of Chicago, 1925.3205

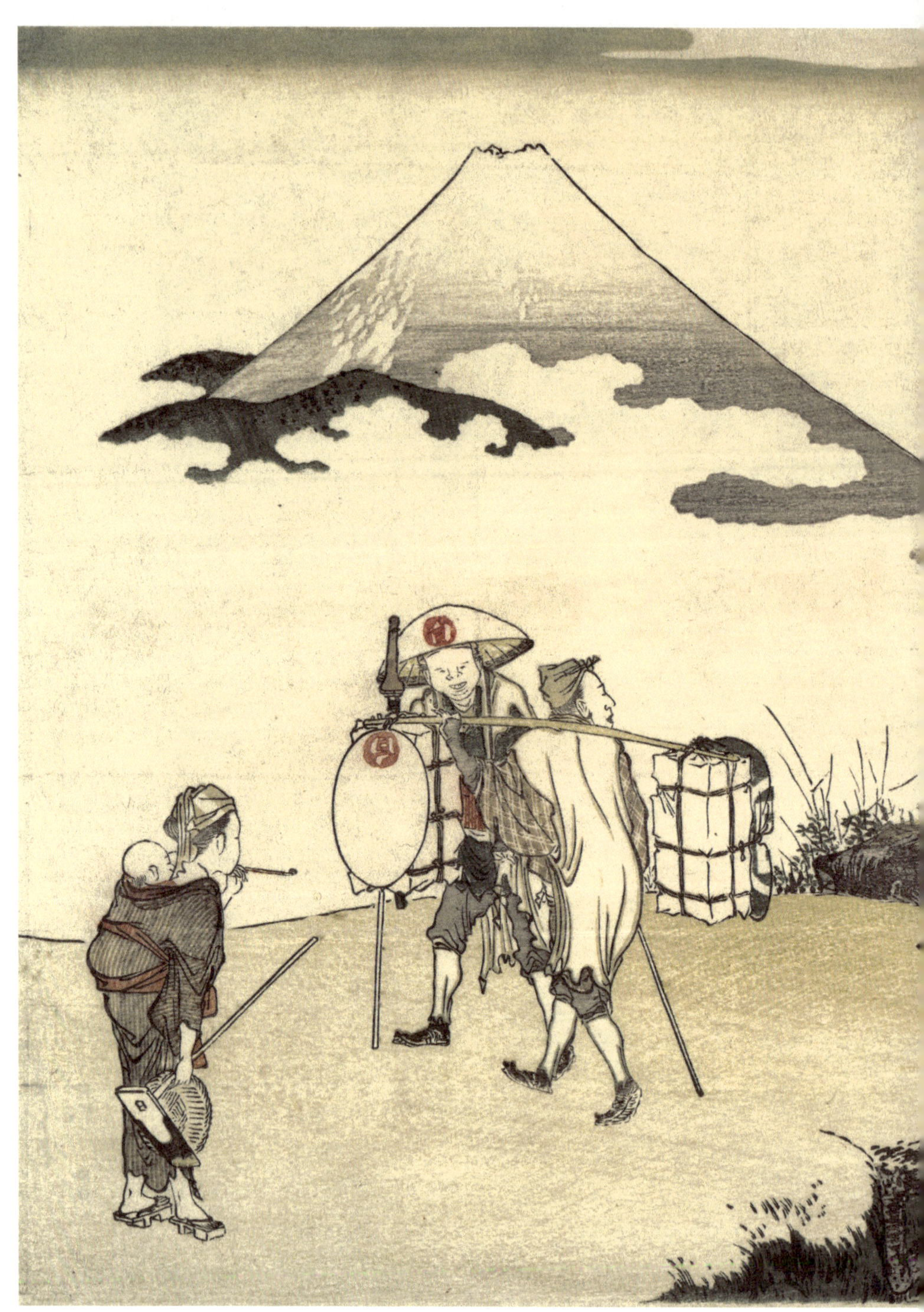

The Top of Mount Fuji
ōban nishiki-e, unsigned

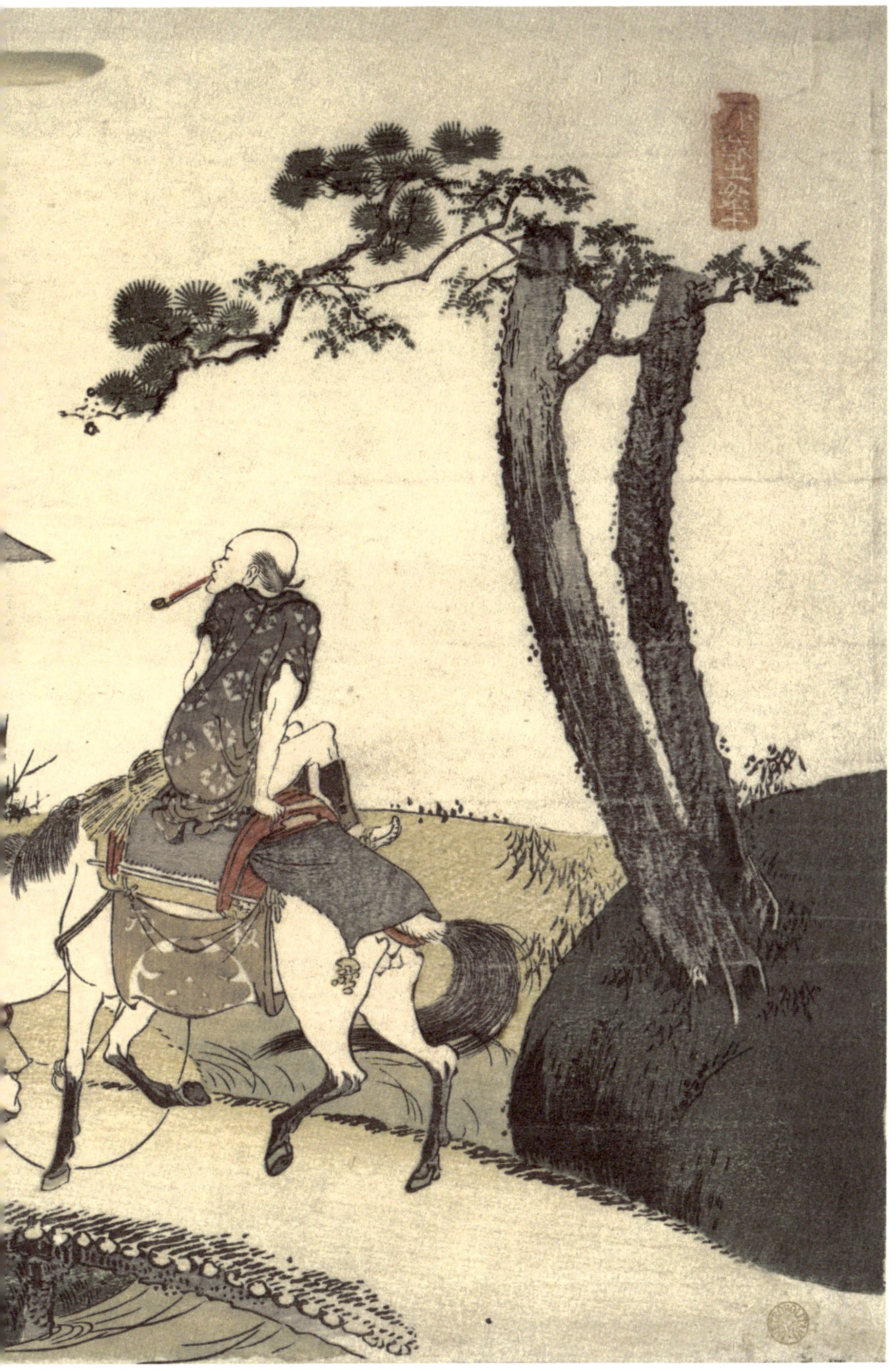

c. 1799. 25.7 × 38.7 cm. Gift of Estate of Samuel Isham, 1914. © 2022 The Metropolitan Museum of Art, New York, JP1012

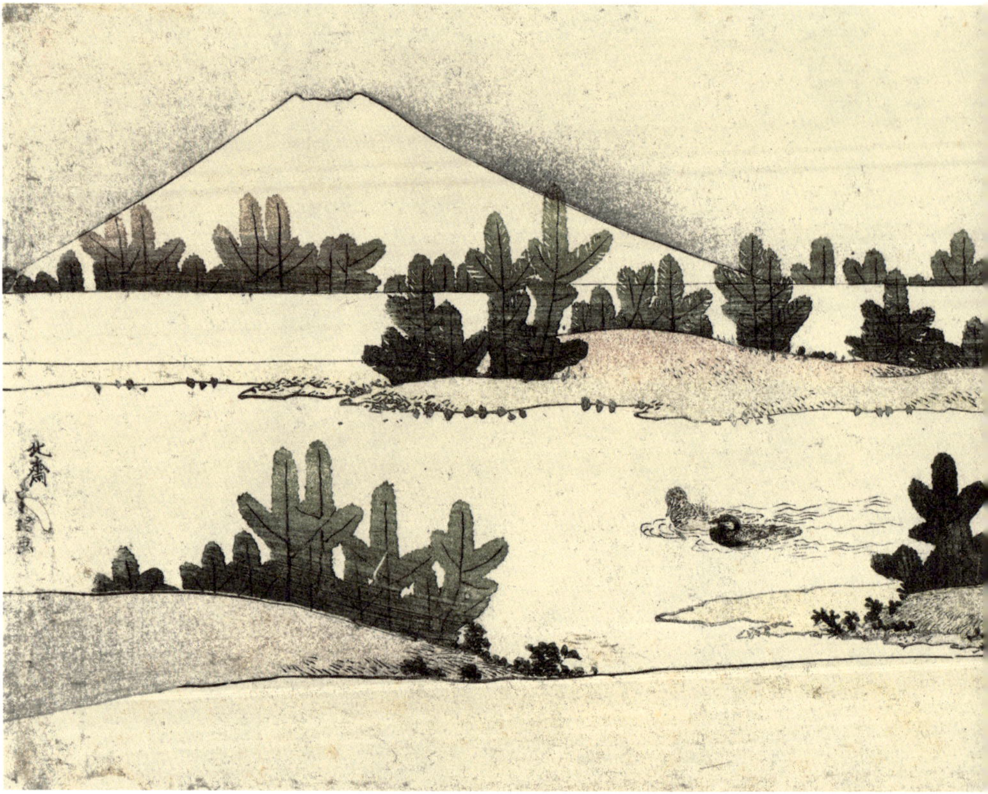

7 *Ladies with Young Pine Trees and Mount Fuji*
surimono (nagaban yoko-e), signed Hokusai Sōri ga

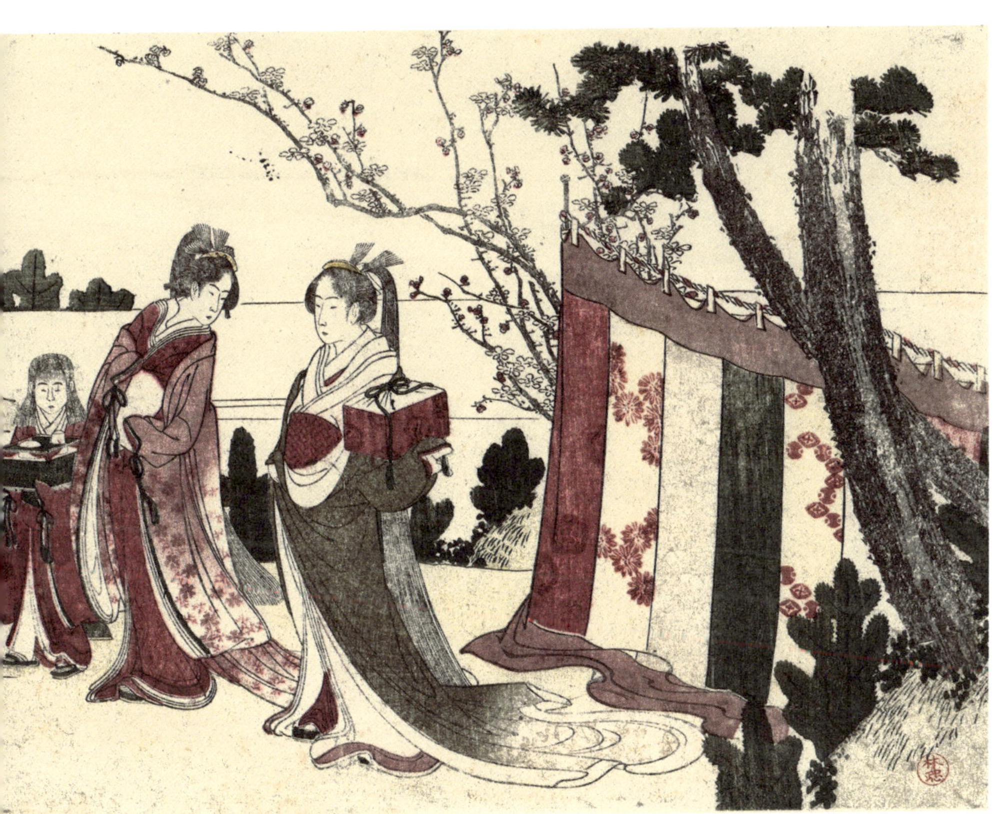

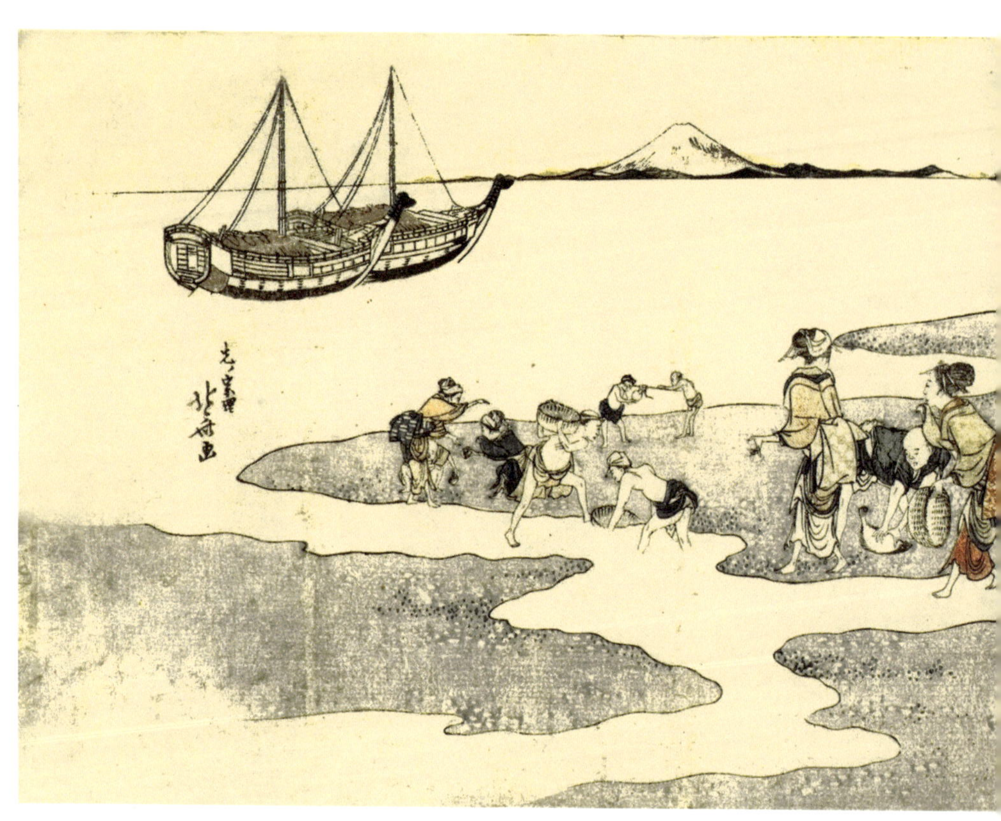

Gathering Shellfish
surimono (nagaban yoko-e), signed Saki no Sōri Hokusai ga

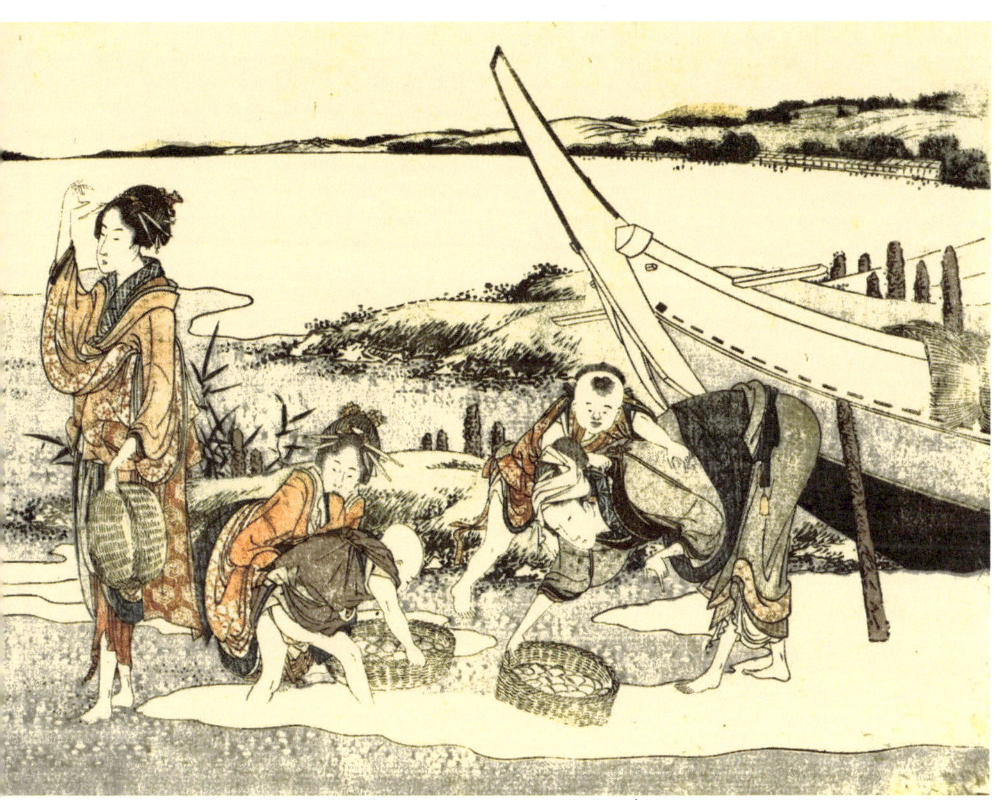

c. 1795–1805. 20.9 × 57.2 cm. Clarence Buckingham Collection, The Art Institute of Chicago, 1925.3205

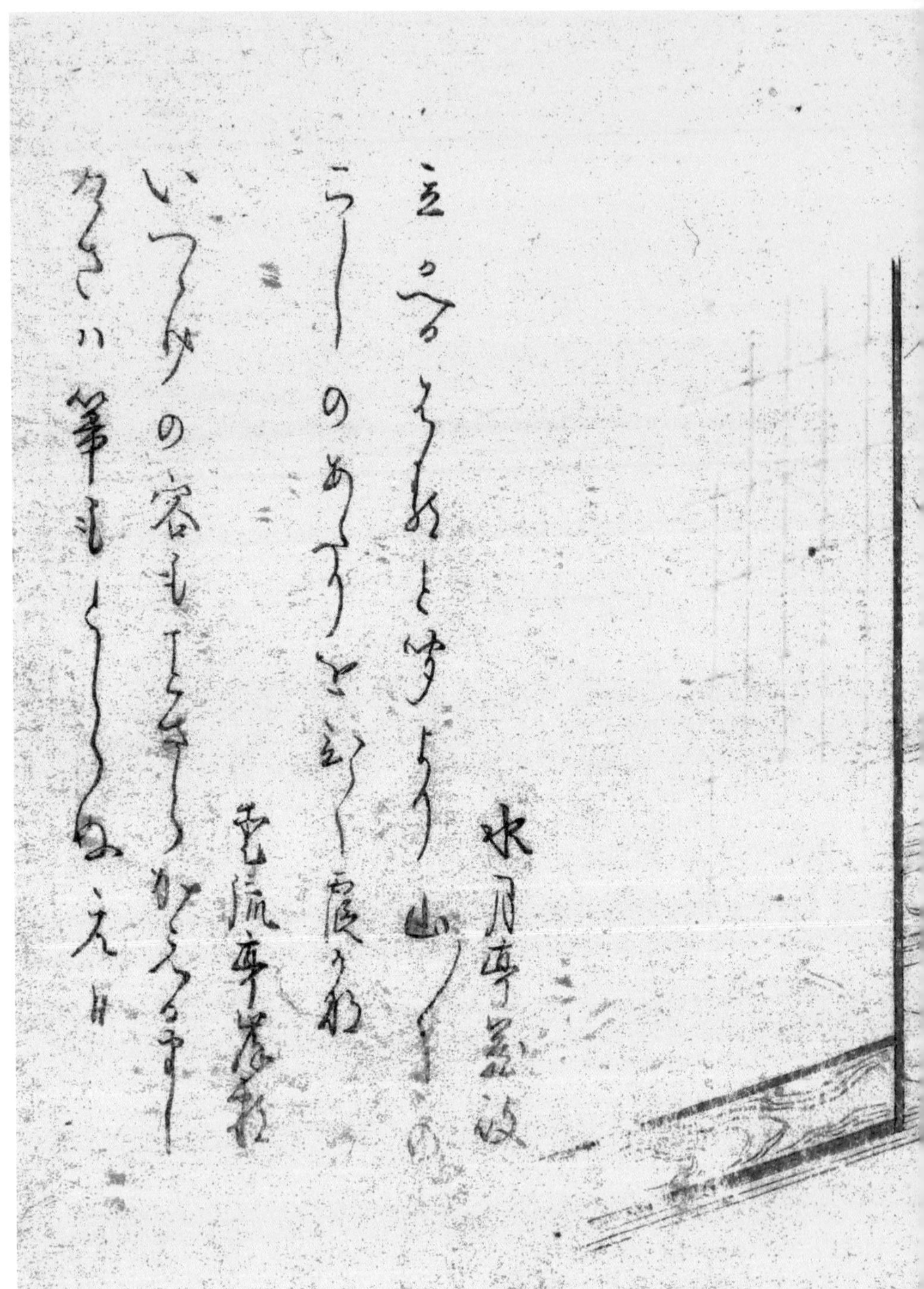

9 *Untitled*
kyōka surimono, signed Saki no Sōri Hokusai ga

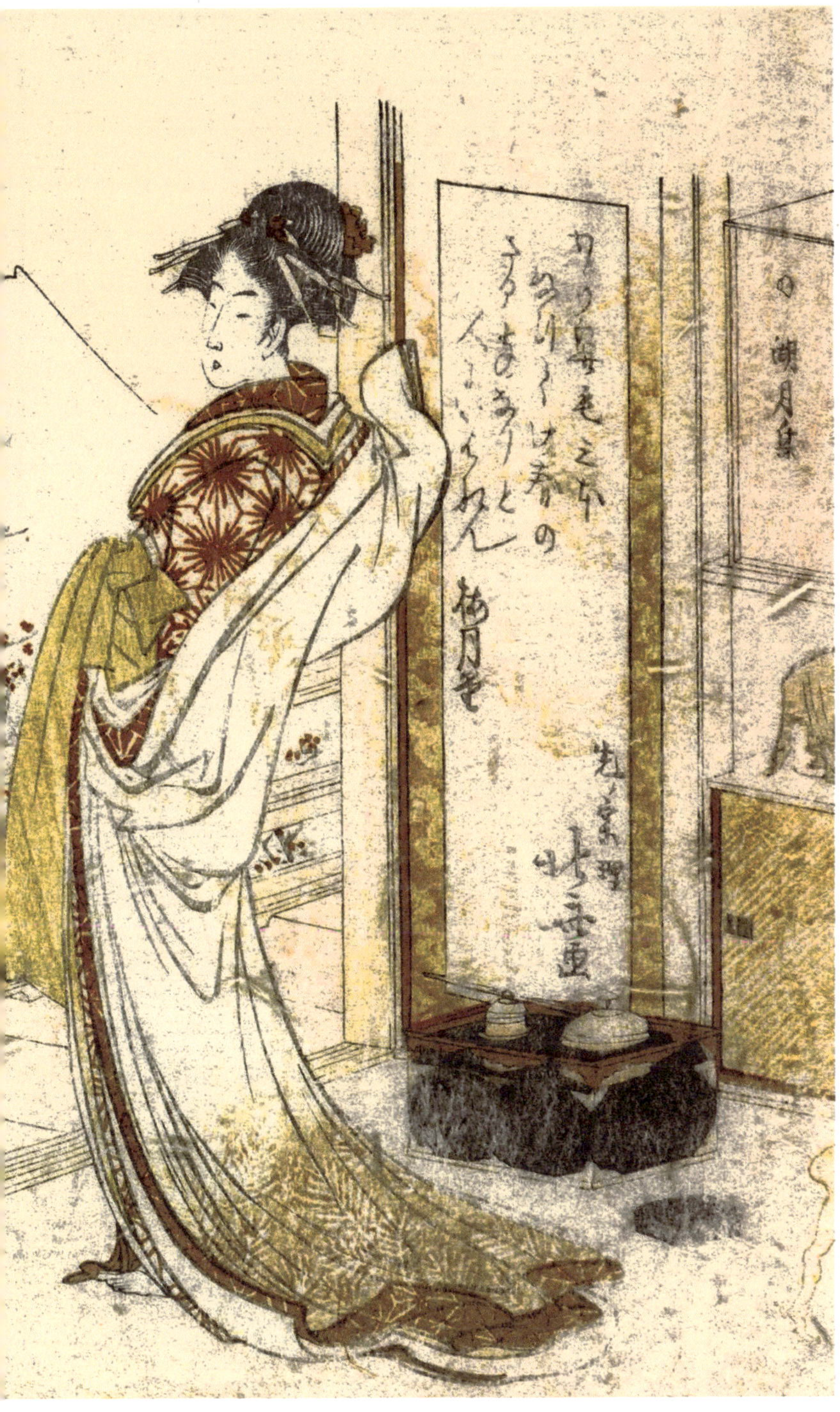

c. 1796–1800. Size unspecified. © The Trustees of the British Museum, 1907,0531,0.561

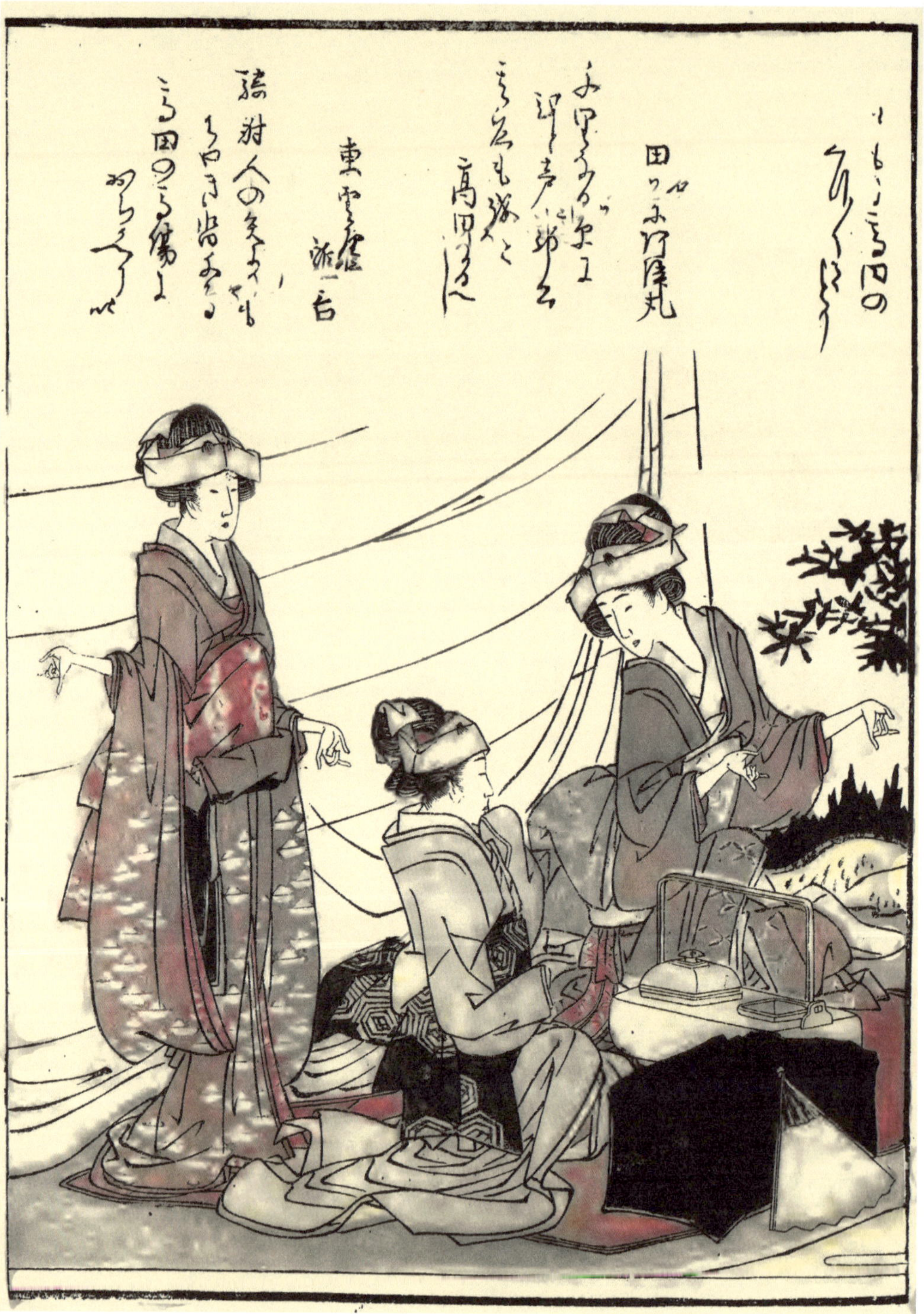

Pages from the book *Mountains upon Mountains*
kyōka ehon, signed Hokusai ga

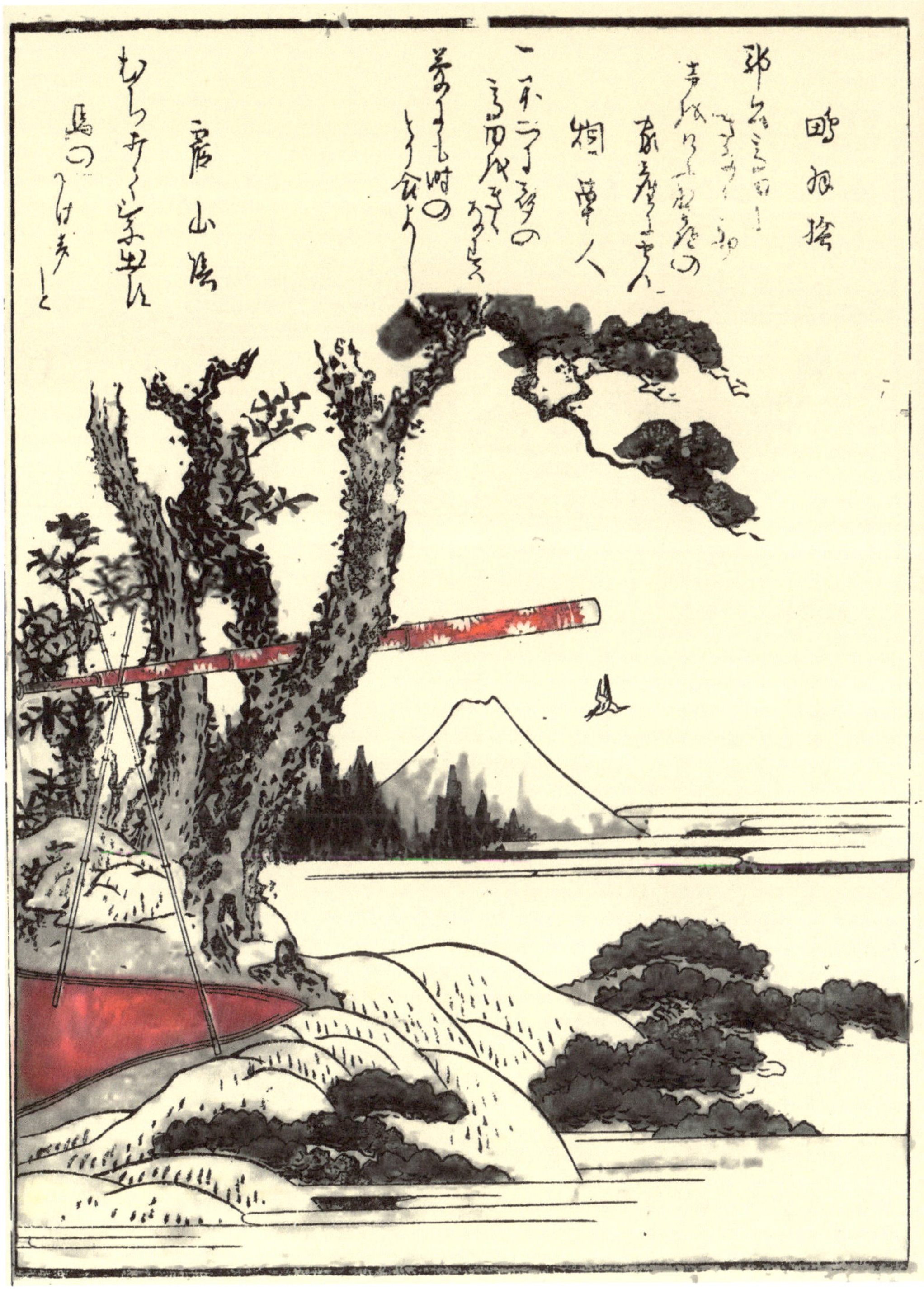

1804. 26.5 × 17.5 cm. Purchase, Mary and James G. Wallach Family Foundation Gift, 2013.
© 2023 The Metropolitan Museum of Art, New York, 2013.714

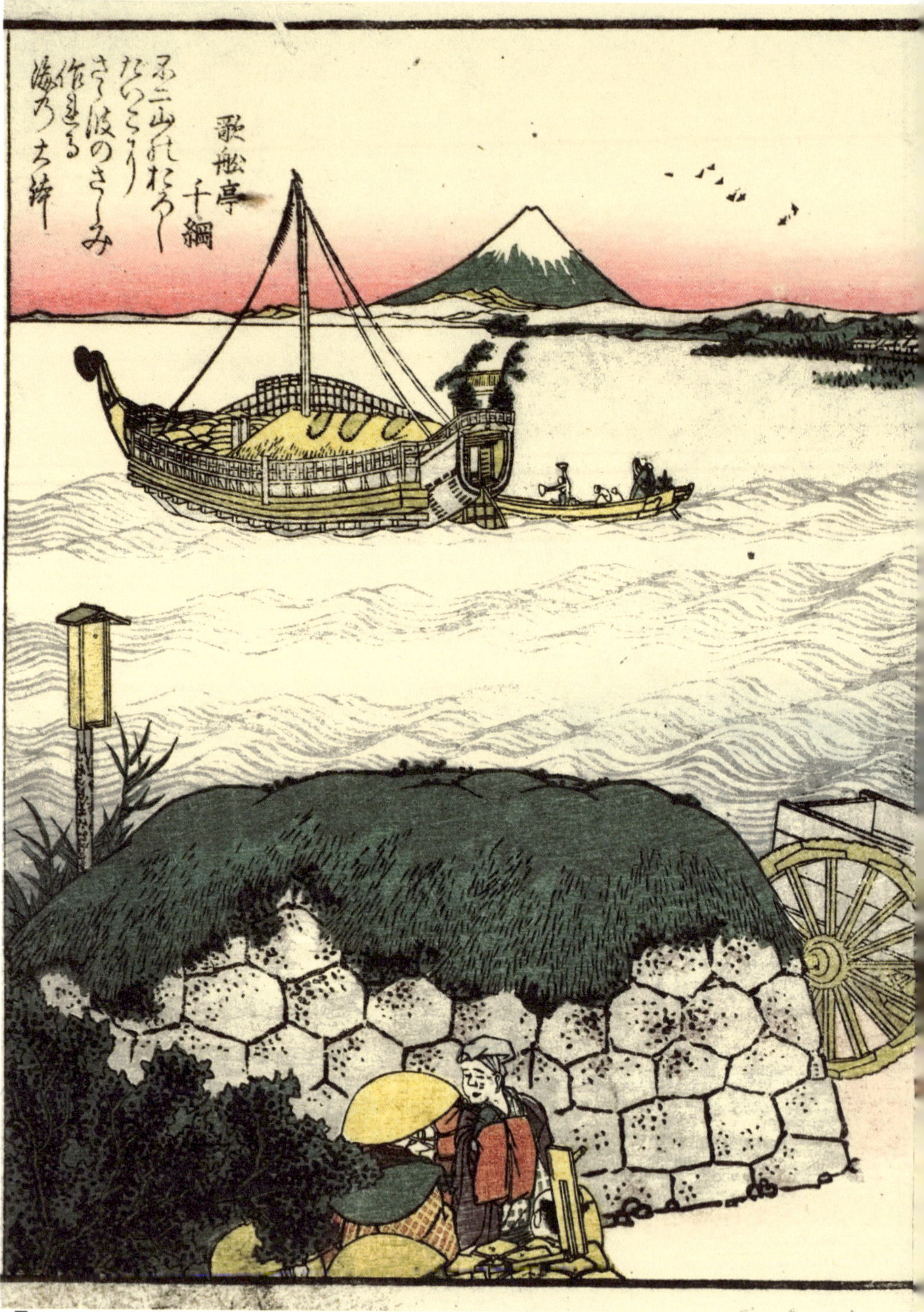

11 Pages from the book *Panoramic Views along the Banks of the Sumida River*
kyōka ehon, unsigned

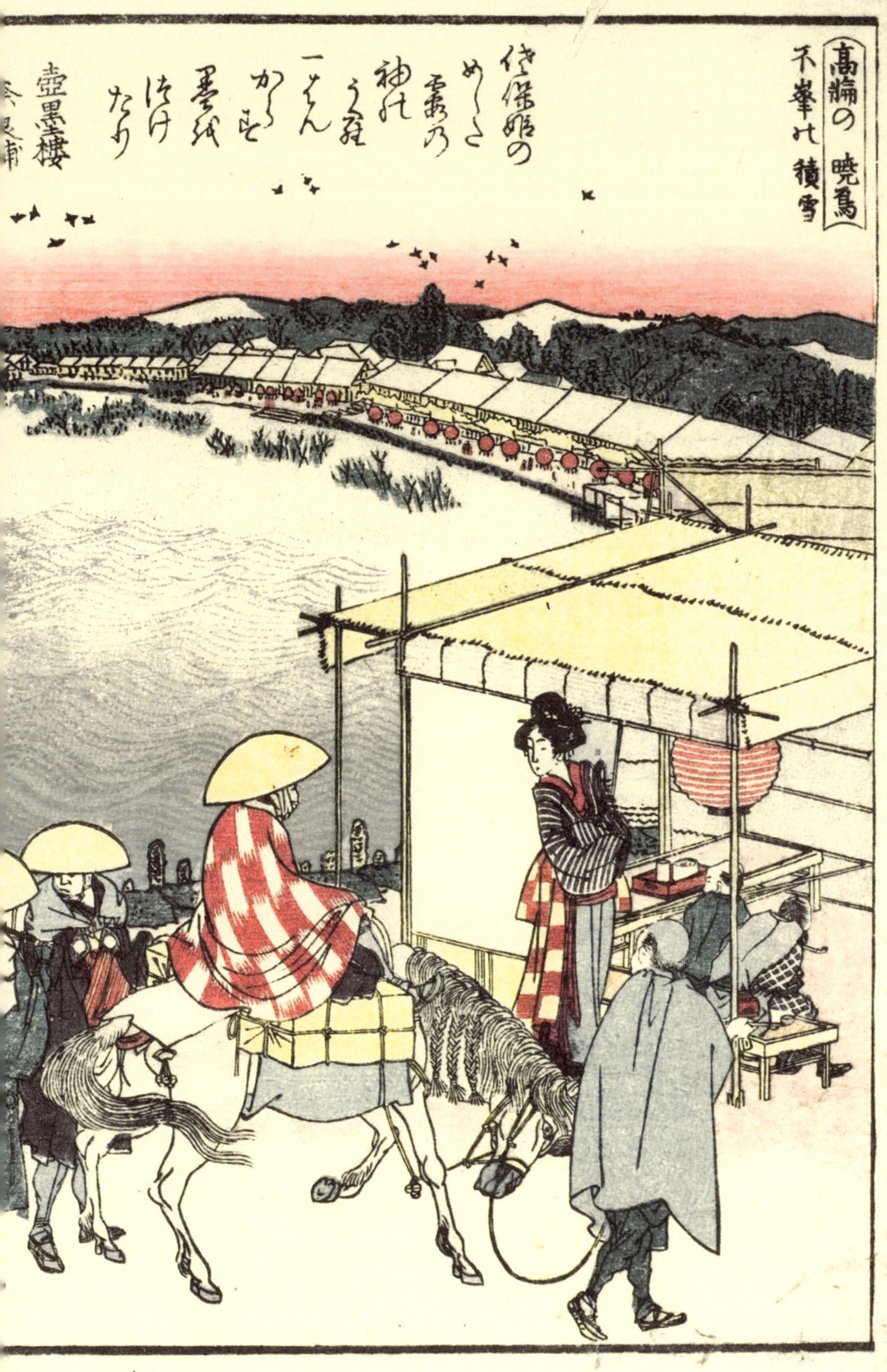

c. 1804–1806. 22 × 15.5 cm. Frederick W. Gookin Collection, The Art Institute of Chicago, 1939.1138

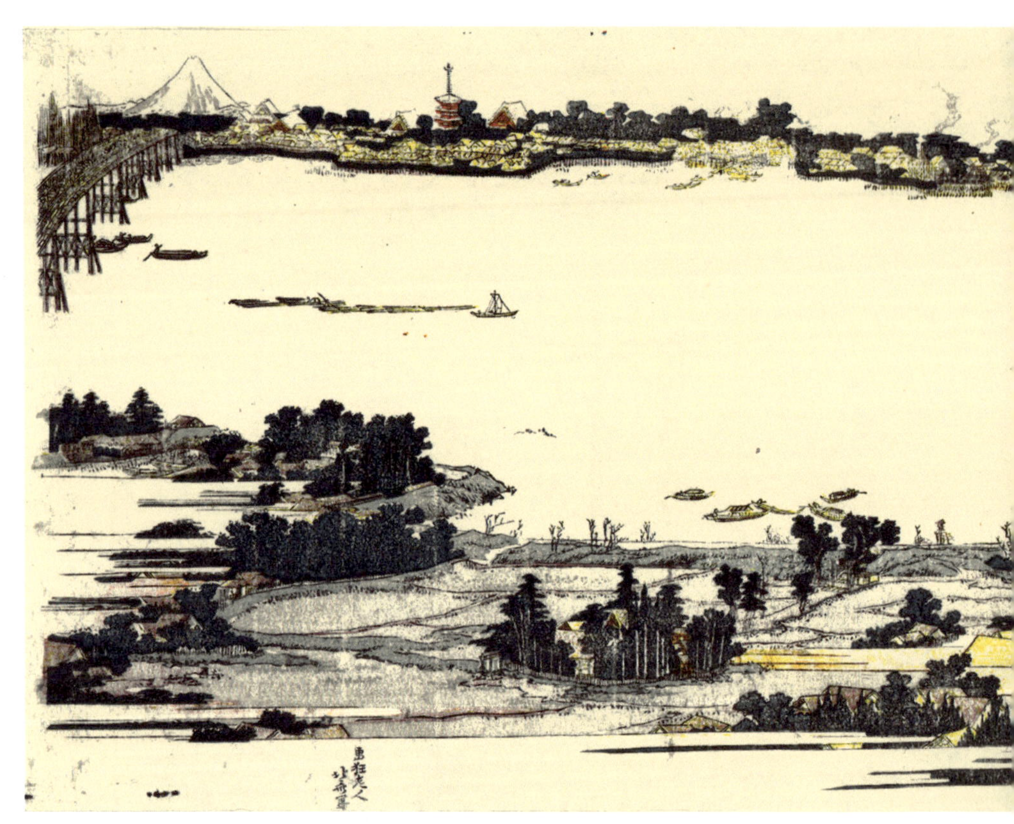

12 *Wide View of Both Banks of the Sumida River, Edo*
surimono (*nagaban yoko-e*), signed Gakyō Rōjin Hokusai utsushi

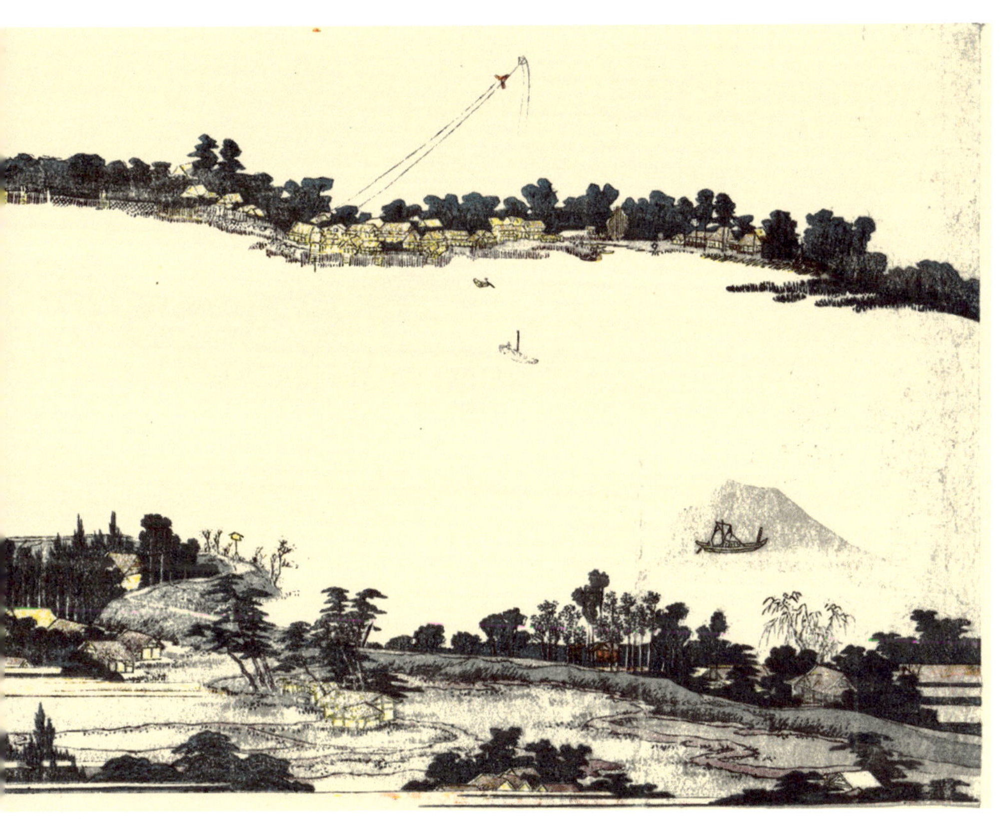

c. 1804. 25.8 × 70.8 cm. Harvard Art Museums/Arthur M. Sackler Museum, Gift of the Friends of Arthur B. Duel, 1933.4.1232

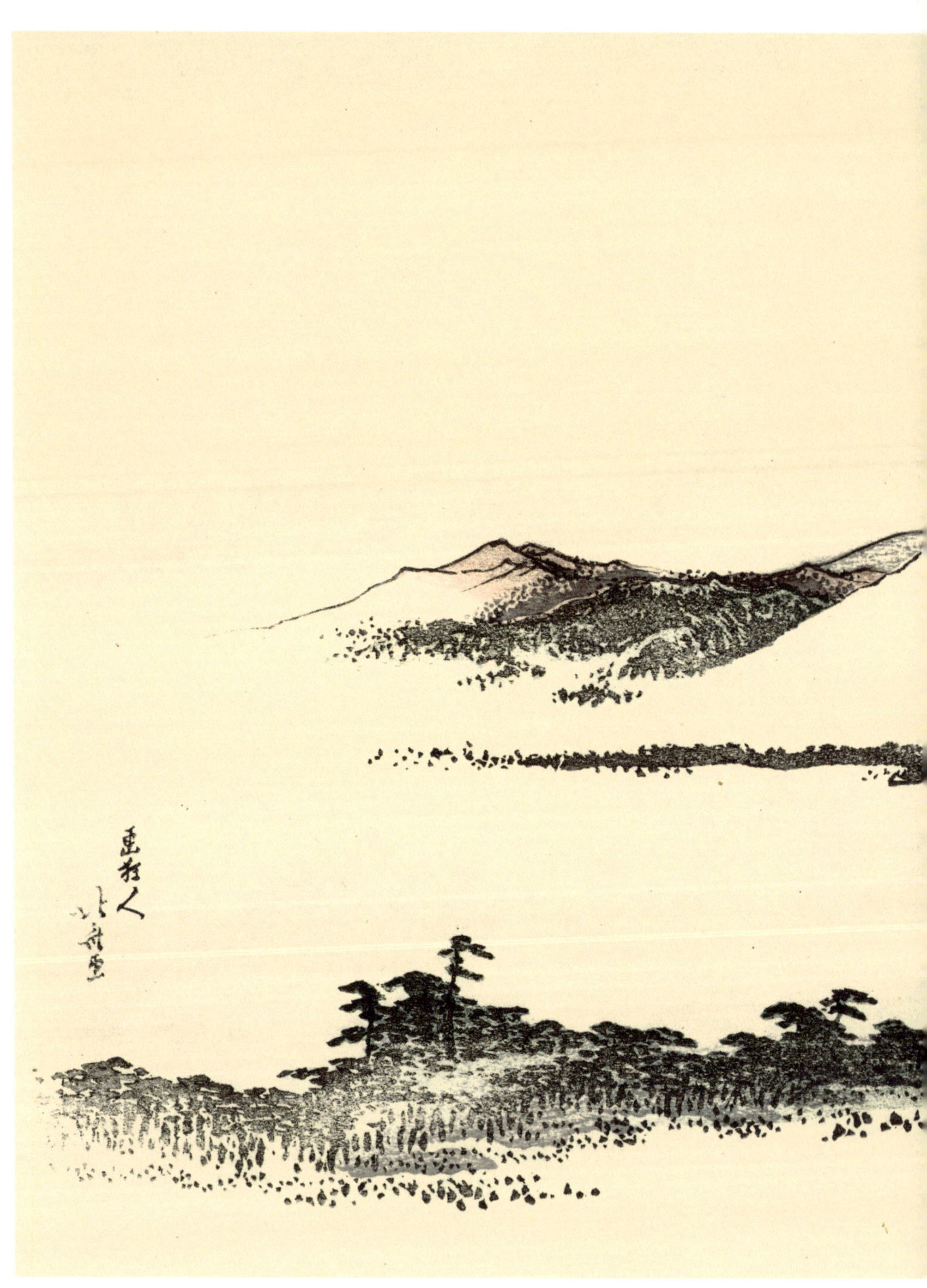

13 *Mount Fuji*
surimono, signed Gakyōjin Hokusai ga

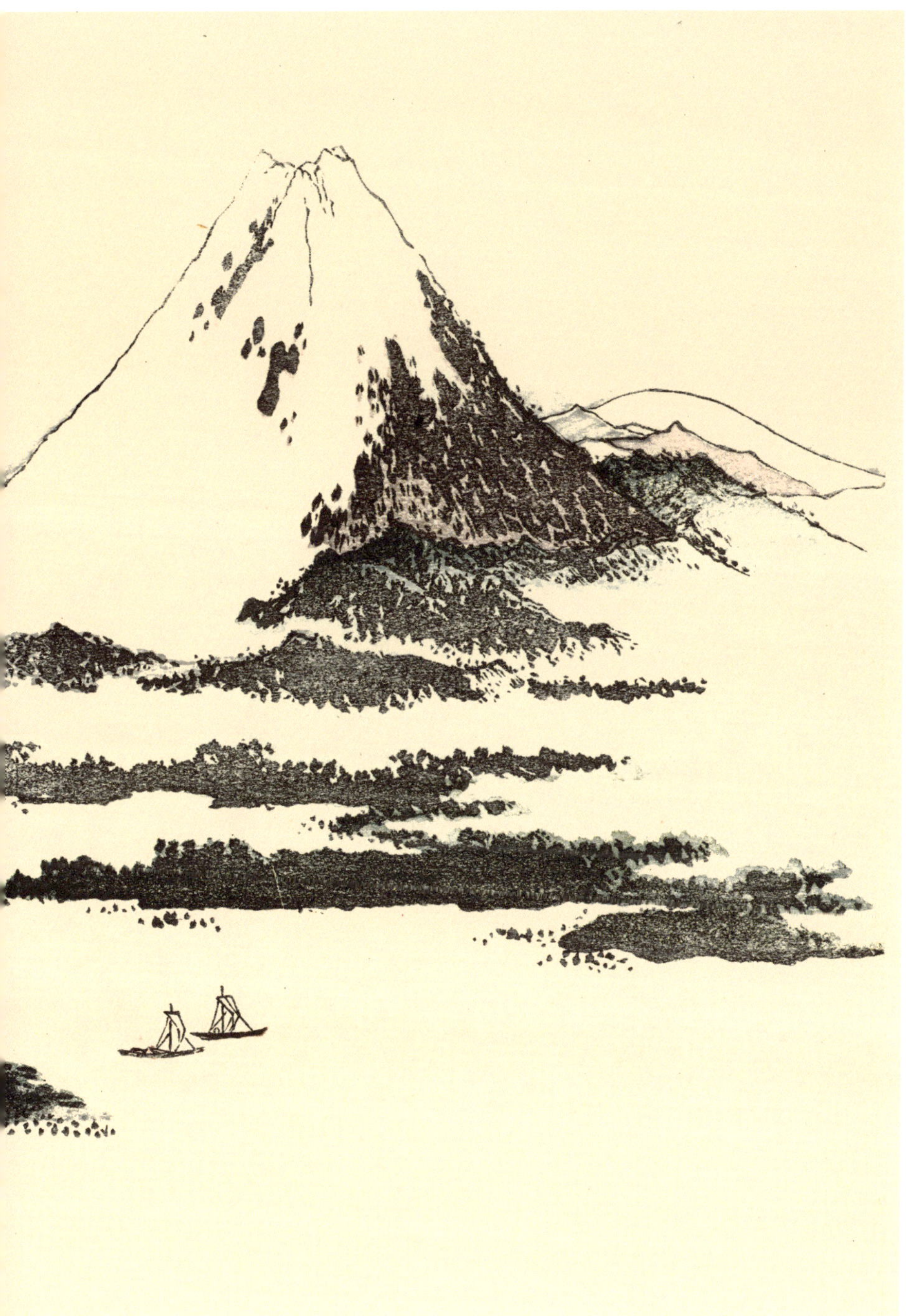

c. 1804–1810. 21.8 × 32 cm. William Sturgis Bigelow Collection. Photograph © 2022 Museum of Fine Arts, Boston, 11.17608

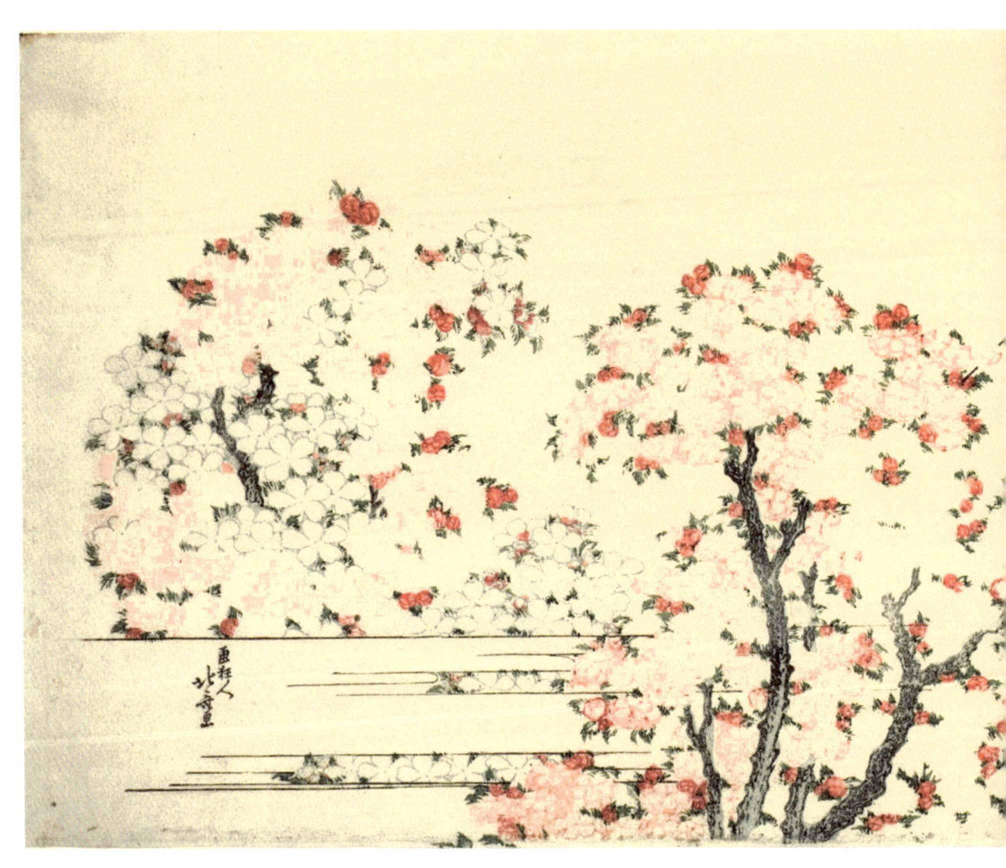

14 *Mount Fuji with Cherry Trees in Bloom*
surimono (nagaban yoko-e), signed Gakyōjin Hokusai ga

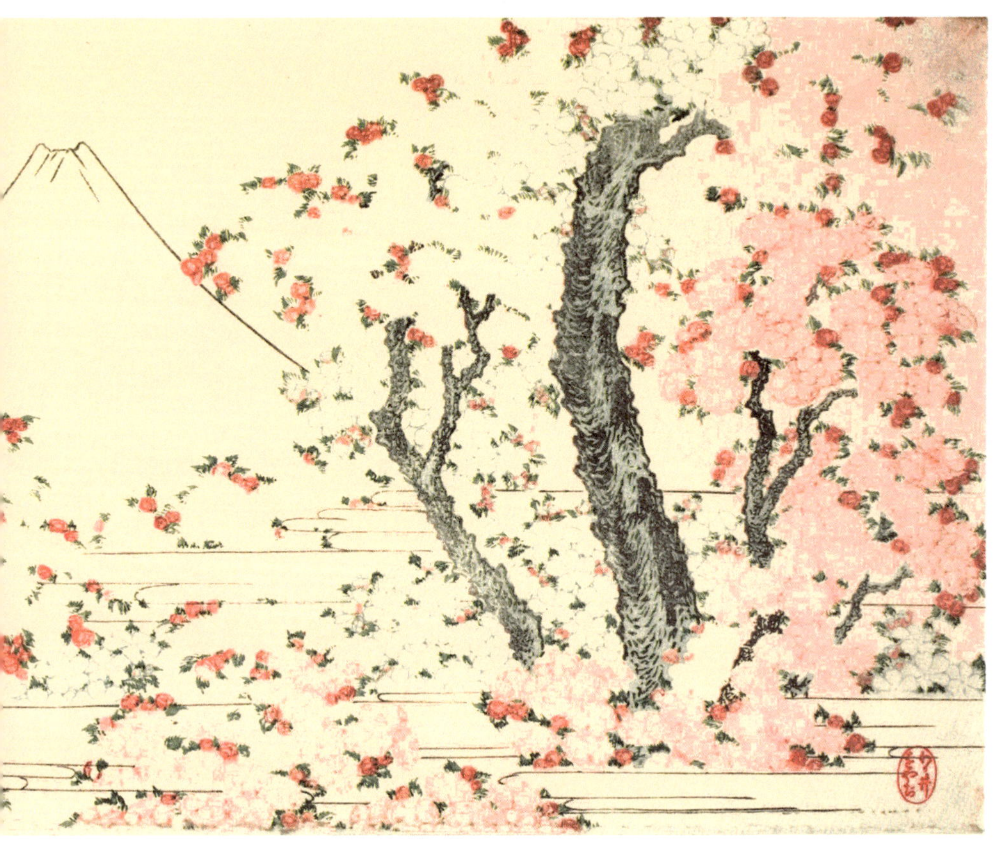

c. 1801 05. 20 1 x 55,4 cm. Gift of Helen C. Gunsaulus, The Art Institute of Chicago, 1954.642

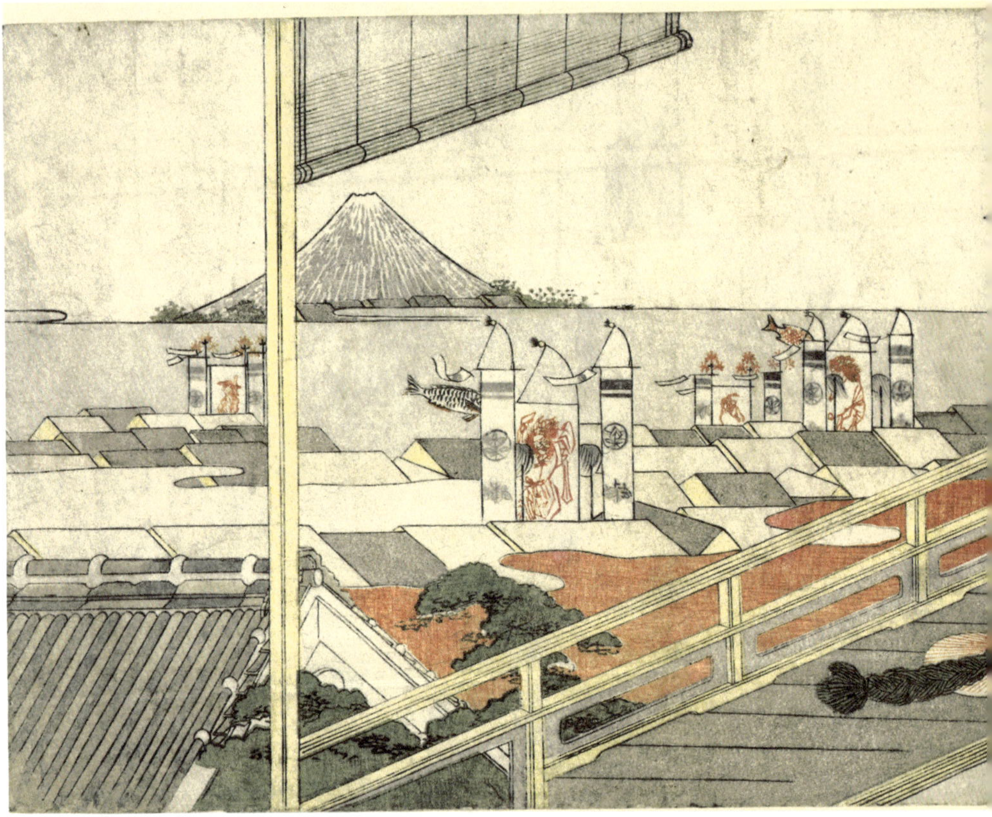

Scene in May: The Boys' Festival
surimono (*nagaban yoko-e*), signed Gakyōjin Hokusai ga

c. 1801–1813. 19.3 × 52.5 cm. Gift of the Friends of Arthur B. Duel, Harvard Art Museums/Arthur M. Sackler Museum, 1933.4.2670

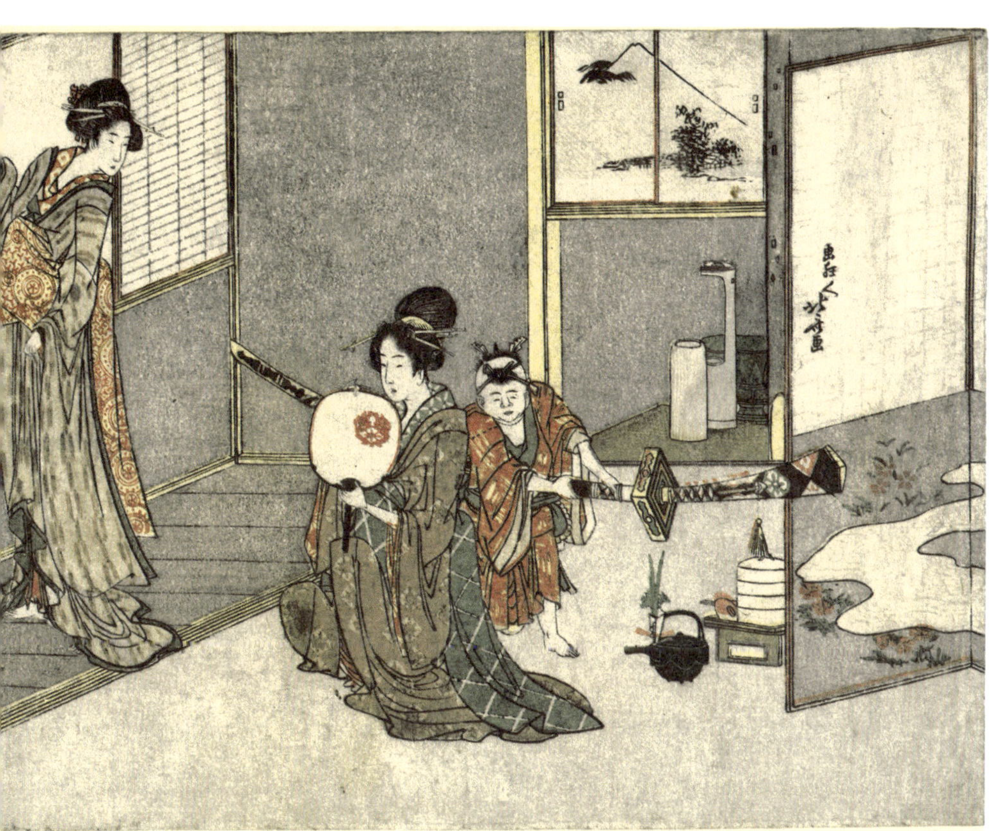

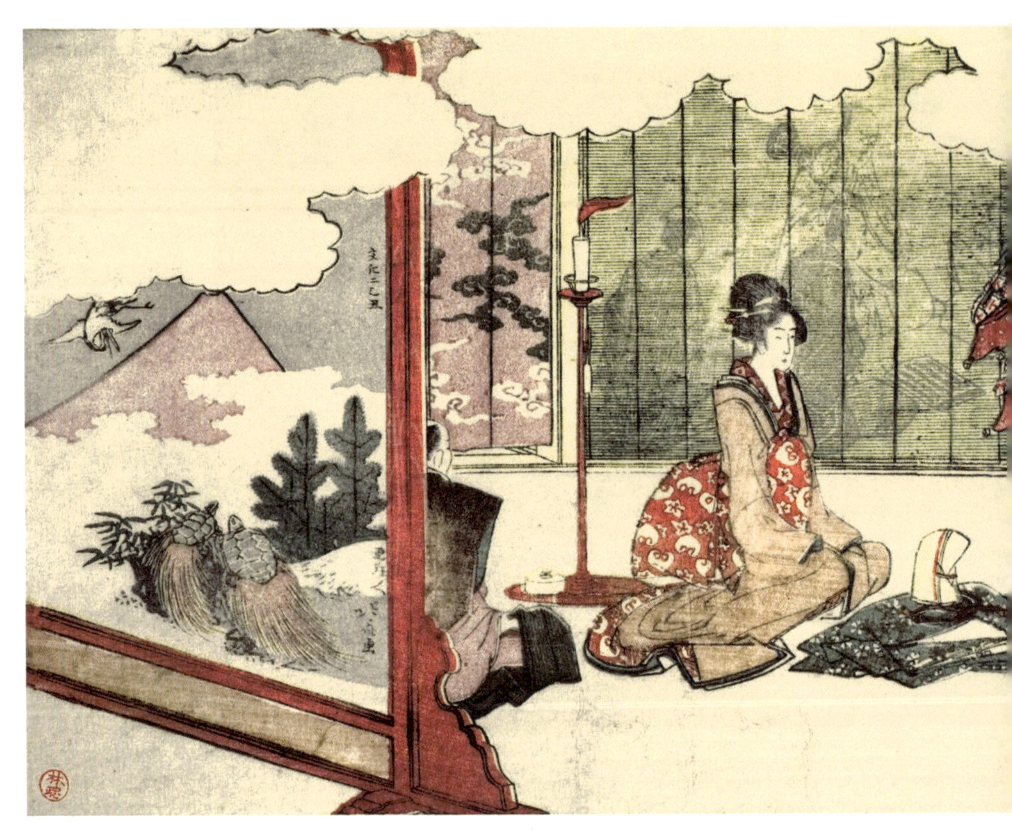

Untitled
surimono (*nagaban yoko-e*), signed Gakyōjin Hokusai ga

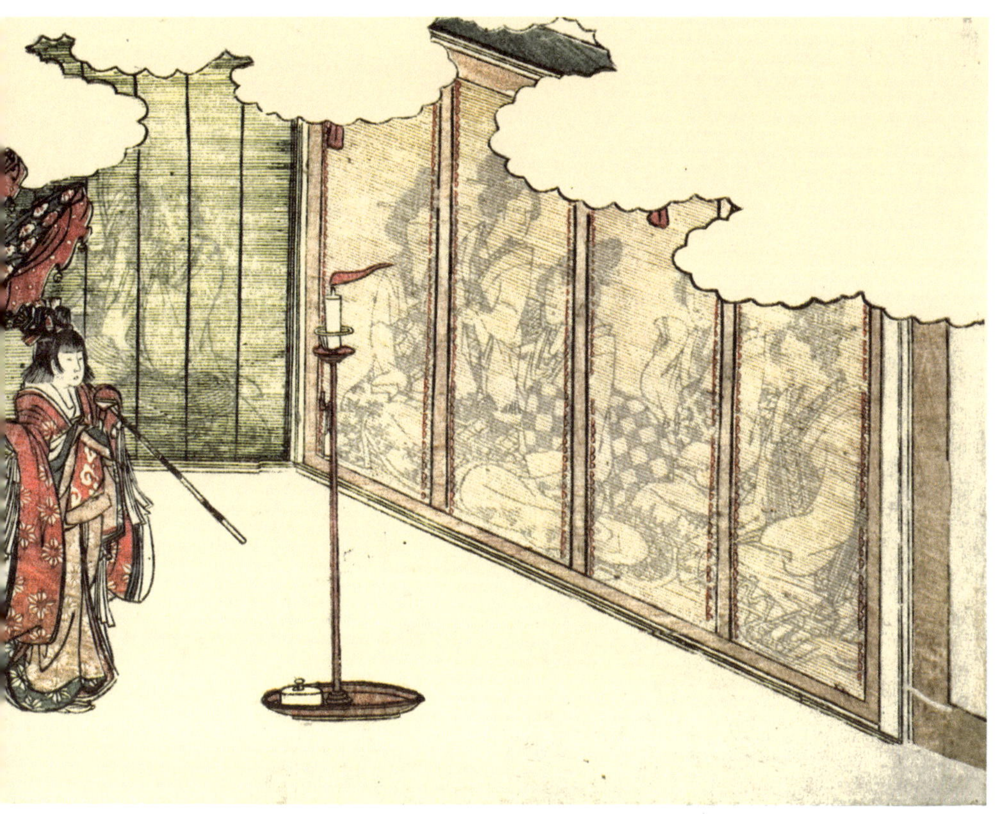

1805. 19.4 × 52.6 cm. Gift of Helen C. Gunsaulus, The Art Institute of Chicago, 1954.644

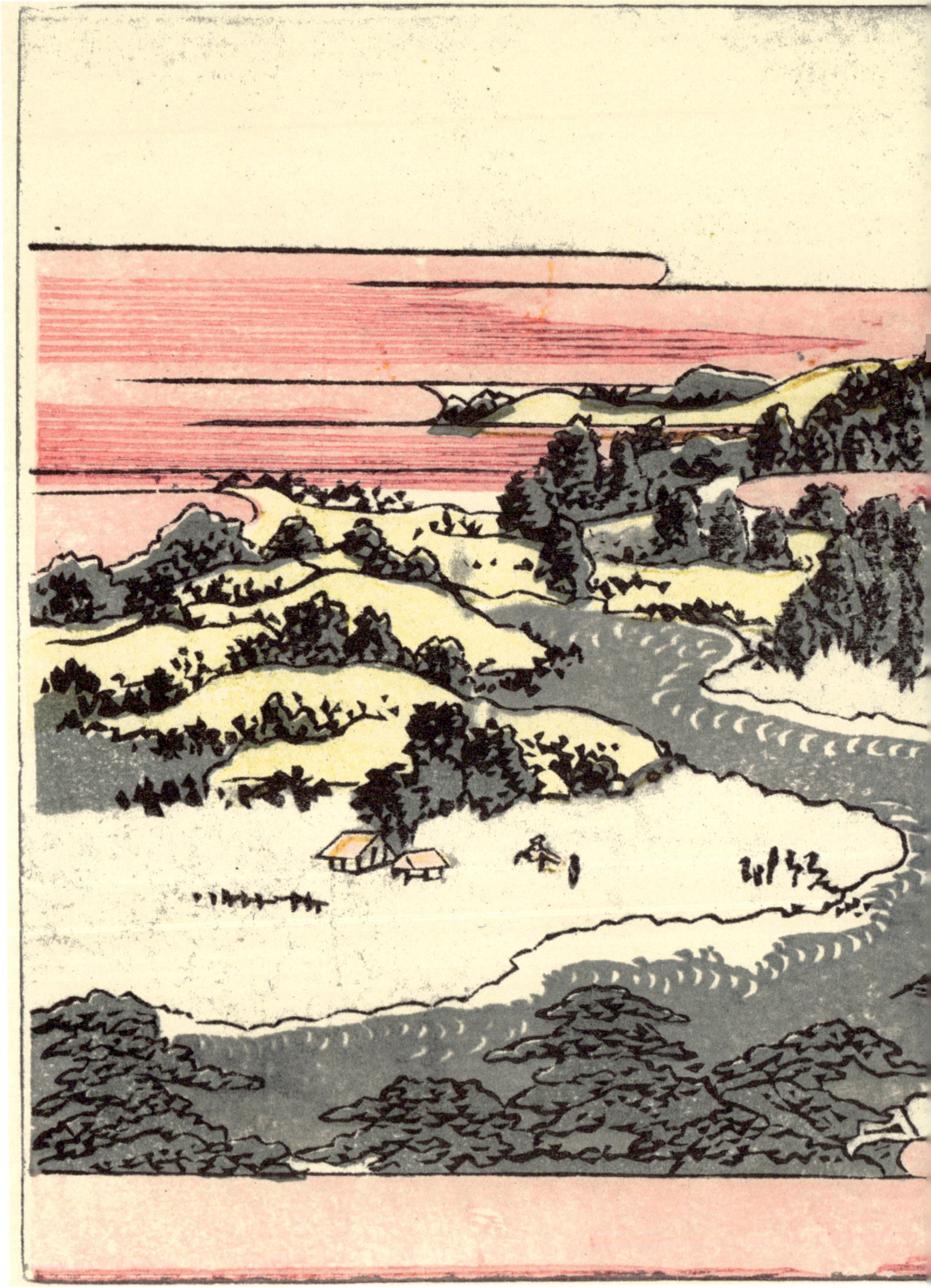

Yoshiwara, no. 15 from the series *Fifty-Three Stations on the Tōkaidō Road*
koban nishiki-e, unsigned

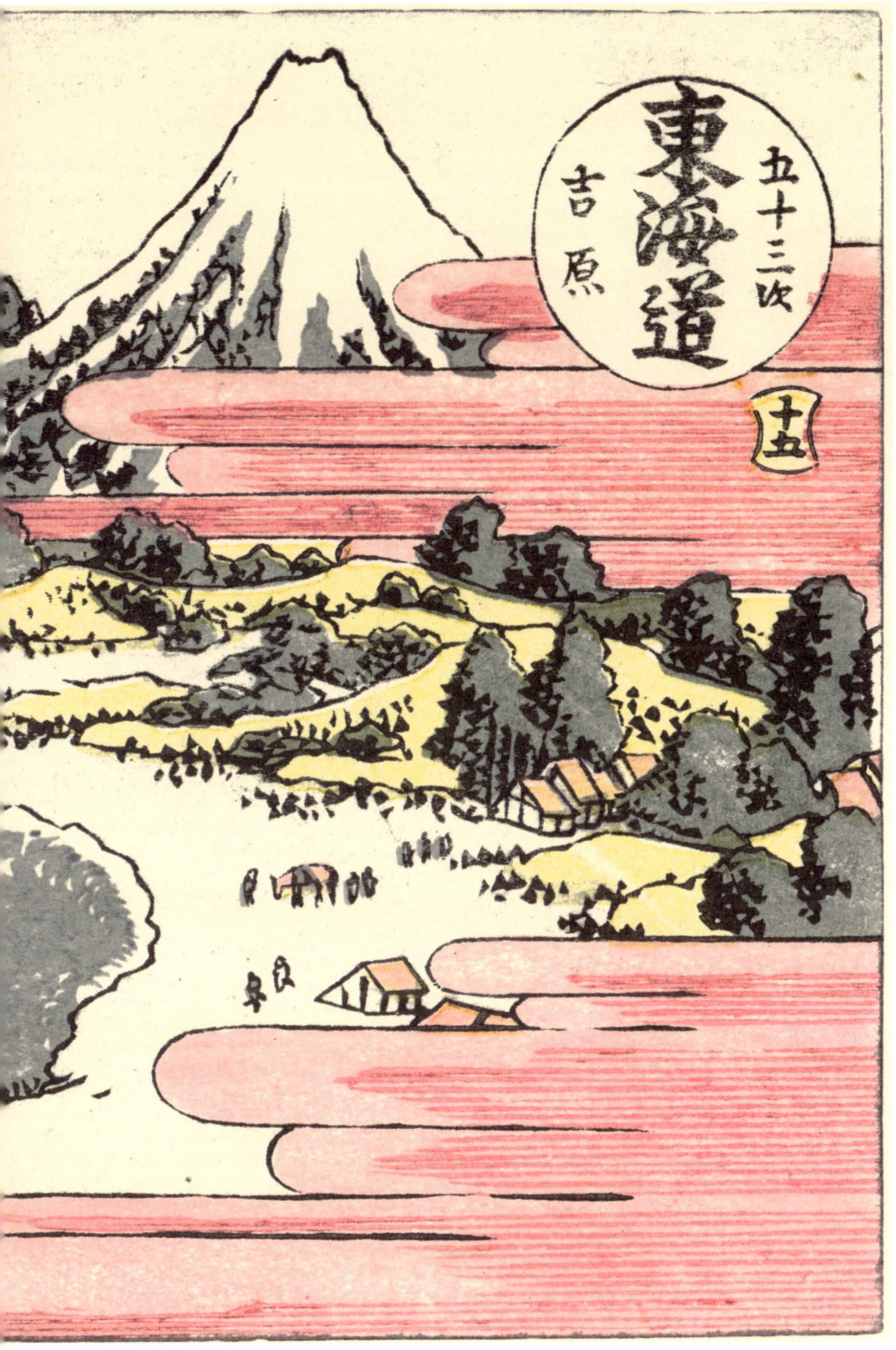

c. 1802. 11.6 × 17.4 cm. William Sturgis Bigelow Collection. Photograph © 2022 Museum of Fine Arts, Boston, 11.20331

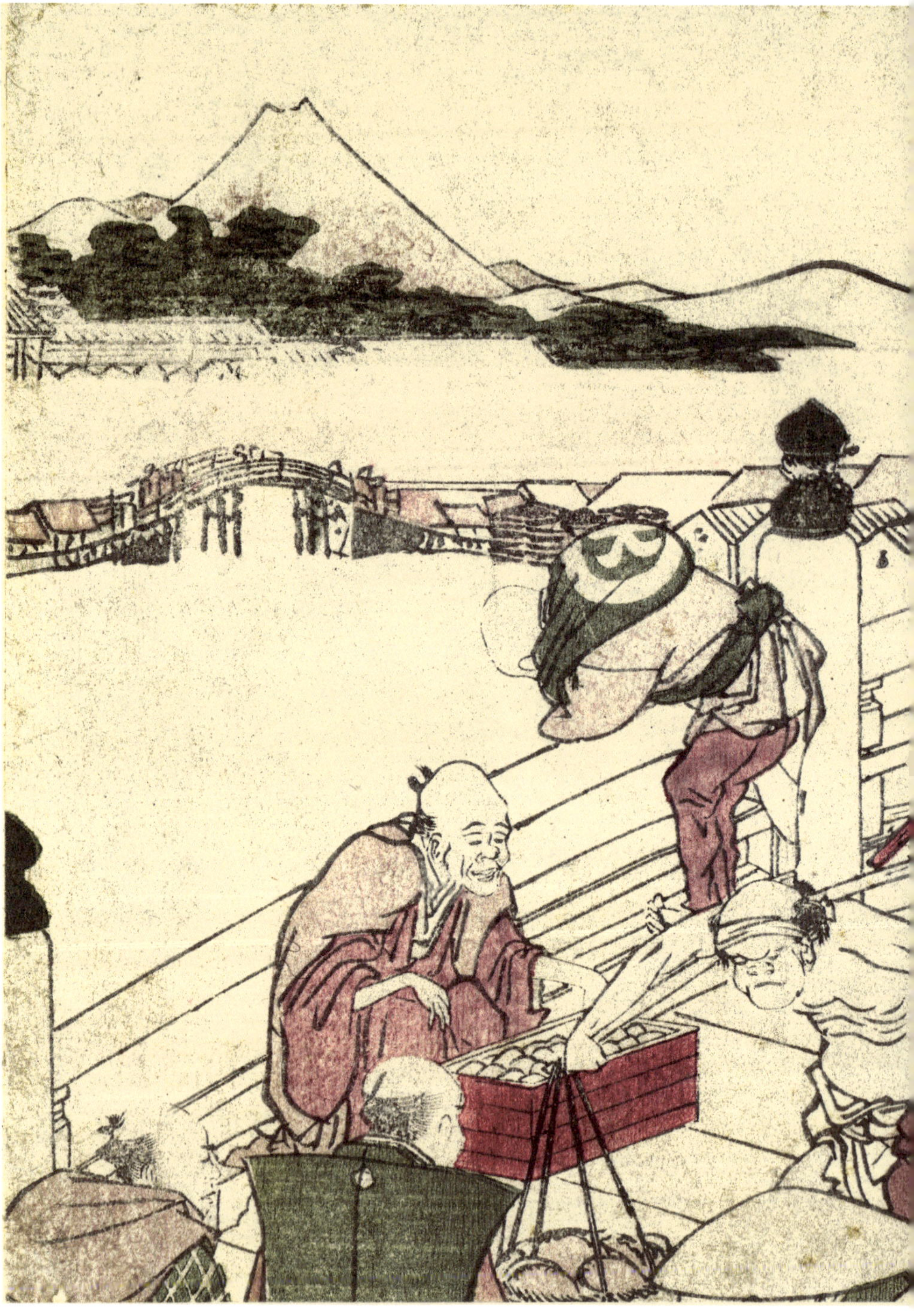

Nihonbashi, from the series *Fifty-Three Stations on the Tōkaidō Road*
koban nishiki-e, unsigned

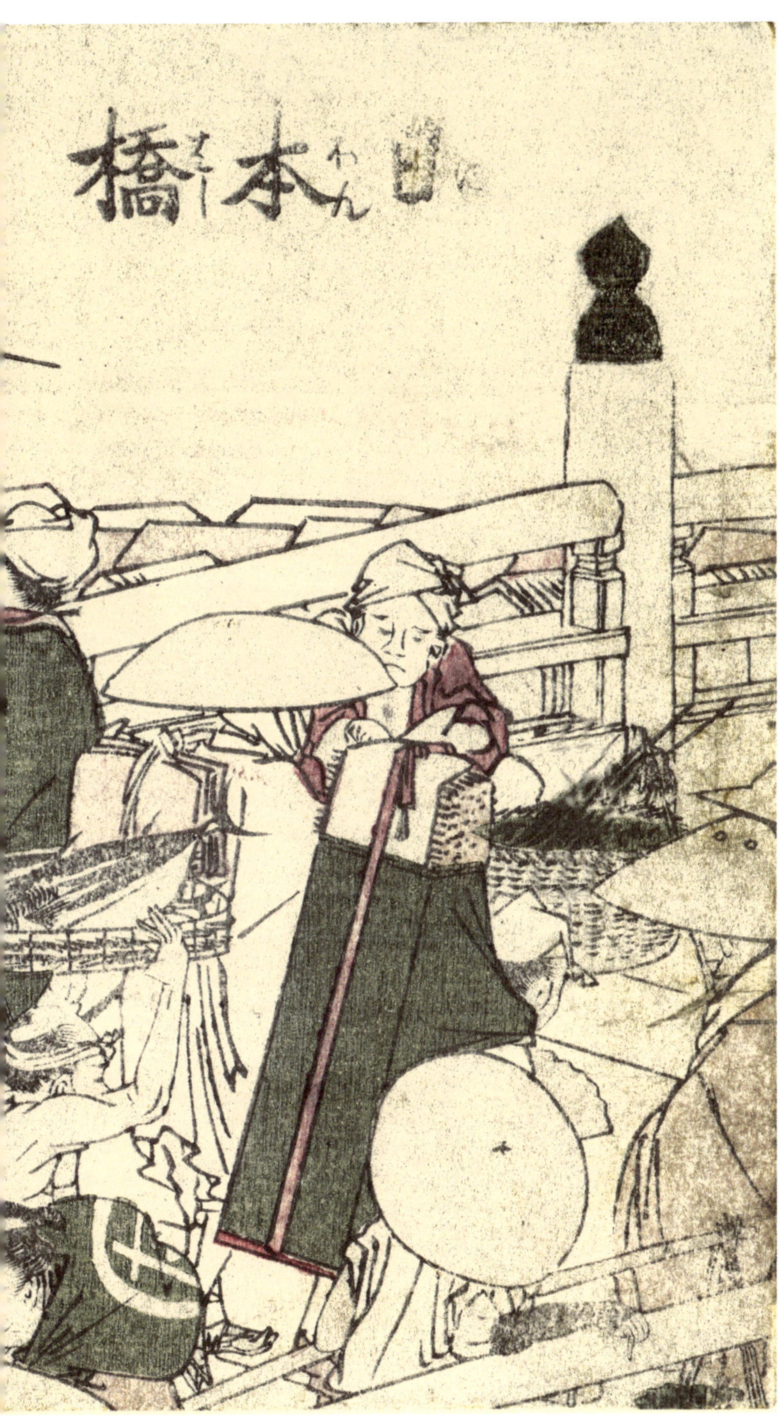

c. 1802. 12.4 × 17.1 cm. Gift of Mrs. Jared K. Morse in memory of Charles J. Morse.
Photograph © 2022 Museum of Fine Arts, Boston, RES.53.261

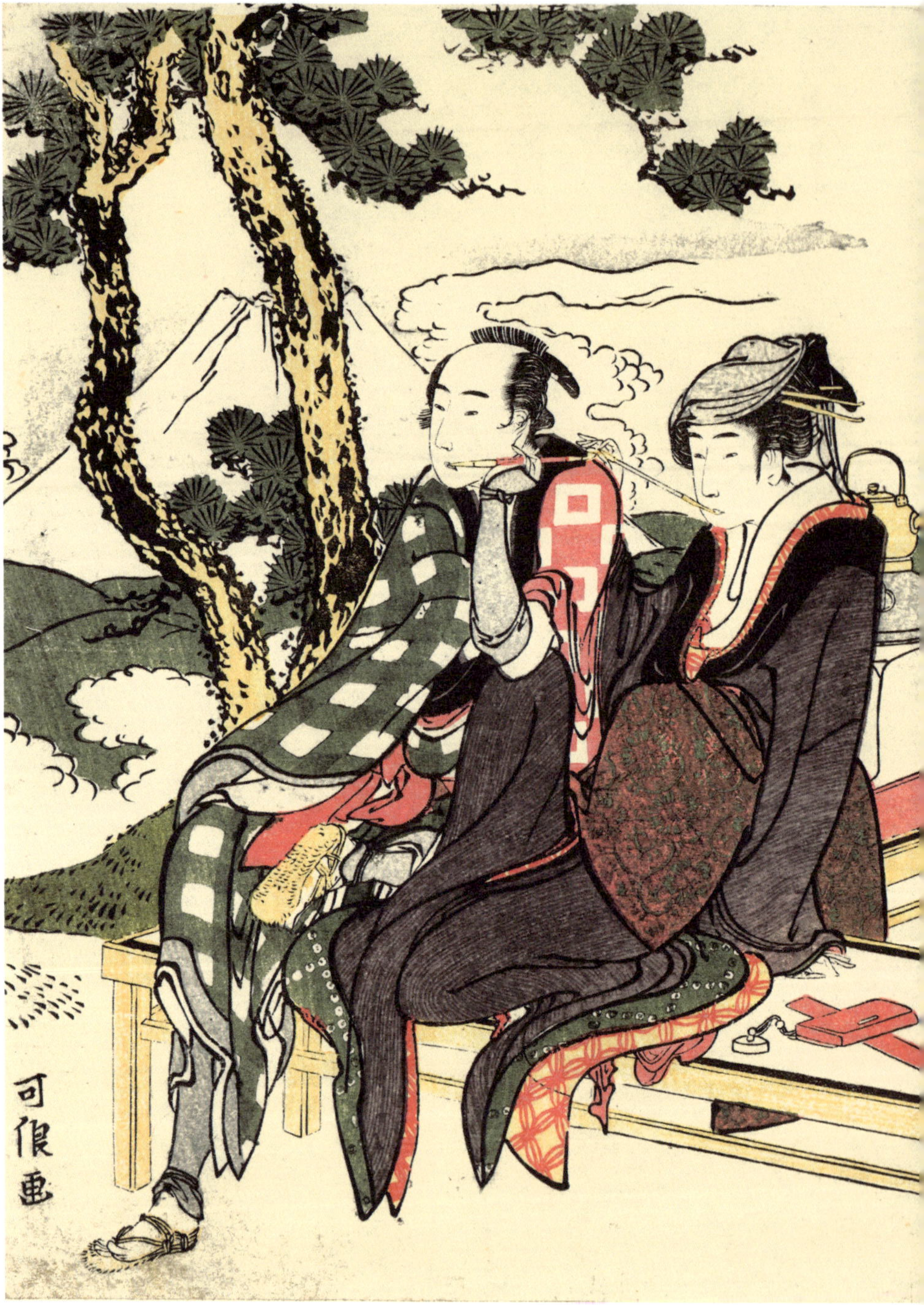

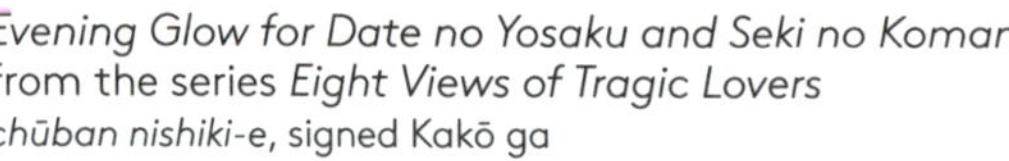

Evening Glow for Date no Yosaku and Seki no Koman
from the series *Eight Views of Tragic Lovers*
chūban nishiki-e, signed Kakō ga

20

c. 1801–04. 23.1 × 17.5 cm. Clarence Buckingham Collection, The Art Institute of Chicago, 1925.3201

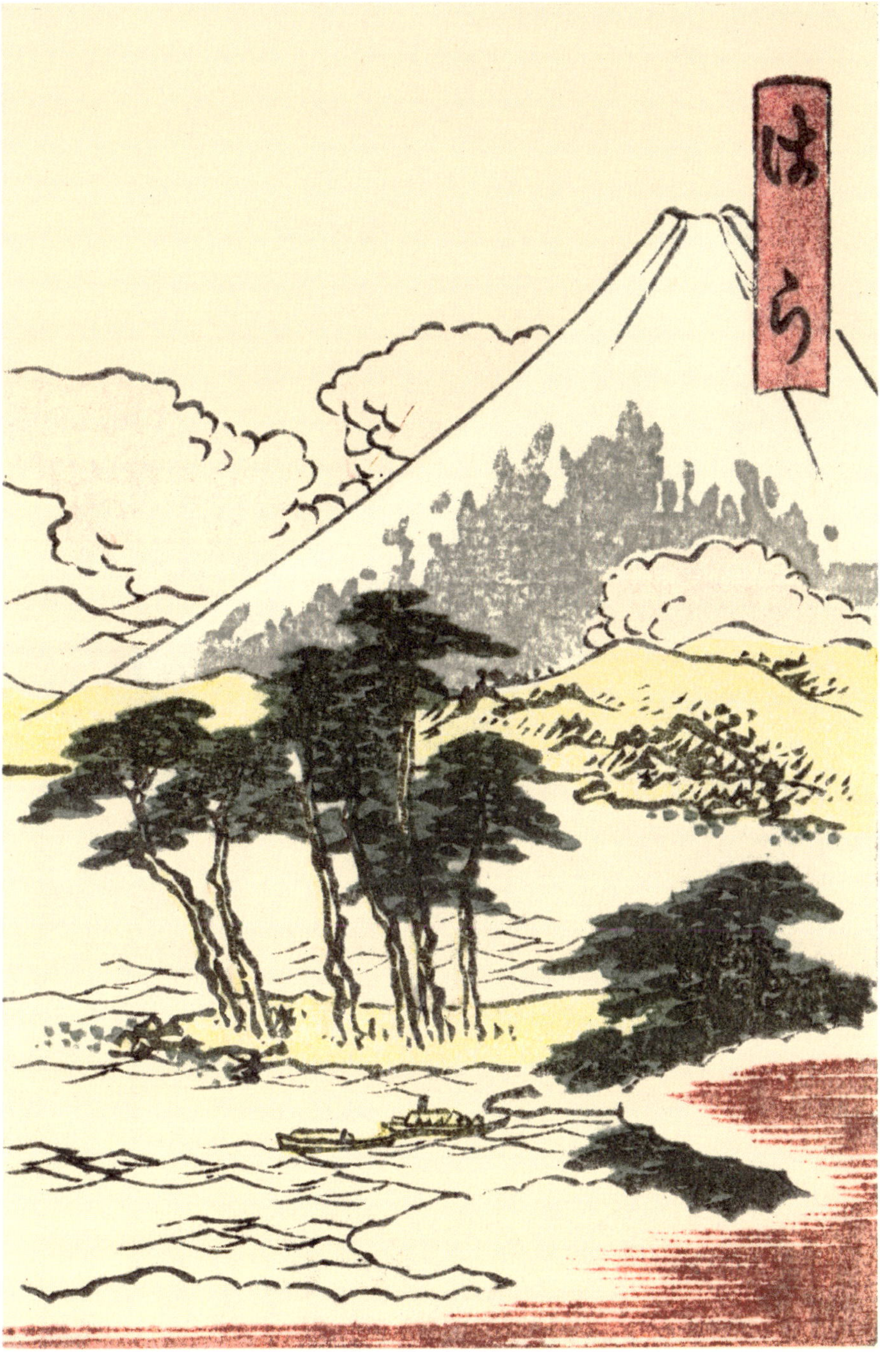

Hara, from the series *Fifty-Three Stations on the Tōkaidō Road, Printed in Colour*   *koban nishiki-e,* unsigned

21 1804. 9.2 × 6.2 cm. William S. and John T. Spaulding Collection; Photograph © 2022 Museum of Fine Arts, Boston, 21.10354

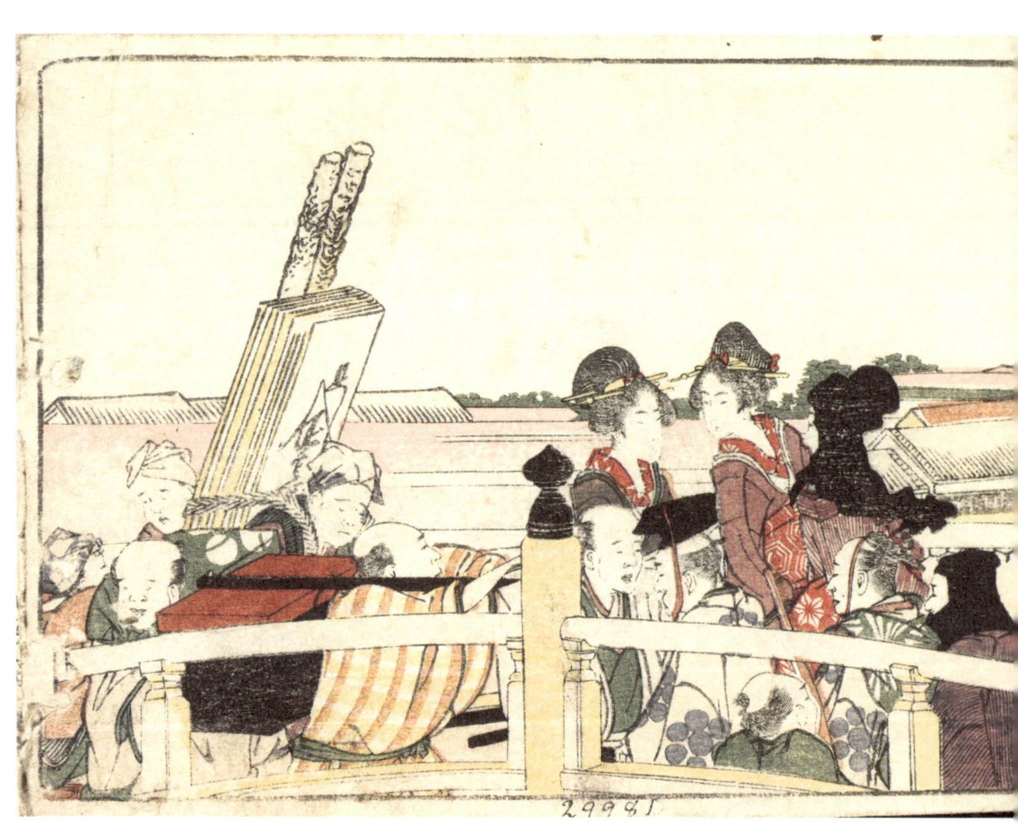

22 *Nihonbashi*, from the series *Fifty-Three Stations on the Tōkaidō Road (Shunkyō)* surimono (nagaban yoko-e), signed Gakyōjin Hokusai ga

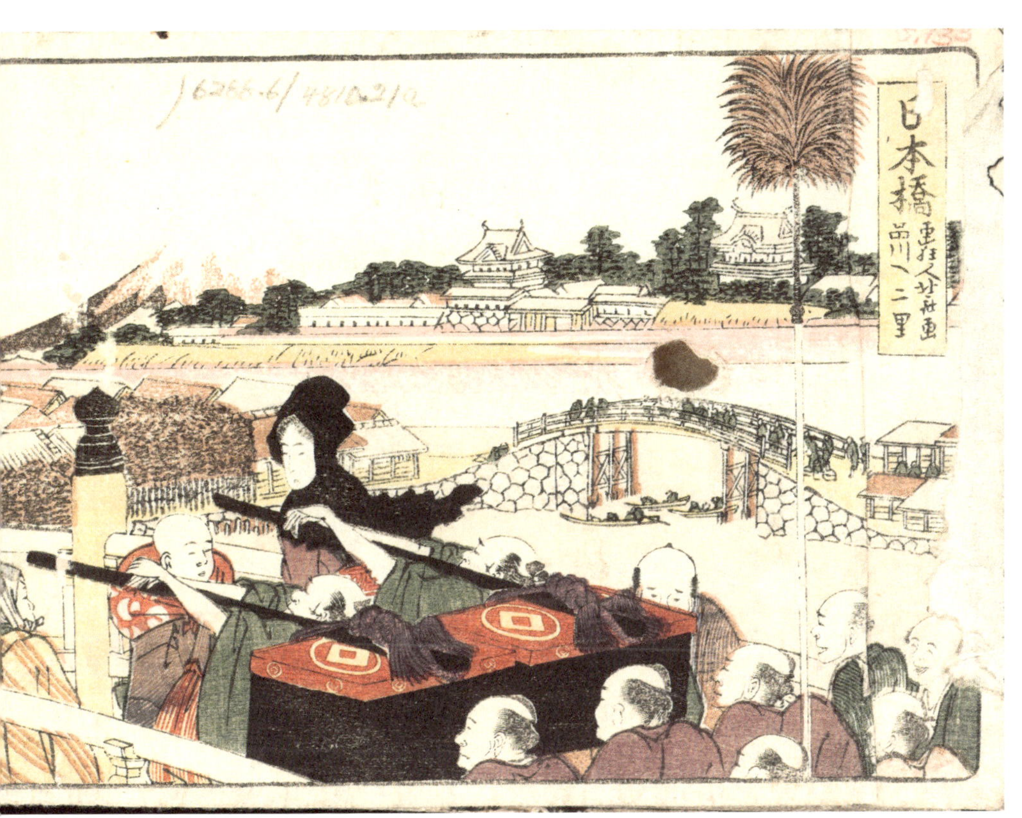

1804. 14.8 × 36.8 cm. William S. and John T. Spaulding Collection. Photograph © 2022 Museum of Fine Arts, Boston, 21.10276

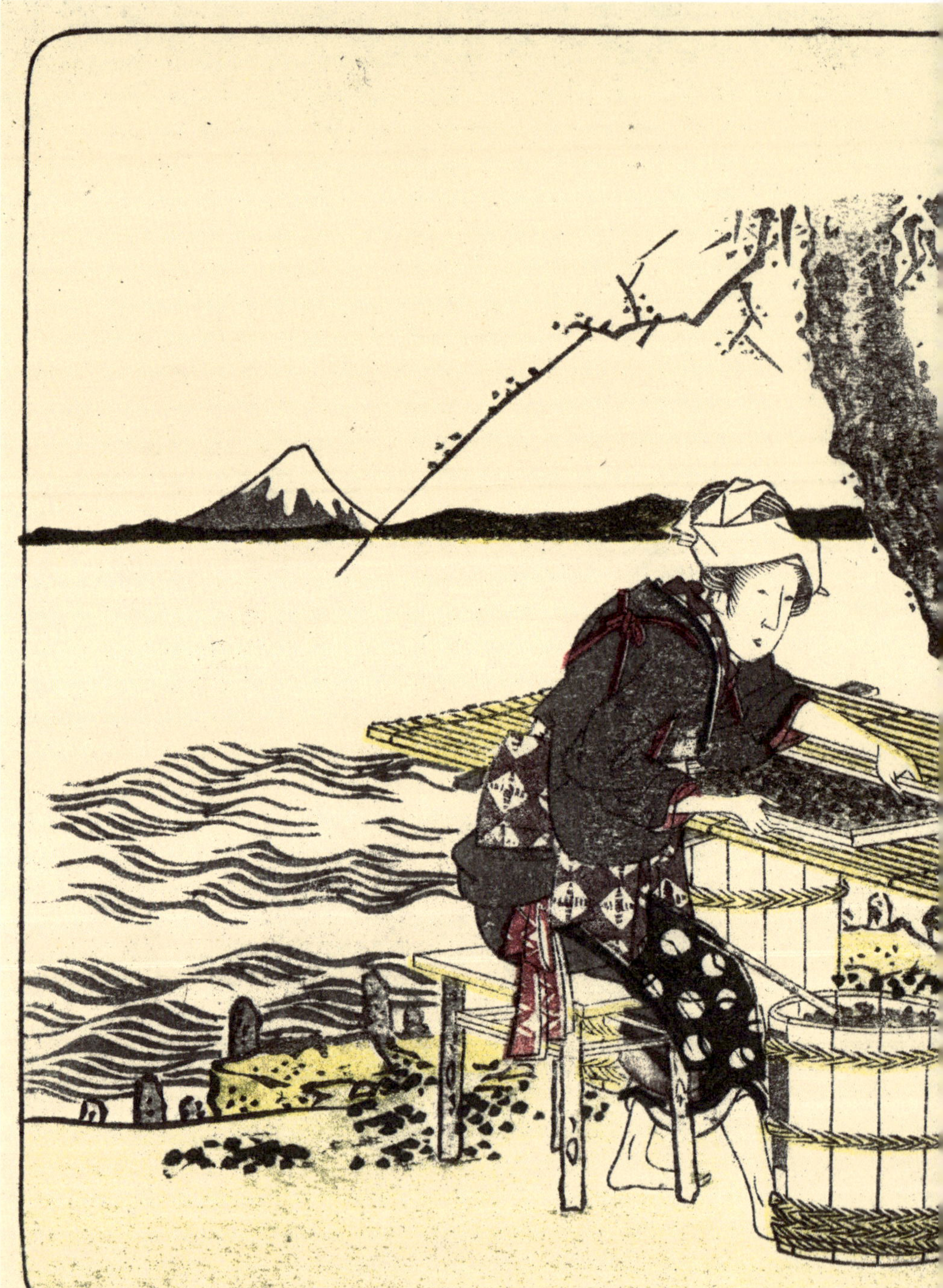

23 *Shinagawa*, from the series *Fifty-Three Stations on the Tōkaidō Road (Shunkyō)* surimono, signed Gakyōjin Hokusai ga

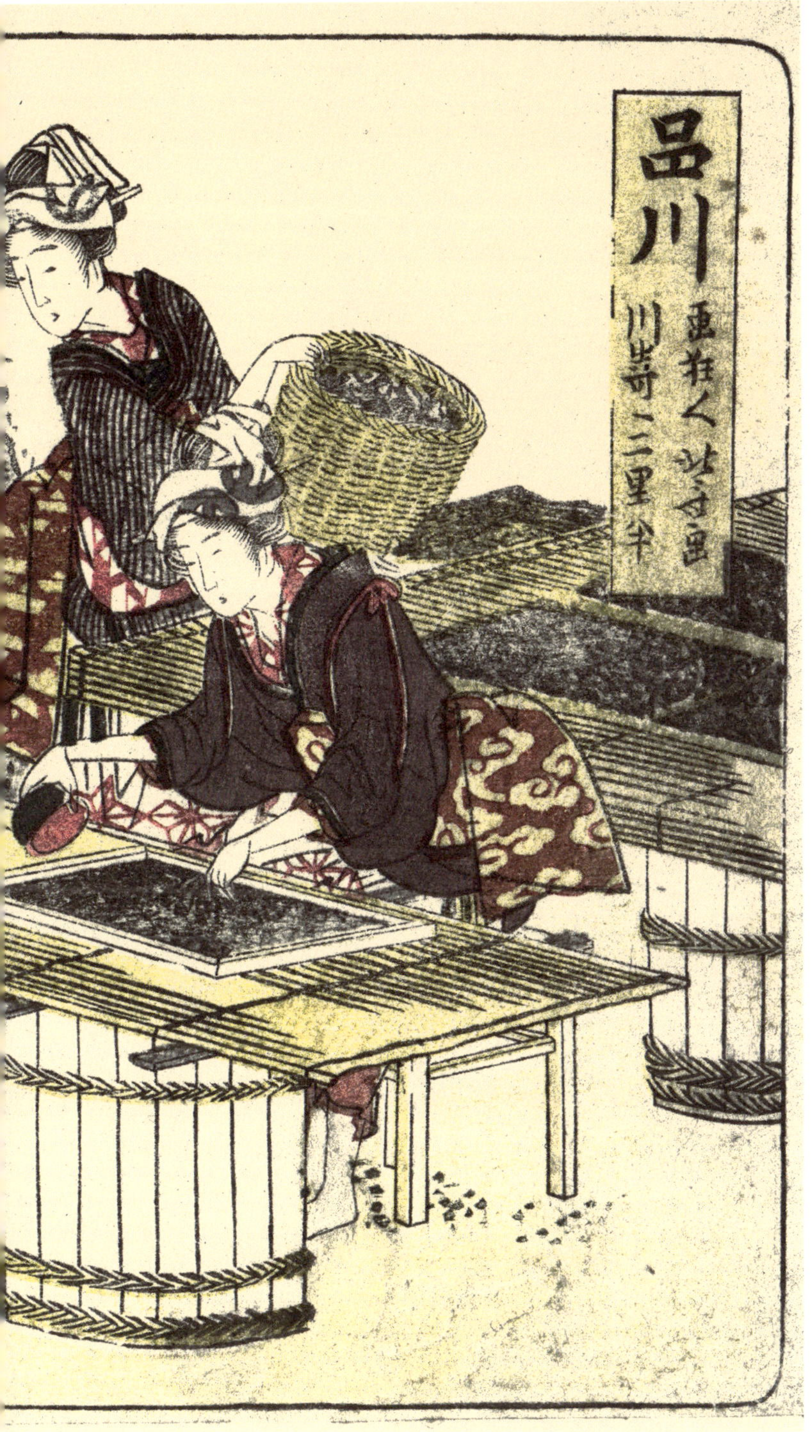

1804. 12.5 × 17.8 cm. William S. and John T. Spaulding Collection. Photograph © 2022 Museum of Fine Arts, Boston, 21.10291

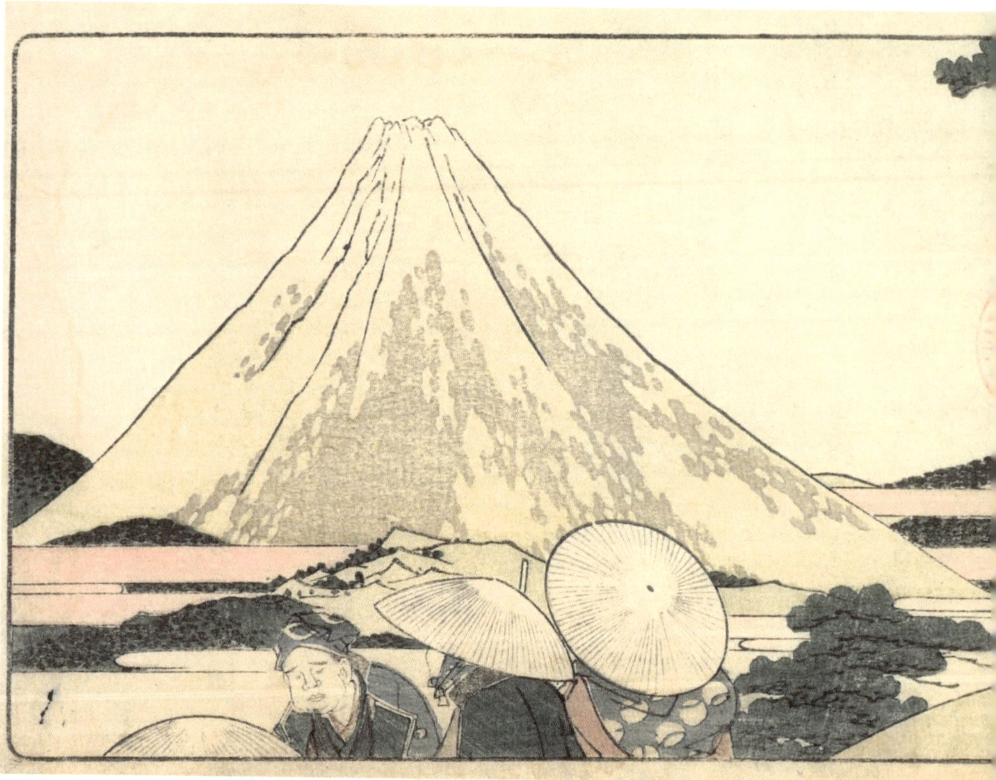

Hara, from the series *Fifty-Three Stations on the Tōkaidō Road (Shunkyō)*
surimono (*nagaban yoko-e*), signed Gakyōjin Hokusai ga

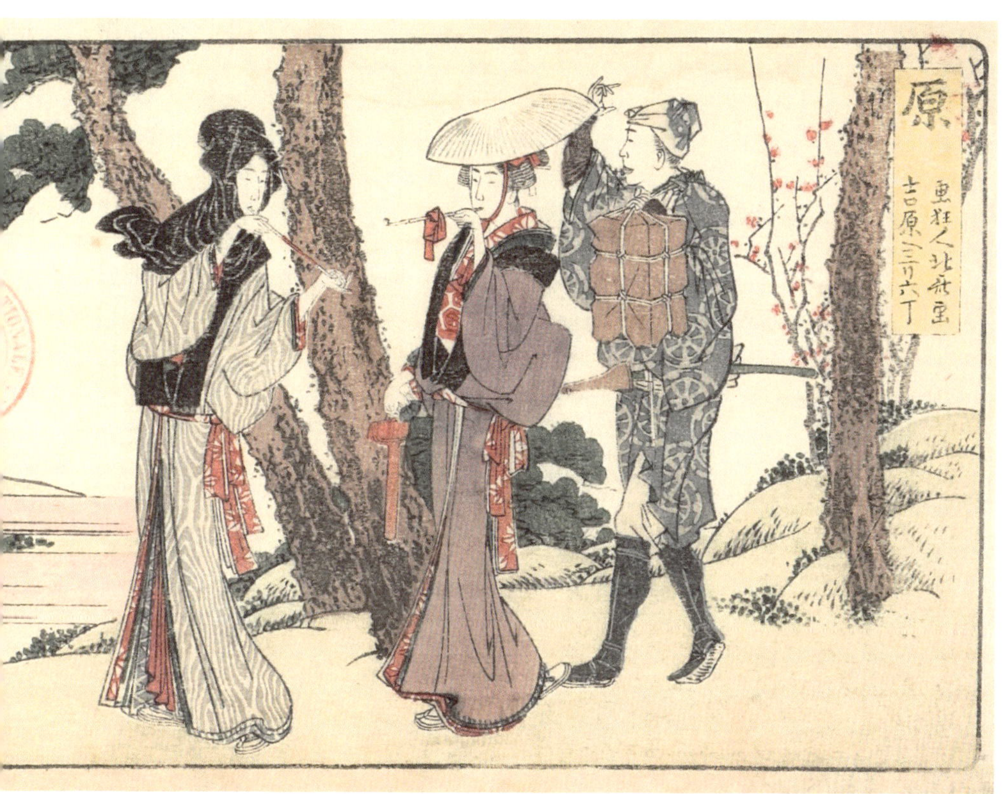

1804. 13.1 × 36.4 cm. Bibliothèque Nationale de France, Japonais 381 (54)

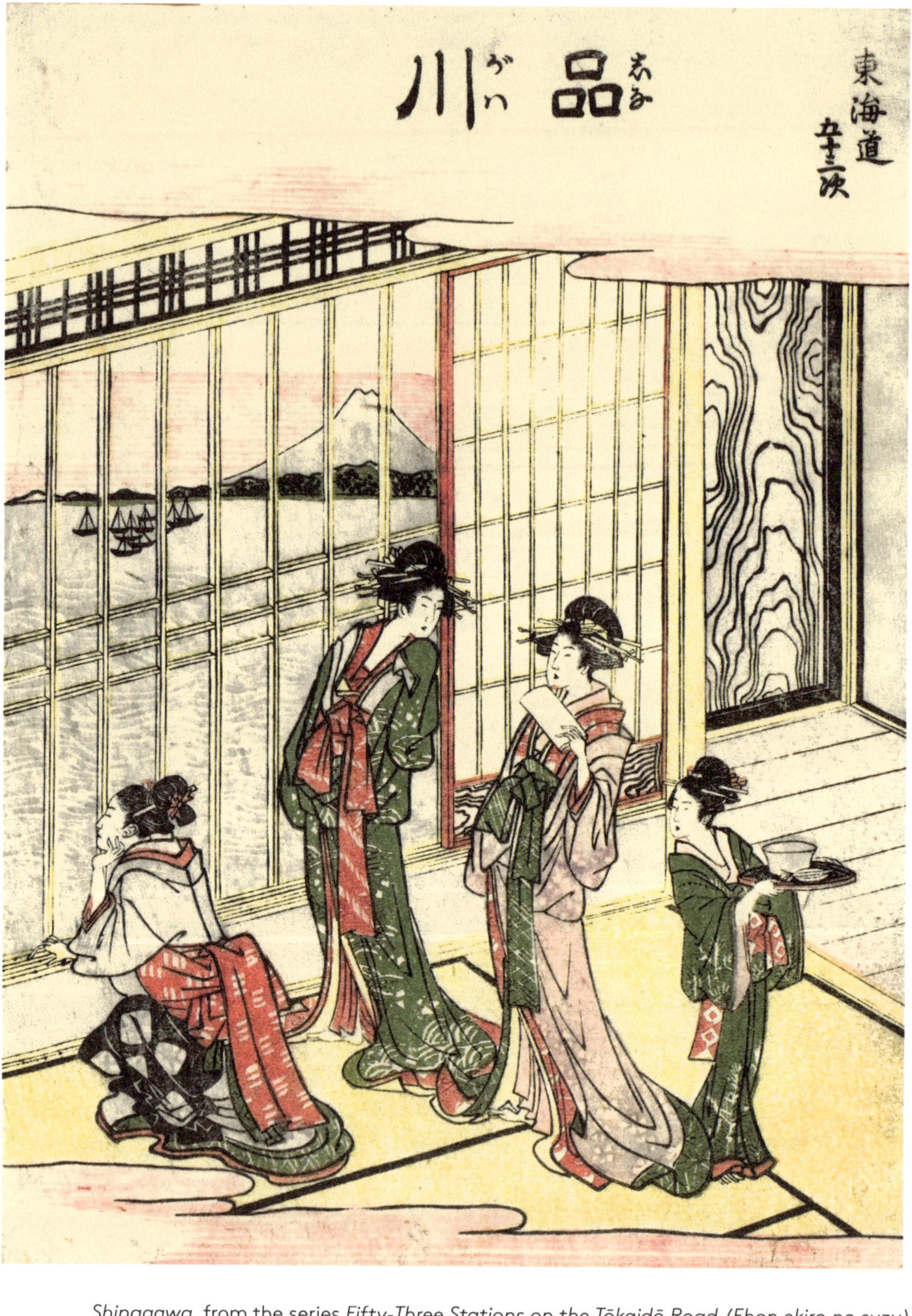

Shinagawa, from the series *Fifty-Three Stations on the Tōkaidō Road (Ehon ekiro no suzu)*
chūban nishiki-e, unsigned

c. 1806. 24 × 18.3 cm. Clarence Buckingham Collection, The Art Institute of Chicago, 1929.499

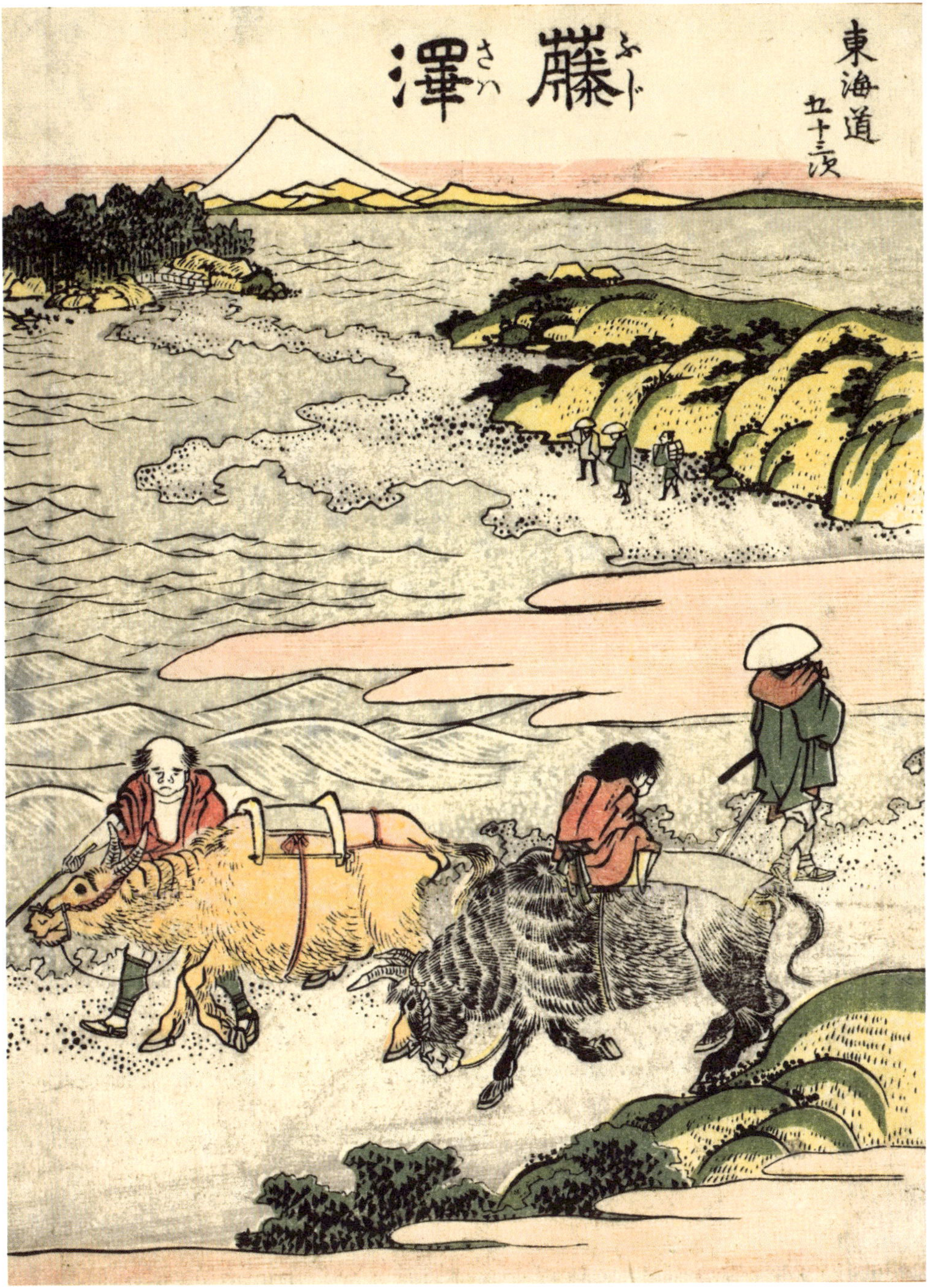

藤澤 ふぢさハ

東海道 五十三次

Fujisawa, from the series *Fifty-Three Stations on the Tōkaidō Road (Ehon ekiro no suzu)*
chūban nishiki-e, unsigned

c. 1806. 24 × 18.3 cm. Clarence Buckingham Collection, The Art Institute of Chicago, 1929.504

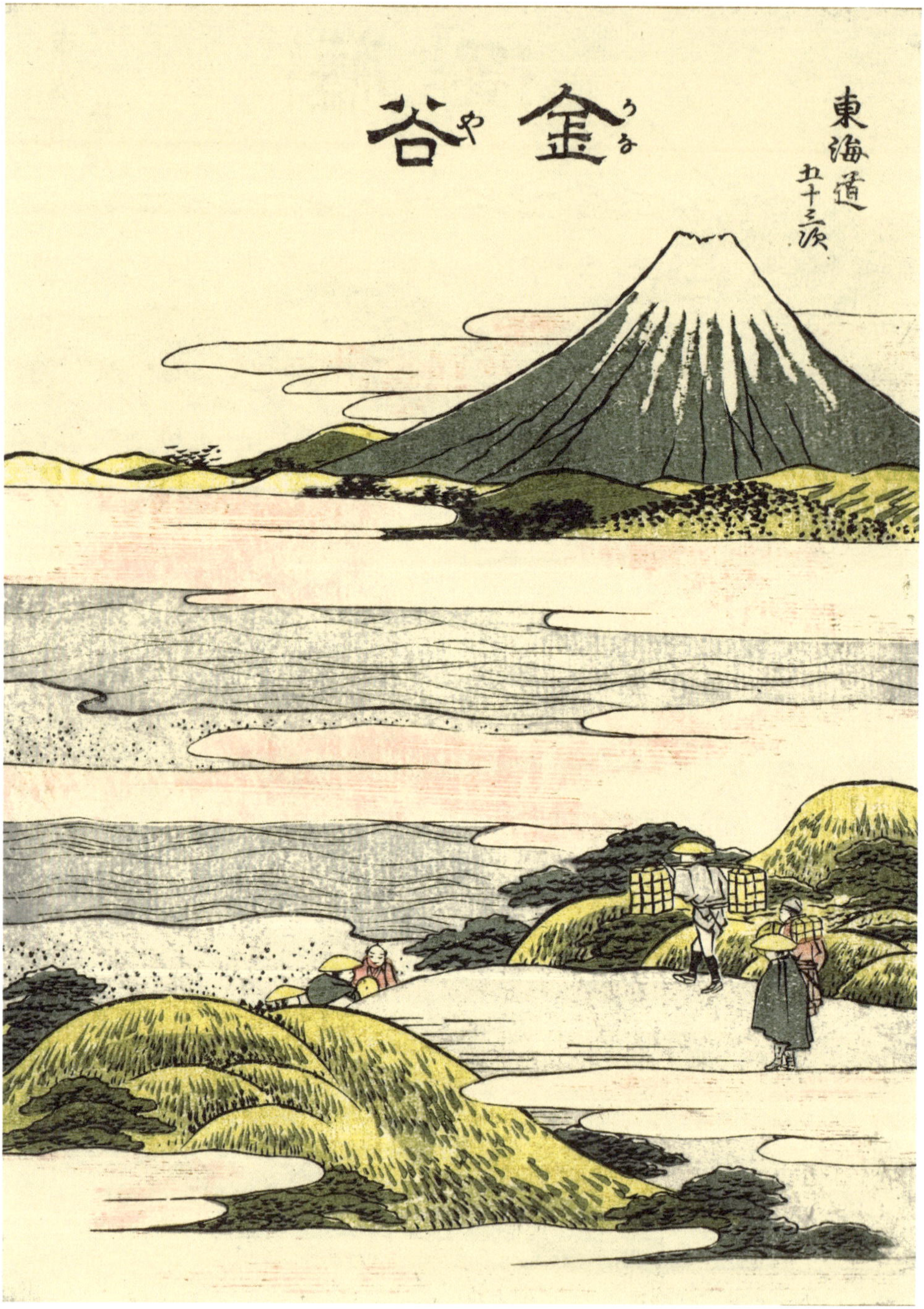

Kanaya, from the series *Fifty-Three Stations on the Tōkaidō Road*
chūban nishiki-e, unsigned

27 c. 1806. 24 × 18.3 cm. Clarence Buckingham Collection, The Art Institute of Chicago, 1929.522

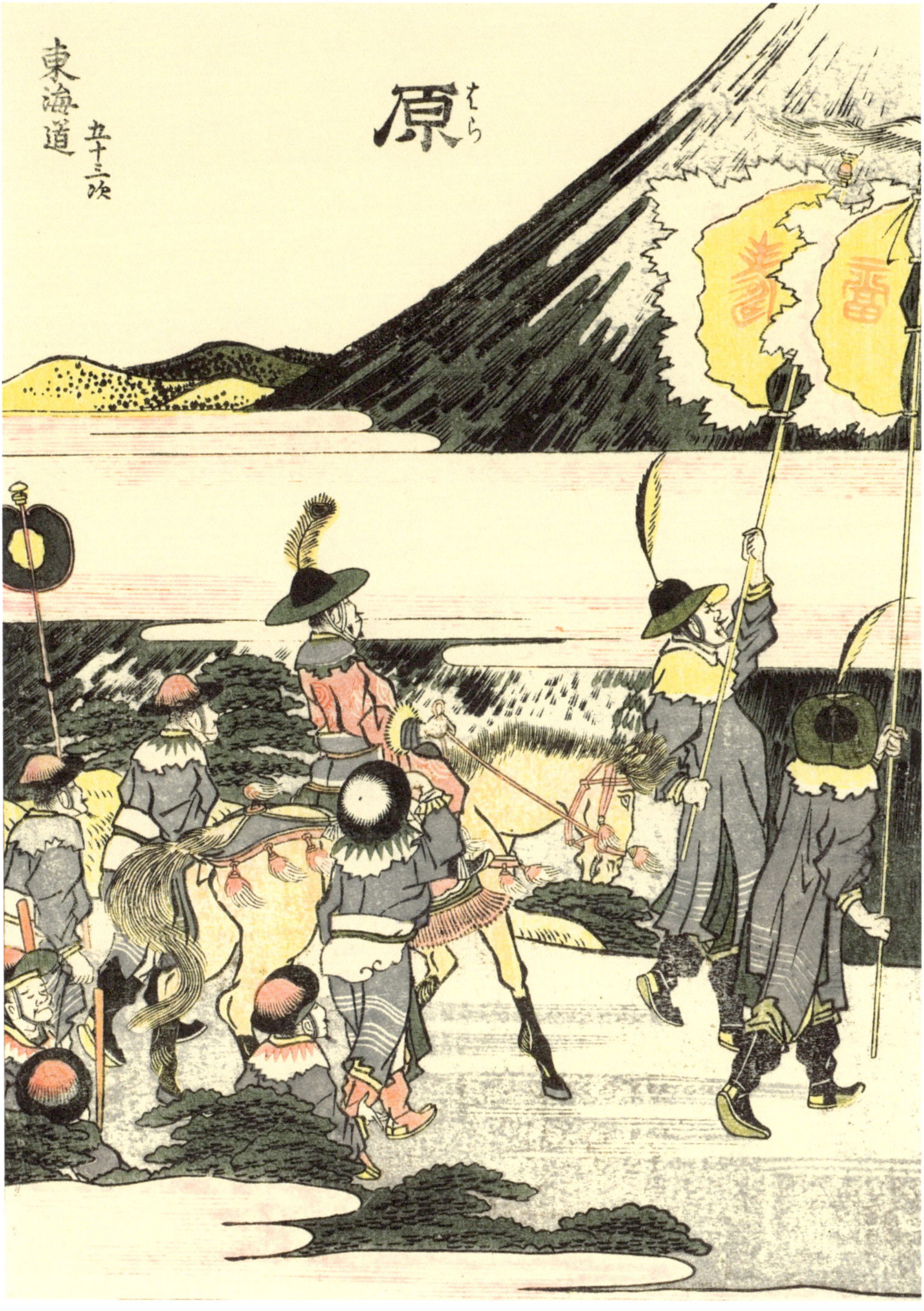

Hara, from the series *Fifty-Three Stations on the Tōkaidō Road*
chūban nishiki-e, unsigned

28

c. 1806. 24 × 18.3 cm. Clarence Buckingham Collection, The Art Institute of Chicago, 1929.511

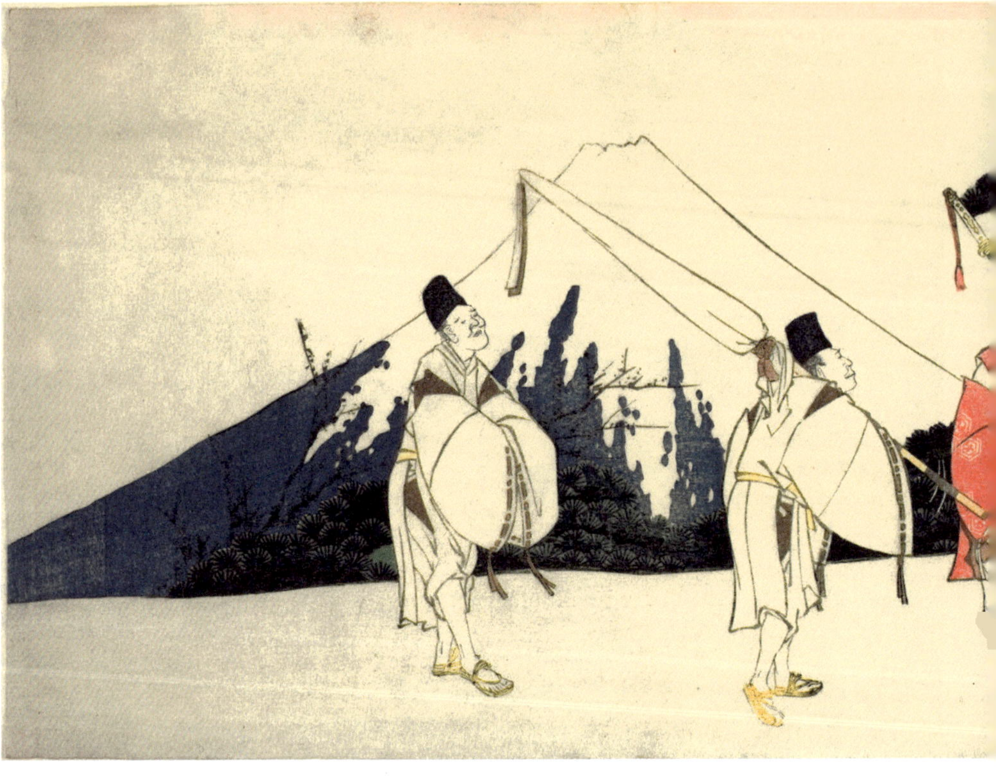

The Eastern Journey of the Celebrated Poet Ariwara no Narihira,
based on the ninth scene from *The Tale of Ise*
surimono (nagaban yoko-e), signed Hokusai ga

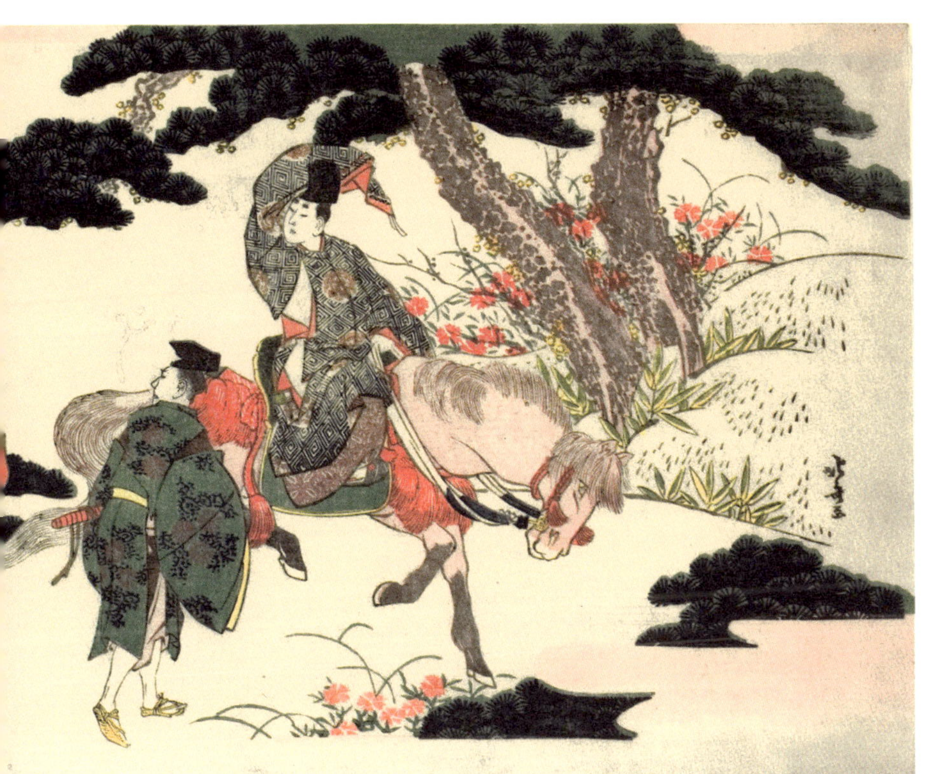

c. 1806. 19.6 × 53.1 cm. Clarence Buckingham Collection, The Art Institute of Chicago, 1925.3215

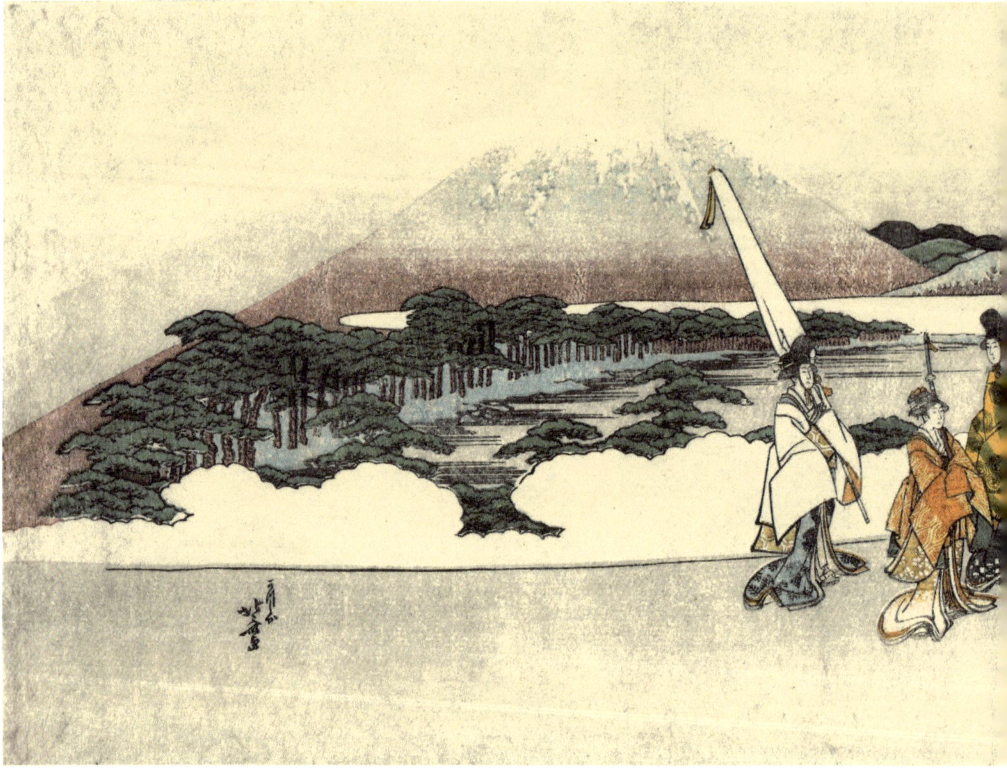

Parody of Narihira's Journey to the East,
based on the ninth scene from *The Tale of Ise*
surimono (nagaban yoko-e), signed Katsushika Hokusai ga

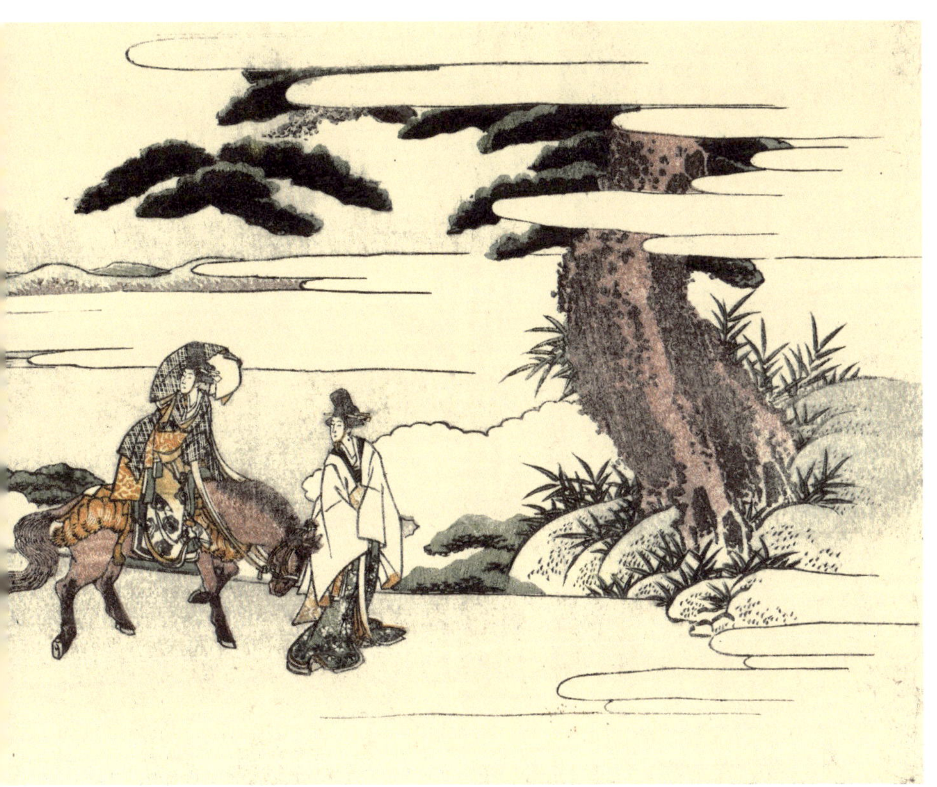

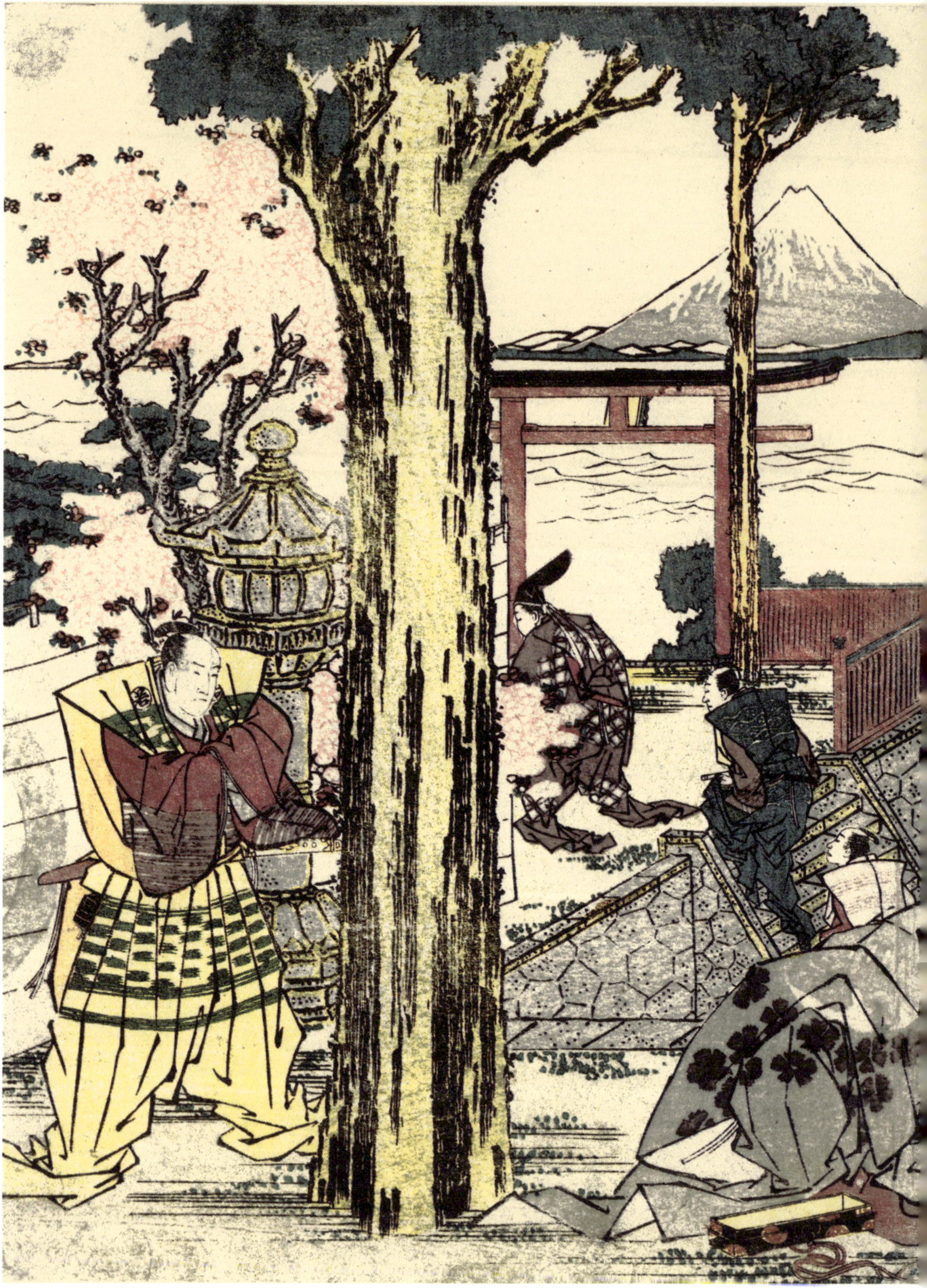

31 Act I, from the series *The Storehouse of Loyal Retainers, a Primer*
ōban nishiki-e, unsigned

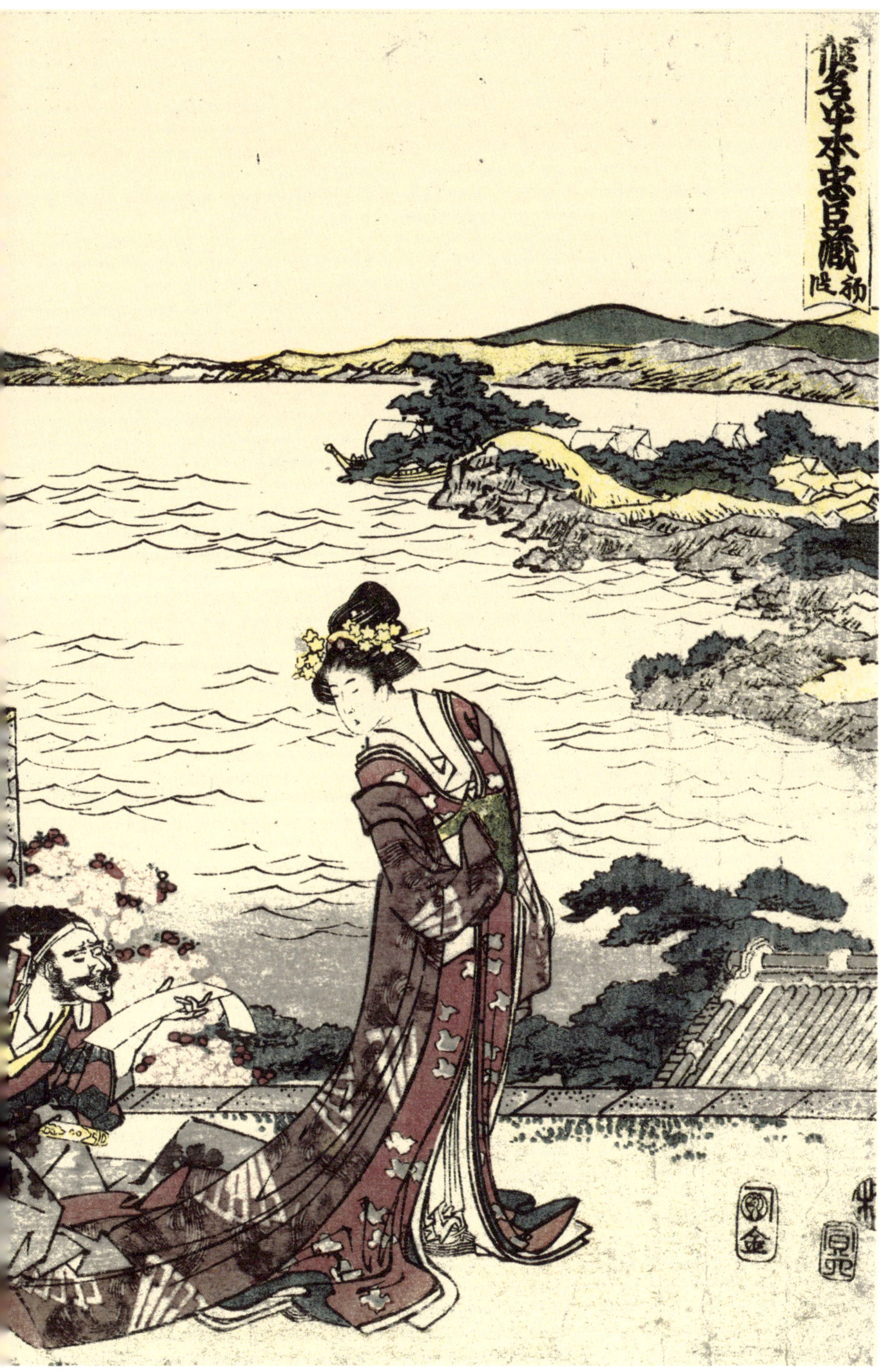

c. 1806. 24.2 × 35.5 cm. William Sturgis Bigelow Collection. Photograph © 2022 Museum of Fine Arts, Boston, 11.17539

Act VIII, from the series *The Storehouse of Loyal Retainers, a Primer*
chūban nishiki-e, signed Hokusai ga

c. 1806. 22.8 × 17.3 cm. Gift of the Friends of Arthur B. Duel,
Harvard Art Museums/Arthur M. Sackler Museum, 1933.4.1829

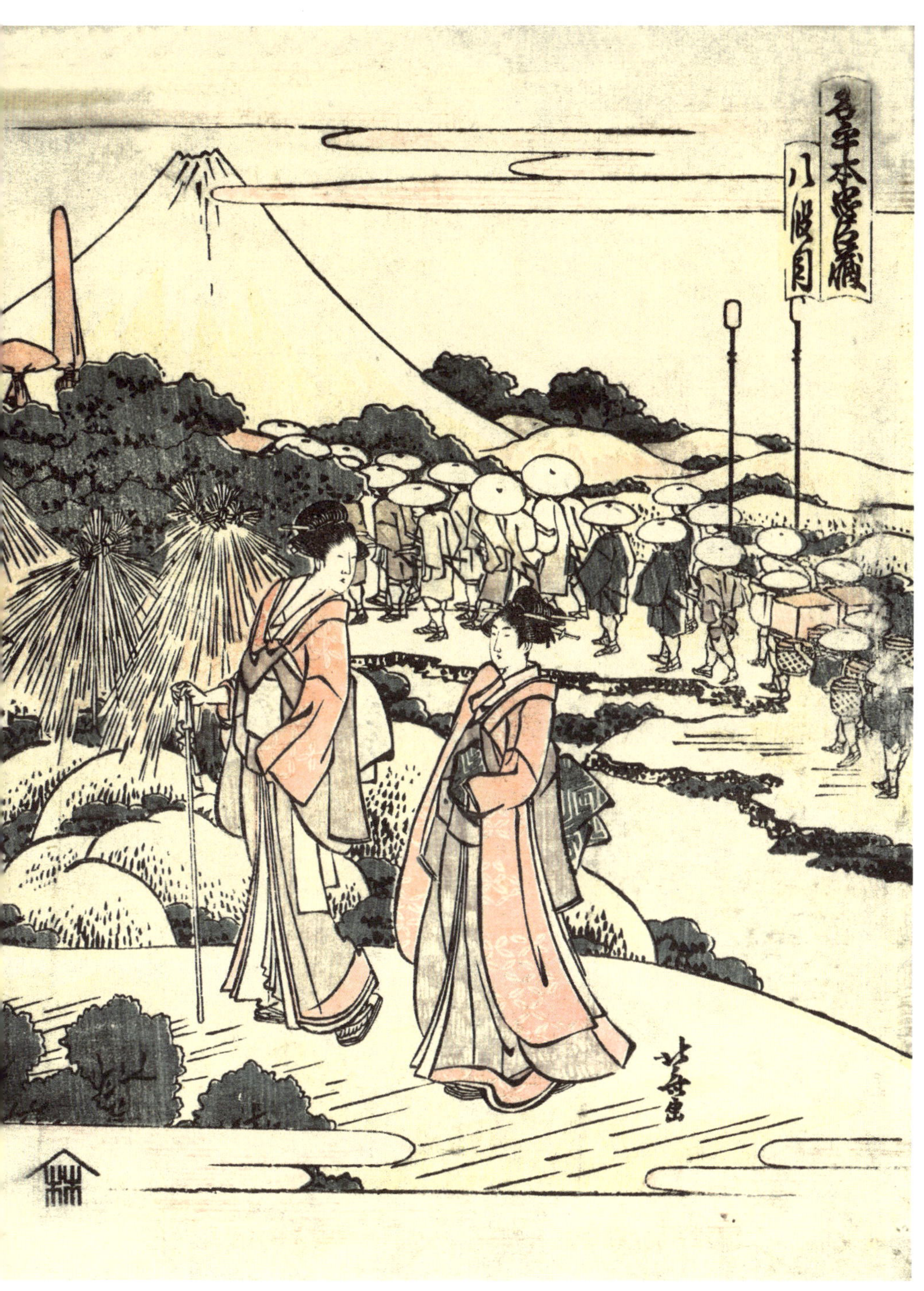

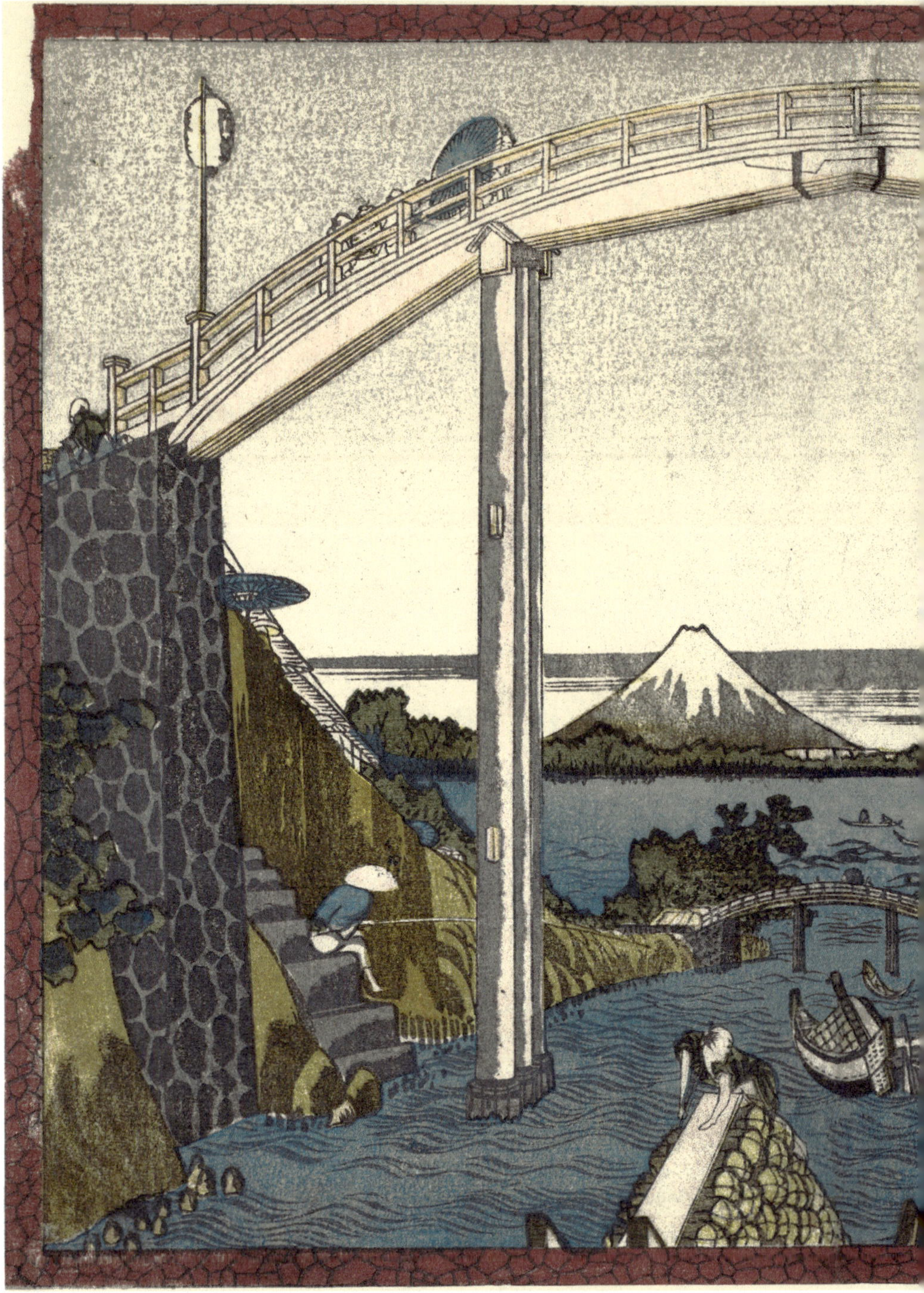

33 *Mount Fuji Under High Bridge,* from a series of landscapes in the Western style
chūban nishiki-e, signed Hokusai ekaku

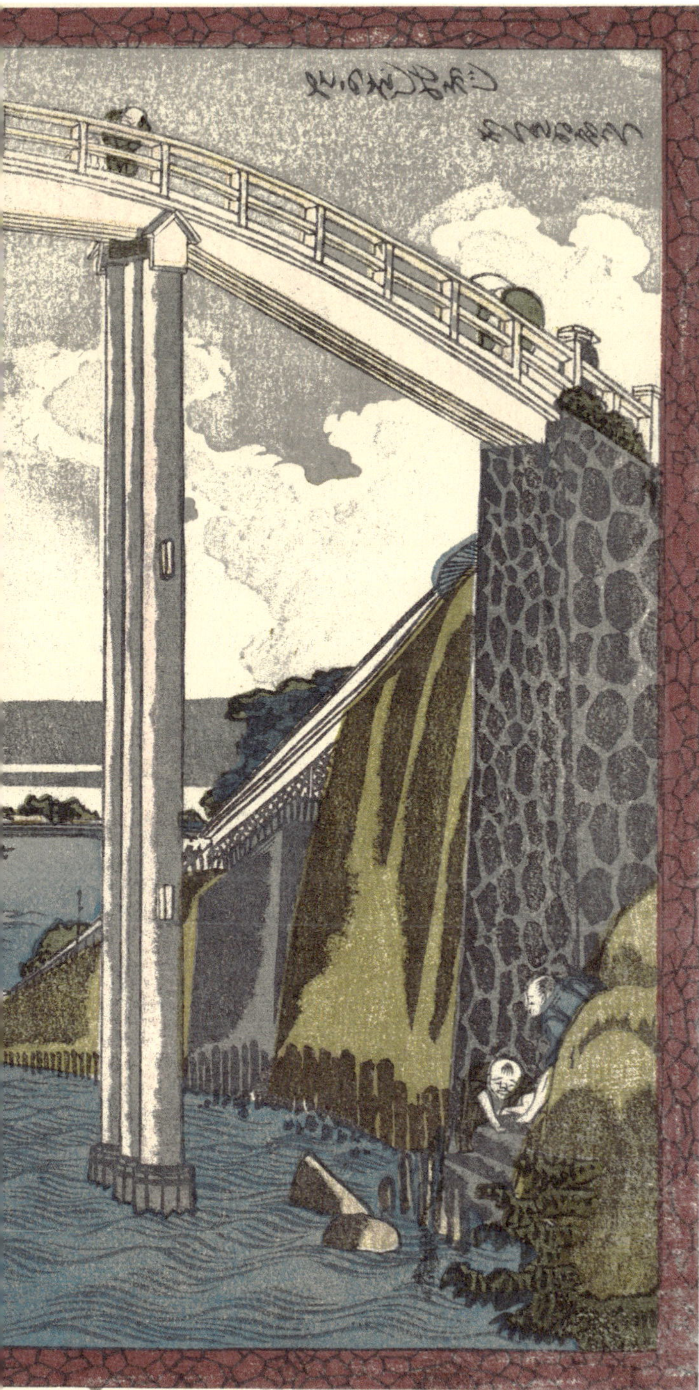

c. 1800–1805. 18.2 × 24.4 cm. William S. and John T. Spaulding Collection. Photograph © 2022 Museum of Fine Arts, Boston, 21.6675

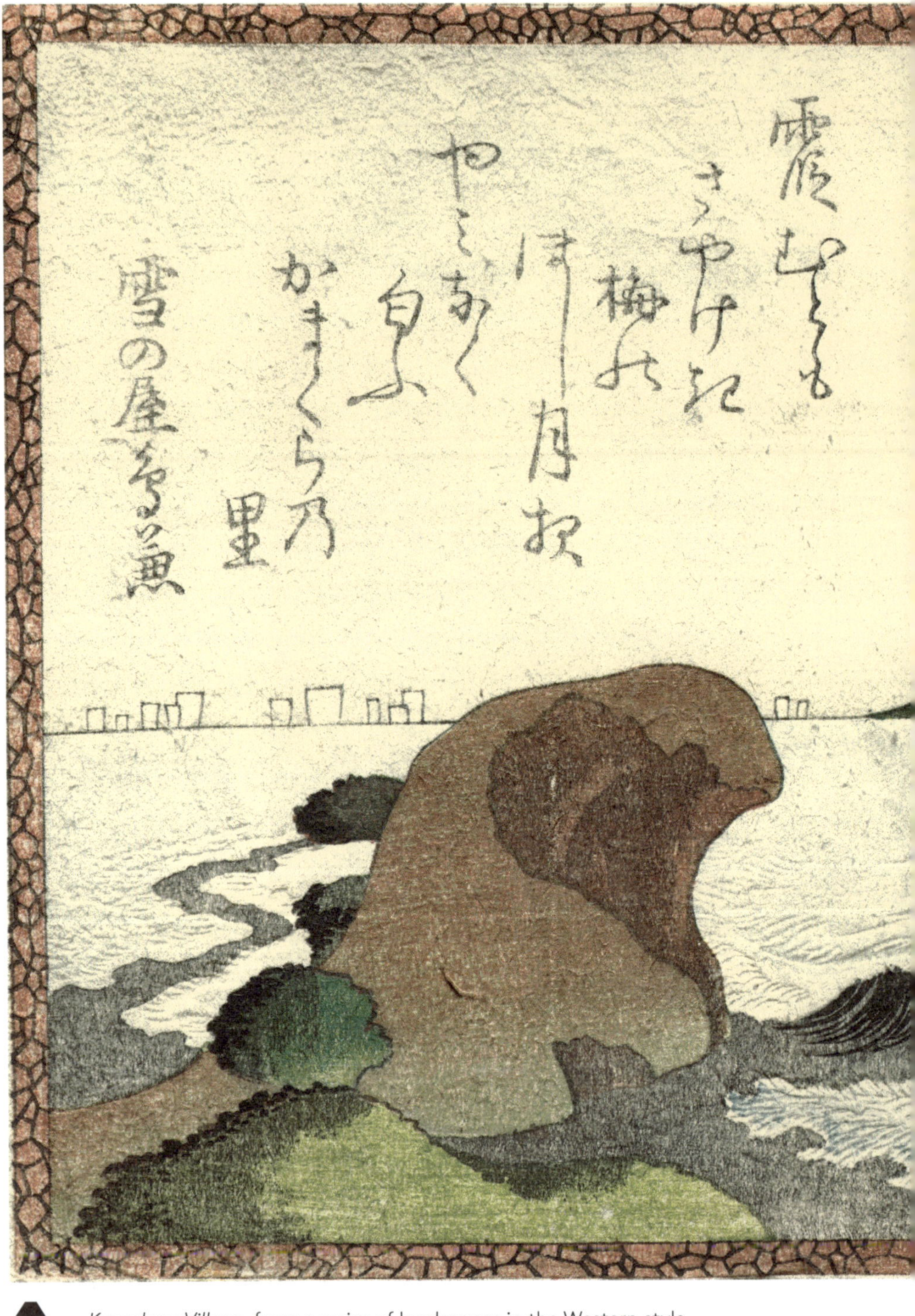

Kamakura Village, from a series of landscapes in the Western style.
kyōka surimono, signed Hokusai utsusu

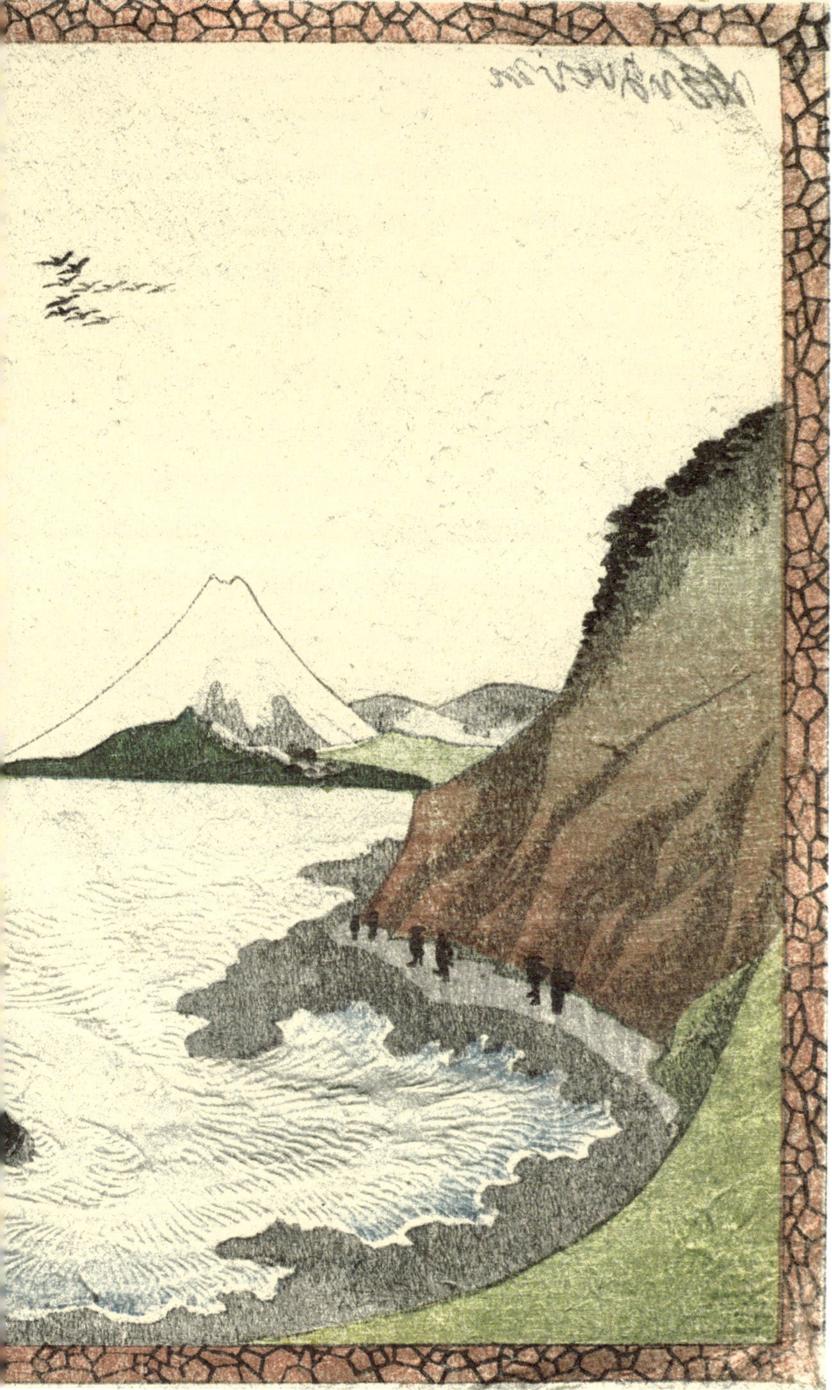

c. 1804–1810. 13.5 × 19.2 cm. William Sturgis Bigelow Collection. Photograph © 2022 Museum of Fine Arts, Boston, 11.16762

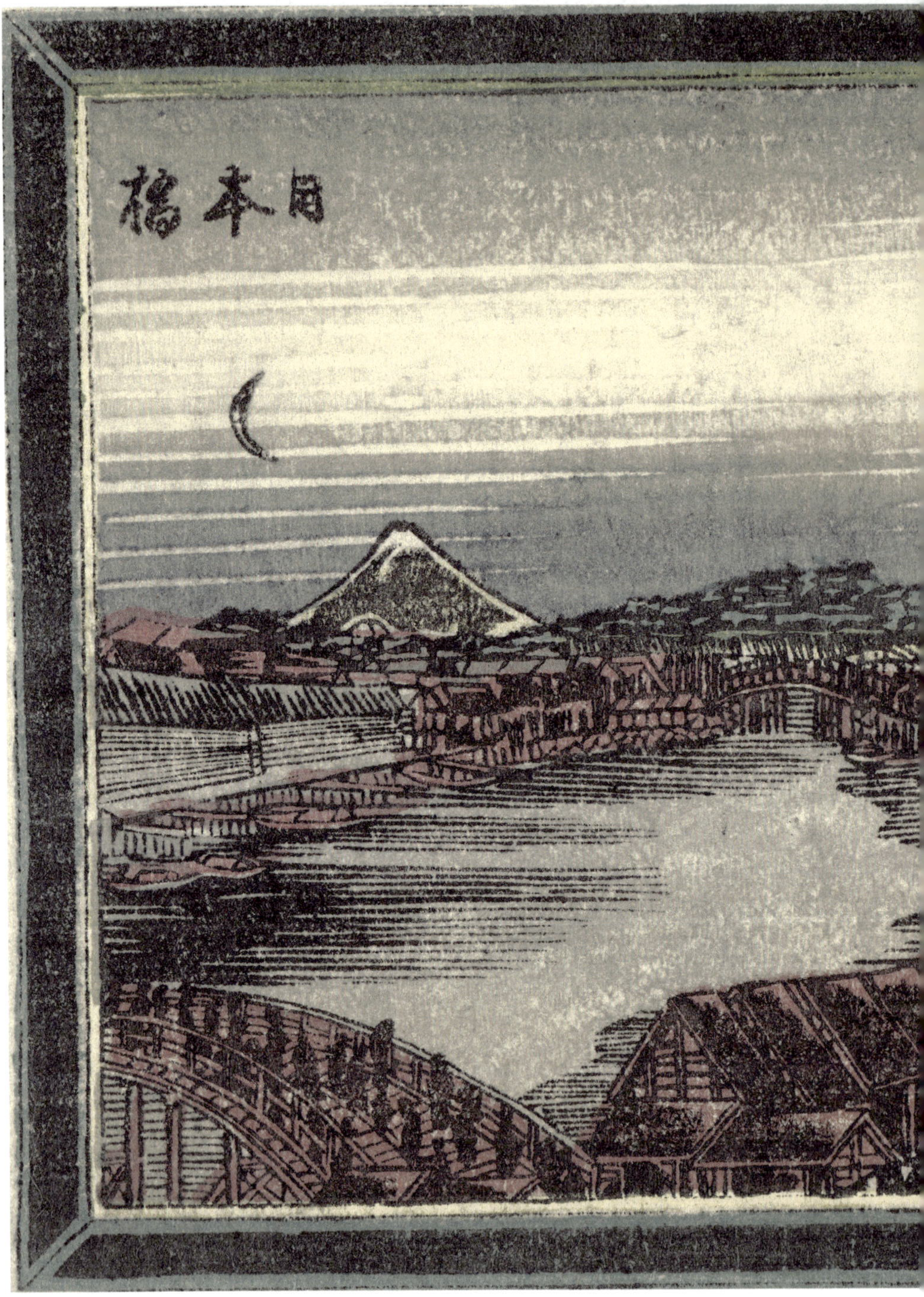

Nihonbashi, from the series *The Dutch Picture Lens: Eight Views of Edo*
koban nishiki-e, signed Hokusai sensei zu

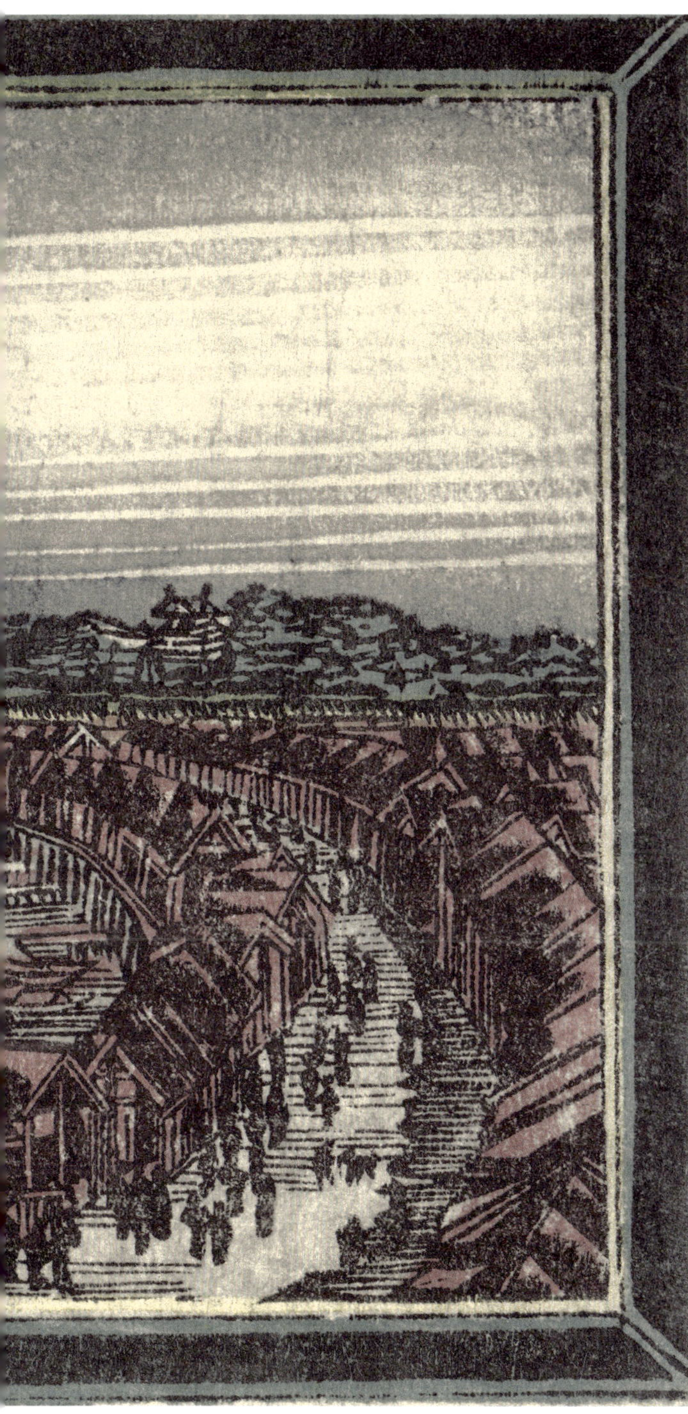

c. 1811–1814. 8.6 × 11.4 cm. William Sturgis Bigelow Collection. Photograph © 2022 Museum of Fine Arts, Boston, 11.20165

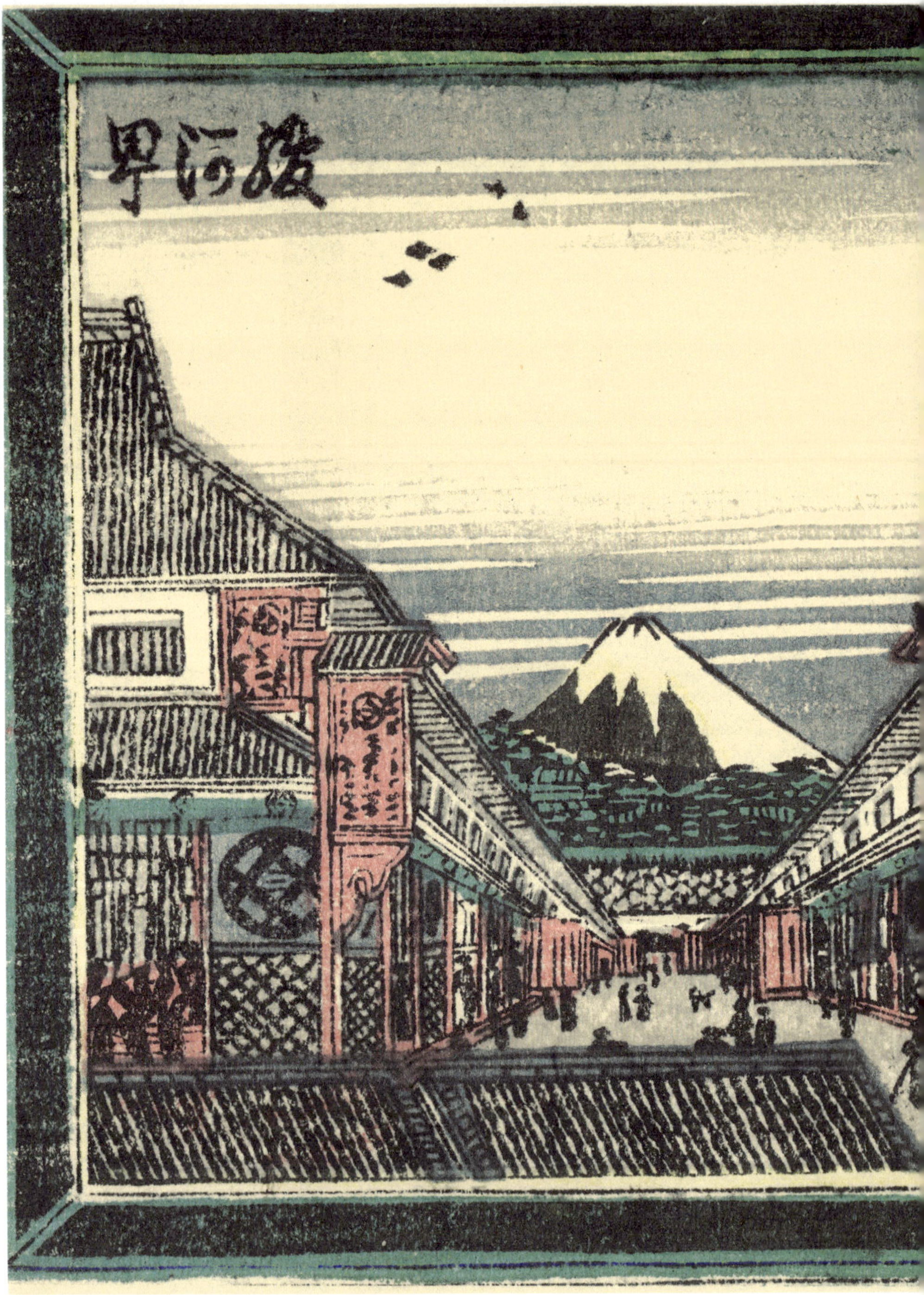

36 *Surugachō*, from the series *The Dutch Picture Lens: Eight Views of Edo*
koban nishiki-e, signed Hokusai sensei zu

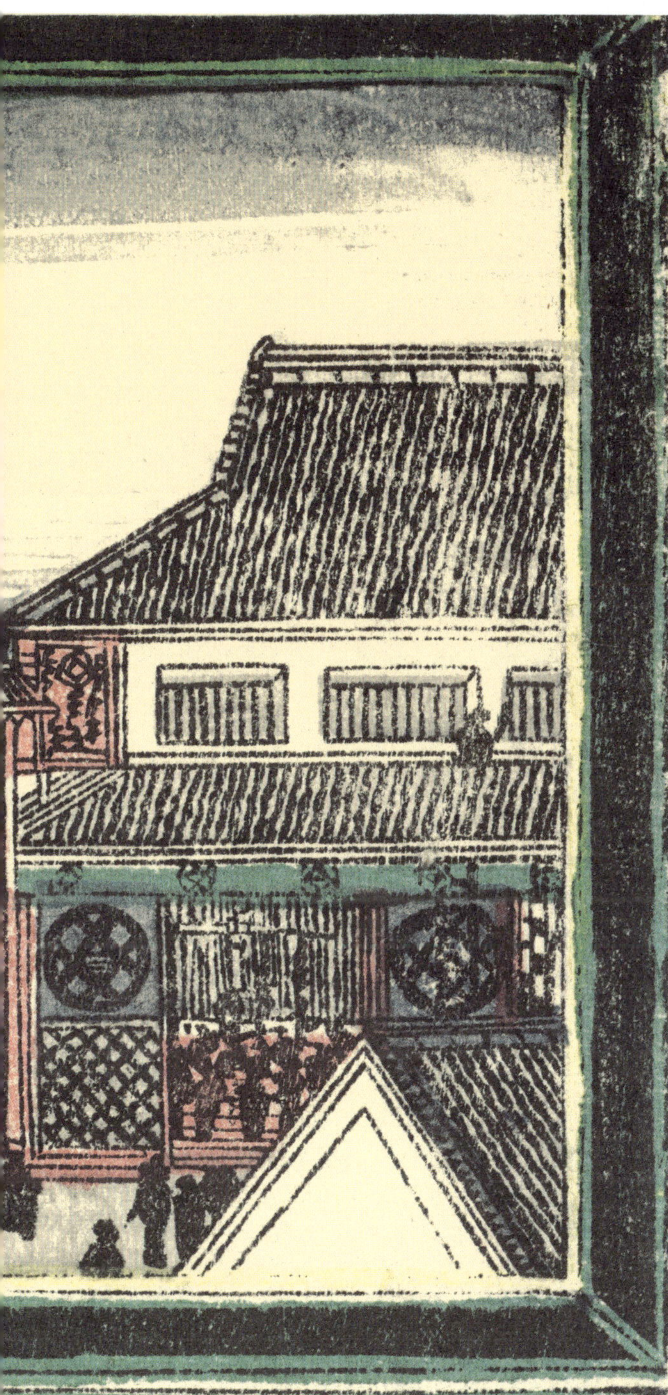

c. 1811–1814. 8.6 × 11.4 cm. William Sturgis Bigelow Collection. Photograph © 2022 Museum of Fine Arts, Boston, 11.20162

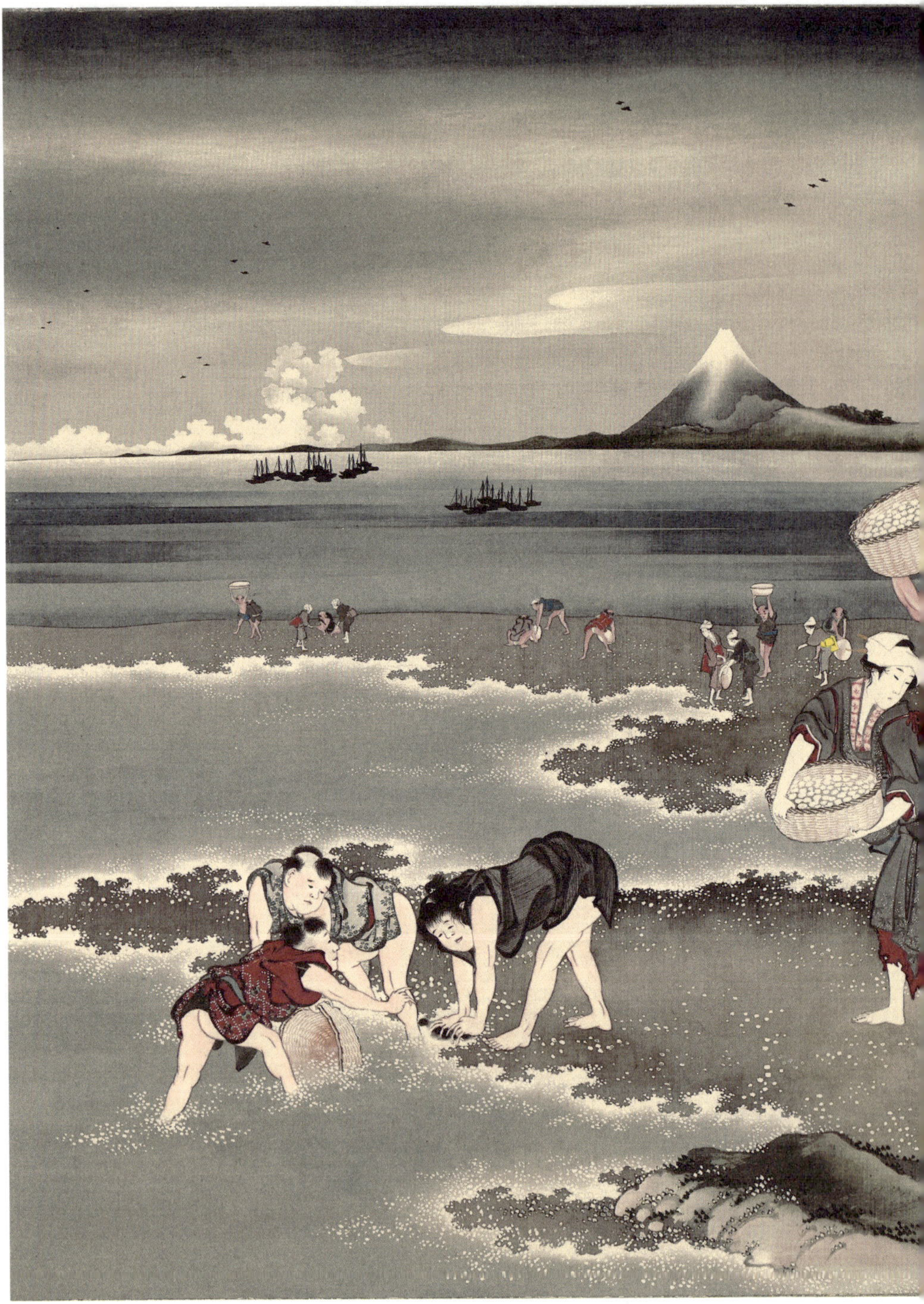

Landscape: Clam-Gatherers on the Shore
colour on silk (*kakejiku*), signed Katsushika Hokusai

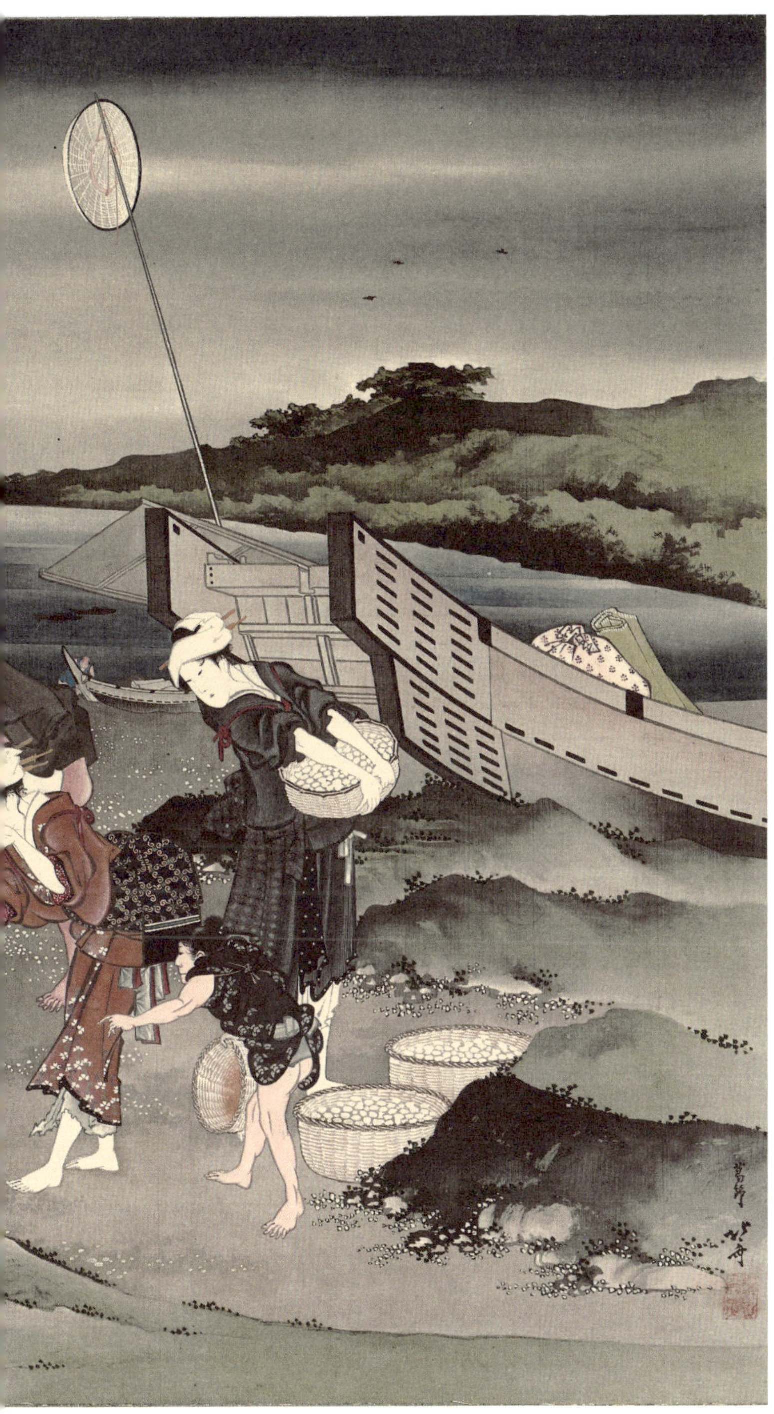

Date unknown. 56.5 × 78.8 cm. National Museum of Asian Art, Smithsonian Institution, Freer Study Collection: Gift of Charles Lang Freer, F1903.2

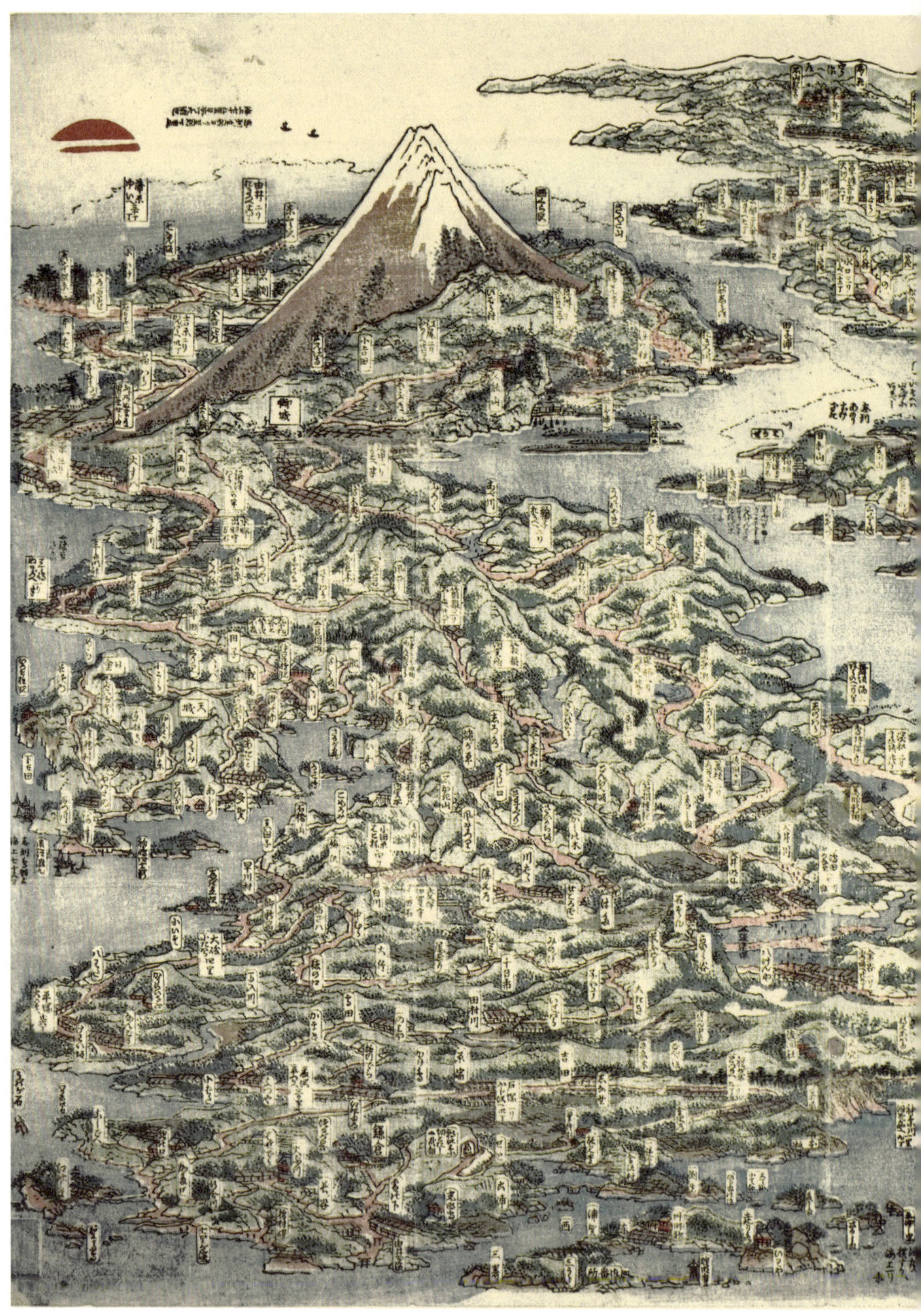

38 *The Famous Places on the Tōkaidō Road in One View*
ōban nishiki-e, signed Katsushika Zen Hokusai Taito hitsu

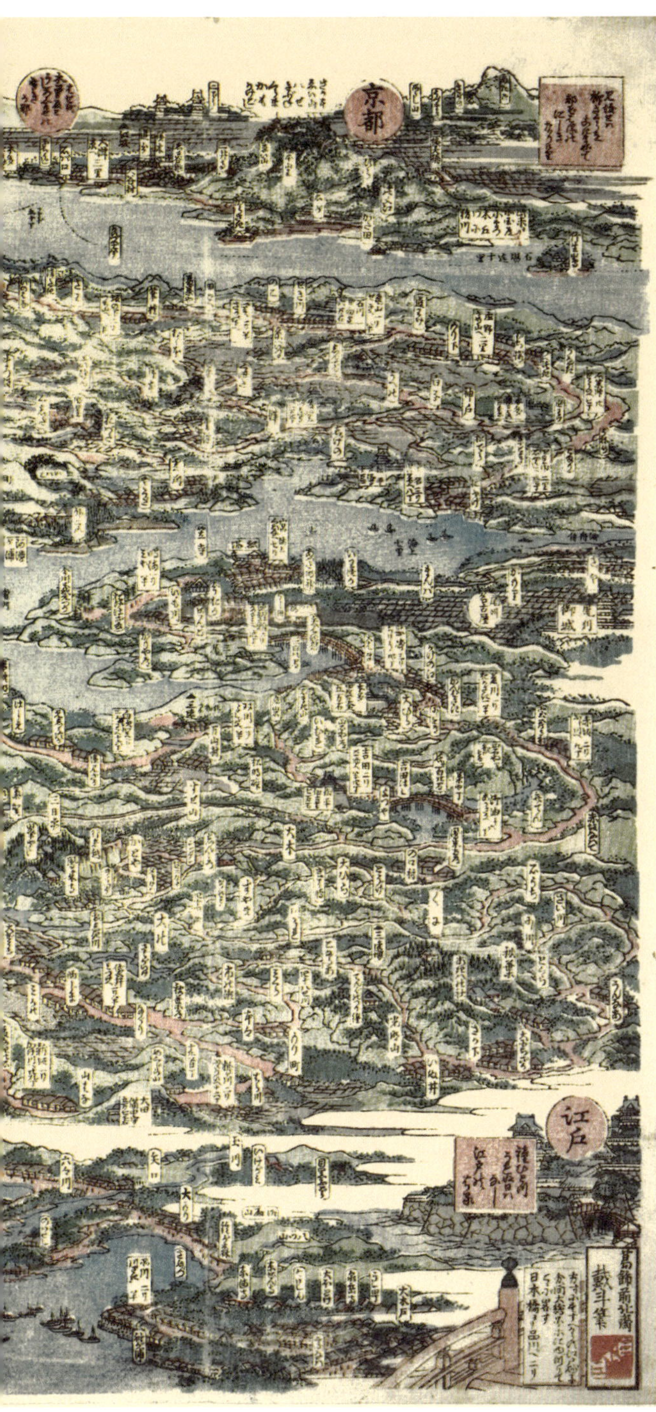

1818. 43 × 58 cm. Frederick W. Gookin Collection, The Art Institute of Chicago, 1939.1107

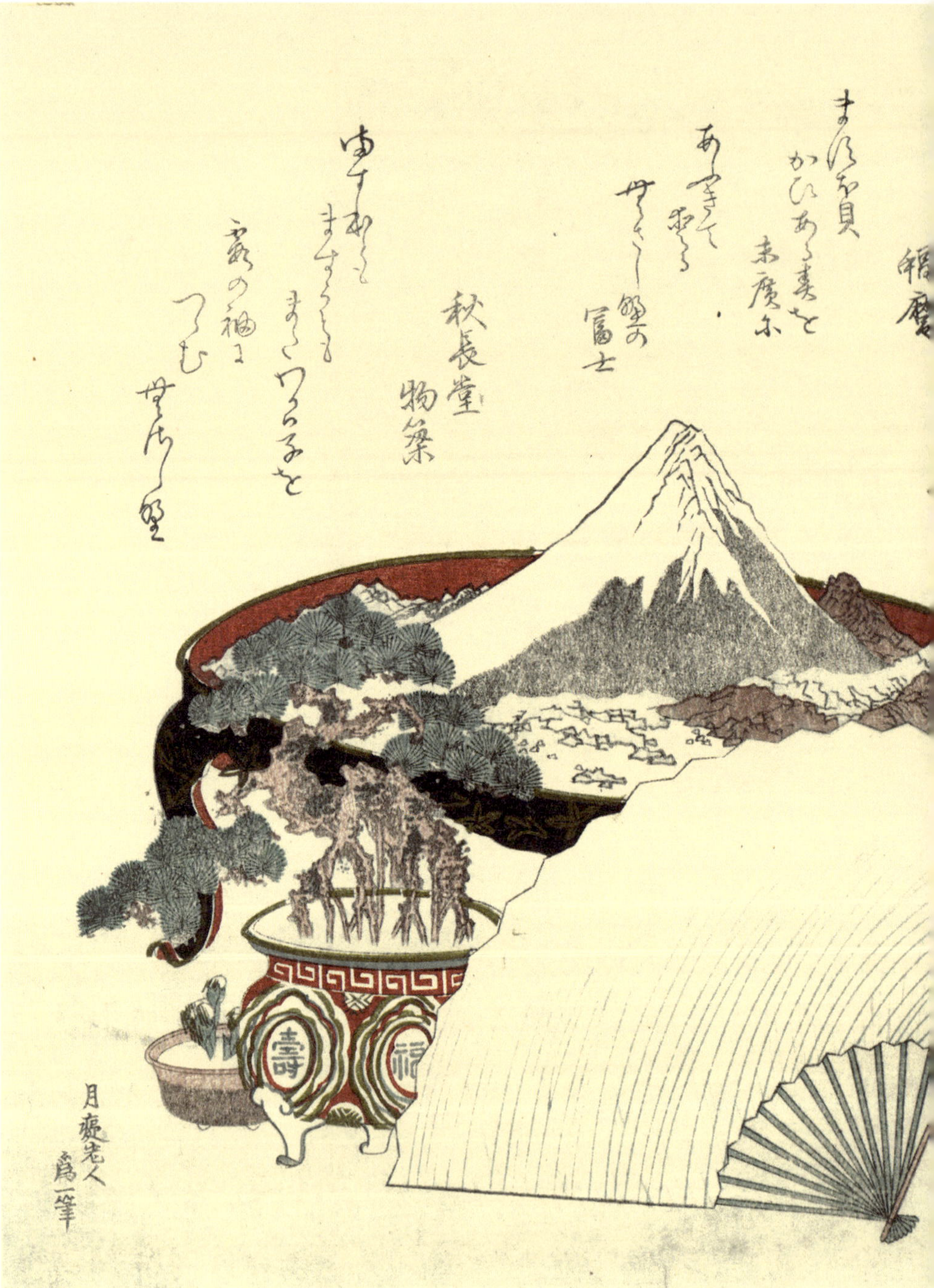

The Pure Red Shell from the series *A Matching Game with Genroku Poem Shells*
surimono, signed Getchi Rōjin Iitsu hitsu

1821. 19.9 × 17.8 cm. Gift of the Friends of Arthur B. Duel, Harvard Art Museums/Arthur M. Sackler Museum, 1933.4.1762

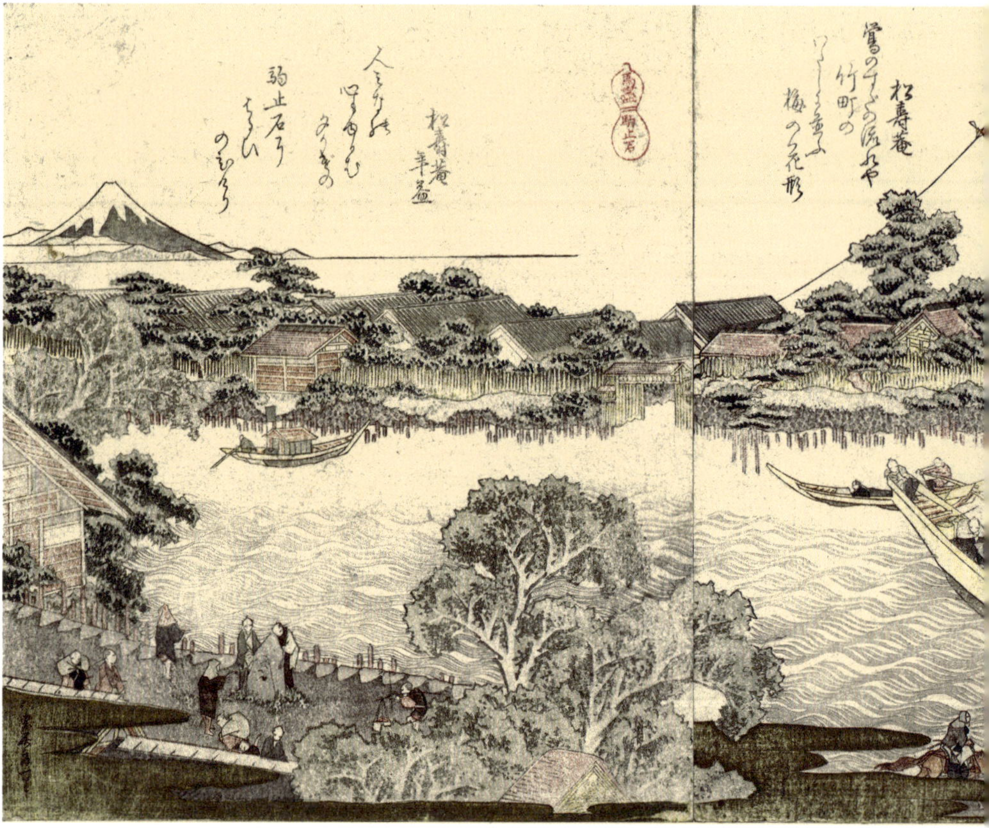

Komagata-dō Temple, Onmaya Embankment, and the Hitching Stone (from right to left), from the series A Set of Horses.
surimono triptych, signed Fusenkyo Iitsu hitsu

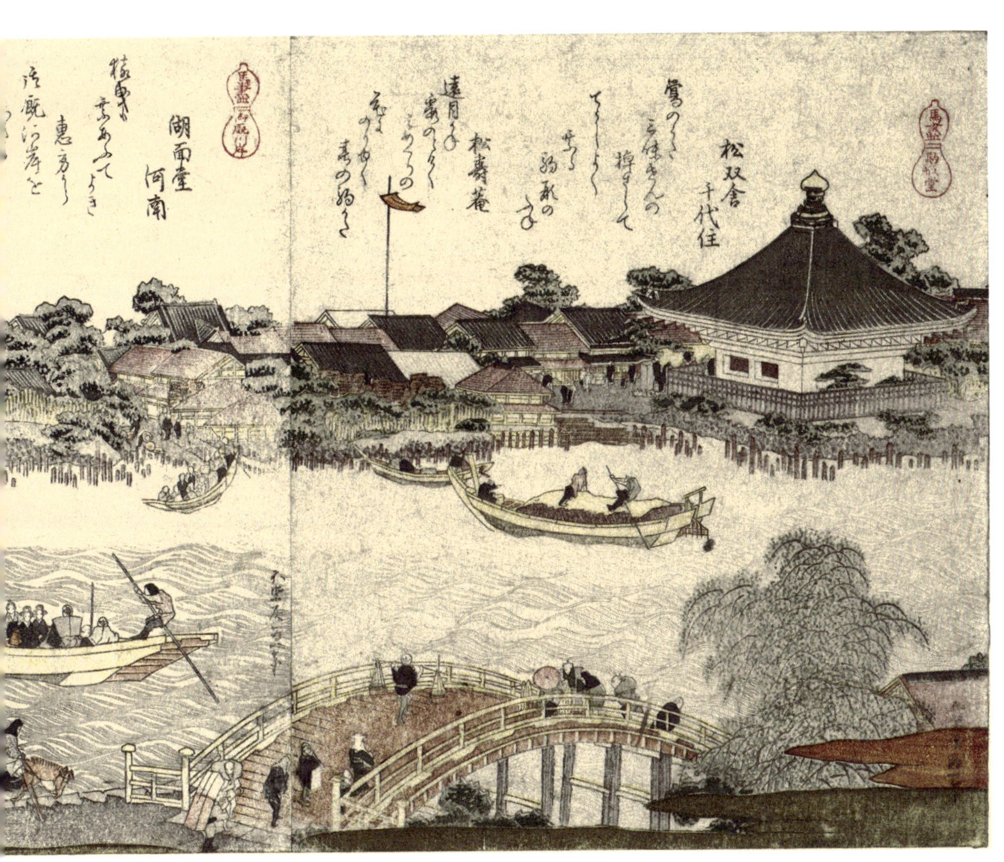

1822. 21 × 55.1 cm. Museum of Fine Arts, Boston – Worcester Art Museum exchange, made possible through the Special Korean Pottery Fund. Museum purchase with funds donated by contribution, and Smithsonian Institution – Chinese Expedition, 1923–24. Photograph © 2022 Museum of Fine Arts, Boston, 54.259-61

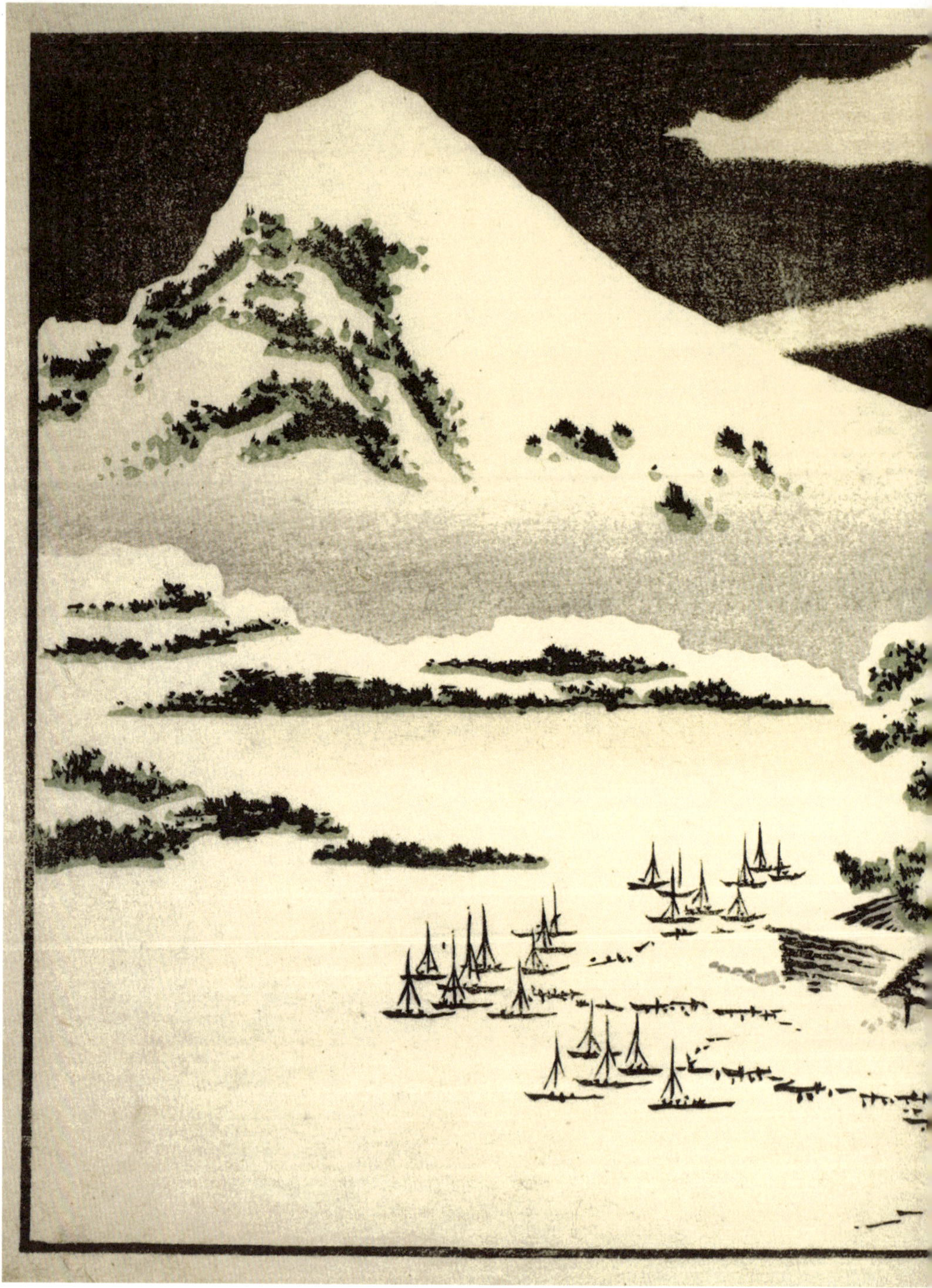

41 *Mount Fuji in Winter*, from the album *Pictures After Nature*
hanshibon, unsigned

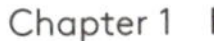

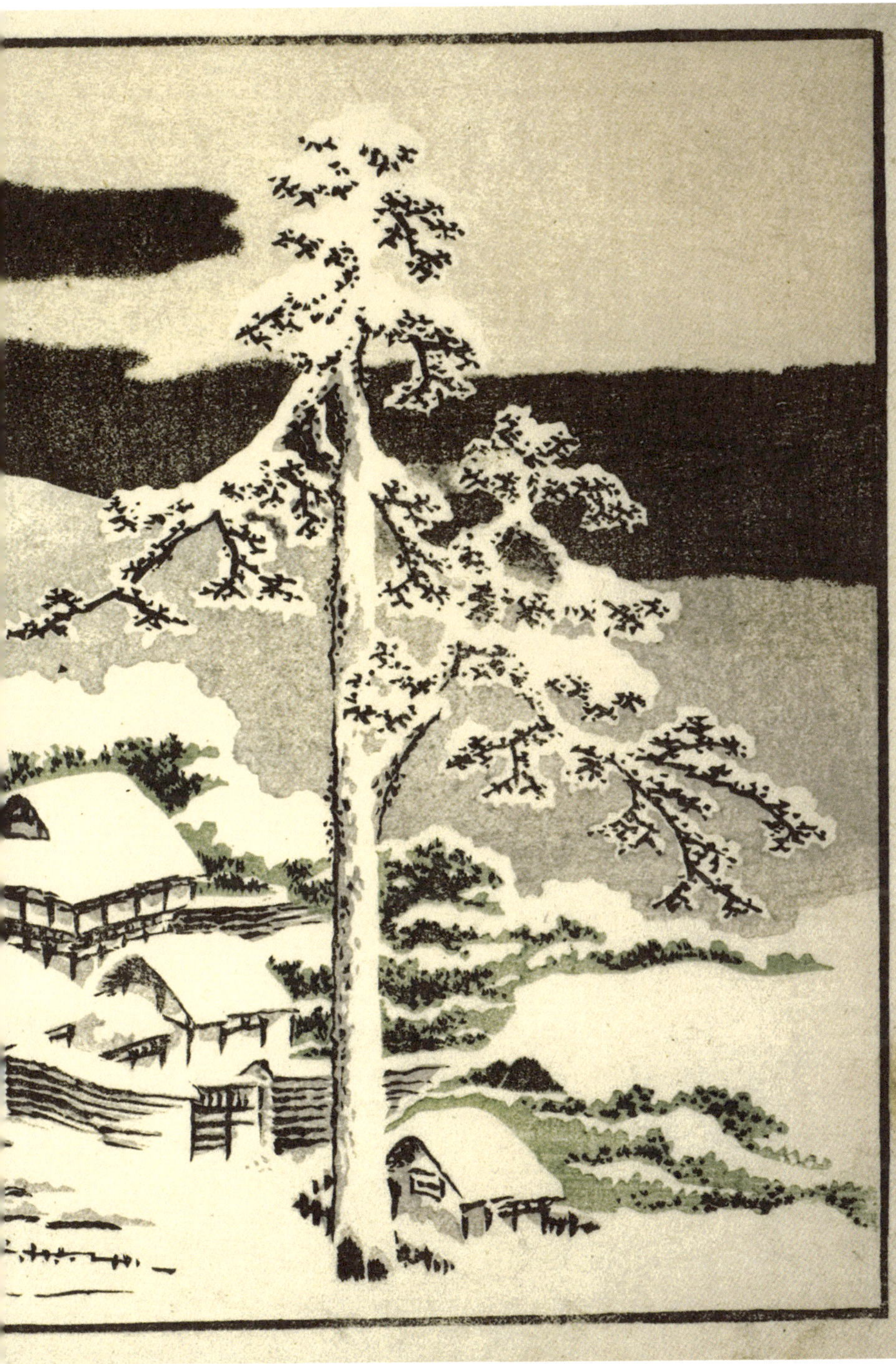

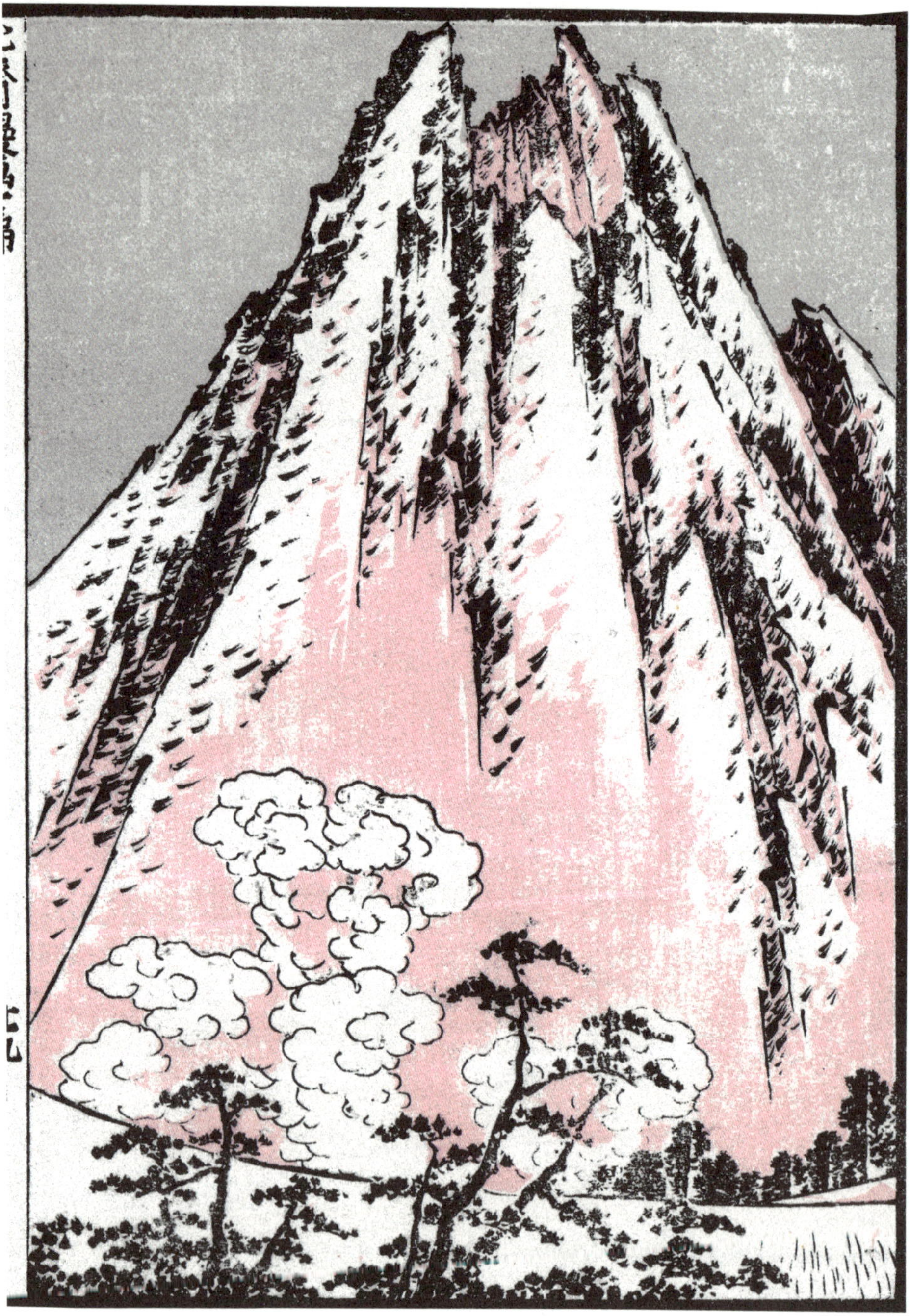

Mishima Pass in Kai Province, from the series *Hokusai Manga*
hanshibon, unsigned

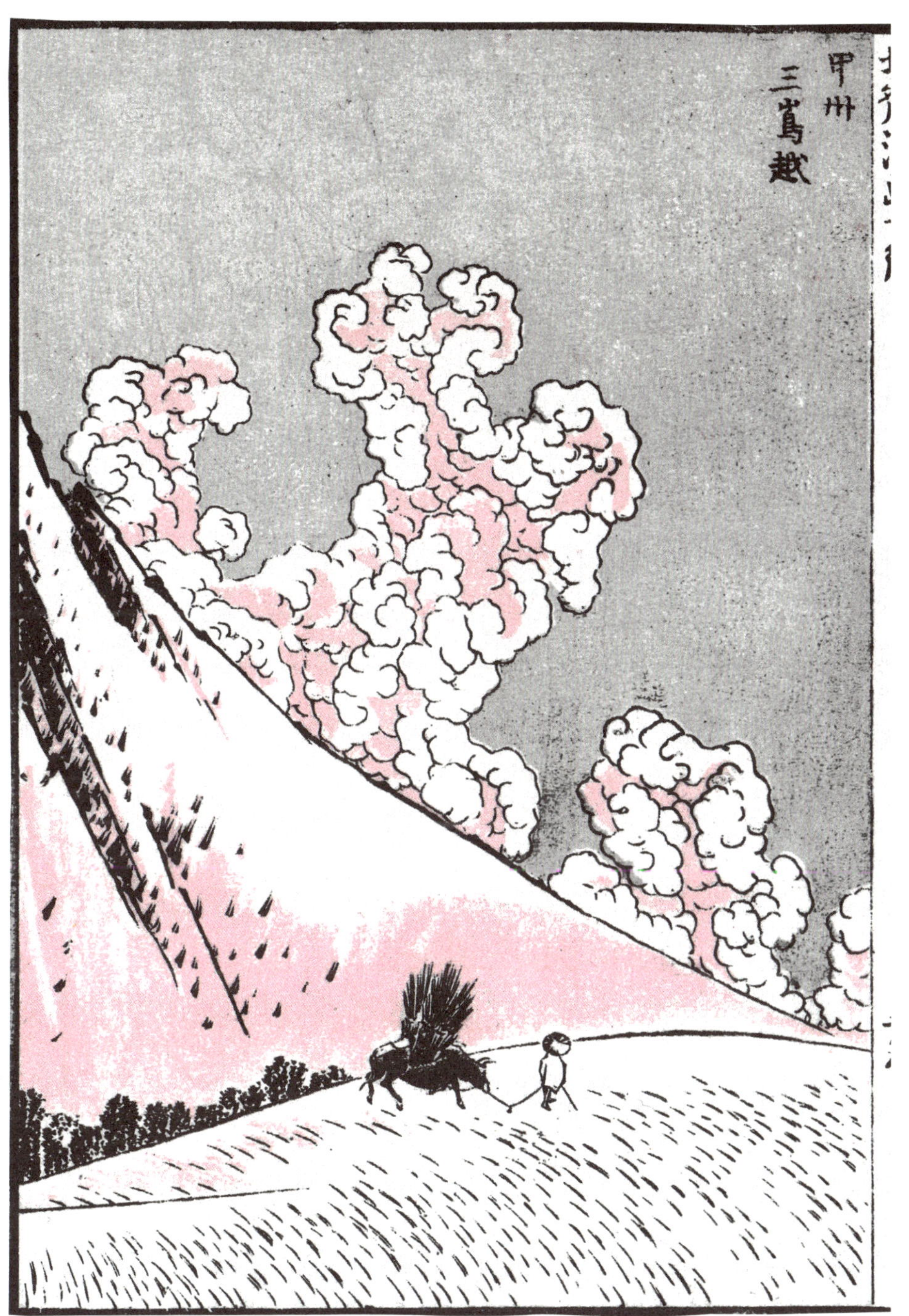

1817. 22.7 × 15.8 cm. The Howard Mansfield Collection, Gift of Howard
Mansfield, 1936 © 2022 The Metropolitan Museum of Art, New York, JIB111a–k

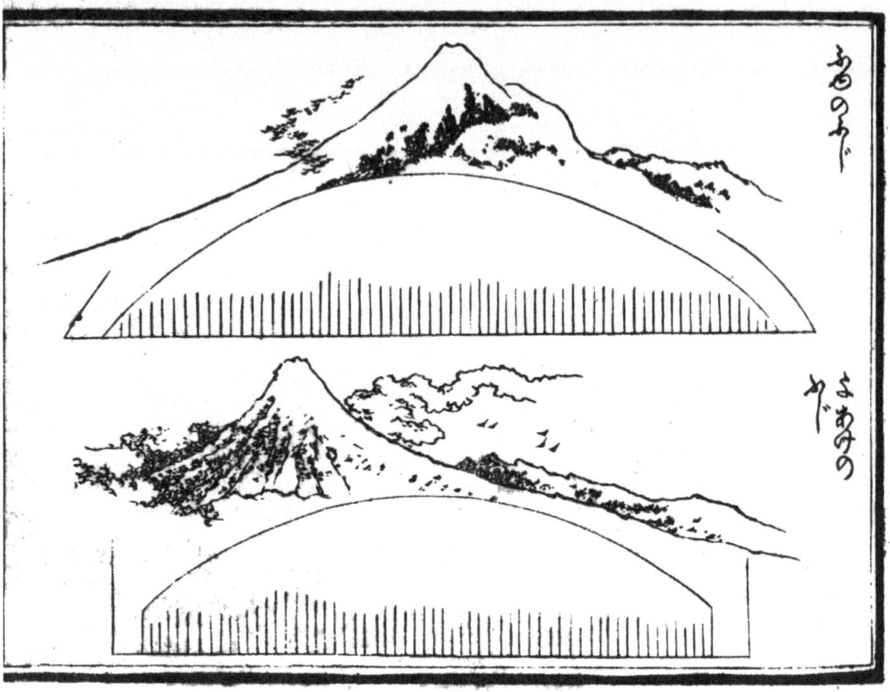

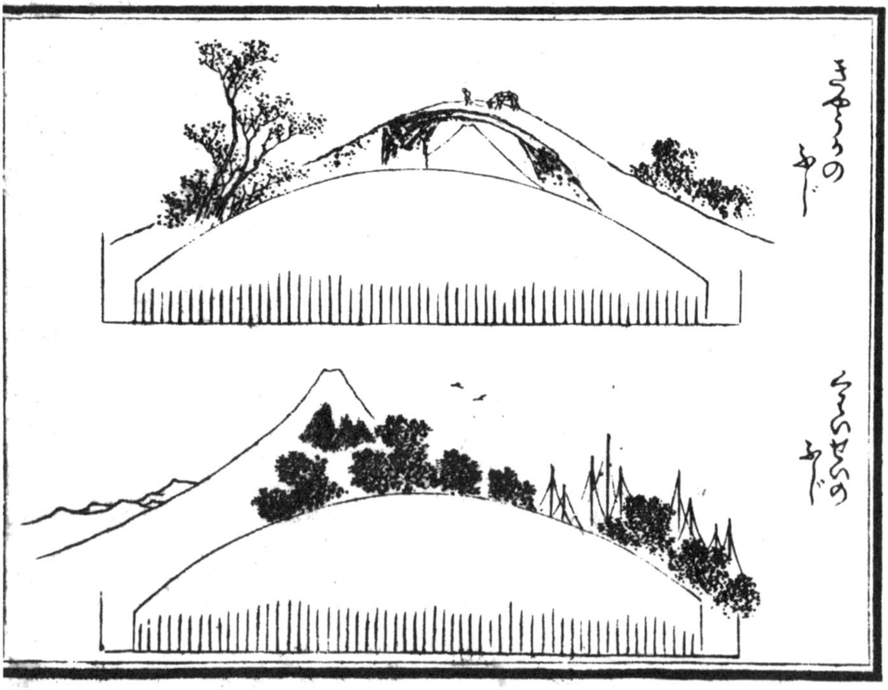

Popular Designs for Combs and Tobacco Pipes, Vol. 2
yokohon, signed Zen Hokusai Iitsu Sensei zu

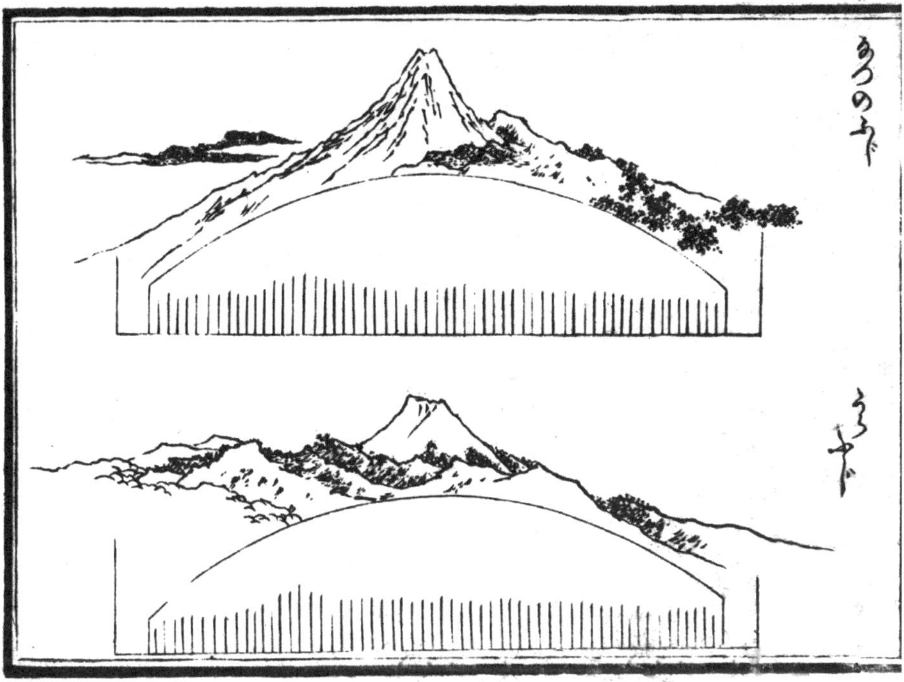

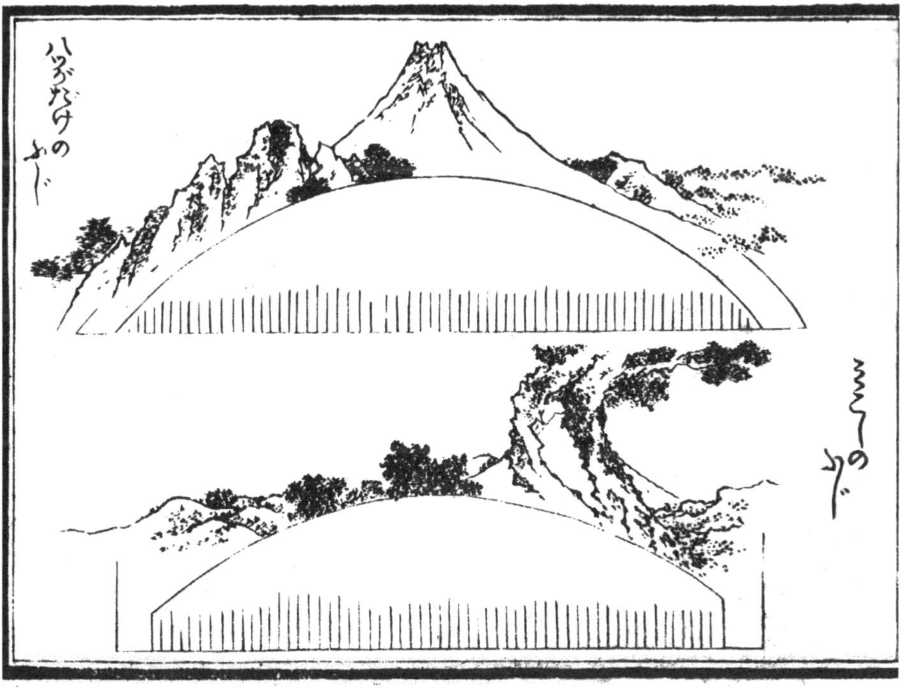

1823. 12.8 × 18.2 cm. National Museum of Asian Art, Smithsonian Institution, Freer Study Collection: Purchase, The Gerhard Pulverer Collection – Charles Lang Freer Endowment, Friends of the Freer and Sackler Galleries and the Harold P. Stern Memorial fund in appreciation of Jeffrey P. Cunard and his exemplary service to the Galleries as chair of the Board of Trustees (2003–2007), FSC-GR-780.240.1–3

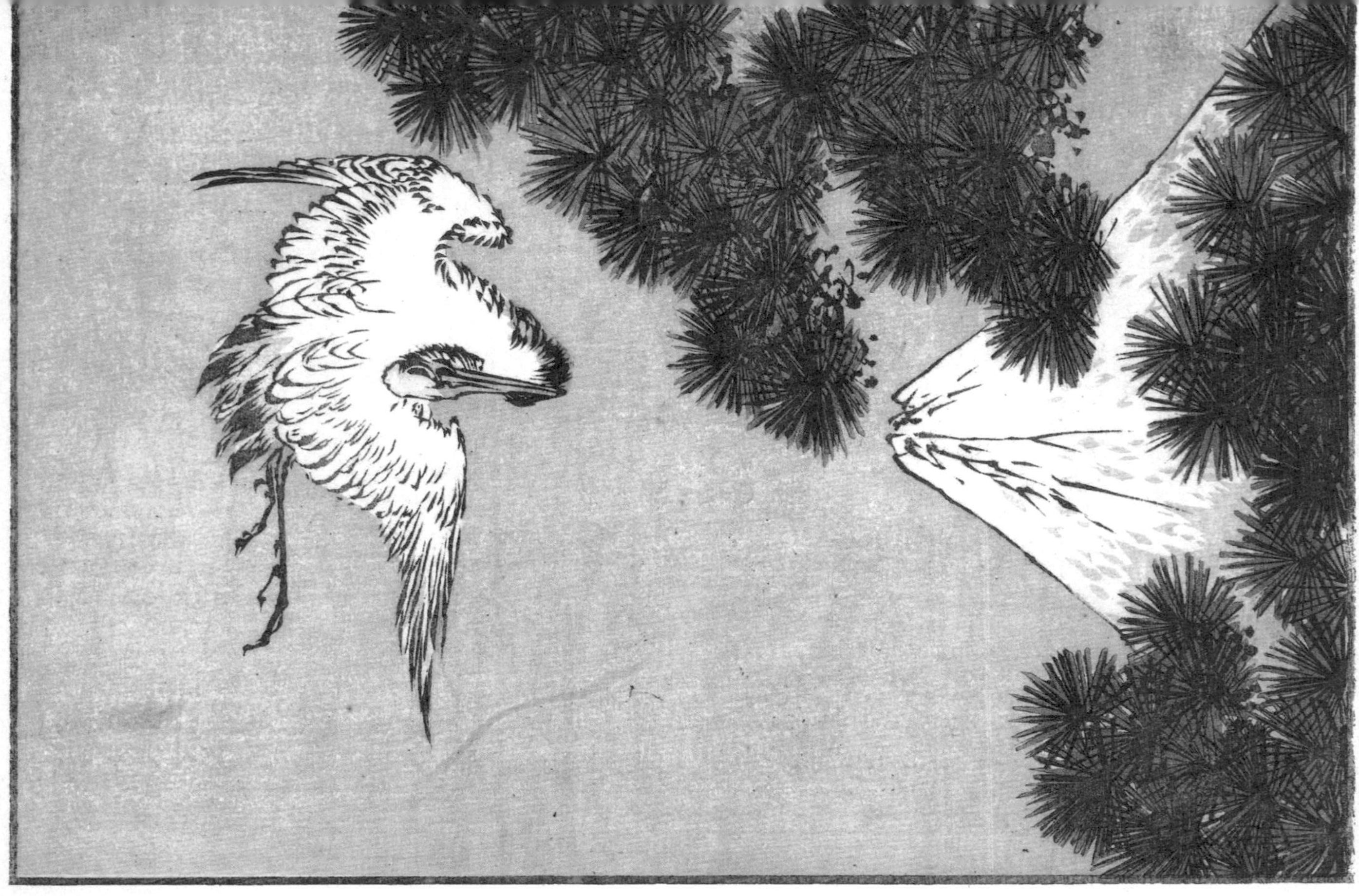

c. 1820. 23.3 × 16 cm. National Museum of Asian Art, Smithsonian Institution, Freer Study Collection: Purchase, The Gerhard Pulverer Collection – Charles Lang Freer Endowment, Friends of the Freer and Sackler Galleries and the Harold P. Stern Memorial fund in appreciation of Jeffrey P. Cunard and his exemplary service to the Galleries as chair of the Board of Trustees (2003–2007), FSC-GR-780.247.1-5

Hokusai Gafu (A Picture Album by Hokusai), Vol. 3
hanshibon, unsigned

Chapter 2

Thirty-Six Views of Mount Fuji

First published 1831–33 by Eijudō Nishimuraya Yohachi

Thirty-Six Views of Mount Fuji is a series of forty-six full-colour prints with the locations added as subtitles. It is thought to have been published from 1831 onwards, at the latest. Hokusai was then seventy-two years old and at the pinnacle of his career.

The following announcement of the publication of *Thirty-Six Views of Mount Fuji* was printed at the back of *Stories in Prompt-book Form* by Ryūtei Tanehiko, published in 1831 by Nishimuraya Yohashi at Eijudō publishing house:

'*Thirty-Six Views of Mount Fuji* by Zen Hokusai Iitsu; single sheet *aizuri*. One view per sheet, to be published one after another. These pictures show how the form of Fuji differs depending on the place, such as the shape seen from Shichirigahama, or the view observed from Tsukudajima: he has drawn them all so that none are the same. These should be useful for those who are learning the art of landscape. If the blocks continue to be cut in this way, one after another, the total should come to more than one hundred, without being limited to thirty-six.'

I have taken the promotional text in the above announcement as the basis for my commentary on *Thirty-Six Views of Mount Fuji*.

At the time, Hokusai had changed his name to Iitsu, but with the immense success of *Hokusai Manga*, the name Hokusai had higher recognition by far. For this reason, the advertisement uses the curious name Zen Hokusai Iitsu (Iitsu, formerly Hokusai). Incidentally, ten prints including *Under the Wave off Kanagawa* in *Thirty-Six Views of Mount Fuji* are signed 'Hokusai aratame Iitsu' (Hokusai, now Iitsu) [136–155].

Aizuri, popularly known as *bero* or 'Berlin blue', refers to *ukiyo-e* prints using shades of blue created with a type of pigment discovered in Prussia in the early 18th century. The original form of this pigment was expensive, but by the mid-19th century a cheaper alternative pigment imported from China was adopted for *ukiyo*-e woodblock prints. Hokusai must have been aware of the unprecedented beauty of *aizuri* and how the colour could be used to create depth, particularly in depictions of the sky and water. There are ten striking examples among the early prints for *Thirty-Six Views of Mount Fuji* [116–135].

The promotional text continues, 'One view per sheet, to be published one after another.' At the time landscape painting was not yet an established genre, but this work with its countless variations on Fuji 'should be useful for those who are learning the art of landscape' because it incorporates perspectives and com-positions that differ from conventional images of famous places. In other words, the advertisement describes the work as a manual for landscape painting.

Popular Designs for Combs and Tobacco Pipes [108–109], published eight years earlier in 1824, included an announcement for the forthcoming publication of 'Eight Views of Mount Fuji' [31], stating that the series would depict the ways that the landscape varies with the seasons, the weather, rain or shine, snow storms in the open air, and other natural phenomena. This never-completed idea was developed further in *Thirty-Six Views of Mount Fuji*, which suggests that this was something Hokusai had been planning for a long time. It is also clear that the intention from the start was to depict Fuji in different moods depending on the season or the weather as seen in *A Mild Breeze on a Fine Day* [138–139], which depicts Fuji tinged by the light of dawn in early summer, or *Shower Below the Summit* [140–141] with its lingering lightning bolts.

Finally, the text says, 'If the blocks continue to be cut in this way ... without being limited to thirty.' In actual fact, since the work was well received, another ten images, popularly known as

'Fuji from the Rear' [188–207], were added to the series, making a total of forty-six prints. Unlike the first thirty-six pictures, Hokusai used black *sumizuri* ink, not blue *aizuri*, for the key block used to print the outlines of 'Fuji from the Rear'.

On its own, the promotional text reflects Hokusai's extraordinary mind and the characteristics of this series, but there is much more to be said about this group of works. Recollecting his age when he produced this series, Hokusai also referred to the challenges he had overcome since then. Chapter 1 describes how he experimented and absorbed a great variety of motifs, styles, and techniques, including Western perspective and the Chinese style of painting, to arrive at *Thirty-Six Views of Mount Fuji,* the receptacle into which he poured everything he had learnt.

The carefully thought-out compositions demonstrate his skill. In *Quick Lessons in Simplified Drawing Part 1* [30], Hokusai explains that geometric shapes such as circles and squares are the basic elements of drawing pictures, but in this series, Mount Fuji, a geometric triangle, is the main motif. This triangular shape is repeated in a clever rhythm, echoing the slant of a house roof [130–131, 176–177, 184–185, 194–195], or contrasting with a round barrel or a water wheel, the curve of a large bridge or a ship's hull [142–143, 152–153, 178–179, 182–183]. The strong lines of the upright trunk of a tall tree, or lumber propped at a diagonal angle emphasize the contours of the mountain [128–129, 134–135, 148–149, 164–165, 188–189], and even fishing lines or kite strings [122–123, 162–163, 176–177] can echo the dramatic triangle of Fuji.

Even when Fuji appears only as a small triangle in the distance, the casual turn of a head towards the mountain, the direction of a pointing arm [156–157, 160–161, 180–181], or the prow of a ship floating in the sea or on a river [118–119] can draw invisible lines that focus attention on the mountain. Moments that look as if they were captured with a high-speed camera further heighten the sense of tension in these bold compositions: a great wave that looks as if it will break apart at any moment [136–137], the lively motion of galloping horses [168–169], or sheets of paper blown into the air by a sudden gust of wind [132–133]. There are too many examples to count, but every single image is witty and ingenious.

The differences in paper formats and print colours suggest that this series was divided into several groups and published at different times. According to one claim, the first group consists of pictures signed 'Hokusai aratame Iitsu' (Hokusai, now Iitsu). In this book, we assume that the series starts with the ten distinctive early *aizuri*-e promoted in the advertisement.

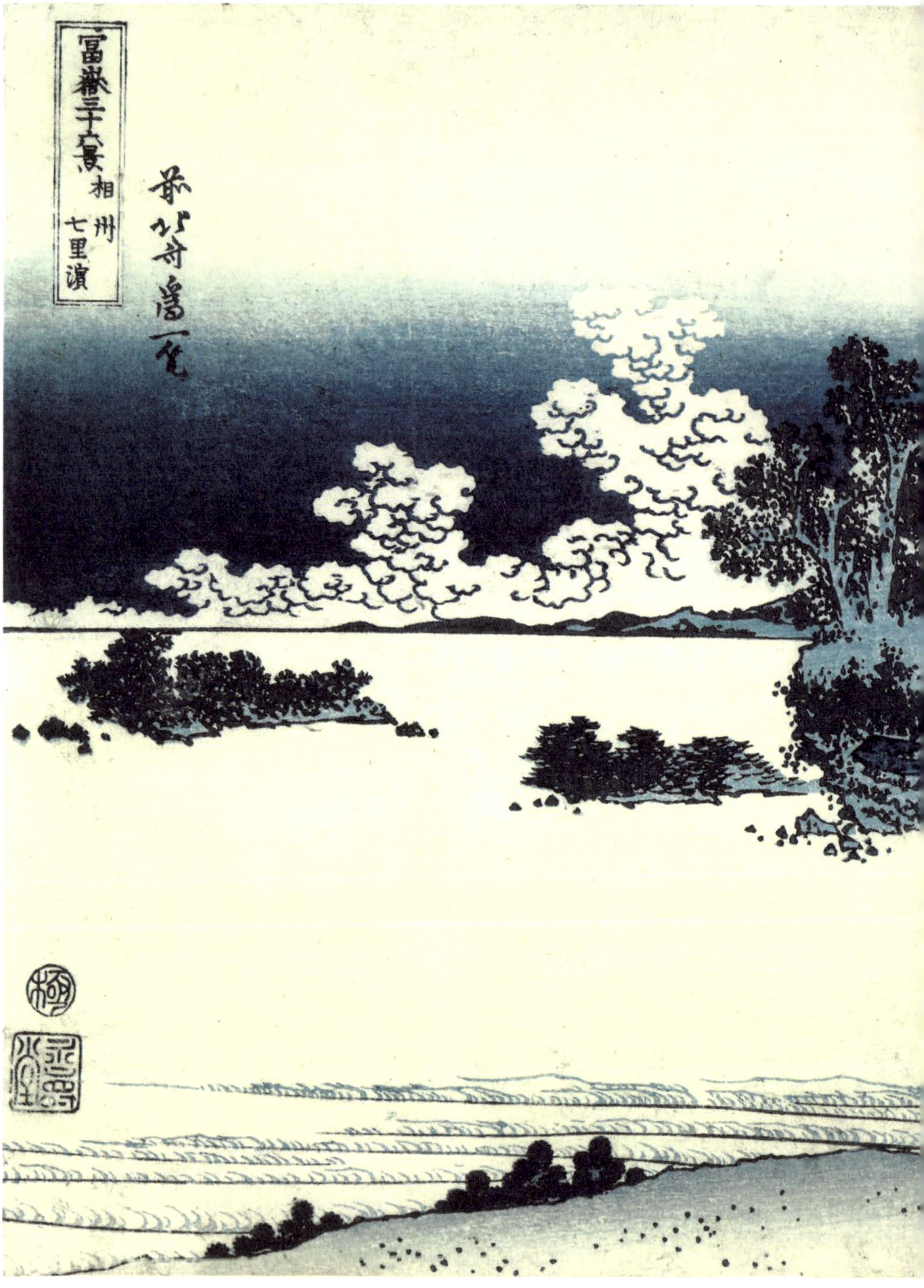

Shichirigahama Beach, Sagami Province
signed Zen Hokusai Iitsu hitsu

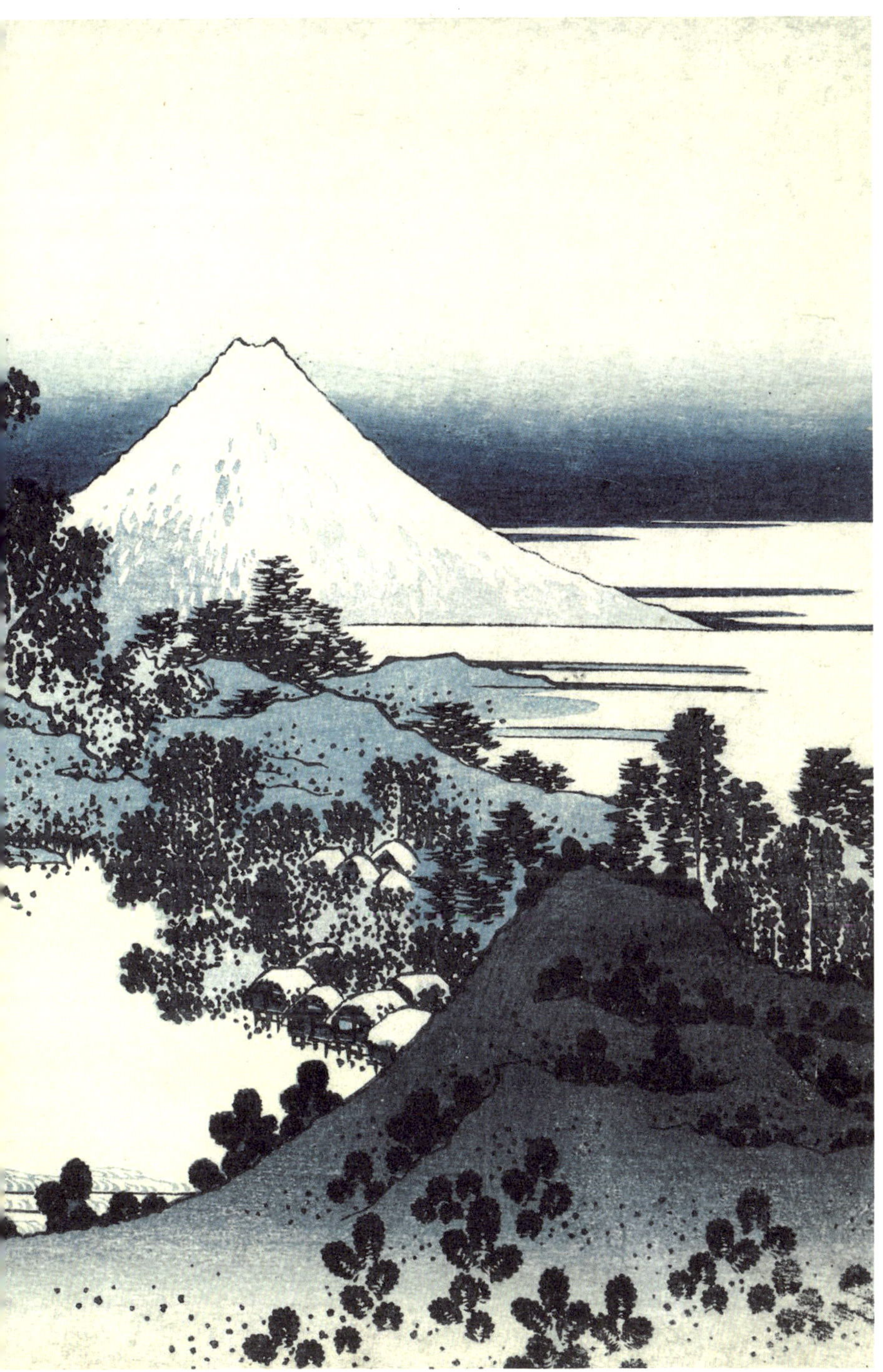

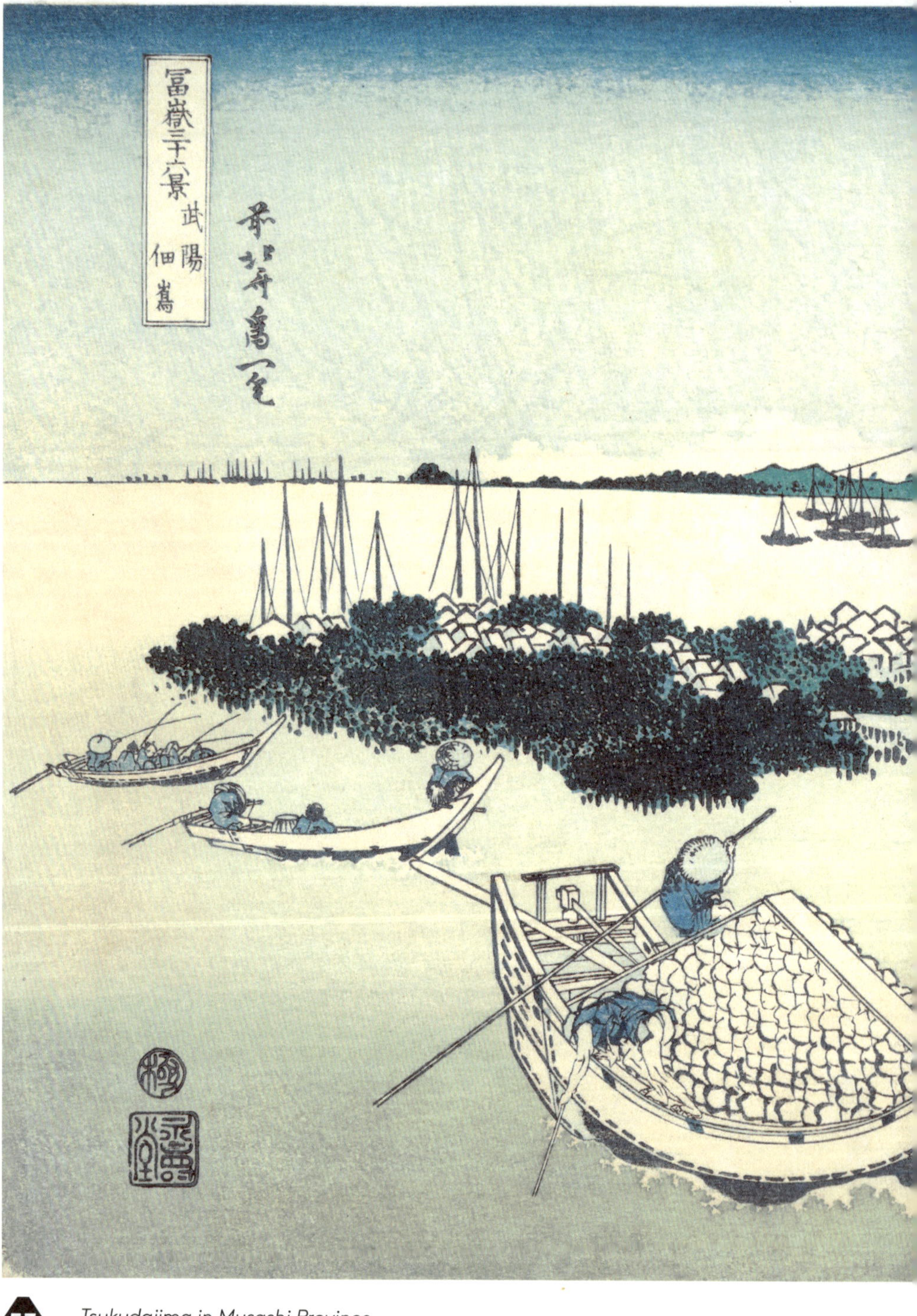

53 *Tsukudajima in Musashi Province*
signed Zen Hokusai Iitsu hitsu

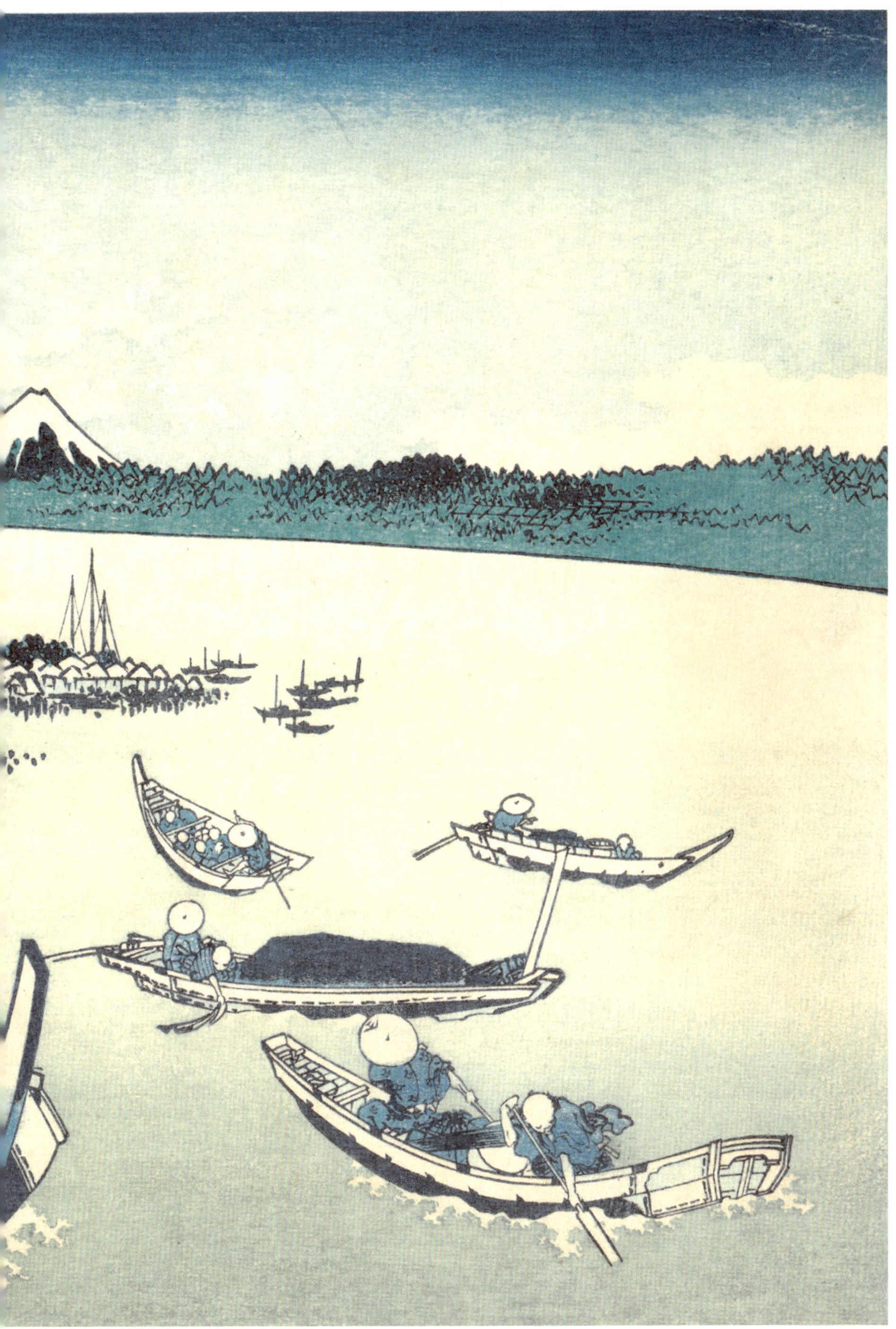

25.4 × 38.7 cm. The Howard Mansfield Collection, Gift of Howard Mansfield, 1936,The Metropolitan Museum of Art, New York, JP2563

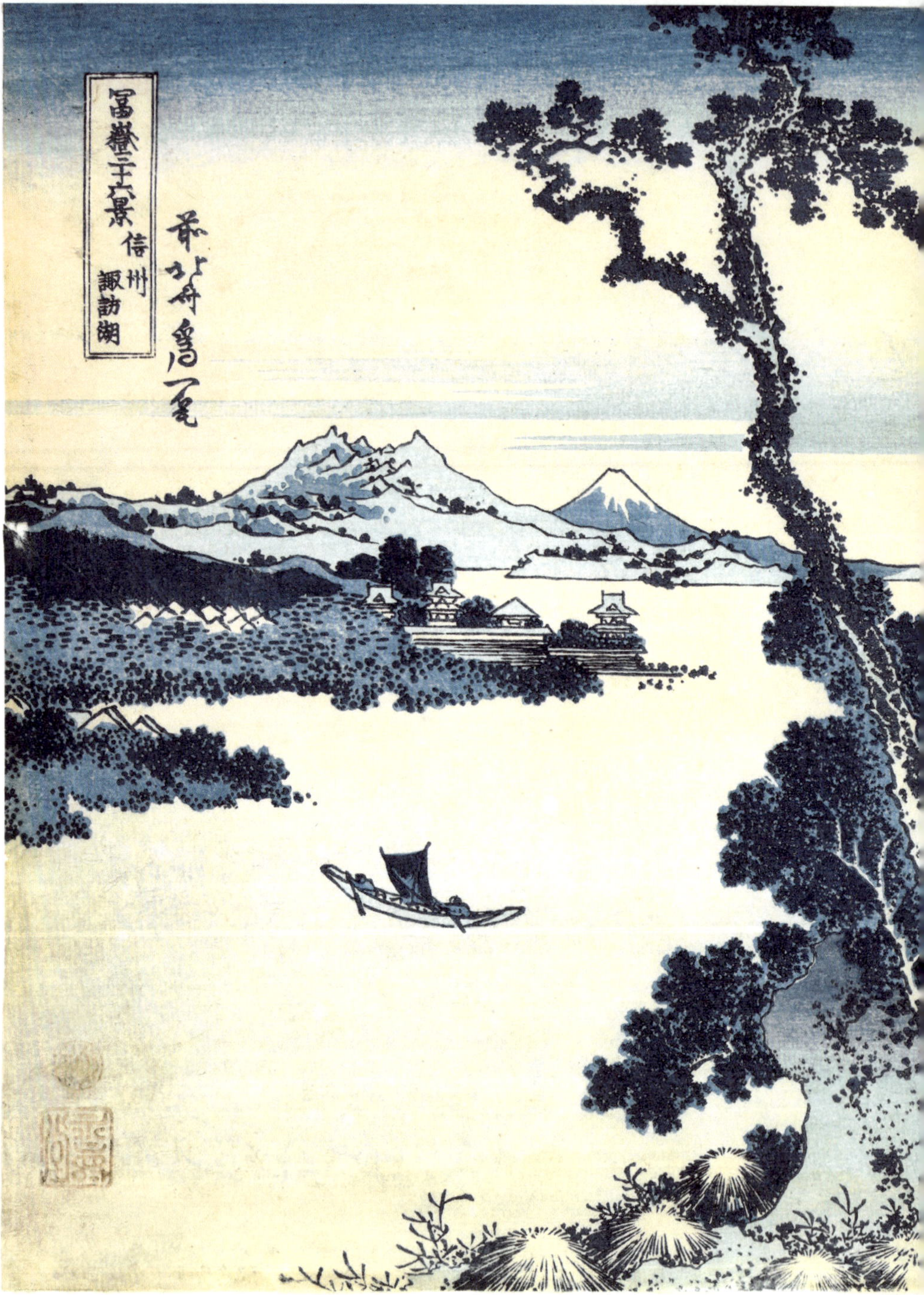

Lake Suwa in Shinano Province
signed Zen Hokusai Iitsu hitsu

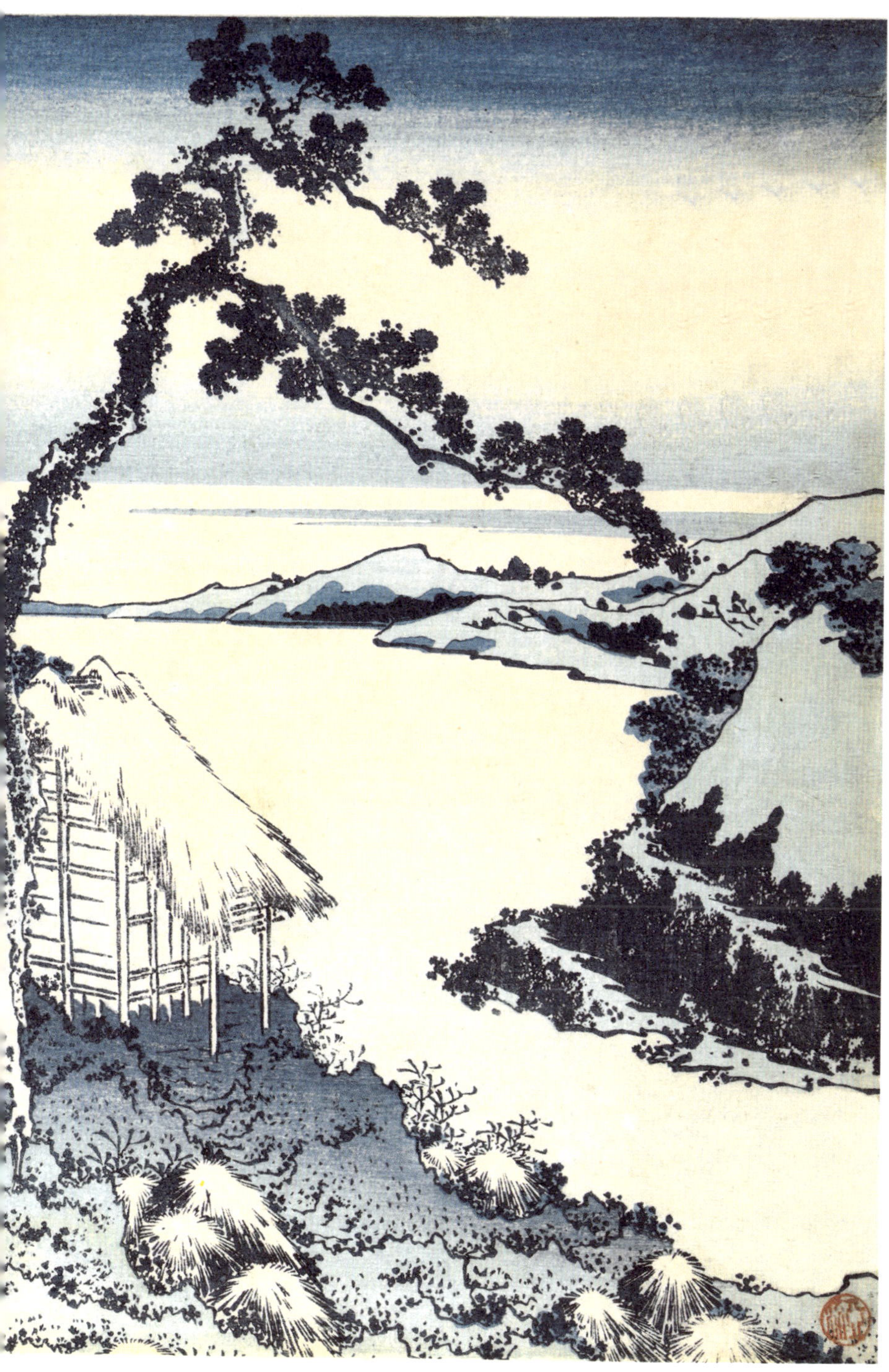

25.5 × 36.5 cm. The New York Public Library: Cadwalader Fund, 89284

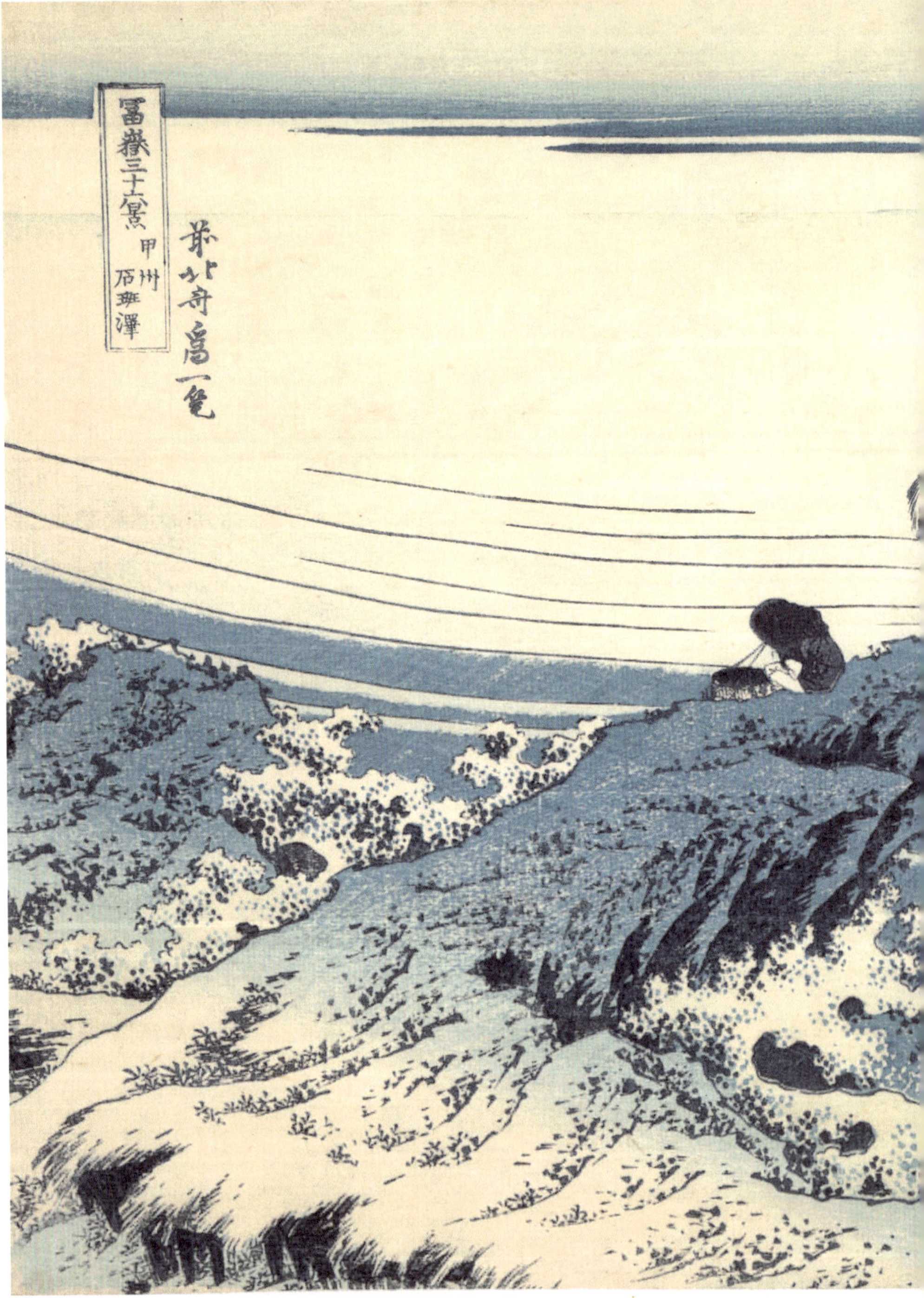

55 *Kajikazawa in Kai Province*
signed Zen Hokusai Iitsu hitsu

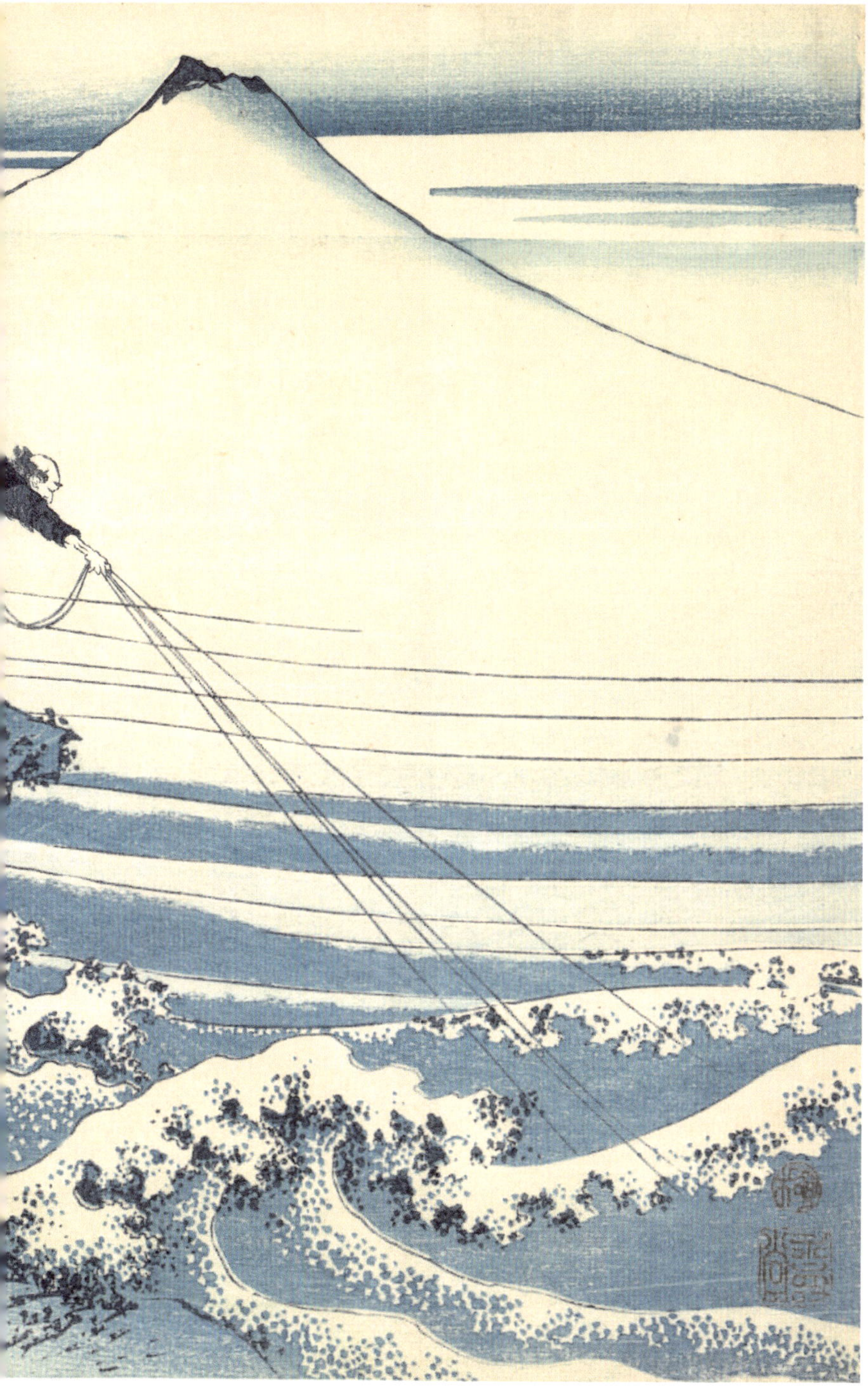

26 × 38.4 cm. Henry L. Phillips Collection, Bequest of Henry L. Phillips, 1939, The Metropolitan Museum of Art, New York, JP2986

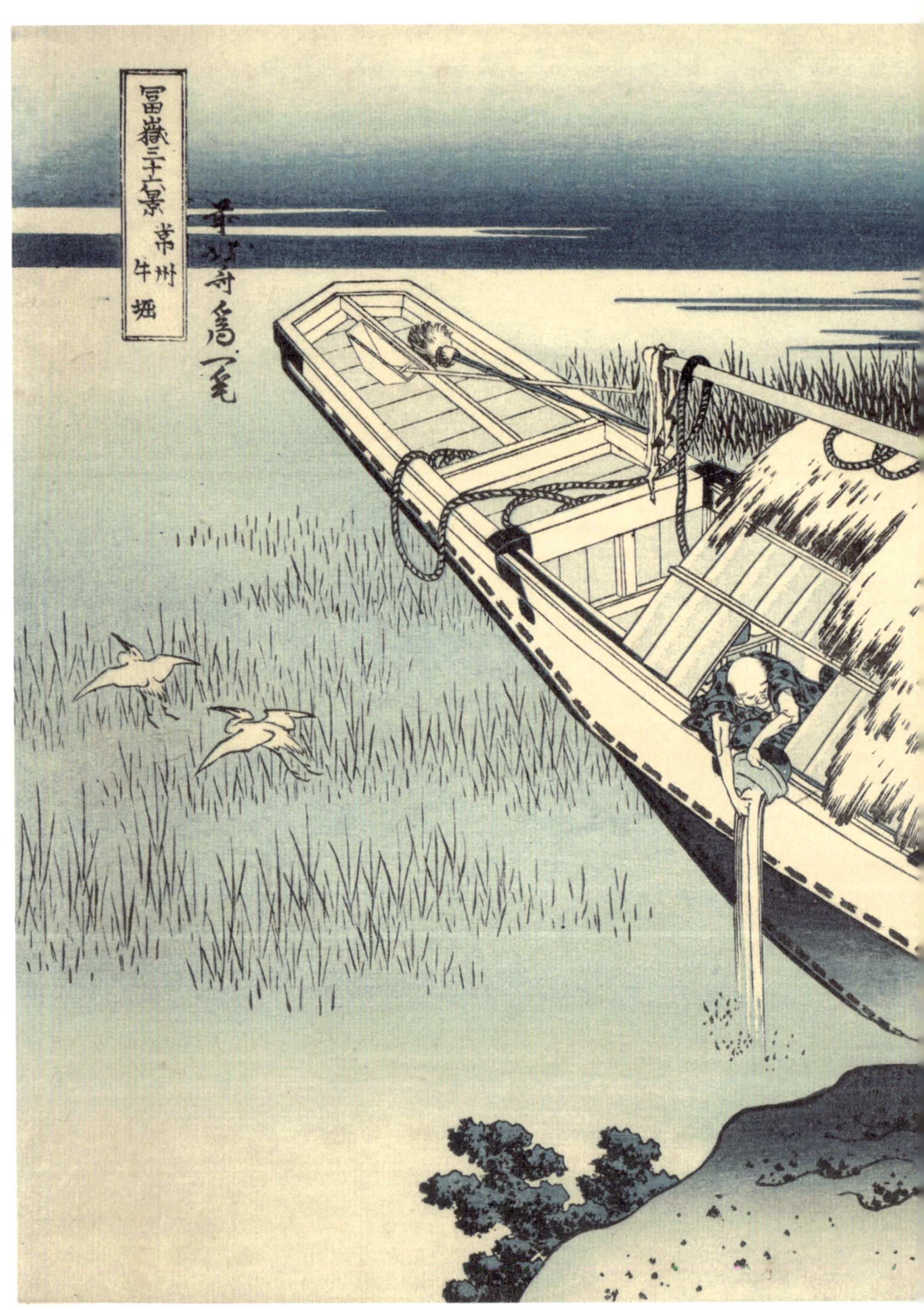

Ushibori in Hitachi Province
signed Zen Hokusai litsu hitsu

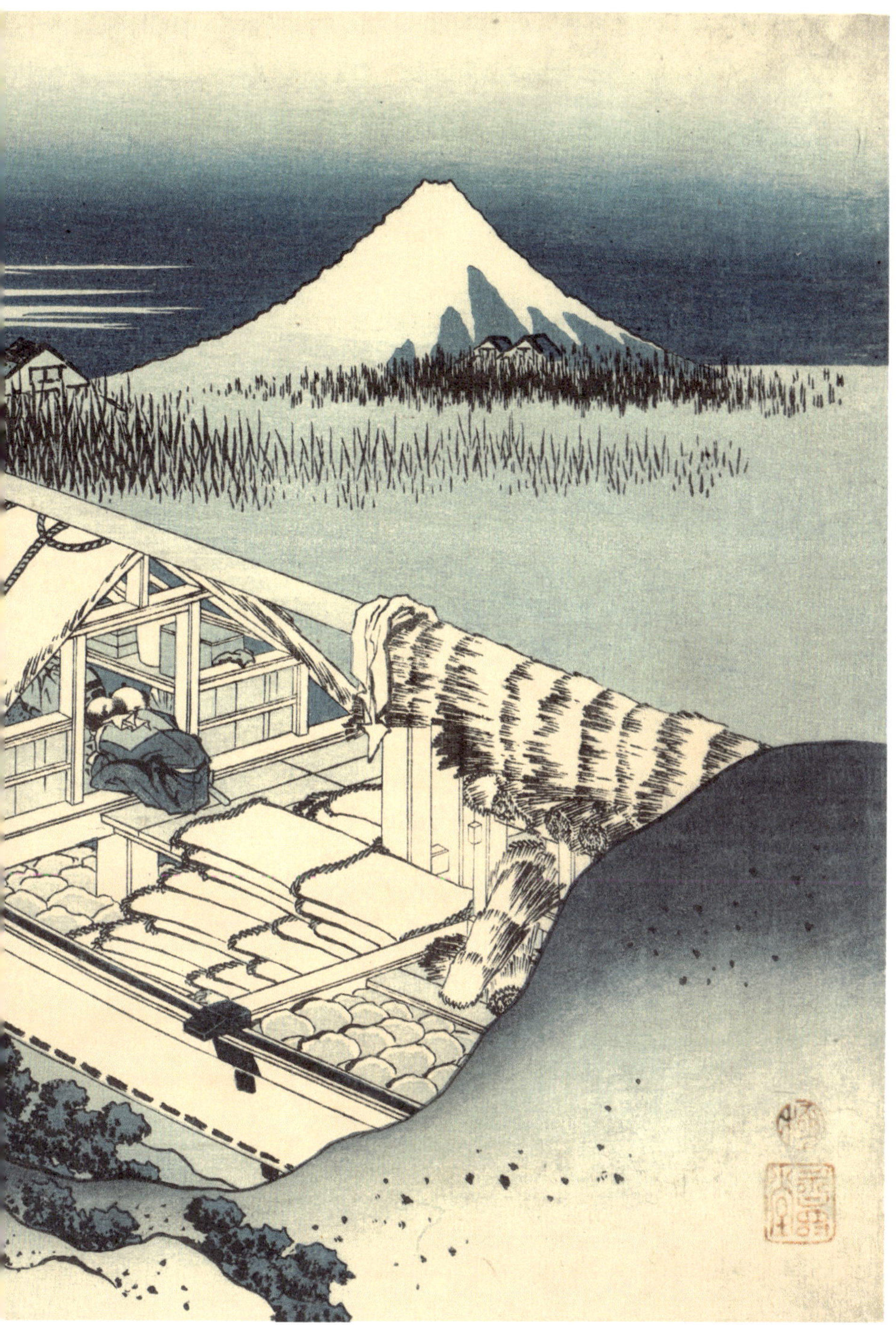

25.9 × 37.5 cm. The Howard Mansfield Collection, Gift of Howard Mansfield, 1936, The Metropolitan Museum of Art, New York, JP2565

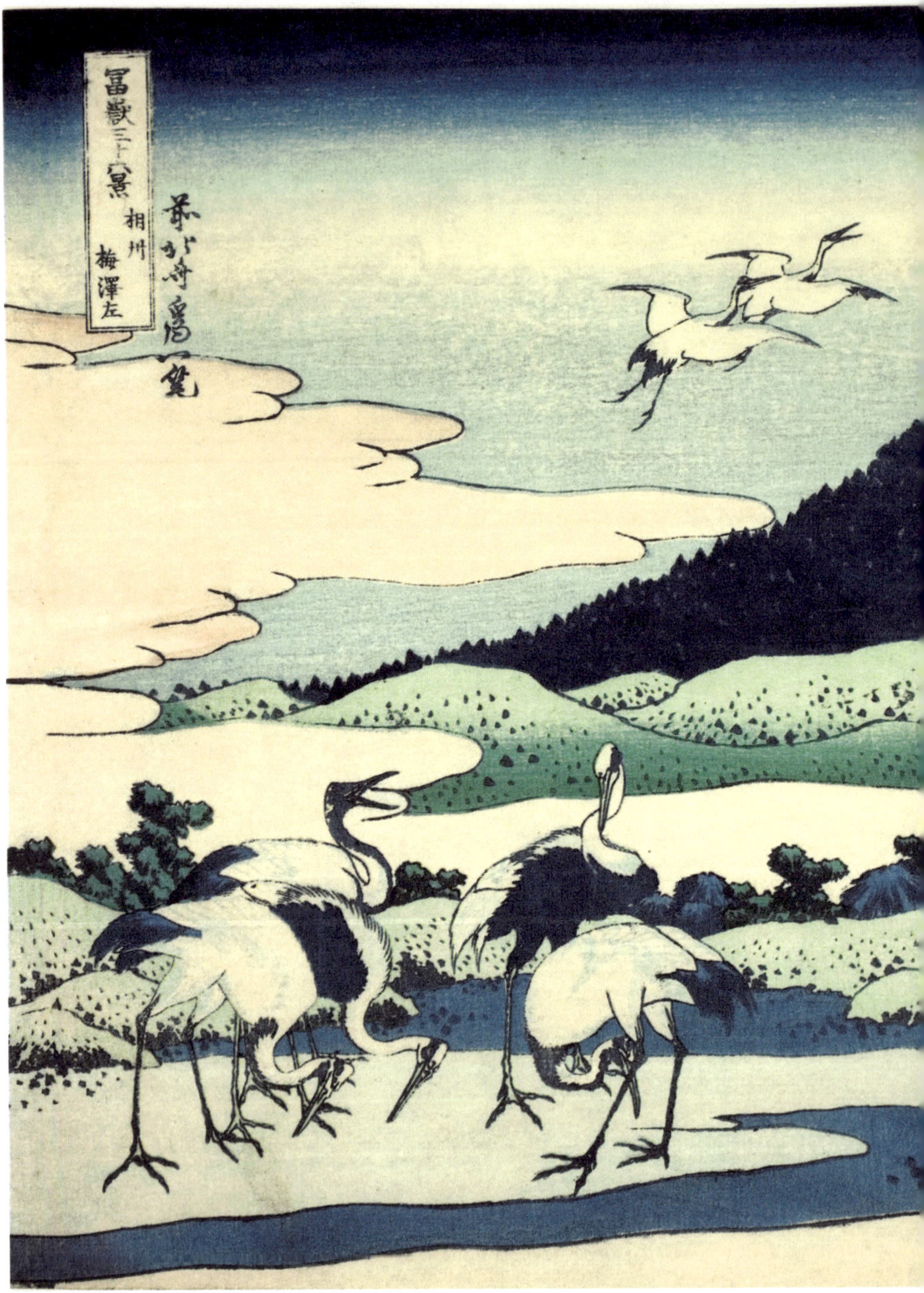

57 *Umezawa Marsh in Sagami Province*
signed Zen Hokusai Iitsu hitsu

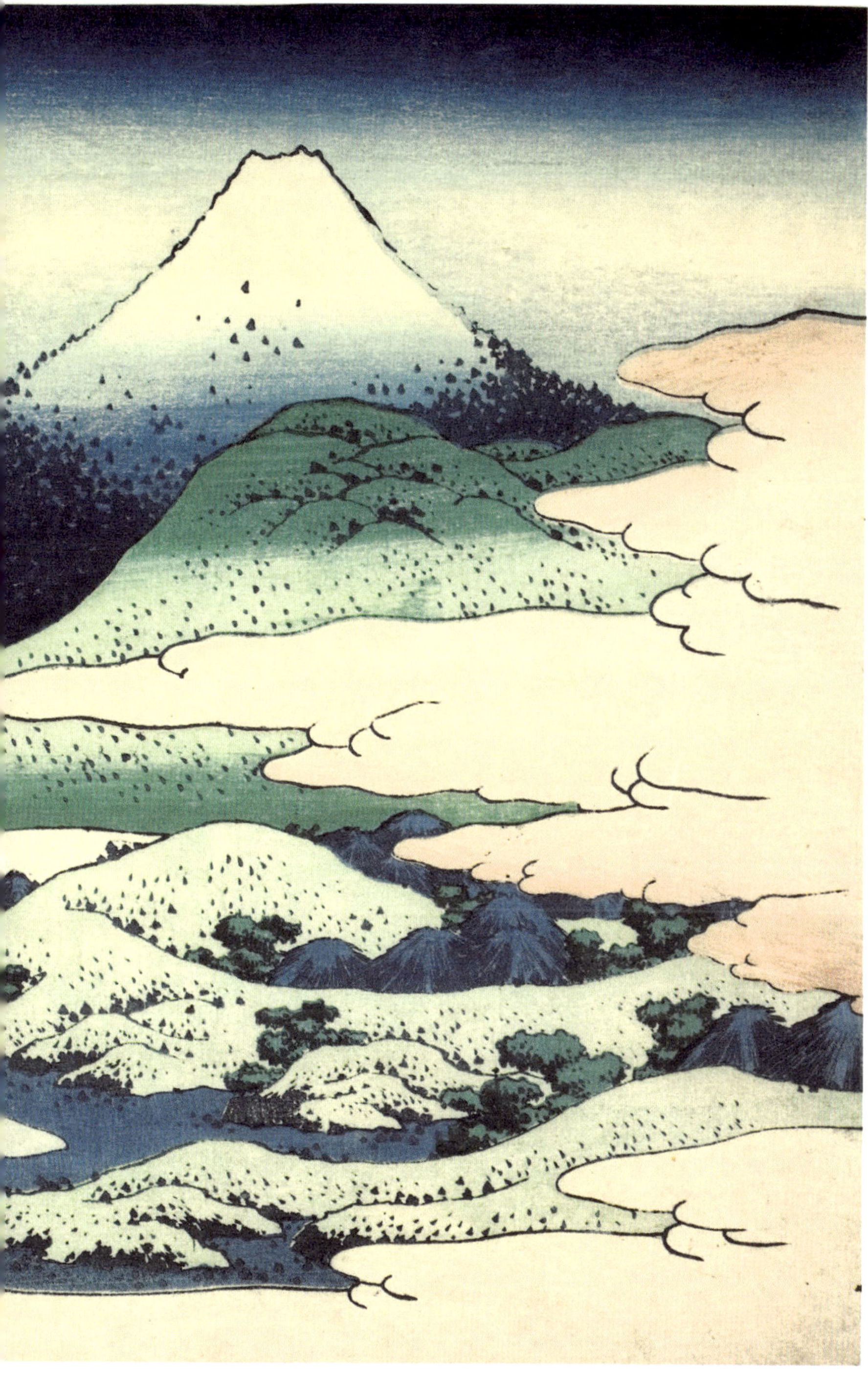

25.7 × 37.8 cm. Clarence Buckingham Collection, The Art Institute of Chicago, 1925.3234

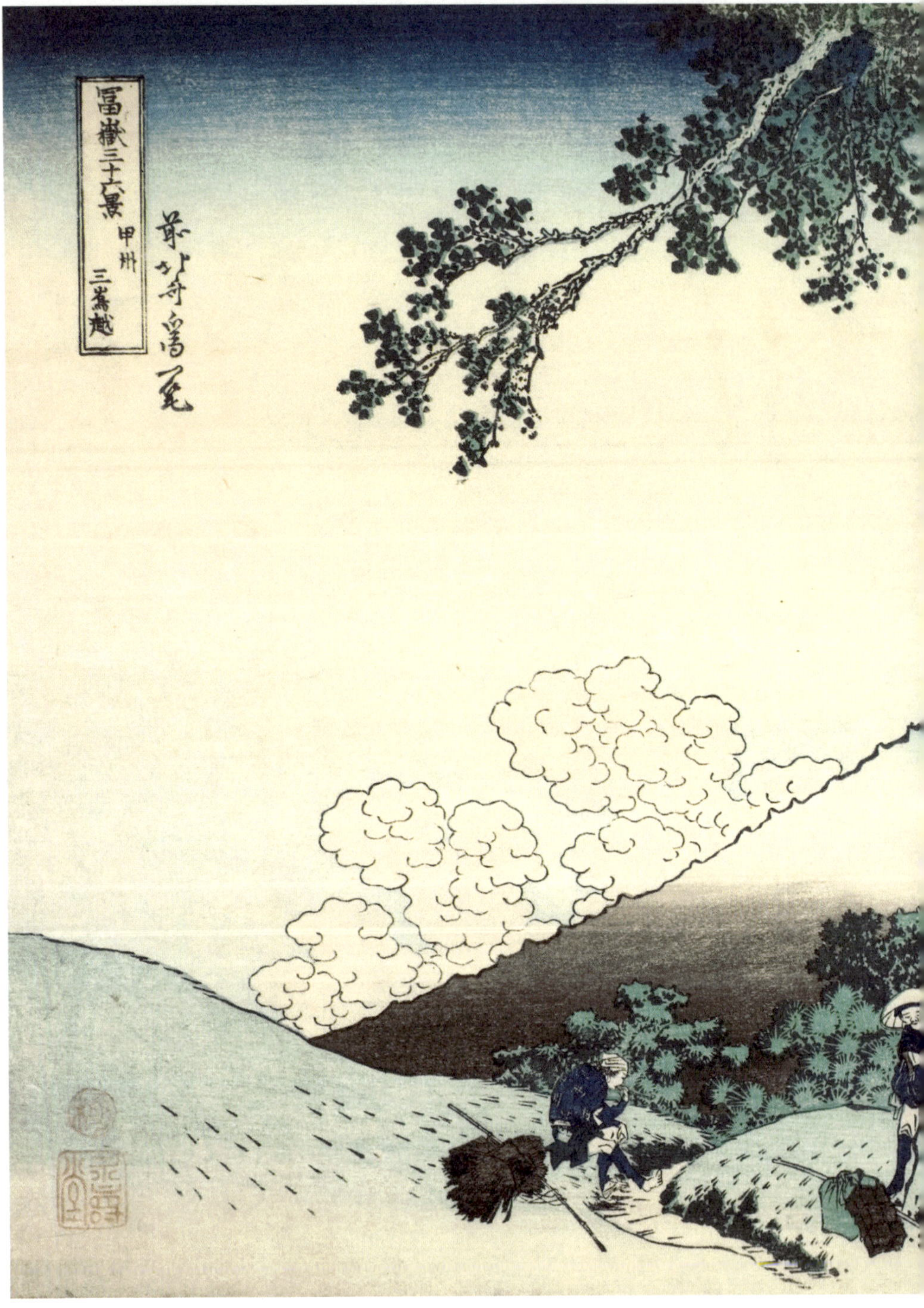

58 *Mishima Pass in Kai Province*
signed Zen Hokusai Iitsu hitsu

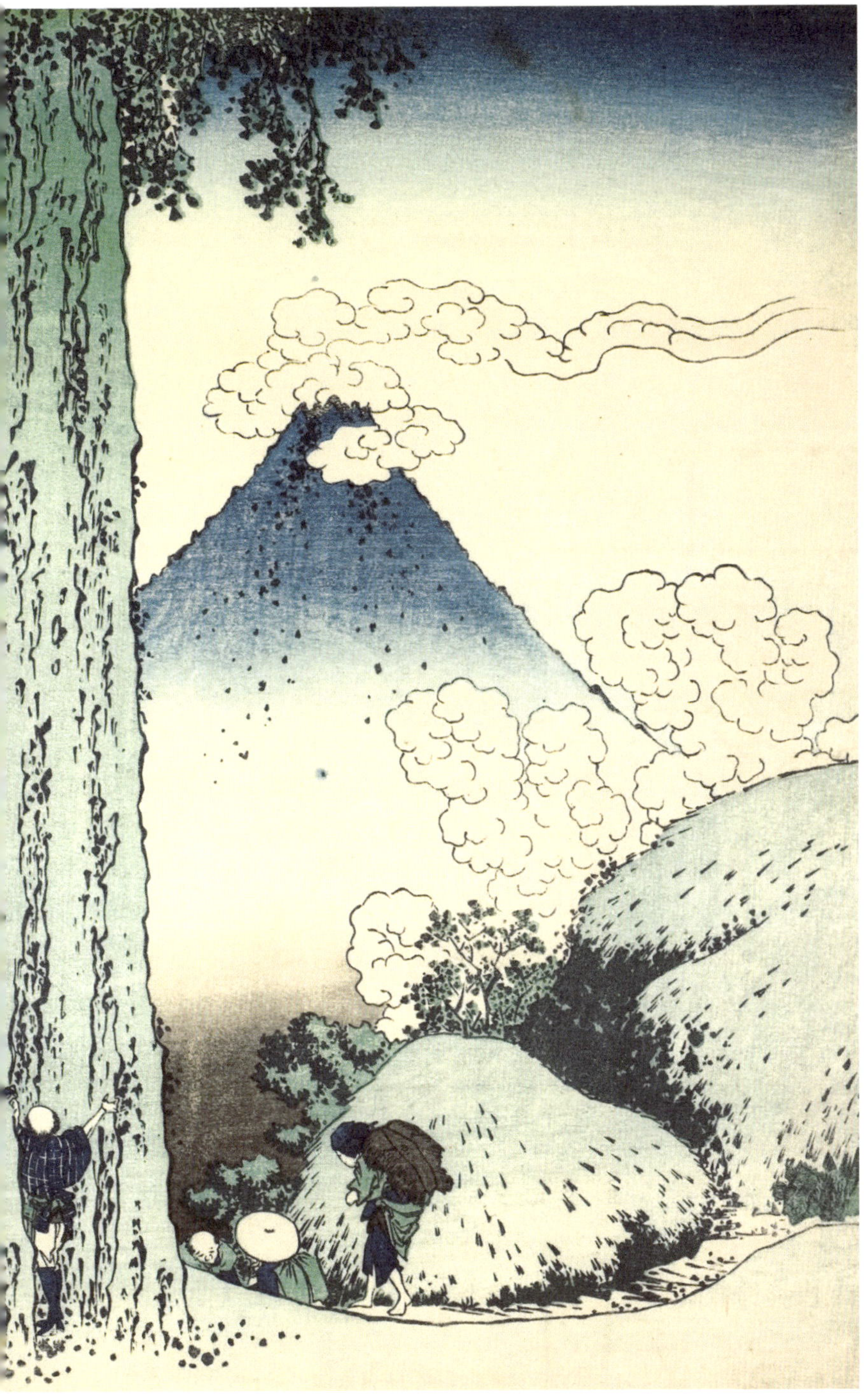

25.7 × 37.2 cm. Clarence Buckingham Collection, The Art Institute of Chicago, 1925.3259

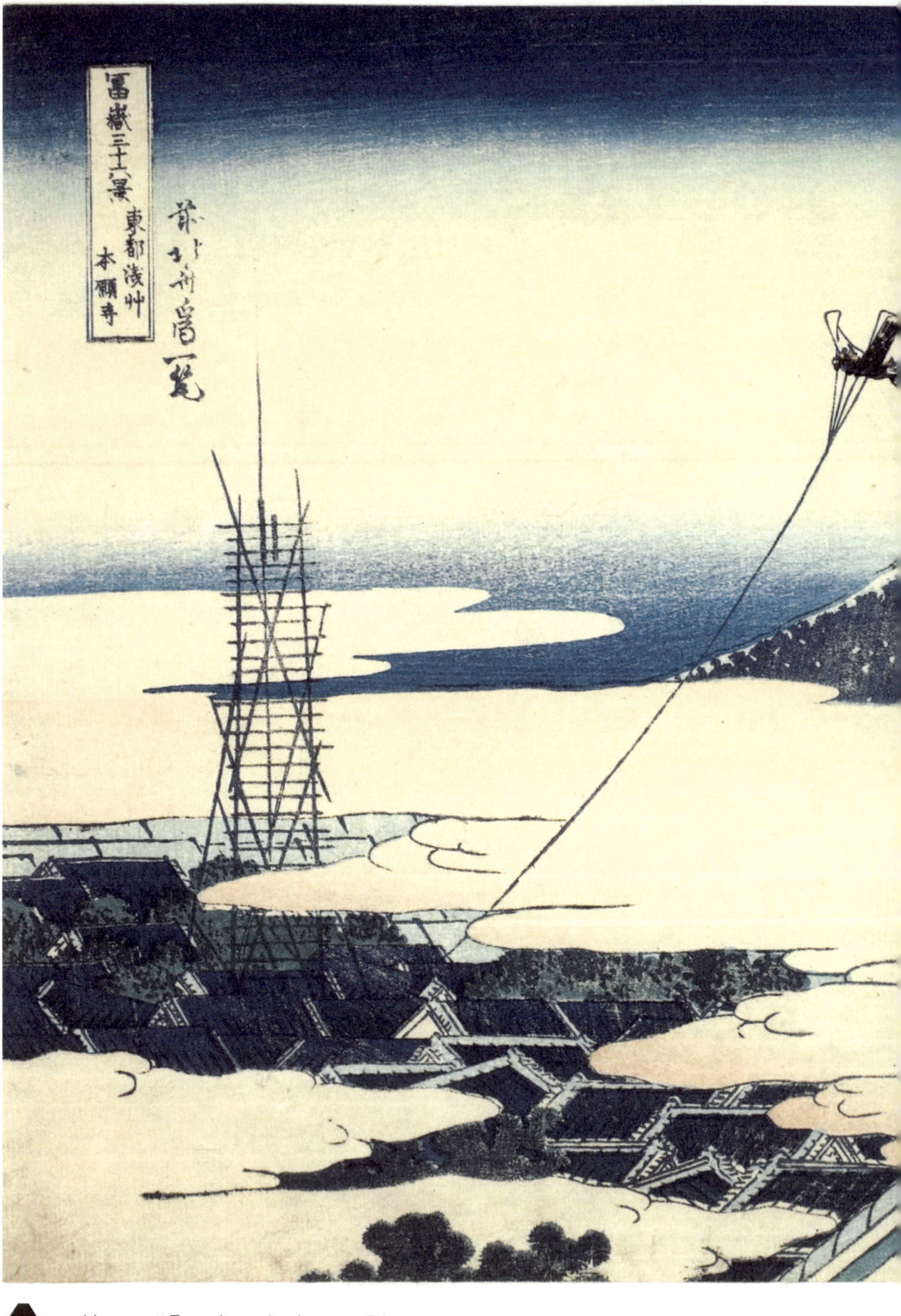

59 *Honganji Temple at Asakusa in Edo*
signed Zen Hokusai Iitsu hitsu

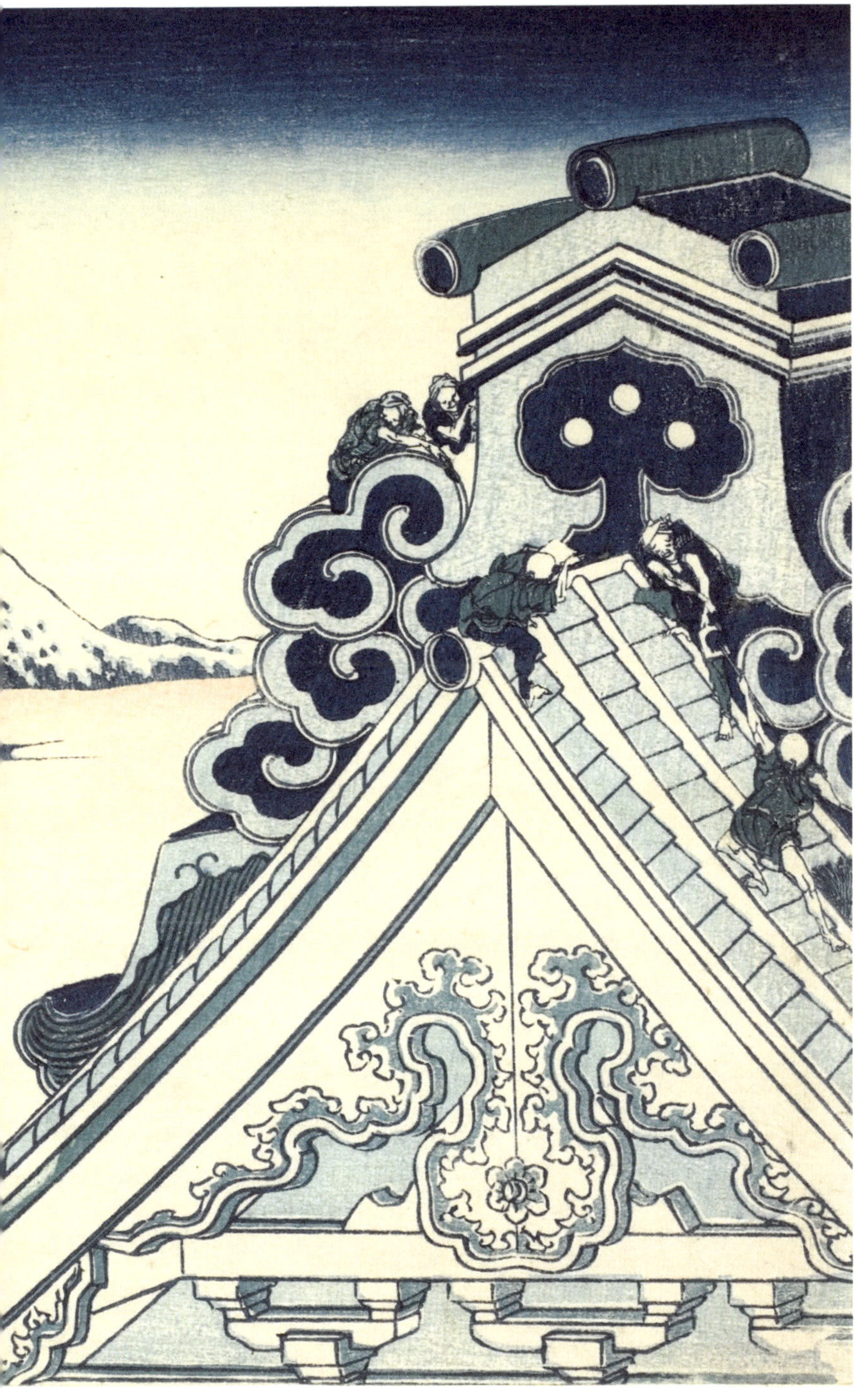

25.7 × 37.2 cm. Clarence Buckingham Collection, The Art Institute of Chicago, 1925.3259

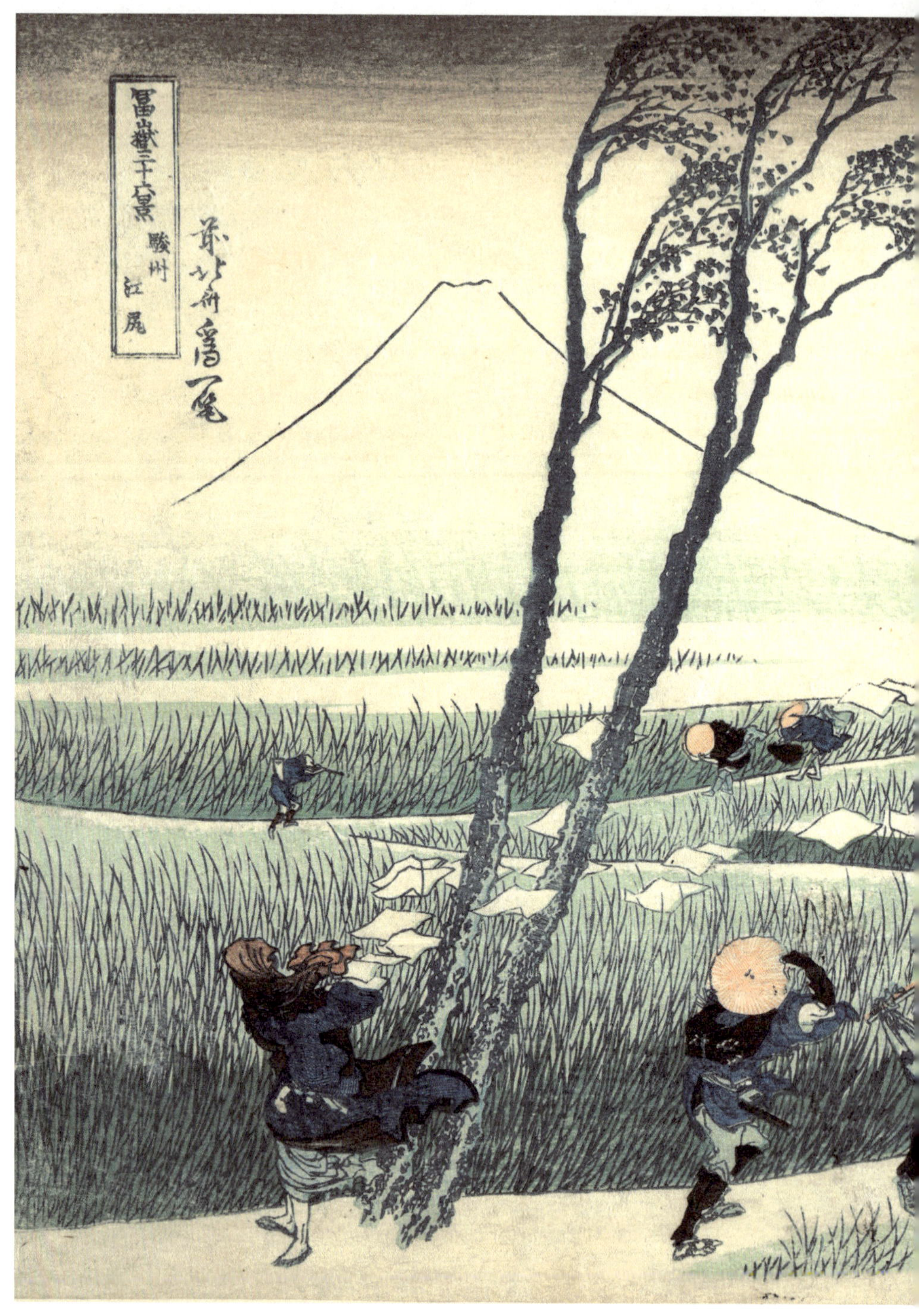

60 *Ejiri in Suruga Province*
signed Zen Hokusai Iitsu hitsu

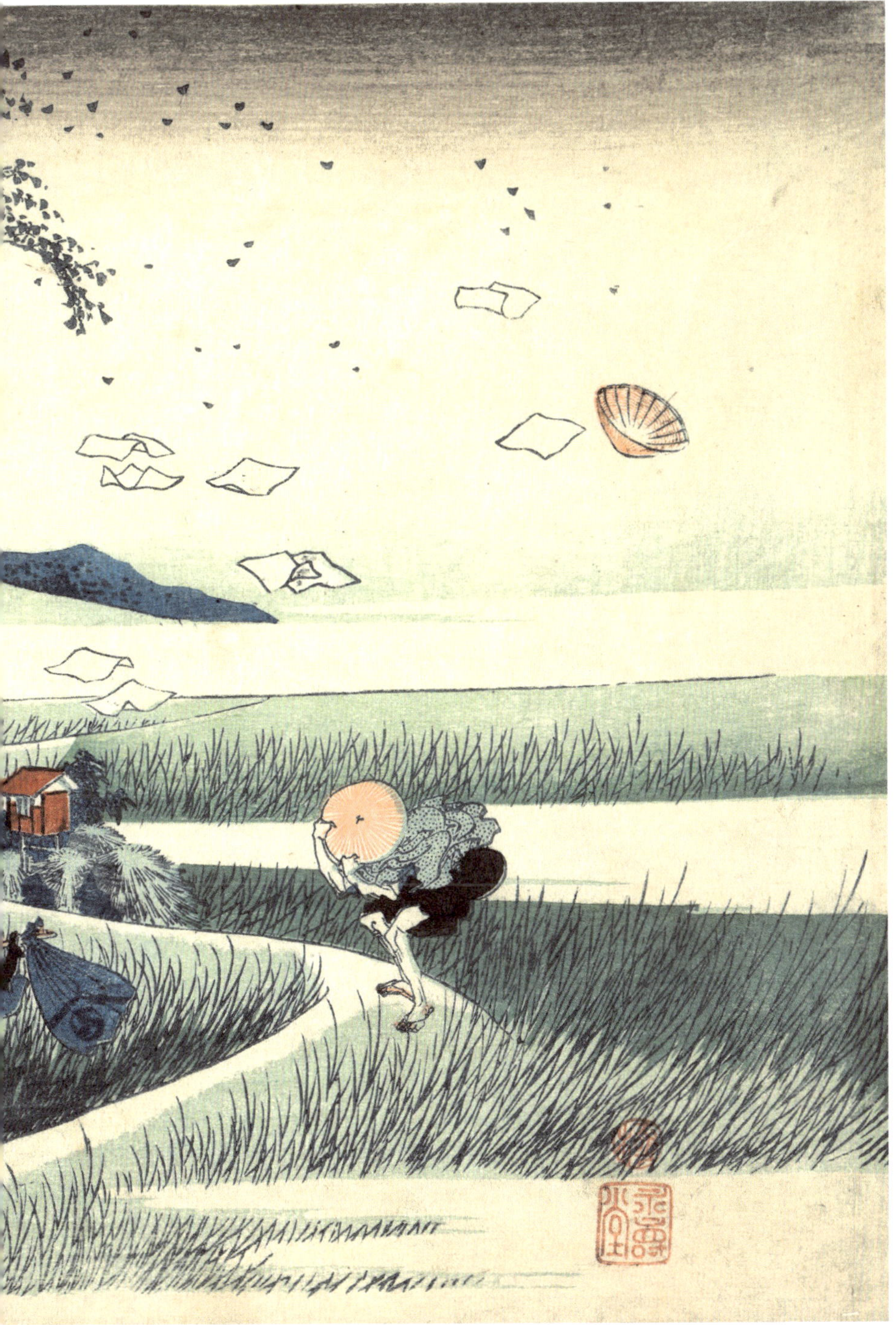

24.4 × 37.5 cm. The Howard Mansfield Collection, Gift of Howard Mansfield, 1936, The Metropolitan Museum of Art, New York, JP2553

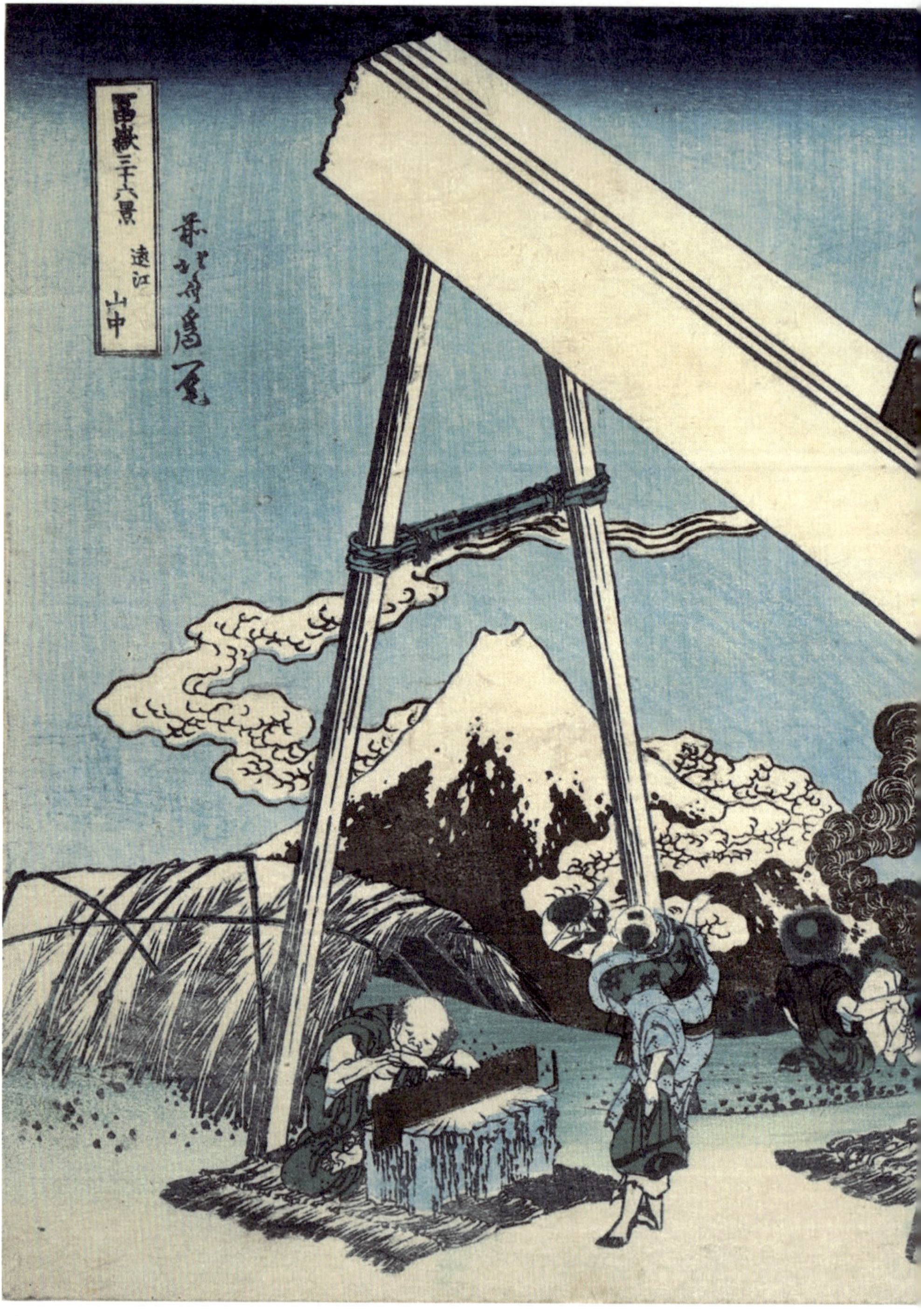

61 *In the Mountains of Tōtōmi Province*
signed Zen Hokusai Iitsu hitsu

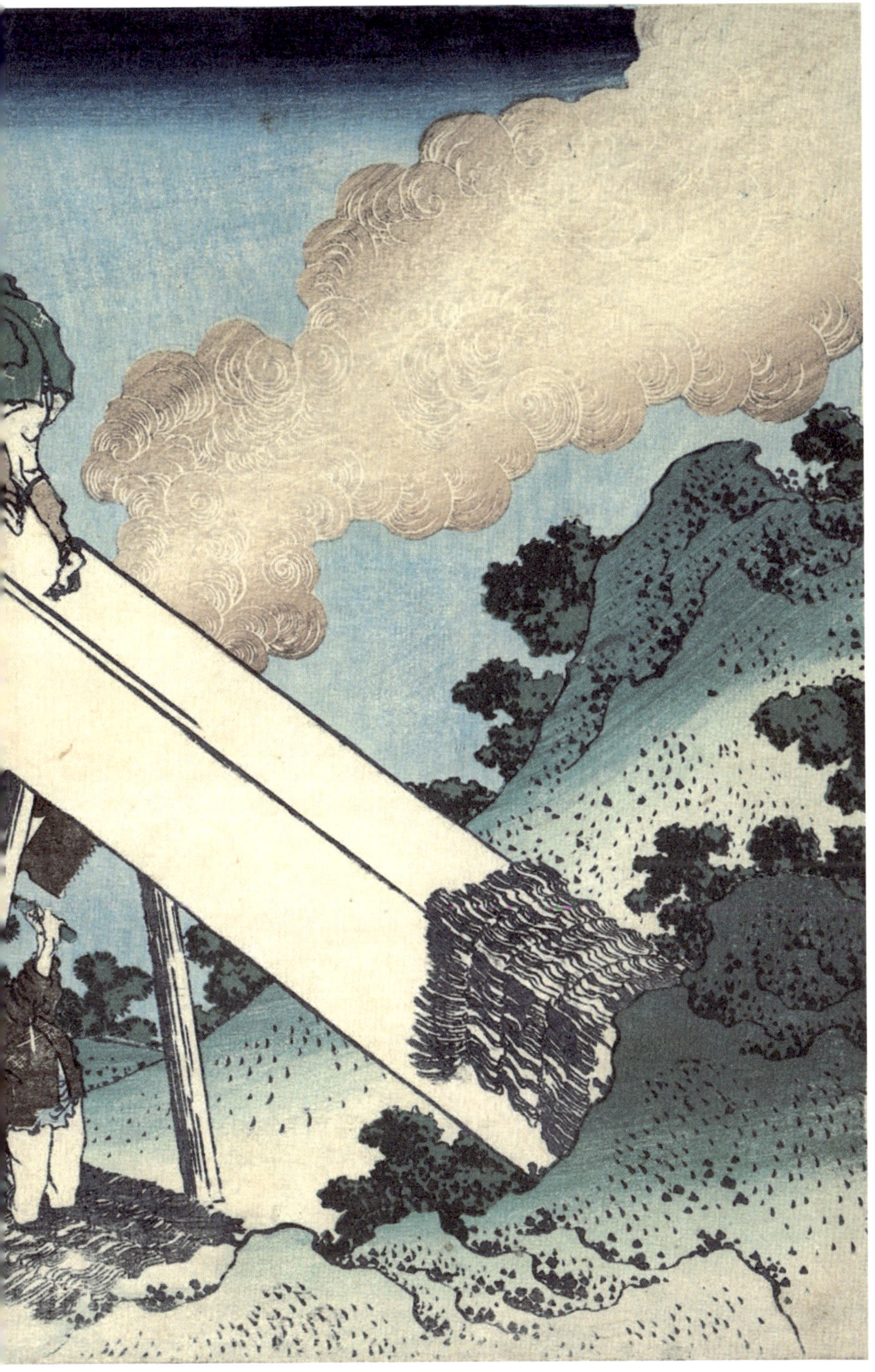

26.4 × 38.4 cm. Henry L. Phillips Collection, Bequest of Henry L. Phillips, 1939, The Metropolitan Museum of Art, New York, JP2966

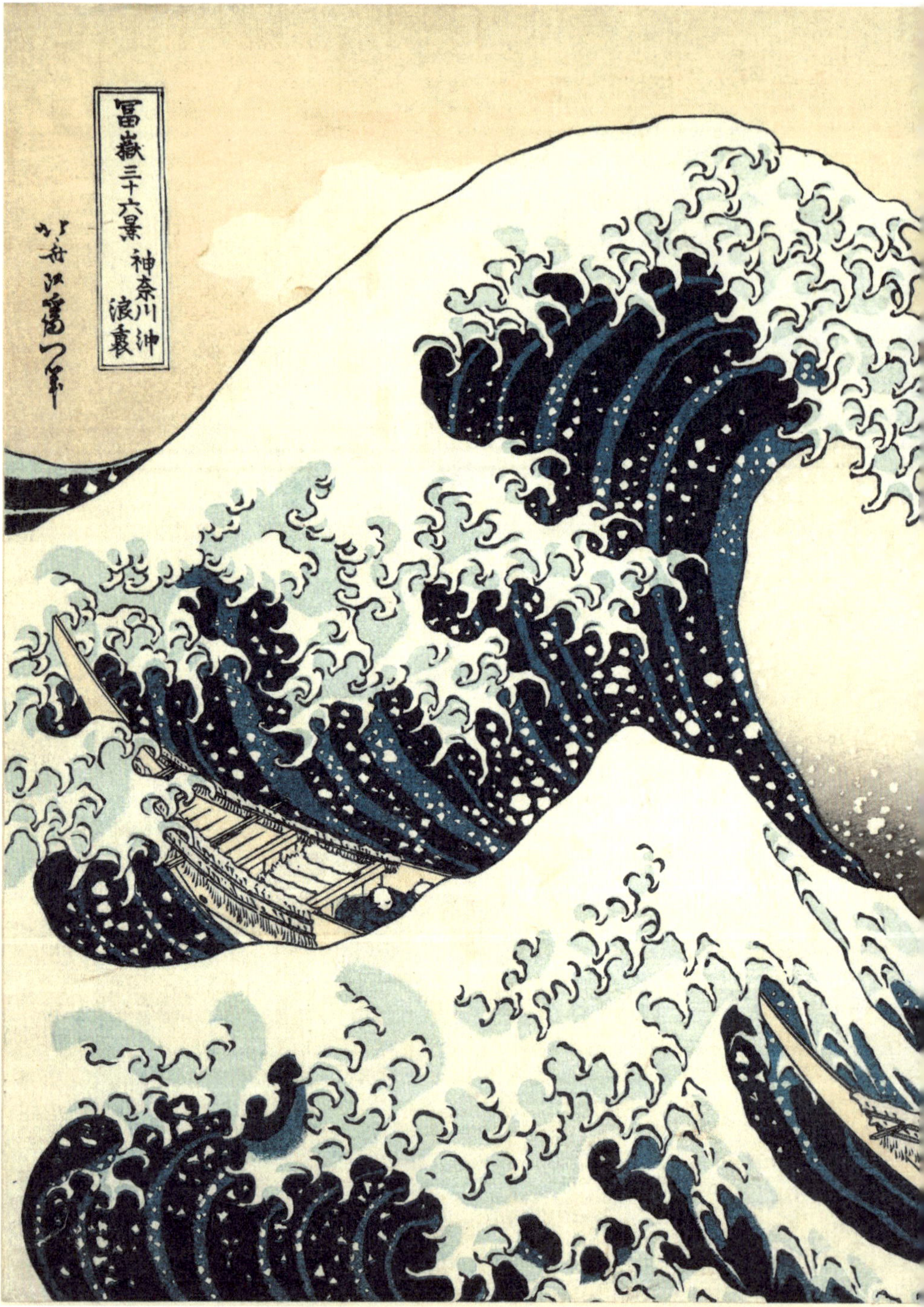

Under the Wave off Kanagawa (The Great Wave)
signed Hokusai Aratame Iitsu hitsu

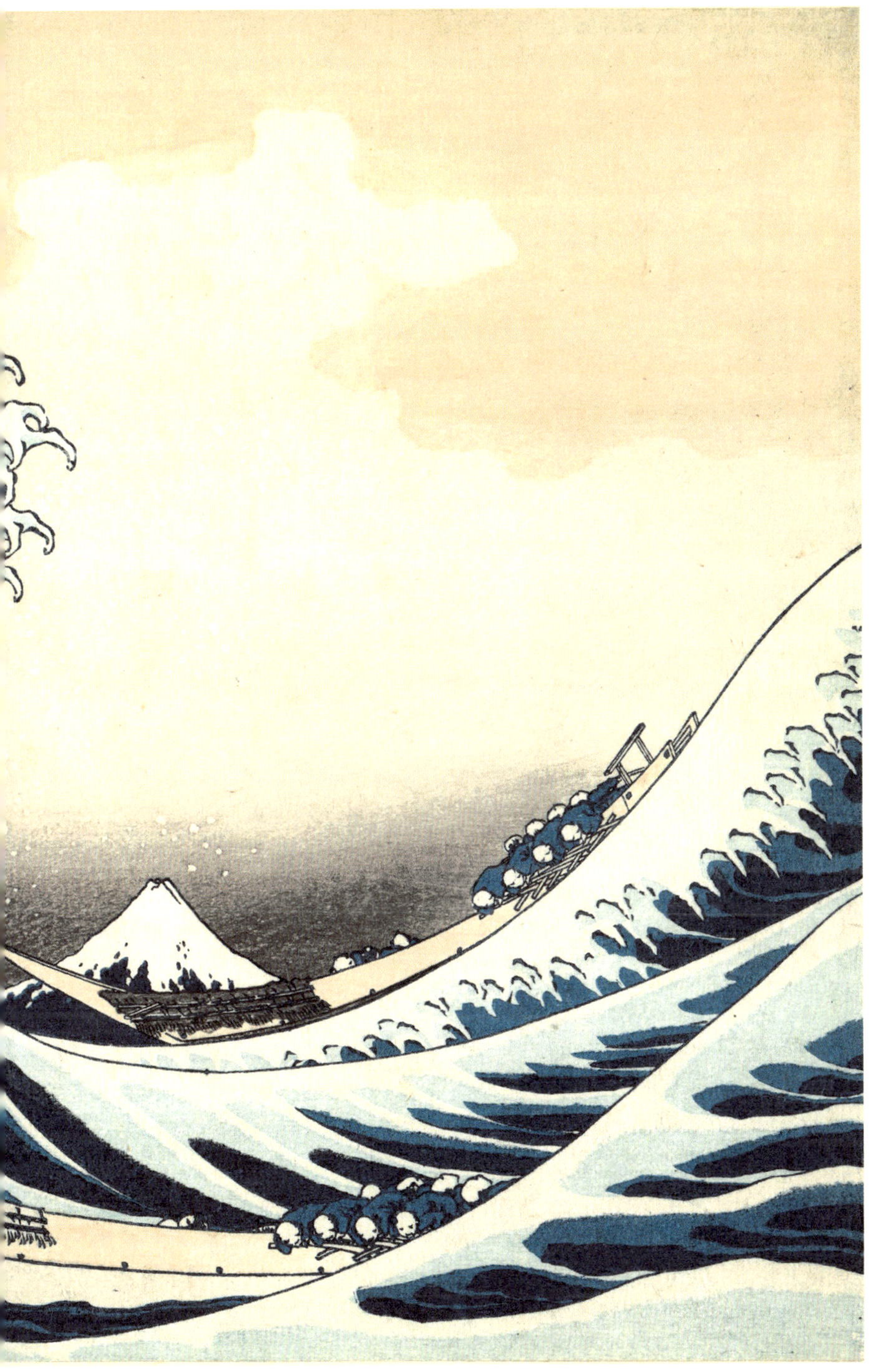

25.4 × 38.1 cm. The Howard Mansfield Collection, Gift of Howard Mansfield, 1936, The Metropolitan Museum of Art, New York, JP2569

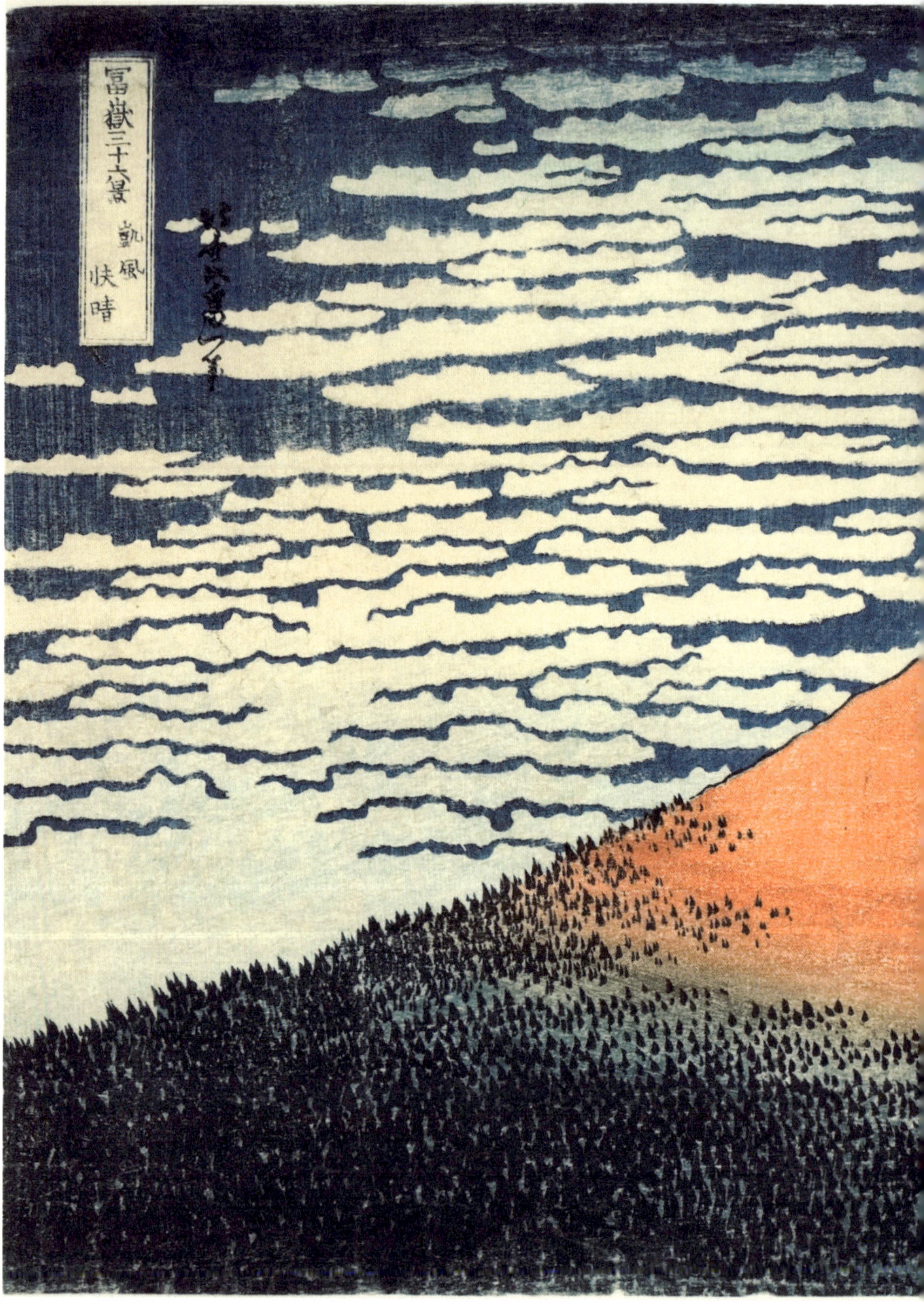

63 *A Mild Breeze on a Fine Day*
signed Hokusai Aratame Iitsu hitsu

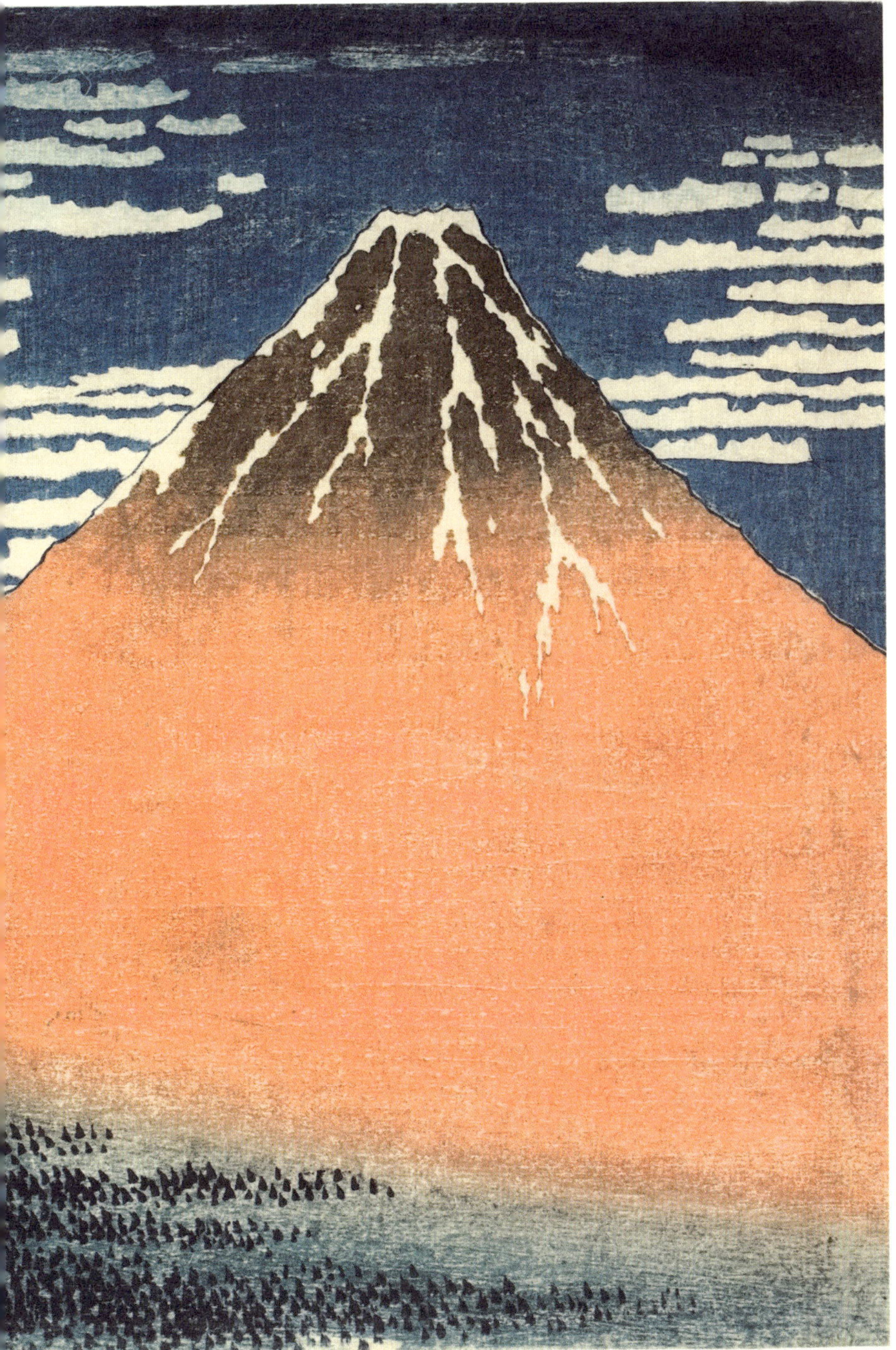

24.2 × 36.5 cm. Clarence Buckingham Collection, The Art Institute of Chicago, 1952.341

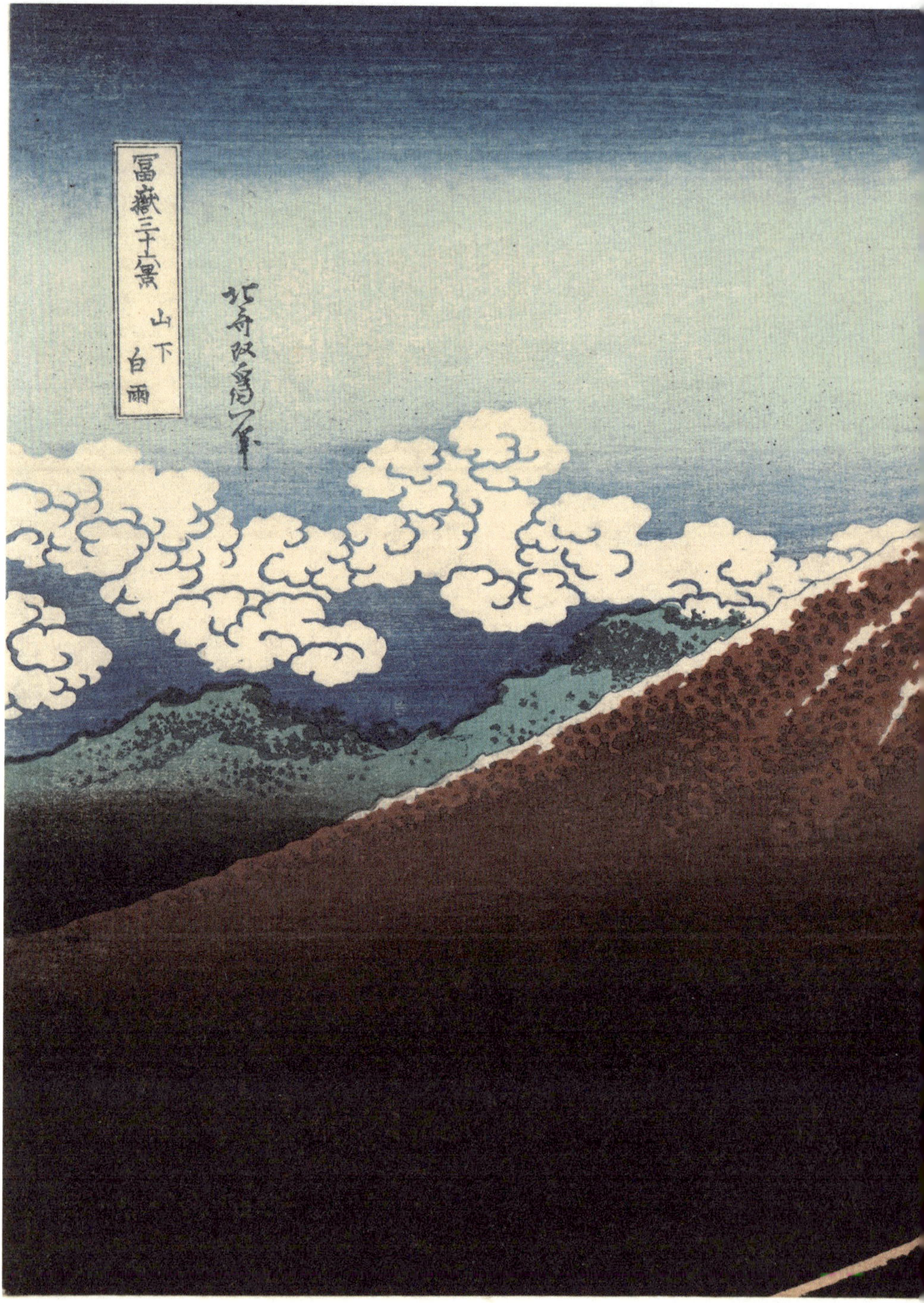

Shower Below the Summit
signed Hokusai Aratame Iitsu hitsu

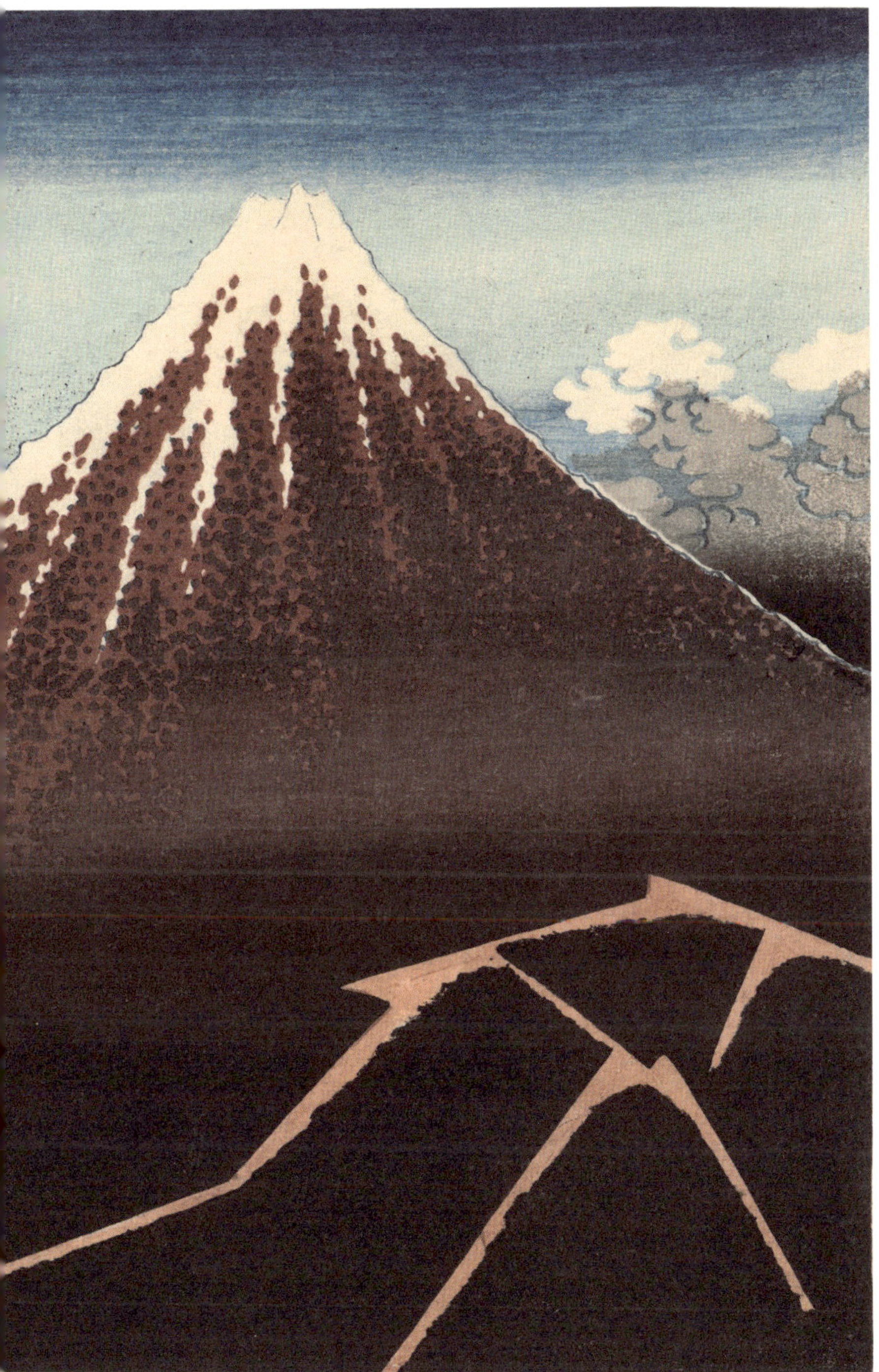

25.7 × 37.6 cm. Clarence Buckingham Collection, The Art Institute of Chicago, 1925.3244

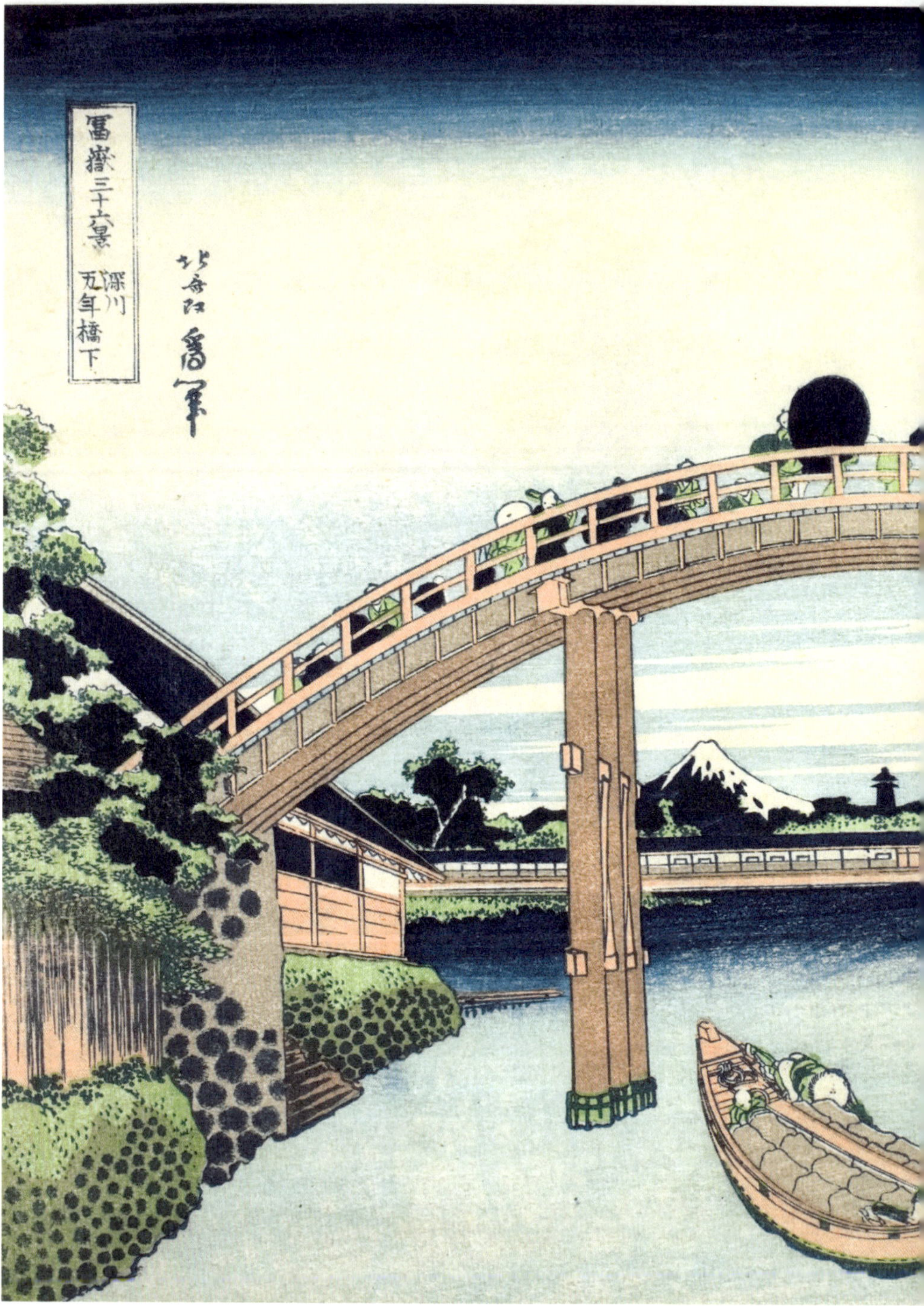

Beneath Mannen Bridge in Fukagawa
signed Hokusai Aratame Iitsu hitsu

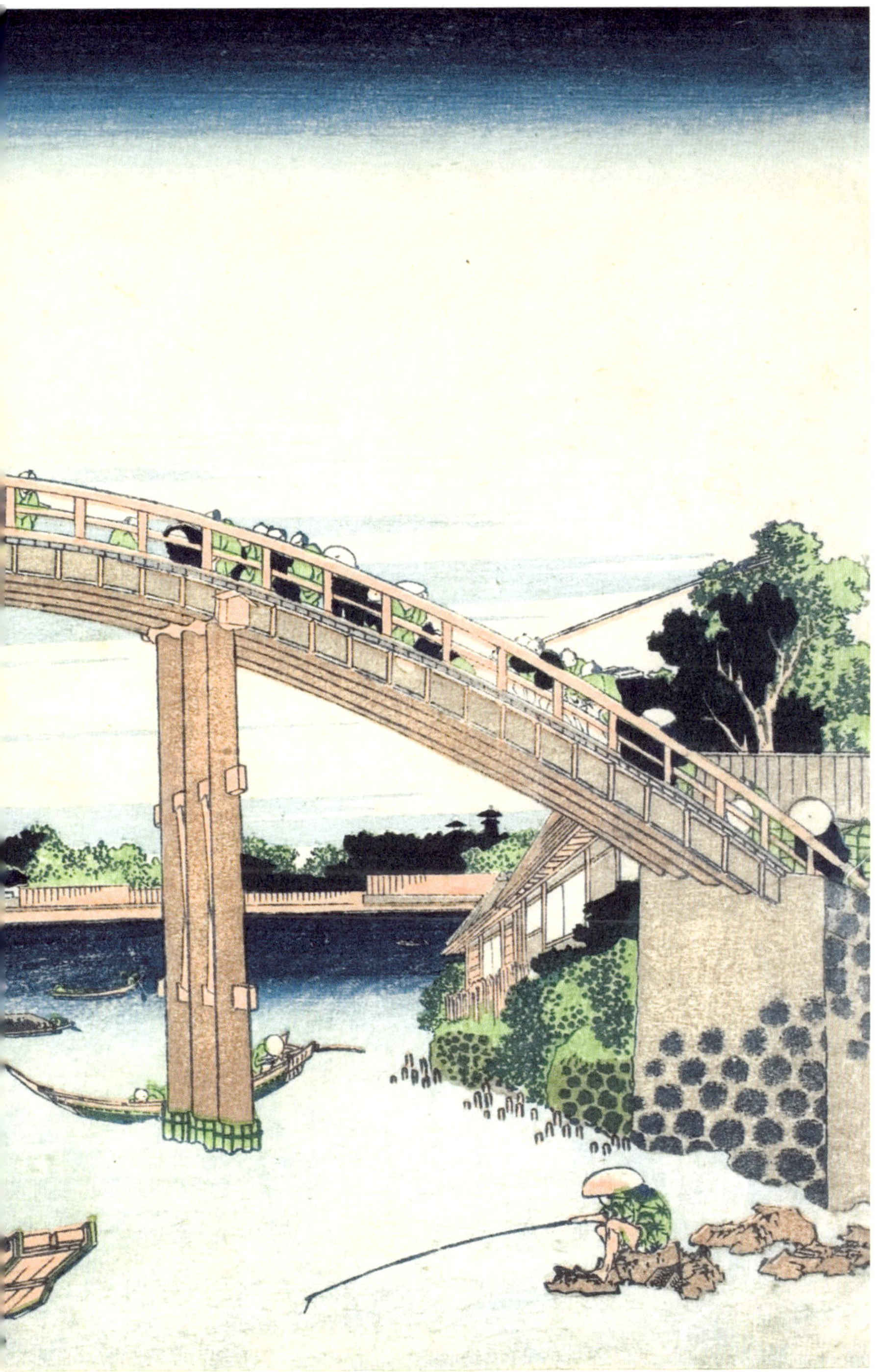

25.8 × 37.2 cm. Clarence Buckingham Collection, The Art Institute of Chicago, 1925.3272

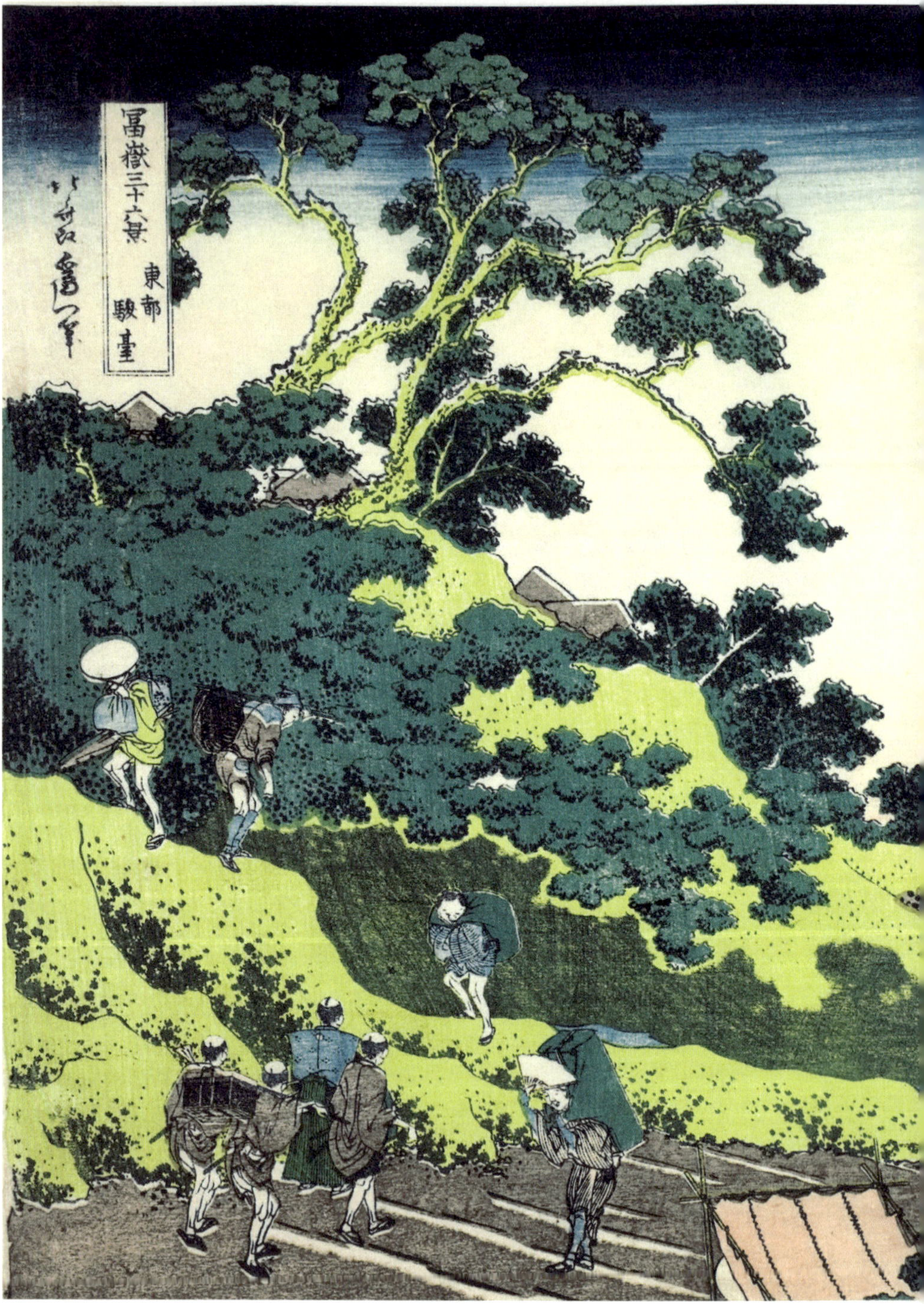

Surugadai in Edo
signed Hokusai Aratame Iitsu hitsu

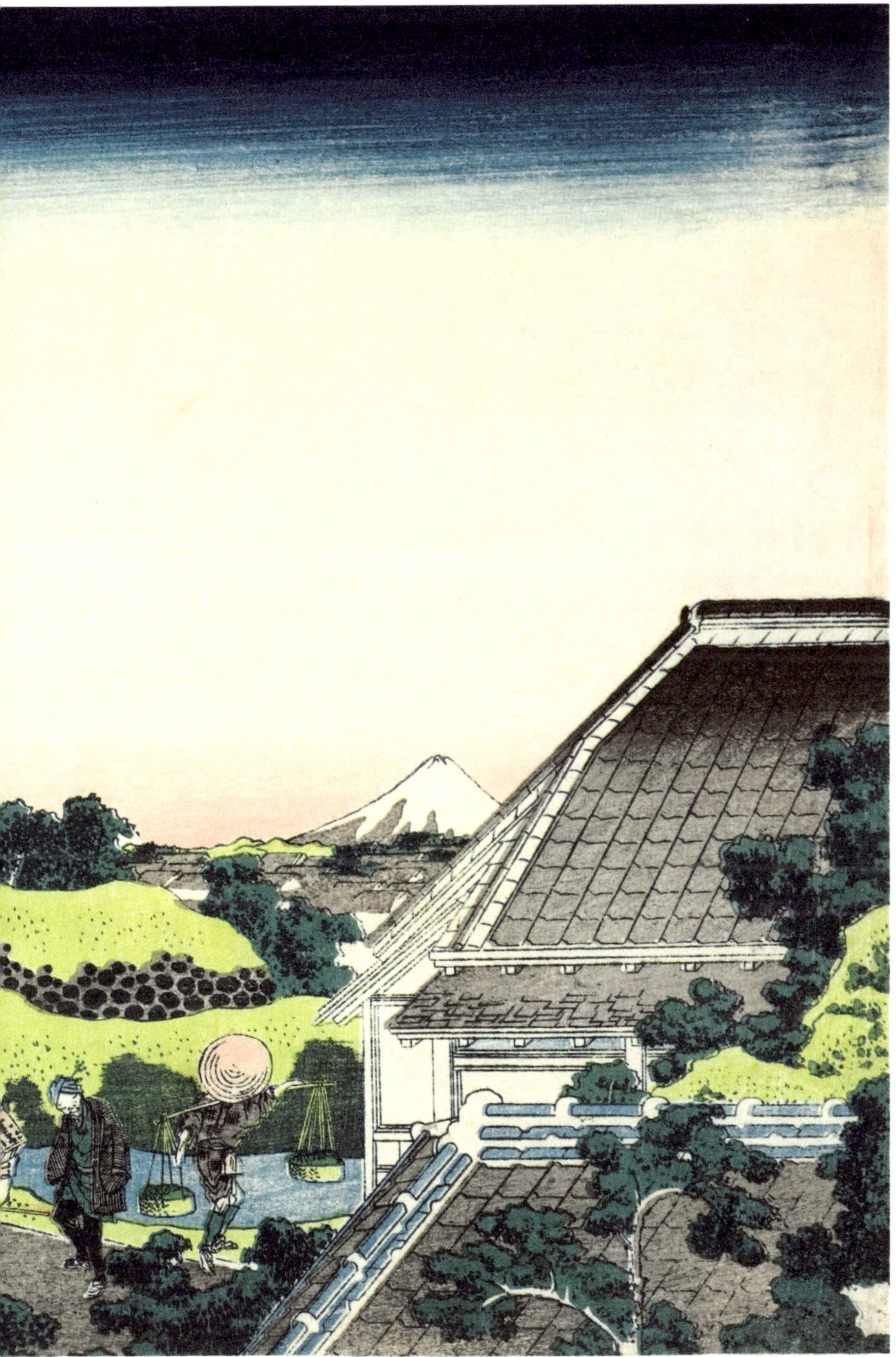

25.9 × 37.5 cm. Clarence Buckingham Collection, The Art Institute of Chicago, 1925.3273

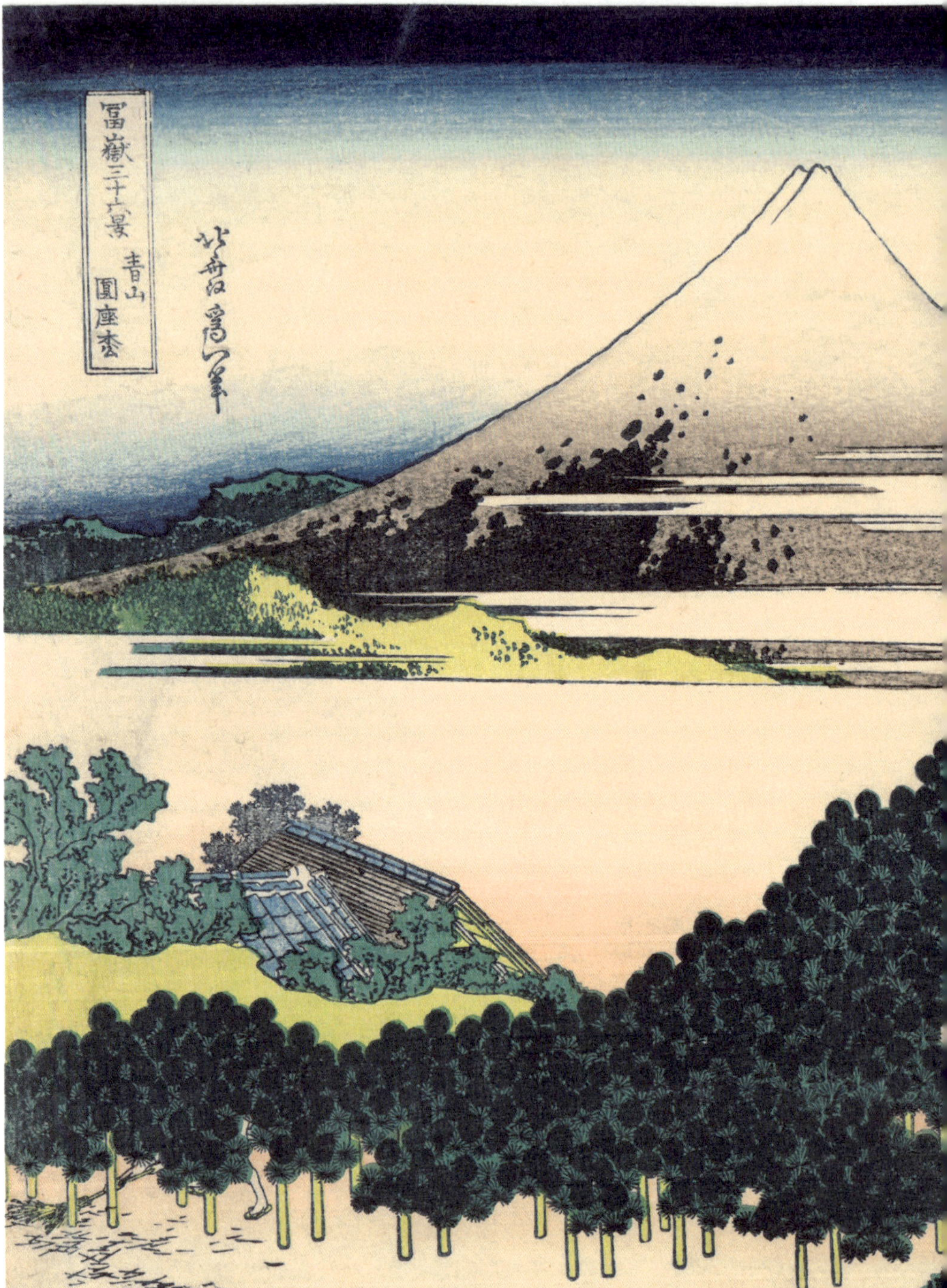

Cushion Pine Tree at Aoyama
signed Hokusai Aratame Iitsu hitsu

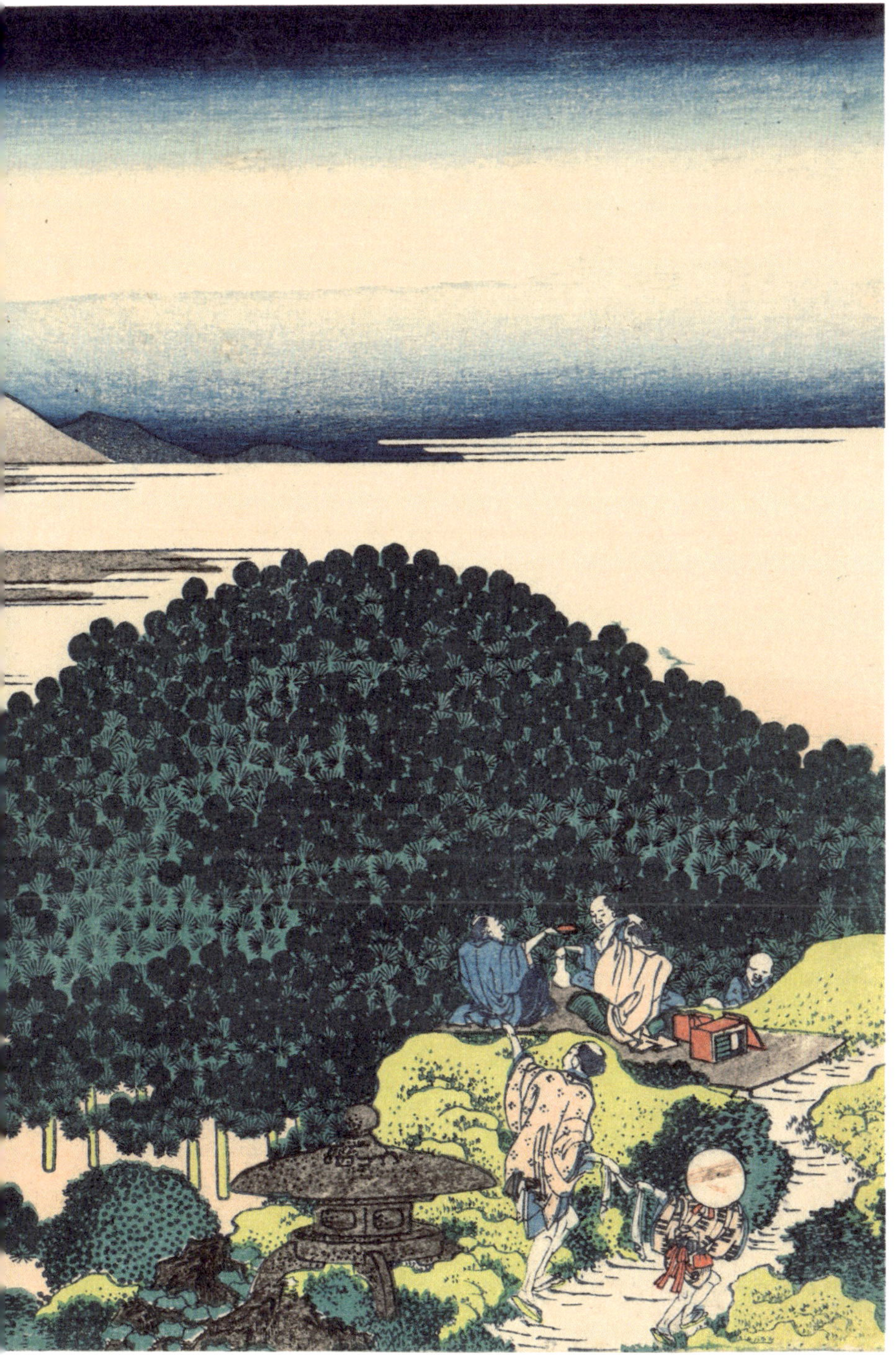

25.5 × 37.5 cm. Clarence Buckingham Collection, The Art Institute of Chicago, 1925.3237

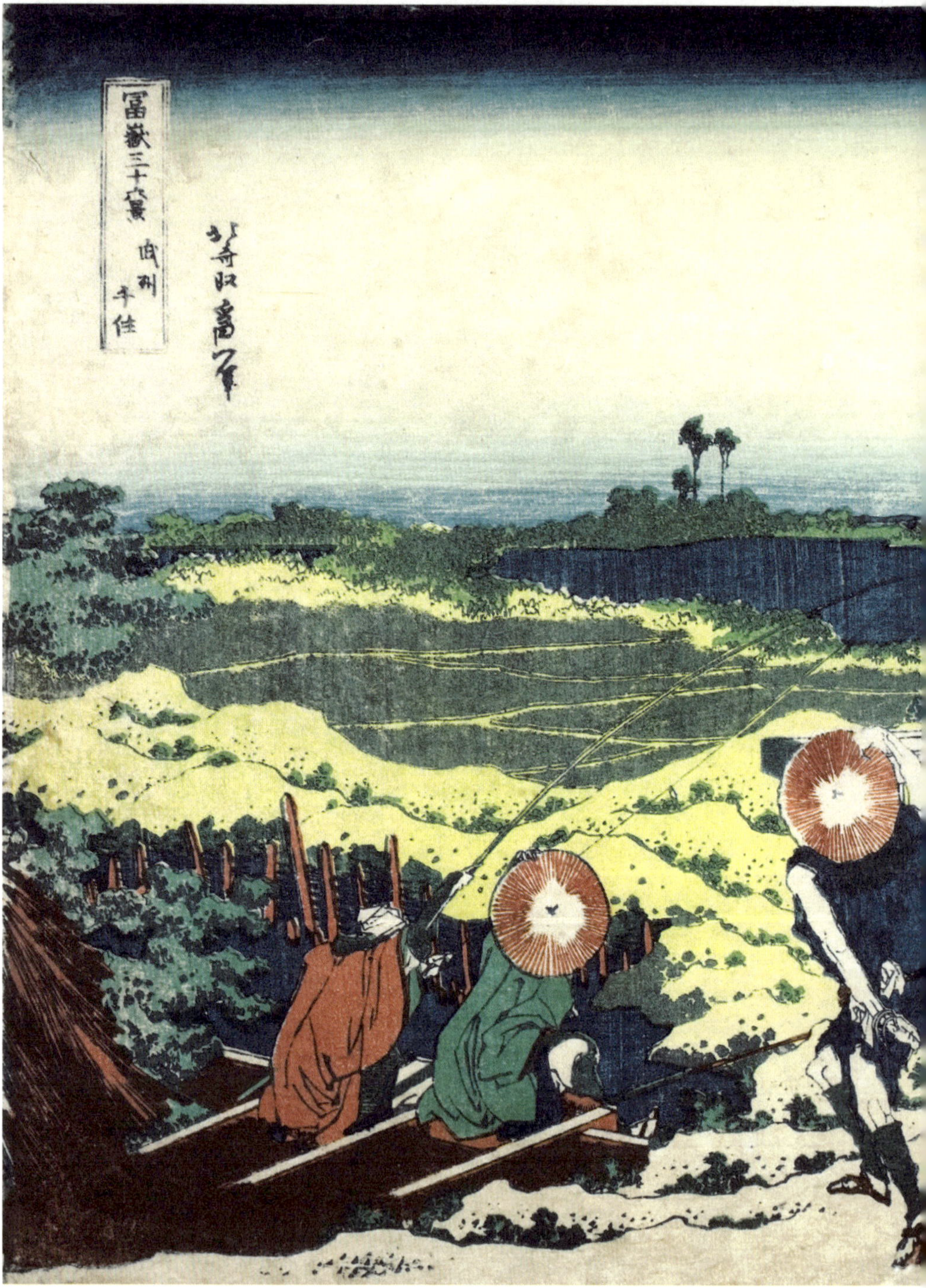

68 *Senju in Musashi Province*
signed Hokusai Aratame Iitsu hitsu

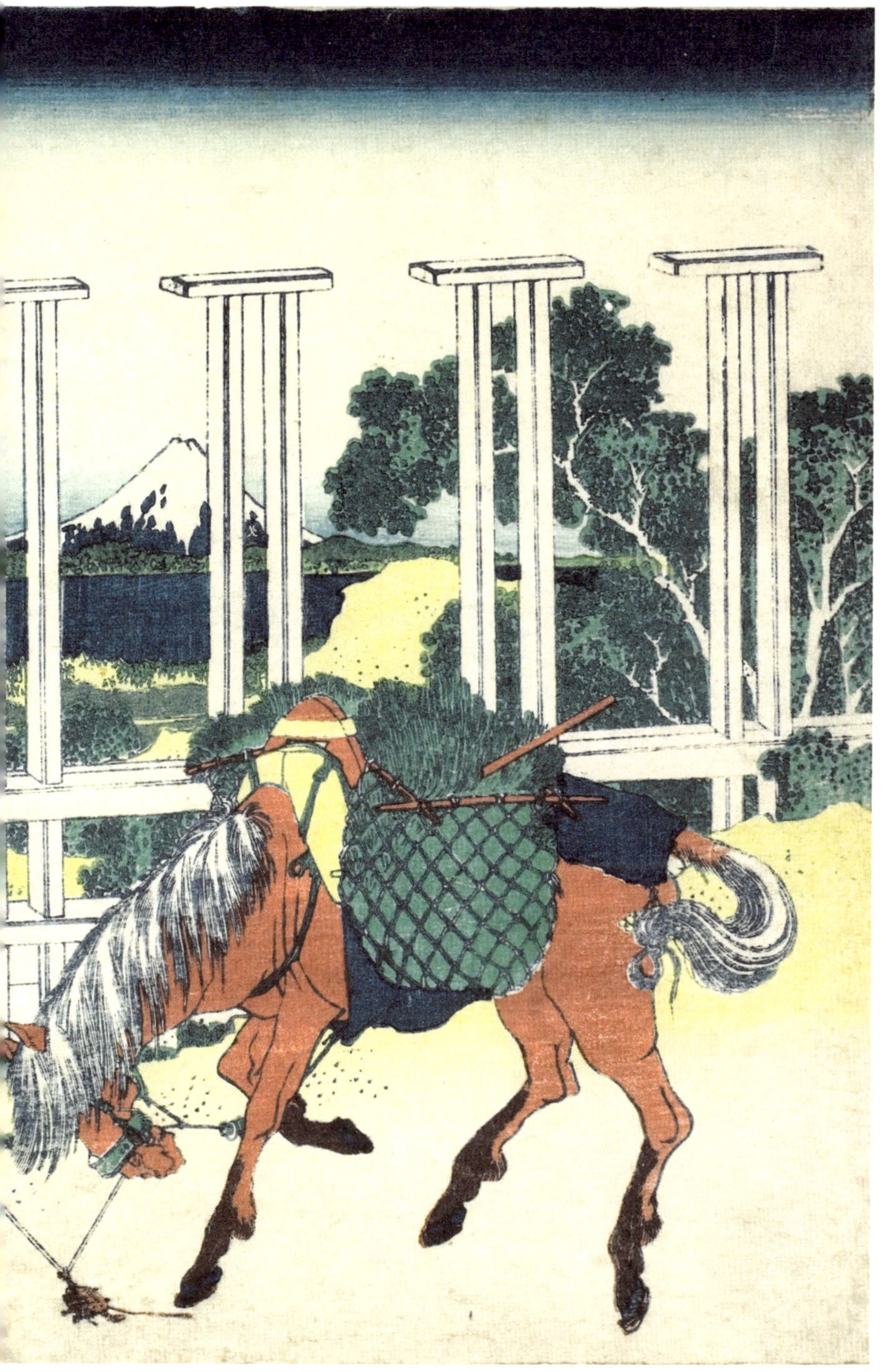

24.6 × 36.5 cm. Rogers Fund, 1922, The Metropolitan Museum of Art, New York, JP1289

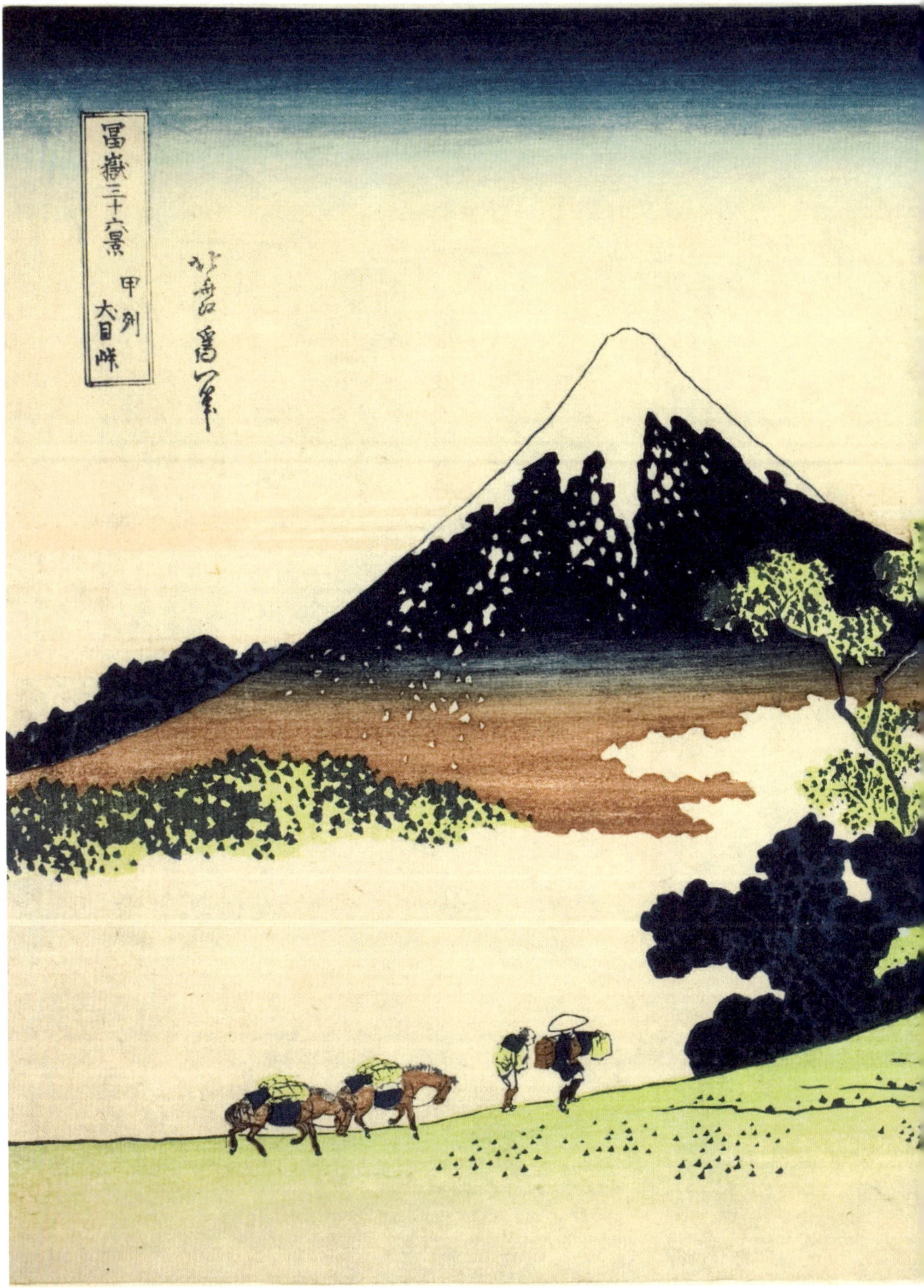

△ **69** *Inume Pass in Kai Province*
signed Hokusai Aratame Iitsu hitsu

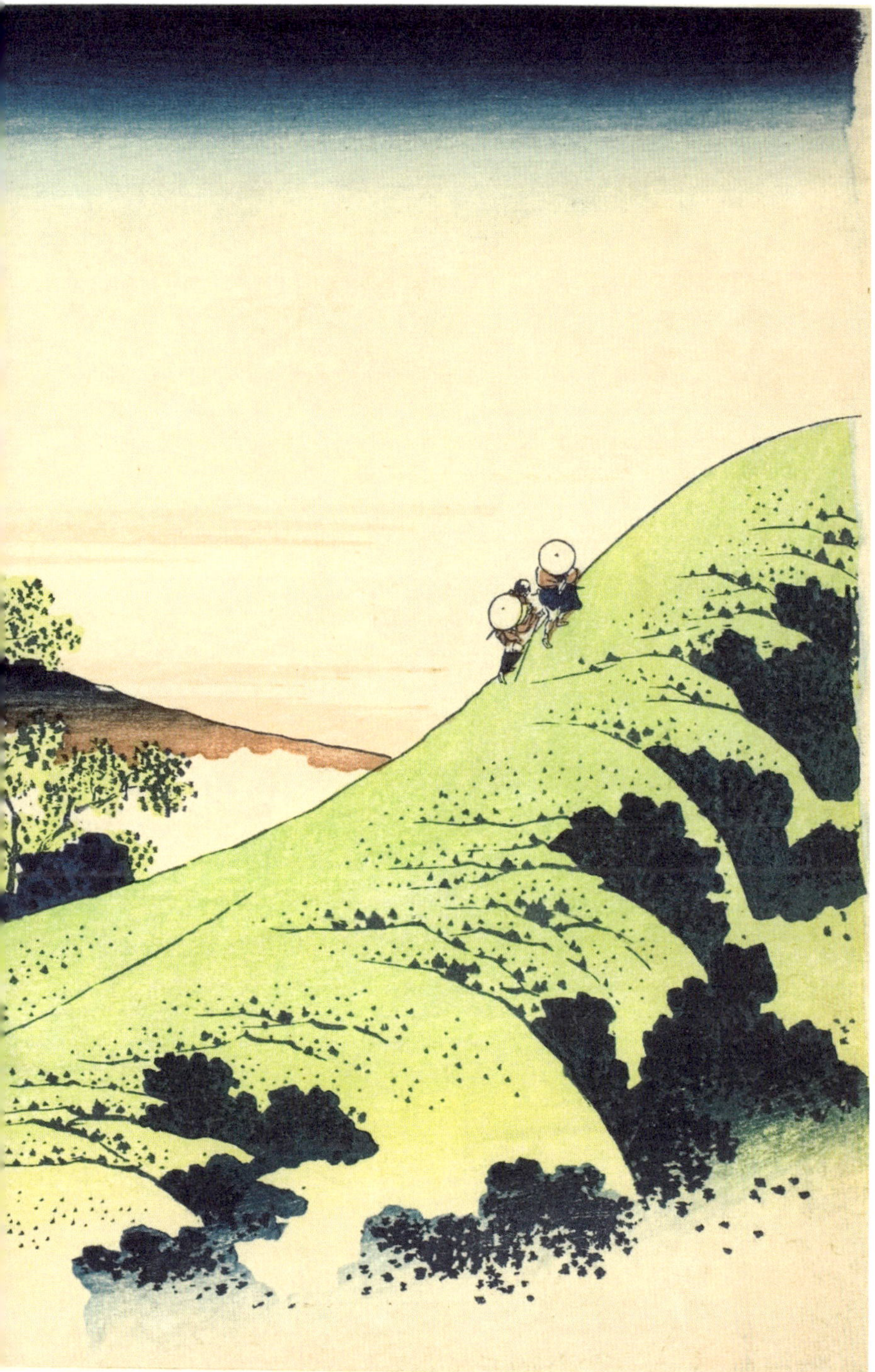

25.7 × 37.5cm. Clarence Buckingham Collection, The Art Institute of Chicago, 1925.3283

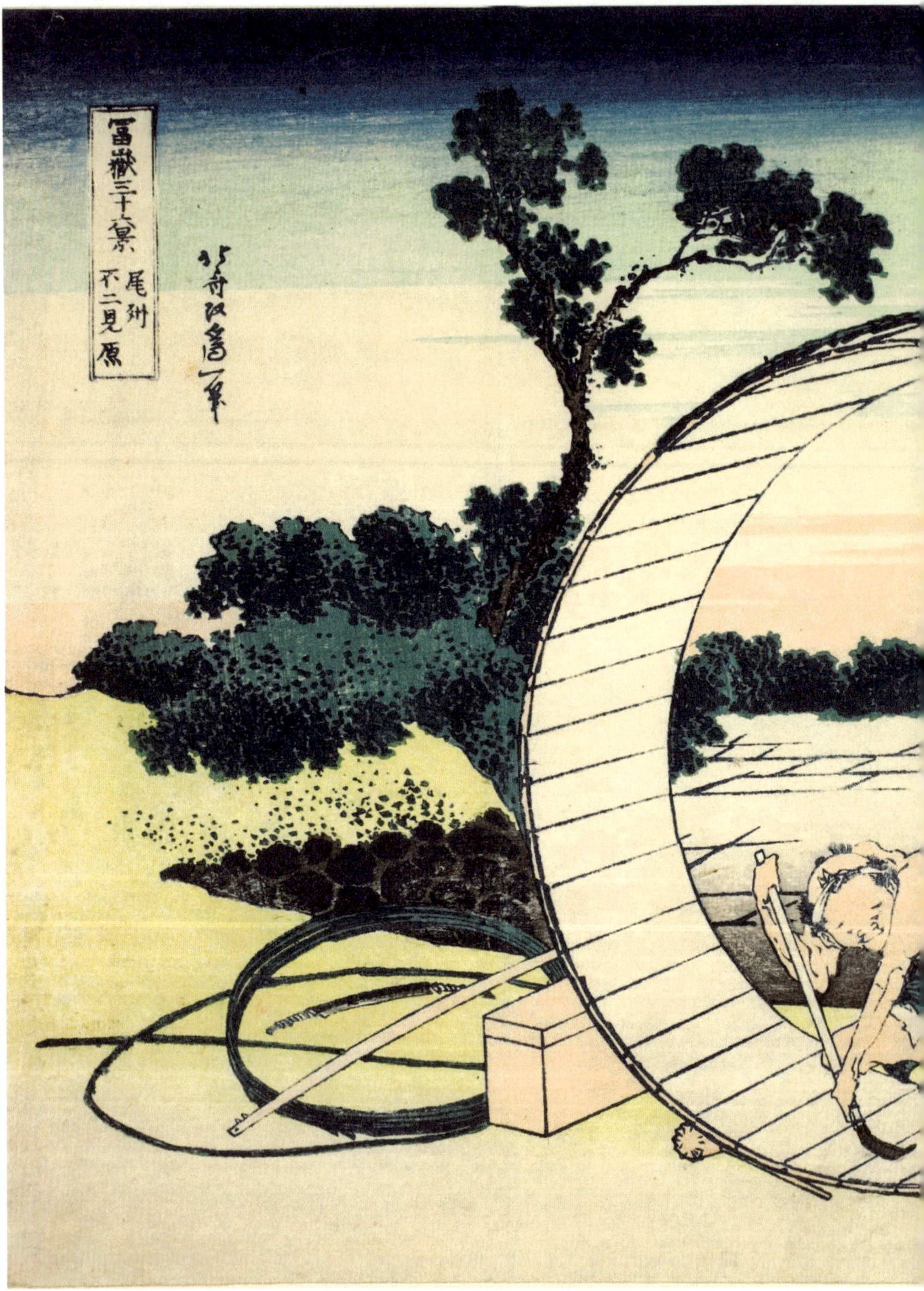

70 *Fujimigahara in Owari Province*
signed Hokusai Aratame Iitsu hitsu

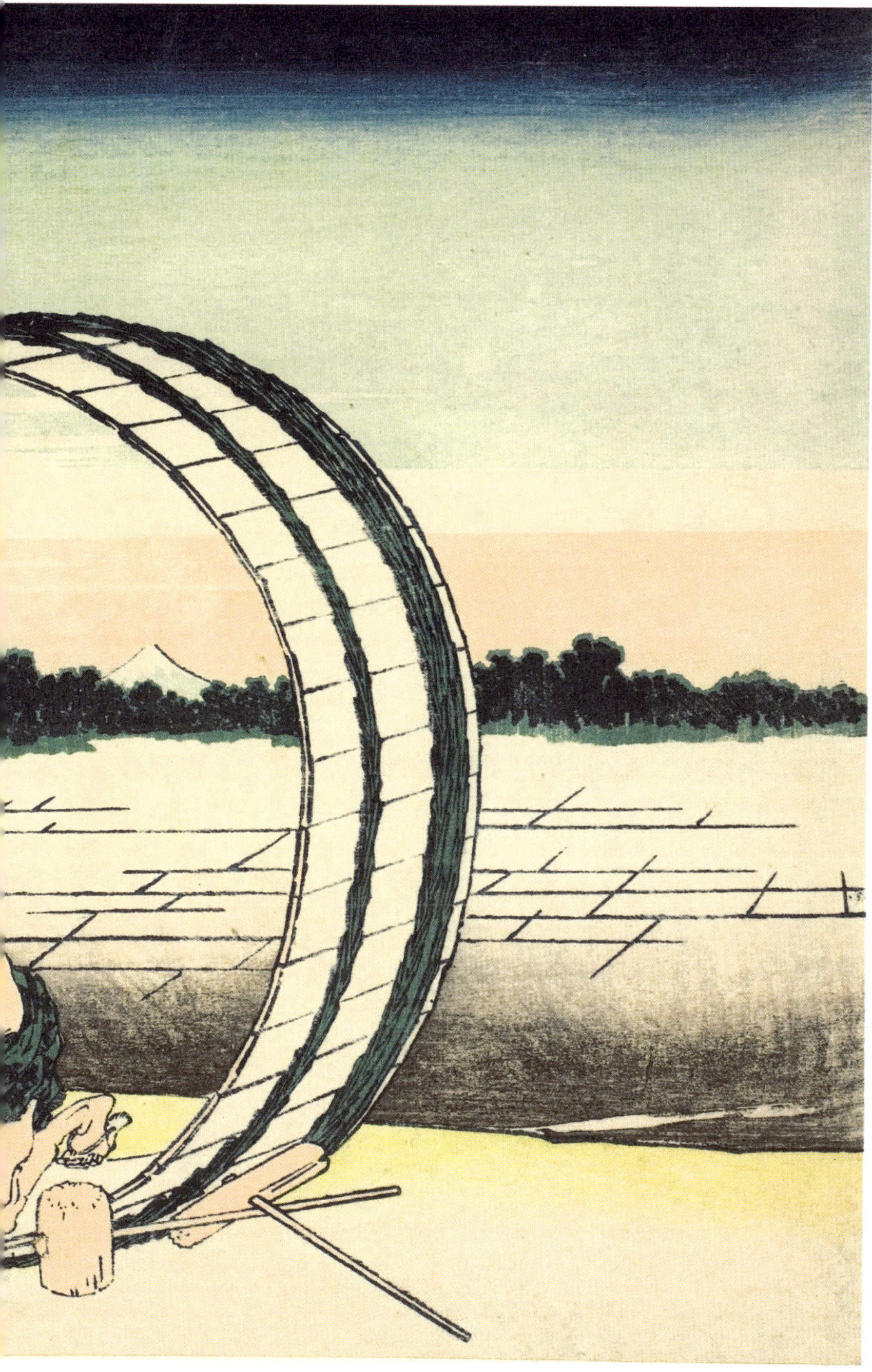

25.6 × 37.2 cm. Clarence Buckingham Collection, The Art Institute of Chicago, 1925.3229

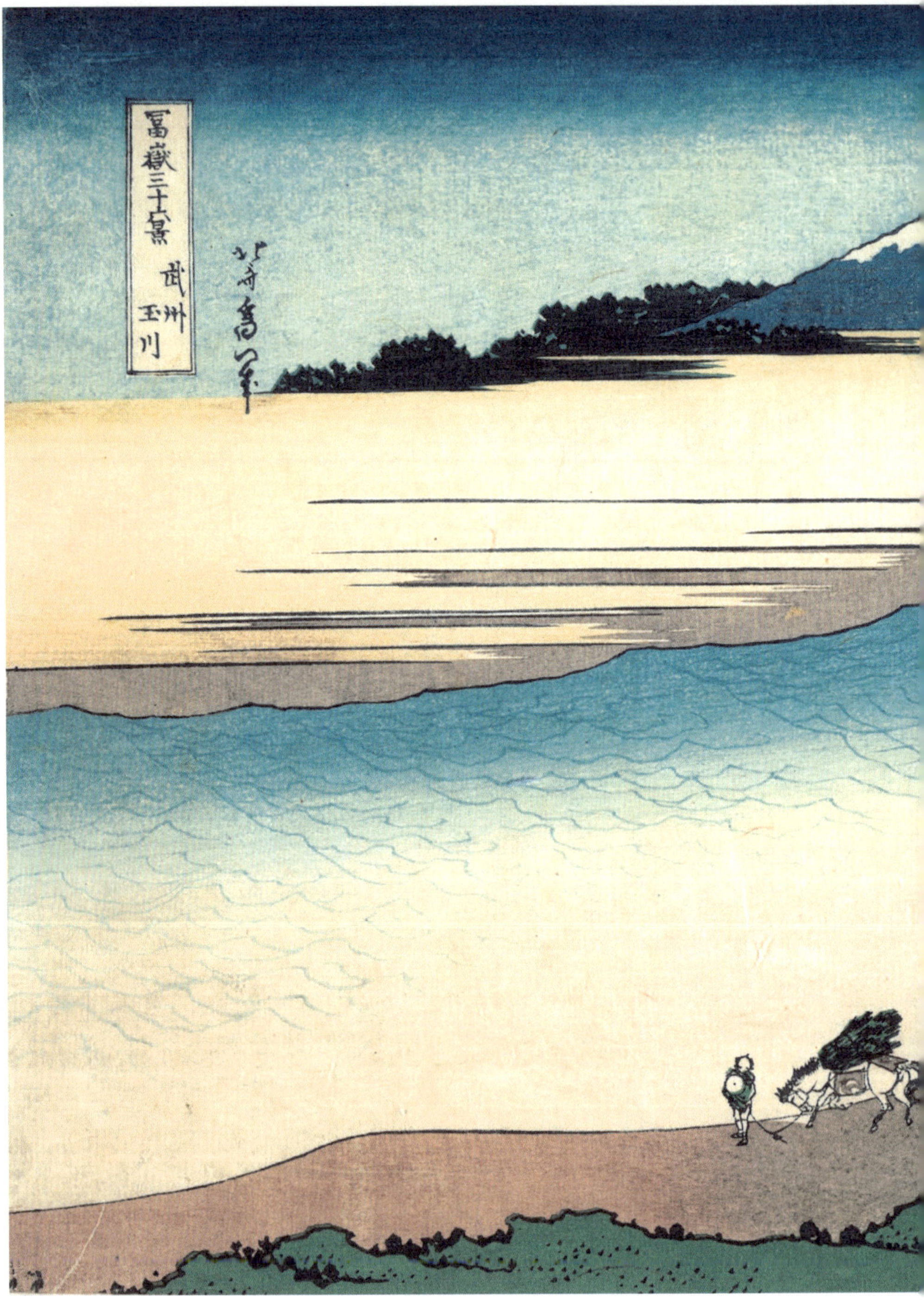

Tama River in Musashi Province
signed Hokusai Aratame Iitsu hitsu

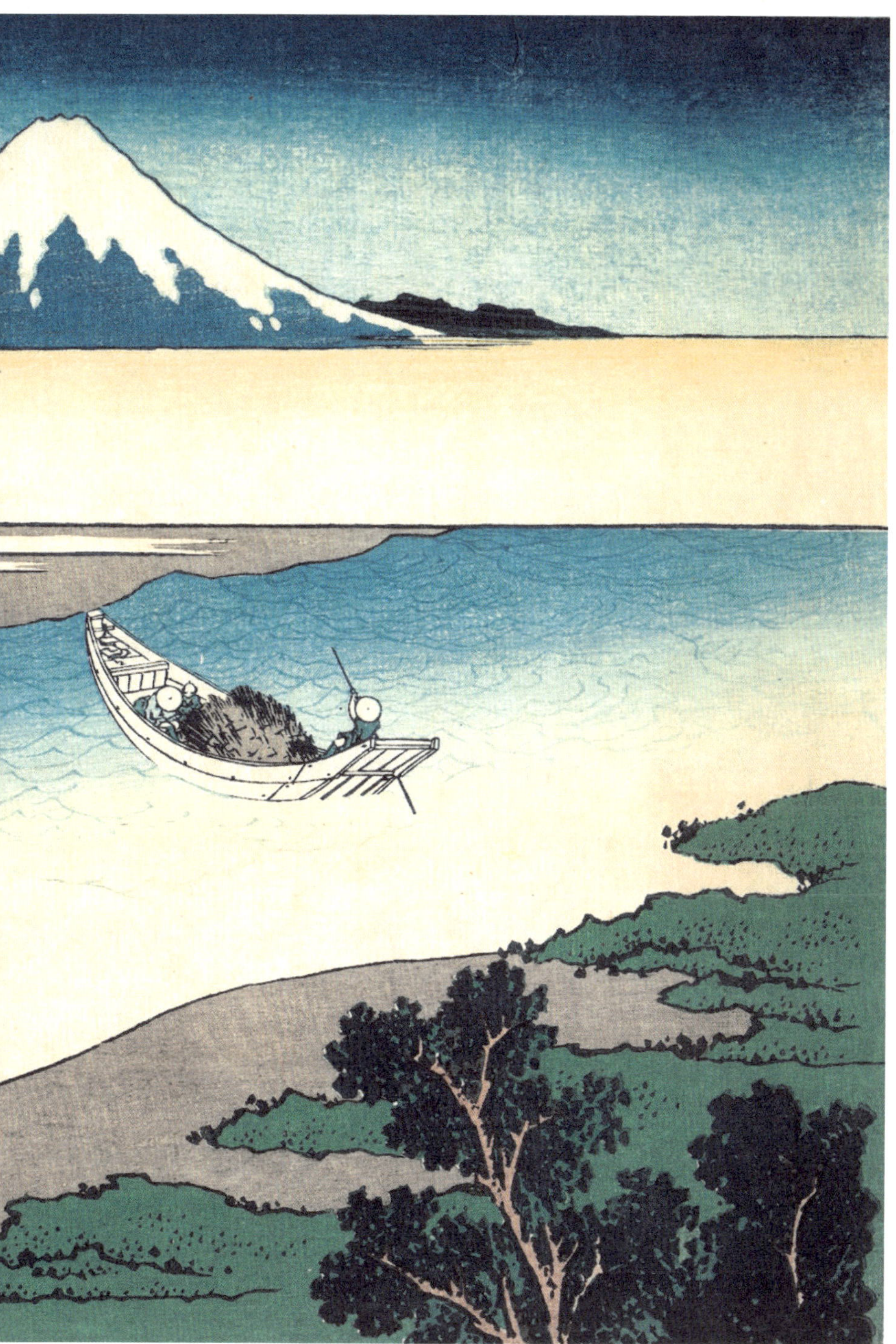

25.4 × 38.1 cm. The Howard Mansfield Collection, Gift of Howard Mansfield, 1936, The Metropolitan Museum of Art, New York, JP2560

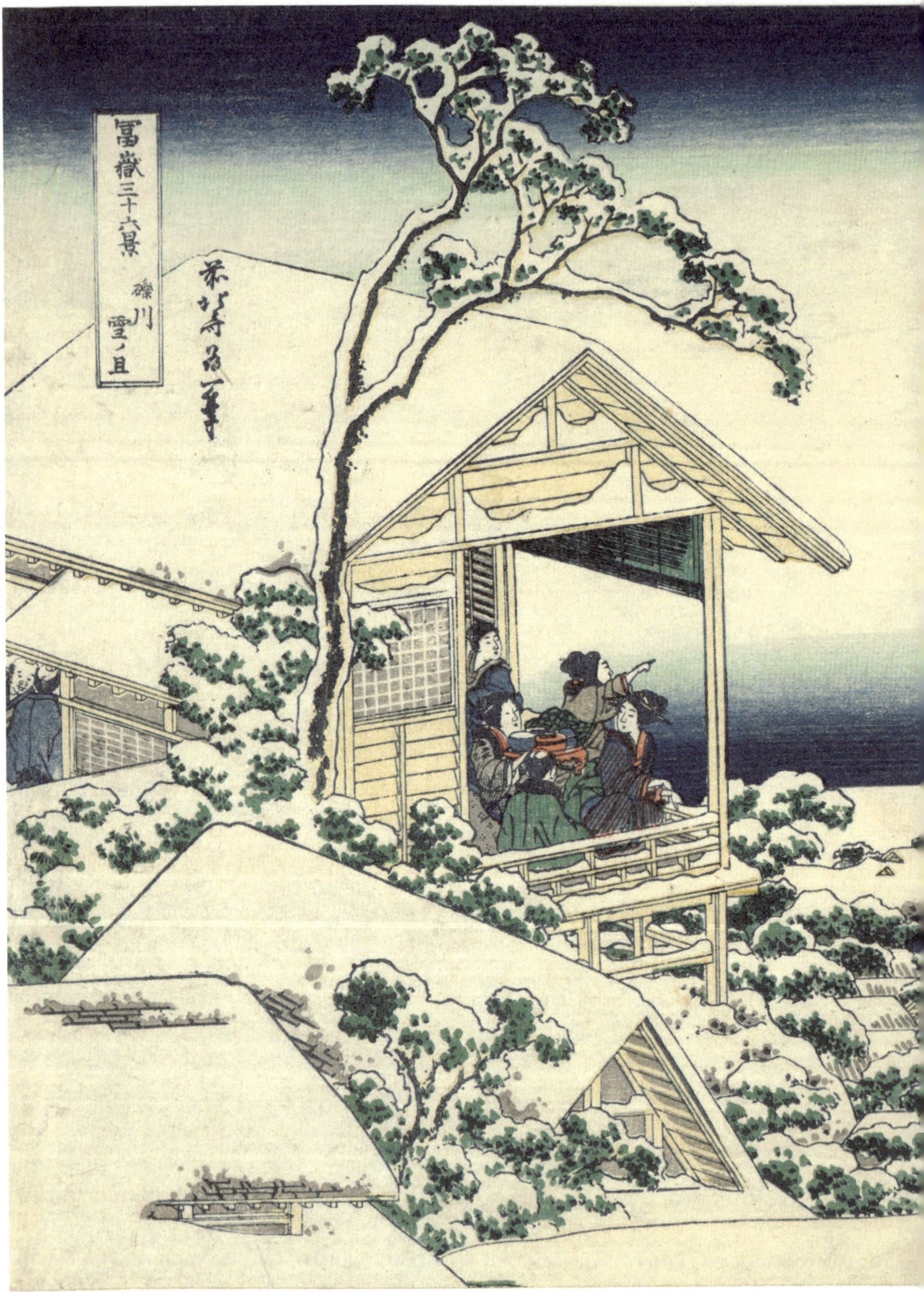

Snowy Morning from Koishikawa
signed Zen Hokusai Iitsu hitsu

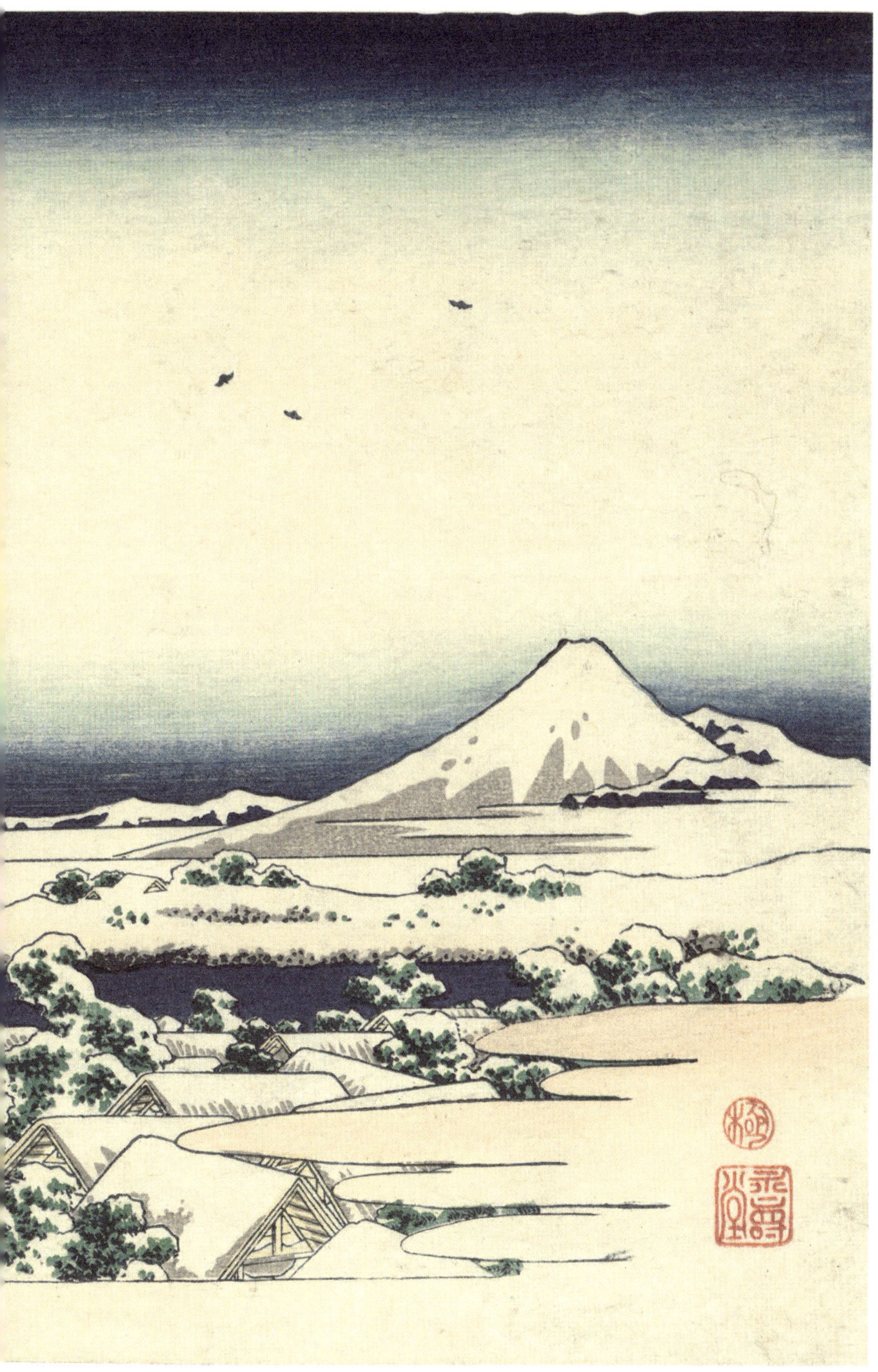

25.6 × 37.5 cm. Clarence Buckingham Collection, The Art Institute of Chicago, 1925.3262

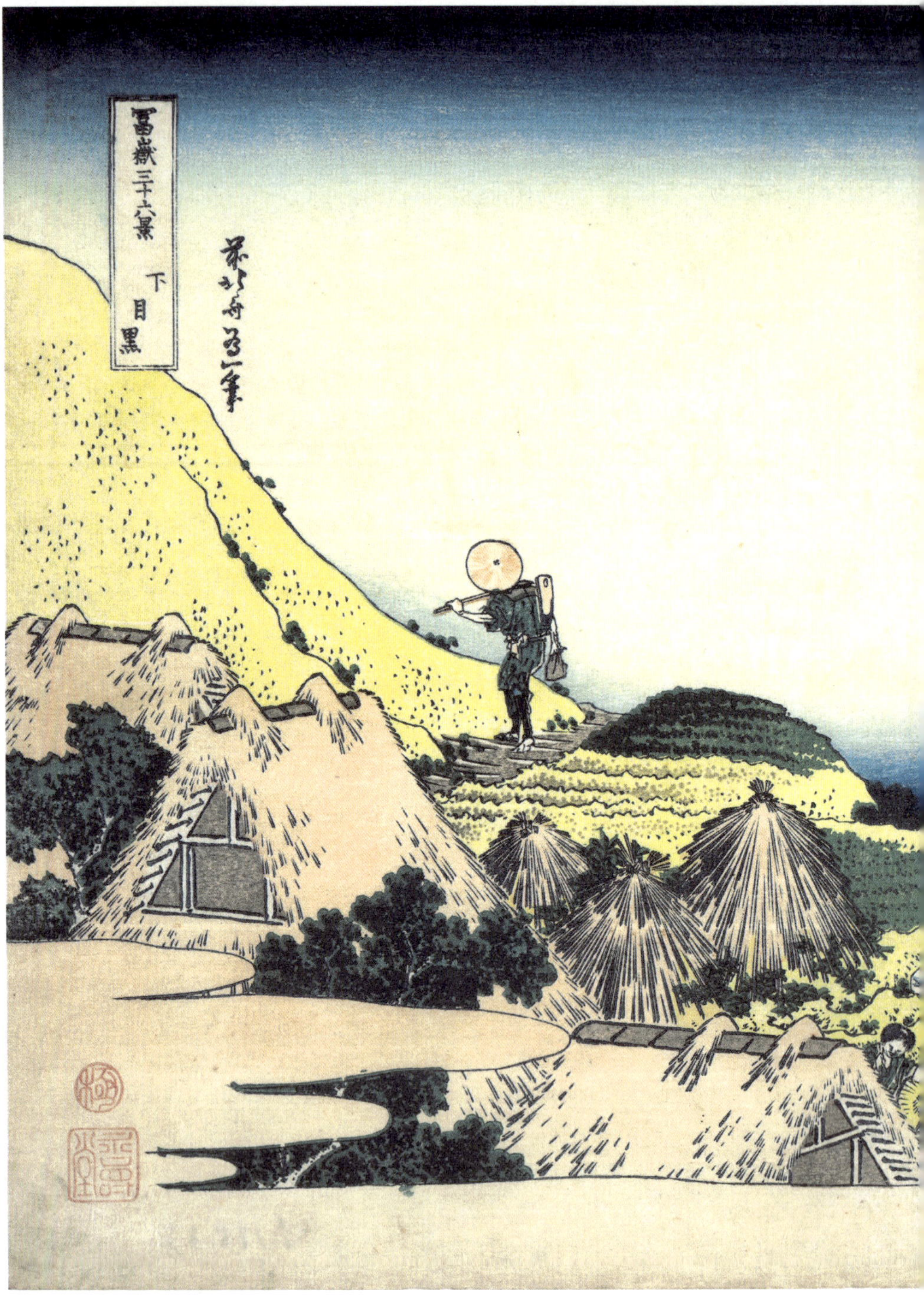

73 *Lower Meguro (Shimomeguro)*
signed Zen Hokusai Iitsu hitsu

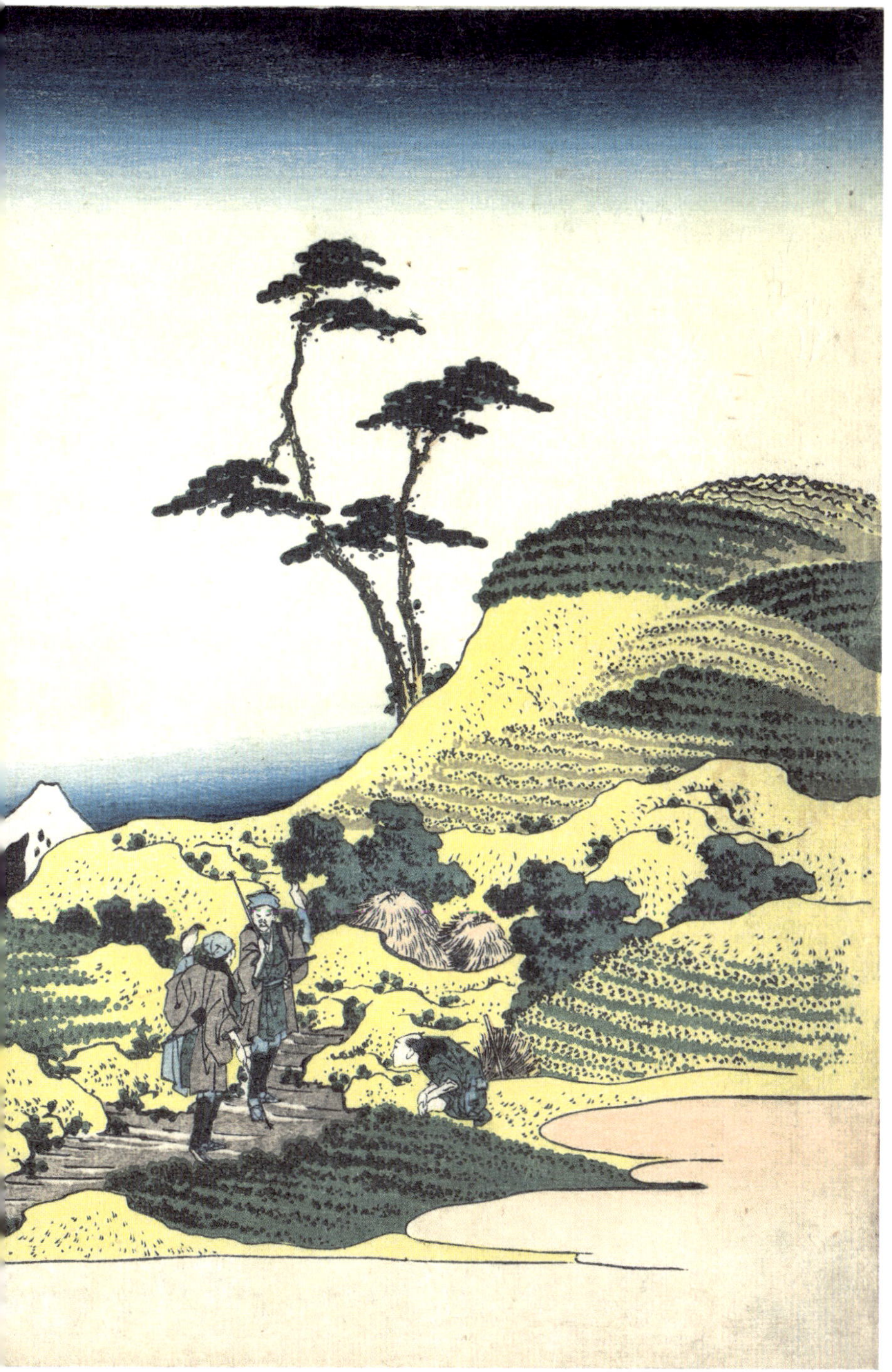

26 × 38.7 cm. Henry L. Phillips Collection, Bequest of Henry L. Phillips, 1939, The Metropolitan Museum of Art, New York, JP2987

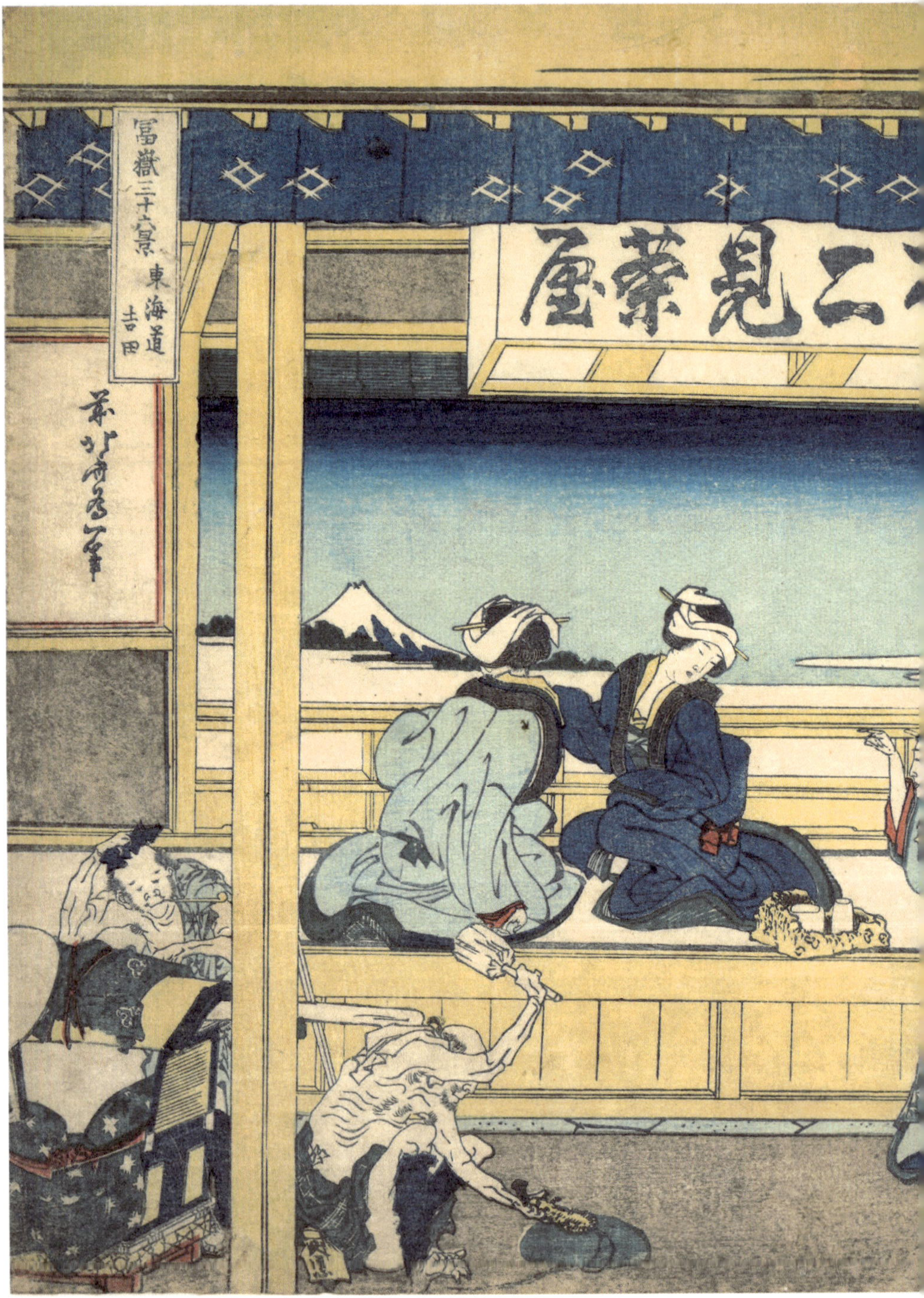

Yoshida on the Tōkaidō Road
signed Zen Hokusai Iitsu hitsu

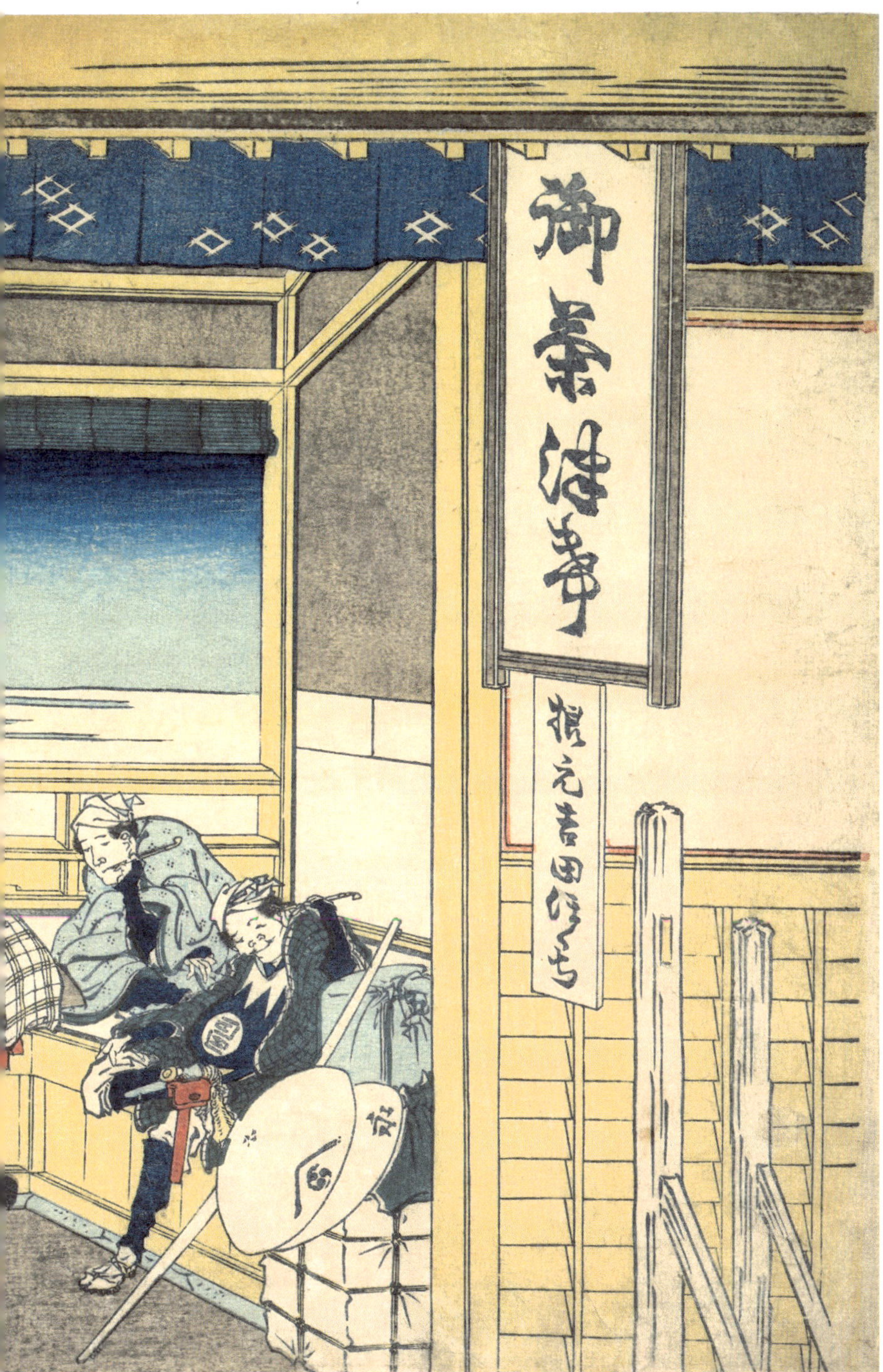

26.4 × 38.4 cm. Henry L. Phillips Collection, Bequest of Henry L. Phillips, 1939, The Metropolitan Museum of Art, New York, JP2974

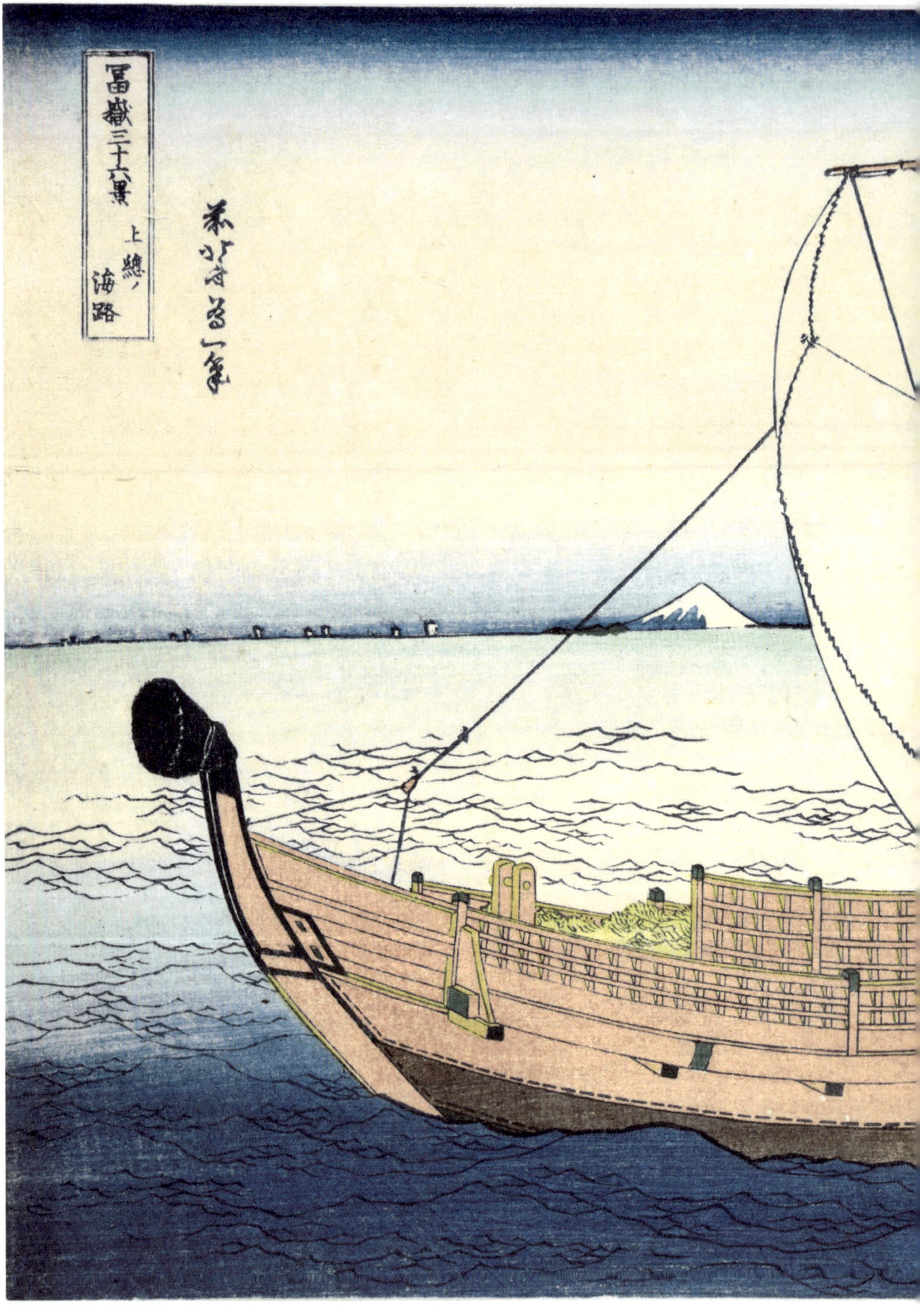

75 *At Sea off Kazusa*
signed Zen Hokusai litsu hitsu

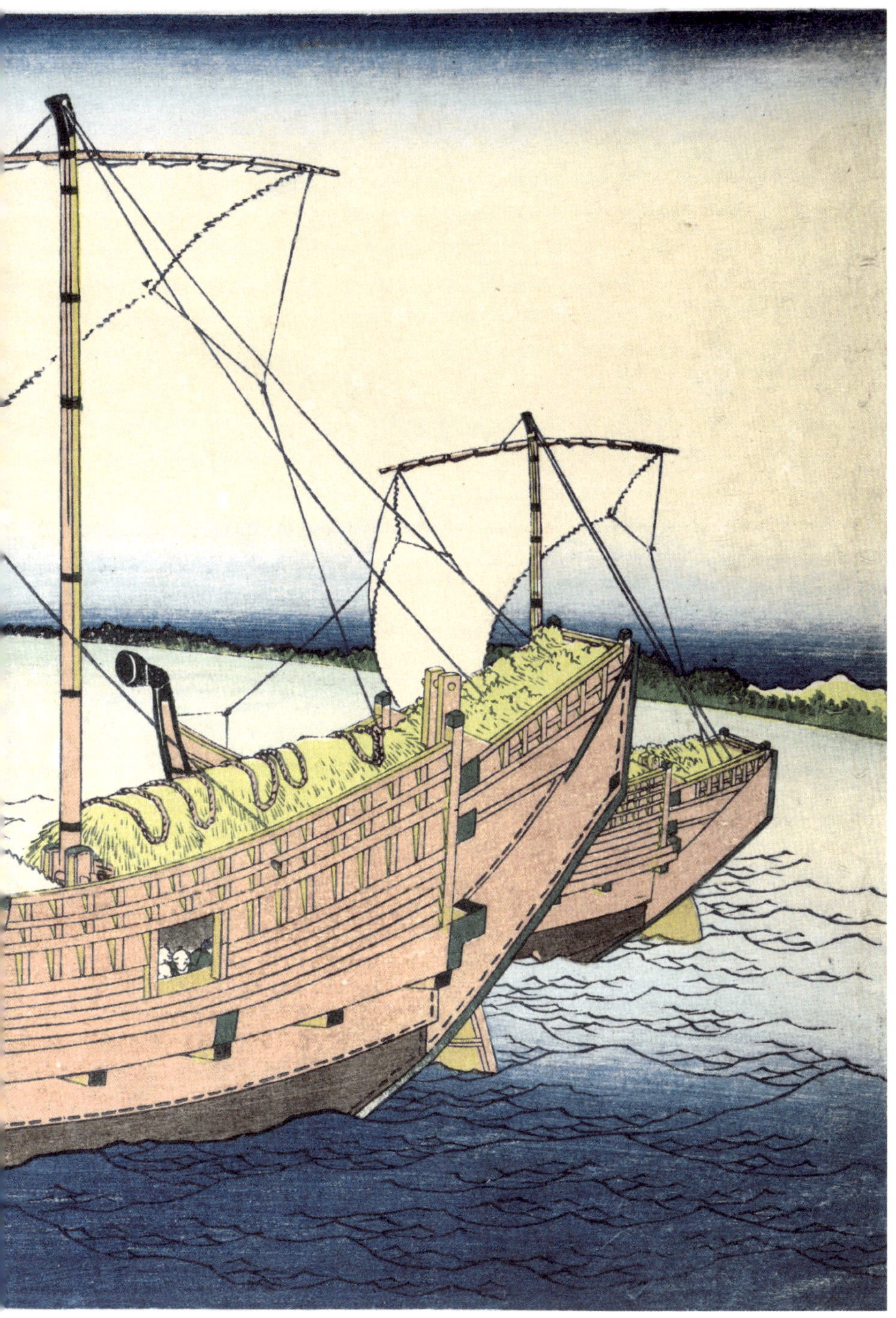

24.4 × 37.5 cm. The New York Public Library: Cadwalader Fund, 89279

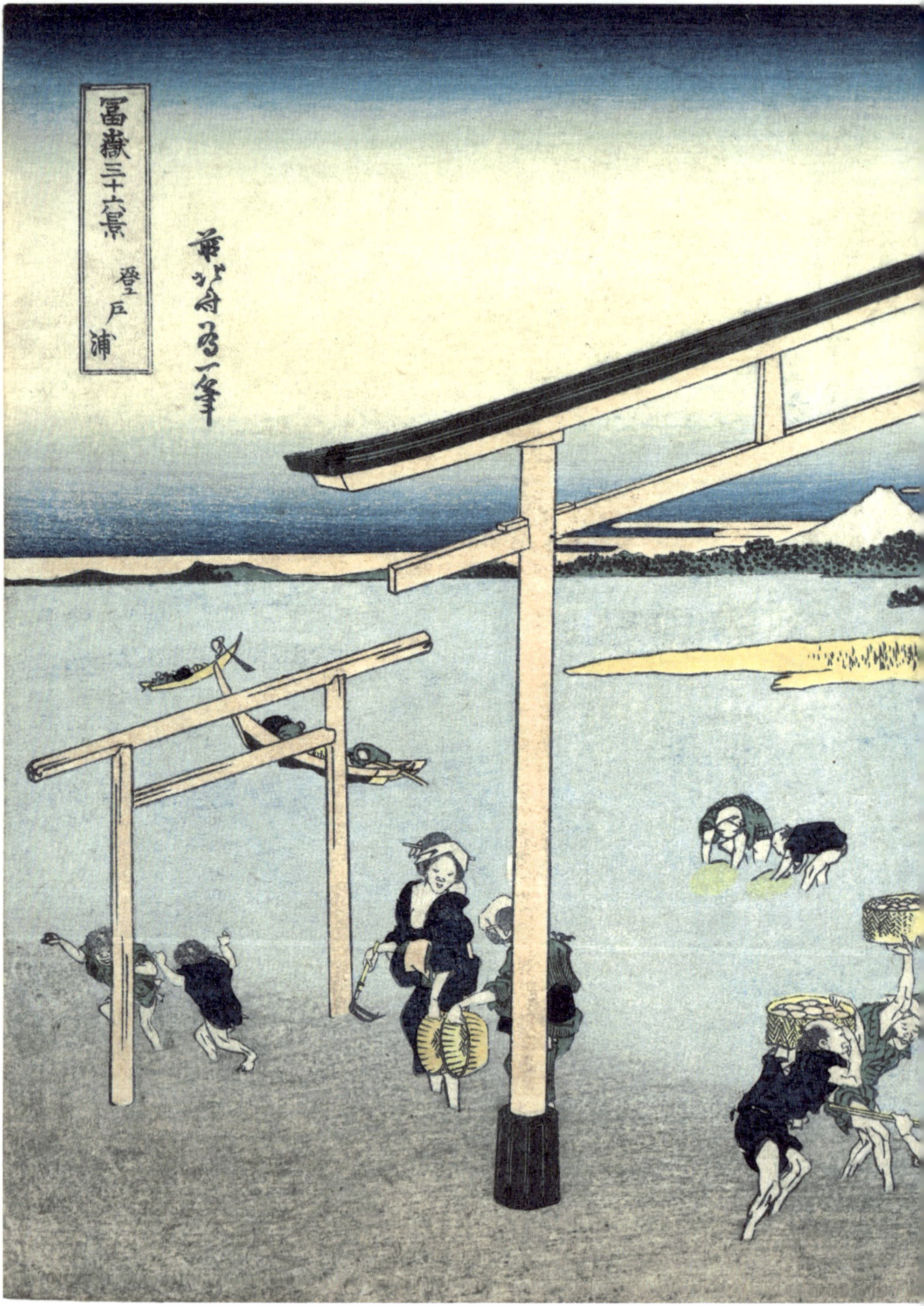

Noboto Bay
signed Zen Hokusai Iitsu hitsu

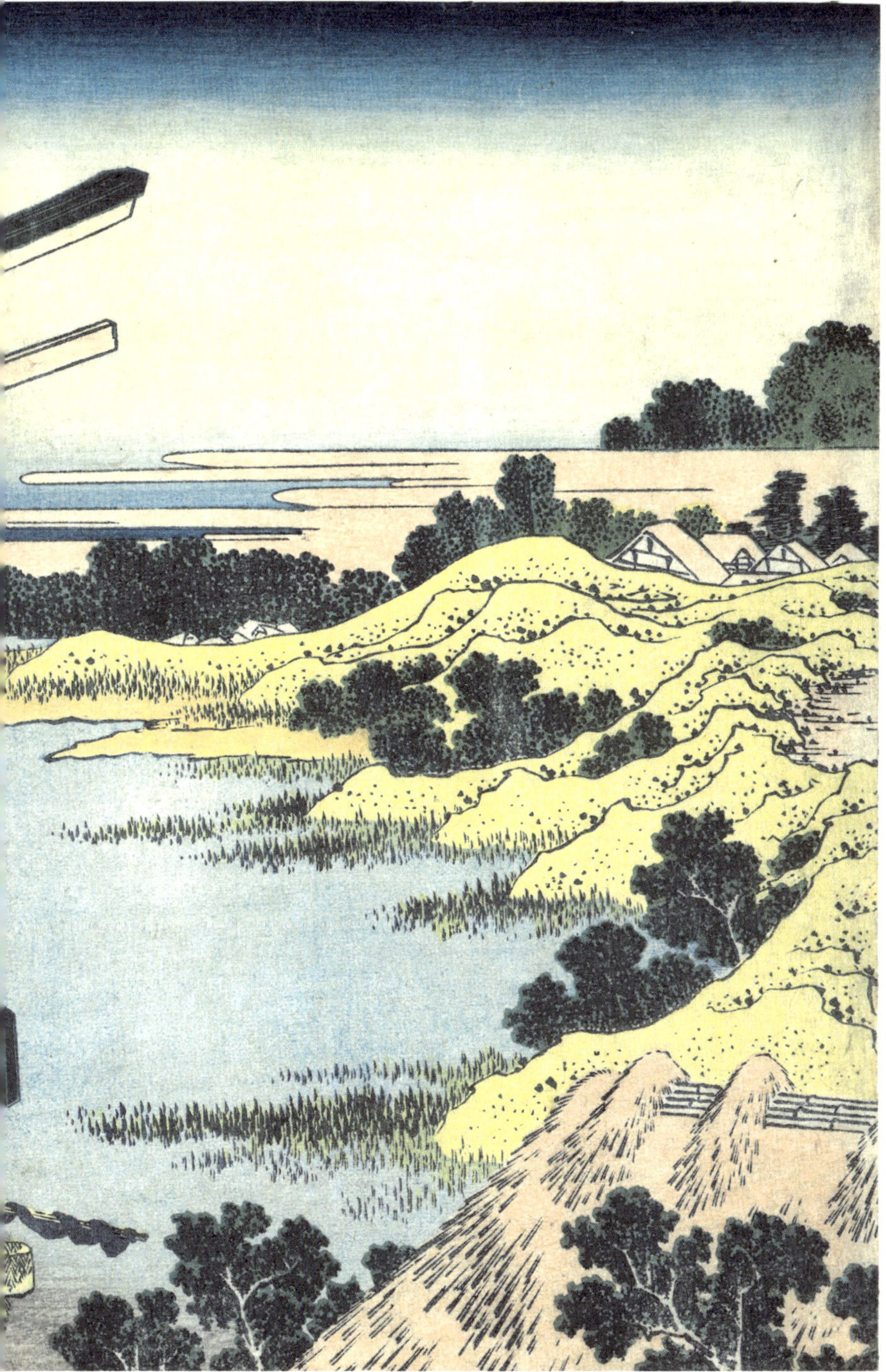

24.8 × 36.5 cm. Henry L. Phillips Collection, Bequest of Henry L. Phillips, 1939, The Metropolitan Museum of Art, New York, JP2958

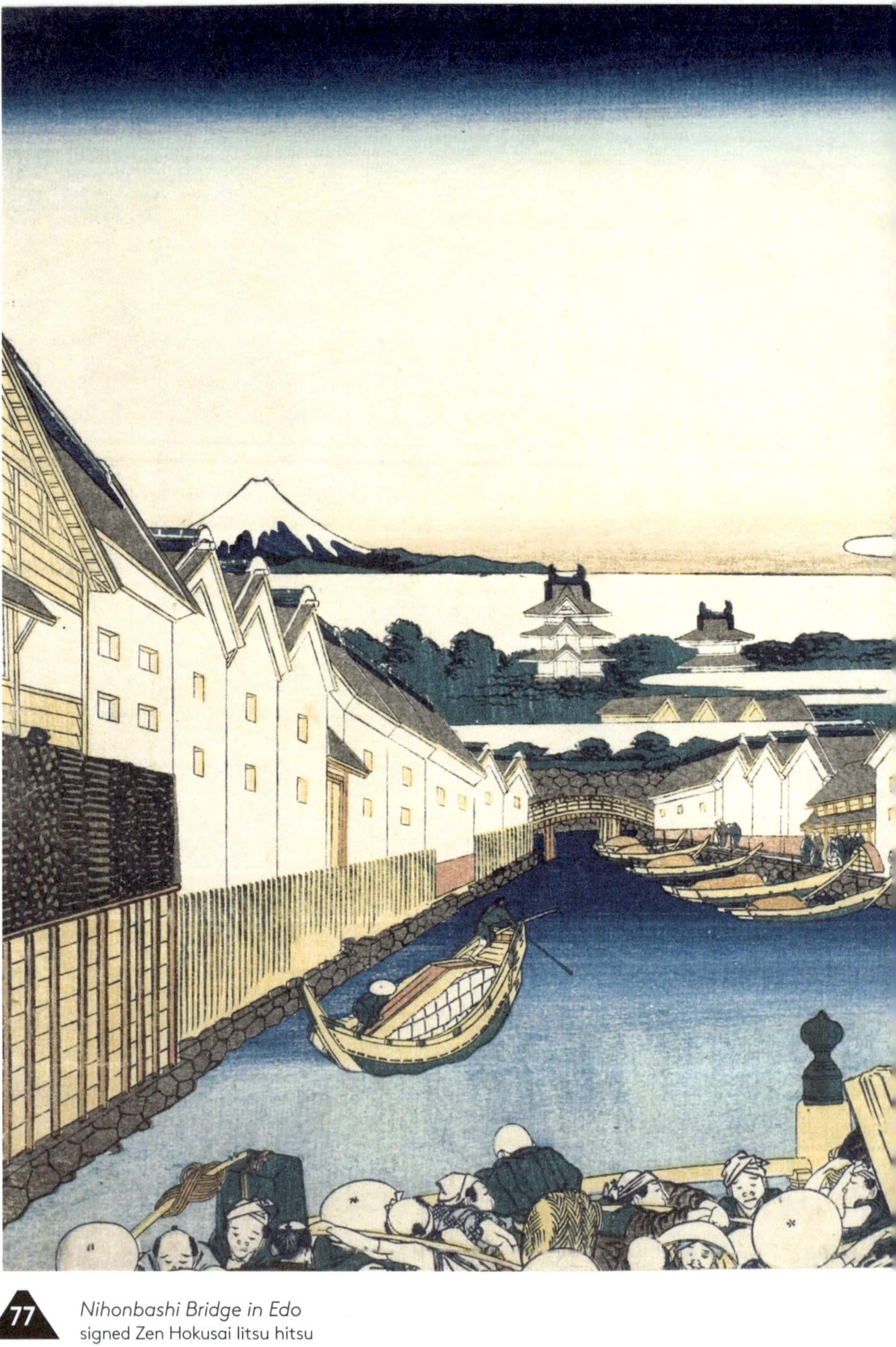

Nihonbashi Bridge in Edo
signed Zen Hokusai Iitsu hitsu

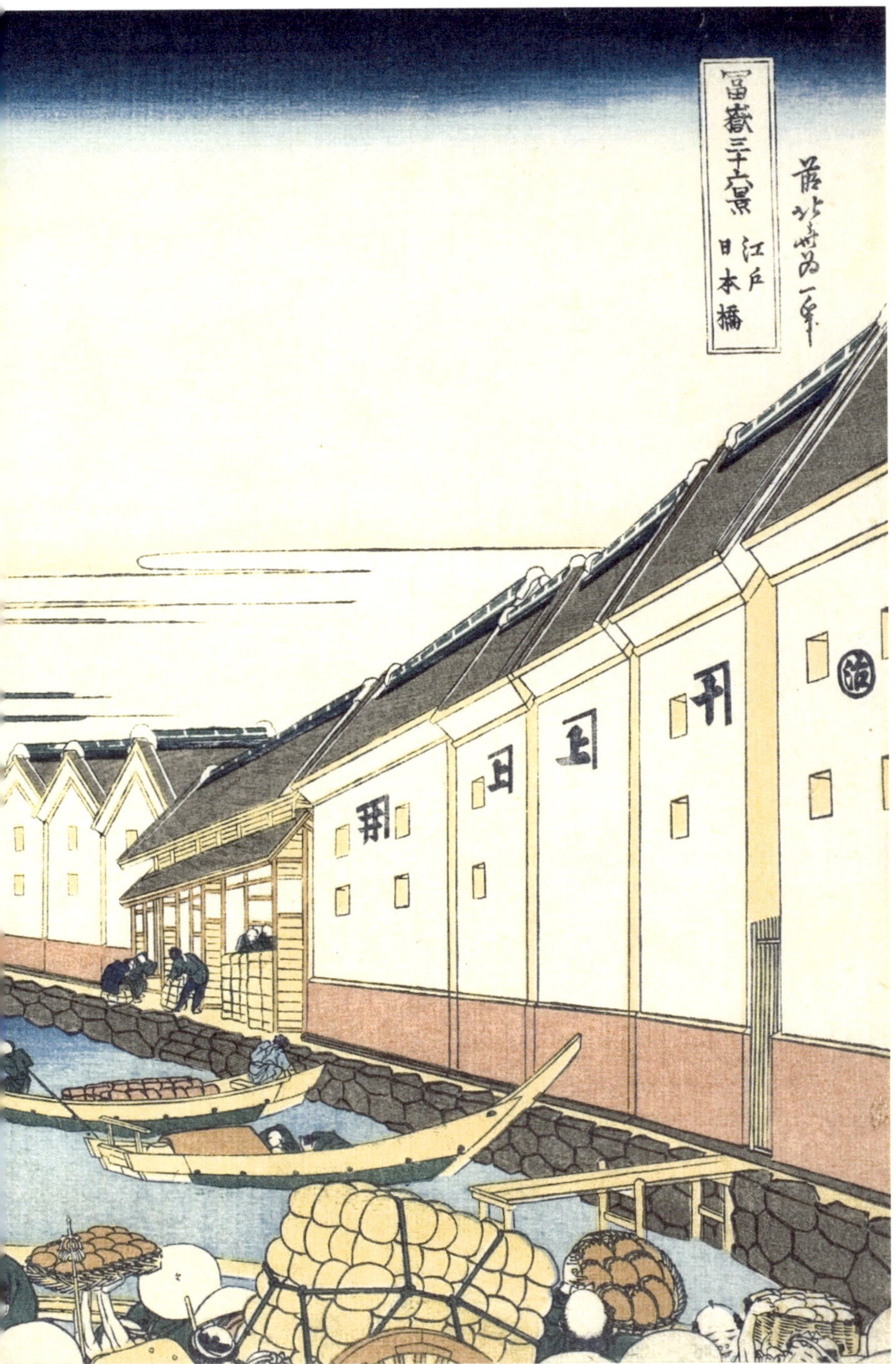

25.6 × 37.5 cm. Clarence Buckingham Collection, The Art Institute of Chicago, 1925.3258

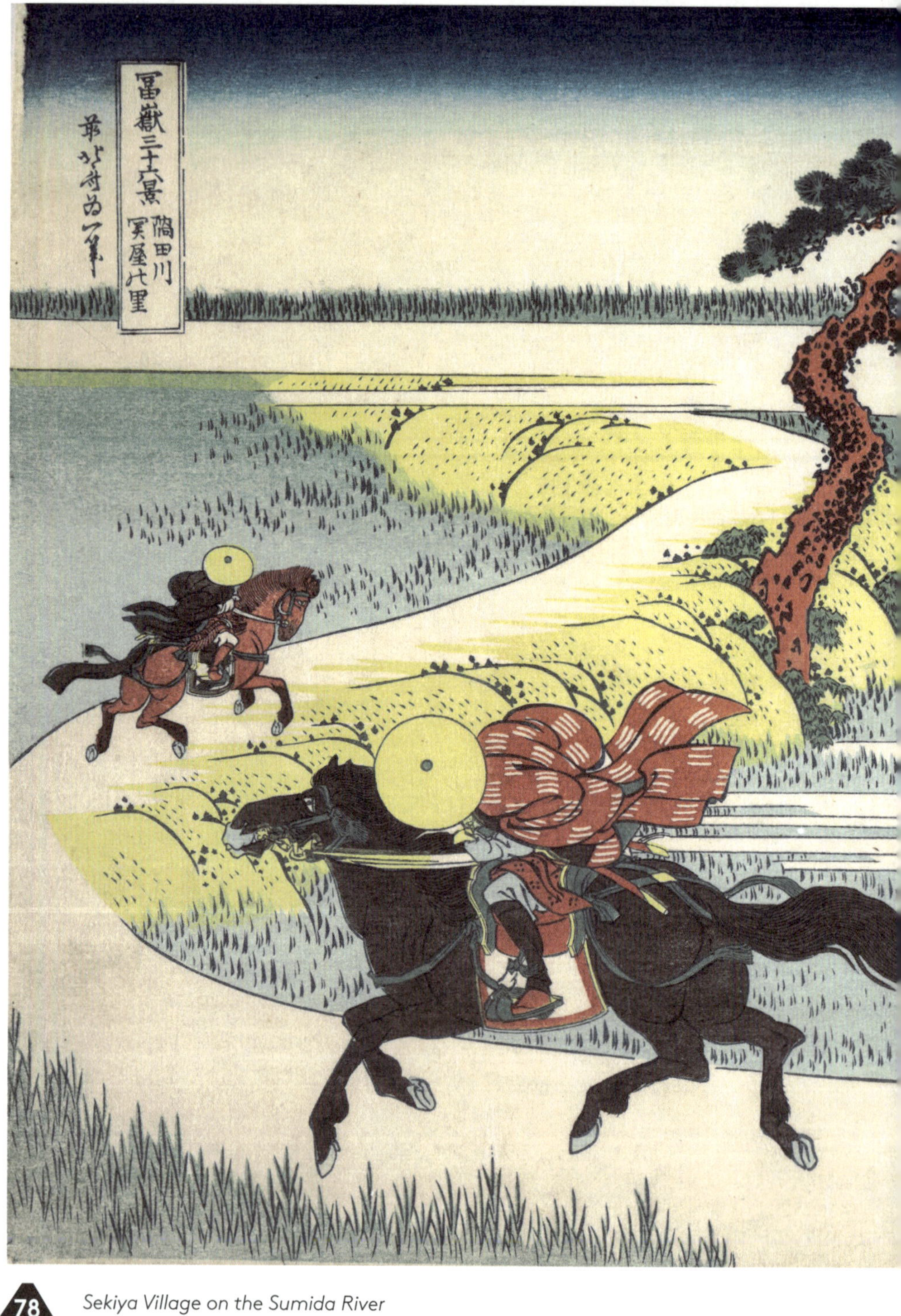

Sekiya Village on the Sumida River
signed Zen Hokusai Iitsu hitsu

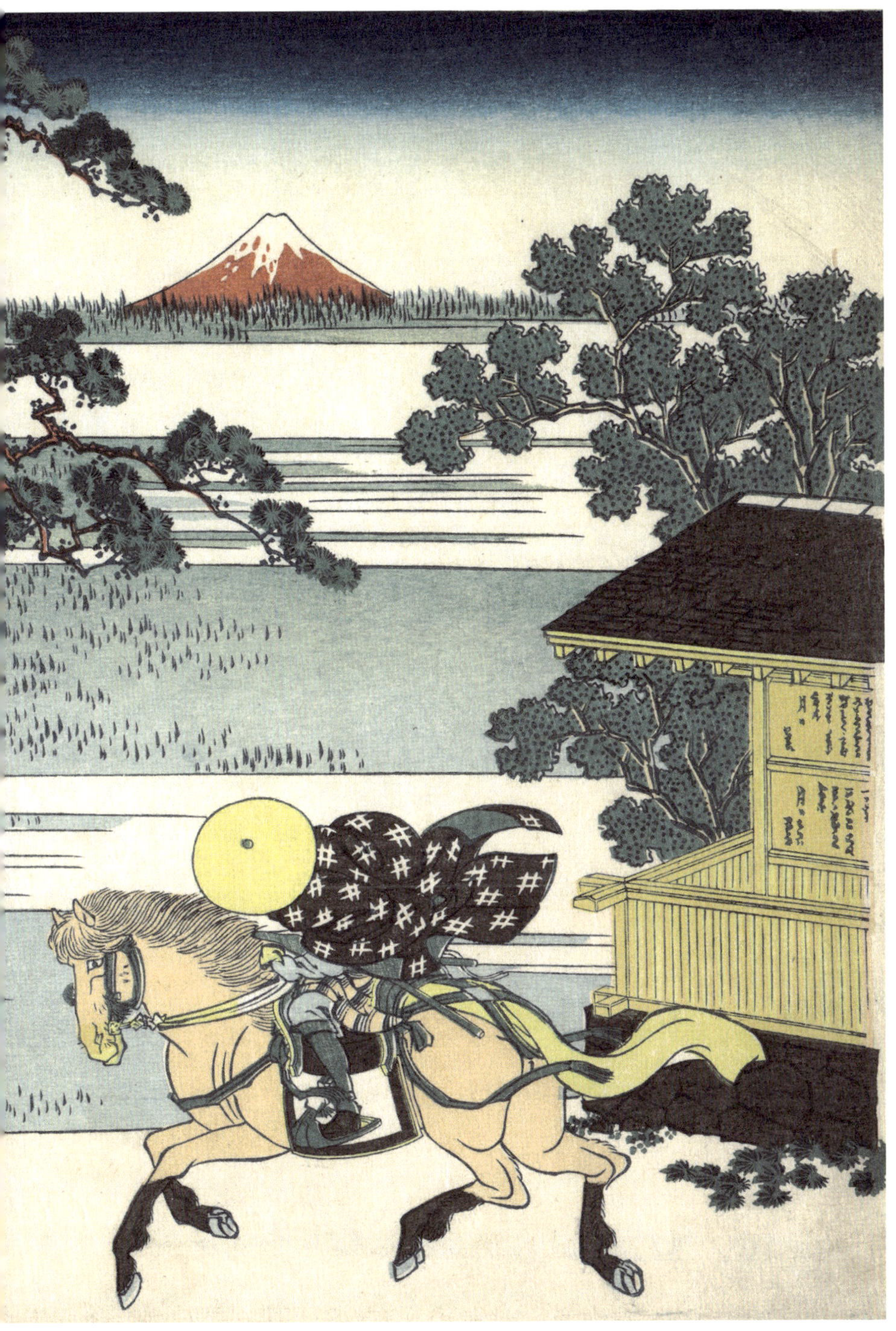

26 × 38.4 cm. Henry L. Phillips Collection, Bequest of Henry L. Phillips, 1939, The Metropolitan Museum of Art, New York, JP2998

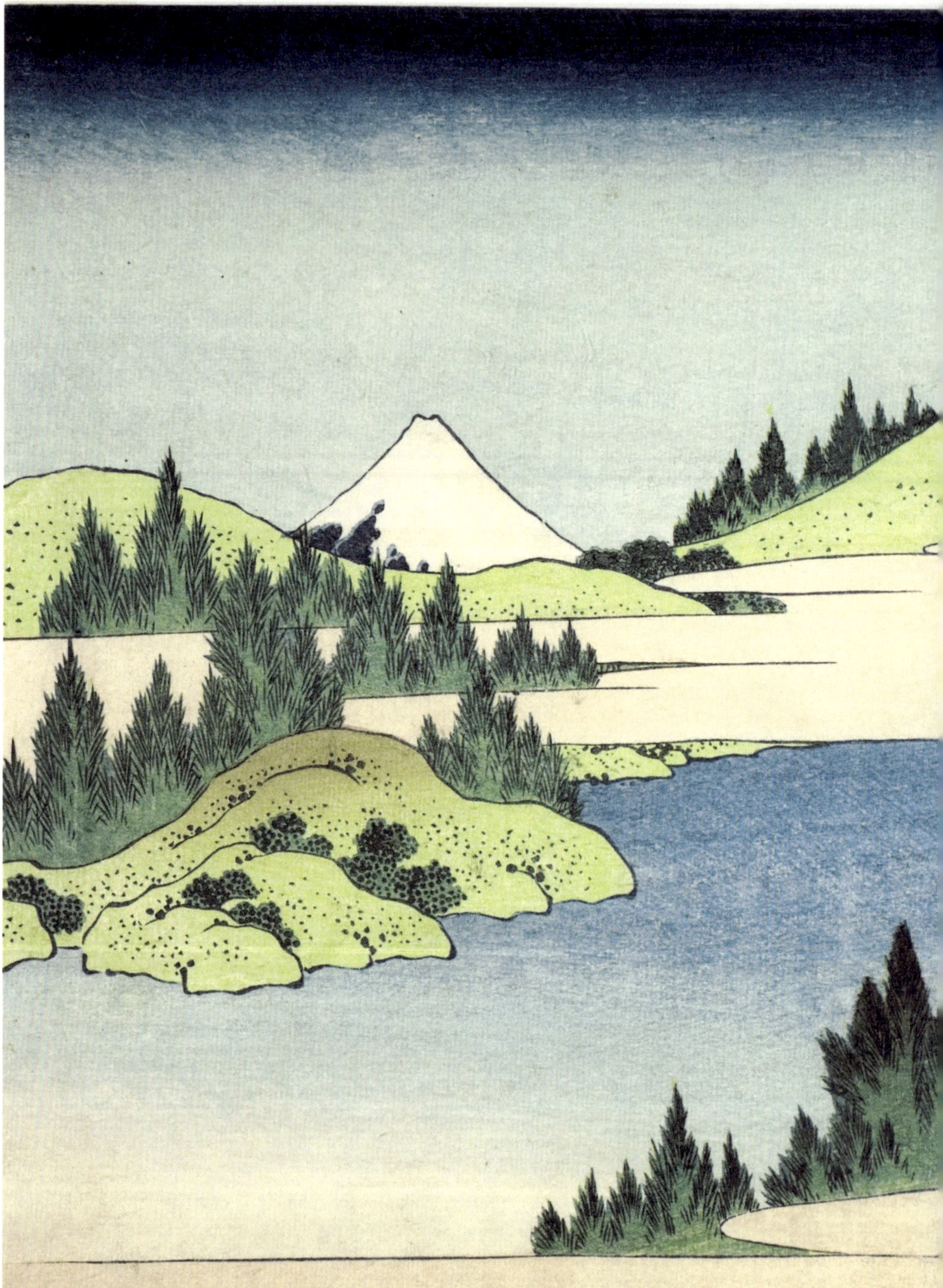

Lake Hakone in Sagami Province
signed Zen Hokusai litsu hitsu

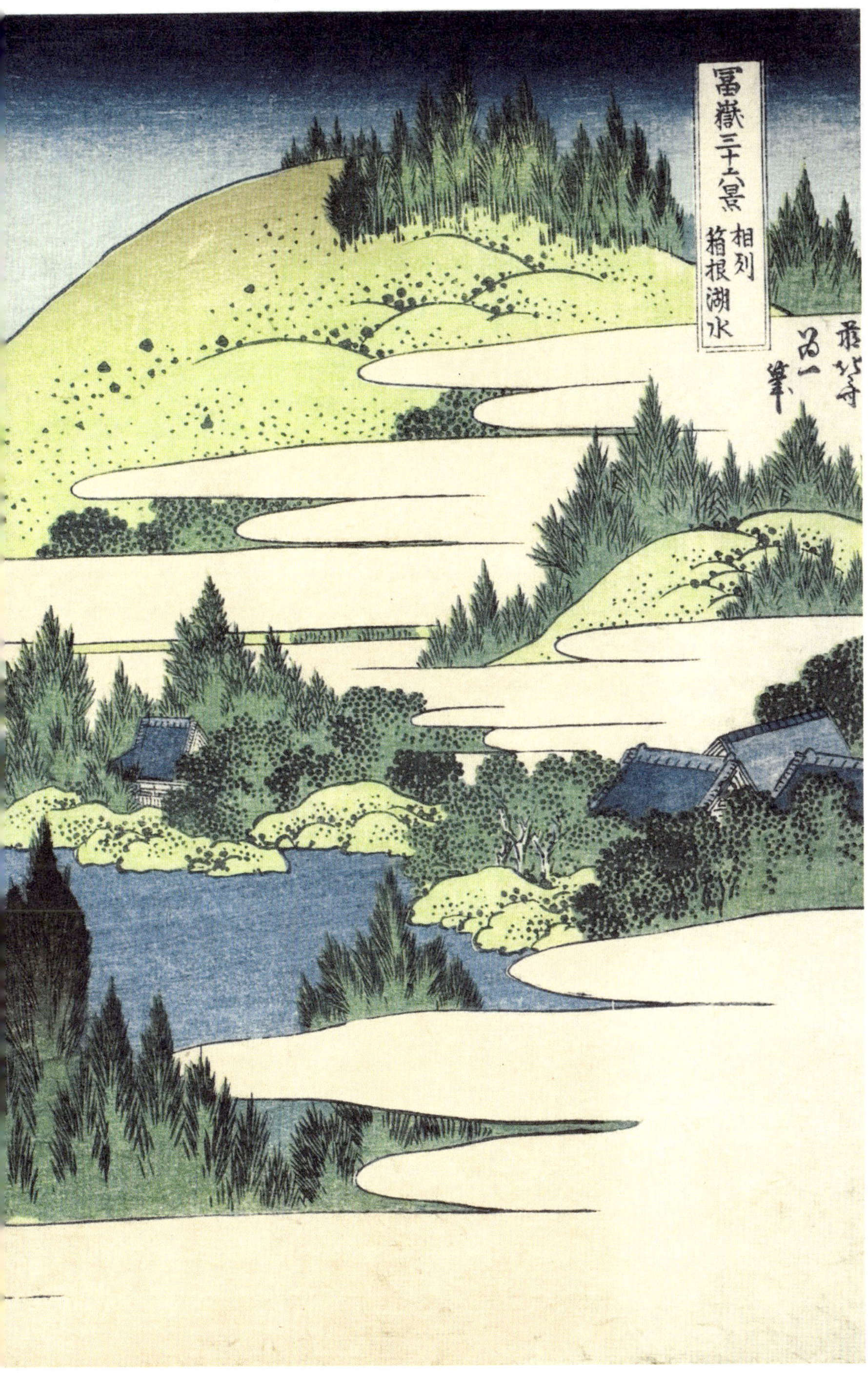

25.6 × 37.5 cm. Clarence Buckingham Collection, The Art Institute of Chicago, 1925.3277

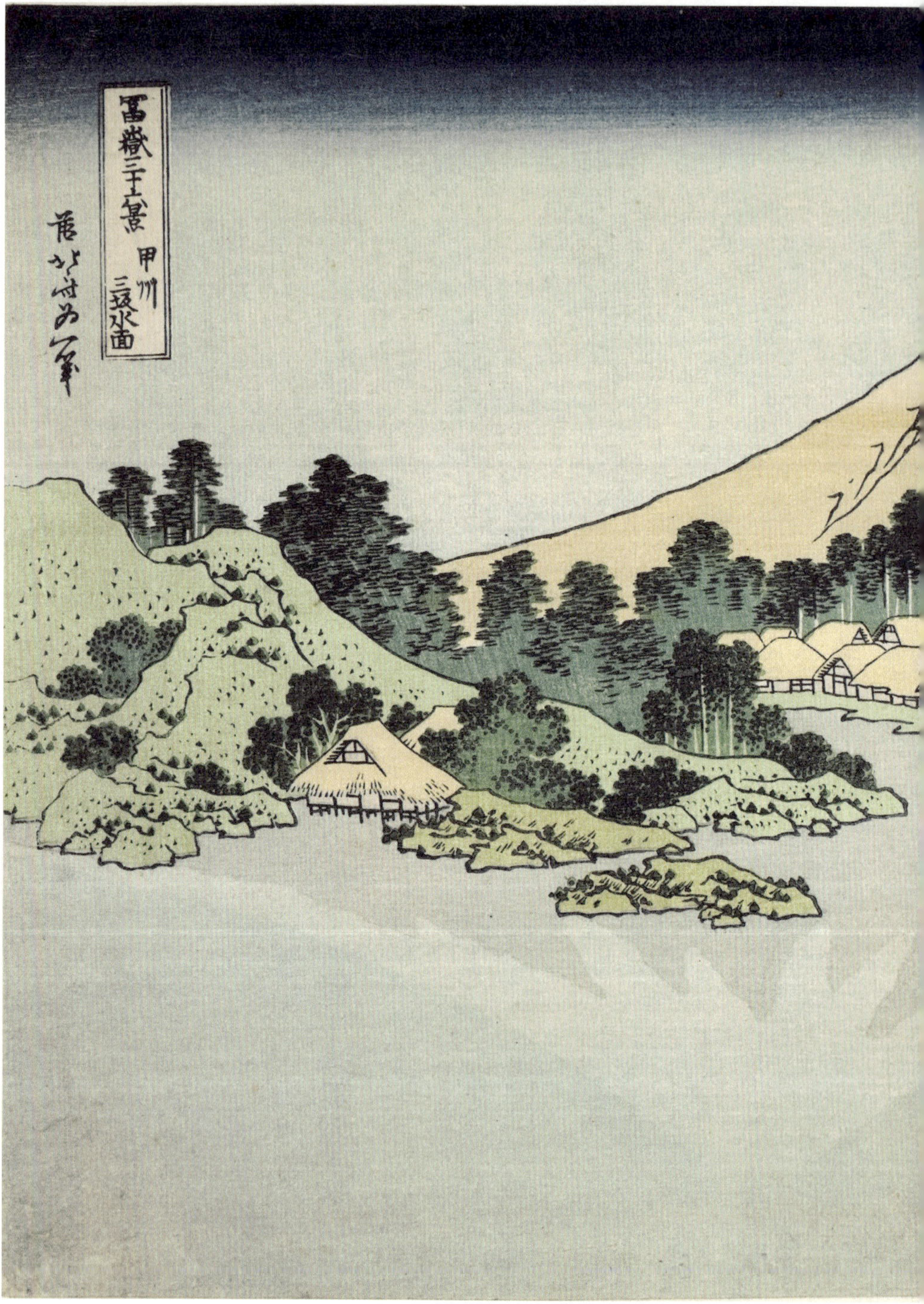

The *Surface of the Water at Misaka in Kai Province*
signed Zen Hokusai Iitsu hitsu

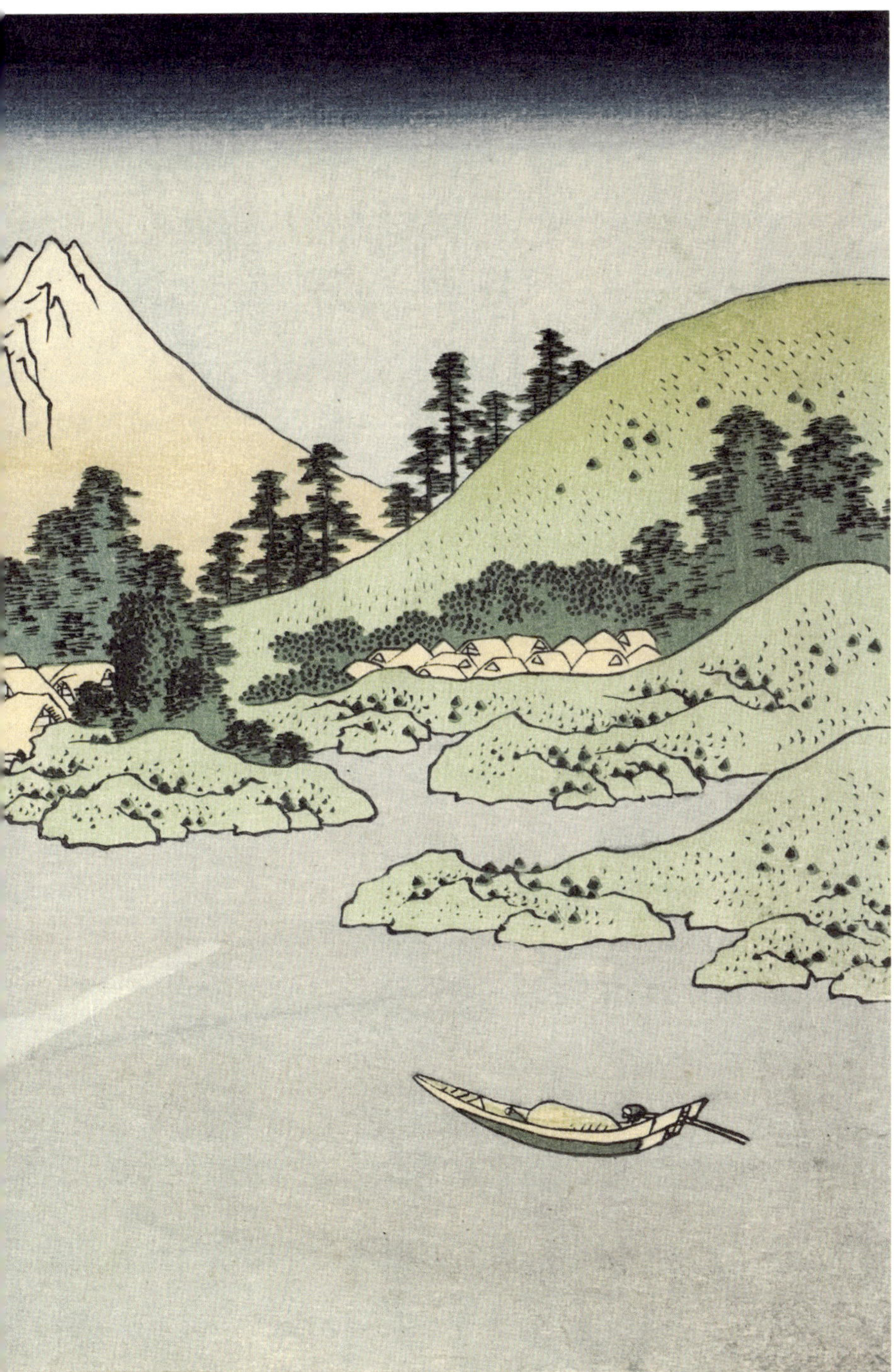

25.7 × 37.5 cm. Clarence Buckingham Collection, The Art Institute of Chicago, 1925.3275

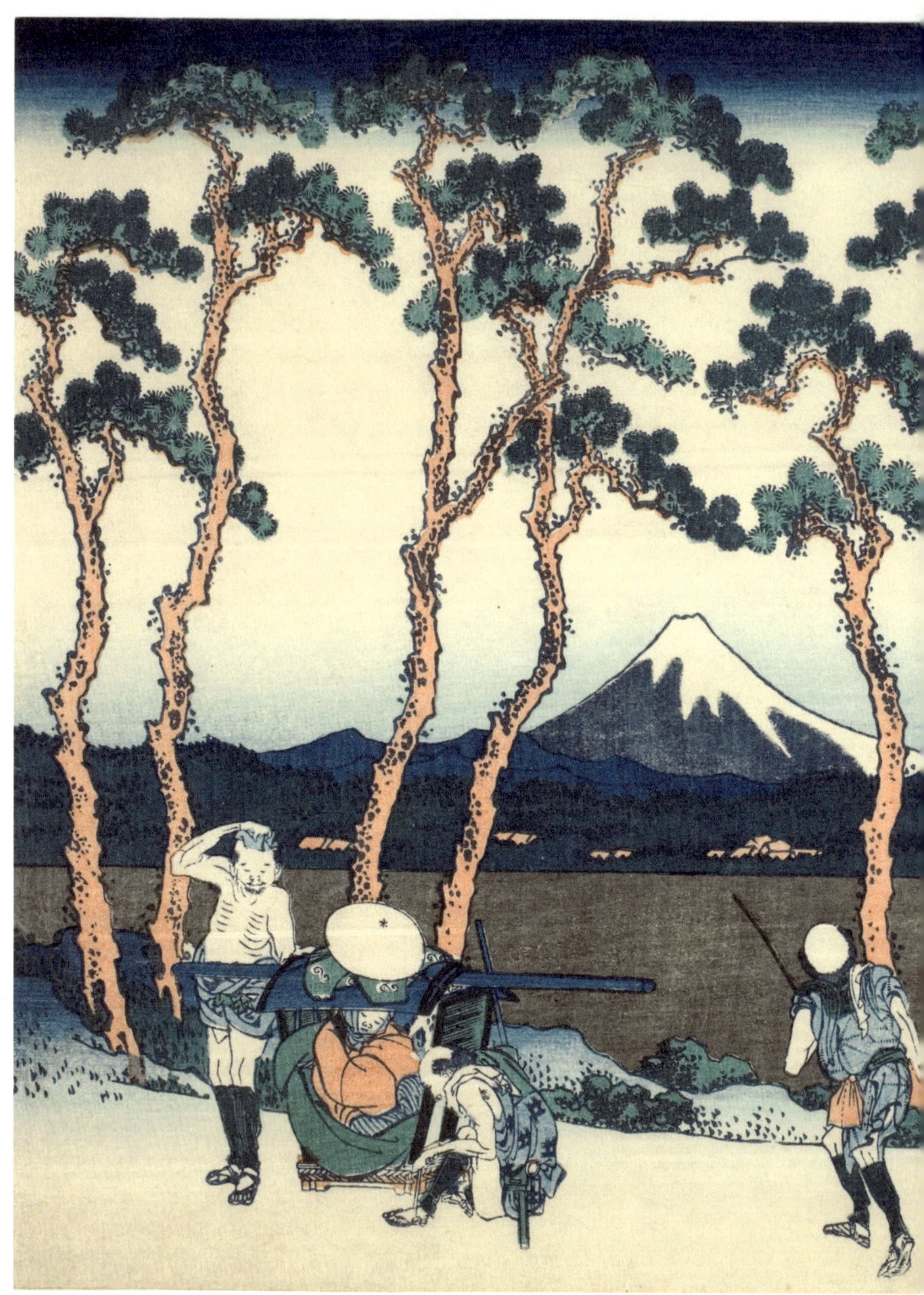

Hodogaya on the Tōkaidō Road
signed Zen Hokusai Iitsu hitsu

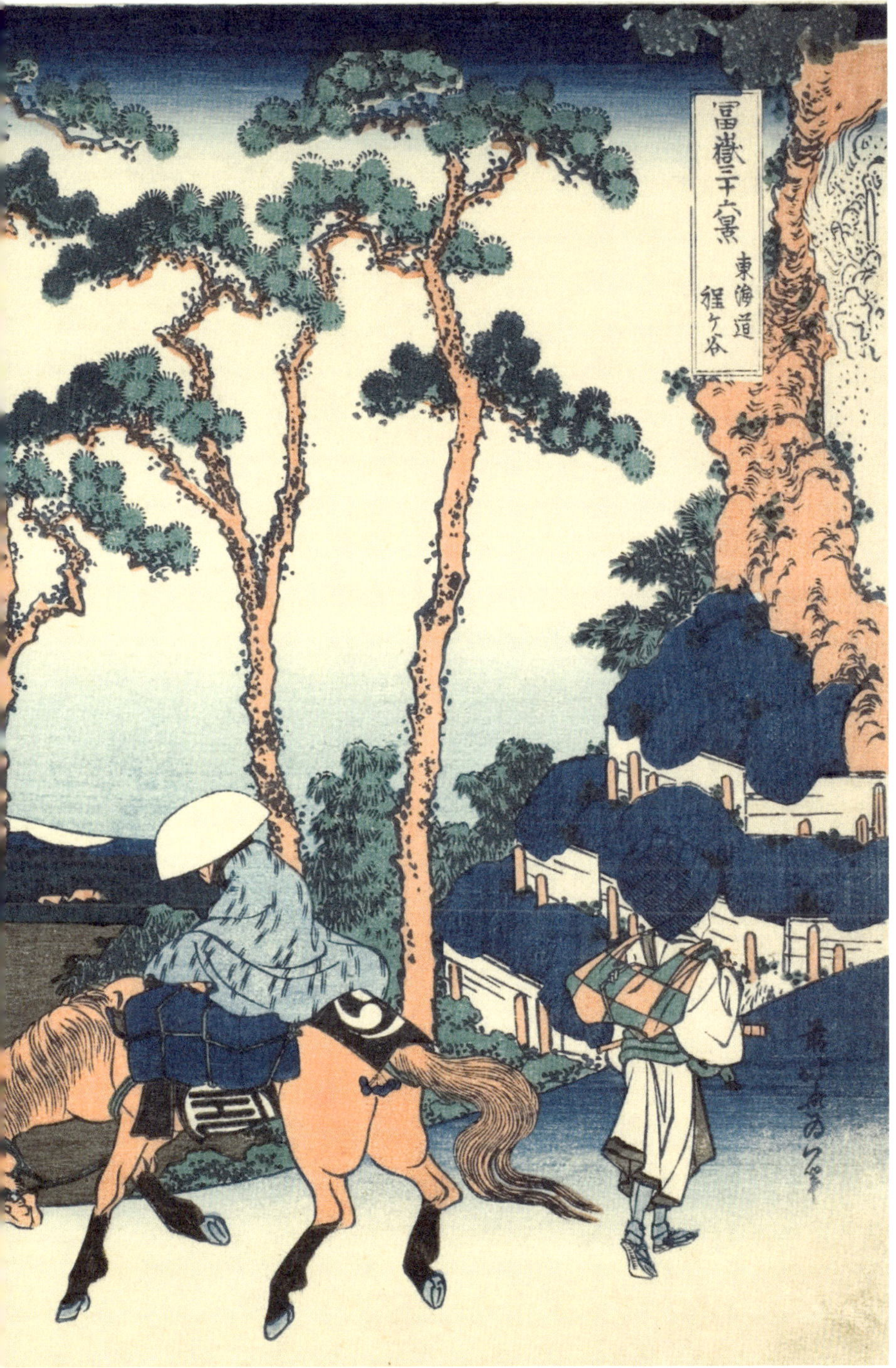

25.8 × 37.7 cm. Clarence Buckingham Collection, The Art Institute of Chicago, 1925.3239

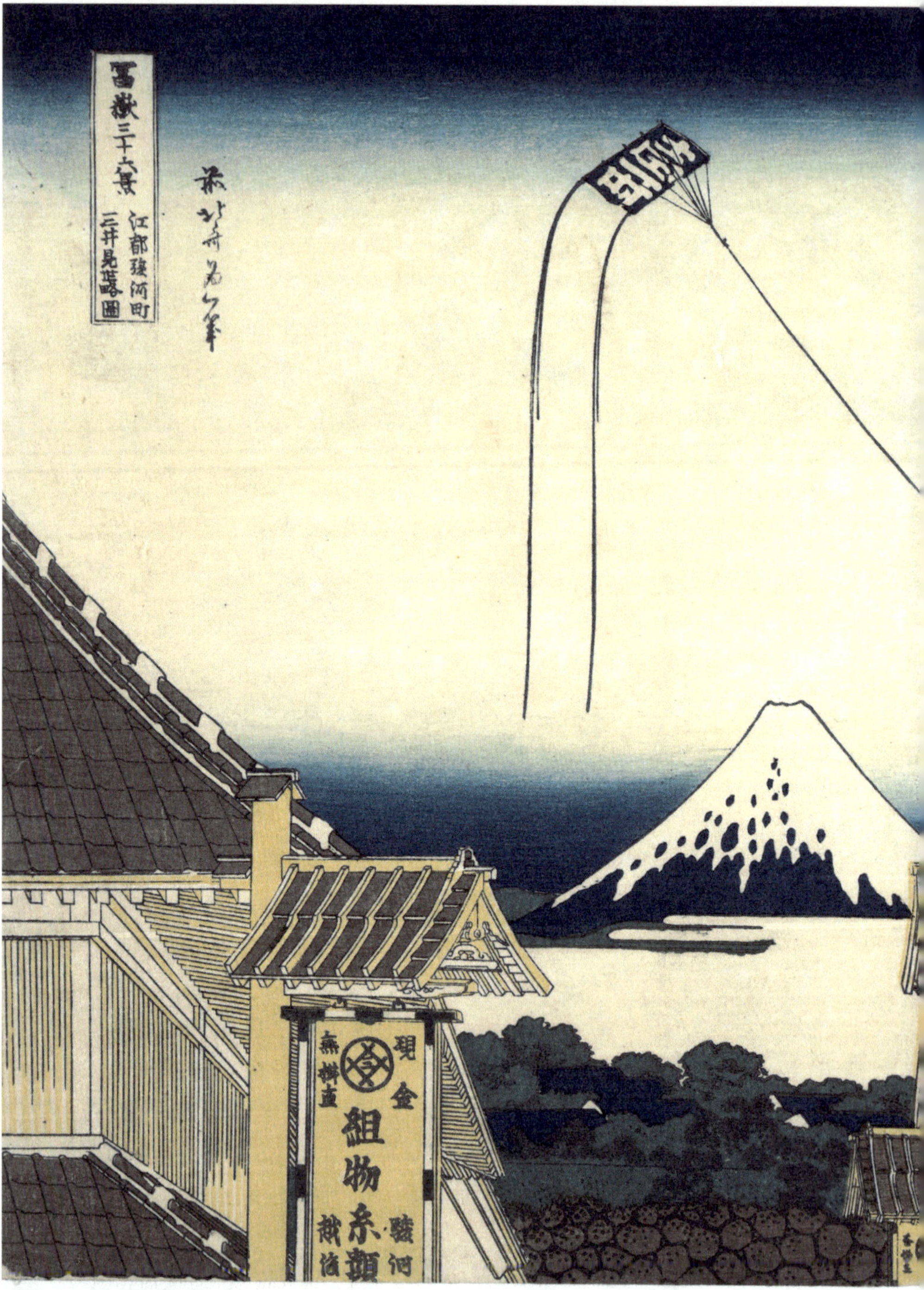

Mitsui Shop at Surugachō in Edo
signed Zen Hokusai Iitsu hitsu

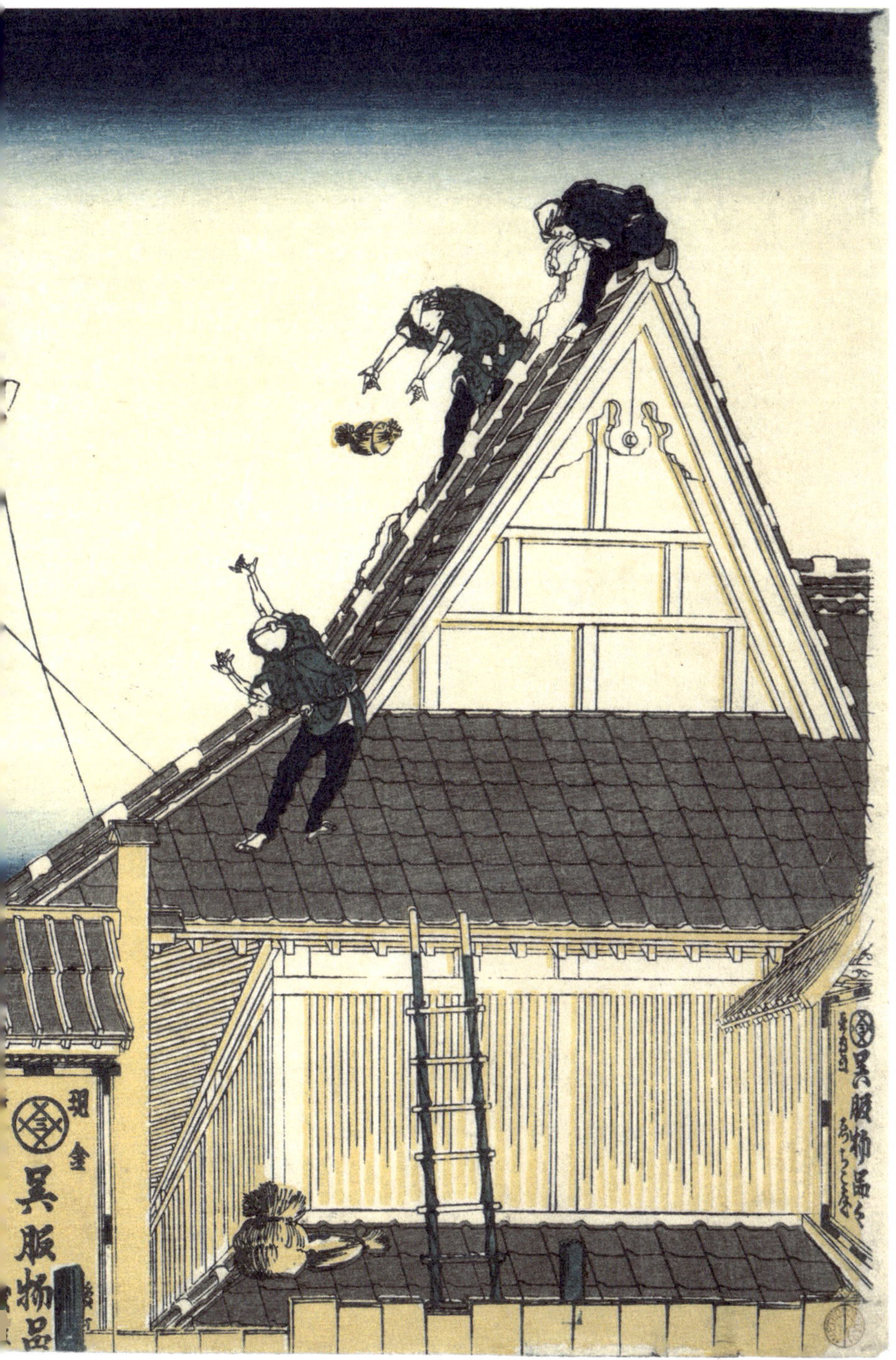

26 × 38.4 cm. Rogers Fund, 1922, The Metropolitan Museum of Art, New York, JP1296

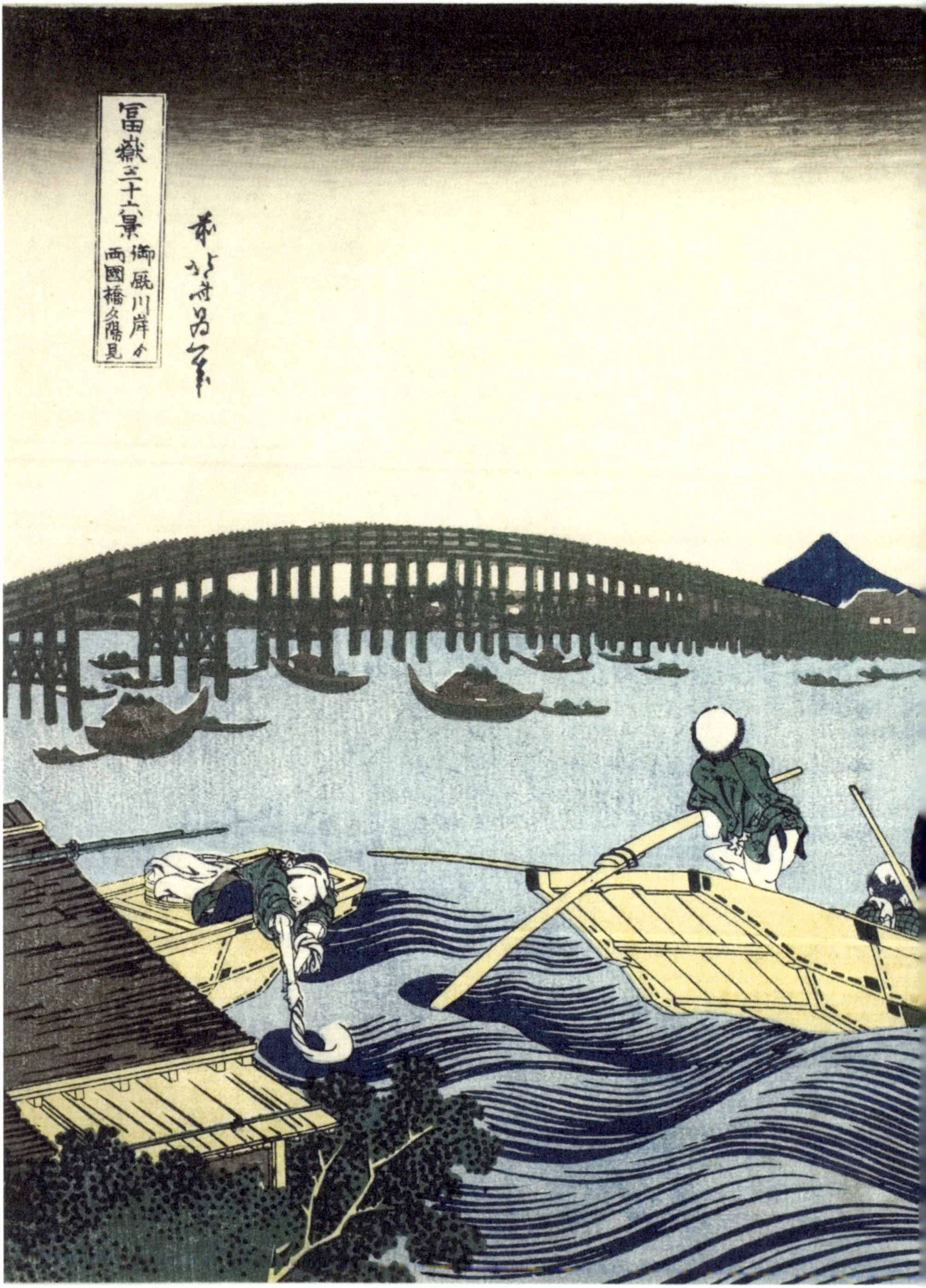

83 *Watching the Sunset over the Ryōgoku Bridge from the Onmaya Embankment*
signed Zen Hokusai Iitsu hitsu

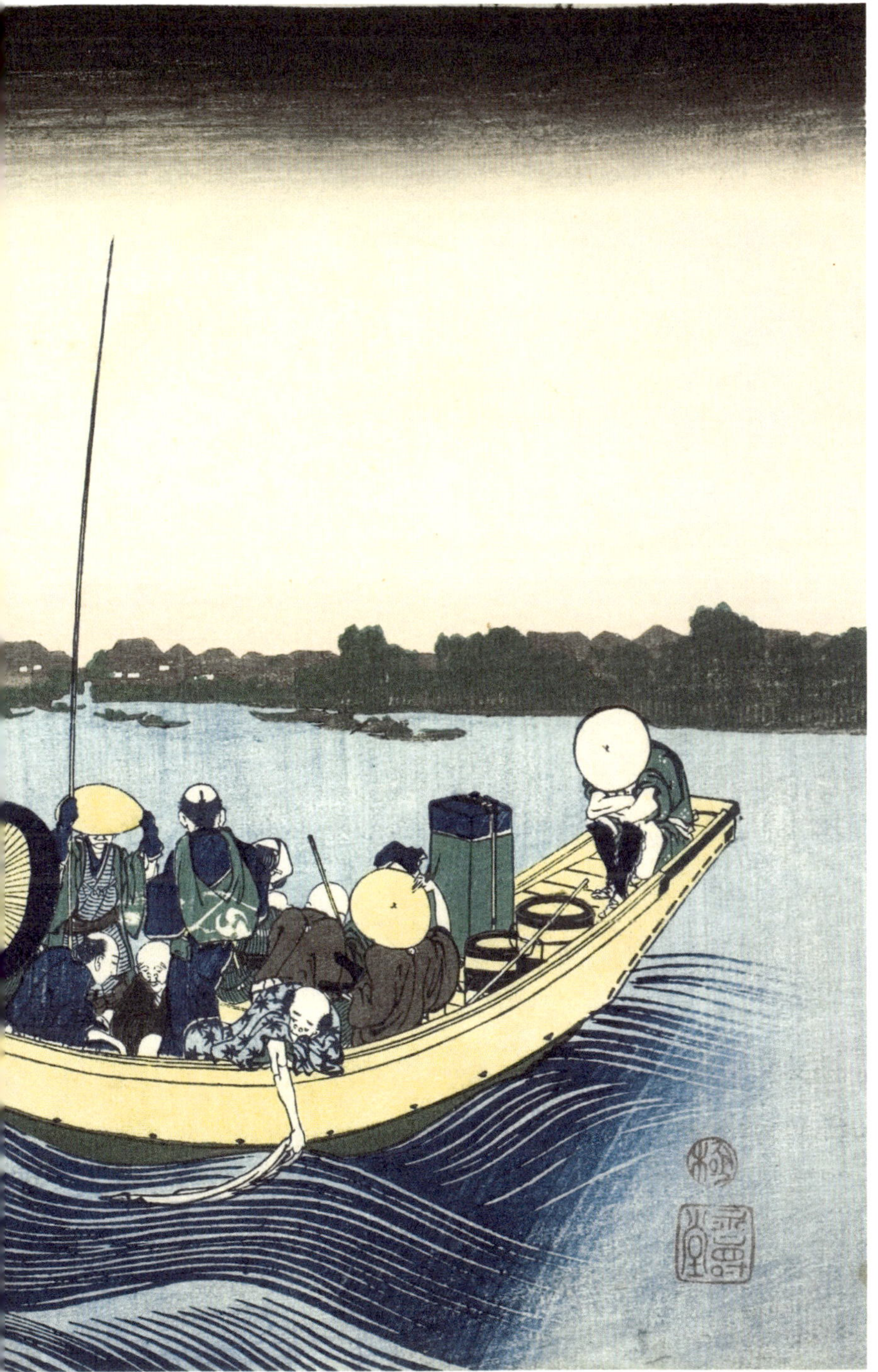

25.4 × 37.5 cm. Gift of H. R. Warner, The Art Institute of Chicago, 1932.166

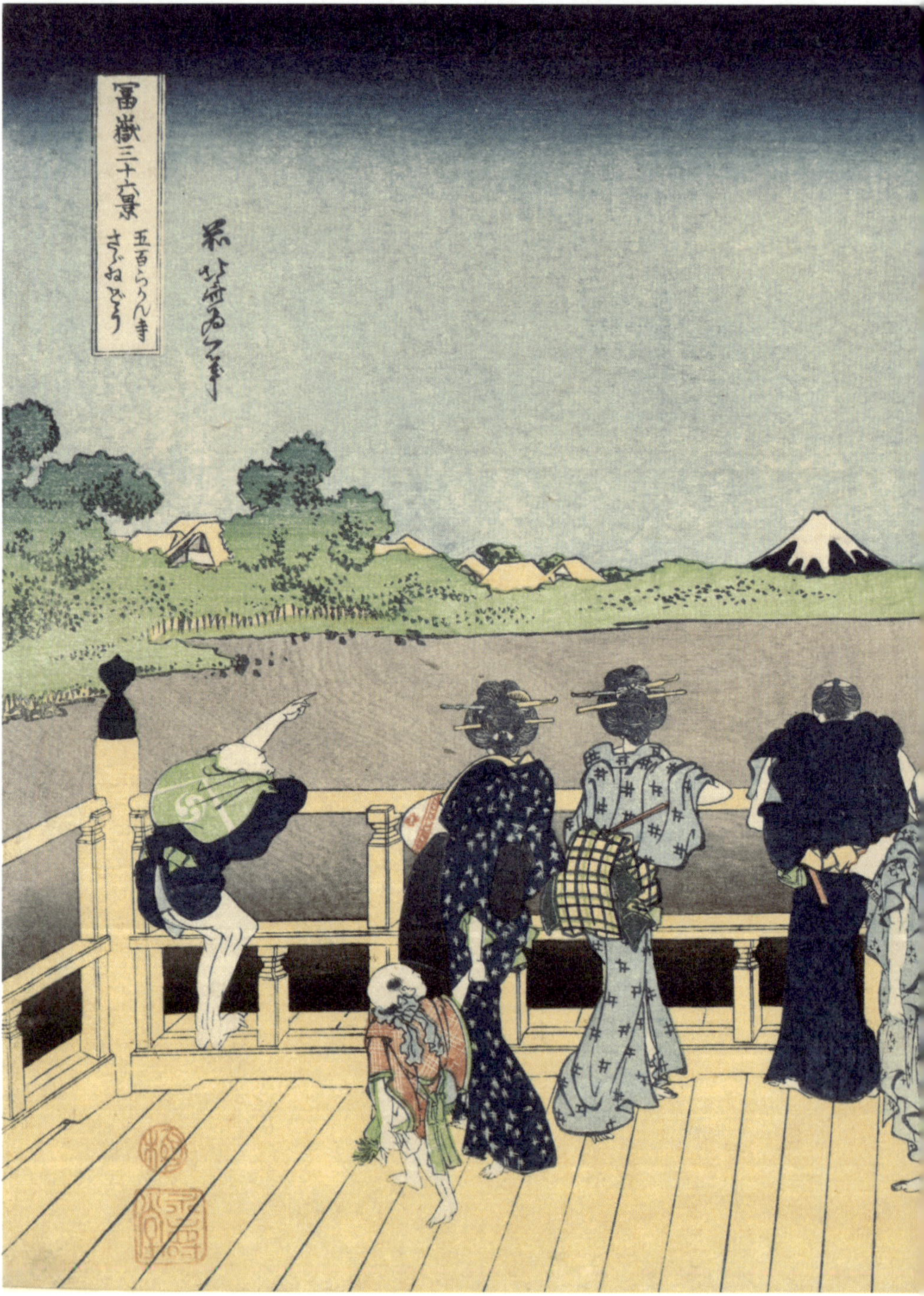

Sazai Hall at the Temple of the Five Hundred Arhats
signed Zen Hokusai Iitsu hitsu

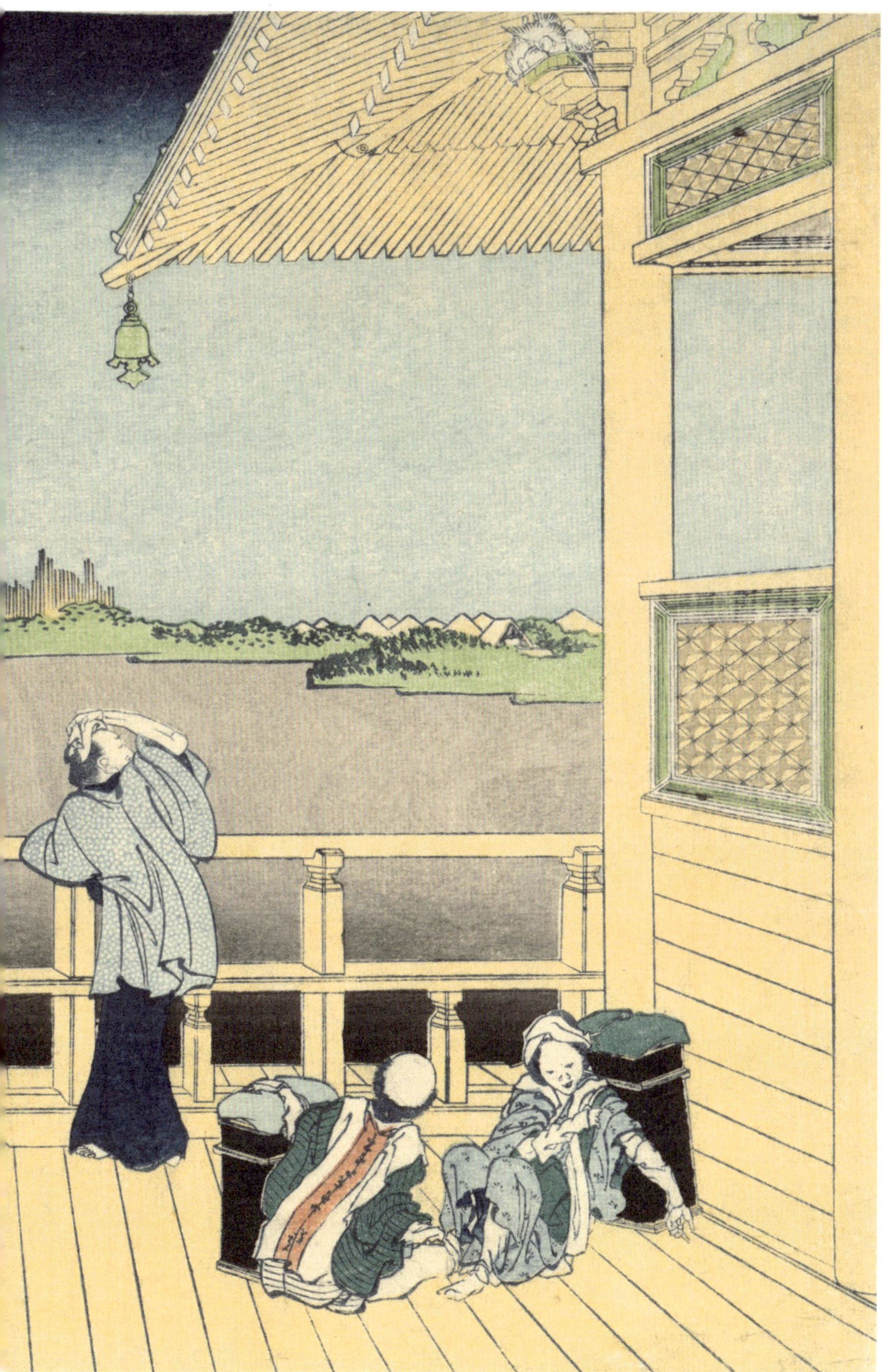

25.7 × 37.4 cm. Clarence Buckingham Collection, The Art Institute of Chicago, 1925.3263

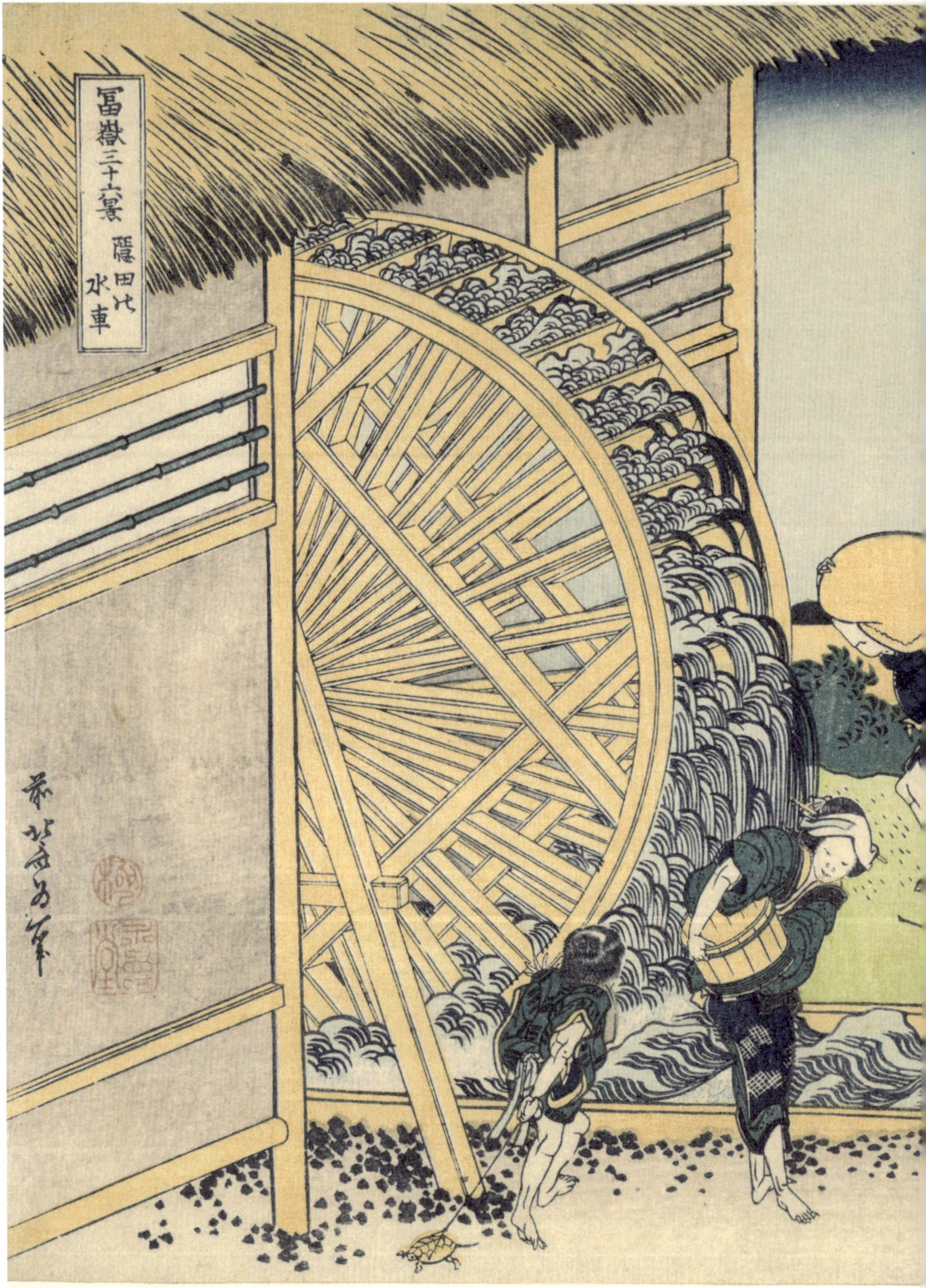

85 *Waterwheel at Onden*
signed Zen Hokusai Iitsu hitsu

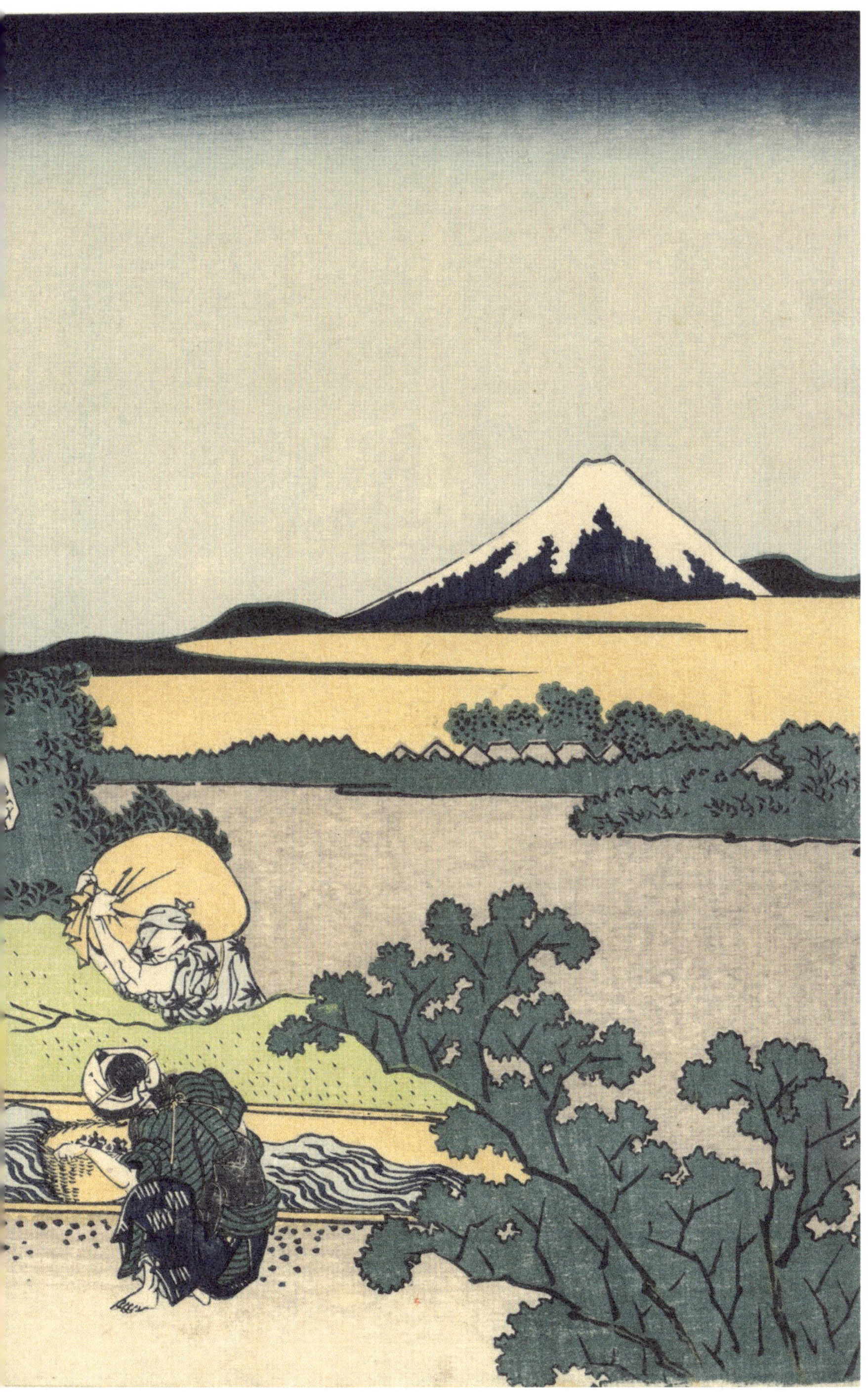

26.1 × 37.3 cm. Clarence Buckingham Collection, The Art Institute of Chicago, 1925.3233

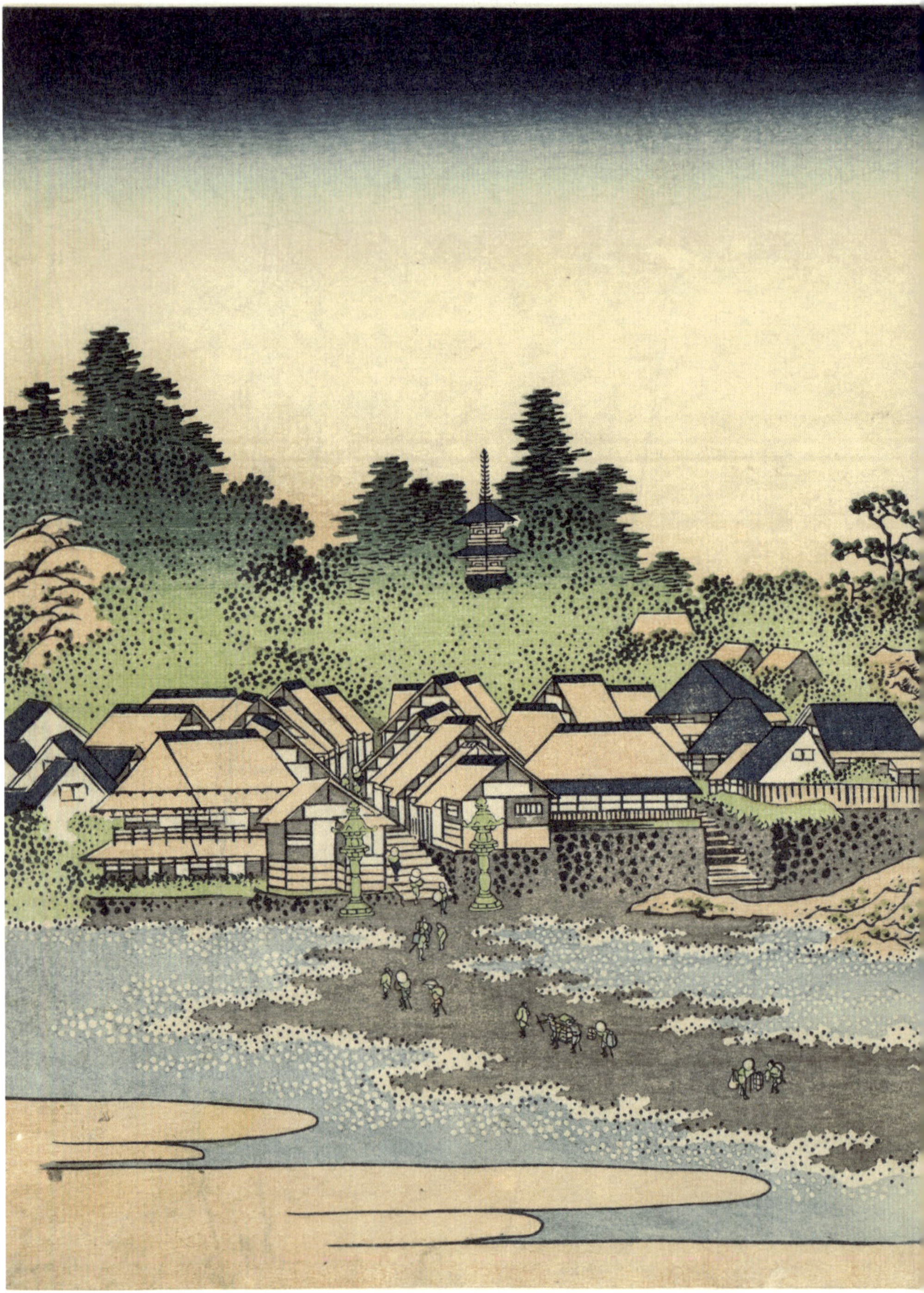

Enoshima Island in Sagami Province
signed Zen Hokusai Iitsu hitsu

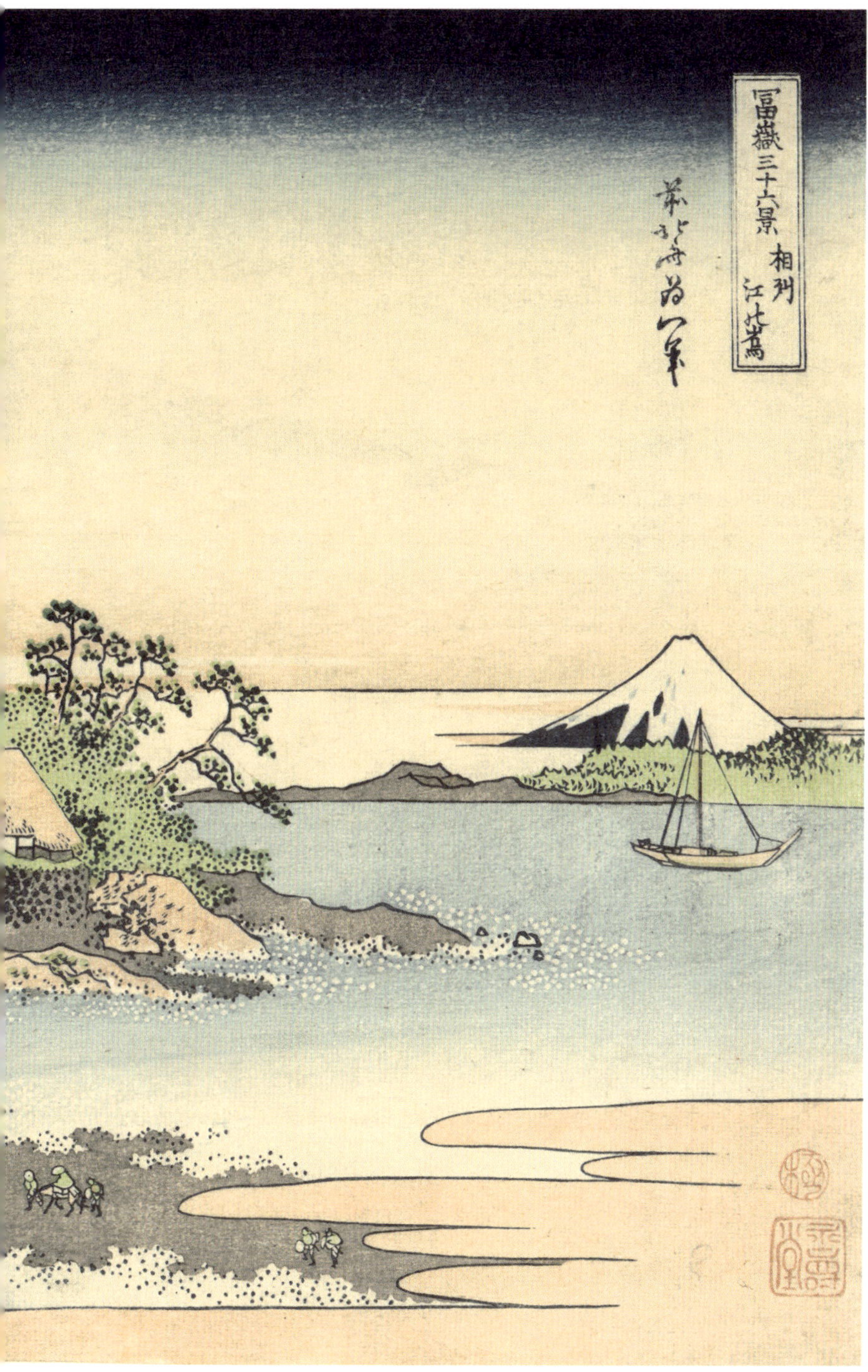

25.7 × 37.5 cm. Clarence Buckingham Collection, The Art Institute of Chicago, 1925.3270

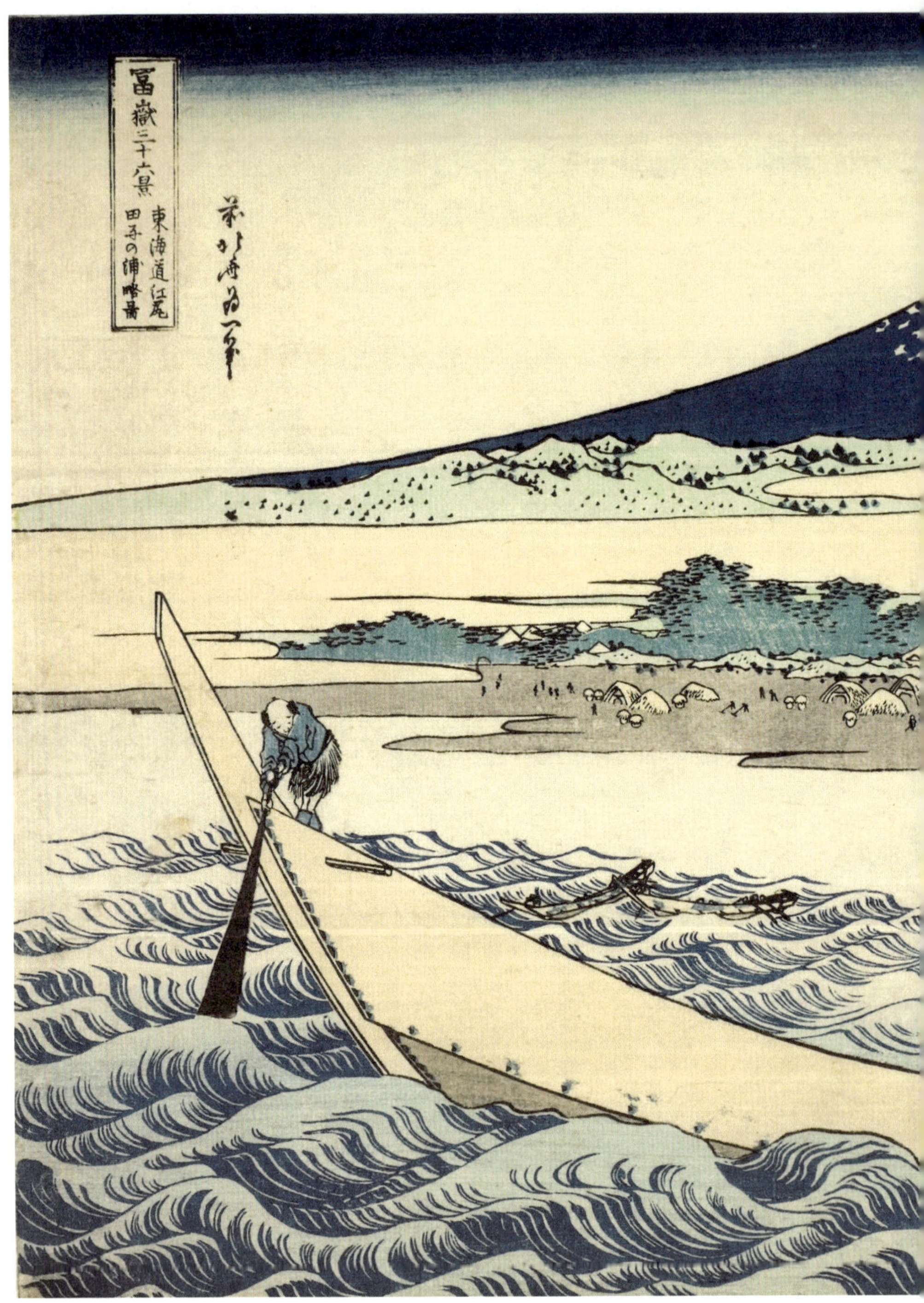

Tago Bay near Ejiri *on the Tōkaidō Road*
signed Zen Hokusai Iitsu hitsu

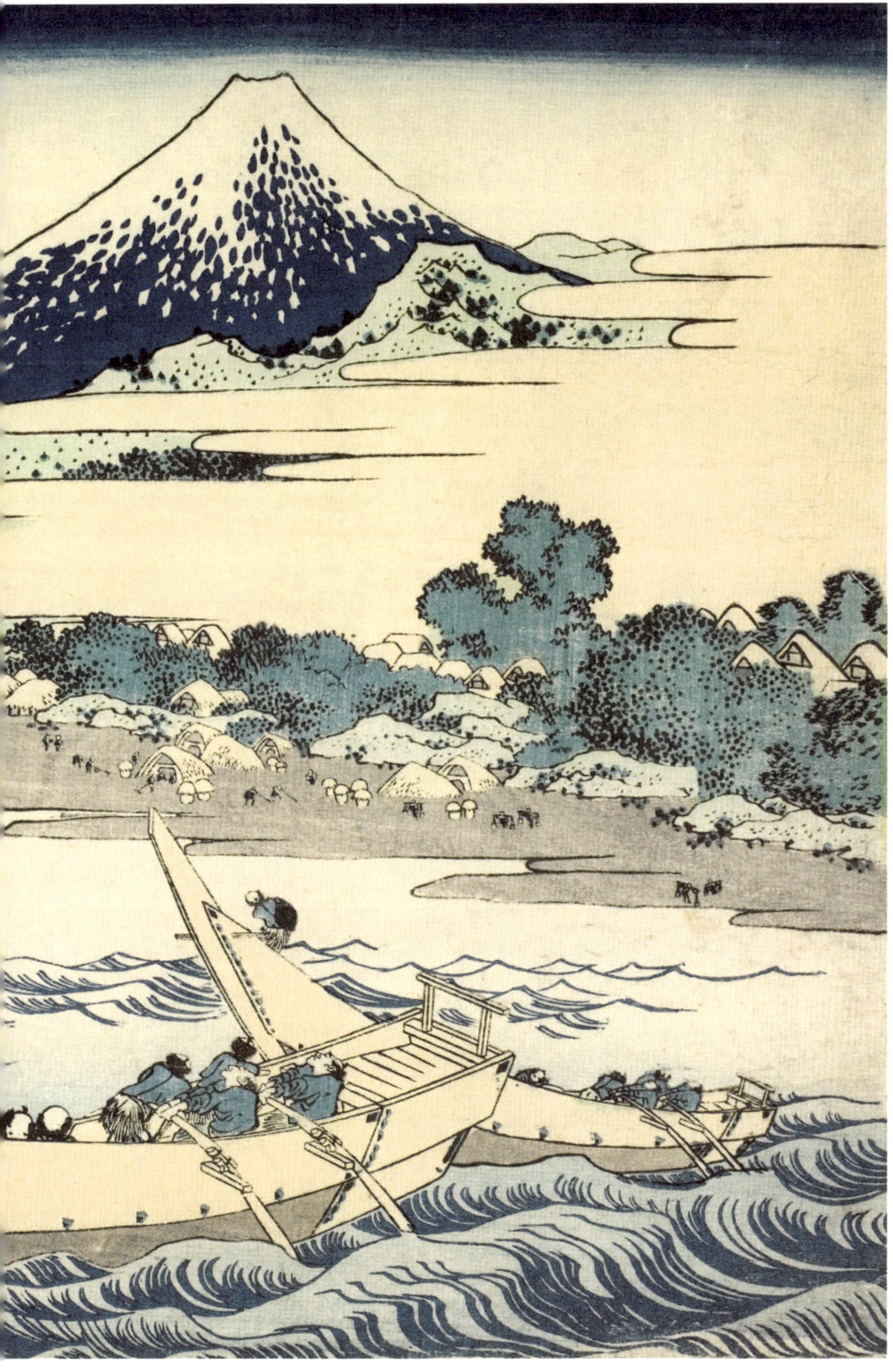

25.9 × 37.7 cm. Bequest of Russell Tyson, 1964, The Art Institute of Chicago, 1058b

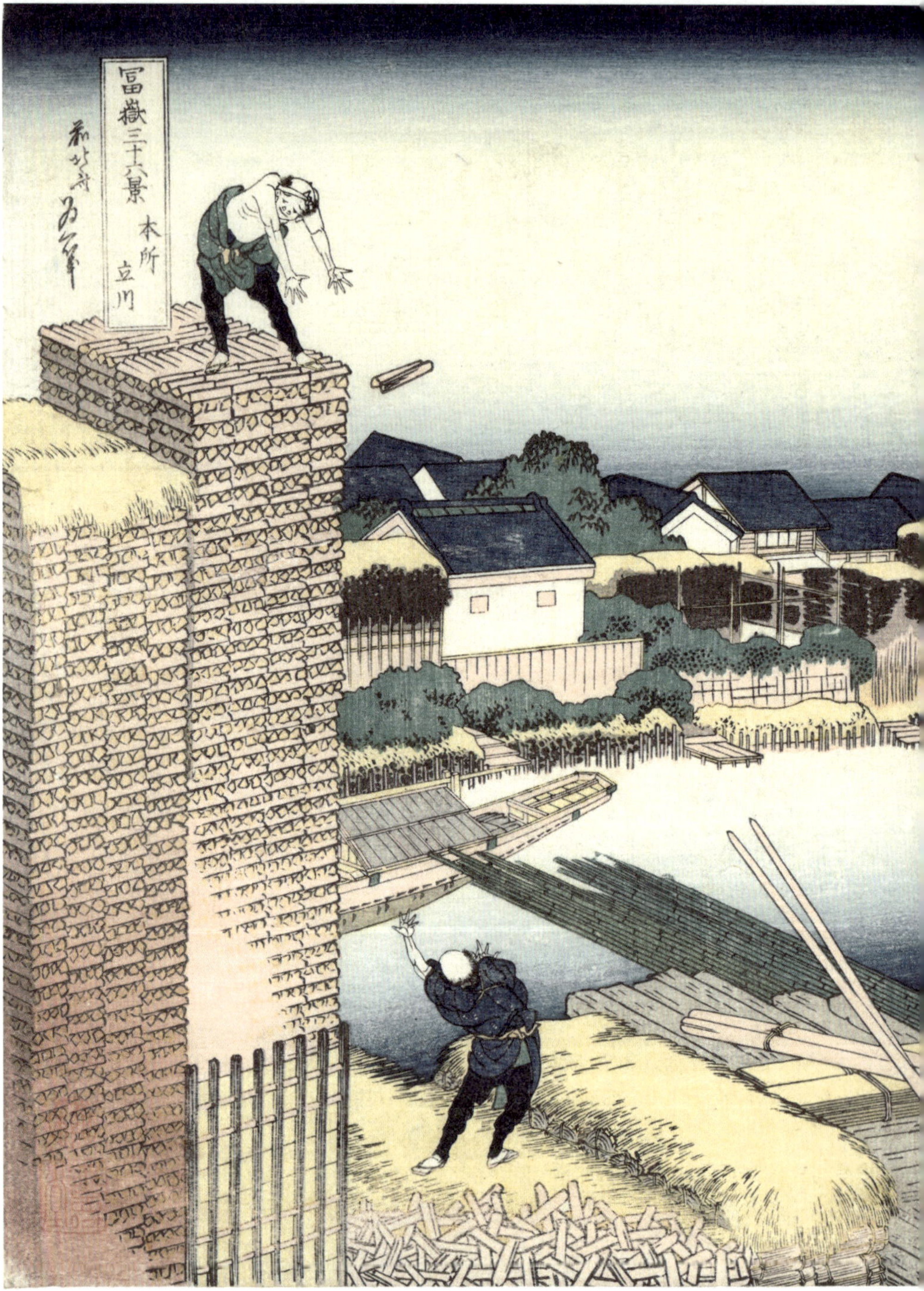

Tatekawa River Lumberyard at Honjo
signed Zen Hokusai Iitsu hitsu

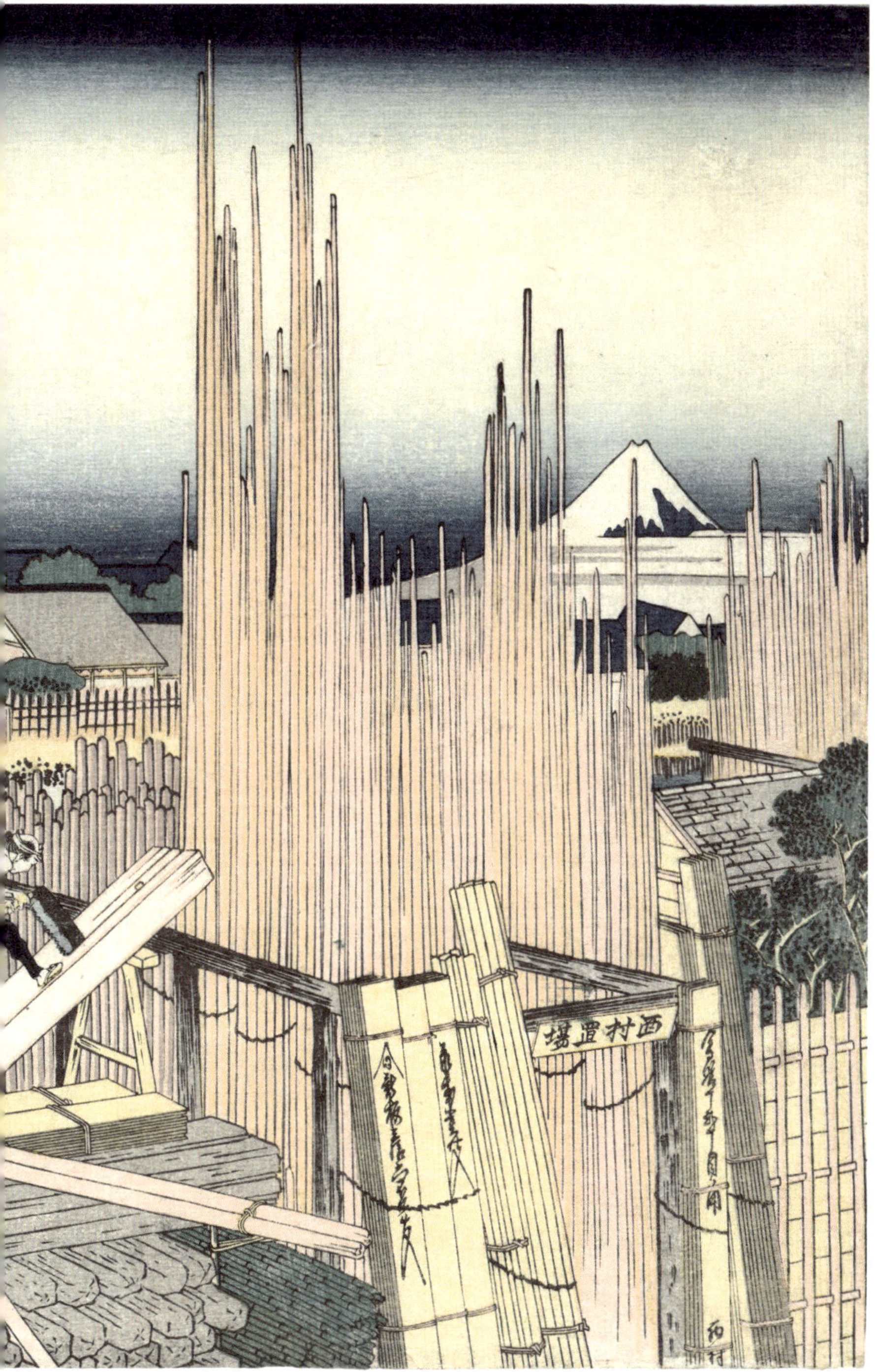

25.4 × 37.5 cm. Gift of Mr and Mrs Gaylord Donnelley, The Art Institute of Chicago, 1971.502

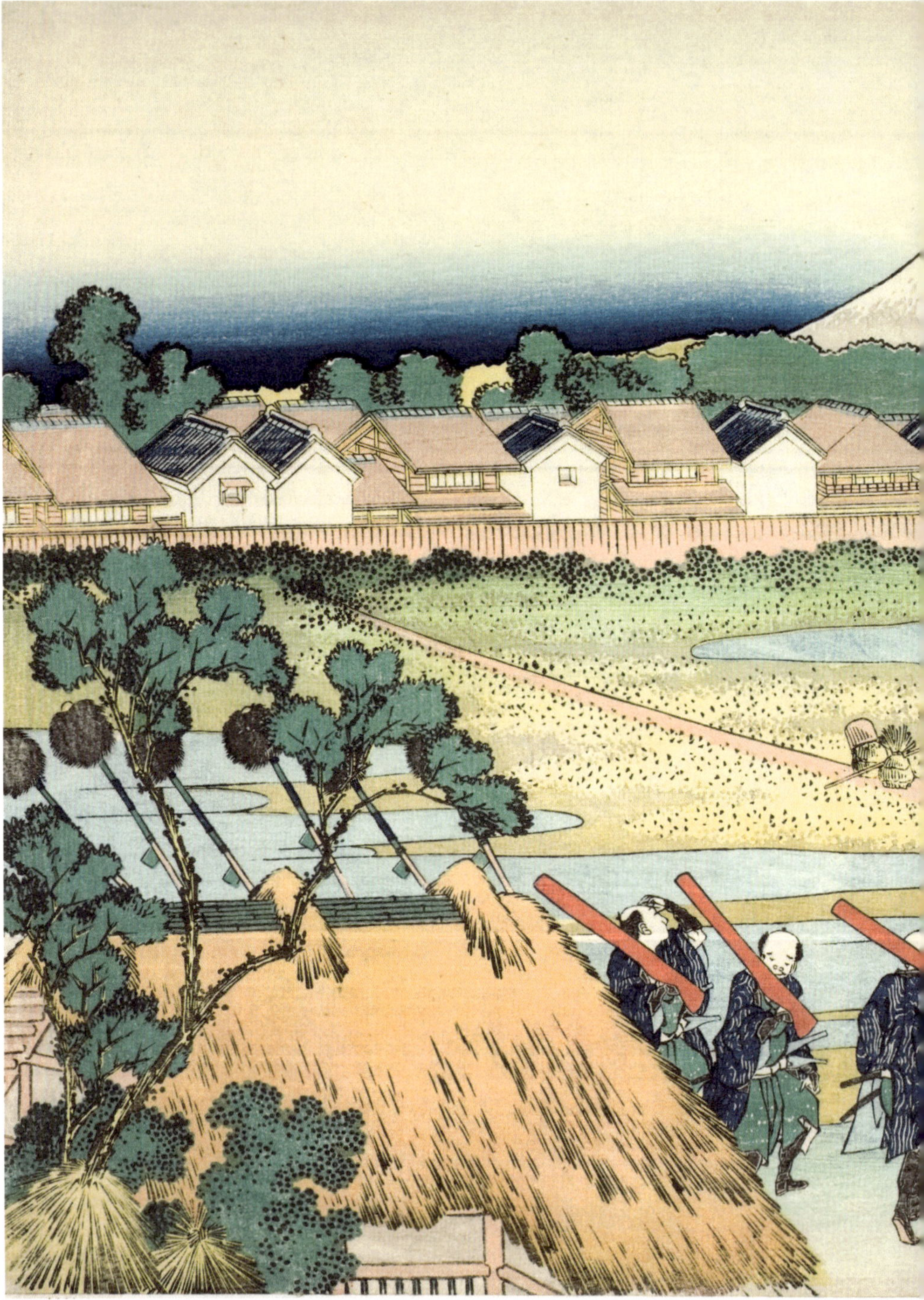

Mount Fuji Seen from the Senju Pleasure Quarter
signed Zen Hokusai Iitsu hitsu

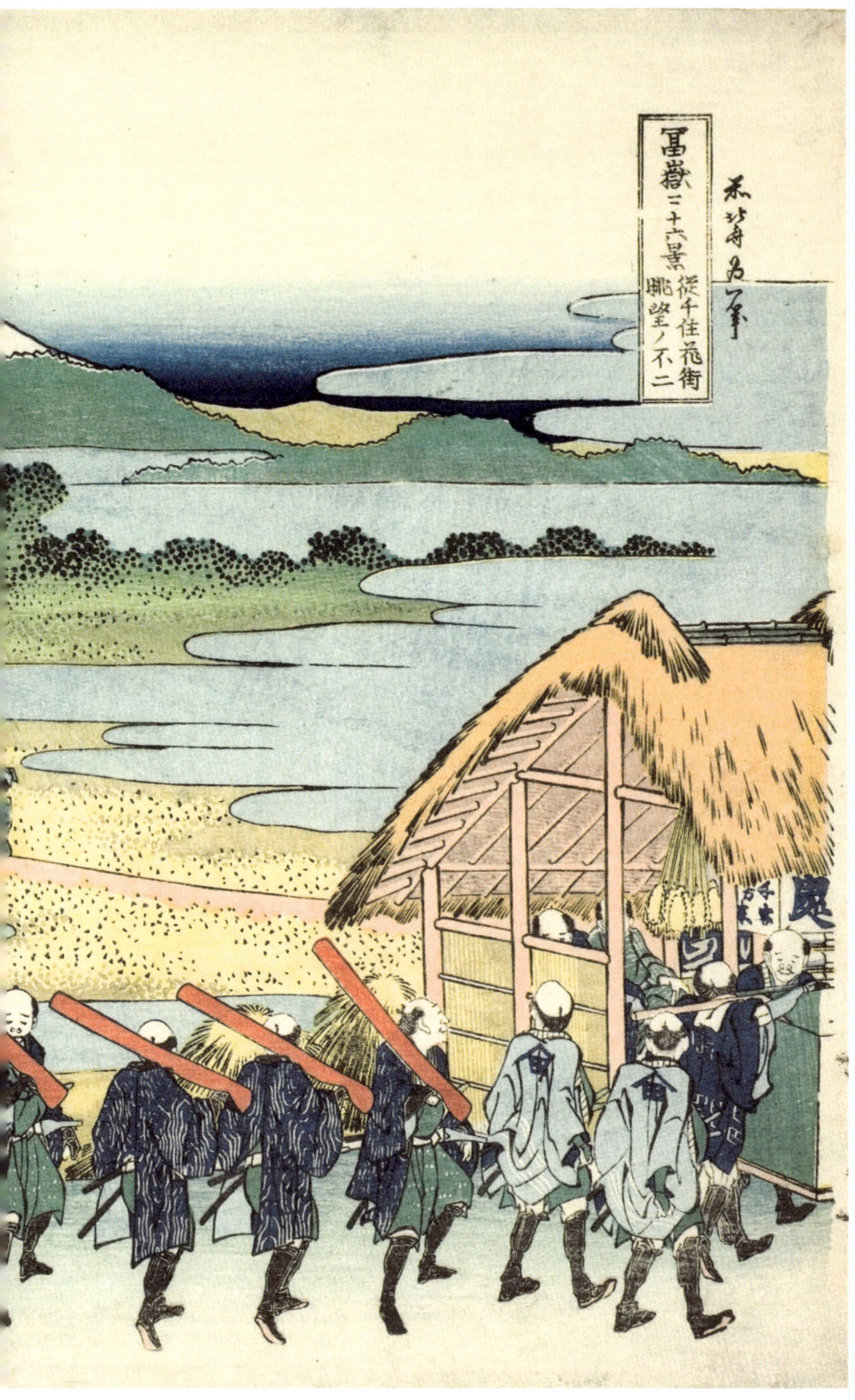

26.7 × 38.4 cm. Clarence Buckingham Collection, The Art Institute of Chicago, 1925.3280

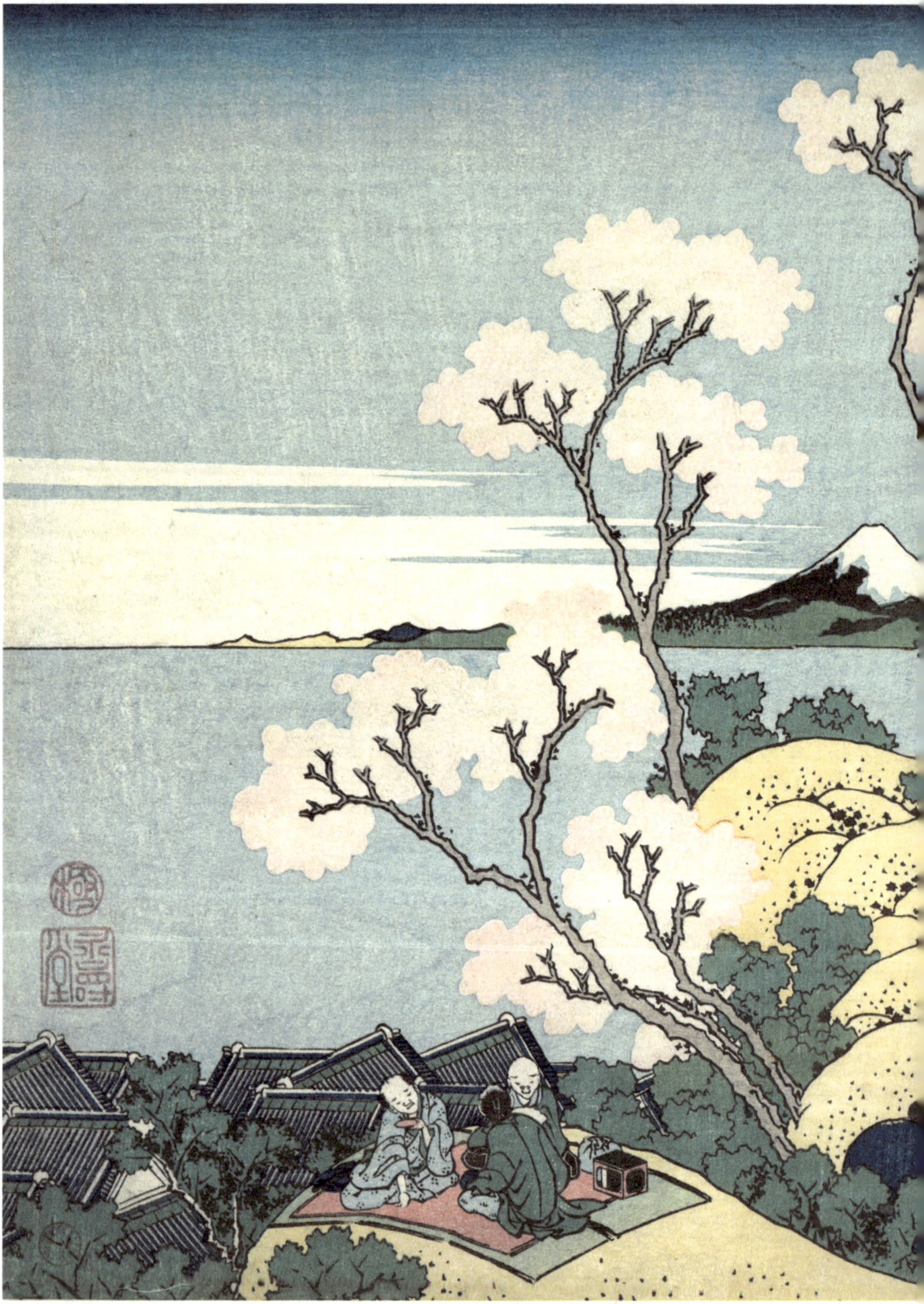

90

Fuji from Gotenyama on the Tōkaidō Road at Shinagawa
signed Zen Hokusai Iitsu hitsu

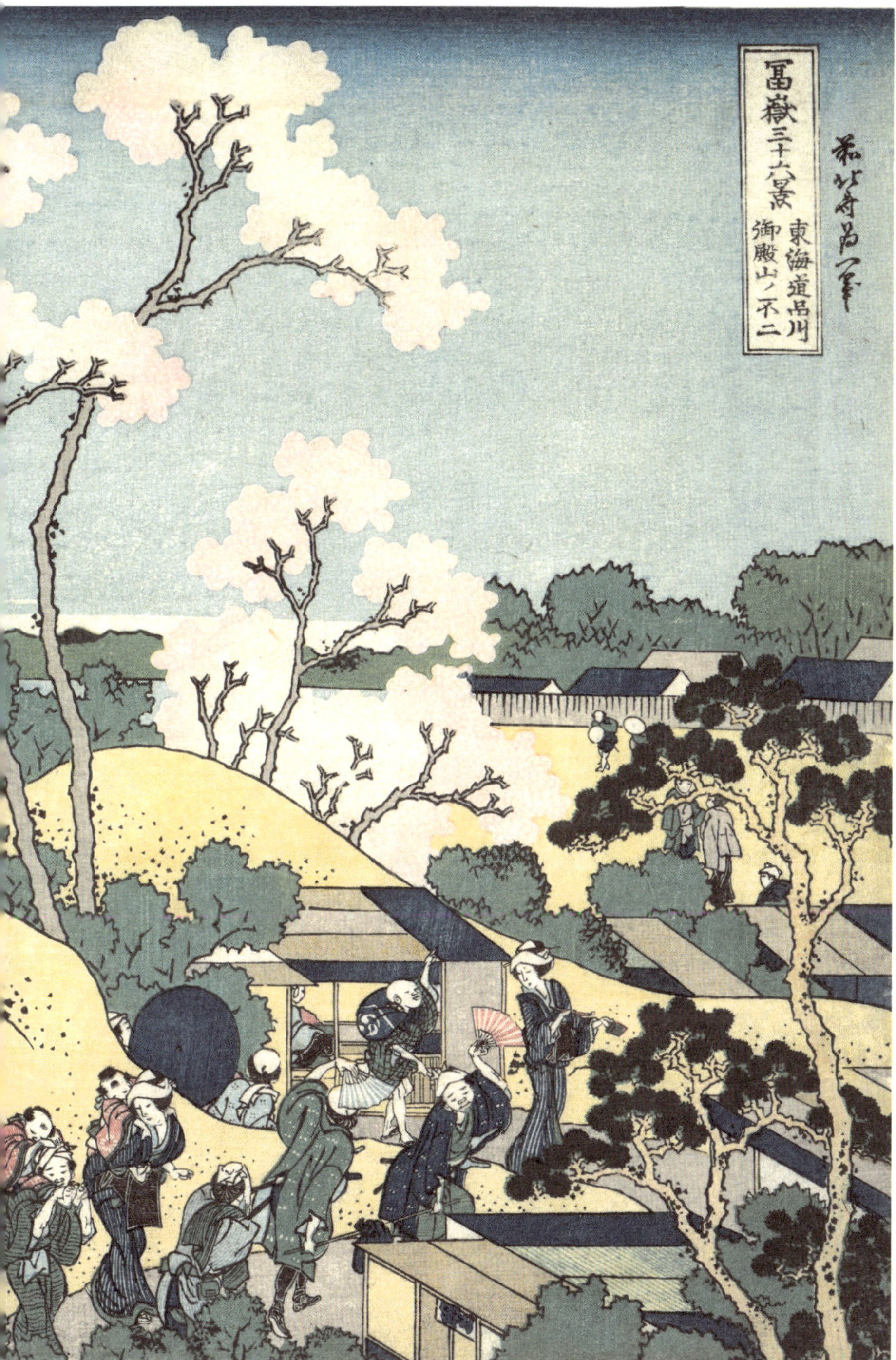

24.8 × 36.7 cm. Rogers Fund, 1922, The DC Museum of Art, JP1284

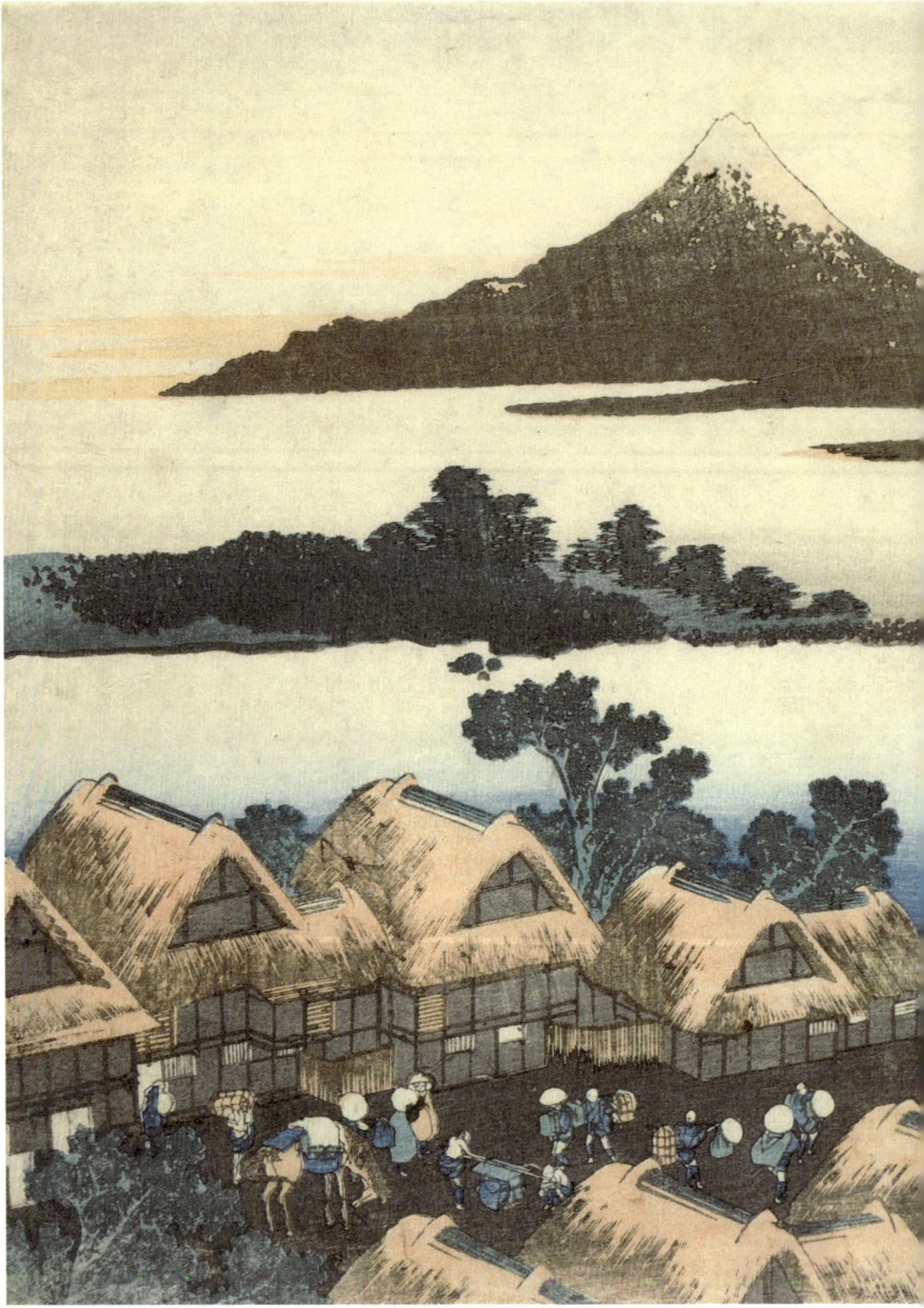

 Dawn at Isawa in Kai Province
signed Zen Hokusai Iitsu hitsu

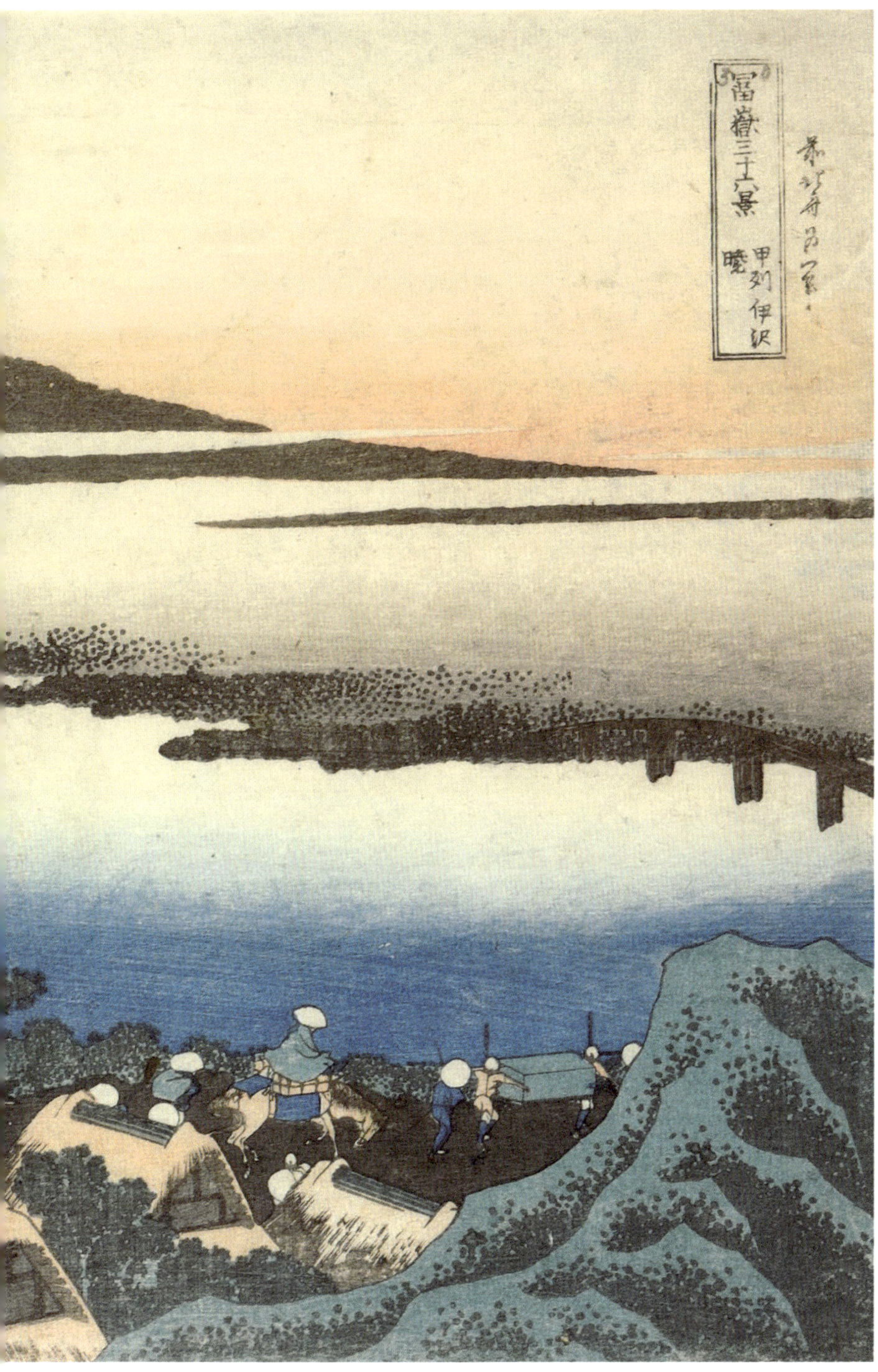
富嶽三十六景　甲州　伊沢
暁

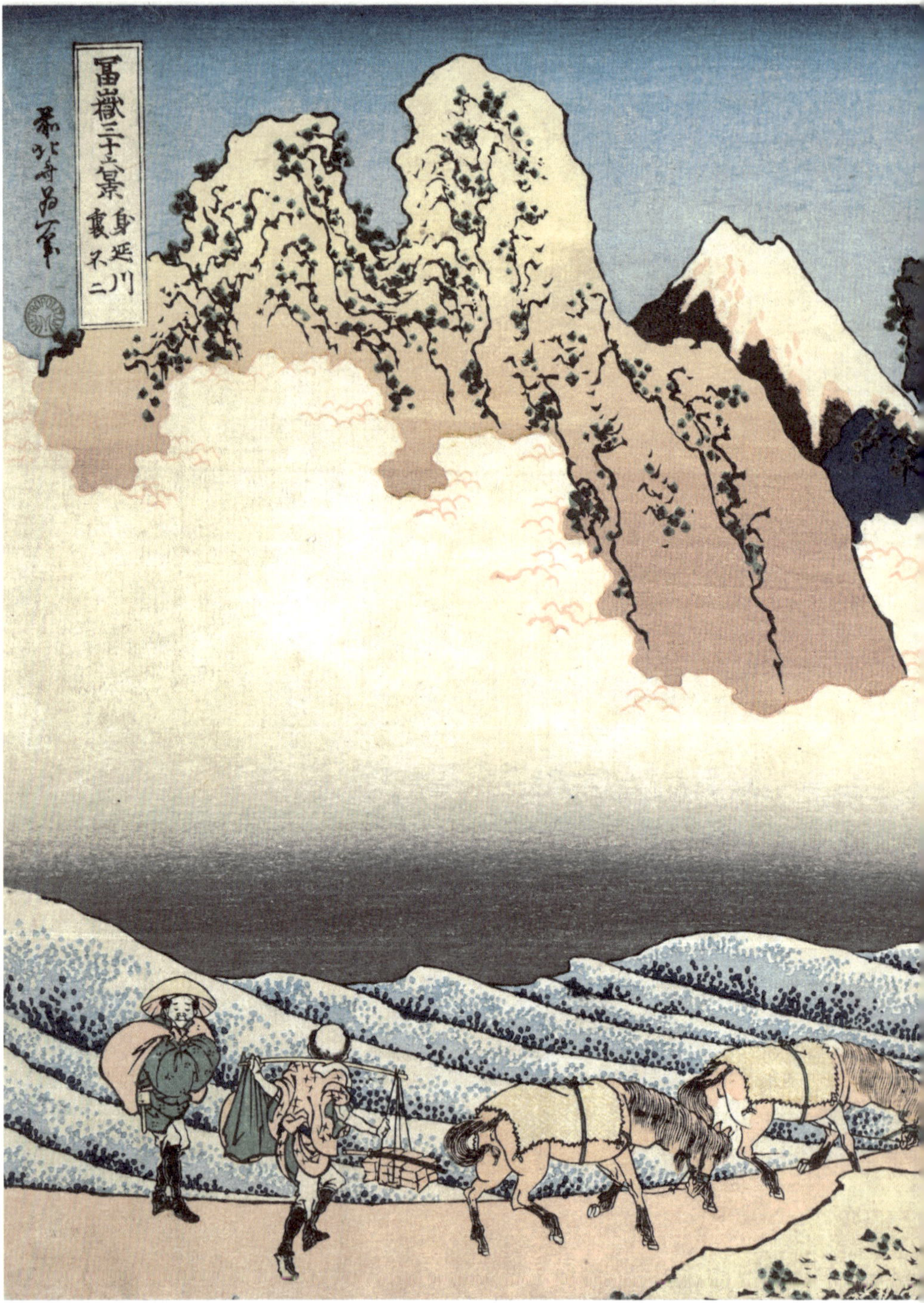

View from the Other Side of Fuji from the Minobu River
signed Zen Hokusai Iitsu hitsu

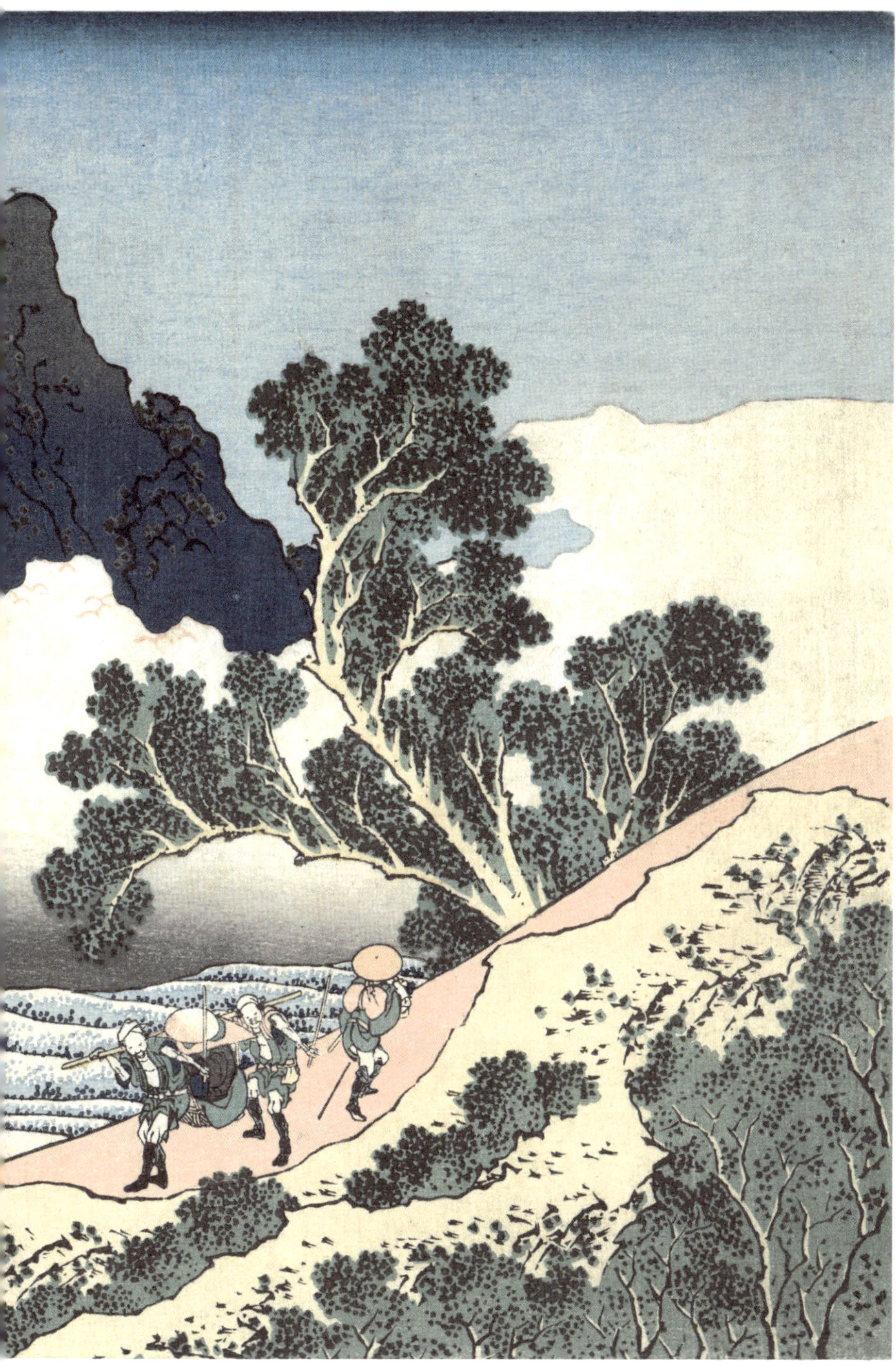

26 × 38.7 cm. Rogers Fund, 1922, The Metropolitan Museum of Art, New York, JP13

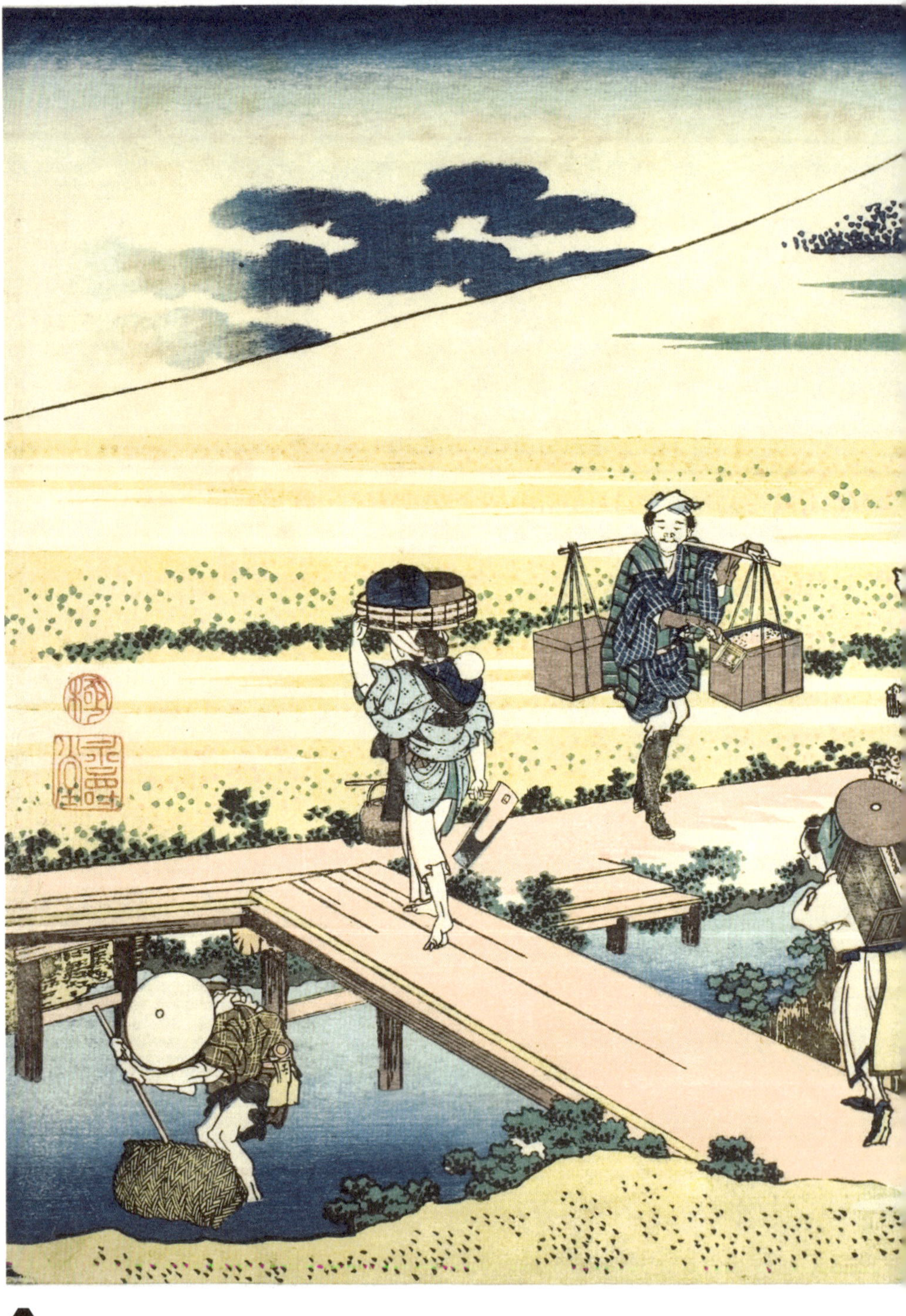

Nakahara in Sagami Province
signed Zen Hokusai Iitsu hitsu

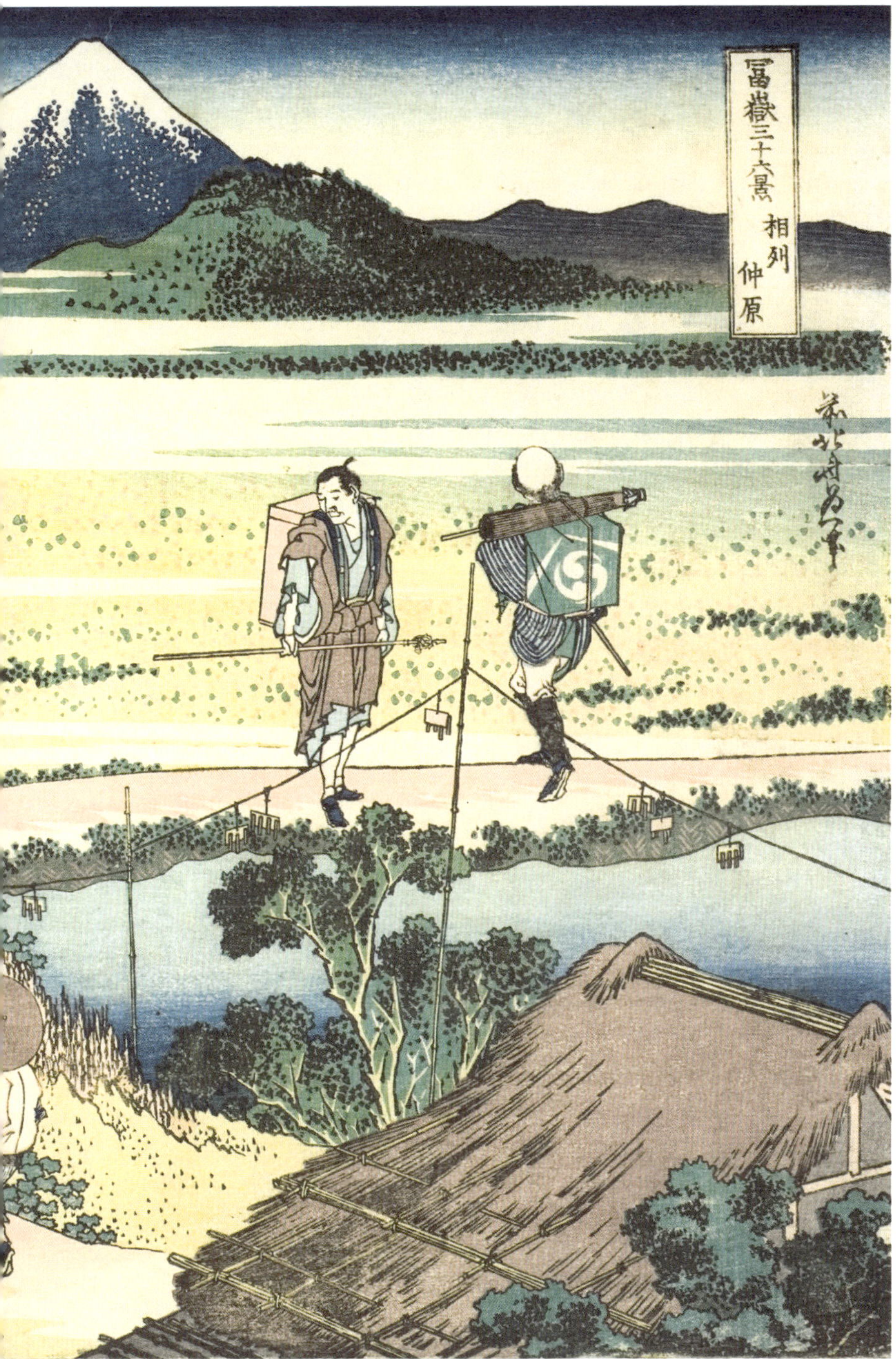

26.5 × 38.8 cm. Clarence Buckingham Collection, The Art Institute of Chicago, 1925.3230

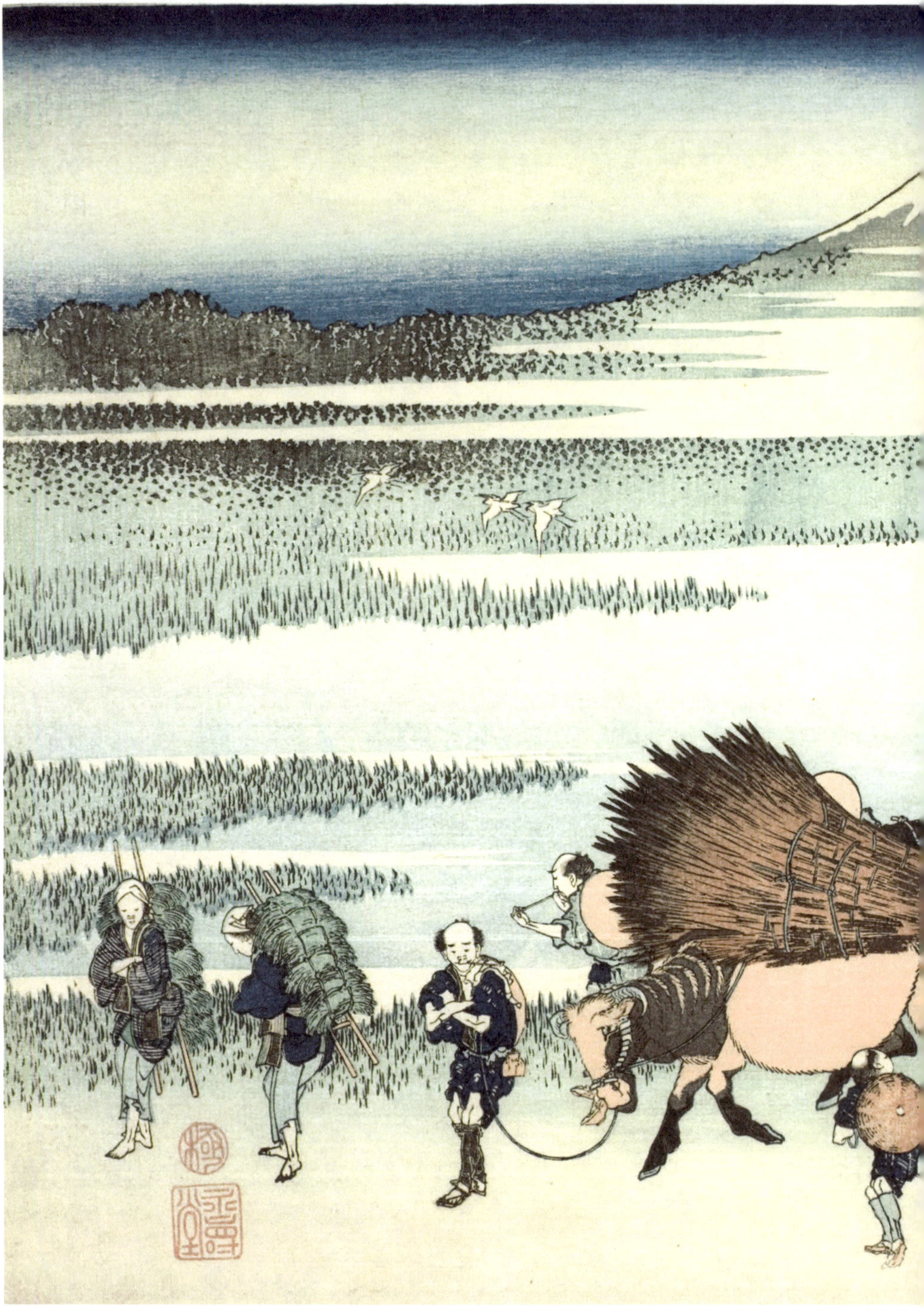

Rice Fields at Ono in Suruga Province
signed Zen Hokusai Iitsu hitsu

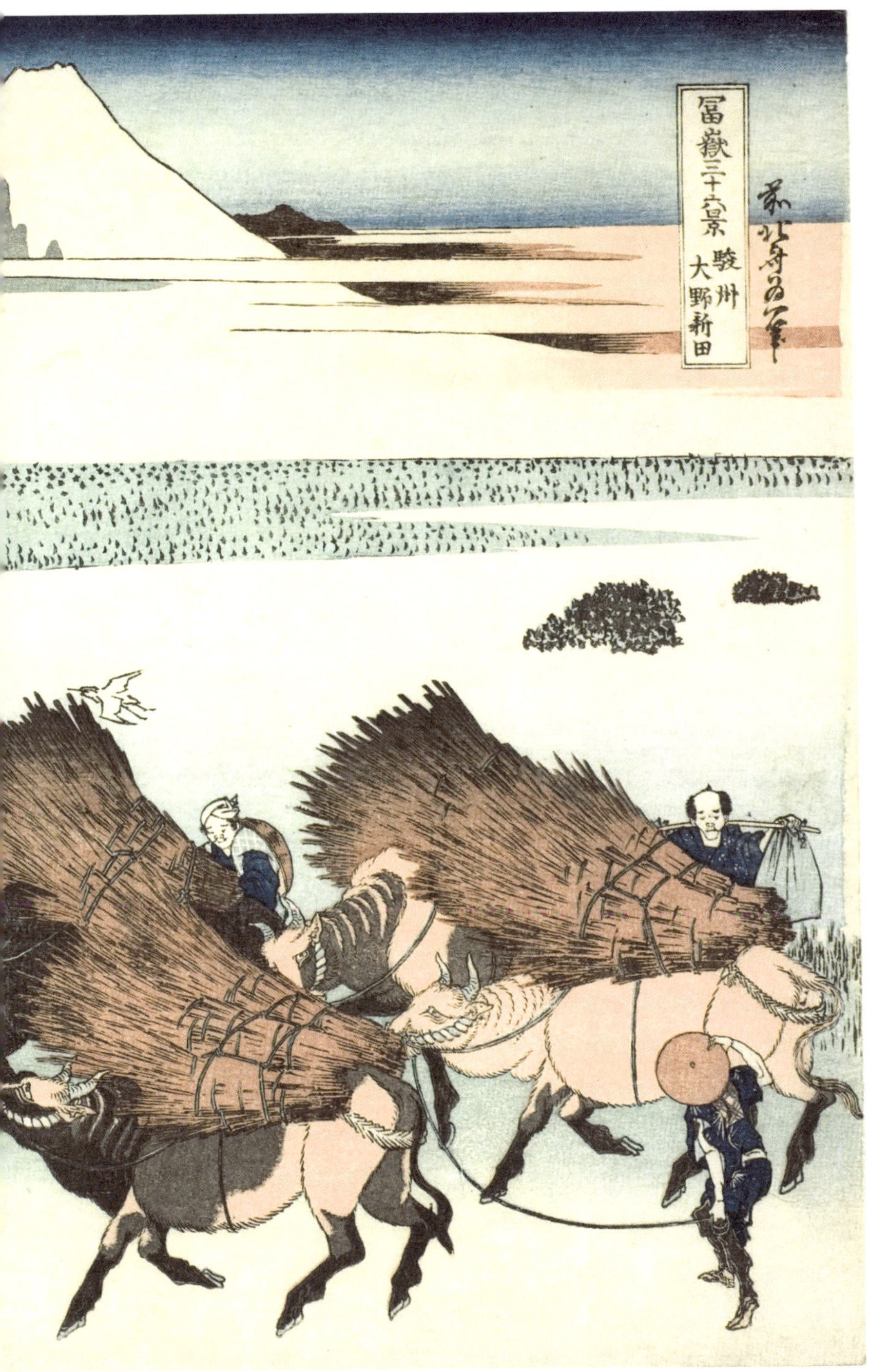

26.5 × 38.3 cm. Clarence Buckingham Collection, The Art Institute of Chicago, 1925.3286

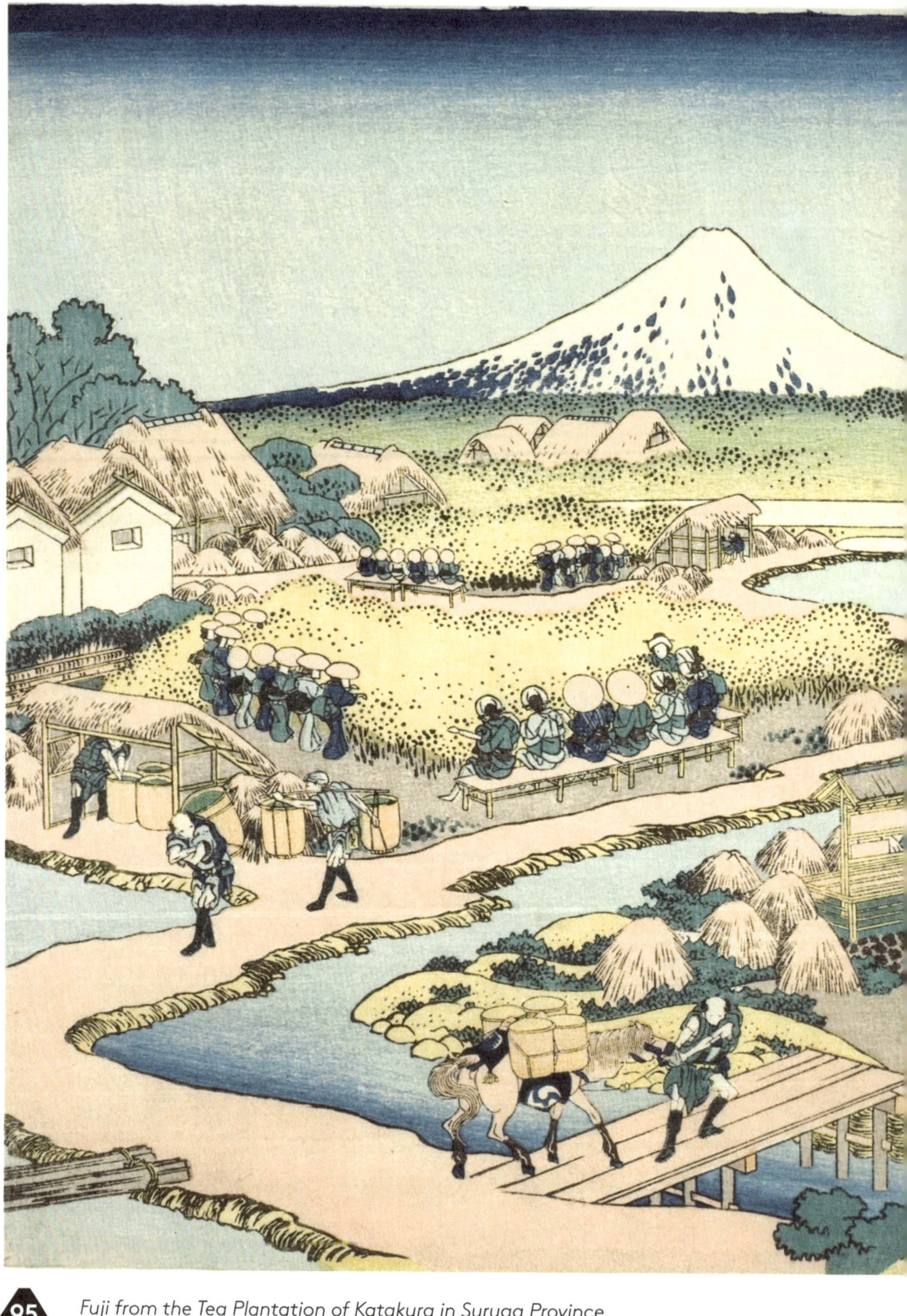

Fuji from the Tea Plantation of Katakura in Suruga Province
signed Zen Hokusai Iitsu hitsu

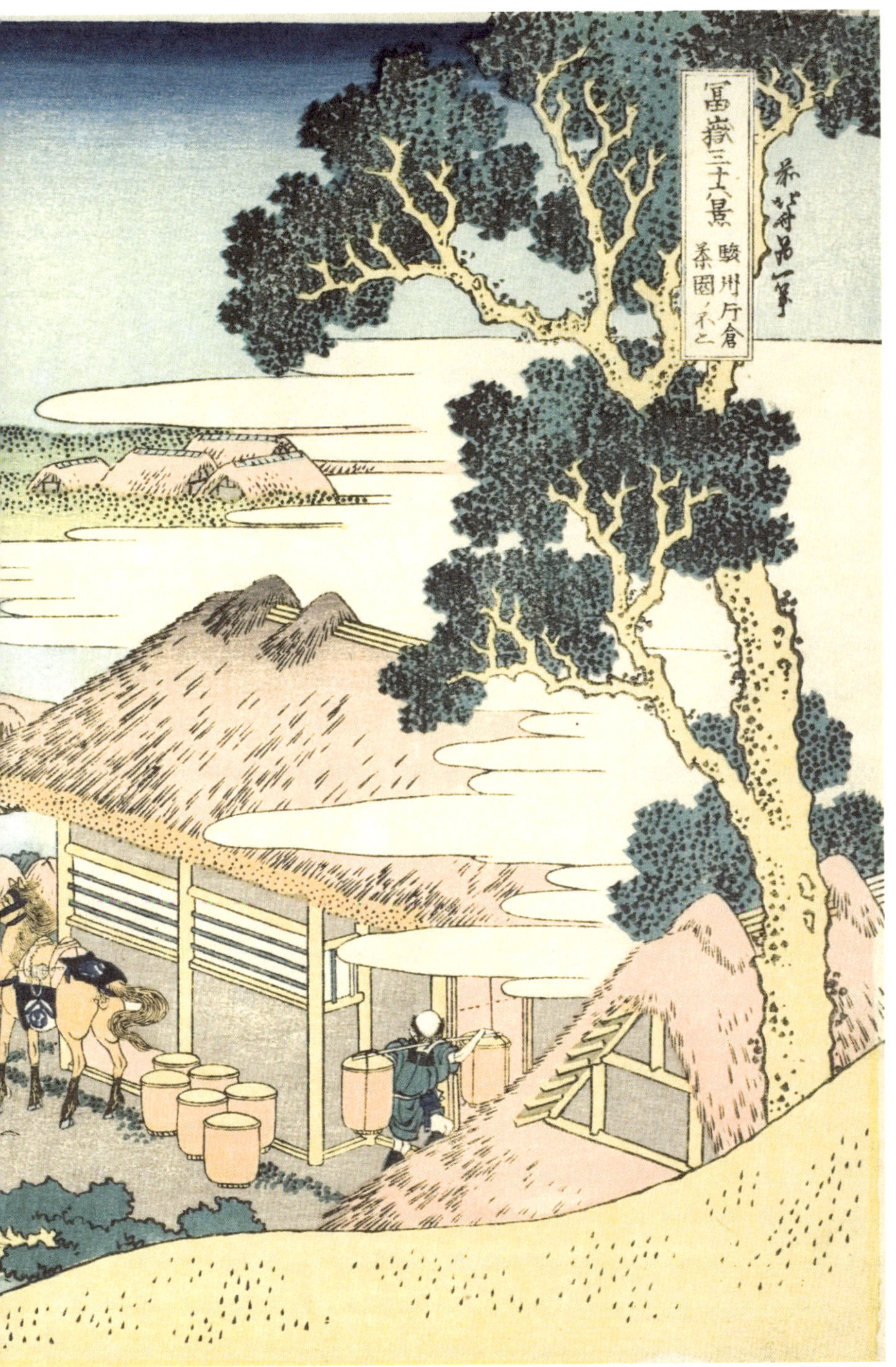

26.5 × 38.1 cm. Clarence Buckingham Collection, The Art Institute of Chicago, 1925.3231

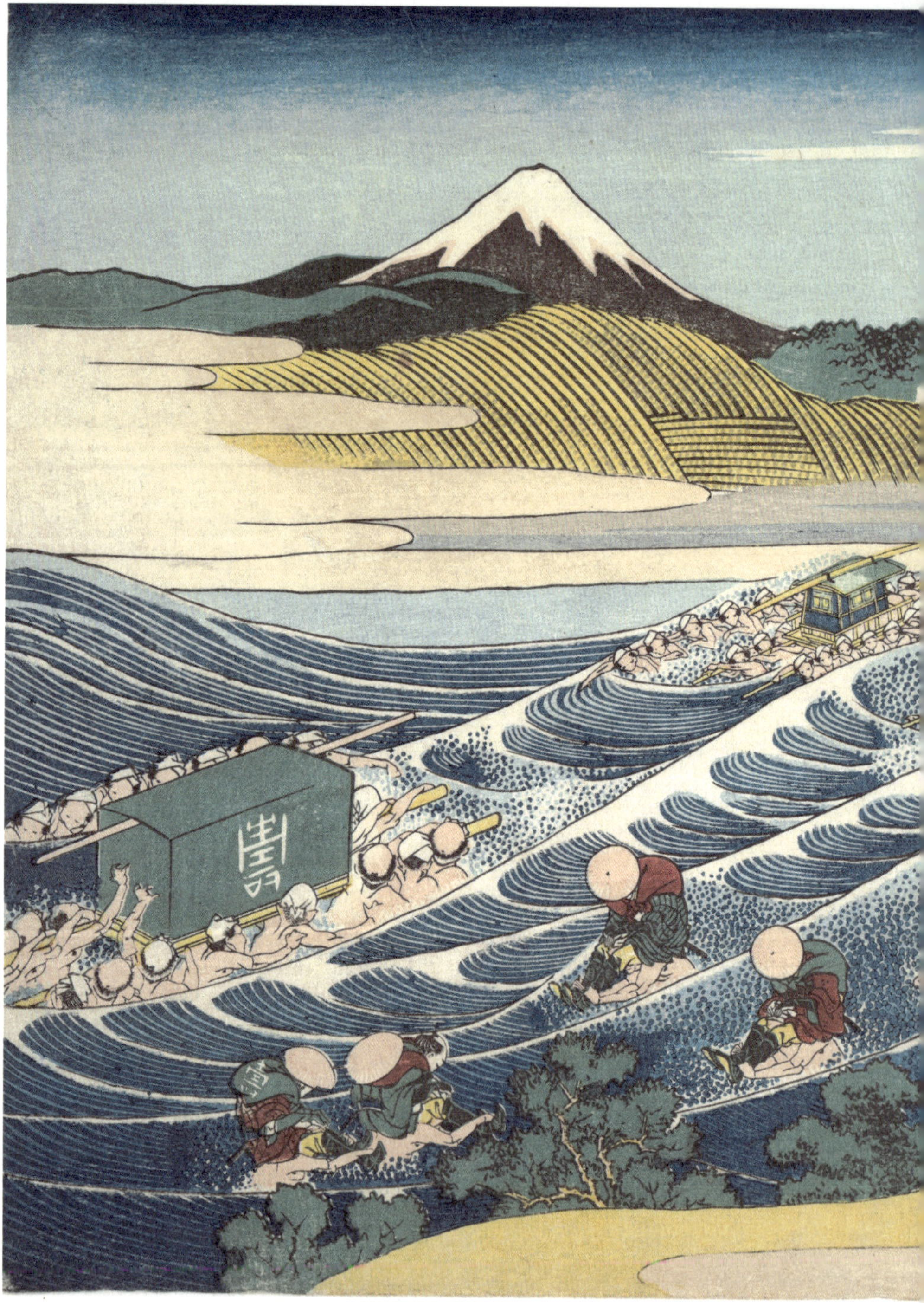

Fuji Seen from Kanaya on the Tōkaidō Road
signed Zen Hokusai Iitsu hitsu

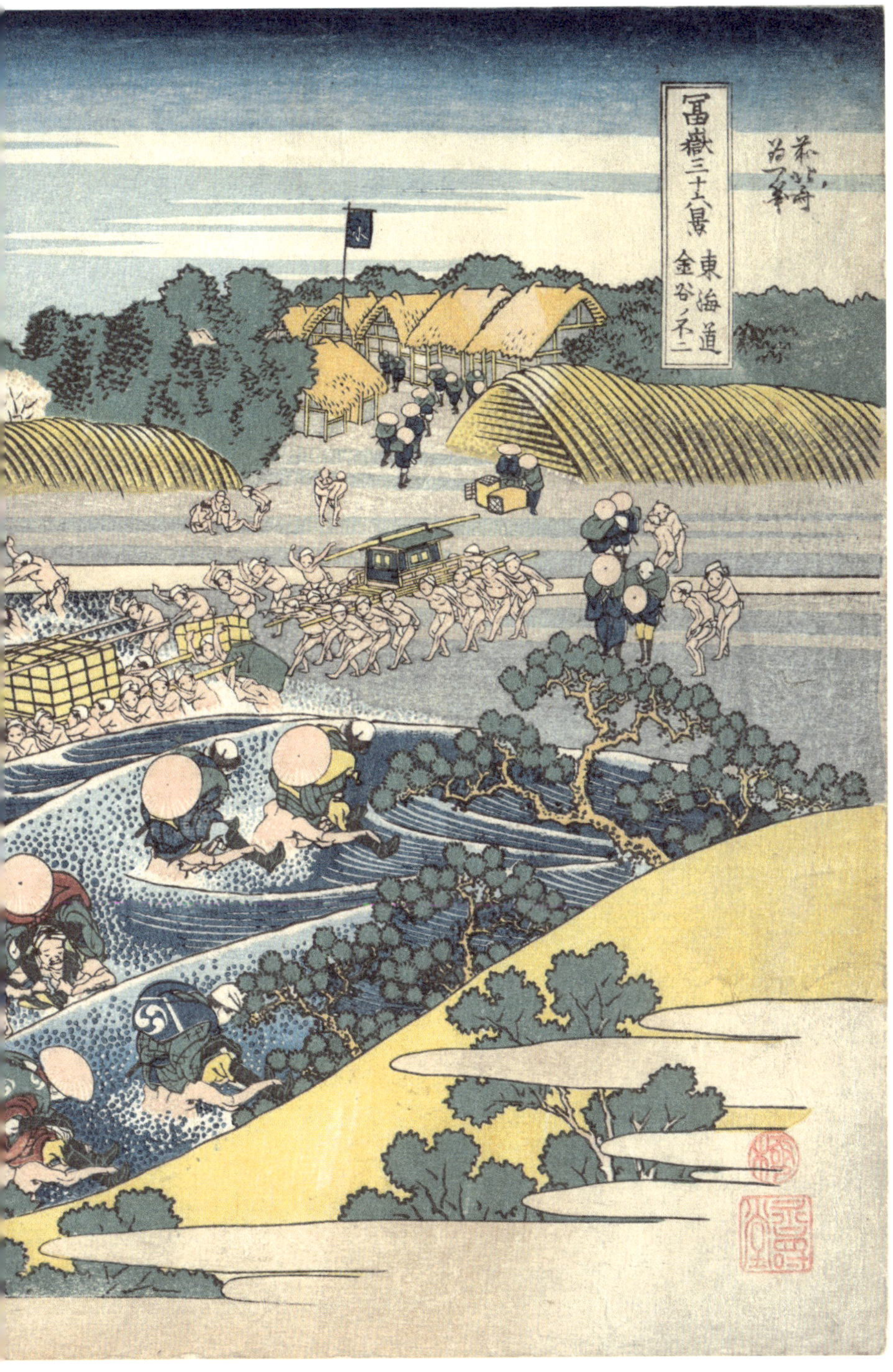

26 × 38.7 cm. Henry L. Phillips Collection, Bequest of Henry L. Phillips, 1939, The Metropolitan Museum of Art, New York, JP2975

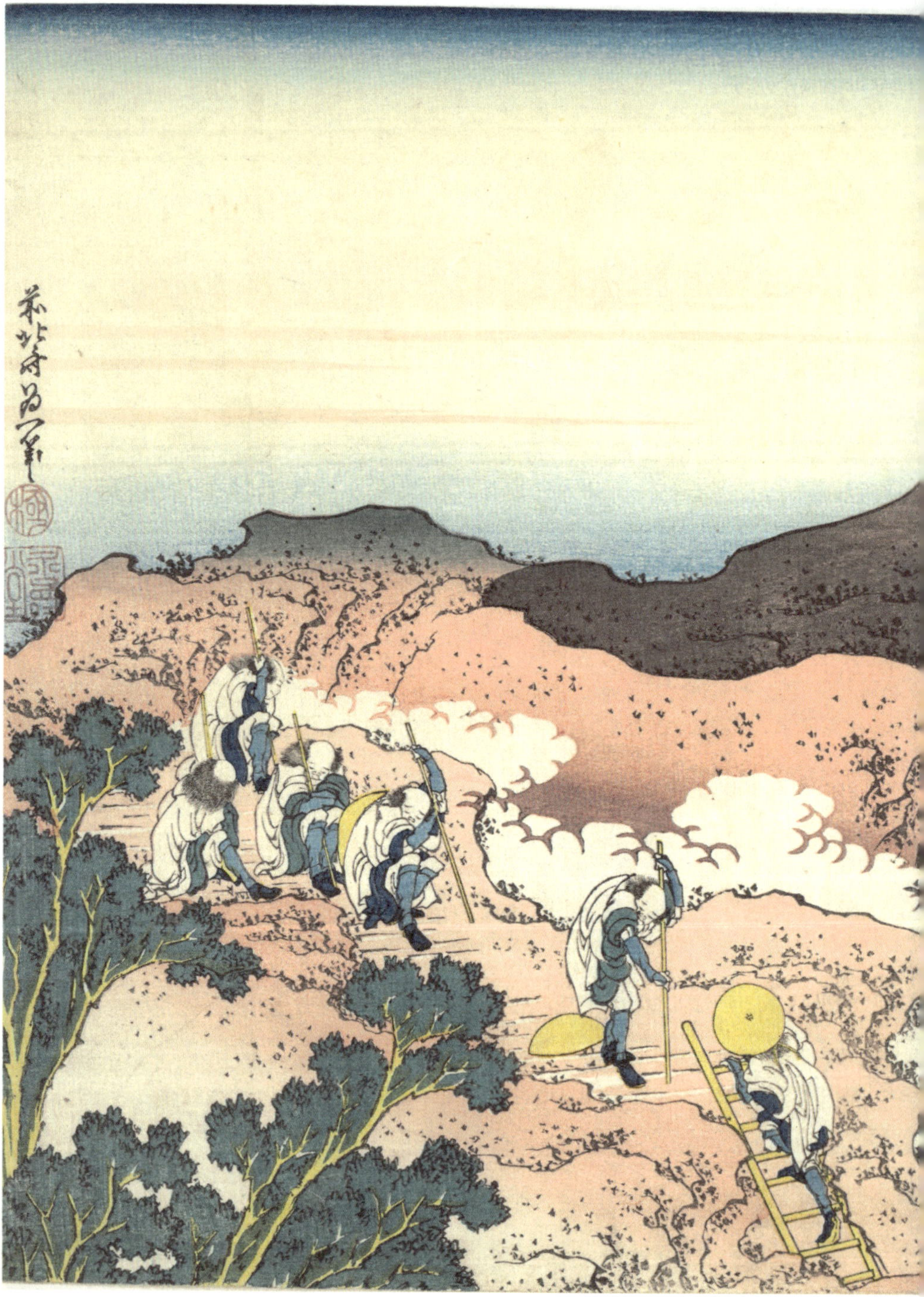

97 *Groups of Mountain Climbers*
signed Zen Hokusai Iitsu hitsu

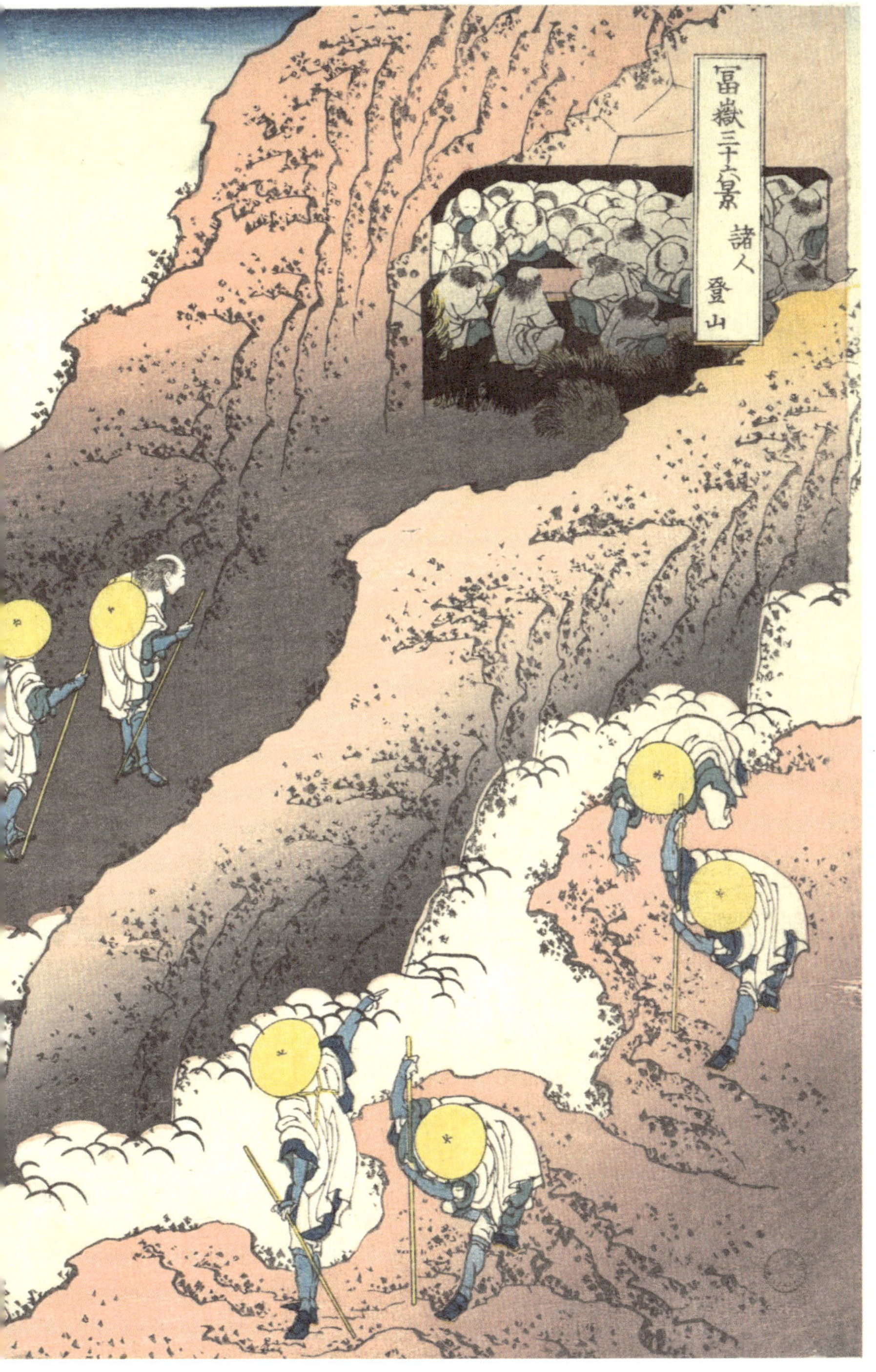

25.4 × 37.5 cm. Rogers Fund, 1922, The Metropolitan Museum of Art, New York, JP1322

Chapter 3

One Hundred Views of Mount Fuji

After completing *Thirty-Six Views of Mount Fuji*, Hokusai started working on *One Hundred Views of Mount Fuji*, which is made up of three volumes. The first volume was published in 1834 when Hokusai was seventy-five. The second volume was published the following year, but it is unclear when the third volume was published.

Since the production periods and the motifs share commonalities, *One Hundred Views of Mount Fuji* is often positioned as a sequel to *Thirty-Six Views of Mount Fuji*, but it is important to remember that Hokusai was a book artist. In other words, *Thirty-Six Views of Mount Fuji* is the culmination of every skill he had at his disposal, but *One Hundred Views of Mount Fuji* is his quintessential achievement as a book illustrator.

During the Bunka era (1804–18), Hokusai produced illustrations for as many as two hundred *yomihon* (illustrated novels), earning a reputation as the foremost artist in the field of book illustration. His unique creativity and talent attracted people to the wild world of *yomihon* stories and the same astonishing powers of expression and description are on full display in *One Hundred Views of Mount Fuji*. Dramatic scenes similar to those that feature in *yomihon* are evident in *The Appearance of Hōeizan* [228–229], in which buildings, people and horses are sent flying through the air by the shock waves from a volcanic eruption.

Hokusai worked on numerous books printed from woodblocks, including drawing manuals, books of comic verse, picture books, and illustrated popular fiction known as *kibyōshi* (meaning 'yellow covers', which is how they were bound). Among his publications, *Hokusai Manga* was a bestseller that enjoyed long-term steady sales. The style of the lively, expressive and dynamic figures in *One Hundred Views of Mount Fuji* is familiar from the figures drawn for *Hokusai Manga*.

Also in evidence are his editing skills that make the most of the characteristics of bound books, which differ from those of single-sheet full-colour woodblock prints. For example, the first volume opens with an image of the principal female deity enshrined at Mount Fuji. The next image refers to the legend of how Mount Fuji appeared overnight, and this is followed by a depiction of the all-powerful founder of mountain asceticism [218–223]. *Fuji Under Clear Skies* [224–225], a solemn image of the sacred mountain, is positioned between these images and another set of images of people making the pilgrimage to Fuji, the object of faith [226–227], followed by *The Appearance of Hōeizan*, before the story continues in the real world with a group of travellers from Edo in *Fuji Under Clear Skies, Part 2* [230–231].

Leading into the book, the sequence that moves from a female deity to worldly affairs and customs is a clever composition. Even though the images all feature Mount Fuji, the series incorporates so many varied motifs that it is clear it was not intended merely as a collection of scenic landscapes to admire. The range of subjects is remarkable, ranging from myths to legends, images of birds and flowers, customs, seasonal landscapes, figures of travellers and labourers. It even includes comic caricatures. In *Hokusai Manga*, the artist drew all of creation in the style of an encyclopaedia. With *One Hundred Views of Mount Fuji*, he may have explored every avenue of comprehensive expression in the attempt to create an encyclopaedia of Mount Fuji.

Assuming that Hokusai manipulates the medium based on its characteristics, we should consider the compositional constraints of drawing landscapes for a book printed from woodblocks, that is, the vertical orientation of the single page. If perspective were employed to draw a landscape with a view of Fuji, the drawings would be all sky. Laid out side by side, the images and the composition would then look very similar. Therefore, Hokusai intentionally made the scenes, people, and objects in the foreground bigger, introducing variation to the compositions. He also emphasized spatial depth by arranging Fuji as a small detail in the distance [238, 254, 255, 286].

The monochrome world of *One Hundred Views of Mount Fuji* is a complete change from the full-colour woodblock prints produced for *Thirty-Six Views of Mount Fuji*, which some people may find a little unsatisfactory. There is a tendency to view the vivid, multicoloured woodblock prints as technically more advanced and more valuable than monochrome prints. However, this is not necessarily true. The early print runs are sharp and detailed since the printer was using newly carved blocks. However, as more print runs followed, the blocks wore down, gradually causing the prints to deteriorate and to lose the appeal of the detailed drawings. Even in cases where the first edition was monochrome, there are quite a few books where later editions were printed in several colours by adding colour blocks to conceal the deterioration of the key blocks. Colour layers were also added to some later editions of *One Hundred Views of Mount Fuji*. In short, the monochrome *One Hundred Views of Mount Fuji* may be lacking colour information, but it is a faithful representation of Hokusai's detailed lines and powers of expression.

Nonetheless, no matter how hard Hokusai worked on his drawings, they would have been nothing without the carver who created the printing blocks and the skills of the printer. Hokusai must have had some bitter experiences as he often complained to his publisher about the poor quality of the carved blocks, or recommended particularly skilled carvers. Egawa Tomekichi, who first worked on *Popular Designs for Combs and Tobacco Pipes*, was one outstanding carver who succeeded in reproducing Hokusai's crisp and delicate lines perfectly. He also carved the blocks for *New Designs for Various Crafts* and volume eleven of *Hokusai Manga*.

Hokusai was extremely particular about the shades of printing ink that were used. He made detailed requests about diluted inks, saying, for example, that since dark colours are ugly, the ink should be diluted to the consistency of clam soup, but he warned against diluting medium black too much. In fact, the heavy fog in *Fuji in Mist* [232–233], the faint outlines of a distant Fuji emerging from the smoke of an open-air fire in *Fuji Through Smoke* [246–247], and the magical mountain of *Fuji in a Dream* [292–293] are the products of advanced printing techniques that pay close attention to the density of the ink. *One Hundred Views of Mount Fuji* is considered the pinnacle of the picture book because of the way the three elements of drawing, carving, and printing work together.

The personal 'manifesto' by Hokusai that was included in the first and second edition of *One Hundred Views of Mount Fuji* became particularly famous. In his own words, Hokusai describes his career as an artist and maps out the prospects for when he is one hundred years old and more [5]. The manifesto is signed with an elegantly carved rendering of Gakyō Rōjin Manji, the new name that he used from that point until his death. The page is also stamped with a red seal in the shape of Fuji. Since the seal is a representation of the self, this marks the moment when Hokusai began to identify himself with Fuji [268].

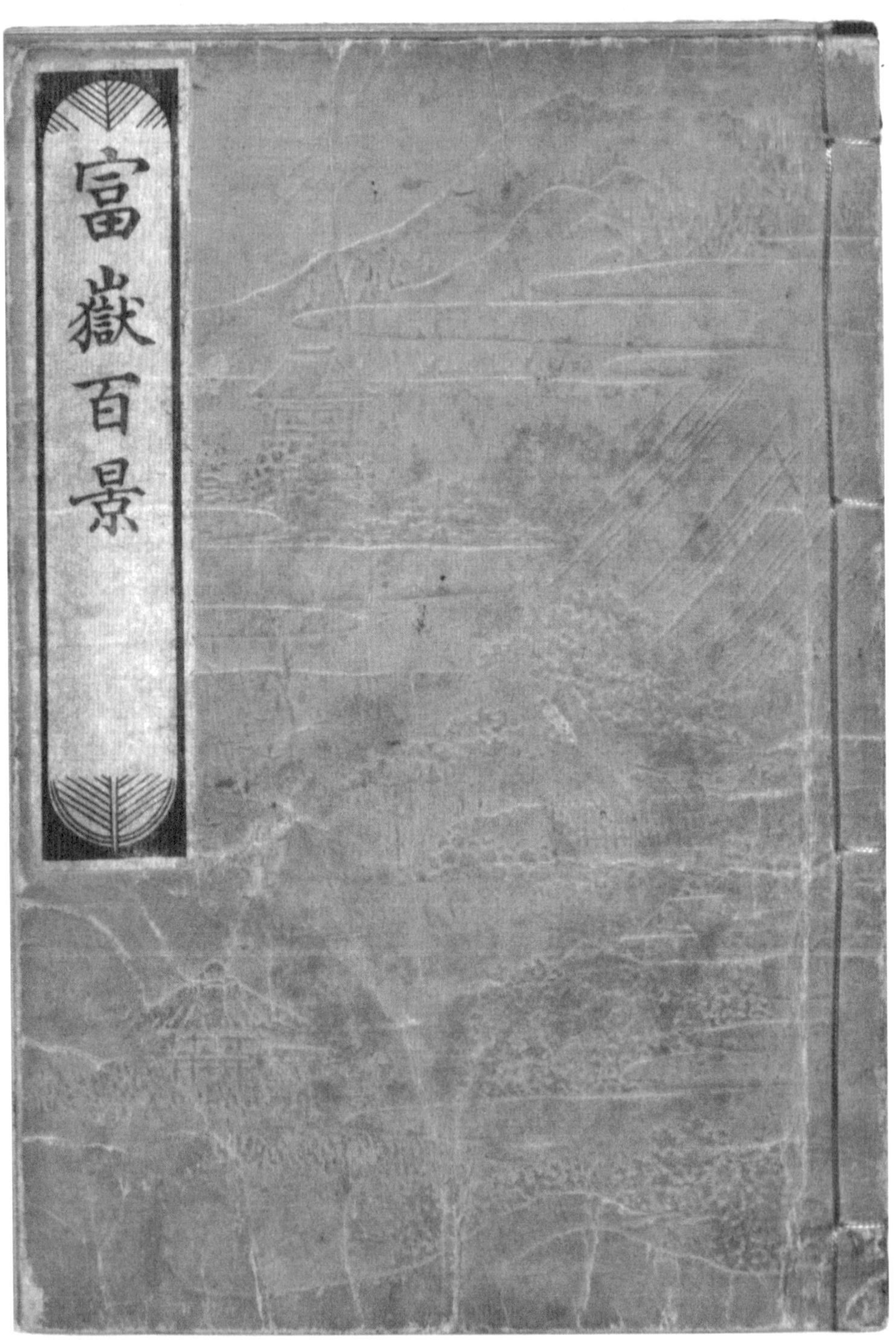

One Hundred Views of Mount Fuji, Volume 1: cover

Note: The images in this section are numbered consecutively as they would be in Western-style books, but in the original Japanese editions, the images were 'read' from right to left.

Volume 1
1834, signed Shichijūgosai ('75 years old') Zen Hokusai Iitsu Aratame Gakyō Rōjin Manji hitsu
Publishers: Nishimura Yūzō, Eirakuya Tōshirō, others

22.7 × 15.8 cm. The Metropolitan Museum of Art, New York. The Howard Mansfield Collection, Gift of Howard Mansfield, 1936, JIB108

Volume 2
1835, signed Shichijūrokusai ('76 years old') Zen Hokusai Iitsu Aratame Gakyō Rōjin Manji hitsu
Publishers: Nishimura Yūzō, Eirakuya Tōshirō, others

22.9 × 15.9 cm. The Metropolitan Museum of Art, New York. The Howard Mansfield Collection, Gift of Howard Mansfield, 1936, JIB108

Volume 3
Unknown date, unsigned
Publishers: Eirakuya Tōshirō

22.7 × 15.8 cm. The Metropolitan Museum of Art, New York. Purchase, Mary and James G. Wallach Family Foundation Gift, 2013, 2013.732a–c

勢冲ら富士百景を窺元せし題其
東滌の不二雨を緑雲より見え窓
峯斬り百嶽を圖をる八蒂此齋家之生山や
獨立し宿峯此嶺半生一峯此畫も又獨立
高峯言名之就事一子云る丈より見む
畫帖諸圖より盤臨蔵を里よる面より圖盛
十五枚の杜観るより也不去此十名を秘藏捕
子載をり先生屬名ら段むらをくなら十名か
壹海勢り挂を紀田凾達八而此峯生る
筆へり近る田子武浦に見を多る三傑を結る

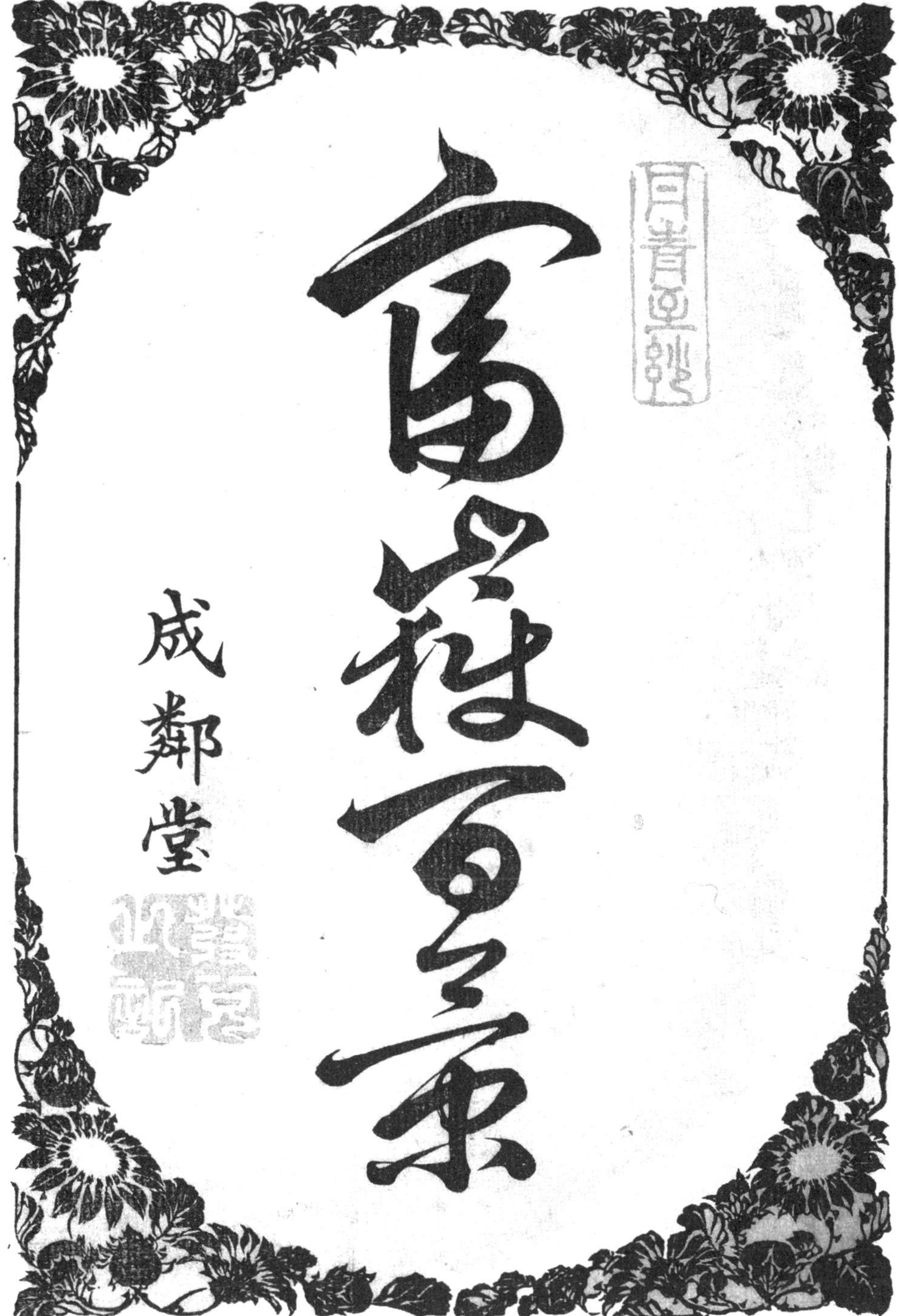
富嶽百景
成鄰堂

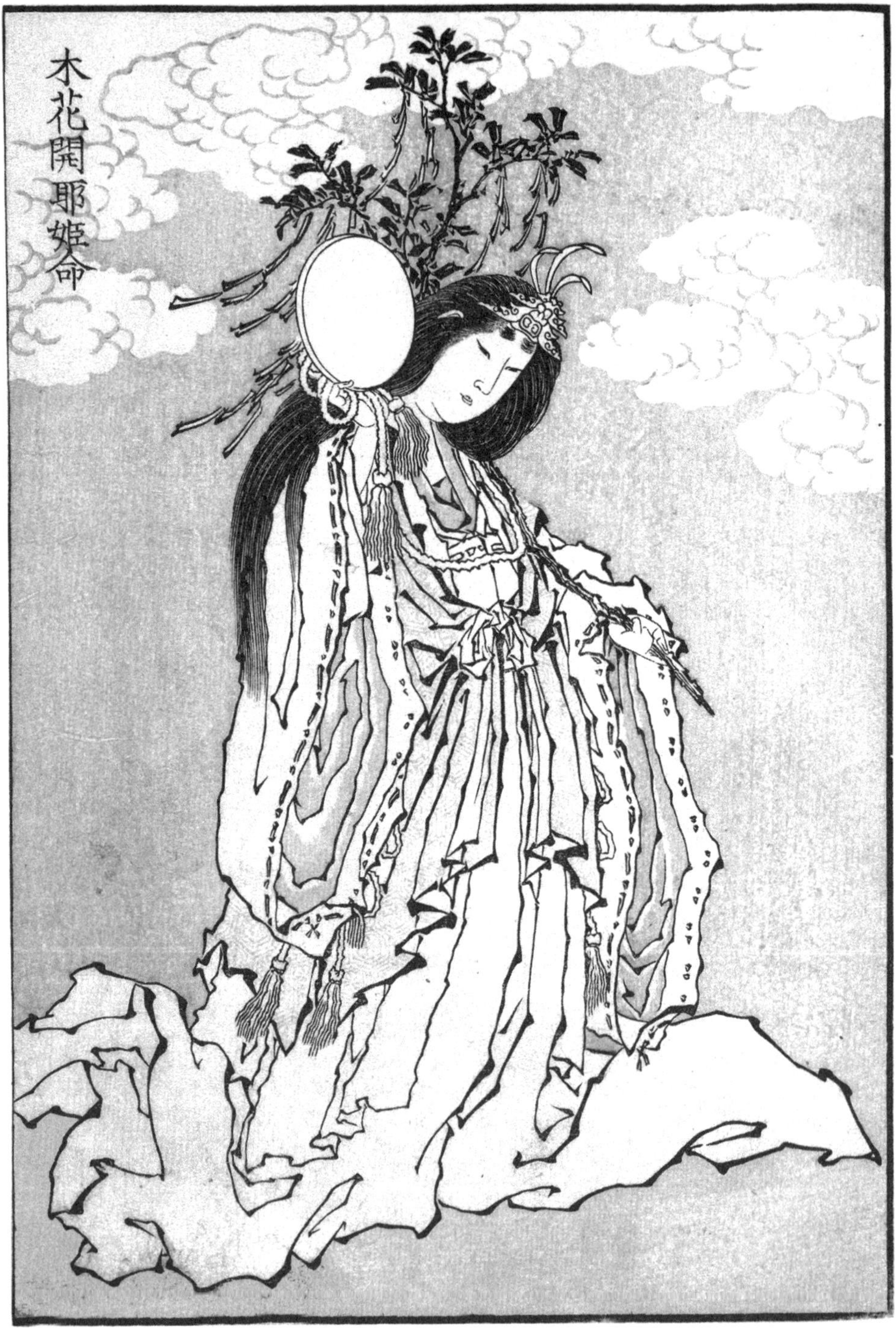

Goddess Konohana Sakuyahime

空（そら）の隈（くま）なき月（つき）生（しょう）をえて四（よ）もの
萩（はぎ）の莟（つぼみ）高（たか）からぬ富士（ふじ）を見（み）る枝（えだ）を花（はな）さ汐（しお）見（み）坂（さか）に
枯（かれ）ゆく木（き）を見（み）れば茂（しげ）りし生（は）ふる稲（いね）葉（ば）の戦（そよ）ぎ
母（はは）高根（たかね）を仰（あお）ぎ蓬（よもぎ）浪（なみ）巌（いわ）を碎（くだ）き大洋（たいよう）の空（くう）谷（こく）に
埋（うず）もる筆（ふで）揃（そろ）へ浪（なみ）阻（はば）むに上（のぼ）つて坐（ざ）を占（し）むる真意（しんい）を寫（うつ）されし
ものとなし精神（せいしん）此（この）峯（みね）に止（とどま）り弾（はず）み出（いで）し生（い）くるもの事（こと）
きり去（さ）り畫（が）本（ほん）の學（がく）顔（がん）を窮（きわ）めて生（い）くる事（こと）
阿（あ）閉（とじ）梨（り）吜（あ）百（ひゃく）荷（か）に為（な）ち久々（ひさびさ）吜（つき）
柳（やなぎ）亭（てい）種（たね）彦（ひこ）永寿（えいじゅ）

天保甲午年　探秀

菫斎（きんさい）　為斎（いさい）敬（けい）書（しょ）

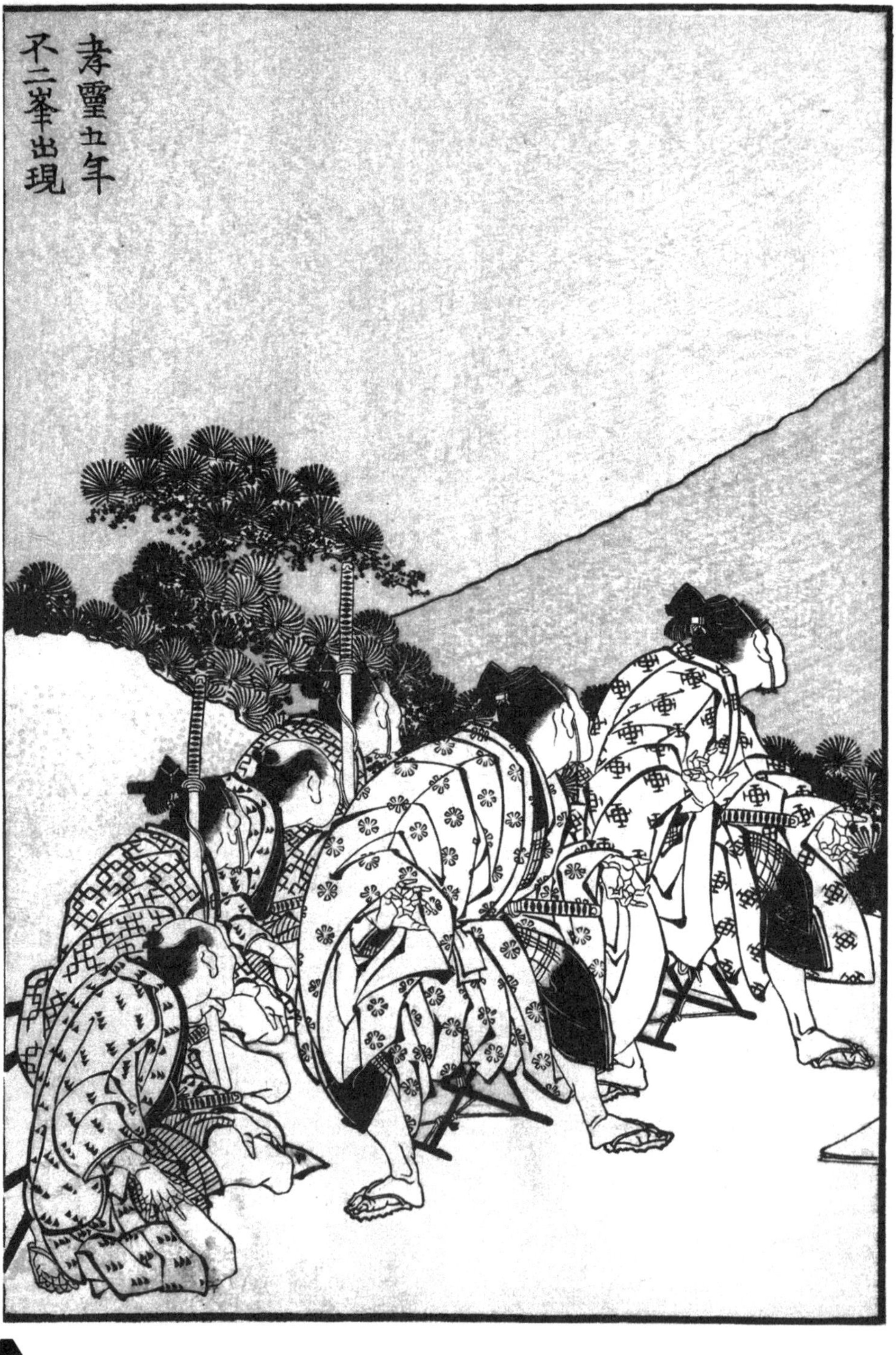

Appearance of Mount Fuji in the Fifth Year of Kōrei

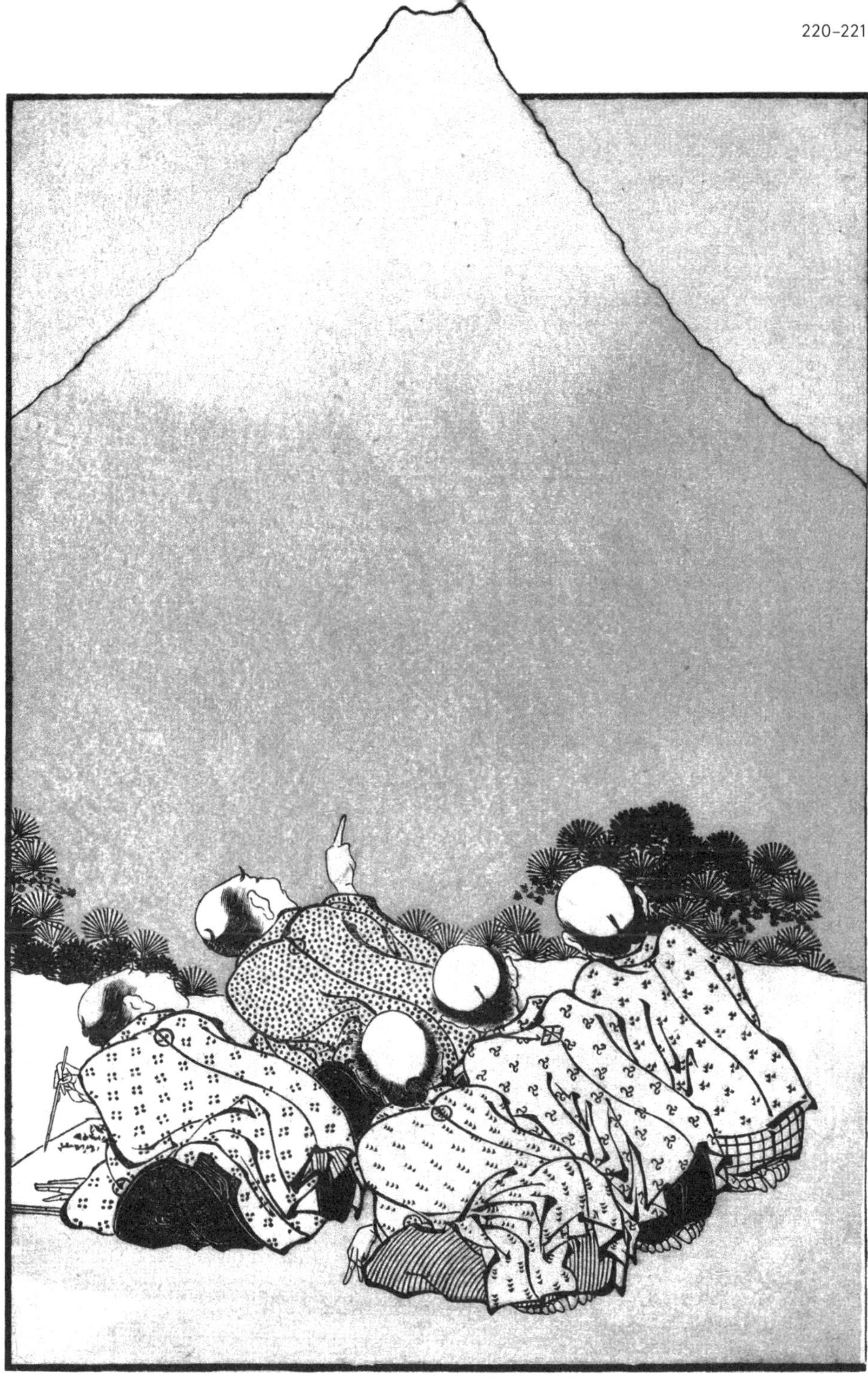

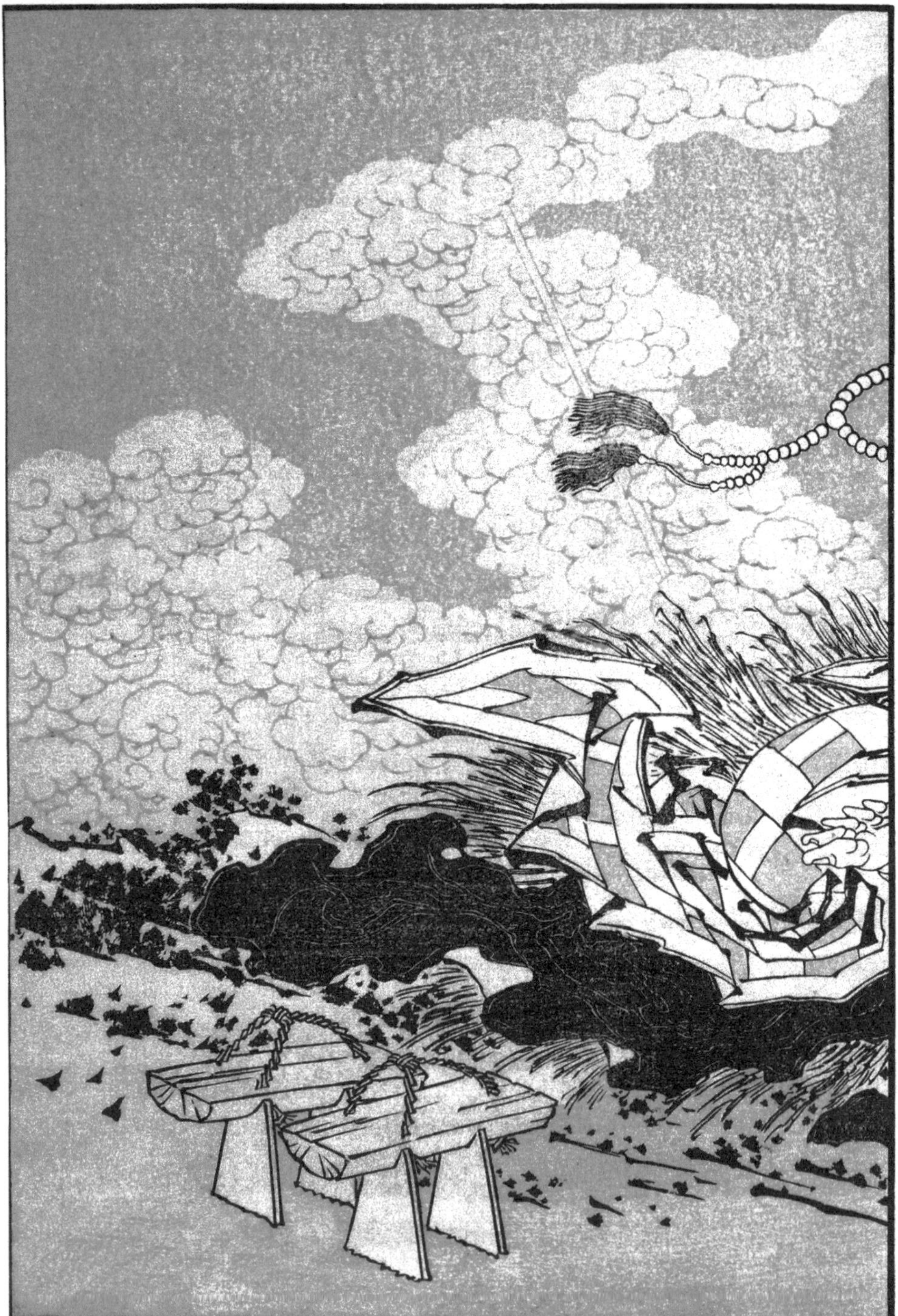

En no Gyōja Opens Mount Fuji

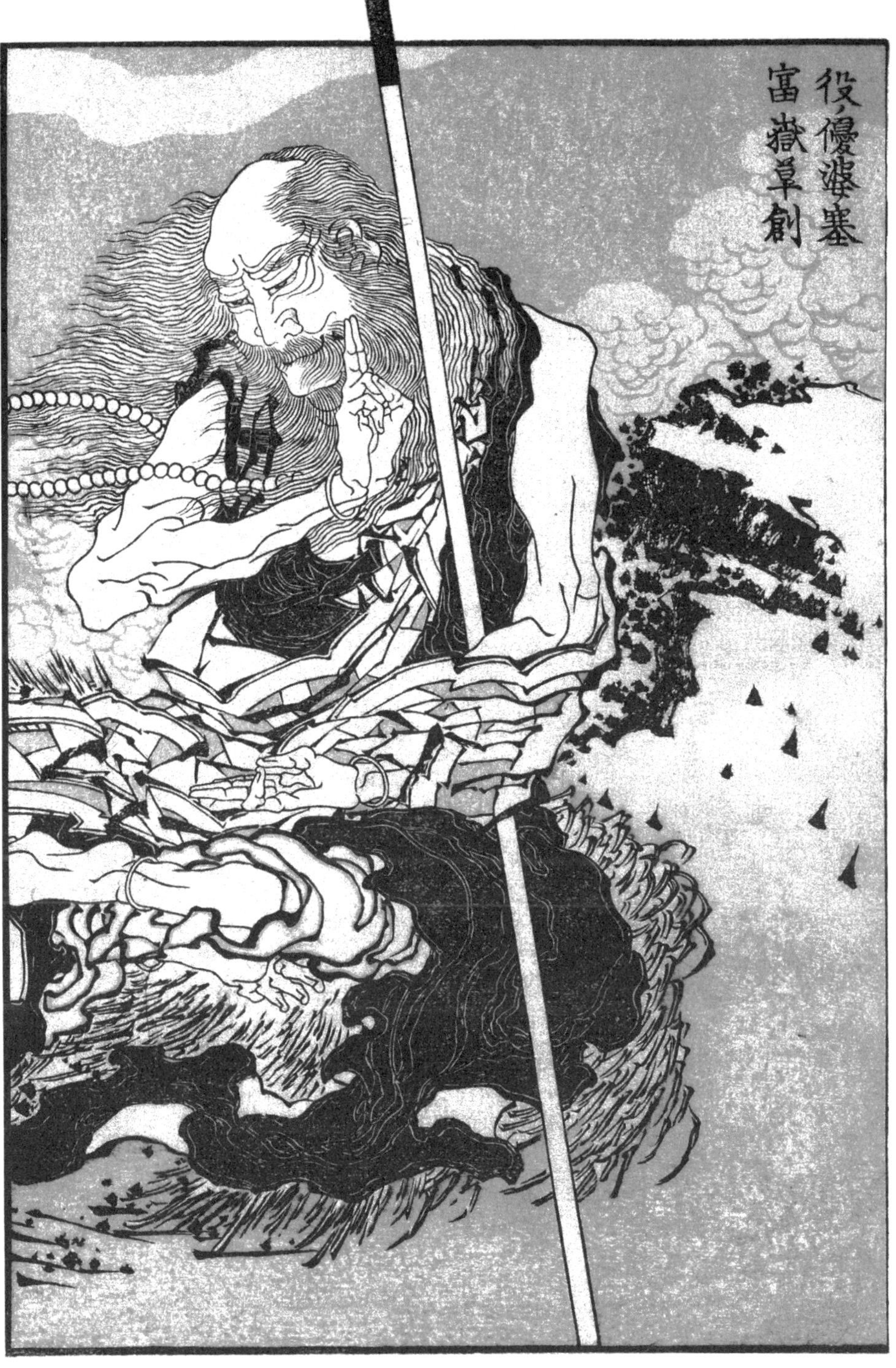
役ノ優婆塞
富嶽草創

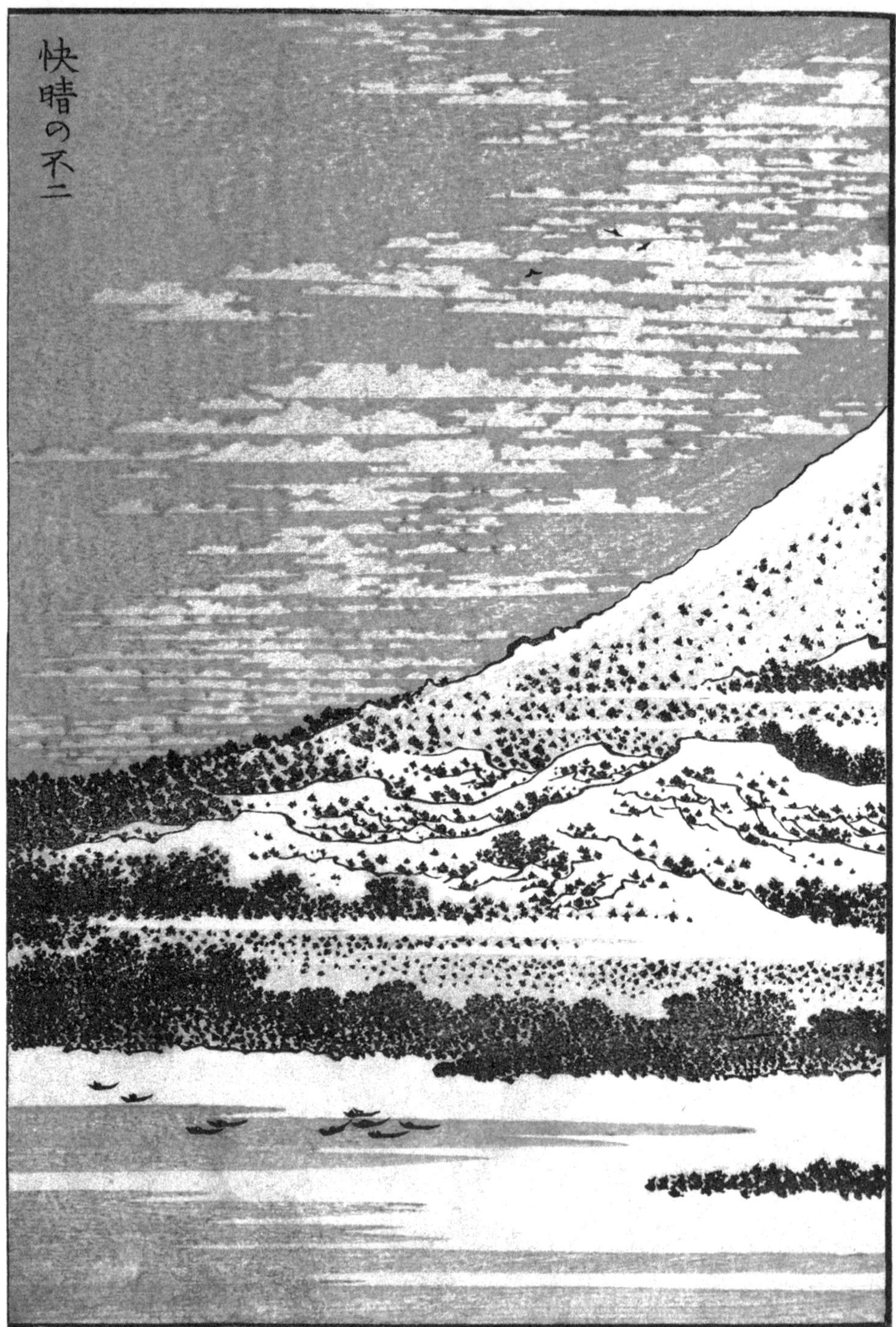

Fuji Under Clear Skies

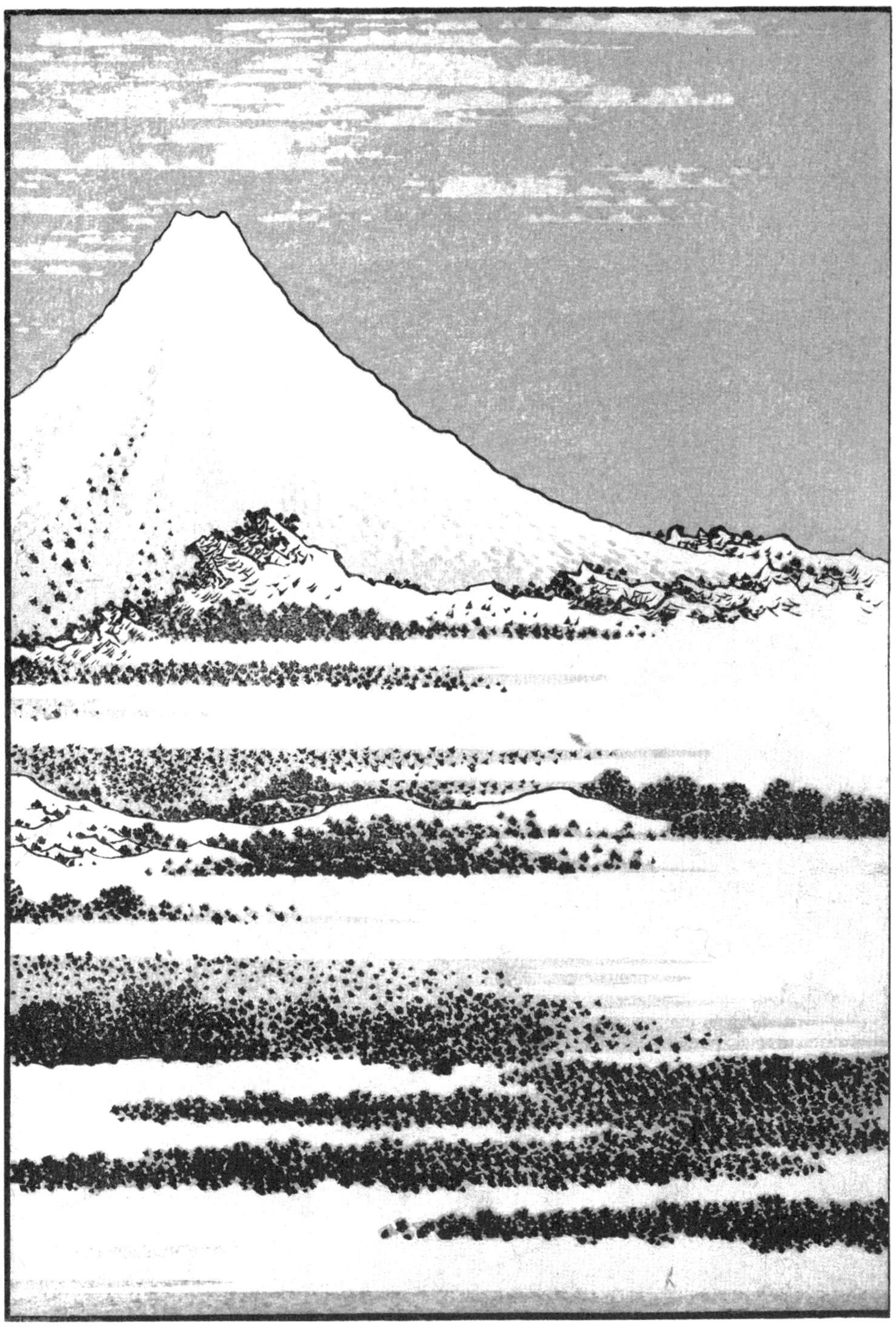

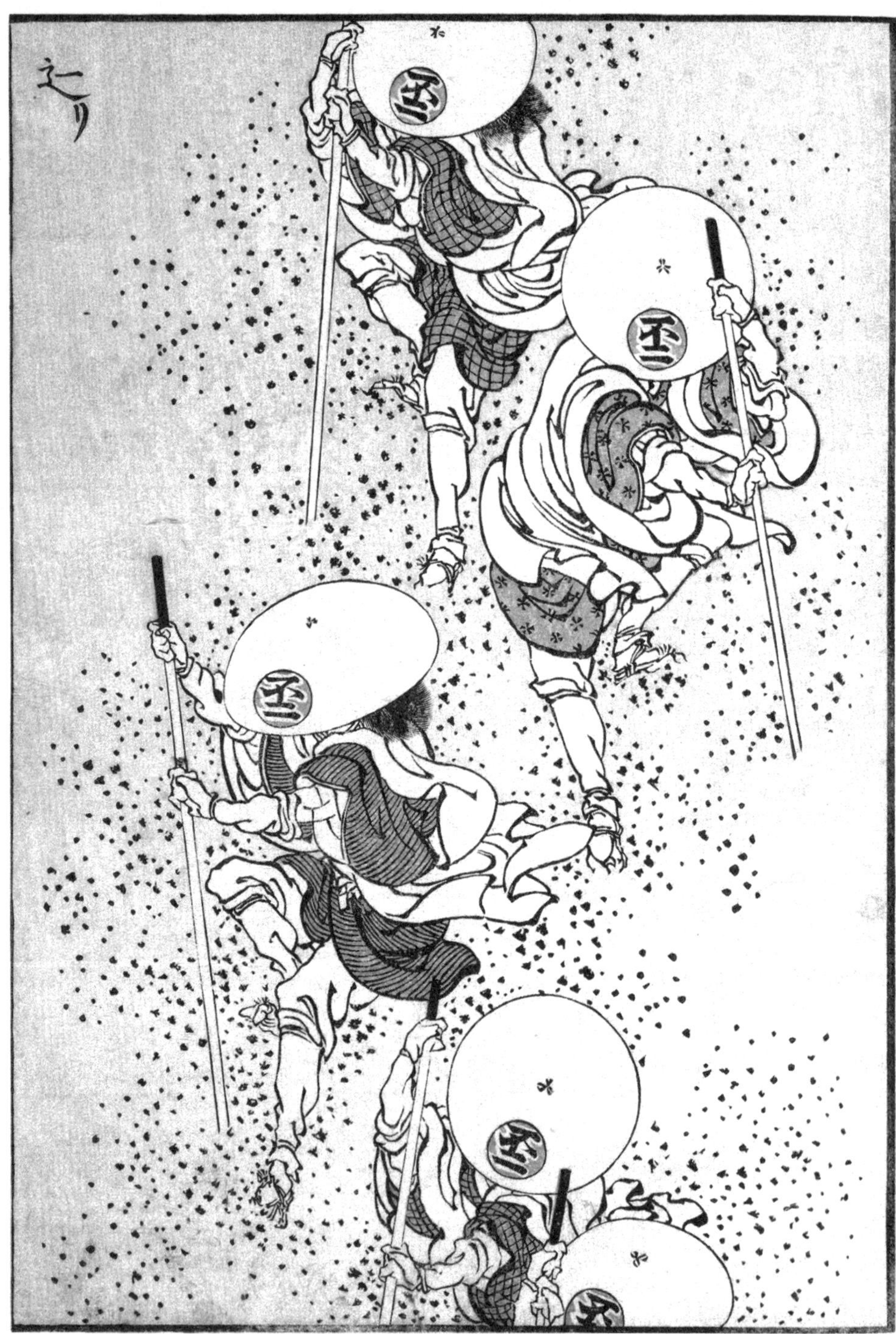

Sliding Down

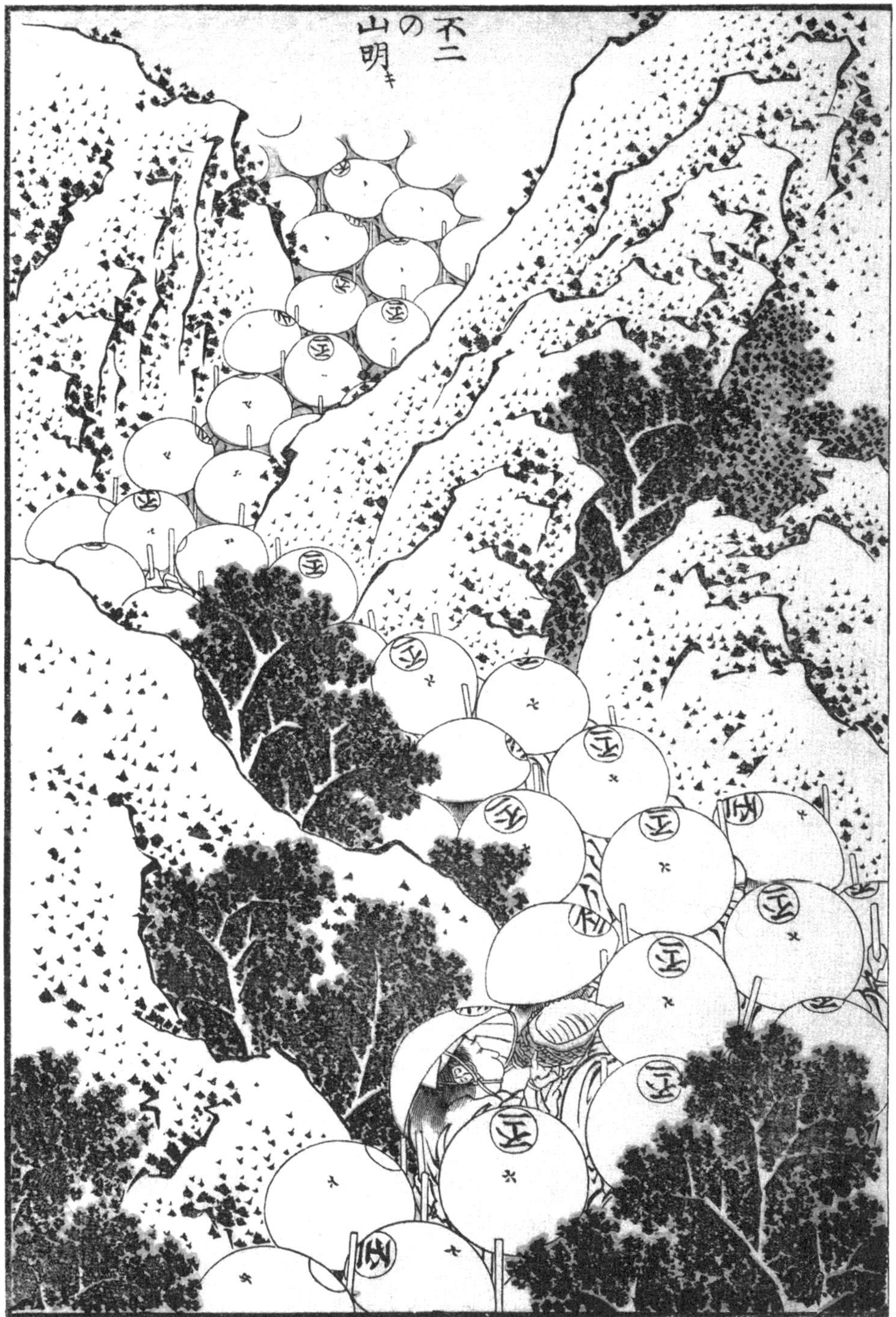

不二の山明キ

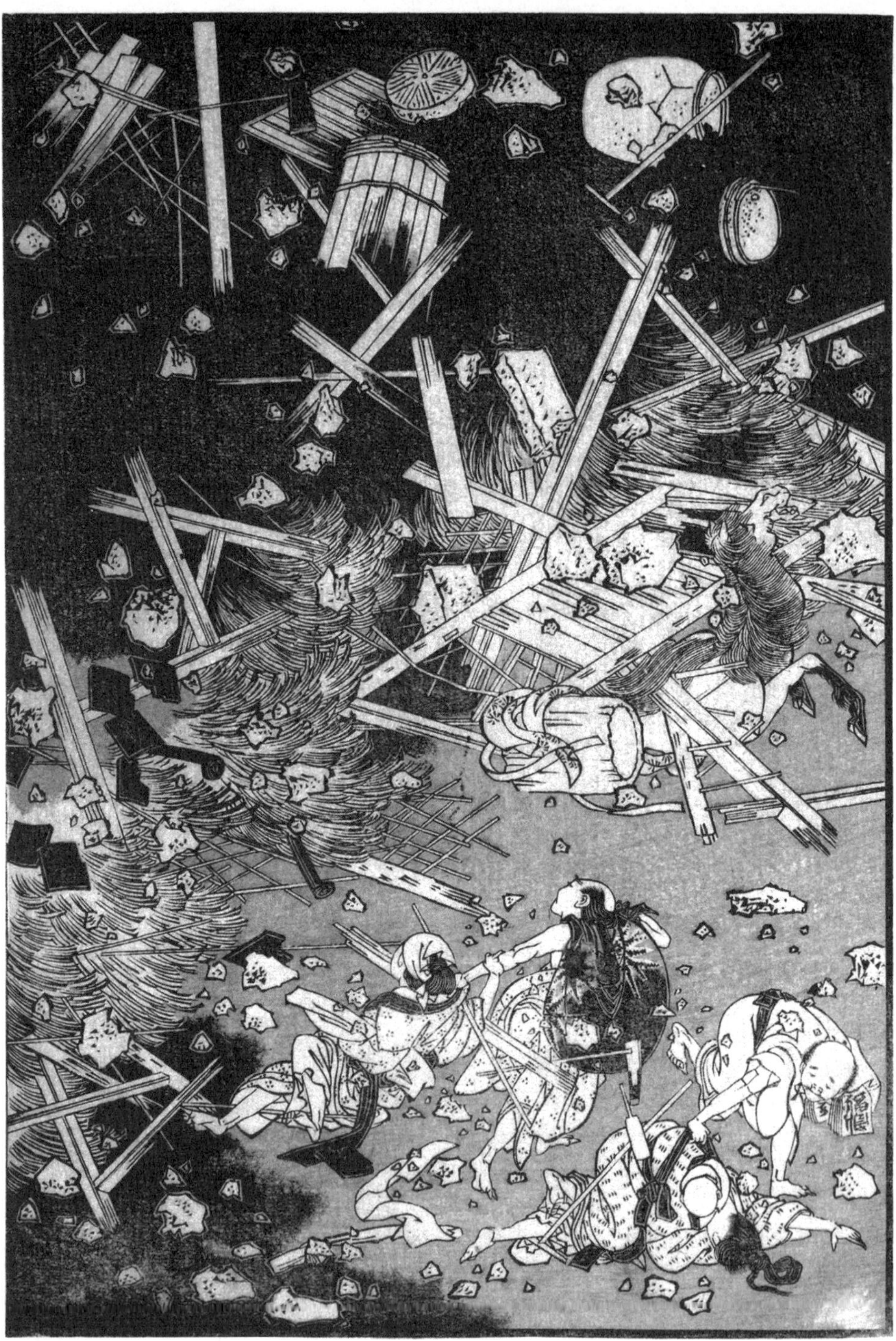

The Appearance of Hōeizan

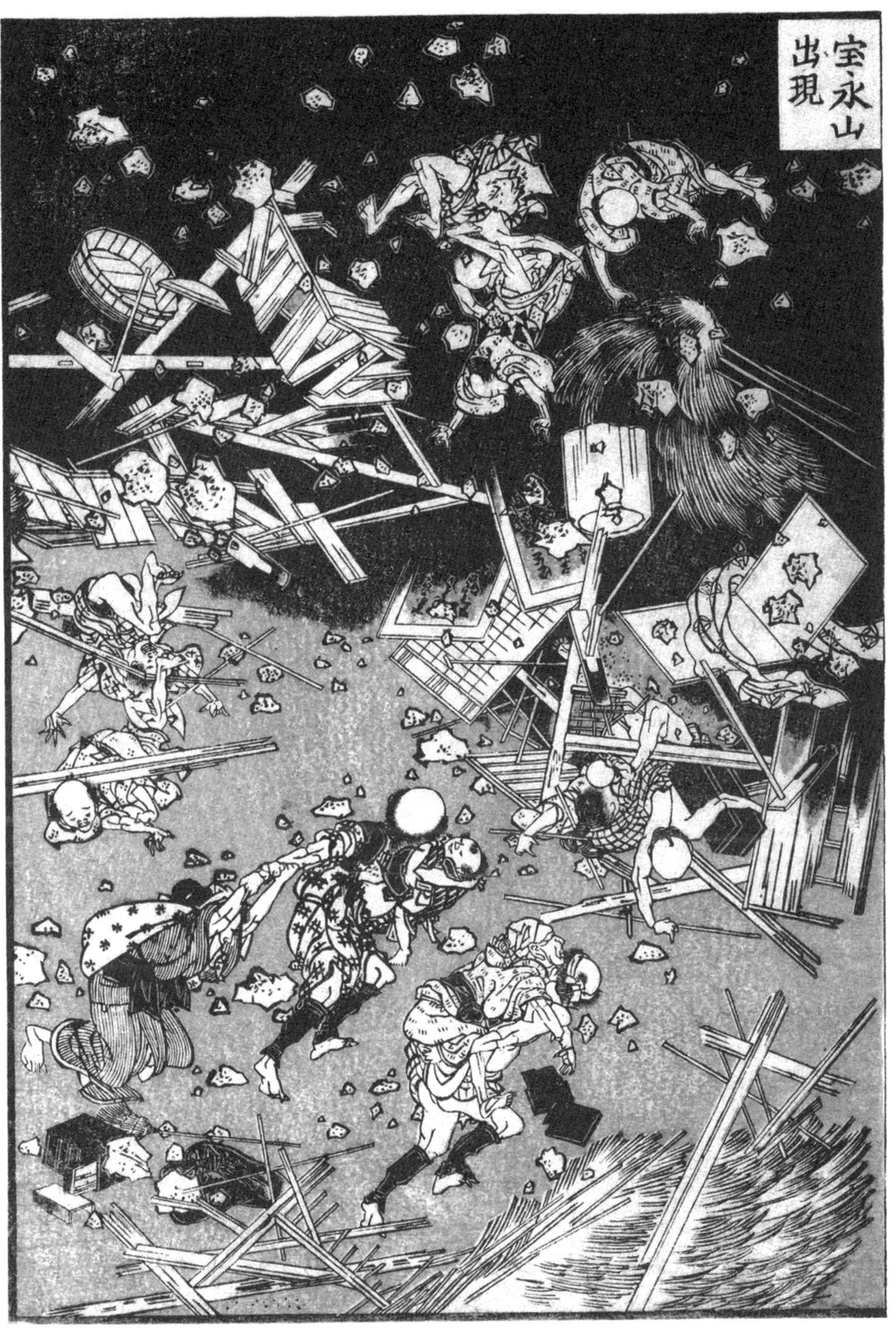
宝永山
出現

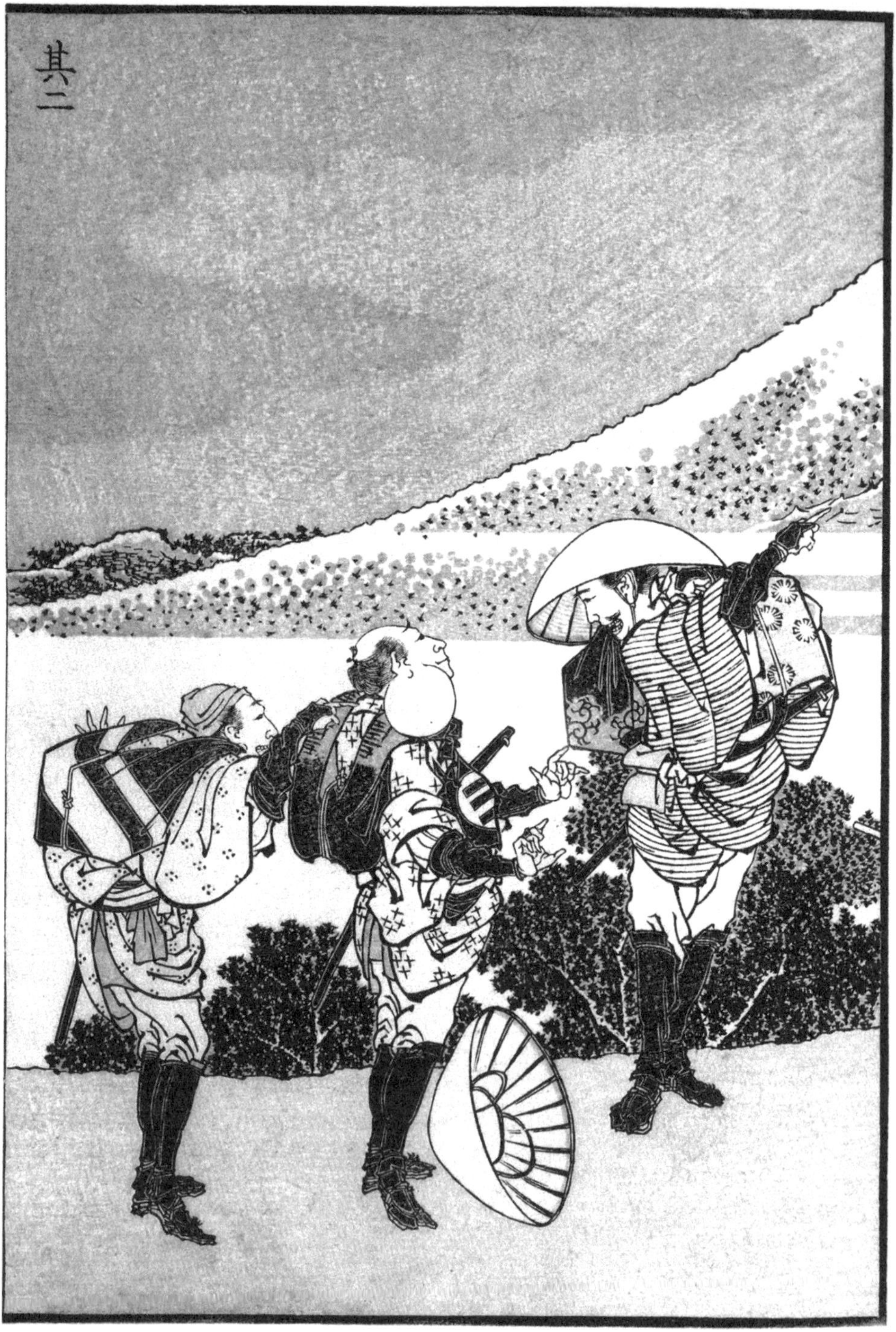

Fuji Under Clear Skies, Part 2

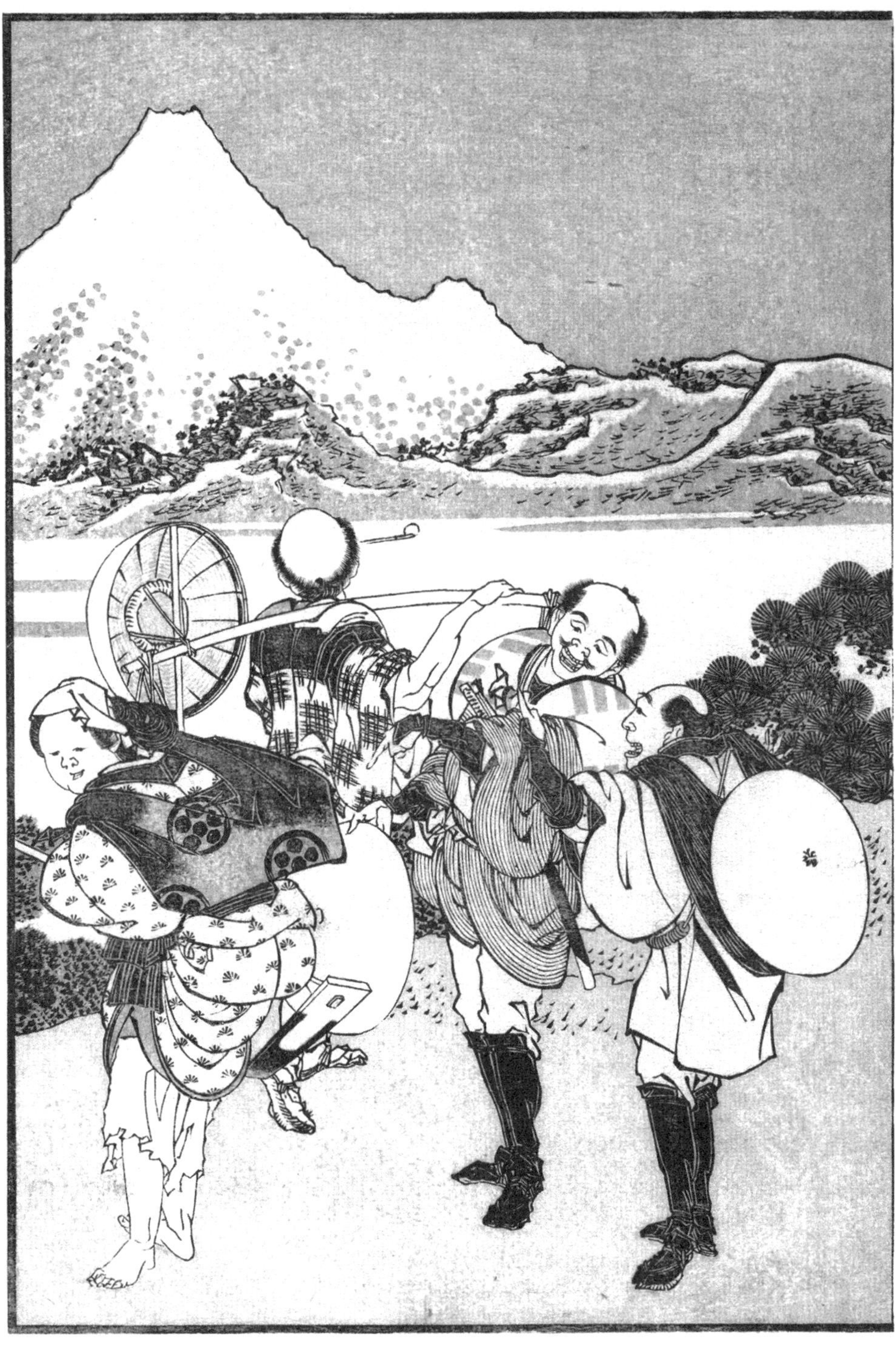

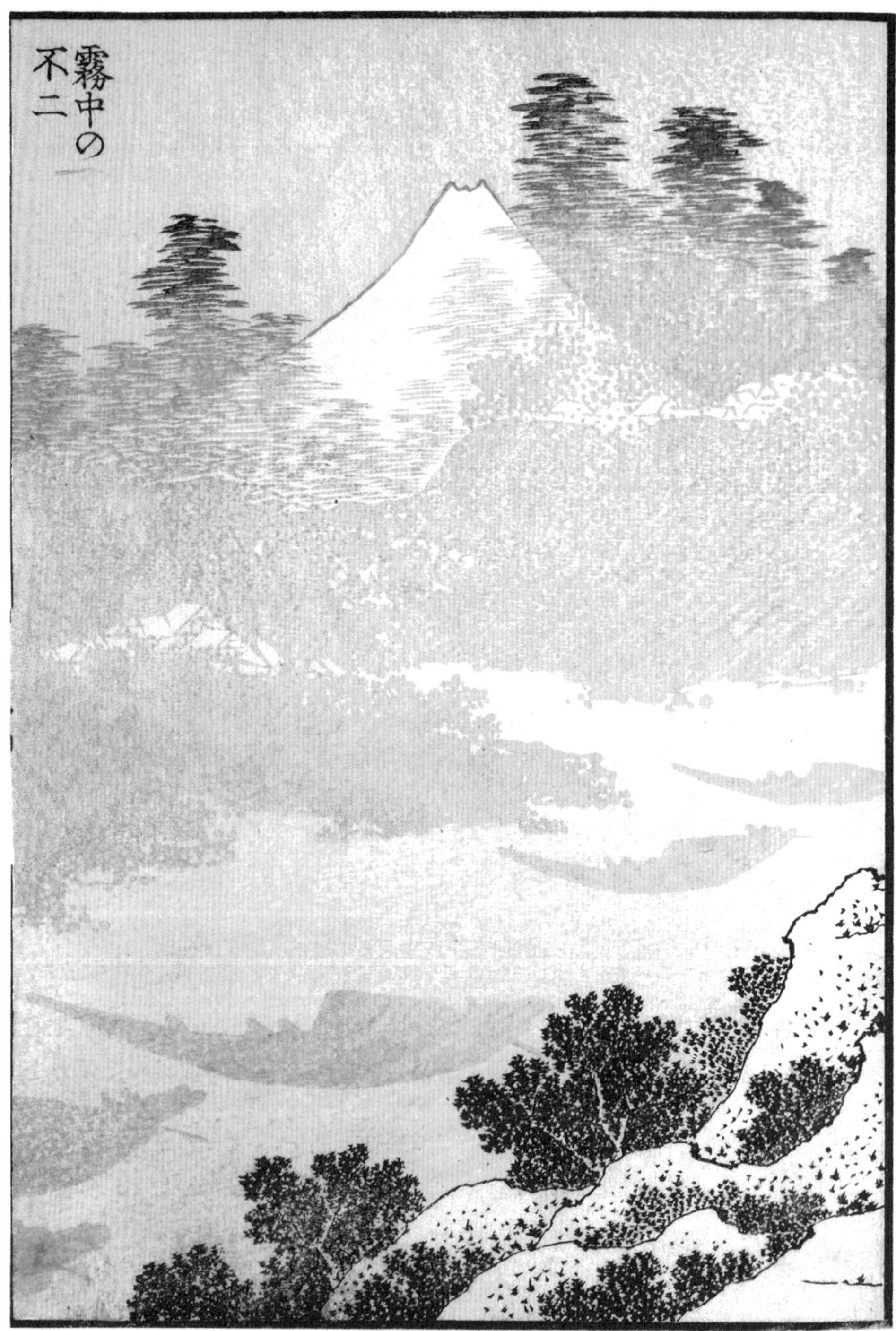

 Fuji in Mist

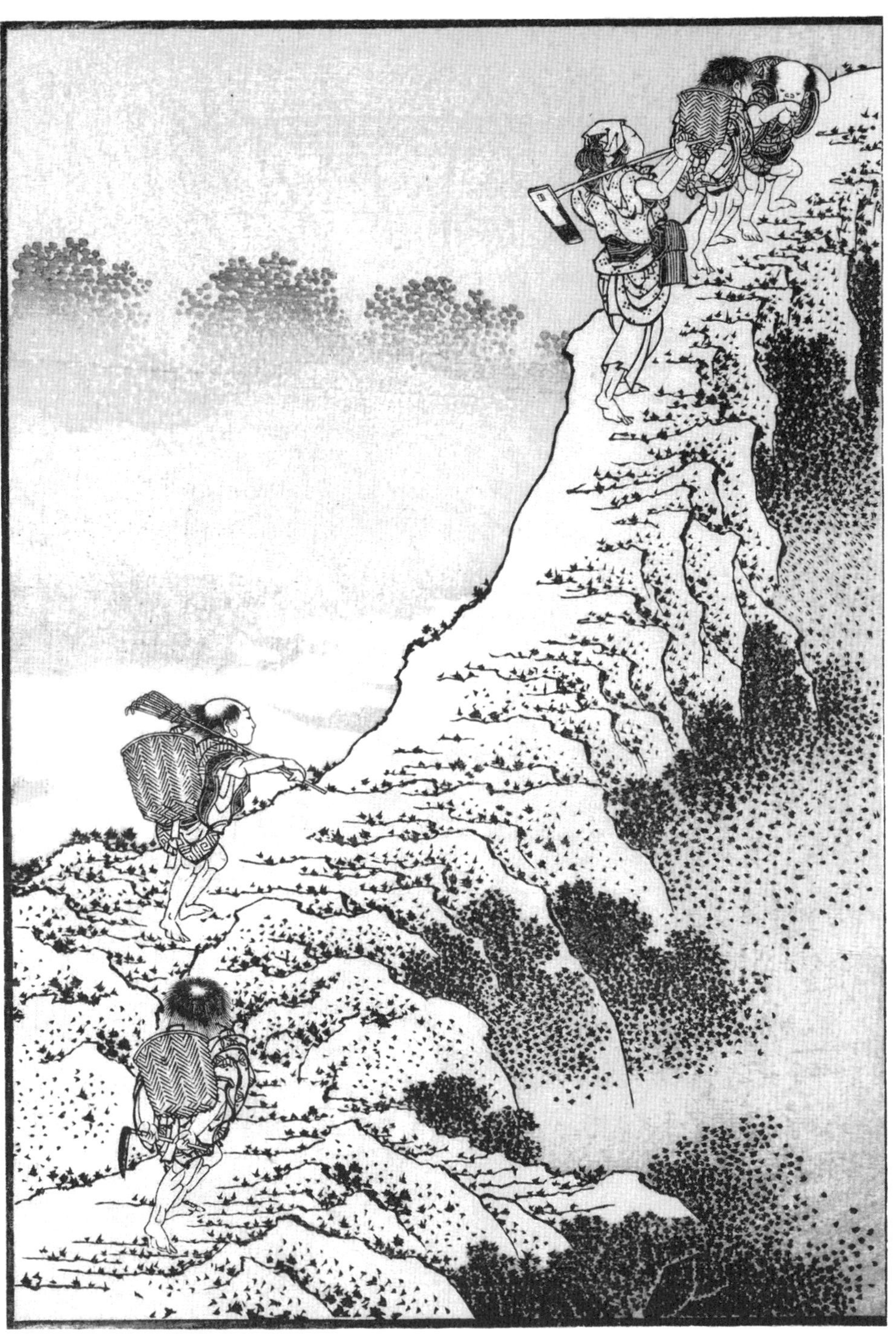

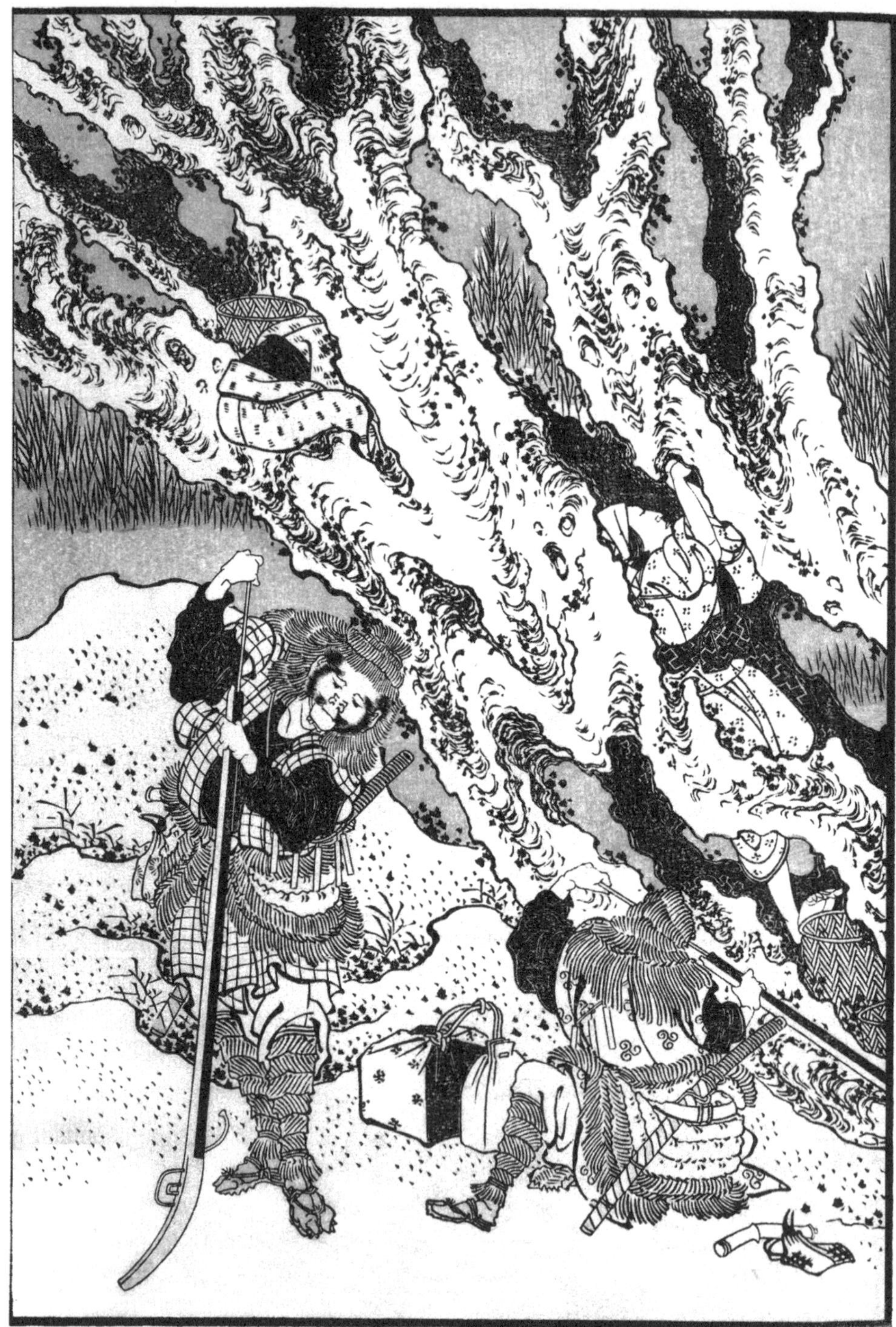

Fuji Among the Mountains

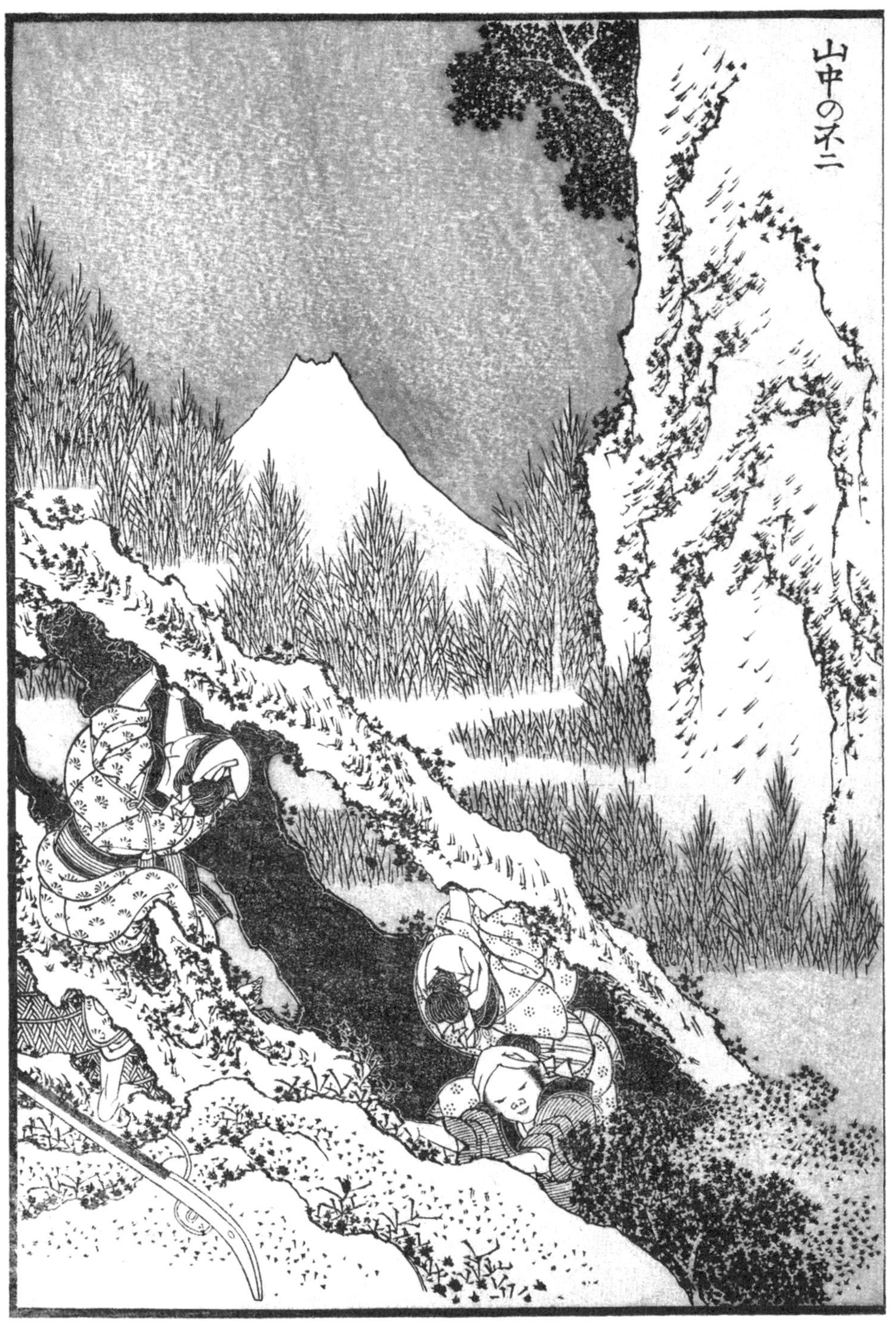
山中のネ二

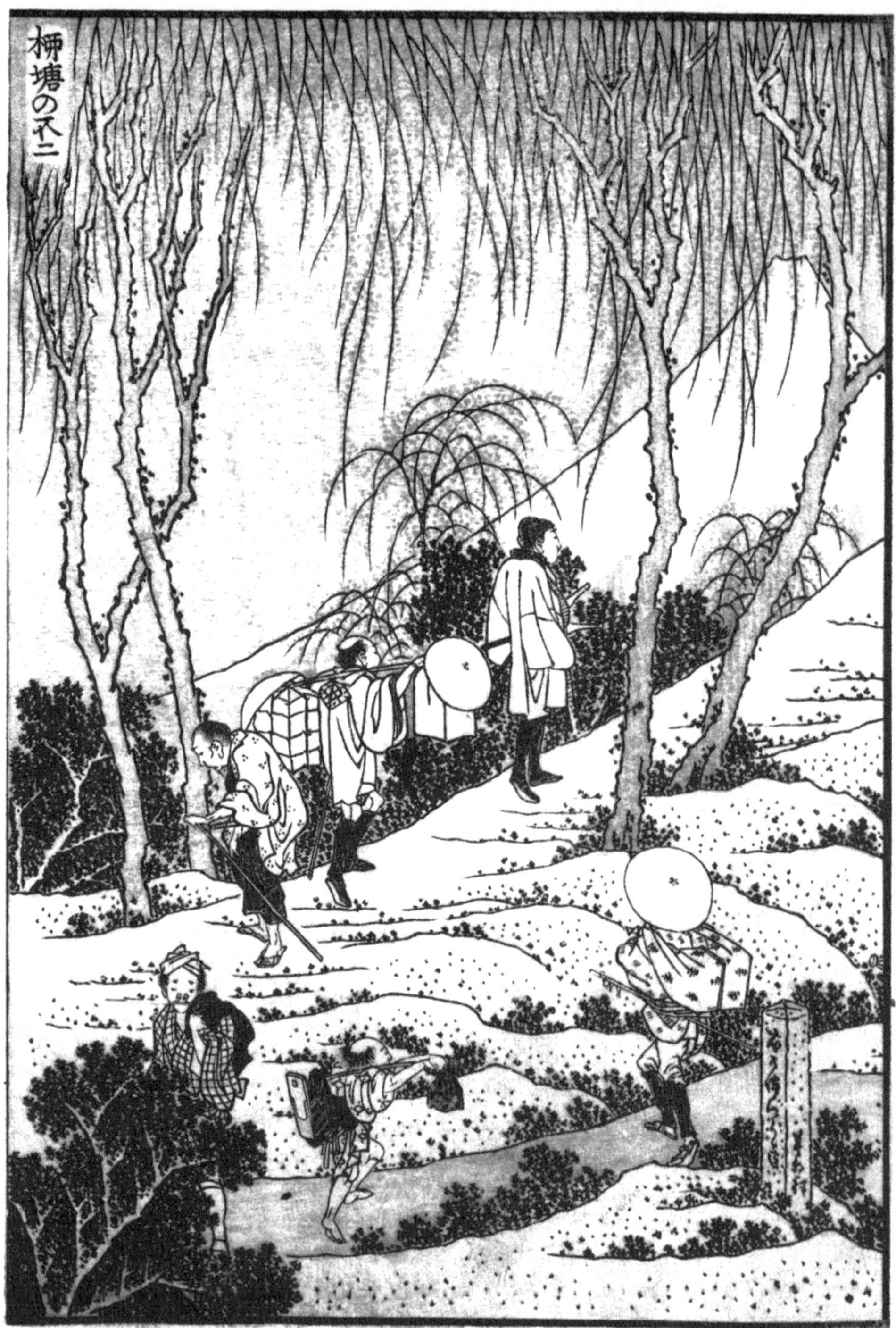

Fuji over a Willow Bank

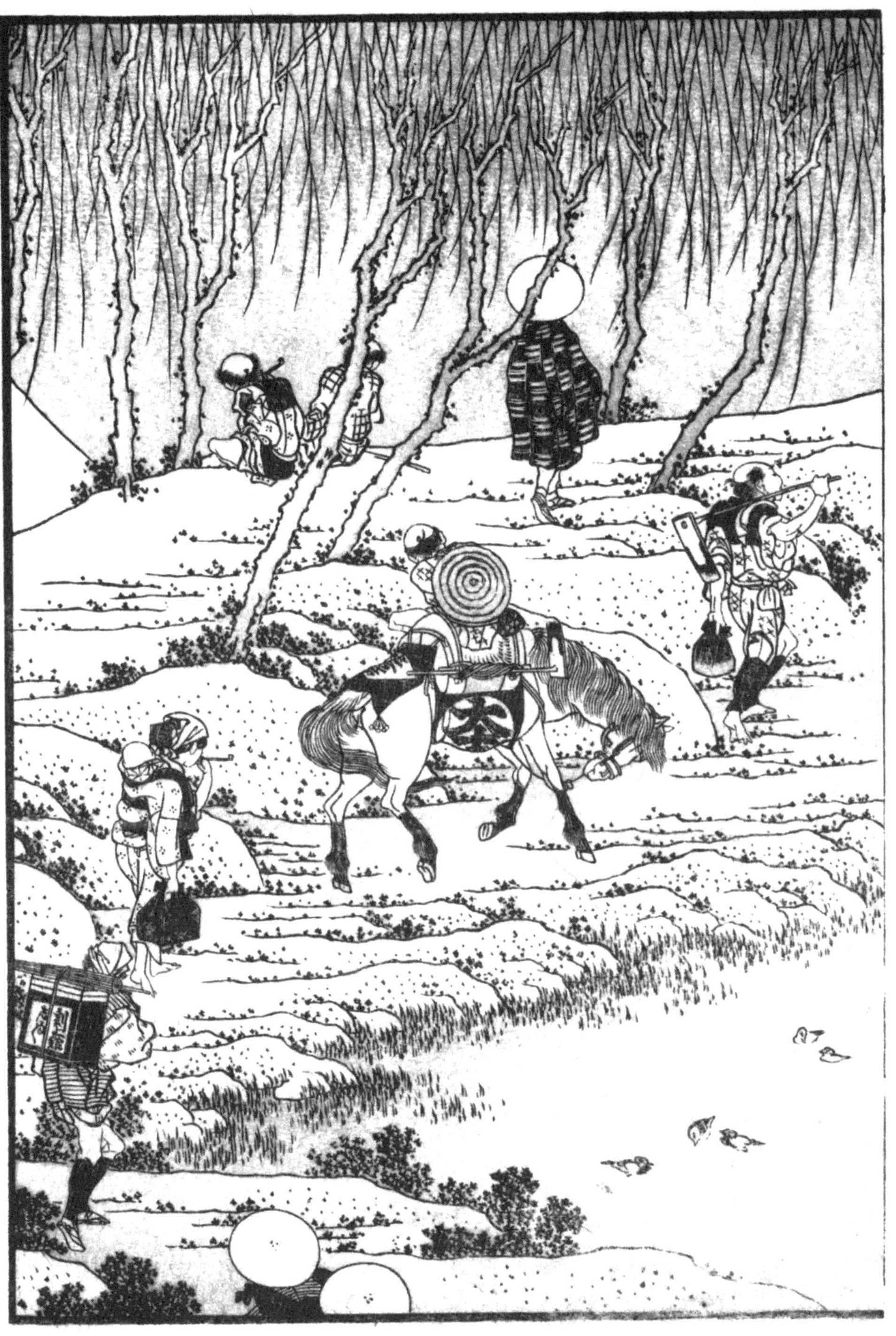

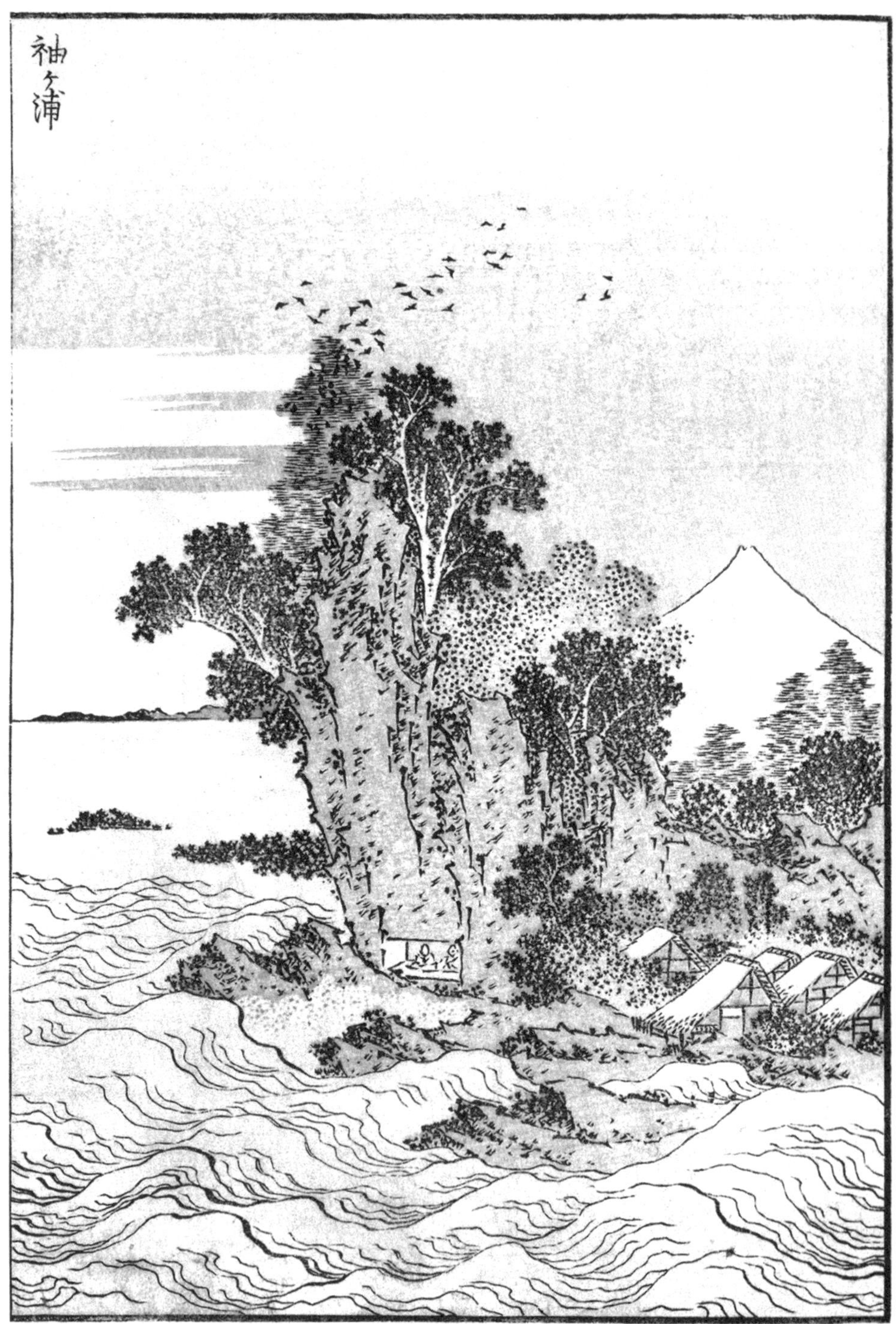

 Sodegaura

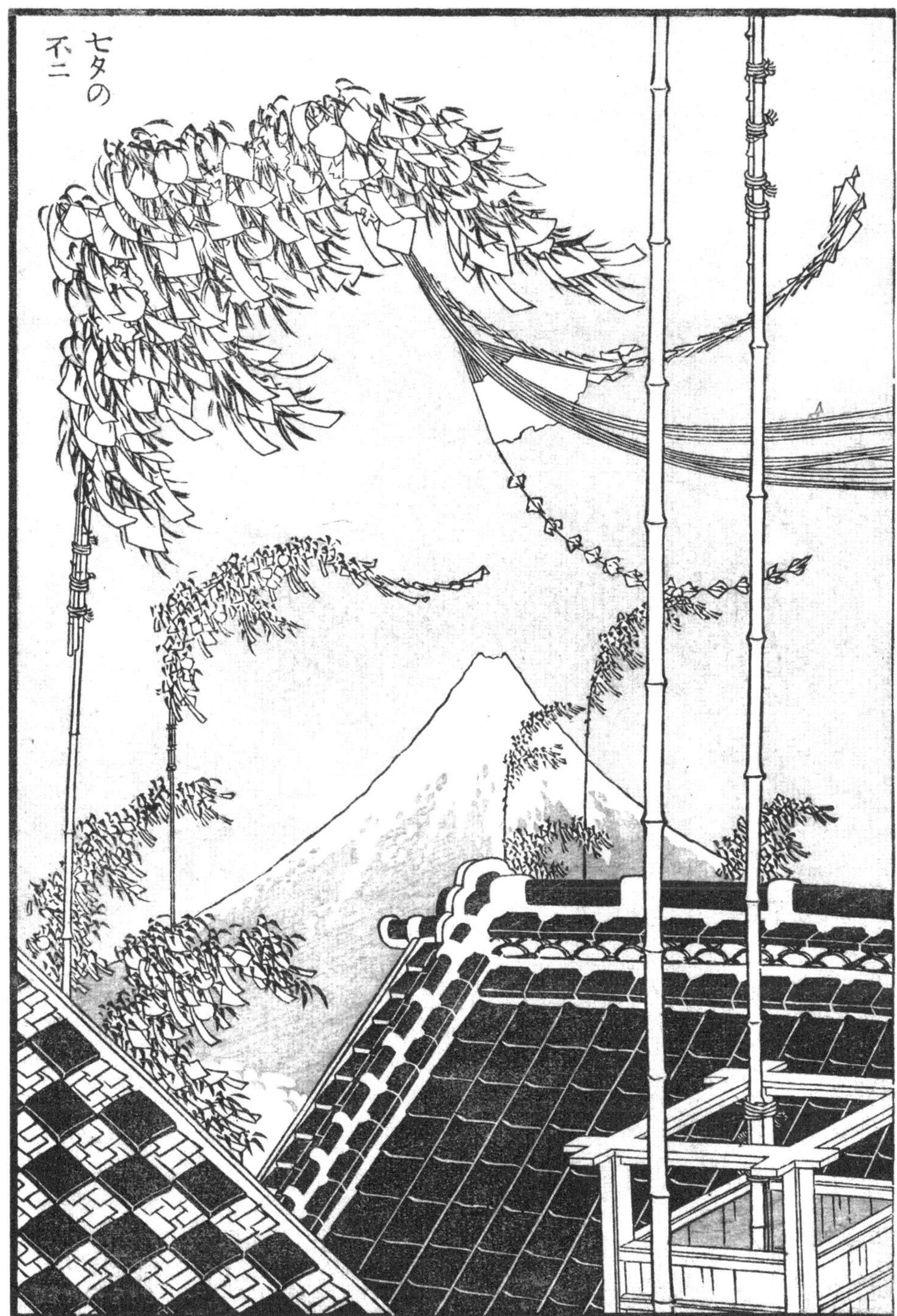

110 *Fuji at Tanabata*

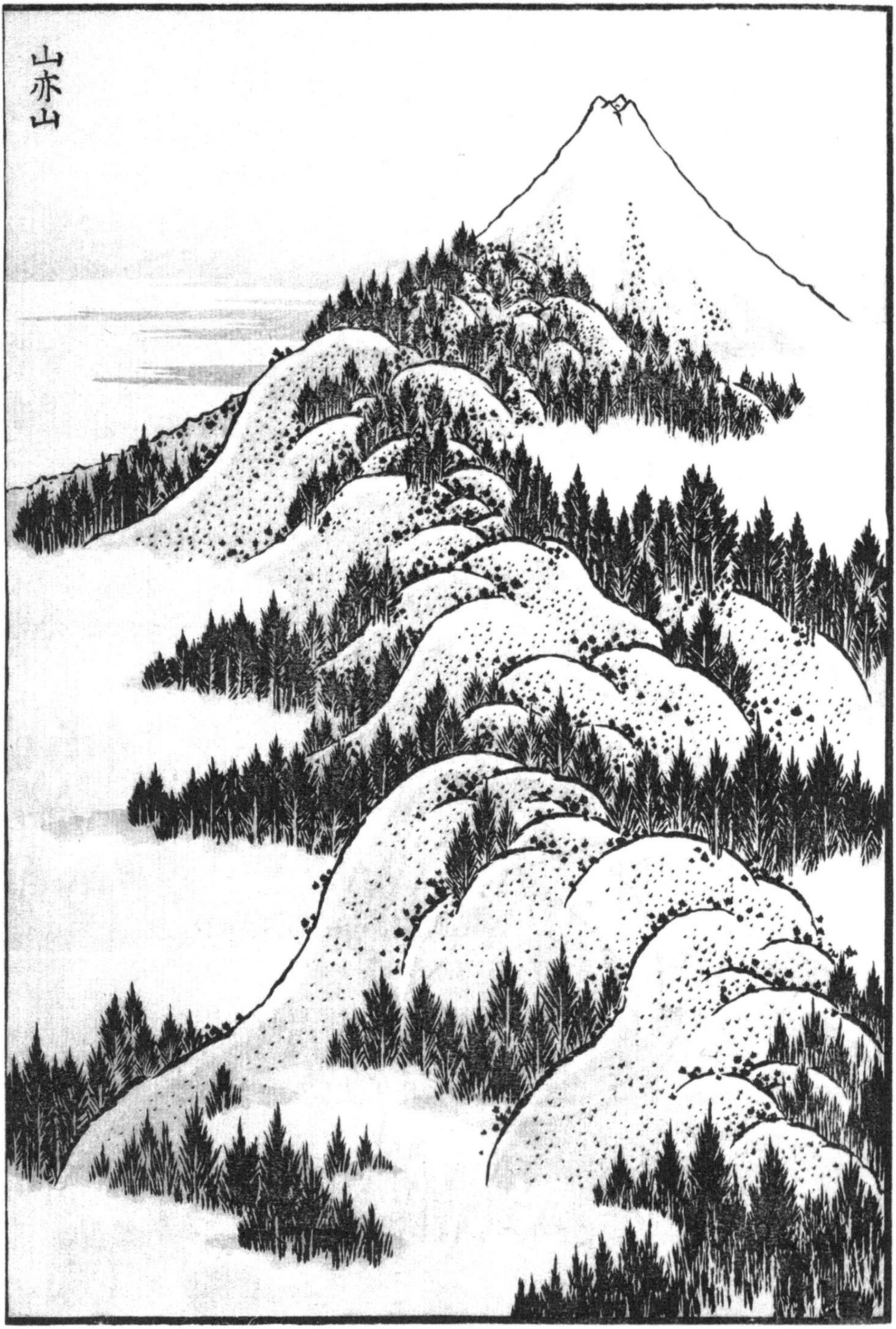

山亦山

Mountains upon Mountains

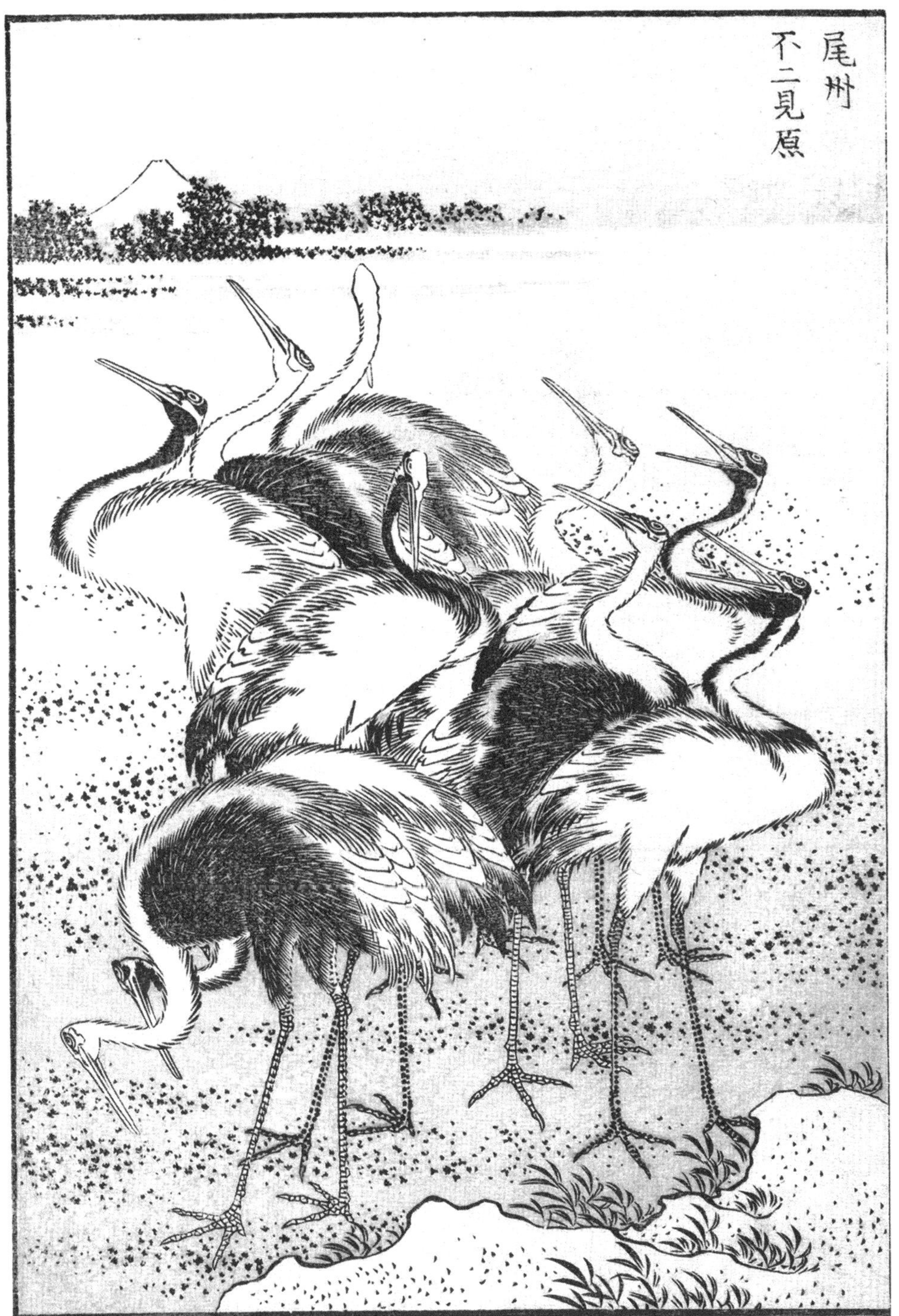

112 *Fujimigahara in Owari Province*

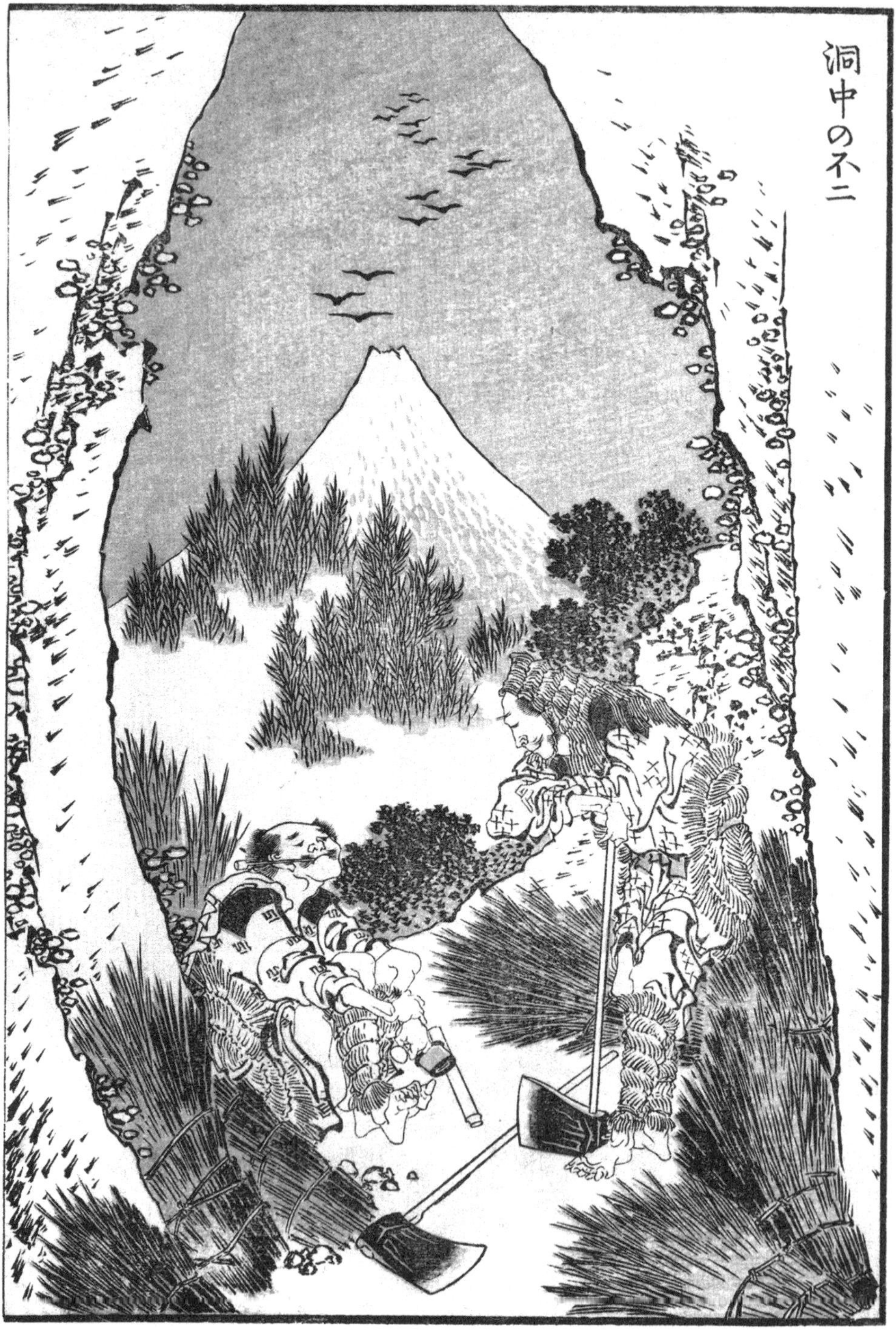

113 Fuji from a Cave

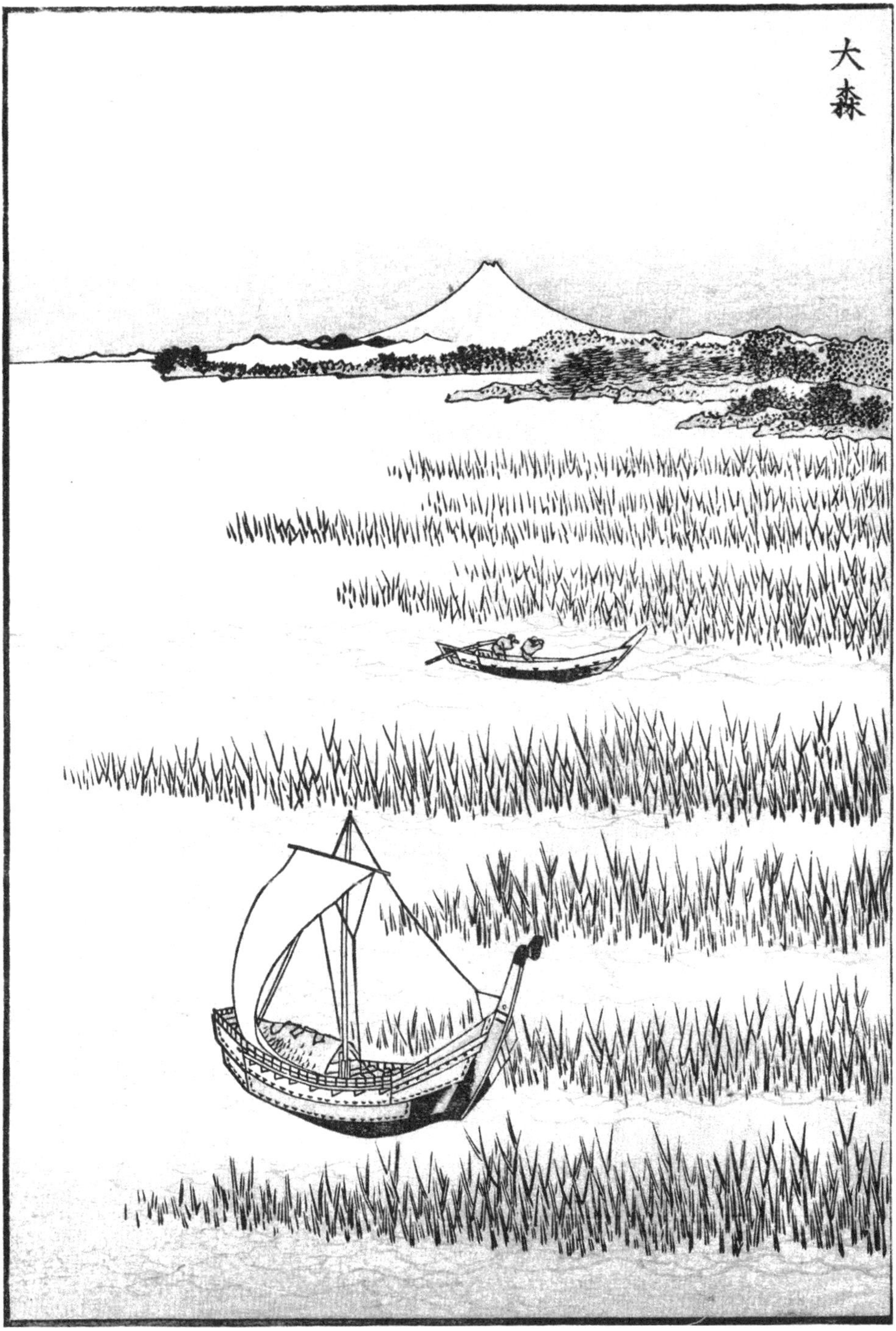

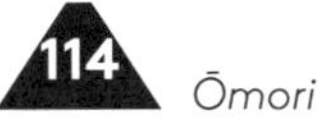

114 *Ōmori*

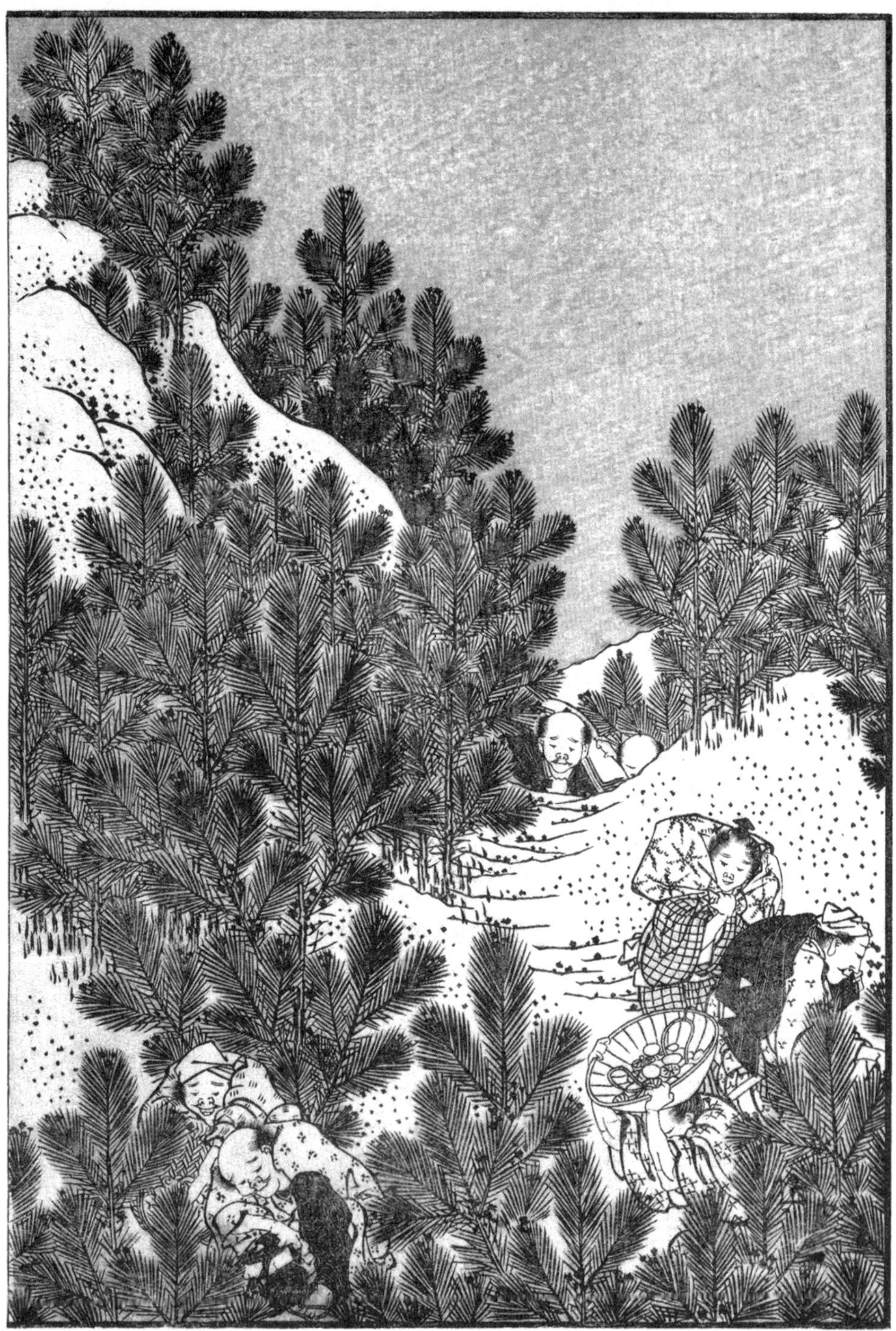

Fuji from a Pine Mountain

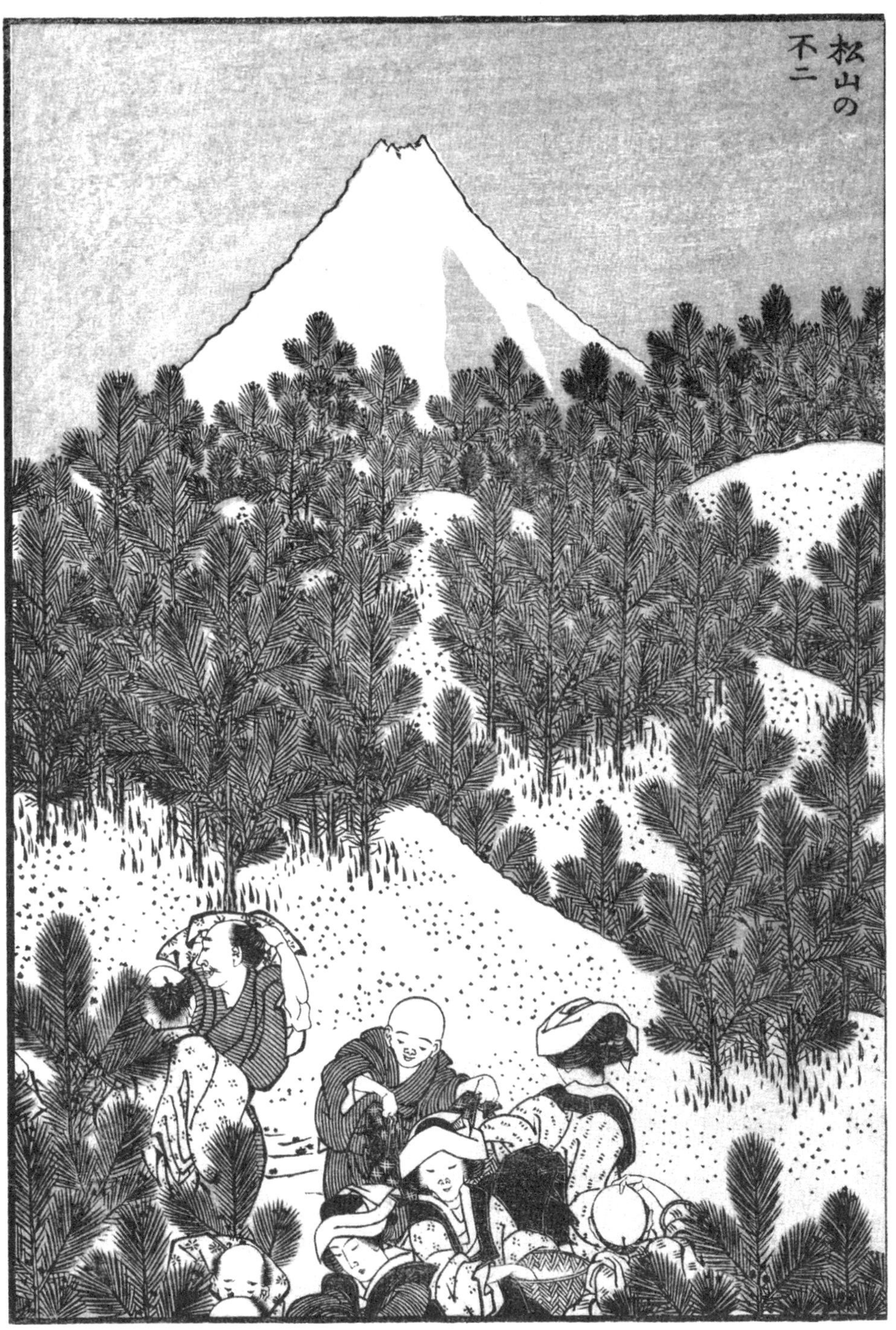

松山の
不二

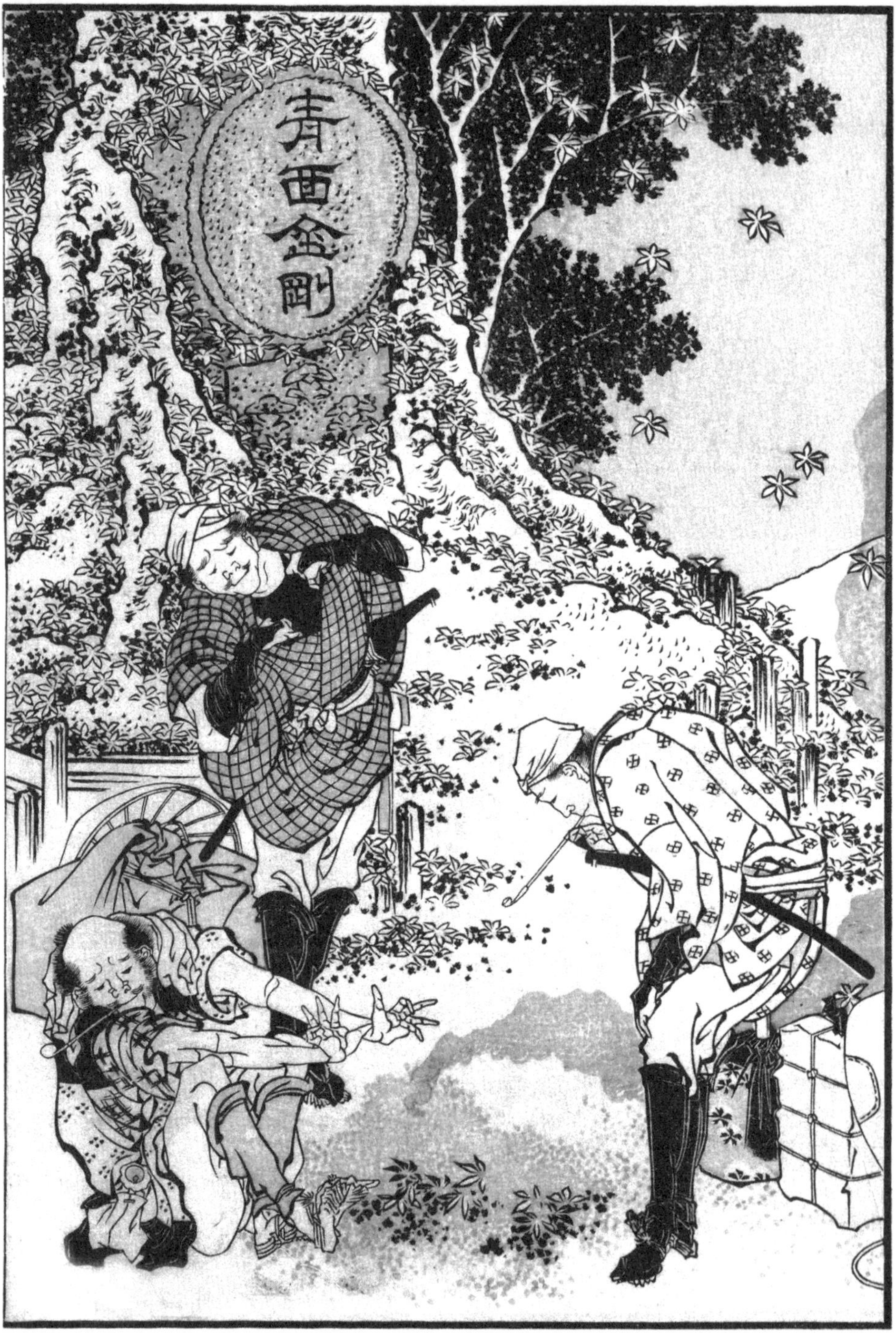

Fuji Through Smoke

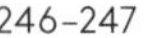

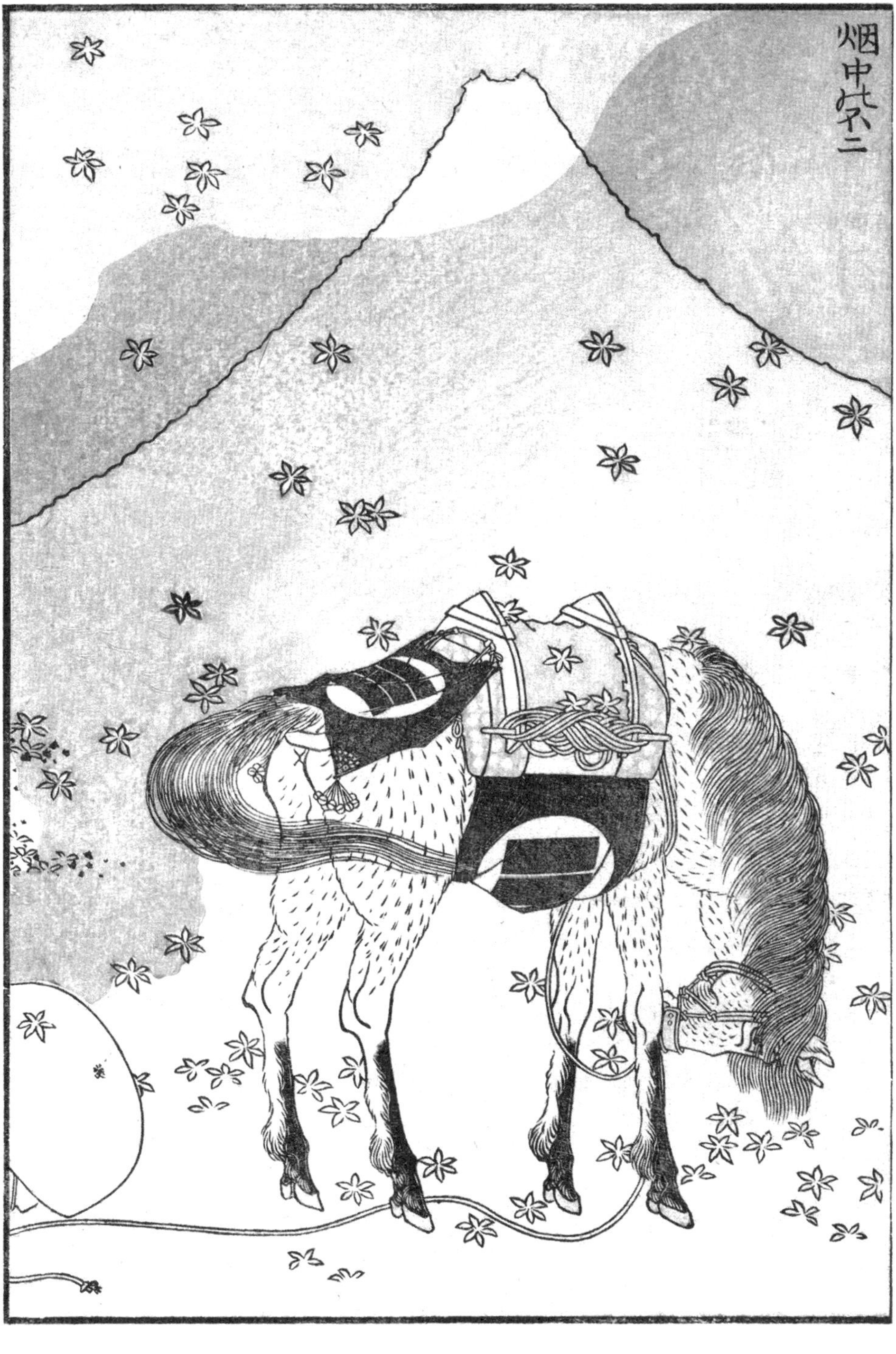

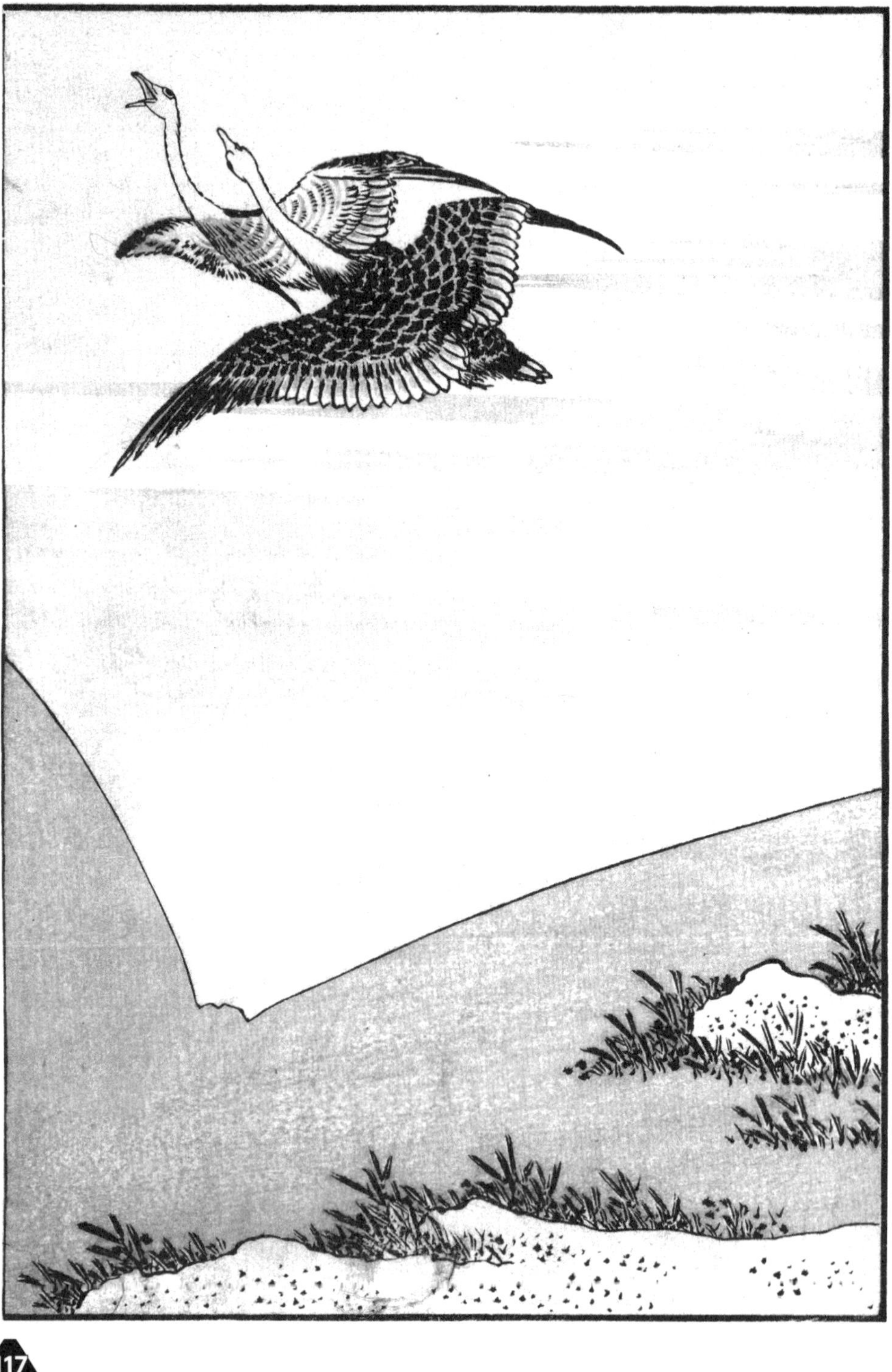

Fuji on the Face of a Rice Field

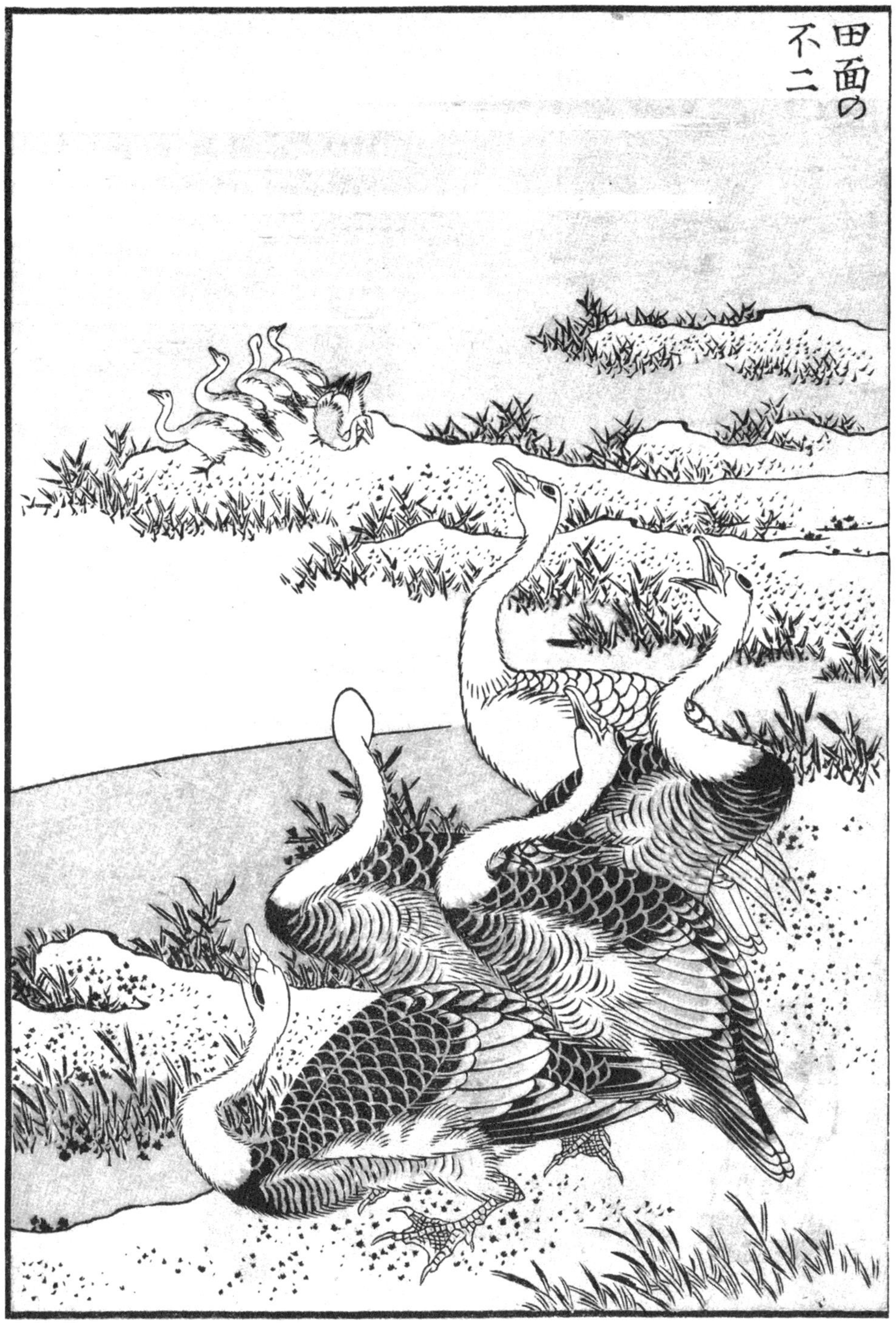
田面の
不二

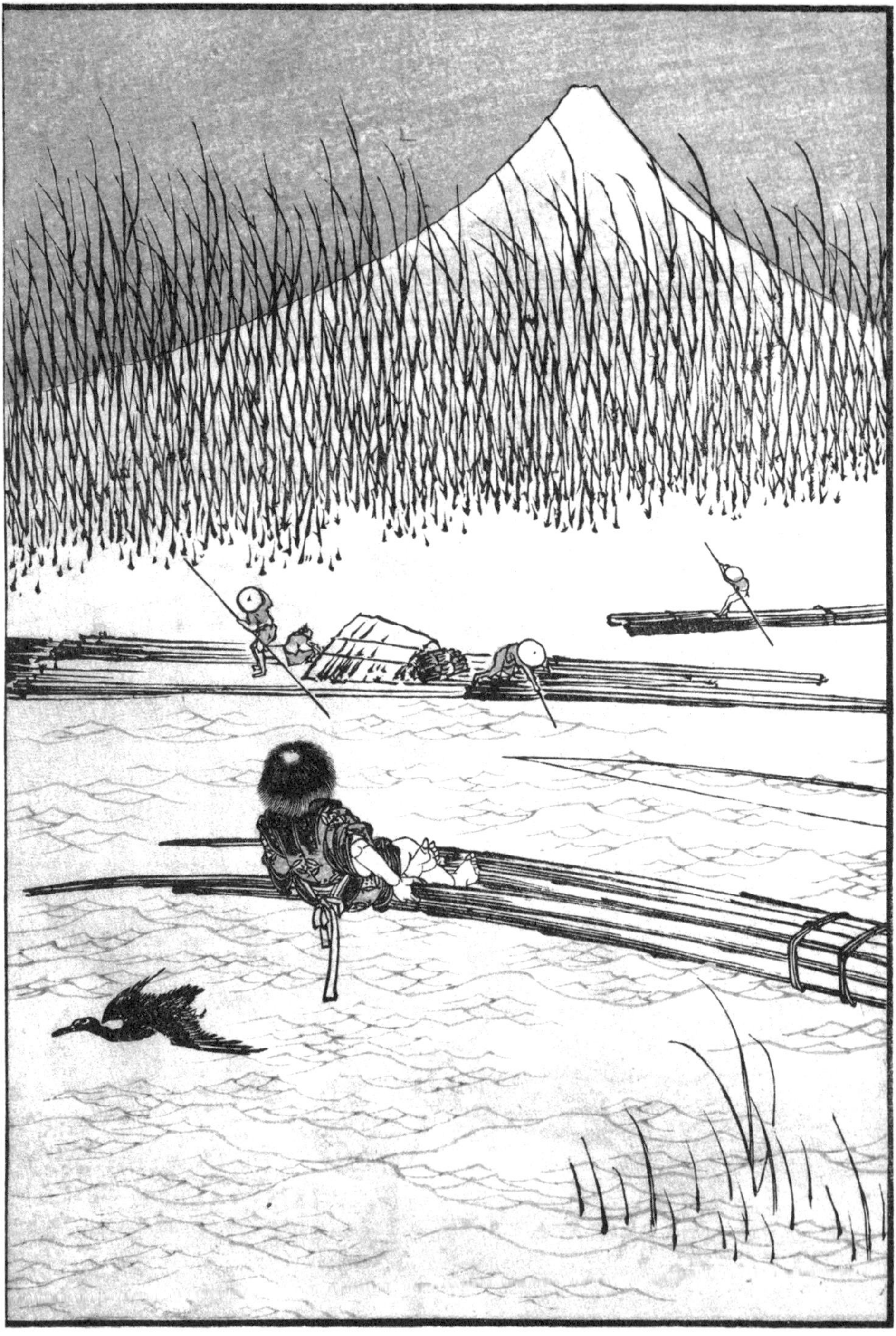

Fuji with Rafts in the Rushes

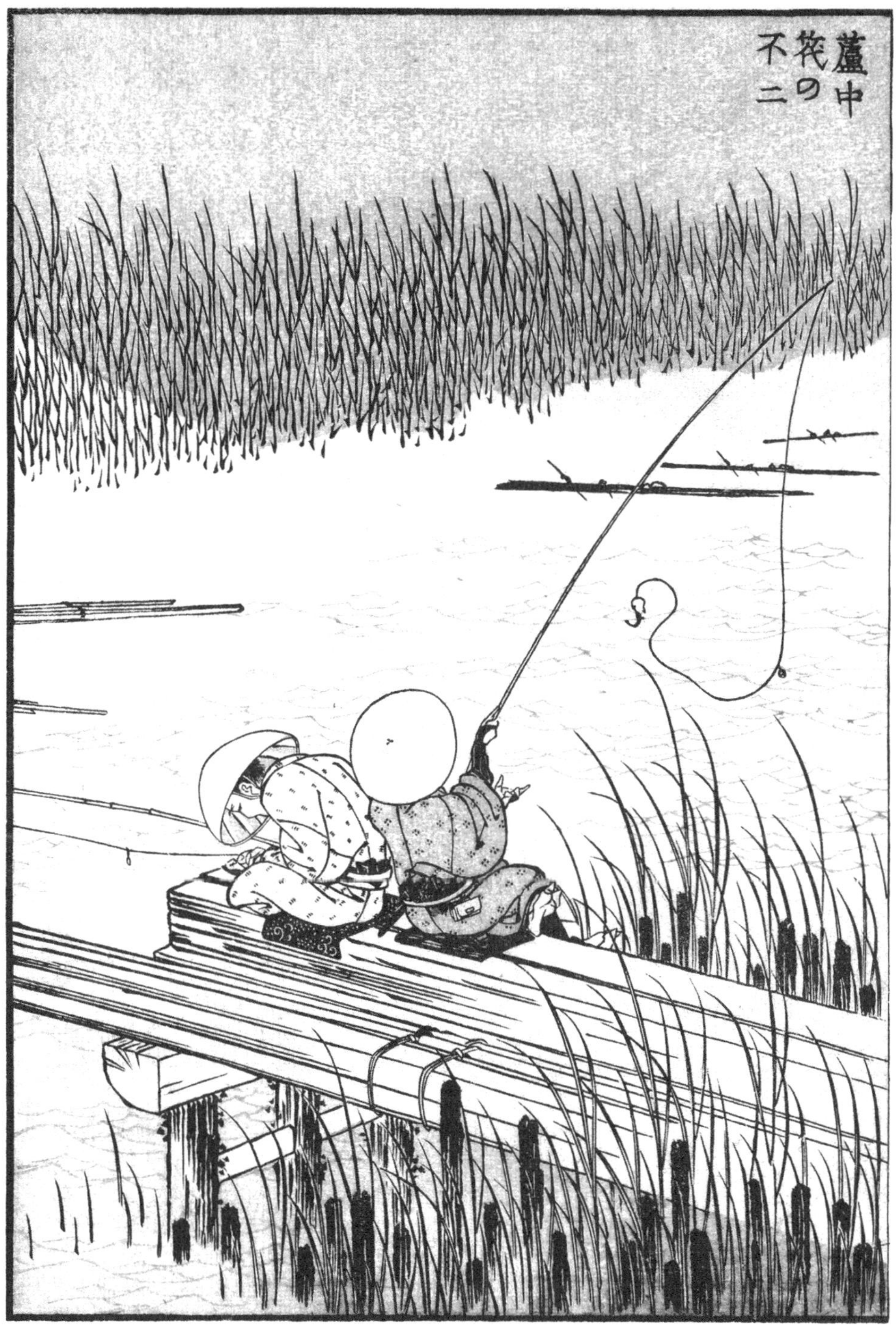
蘆中の不二

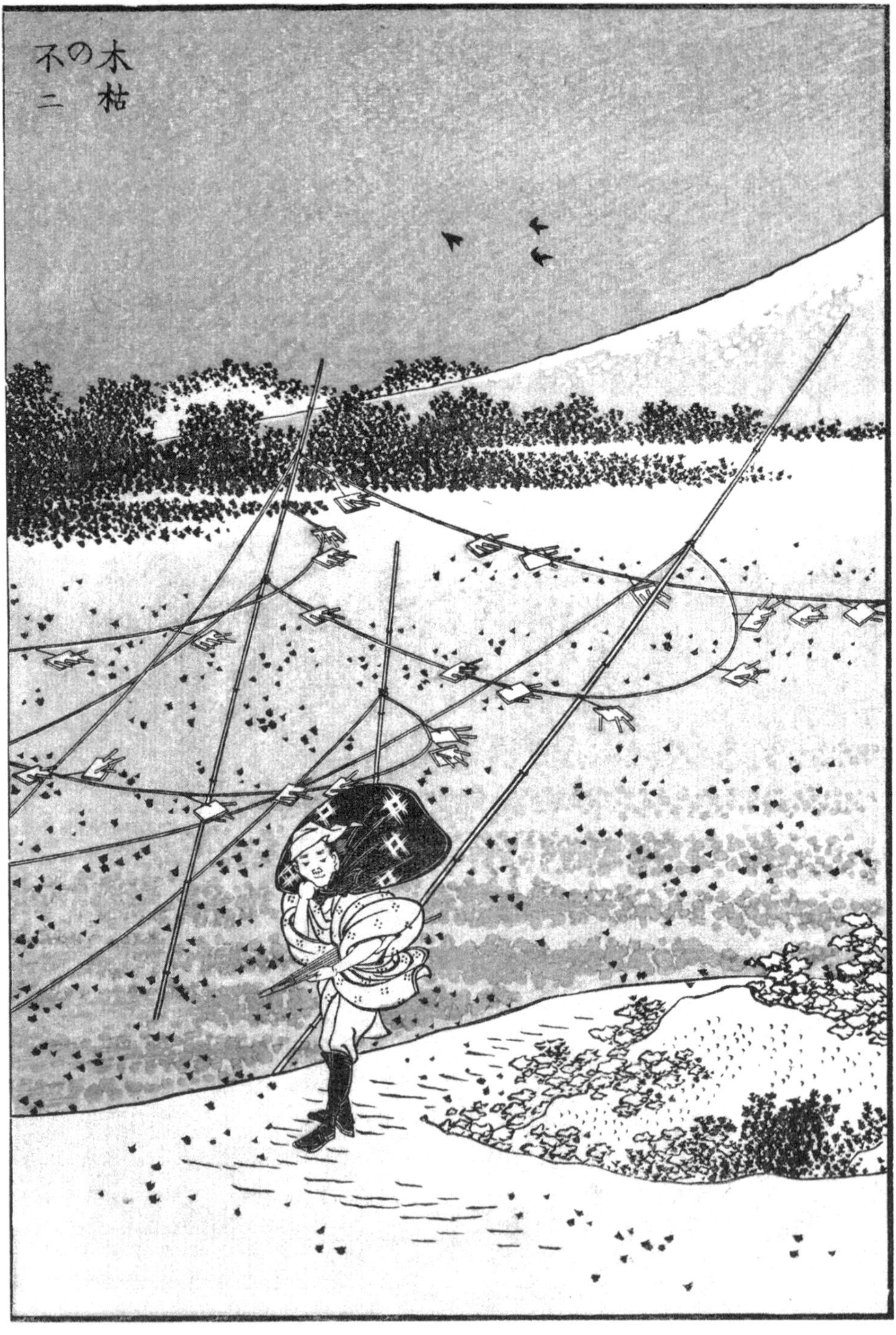

119 *Fuji in a Winter Wind*

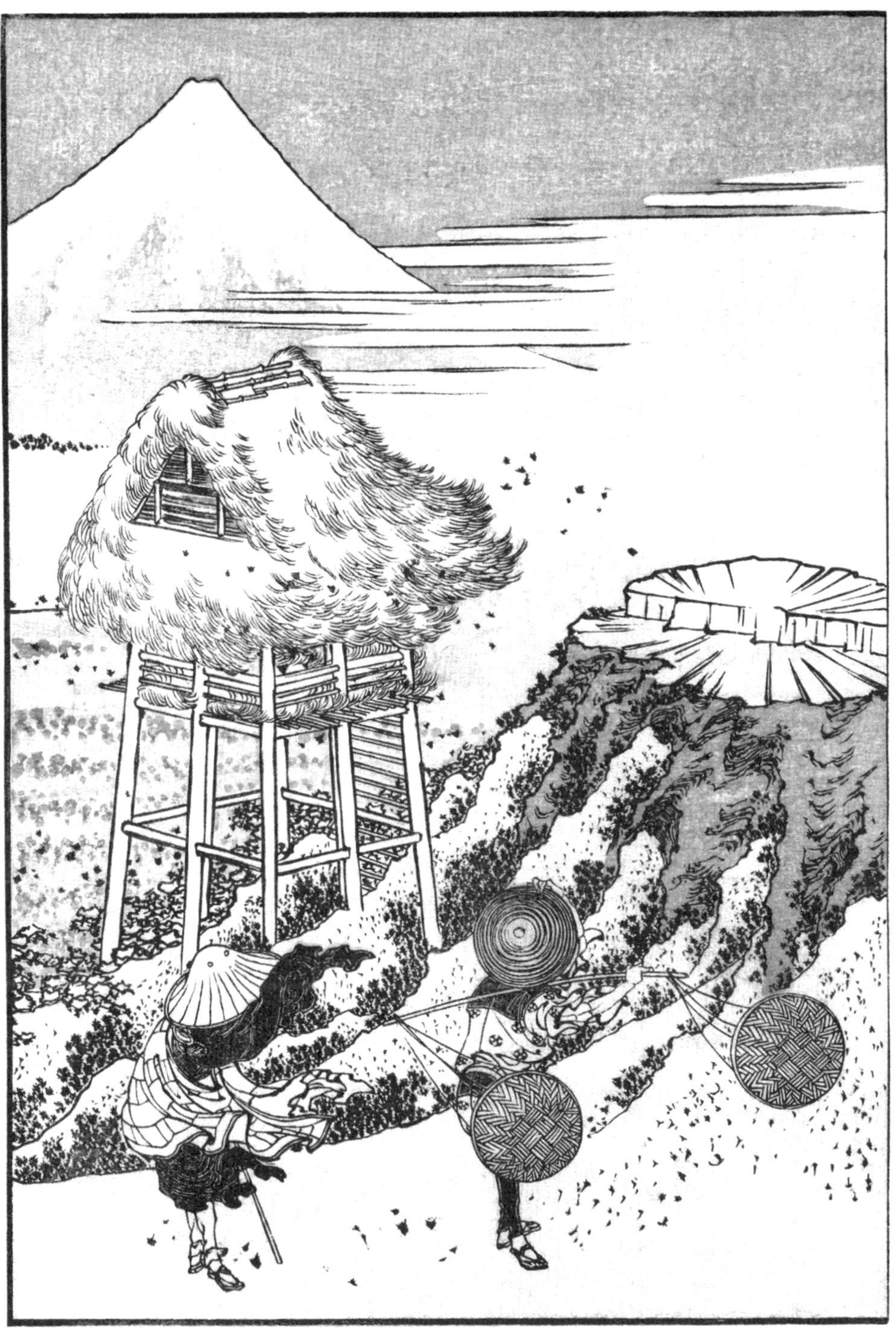

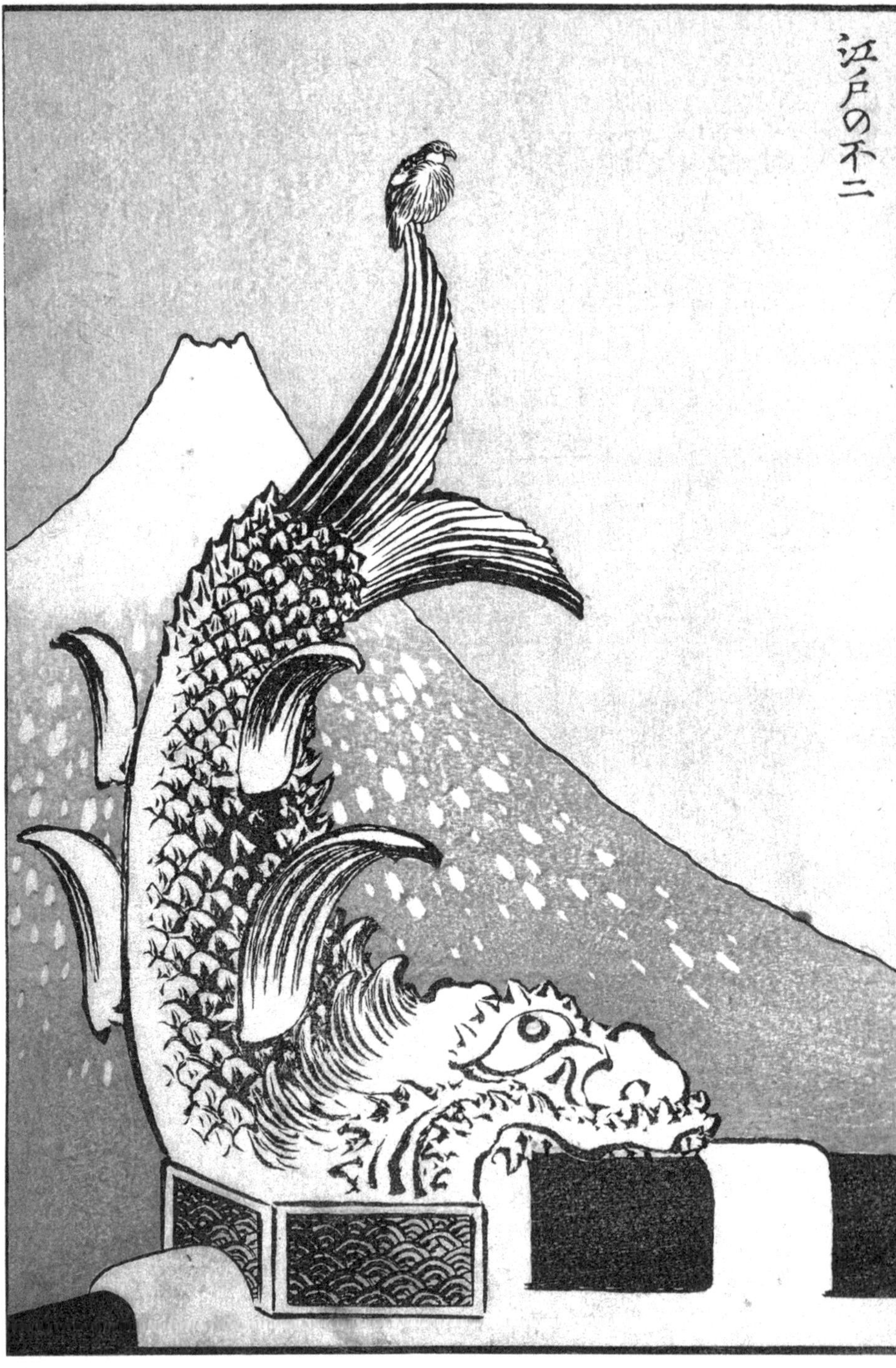

120 *Fuji from Edo*

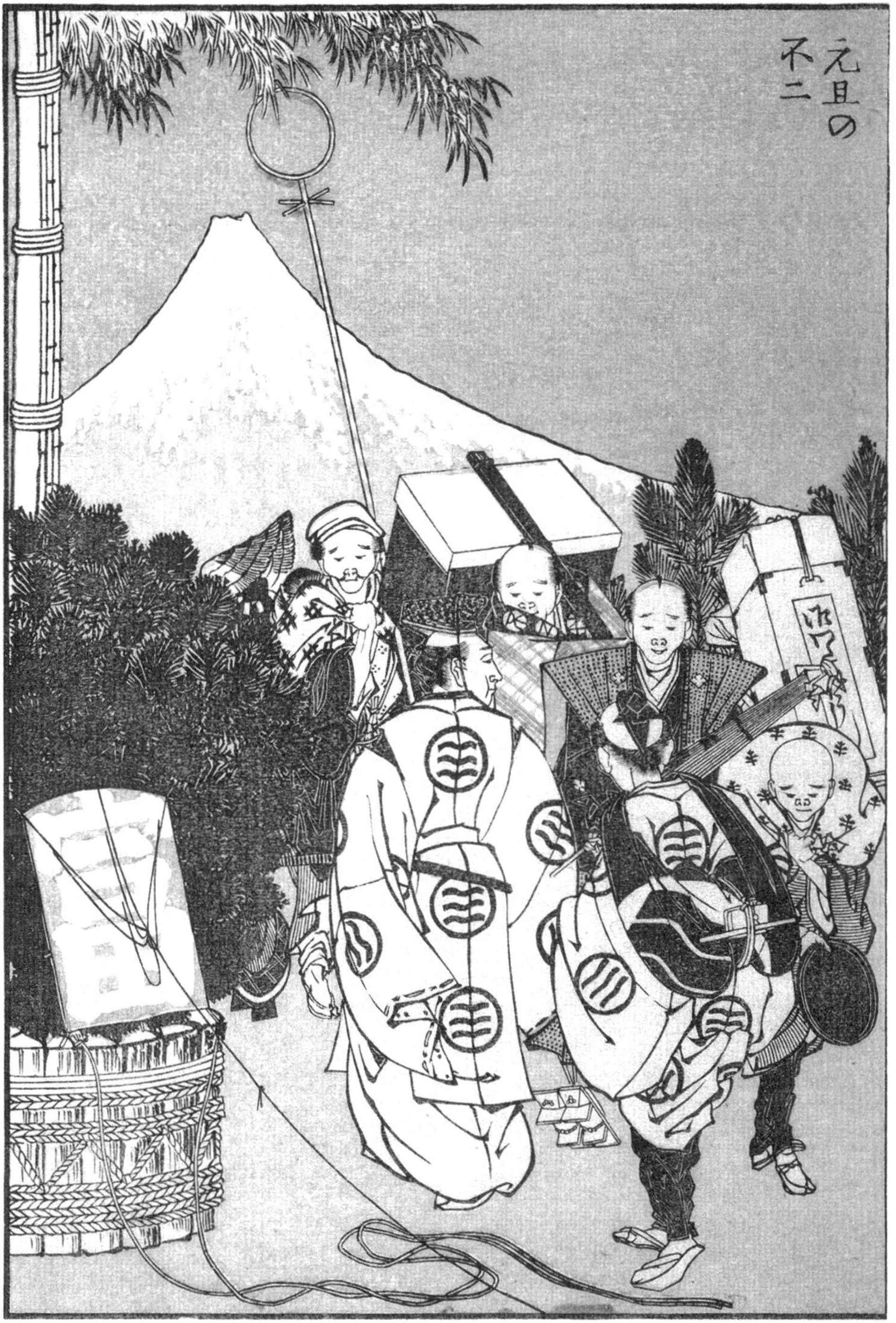

121 *Fuji on New Year's Day*

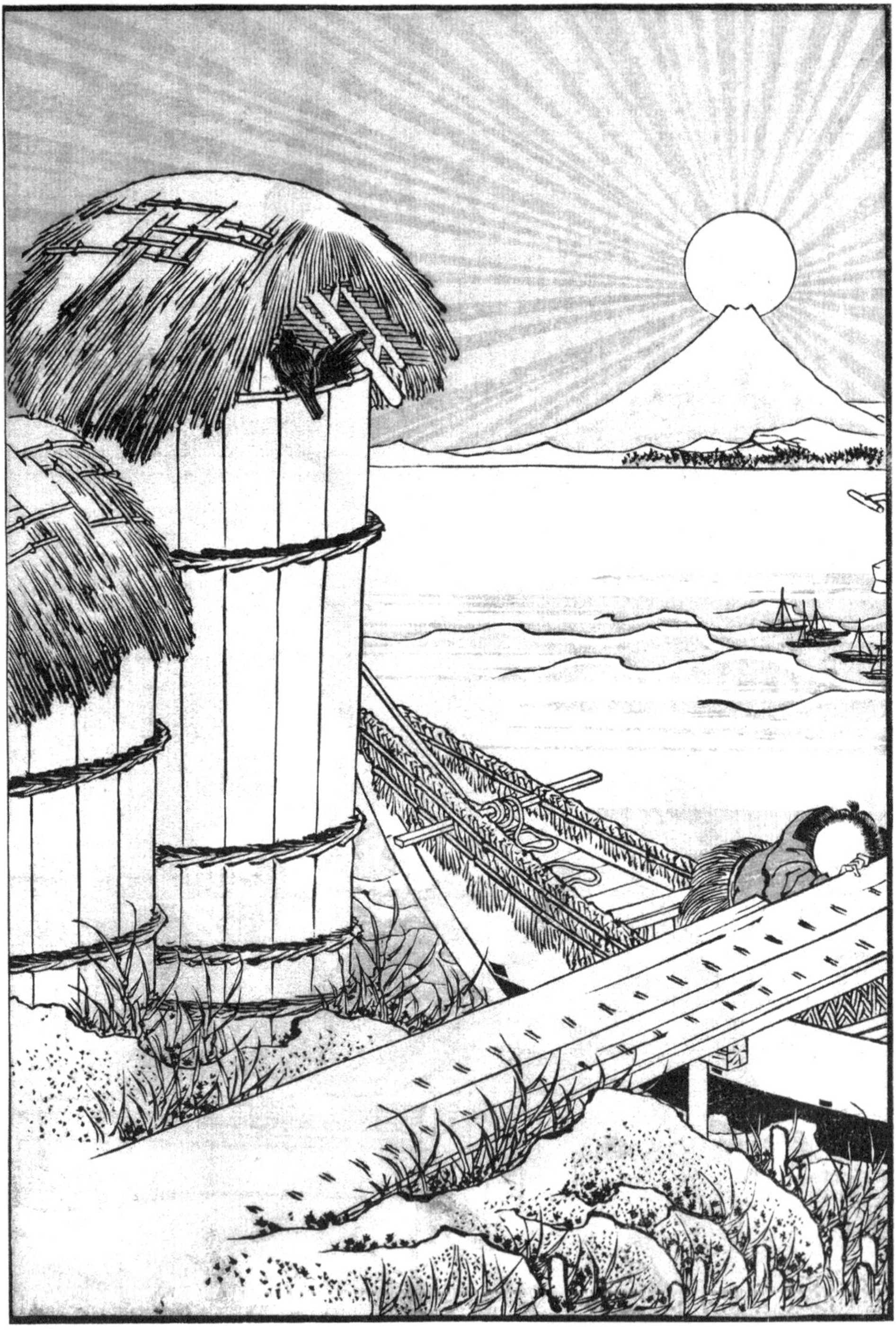

Fuji as a Mirror Stand

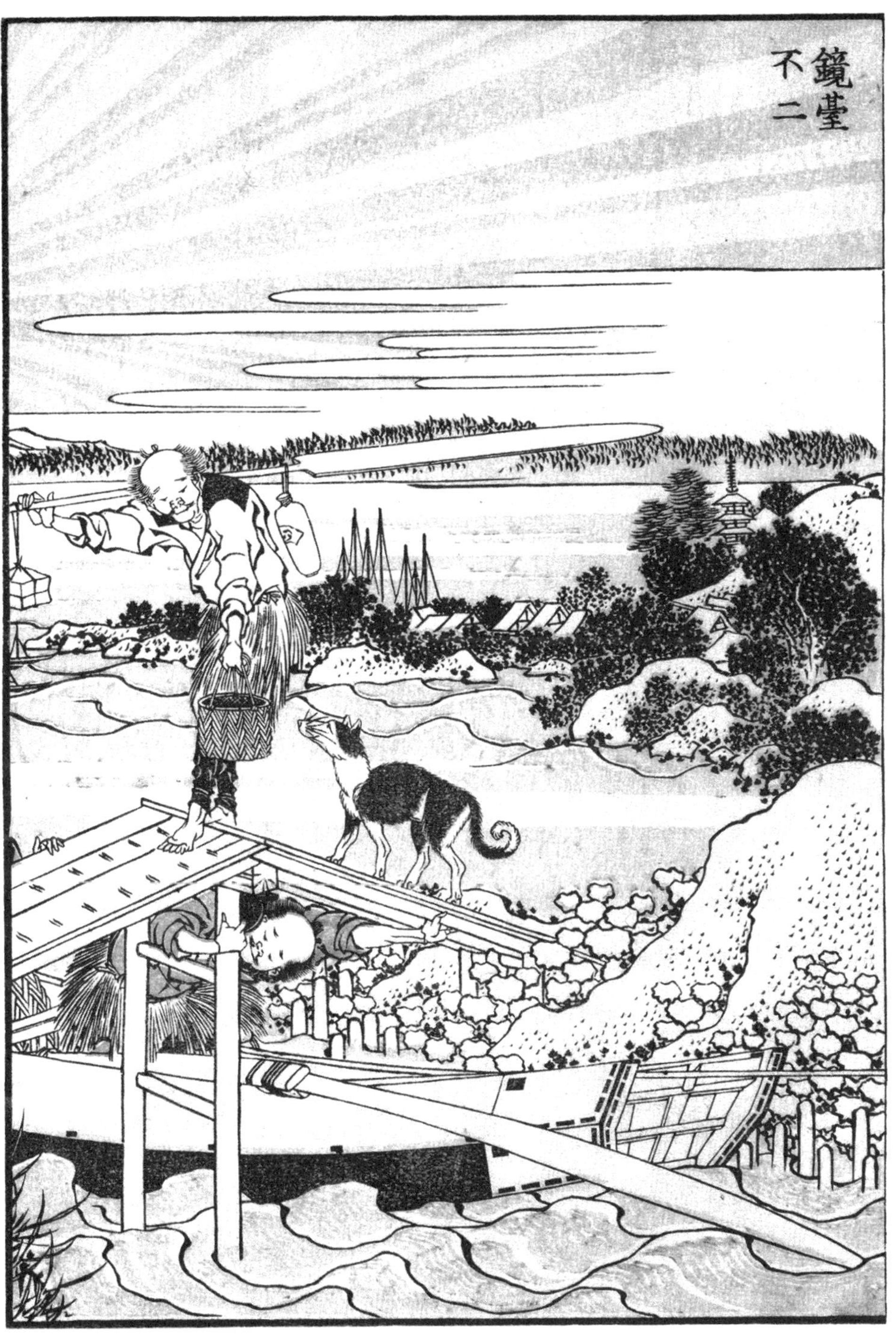

鏡臺
不二

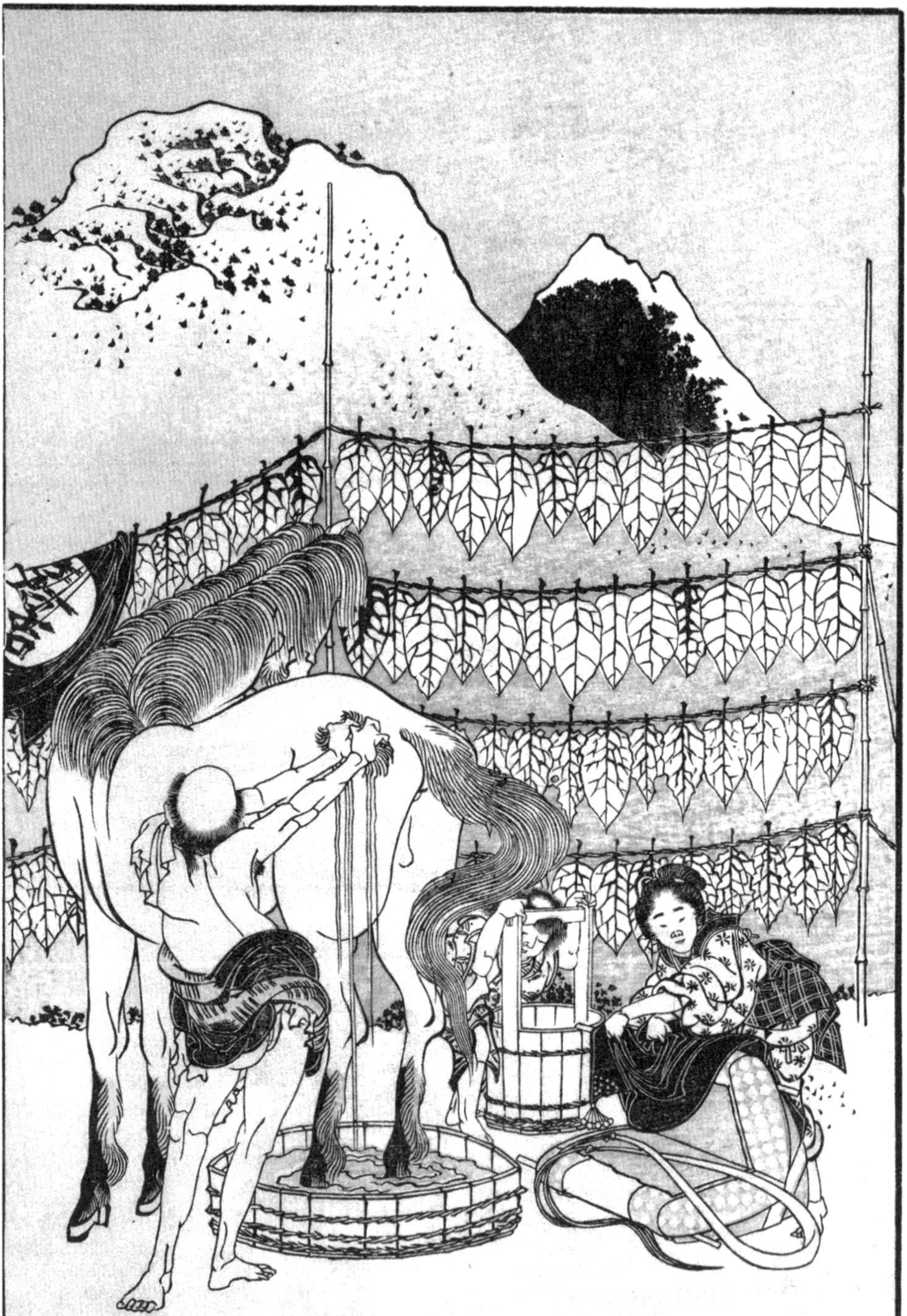

Fuji from Behind

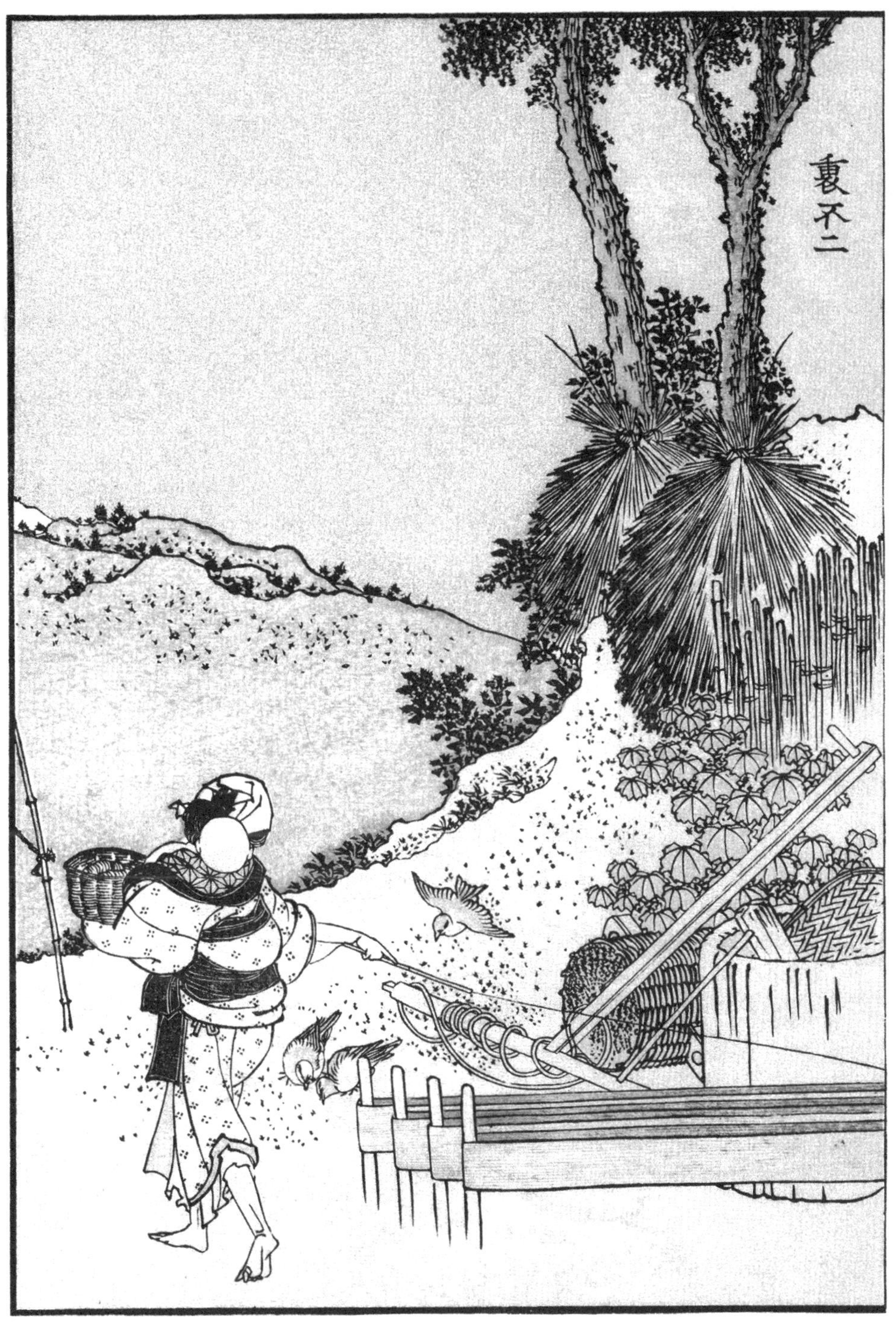
裏不二

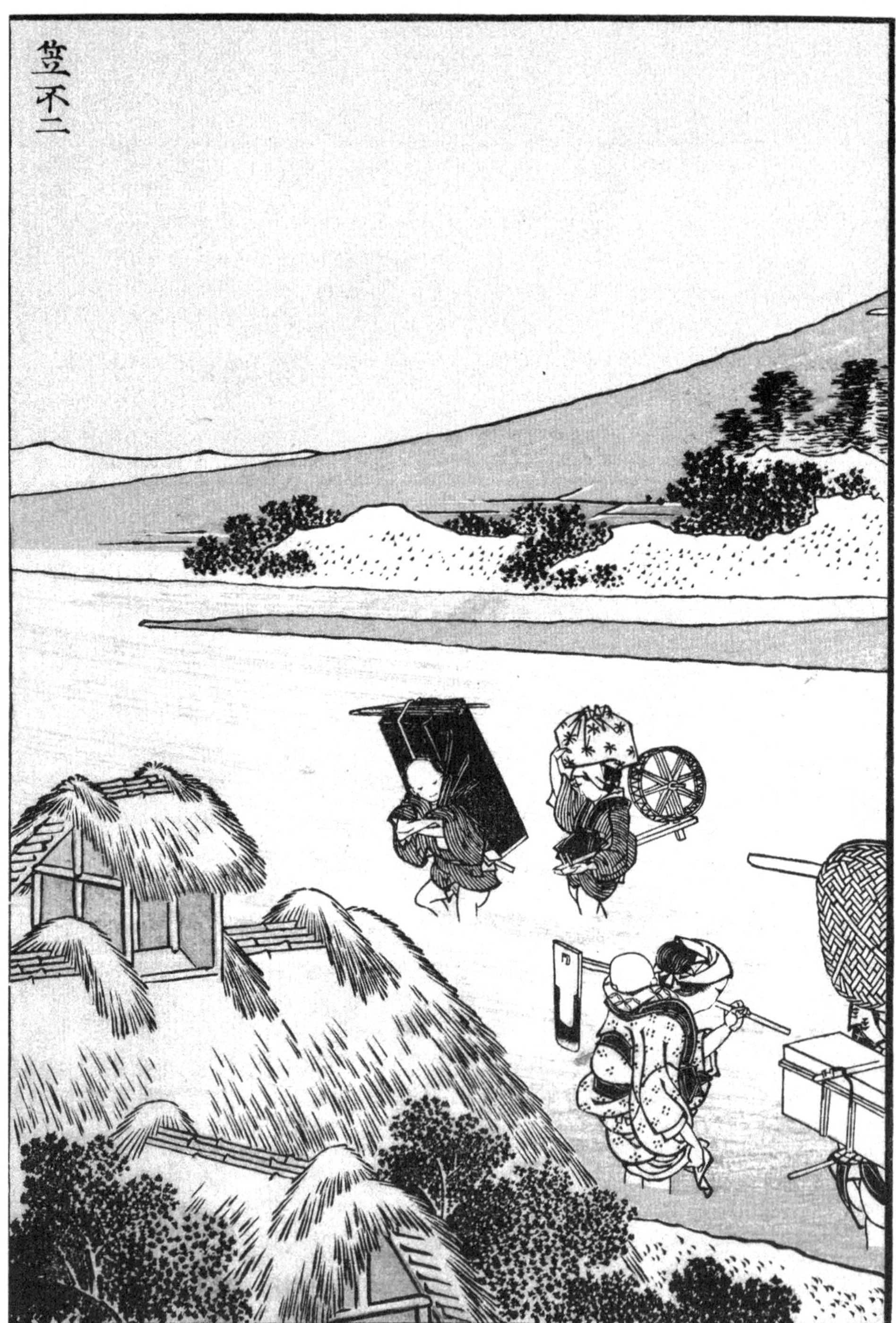

Fuji with a Hat

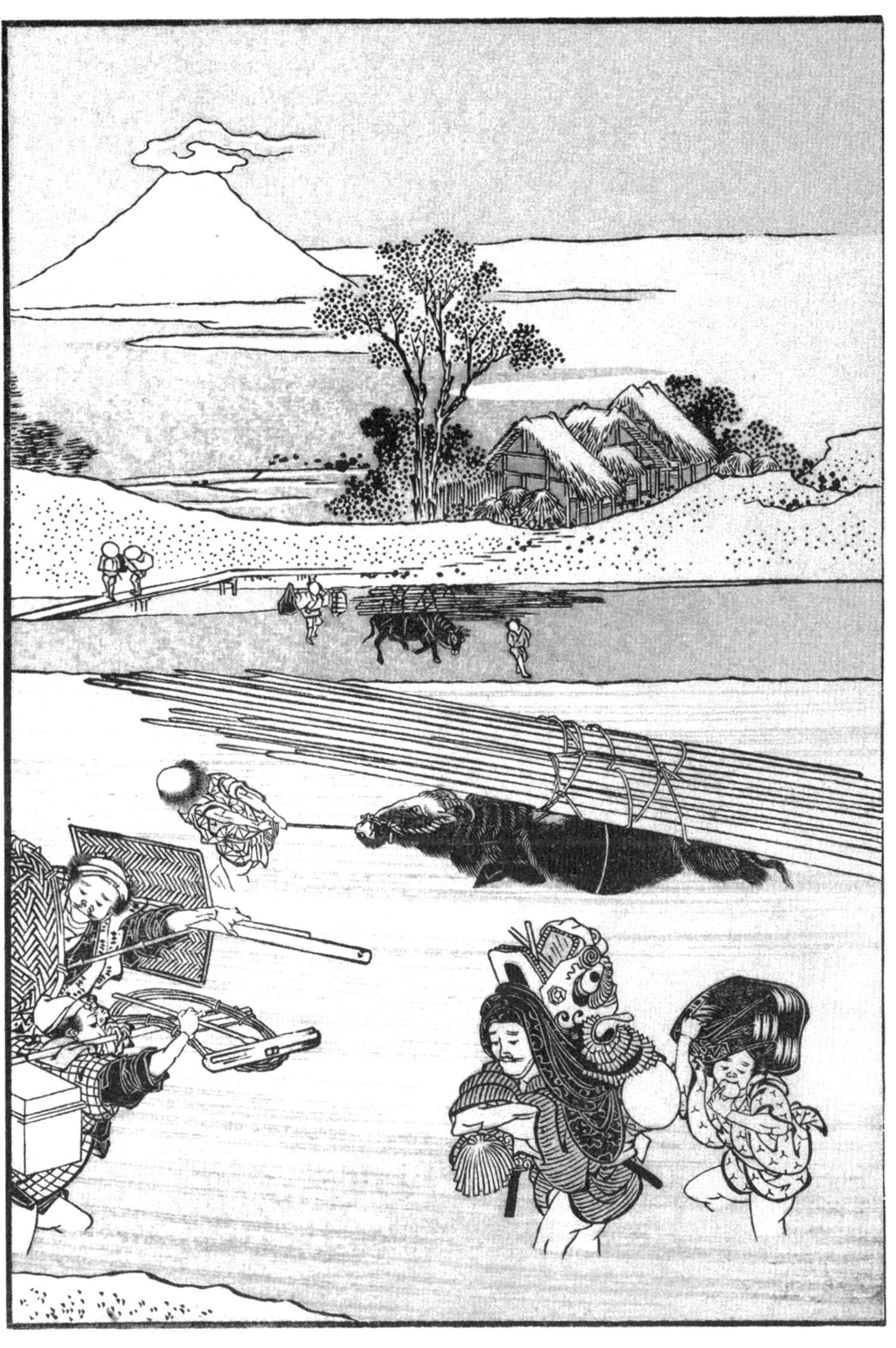

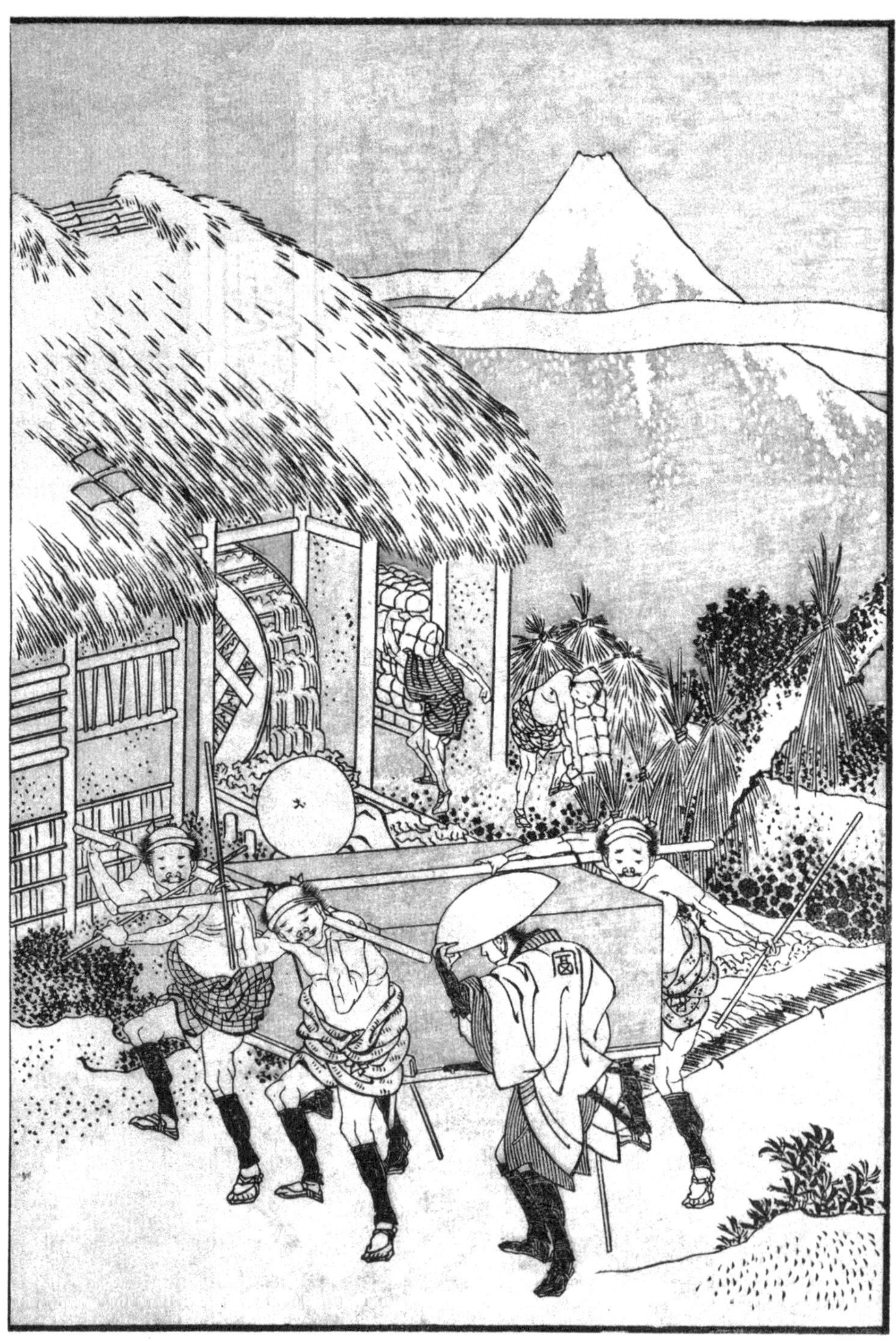

Fuji with a Belt

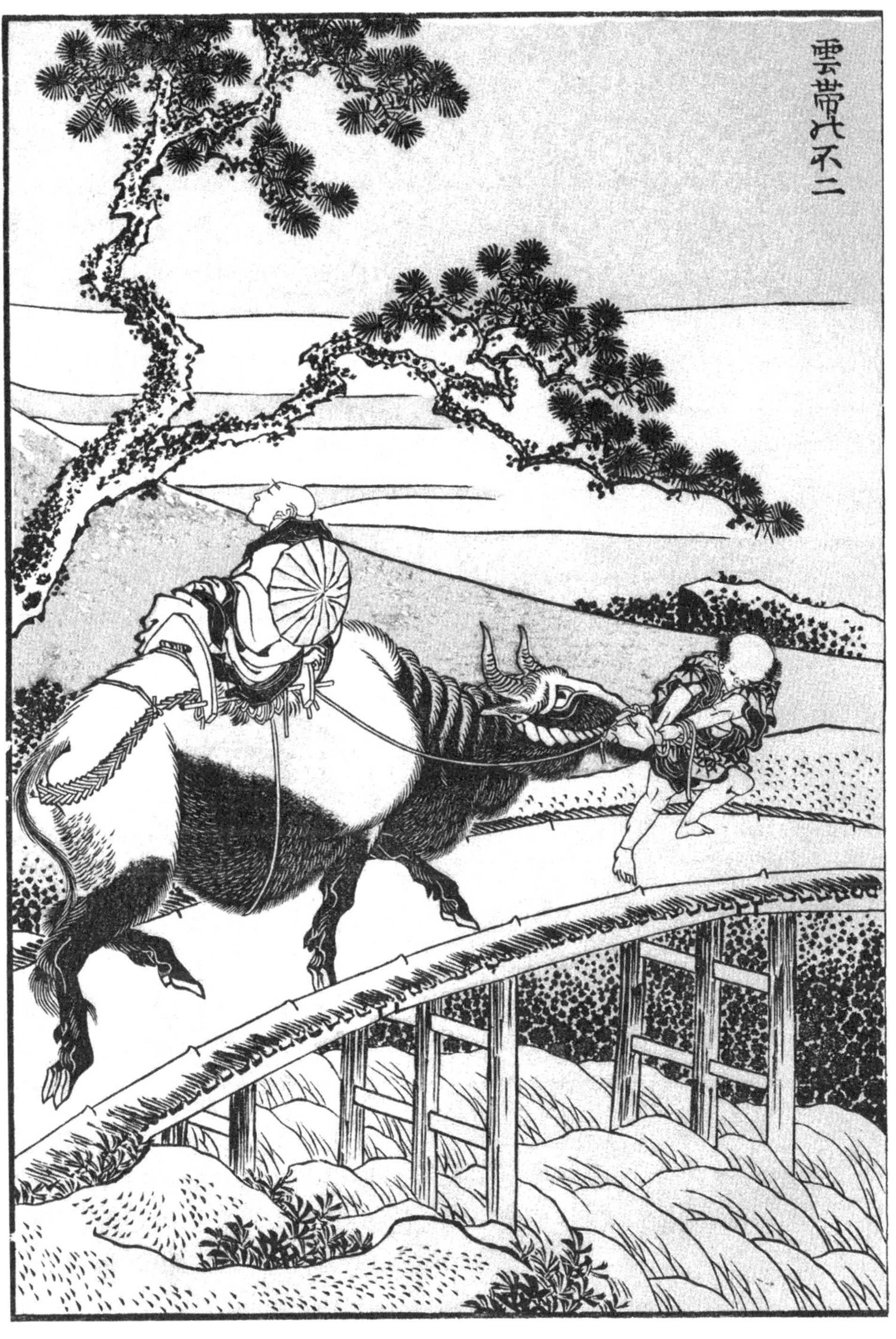

雲帯比不二

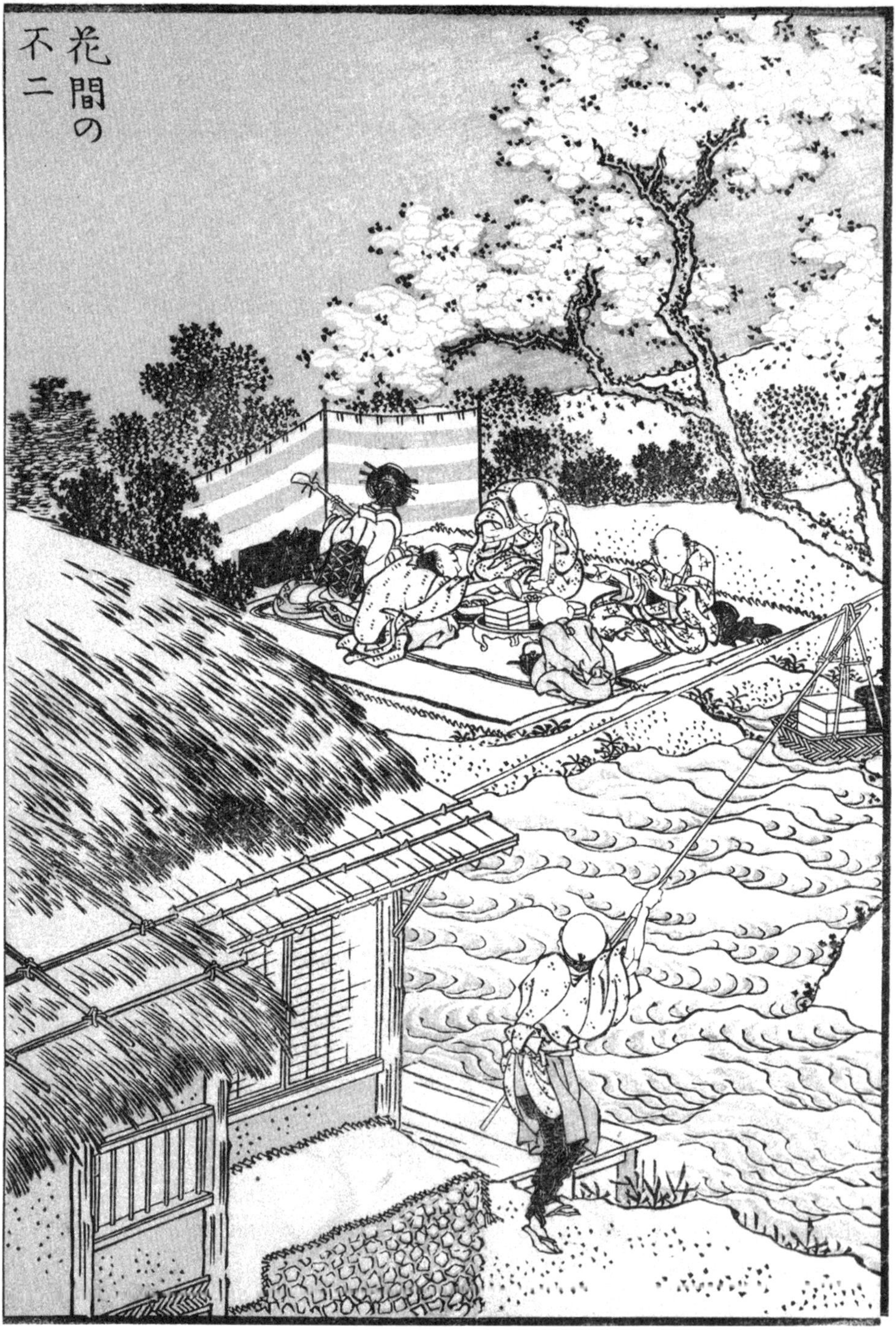

Fuji Through Flowers

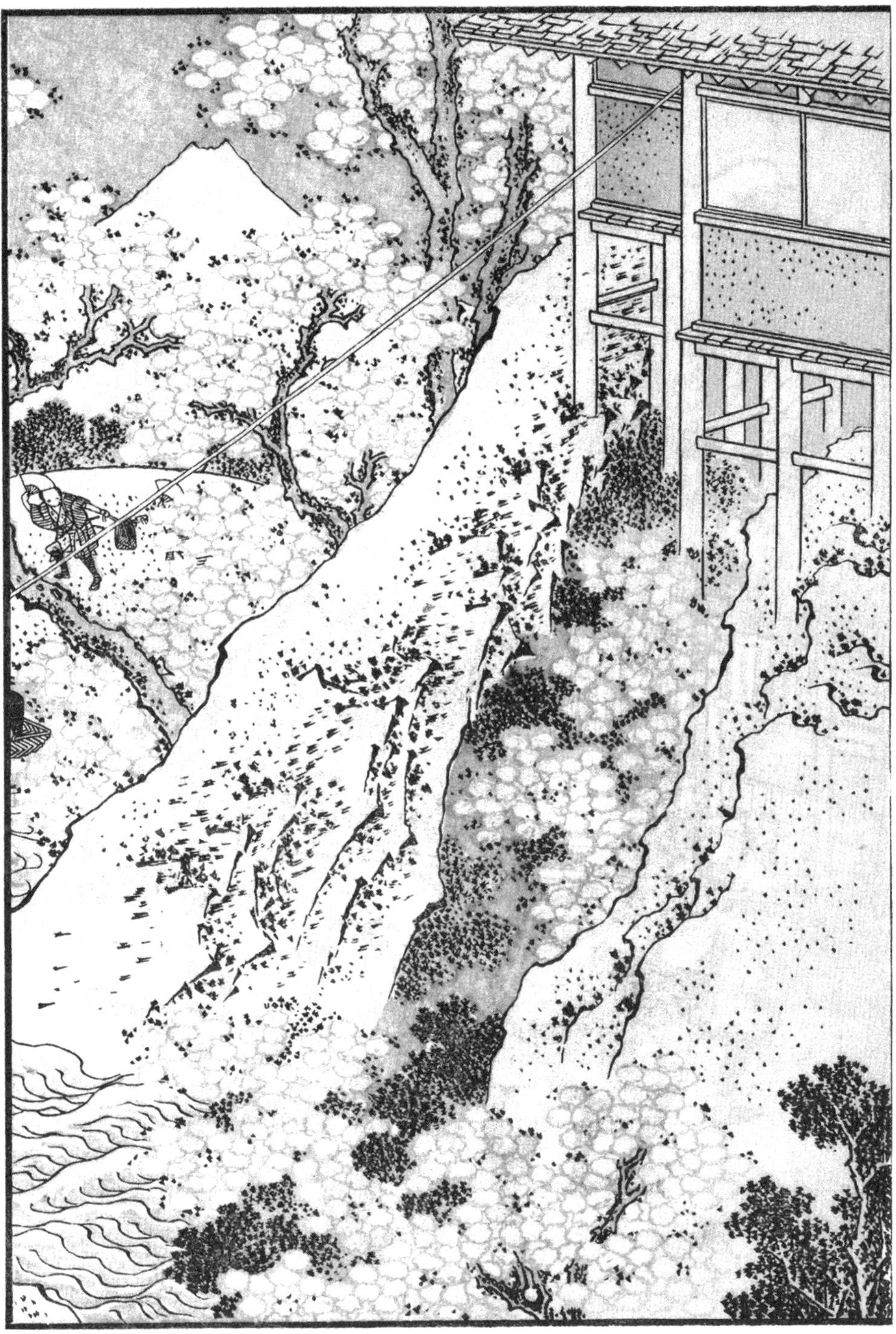

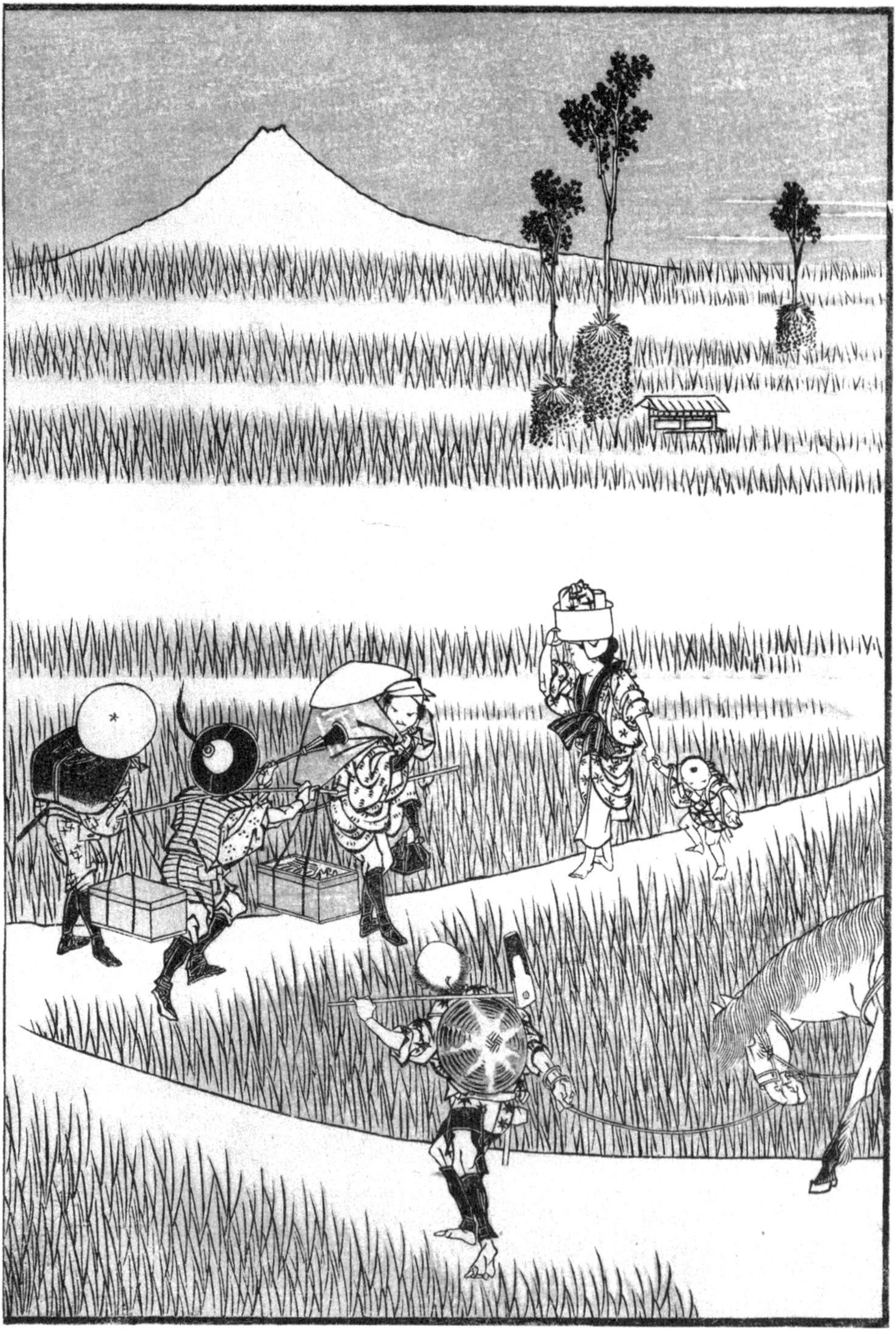

127   *Fuji in a Good Harvest*

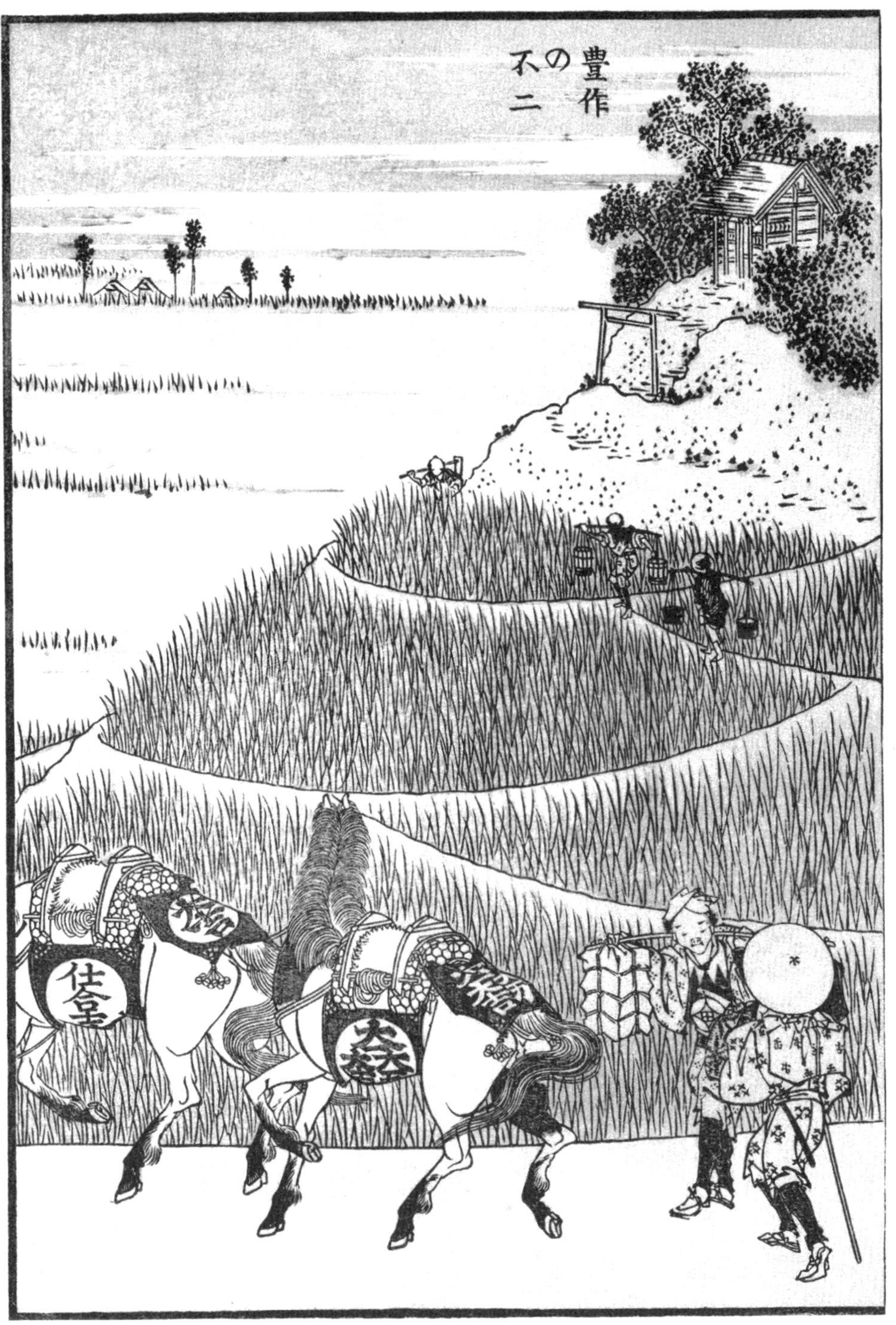
豊作の不二

七十五齢　前北齋爲一改　画狂老人卍筆

己六才より物の形状を写の癖ありて半百の此より數々画圖を顕はすといへども七十年前画く所は實に取るに足るものなし七十三才にして稍々禽獸虫魚の骨格草木の出生を悟り得たり故に八十才にしては益々進み九十才にして猶其奥意を極め一百歳にして正に神妙ならん歟百有十歳にしては一点一格にして生るがごとくならん願くは長壽の君子予が言の妄ならざるを見たまふべし

画狂老人卍述

剞劂　江川留吉　五雲亭

冨嶽百景　初編既刊　二編近刊　三編全近刻

名橋百景　近刻

異草百花撰　近刻

百家奇術　同

狂画草筆百眼　同

百壽百福　同

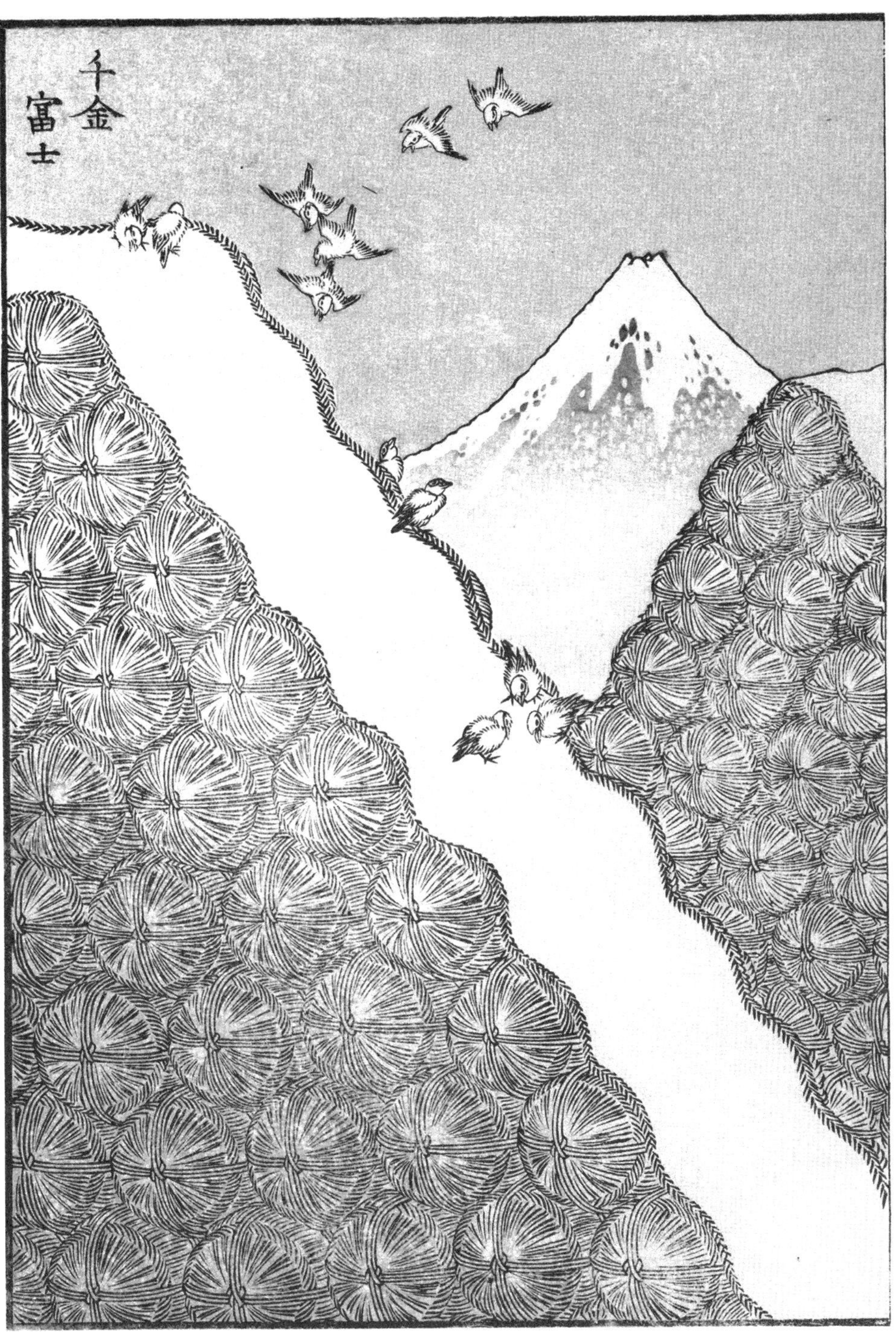

 Fuji Bountiful

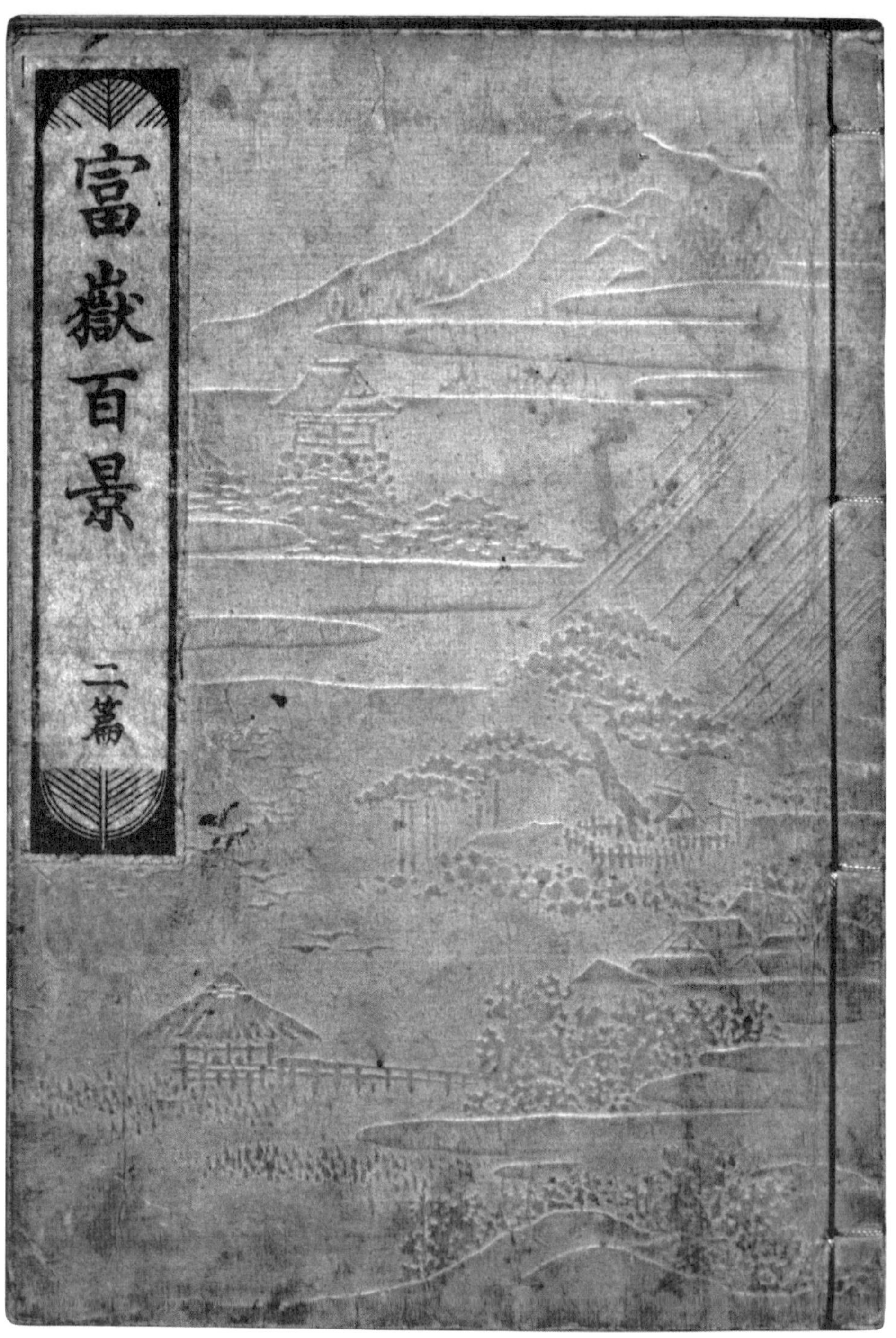

One Hundred Views of Mount Fuji, Volume 2: cover

漁家百景　近刻

圓方／長短　一百自在圖會　近刻

月下百景　同

百馬百牛　同

農家百景　同

百禽百獸　同

天保五甲午年春三月發行

尾州名古屋　永樂屋東四郎

江戶麴町四丁目　角丸屋甚助

金馬喰町二丁目　西村與八

仝　西村祐藏

書林

富士之為山也，其形嵬然，其色蒼
磨銀鑾而為澄，不峙而似一面玲
瓏如芙蓉之出水，而高跨君山撥之
巔，是其所以冠天下也。若夫日
出而皎潔，夕陽薄暮，蒼翠微
茫，變其色，遠望之矣，望至於煙
秋風雲霽，雨歇則其朝暮之變化矣

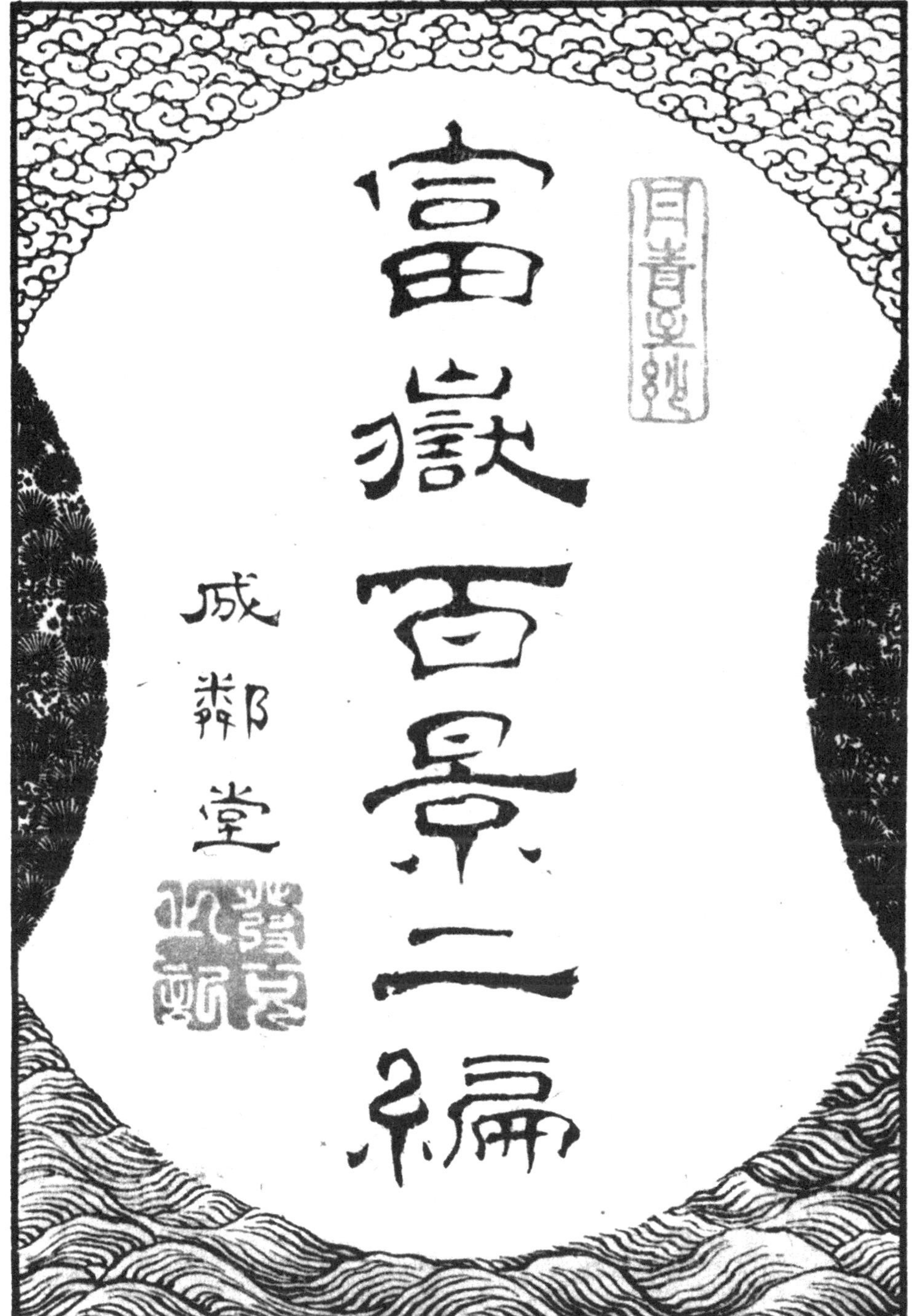
富嶽百景二編
成鄰堂

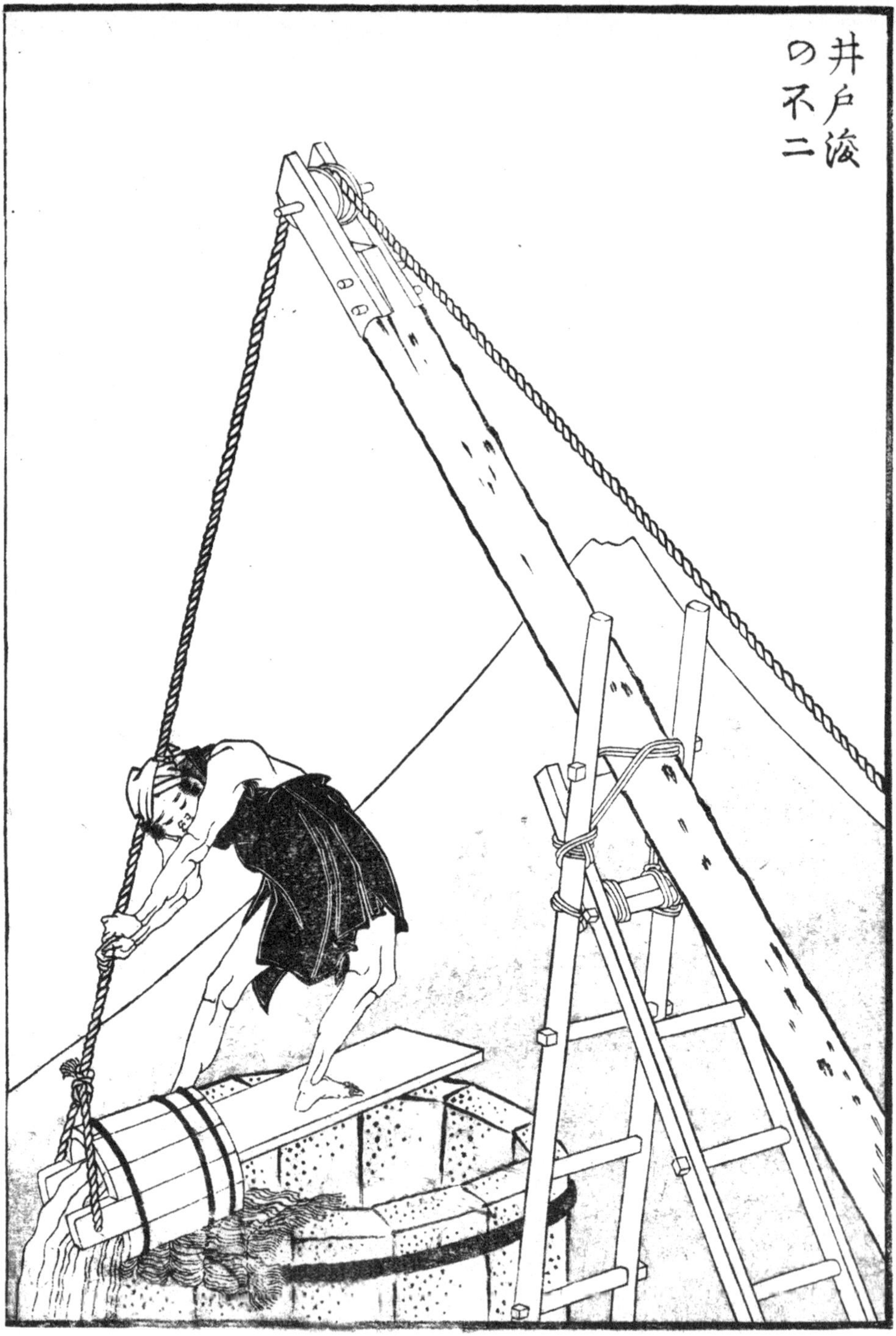

129 *Well-Cleaning Fuji*

冨嶽百景図百景十精工之図
百変之妙観右盡之見矣
天保六乙未正月
廬山孝

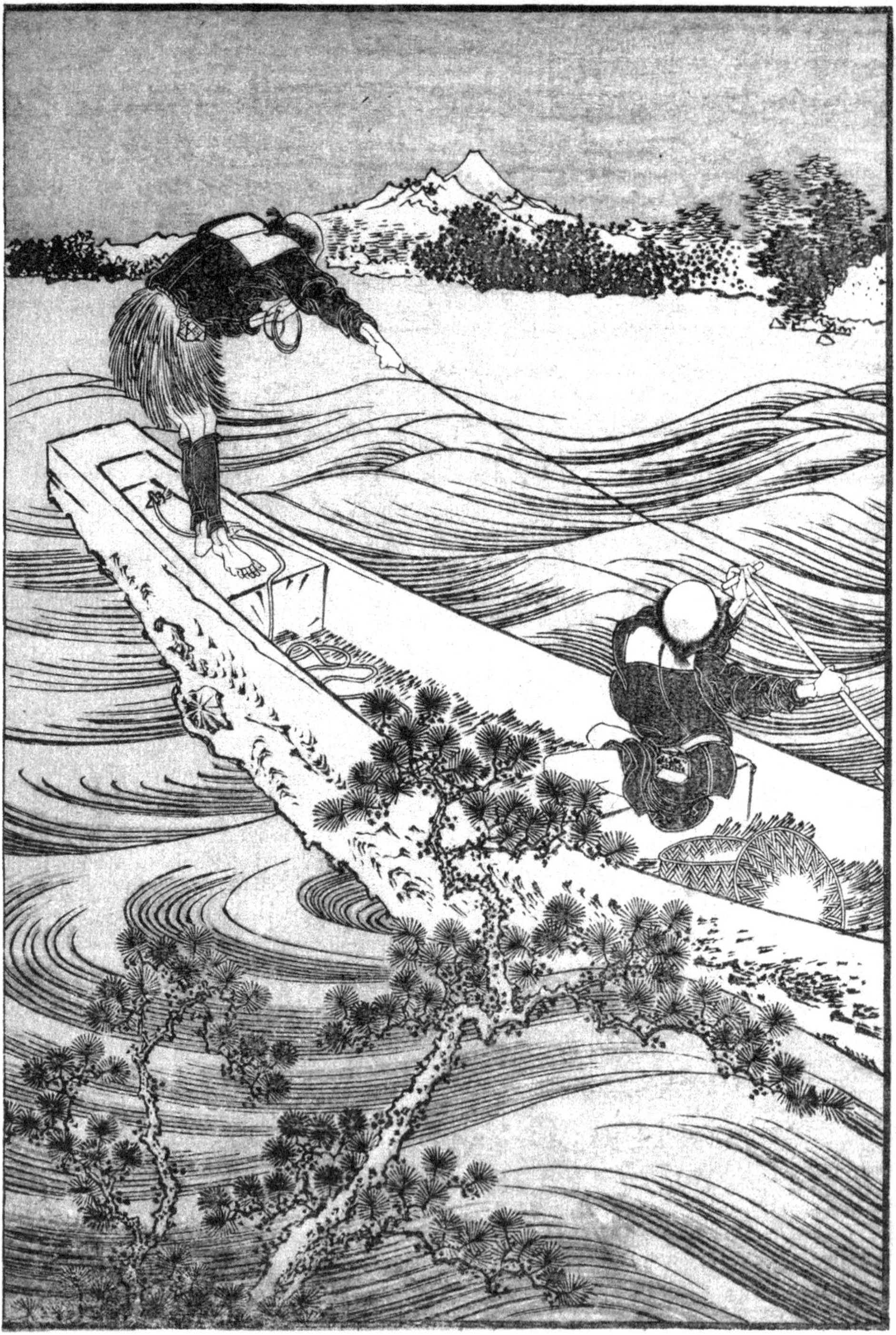

Fuji and Yatsugatake in Shinshū

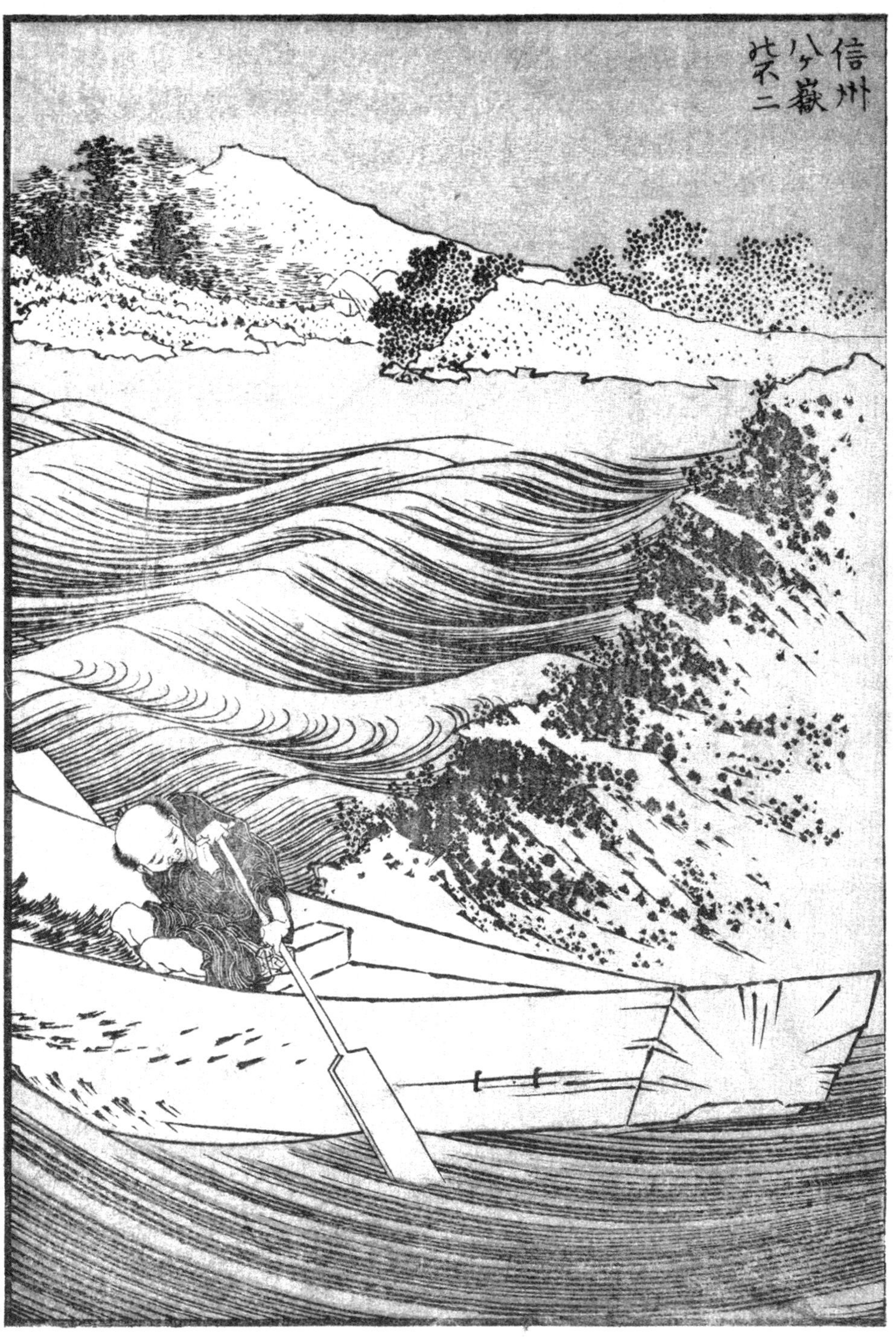
信州
八ヶ
嶽
芙
不
二

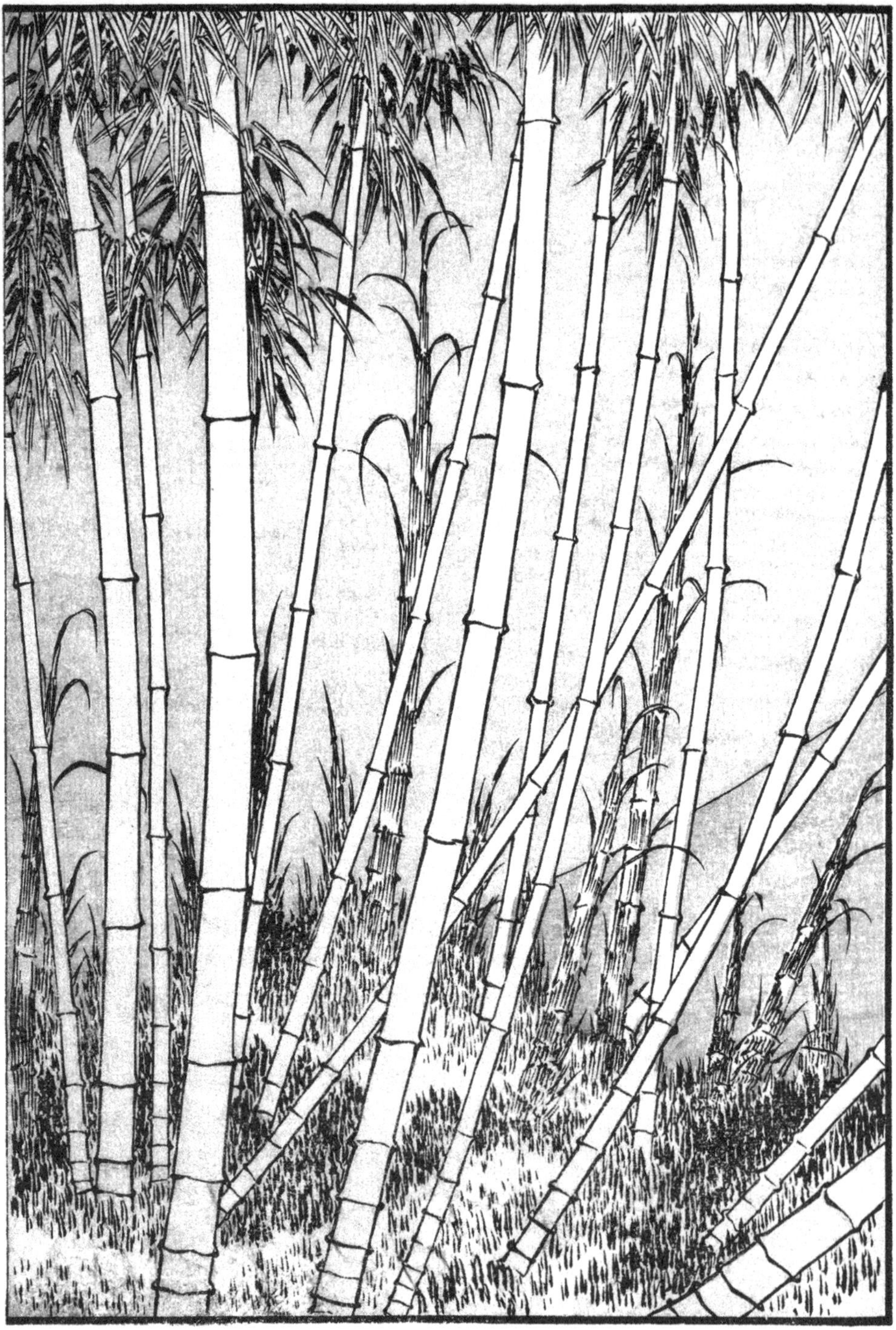

Fuji of the Bamboo Grove

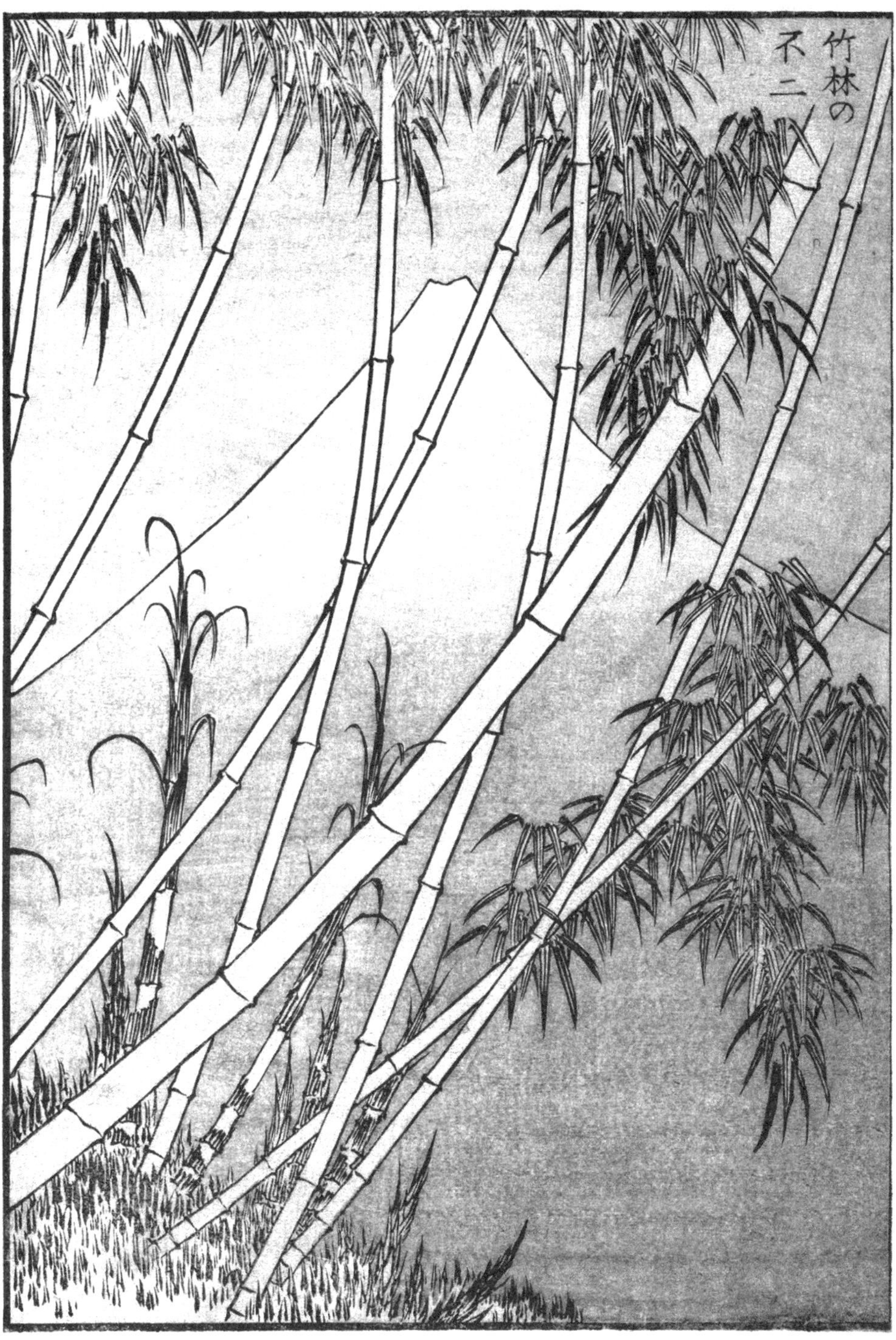
竹林の
不
二

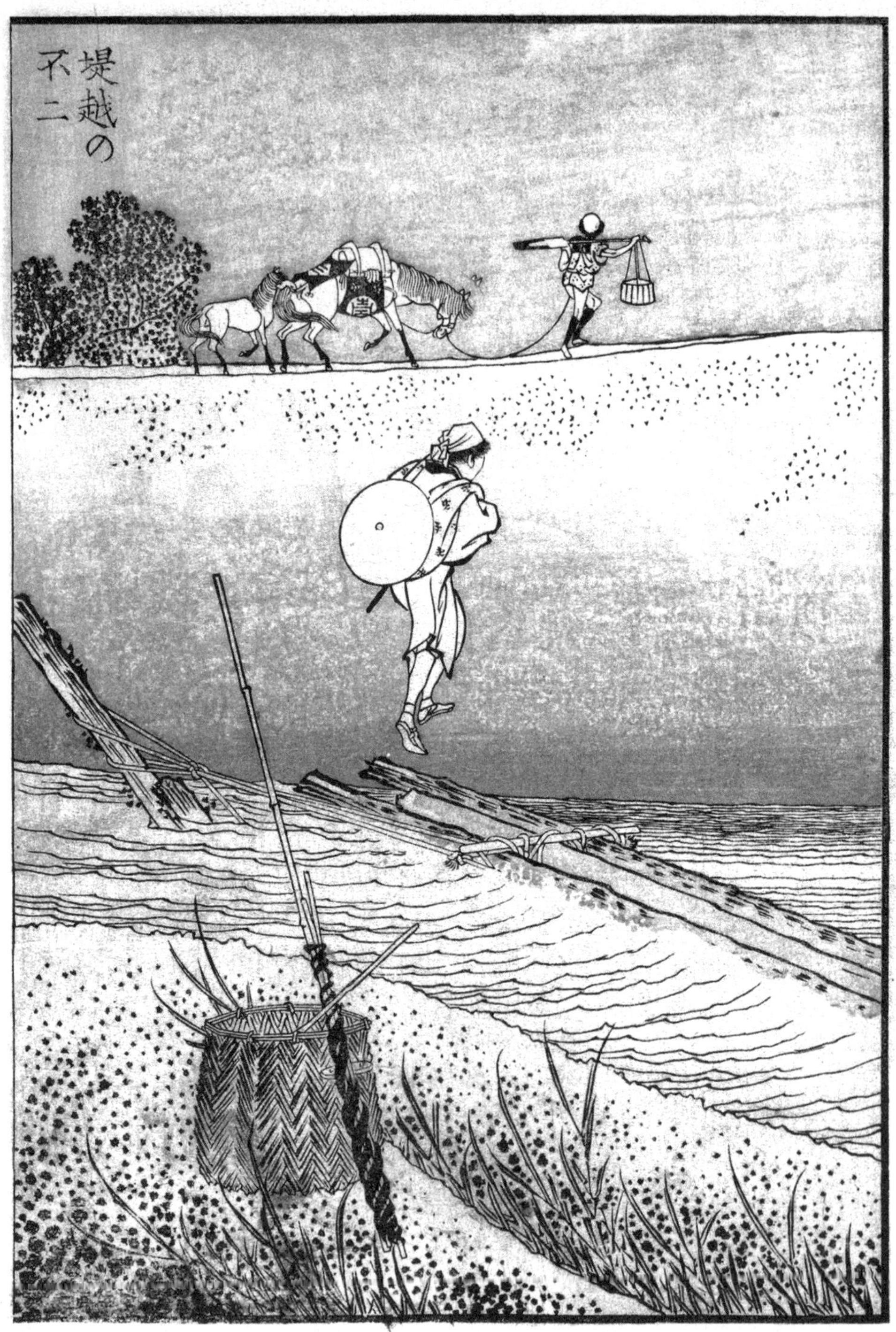

Fuji over a Bank

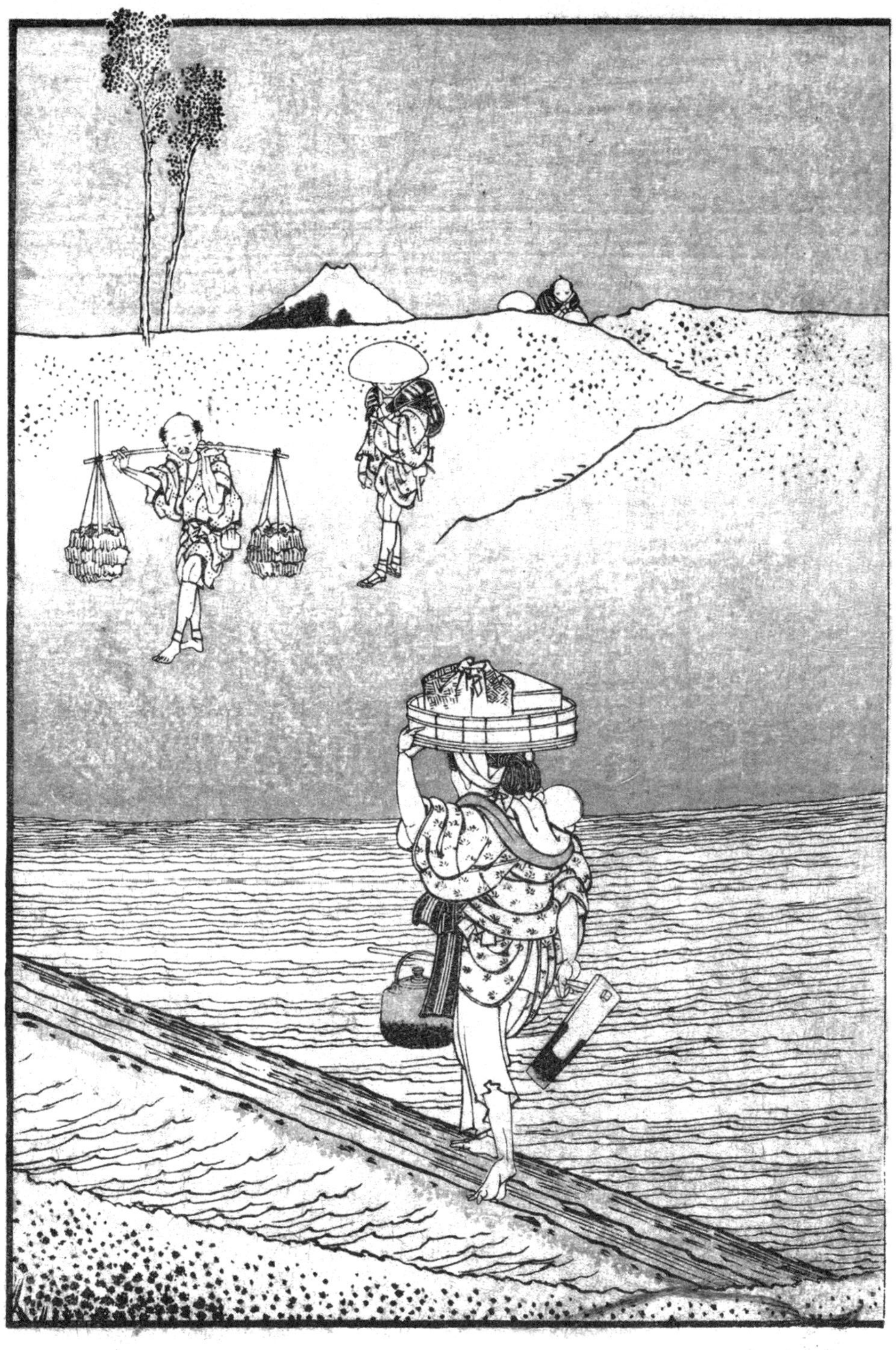

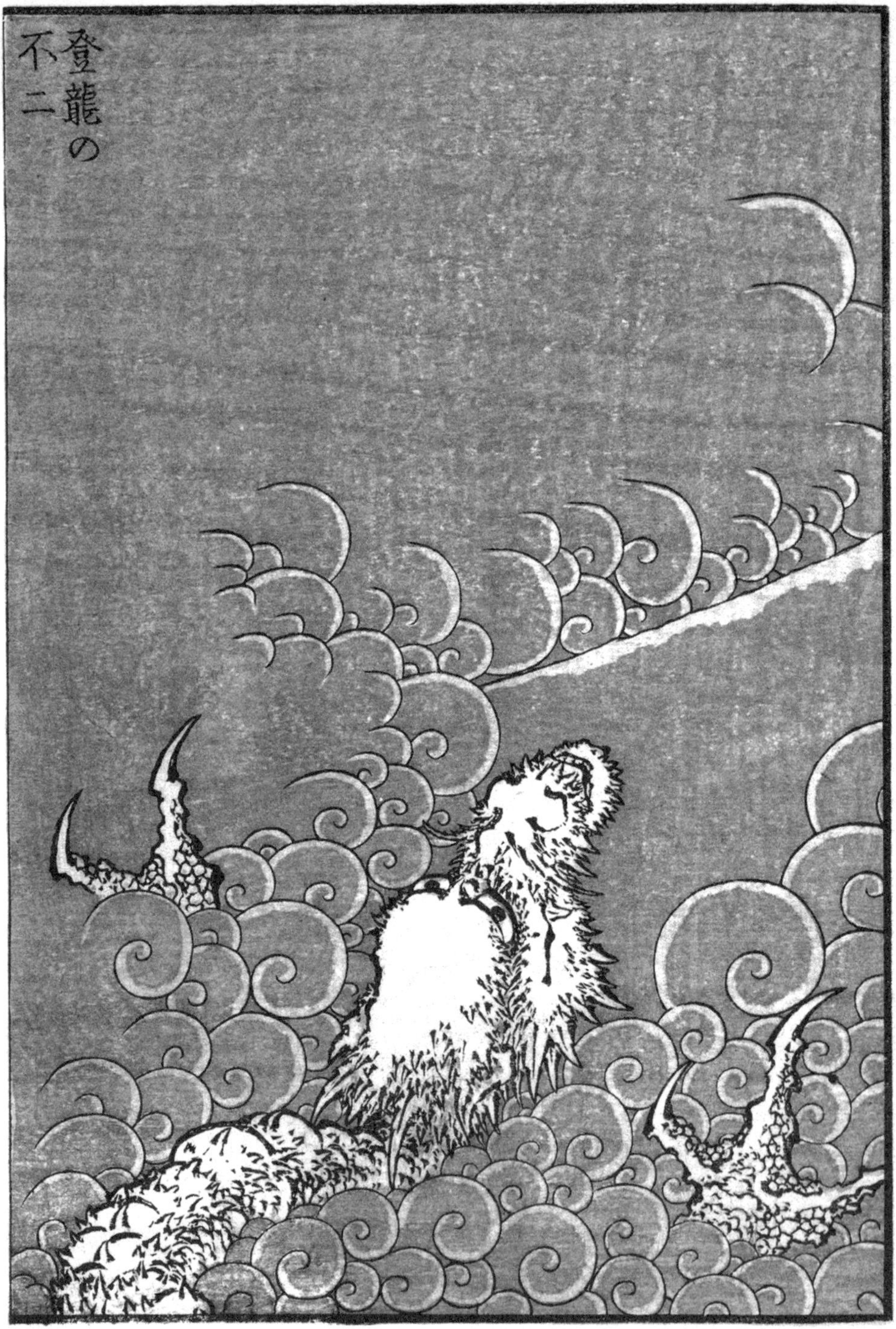

Fuji and Ascending Dragon

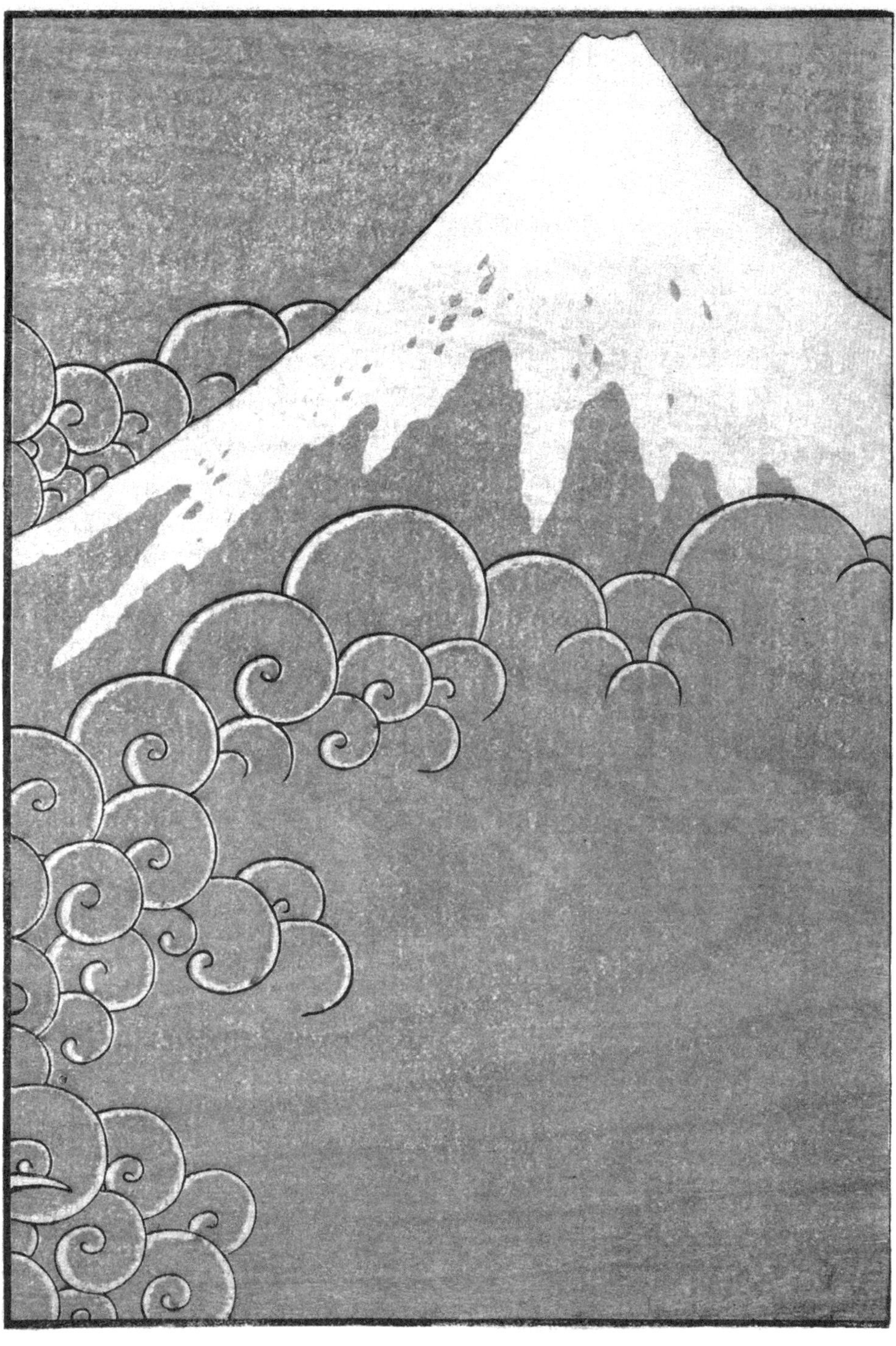

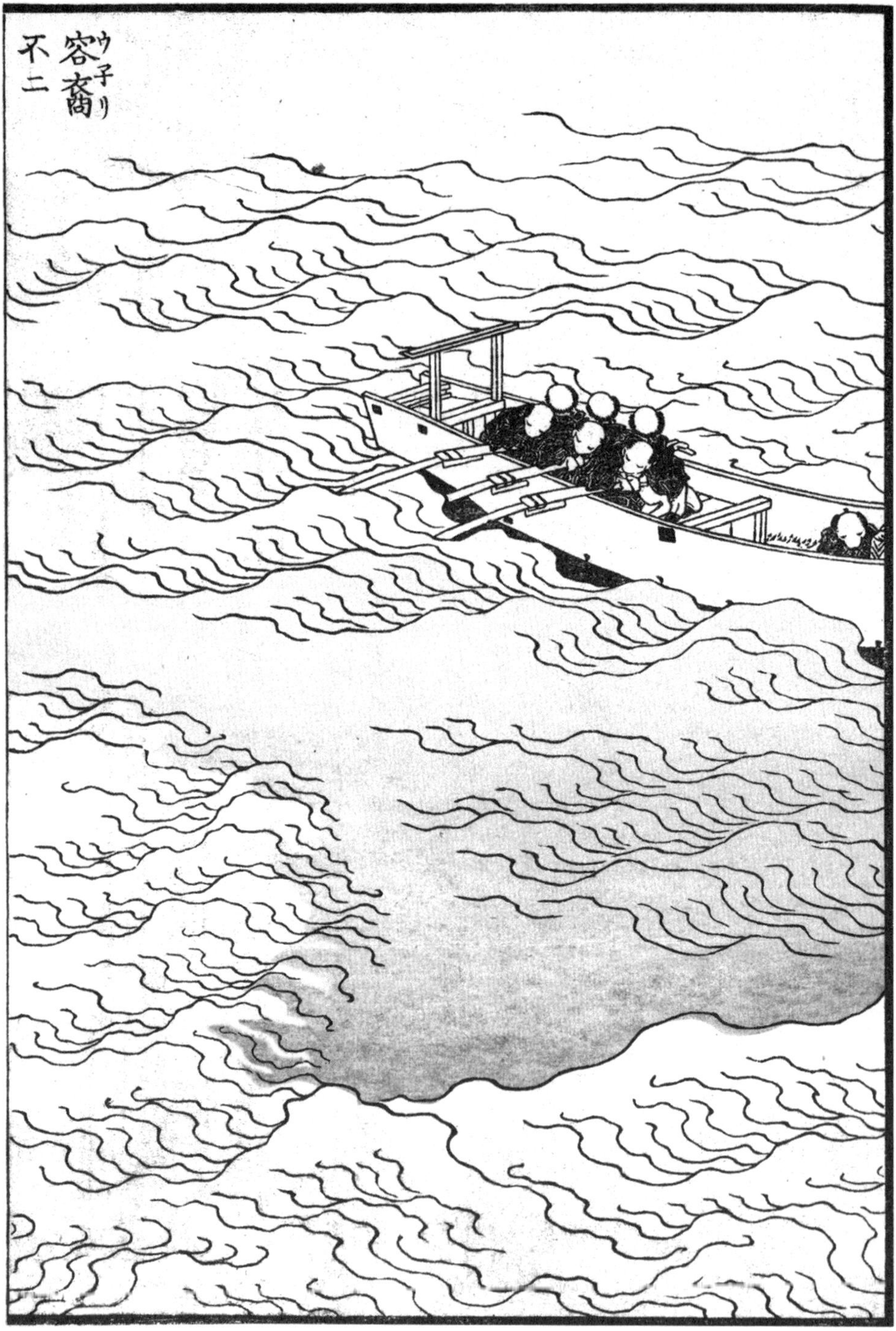

134

Fuji on the Swell

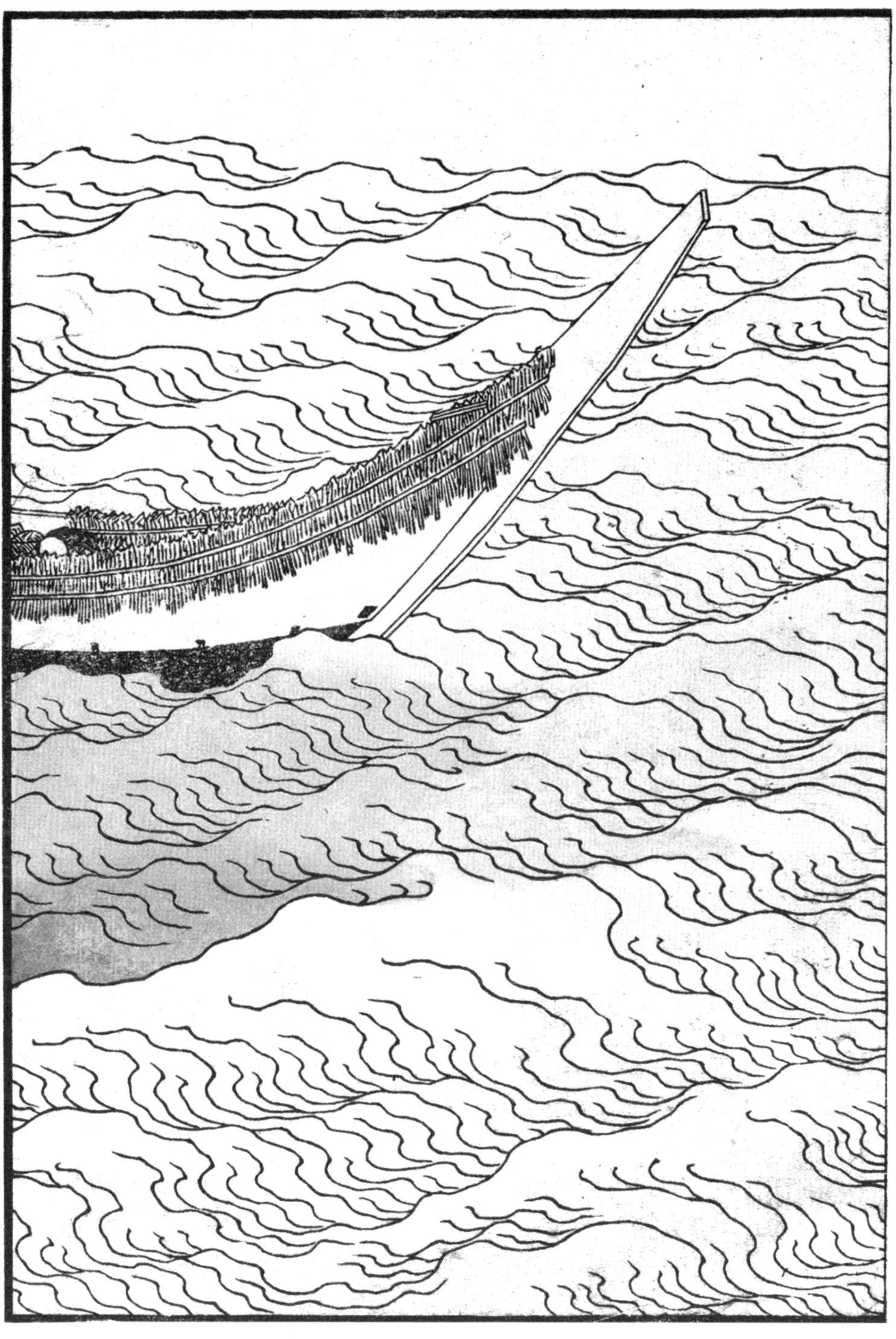

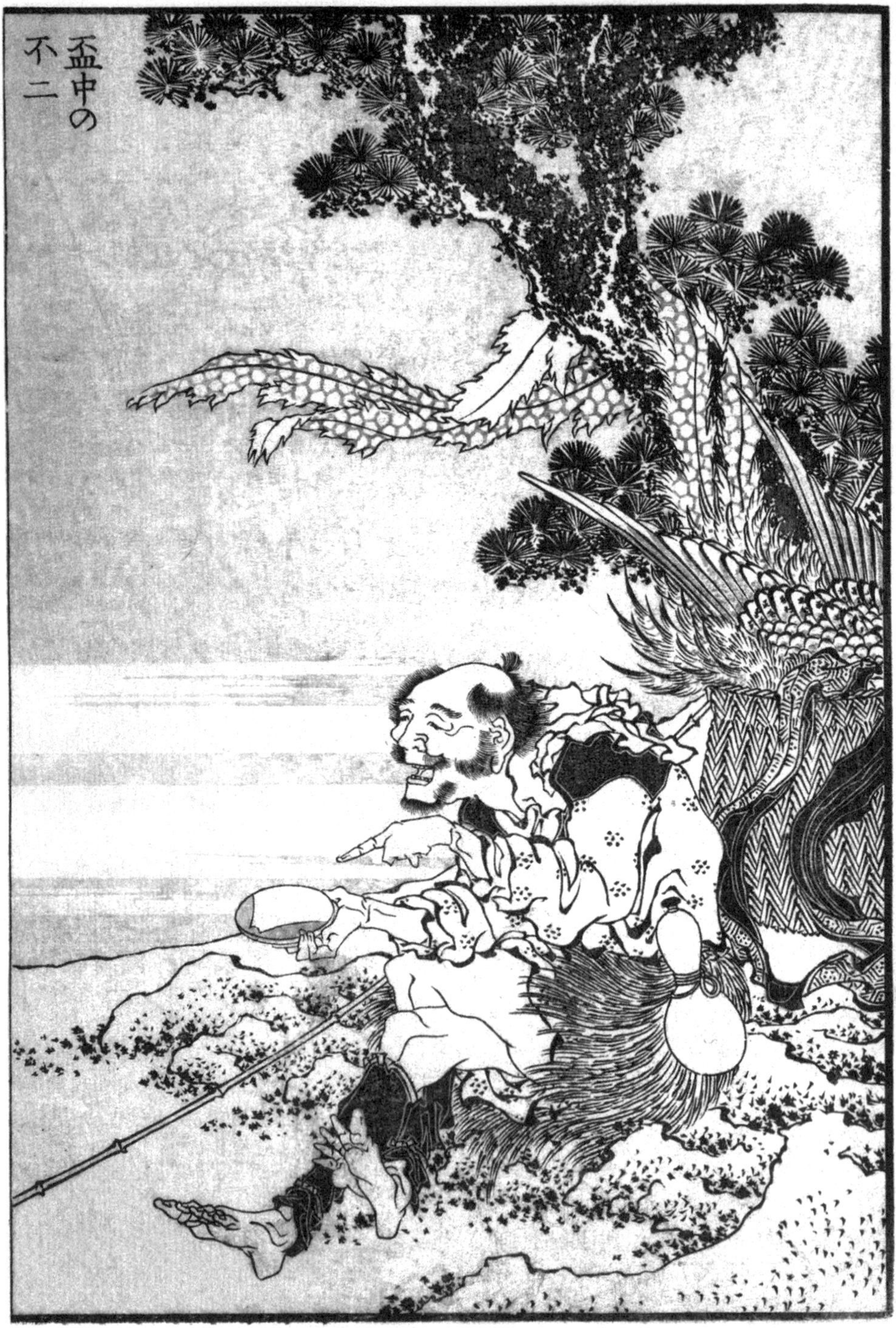

盃中の不二

135

Fuji in a Winecup

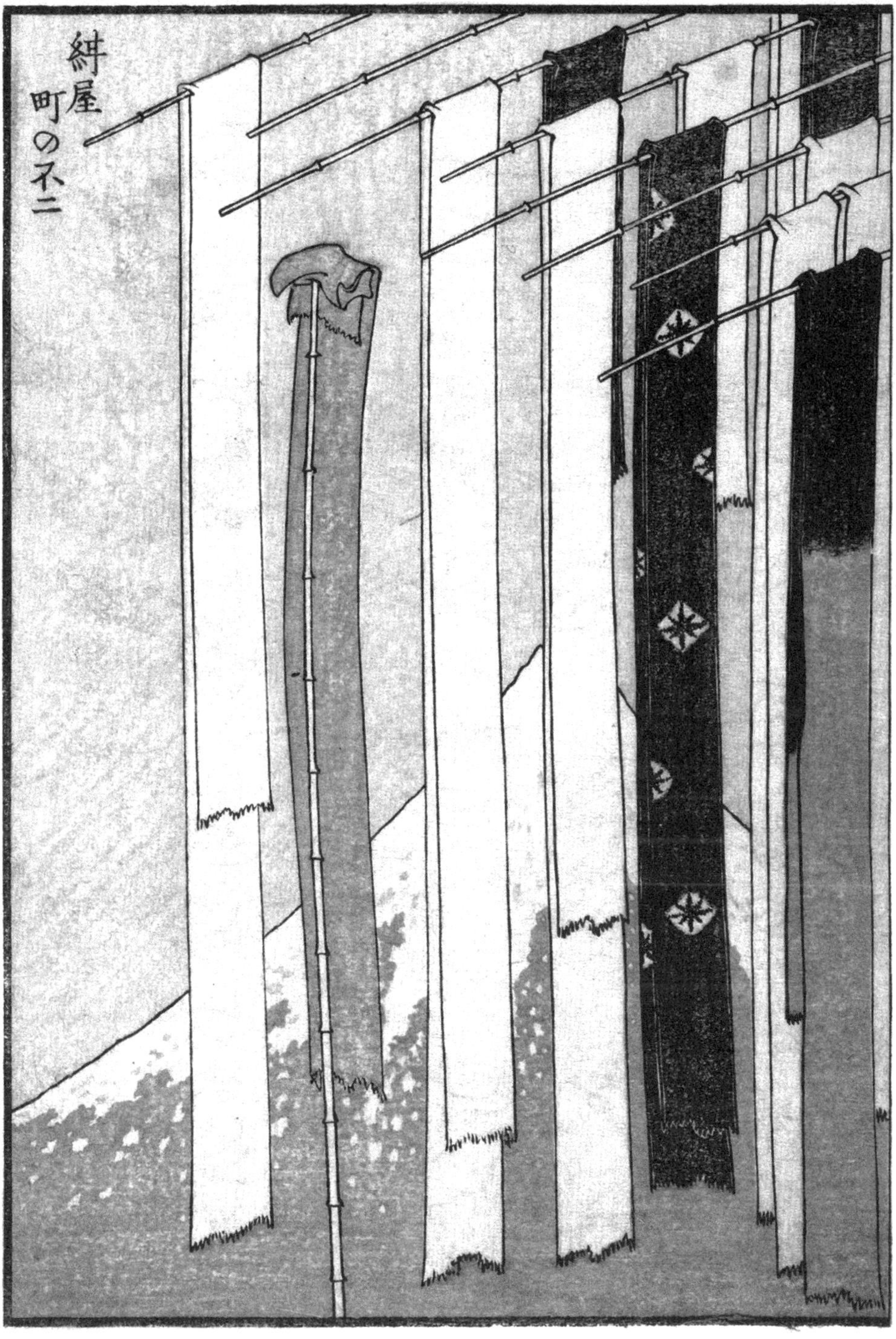

136   *Fuji Seen from the Dyers' Quarter*

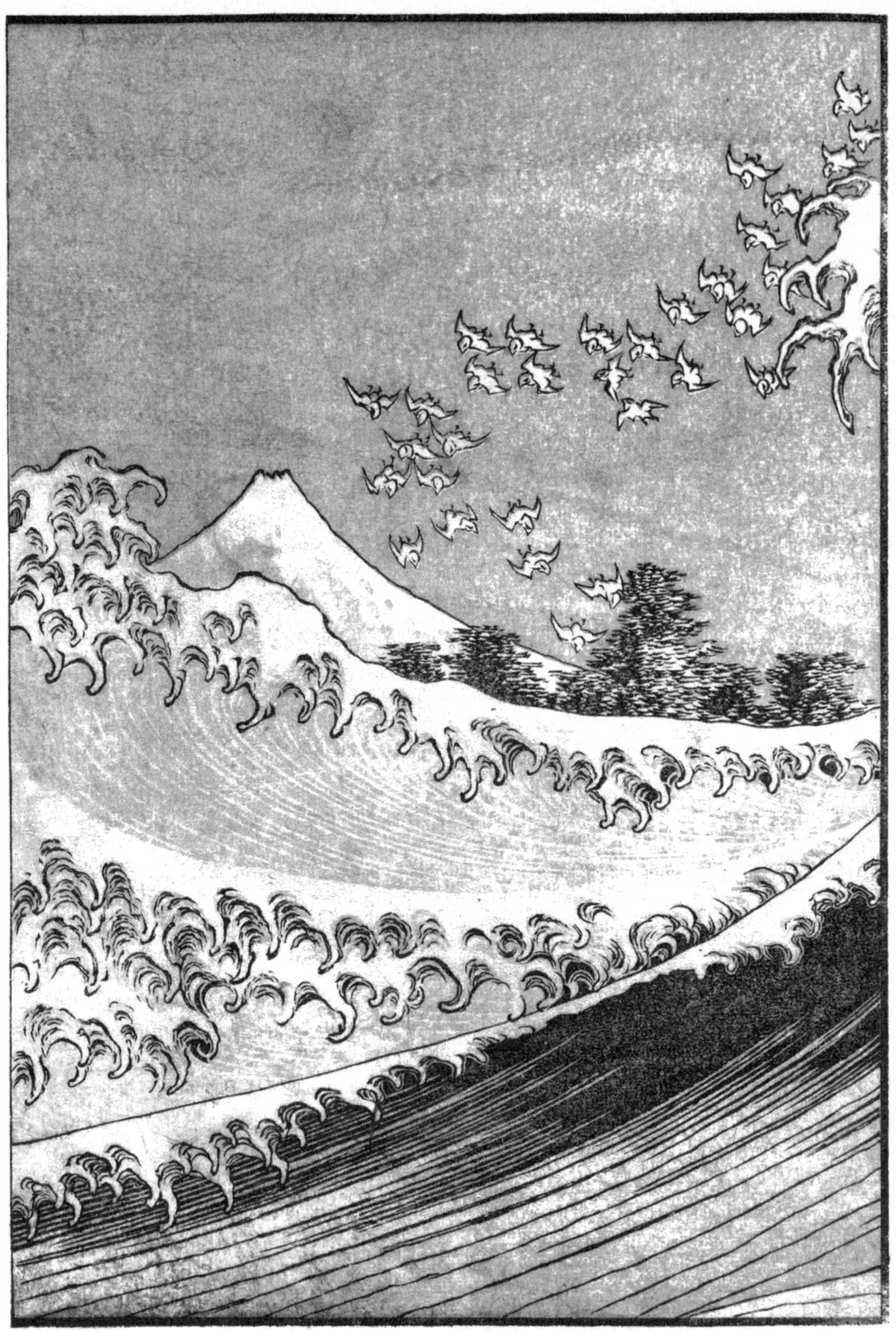

 Fuji at Sea

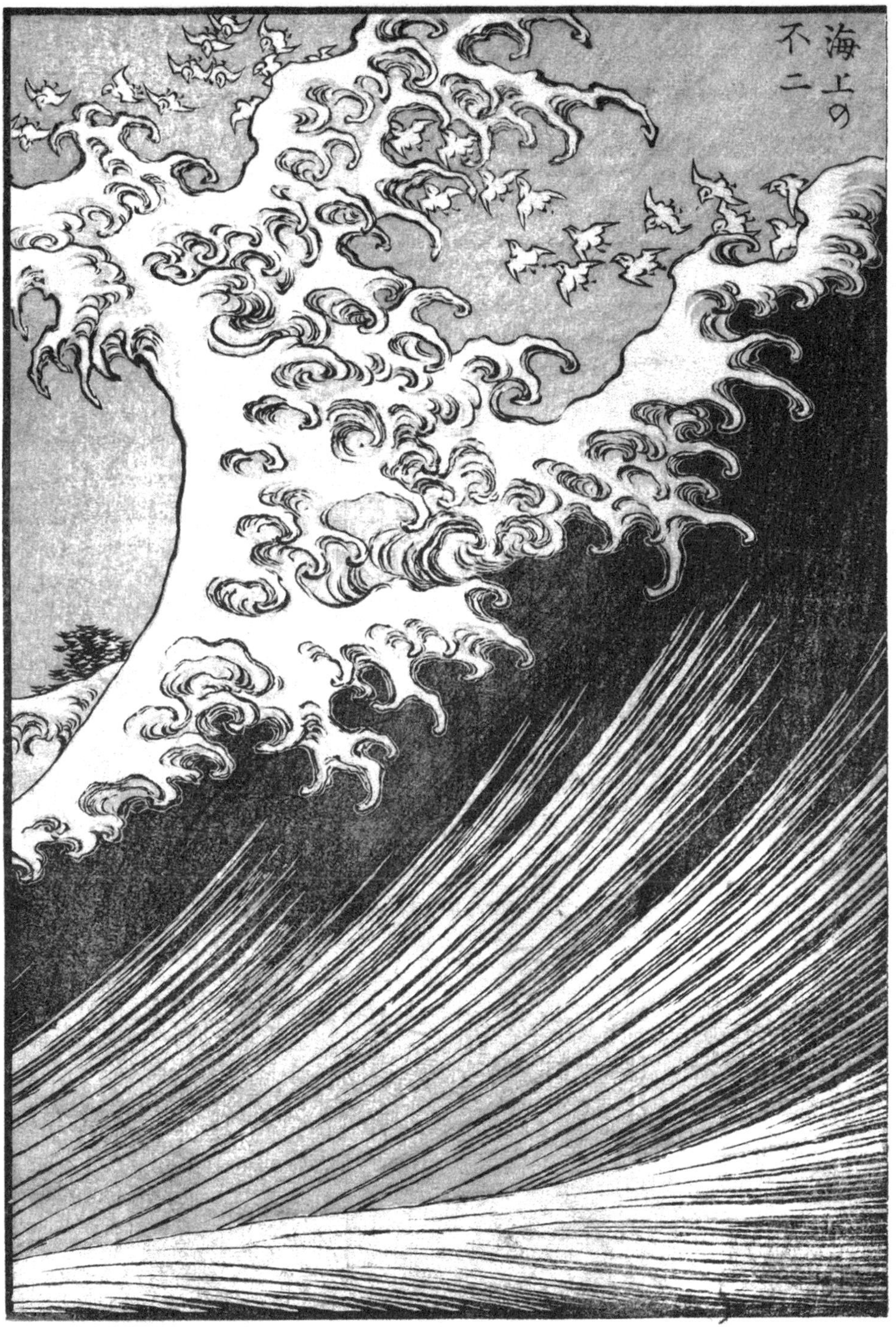
海上の
不二

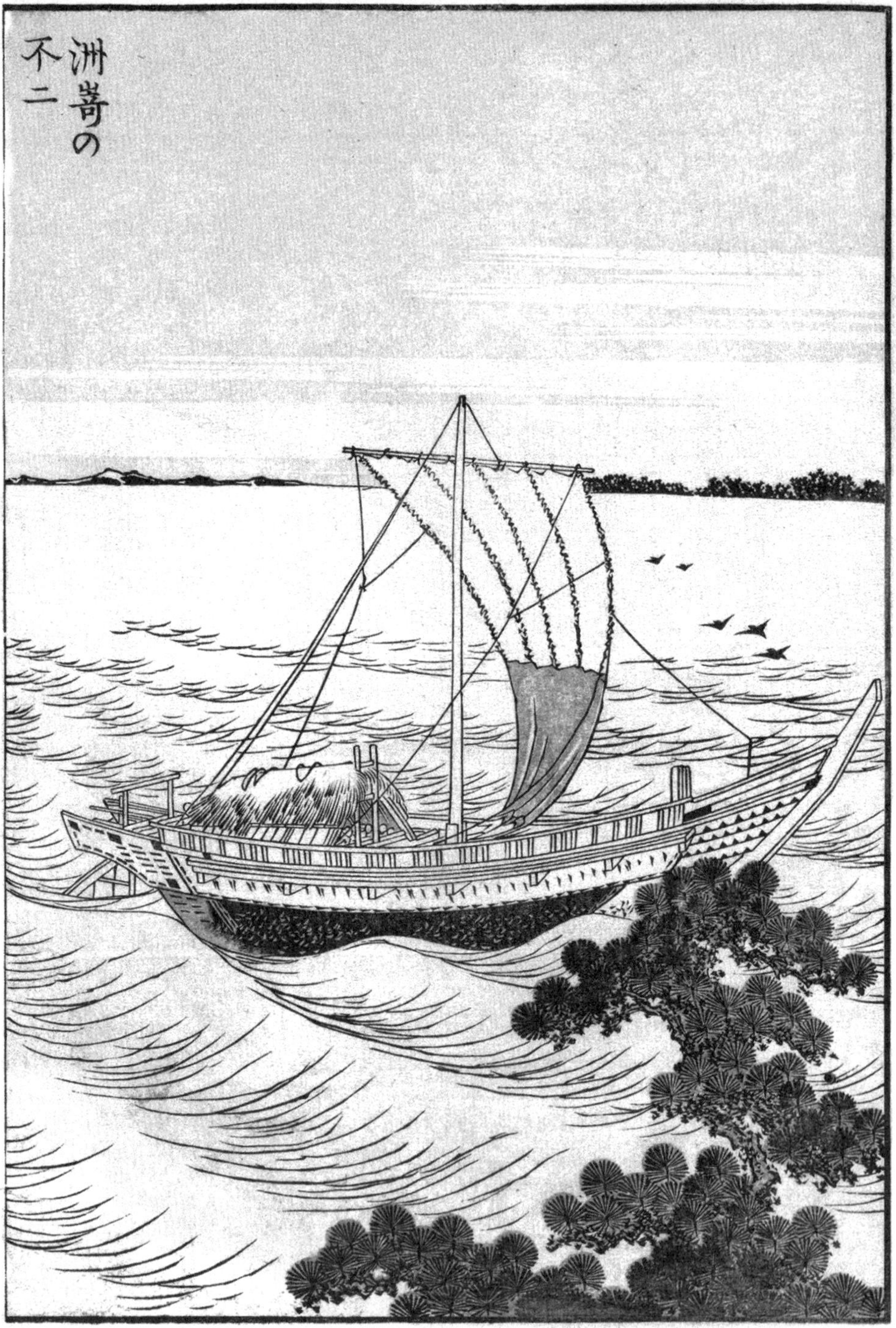

Fuji from Susaki

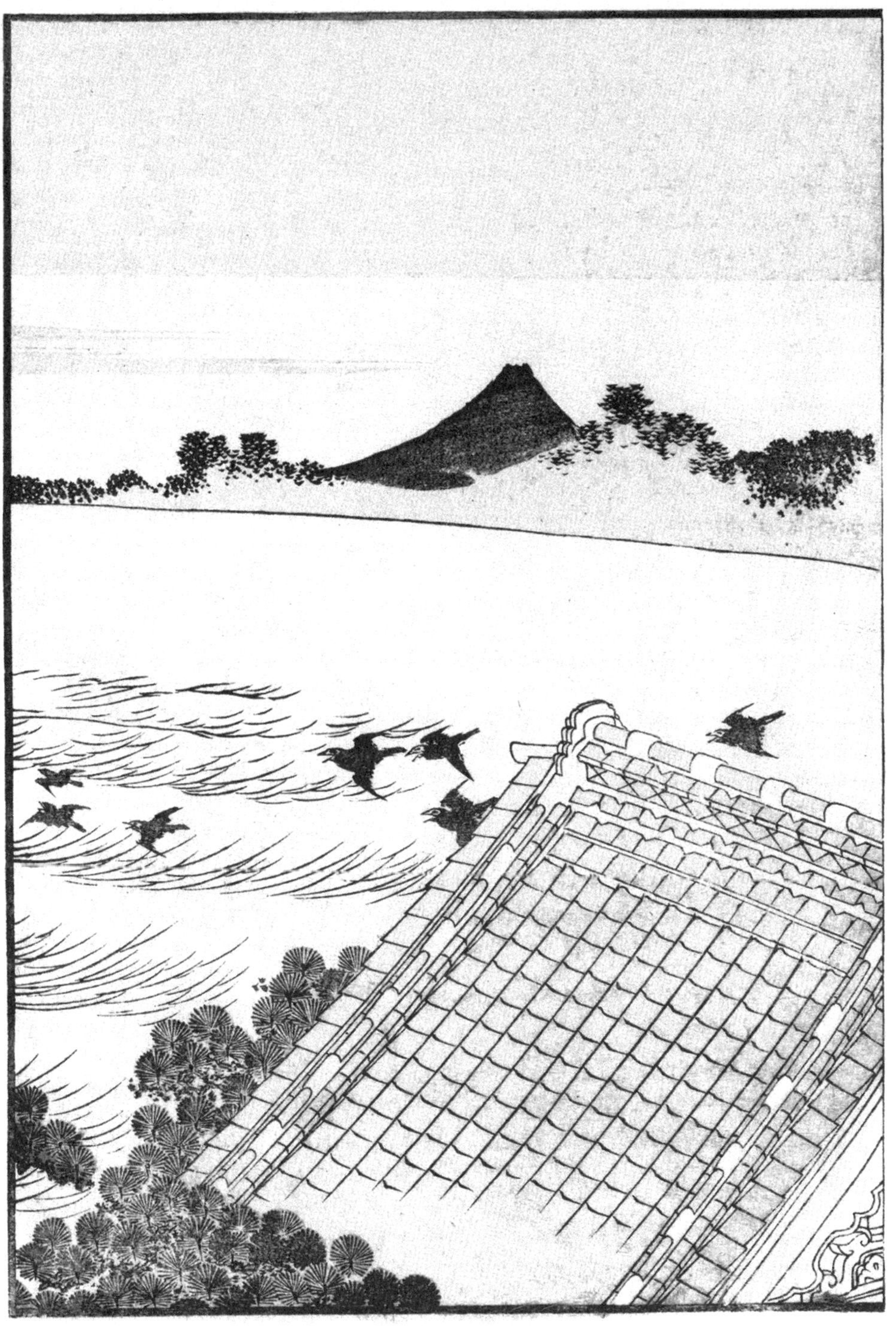

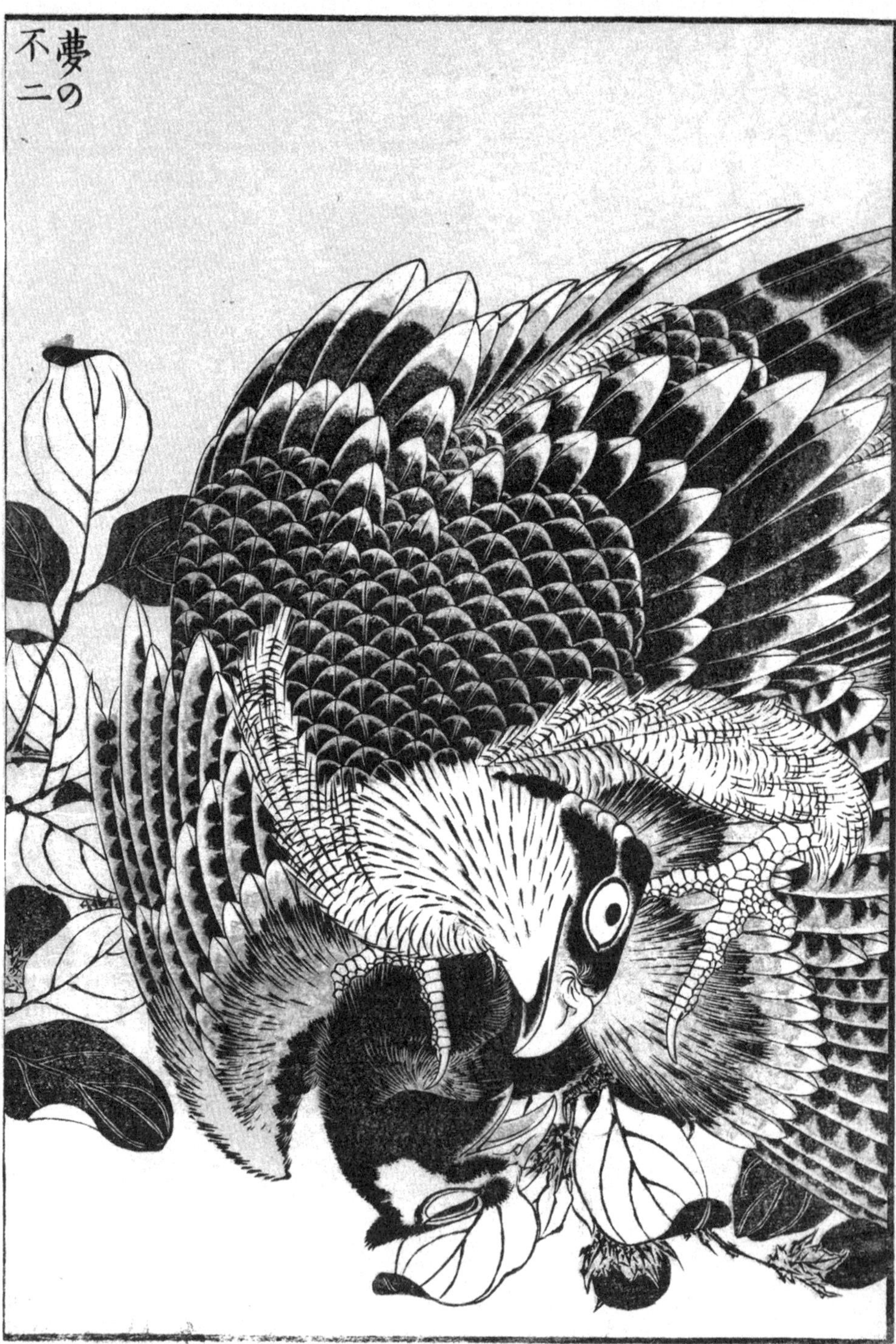

Fuji in a Dream

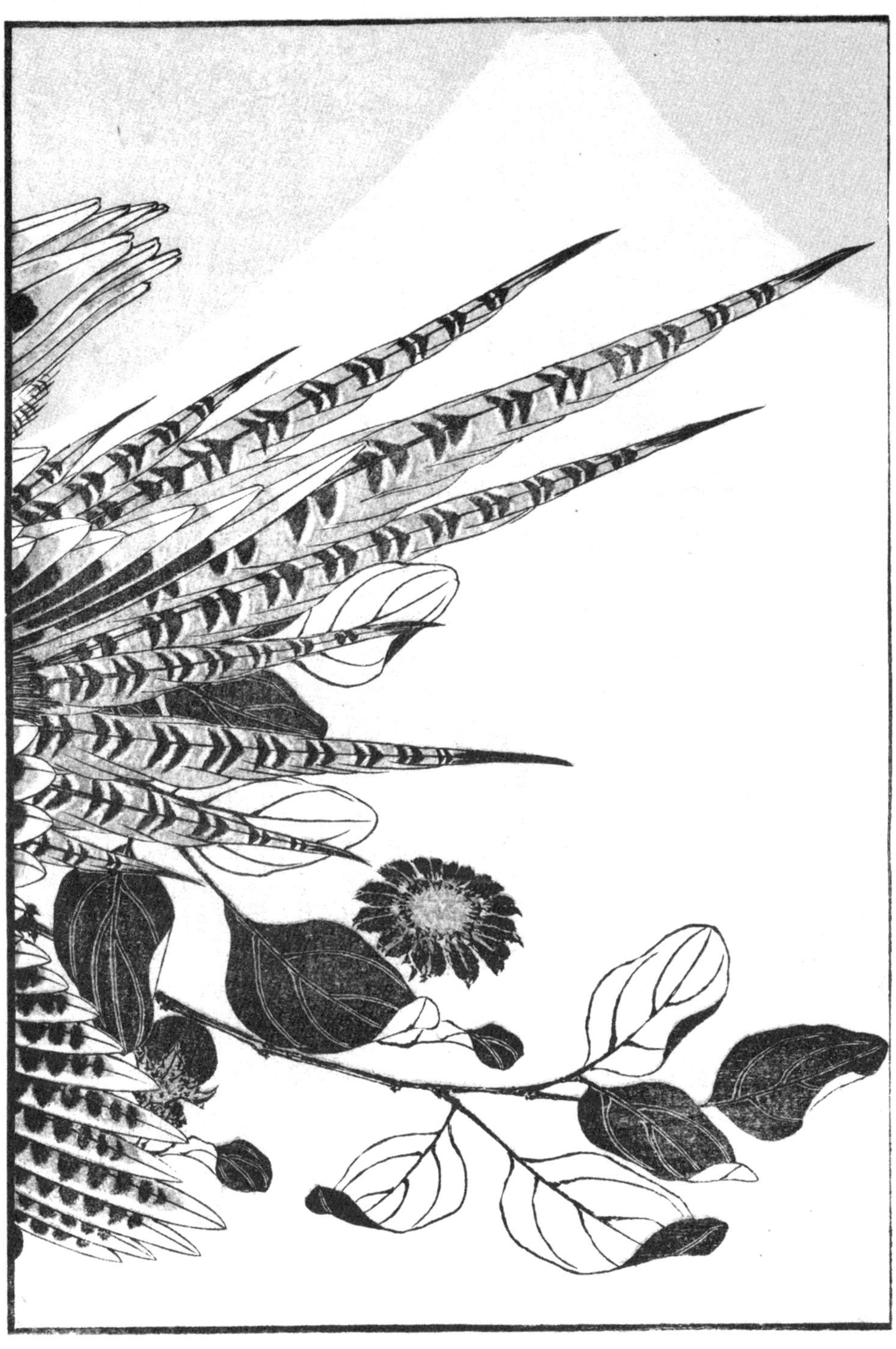

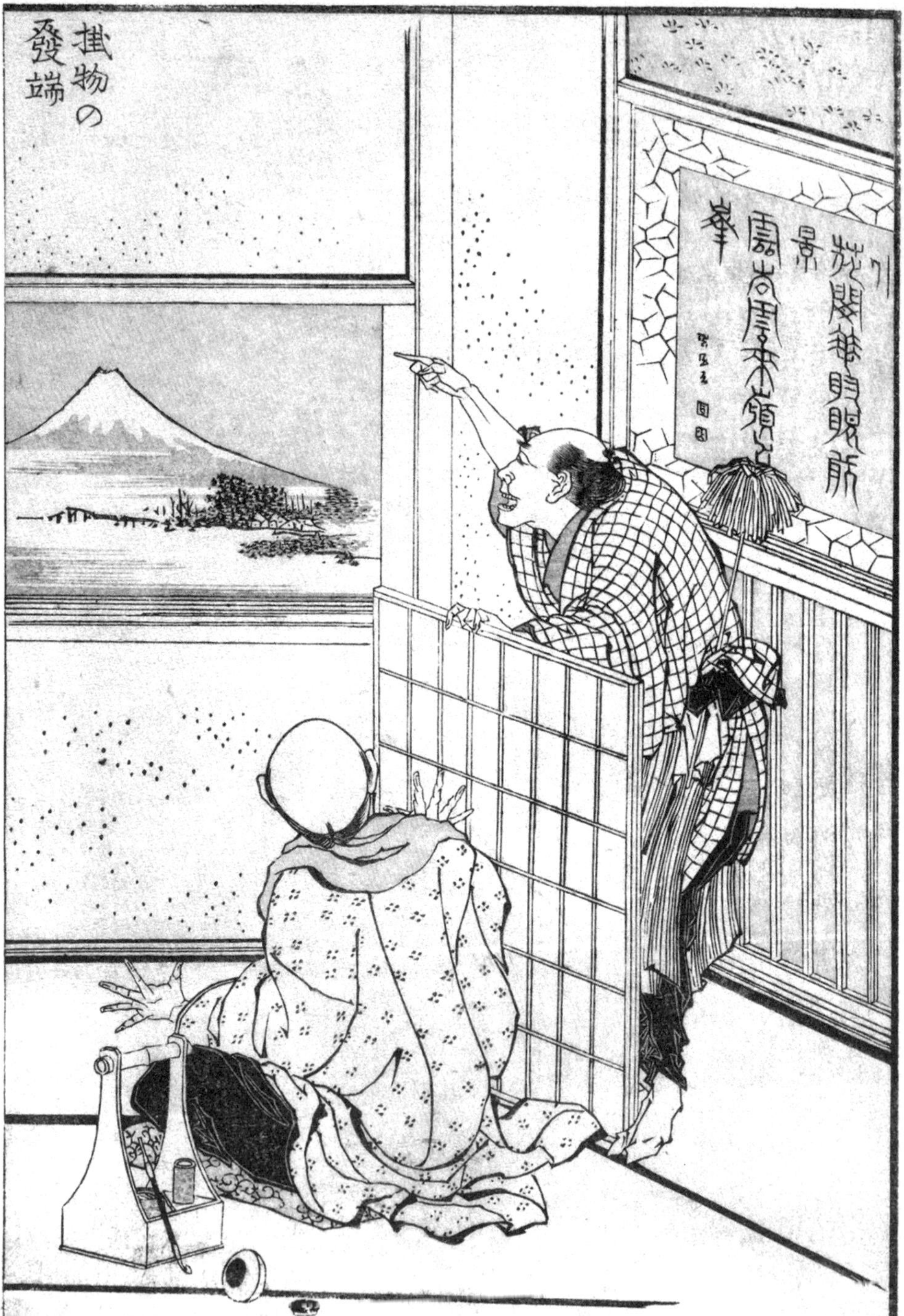

The First Hanging Scroll

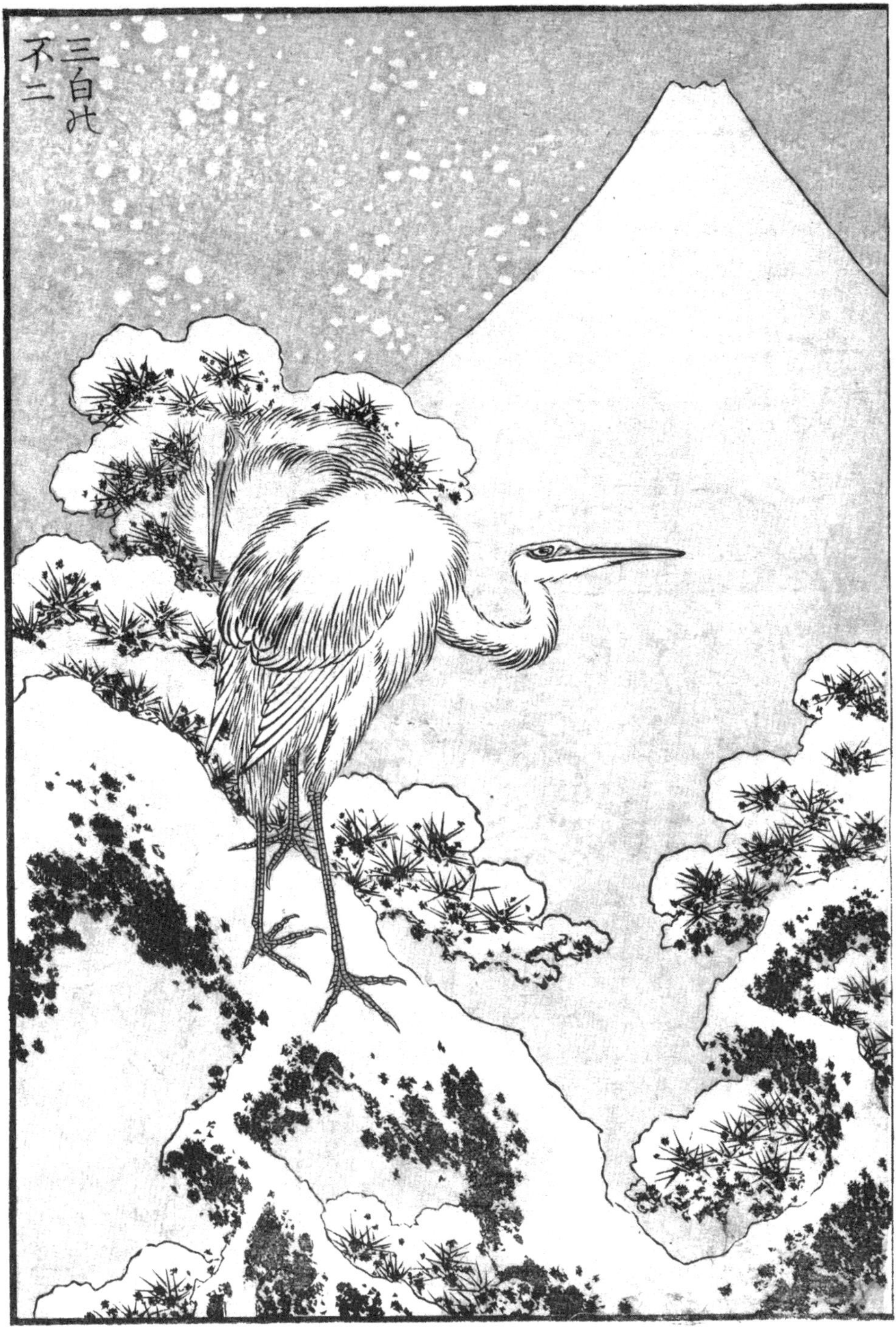

141 *Fuji Under Three Days of New Year Snow*

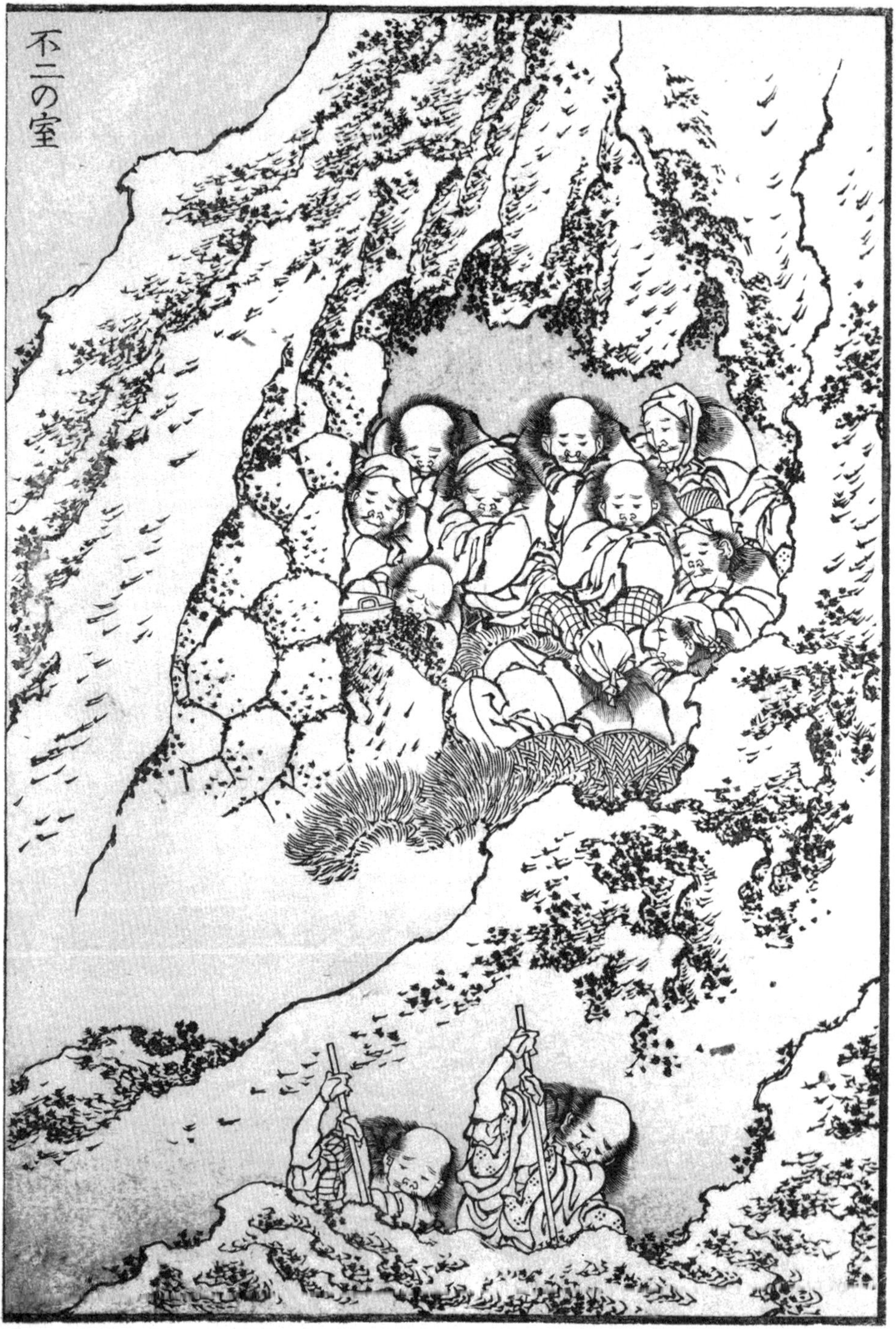

Rock Shelter on Fuji

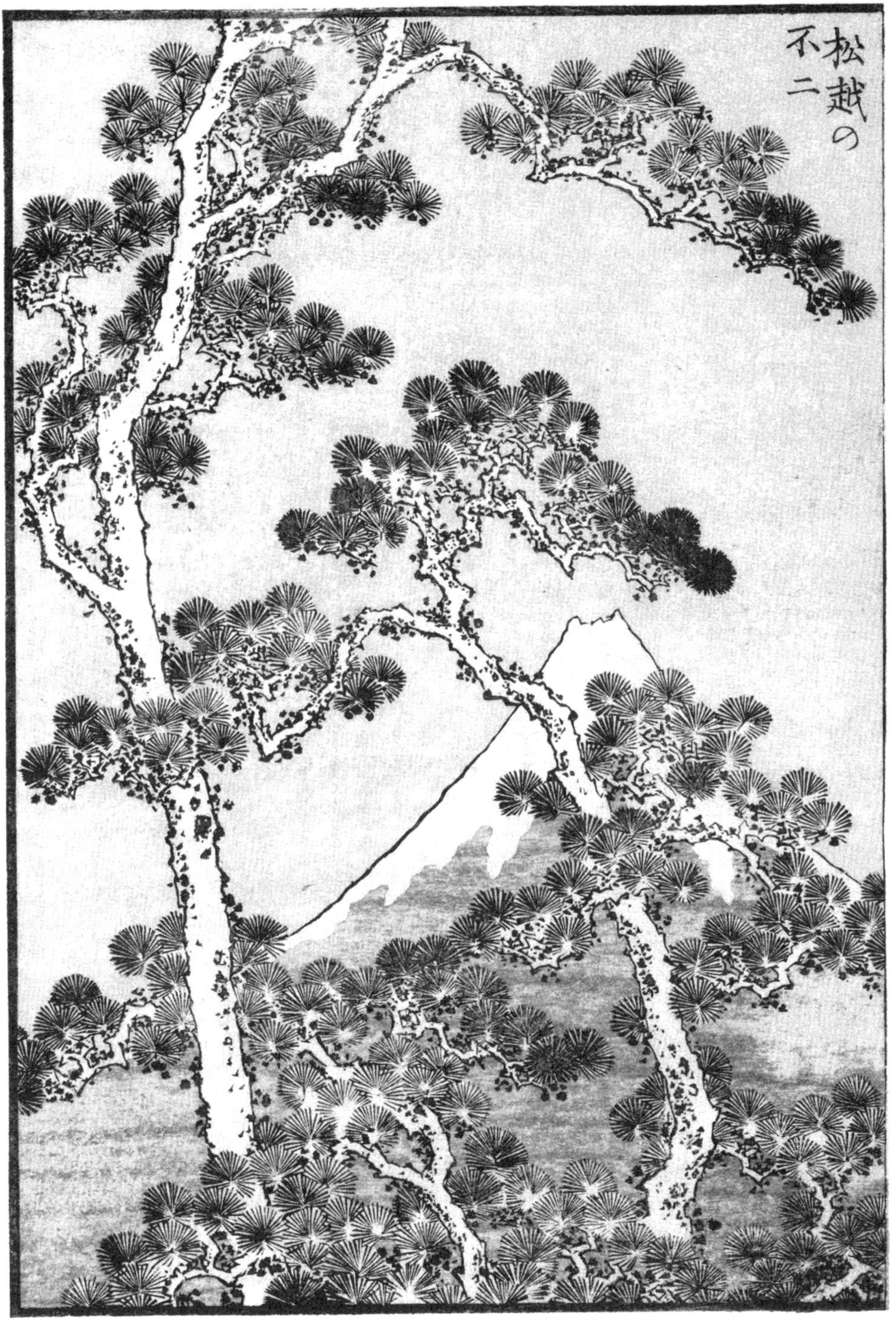

143 *Fuji Through Pine Trees*

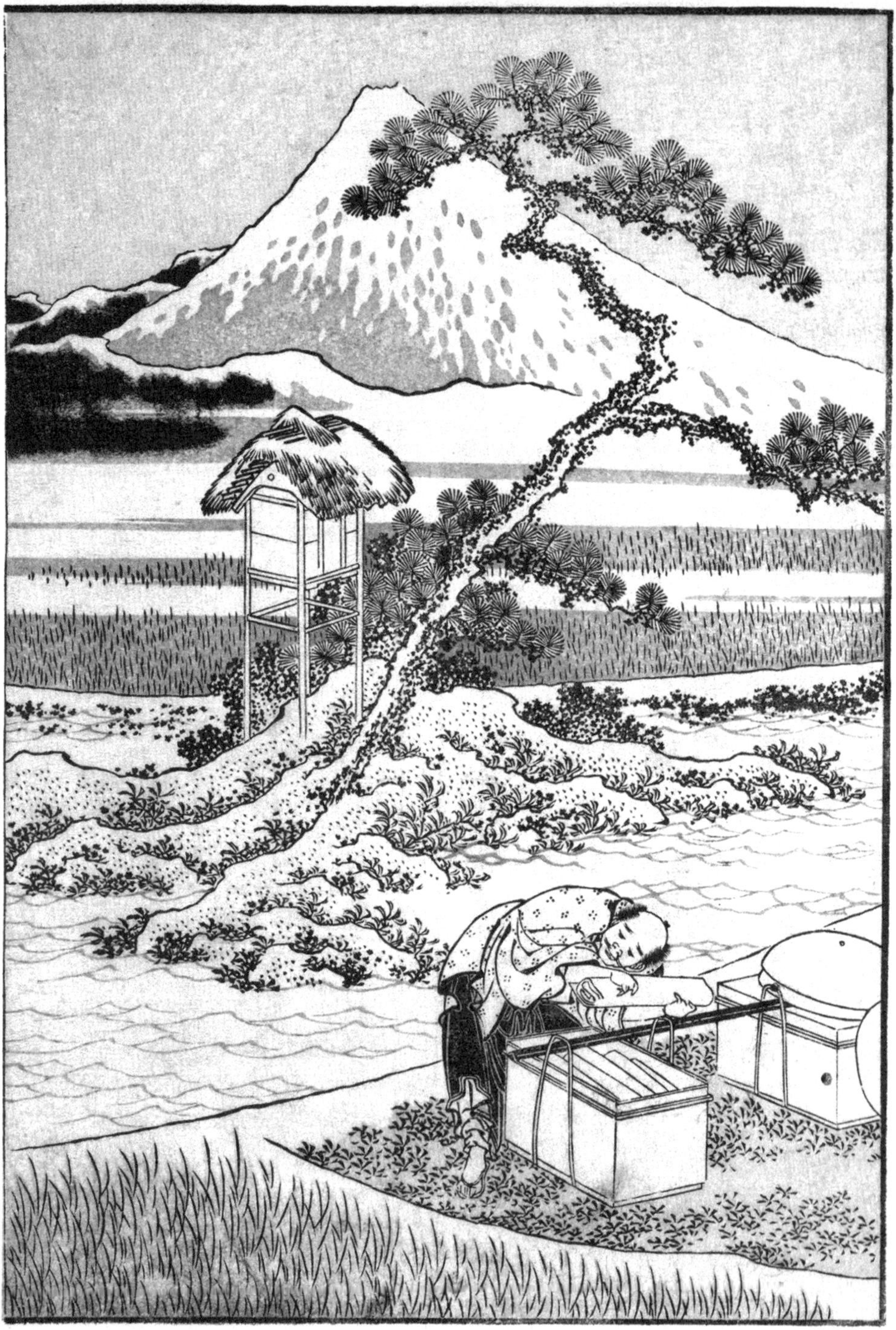

   Drawing Fuji from Life

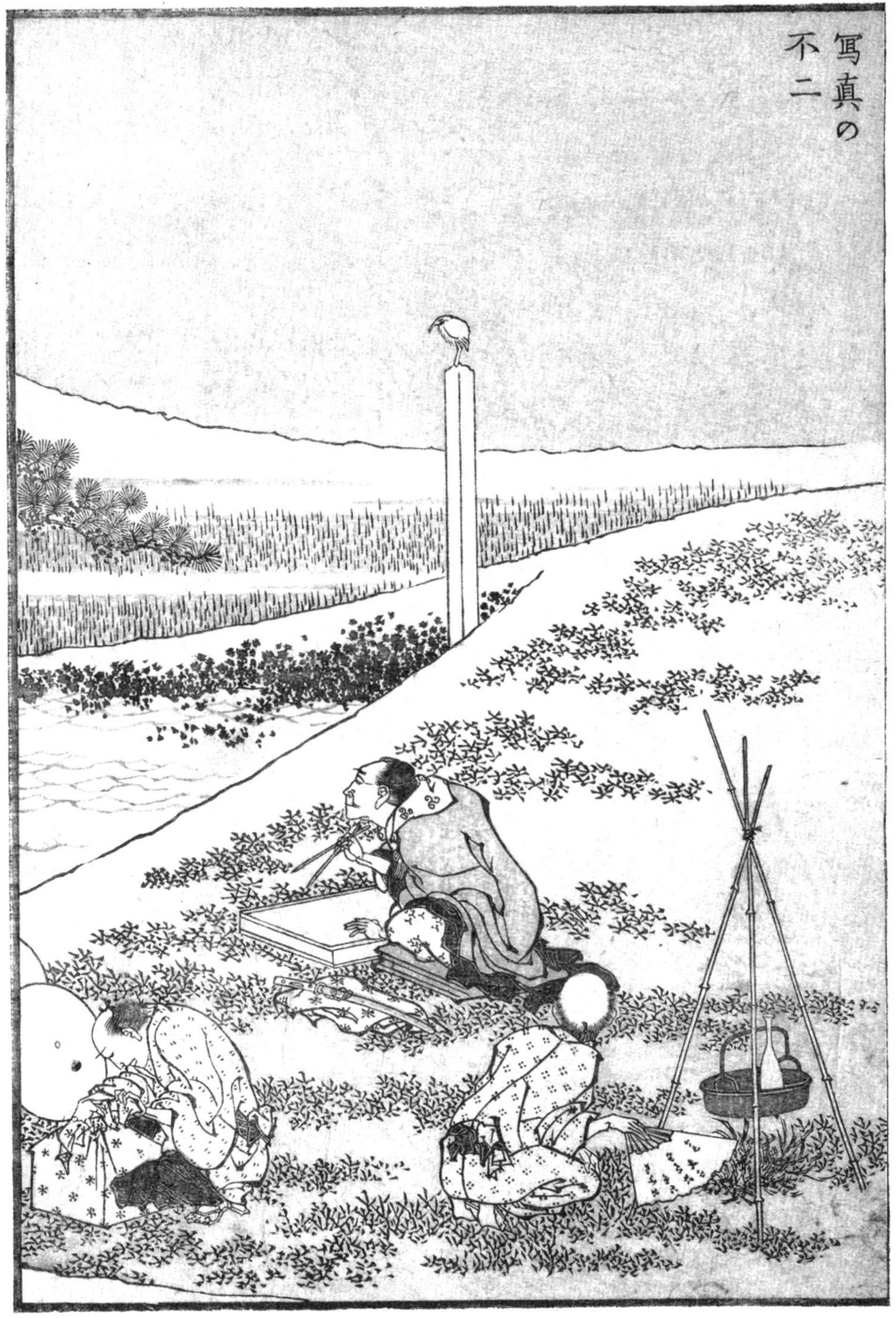
写真の
不二

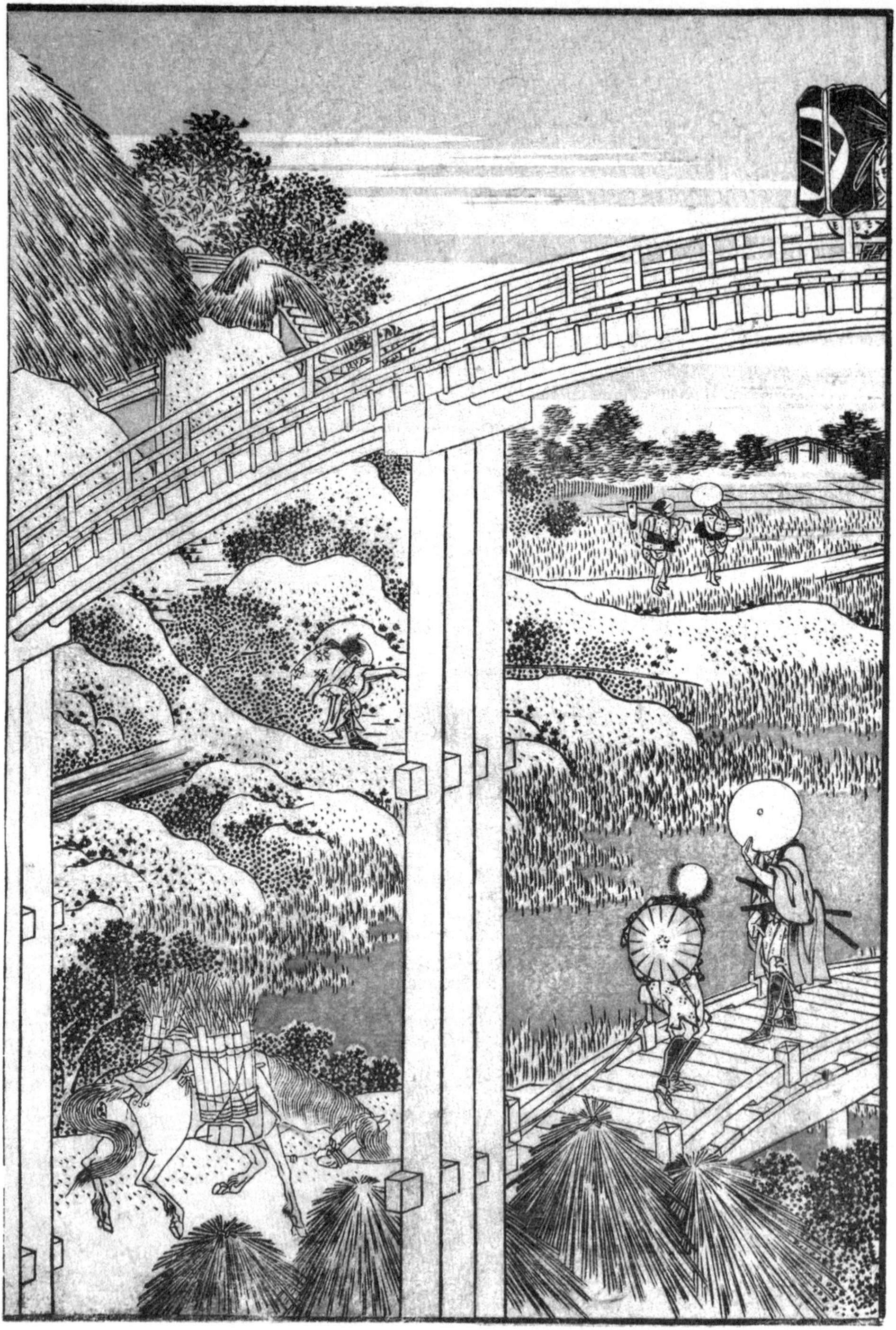

Fuji with Seven Bridges in One View

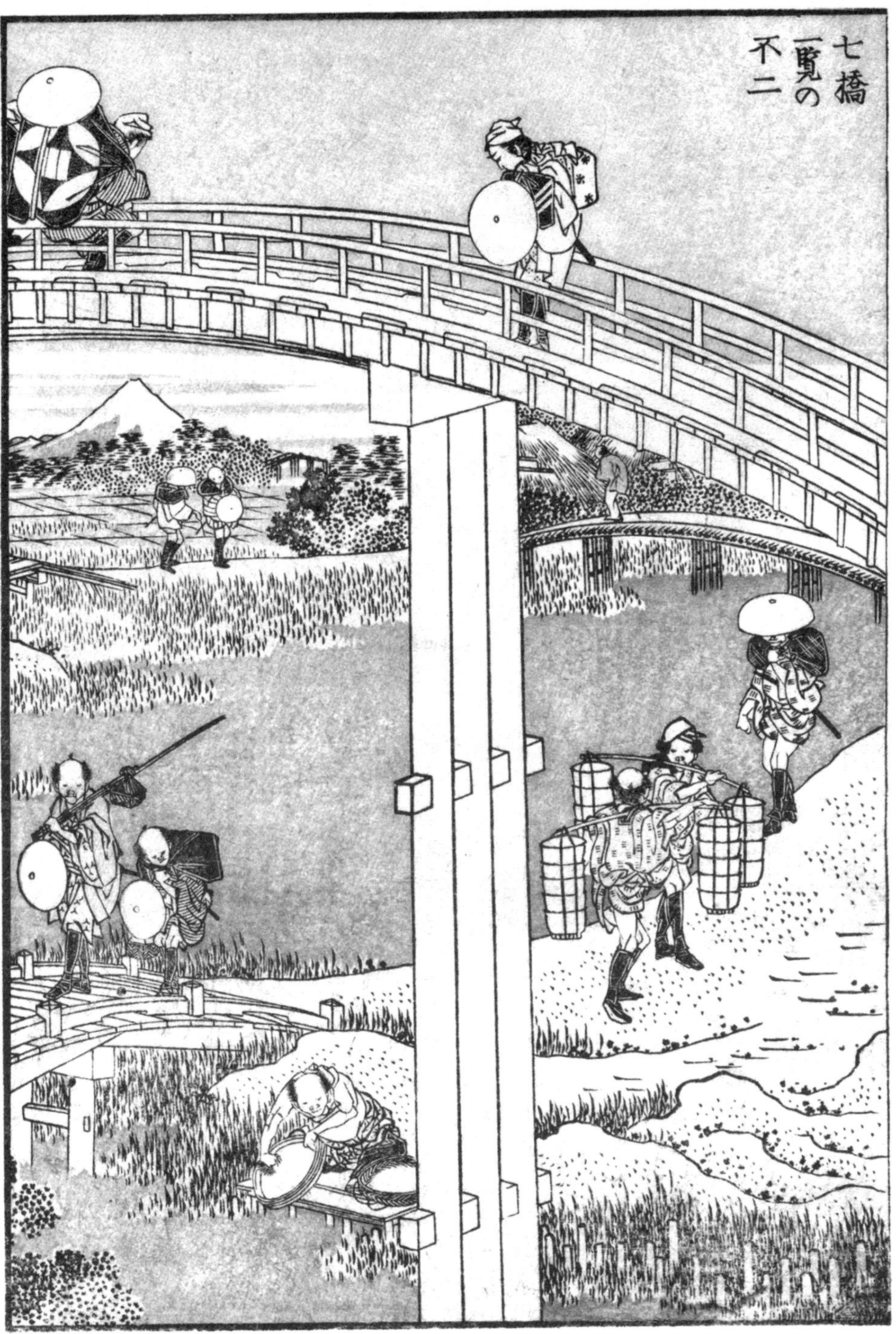

七橋
一覧の
不二

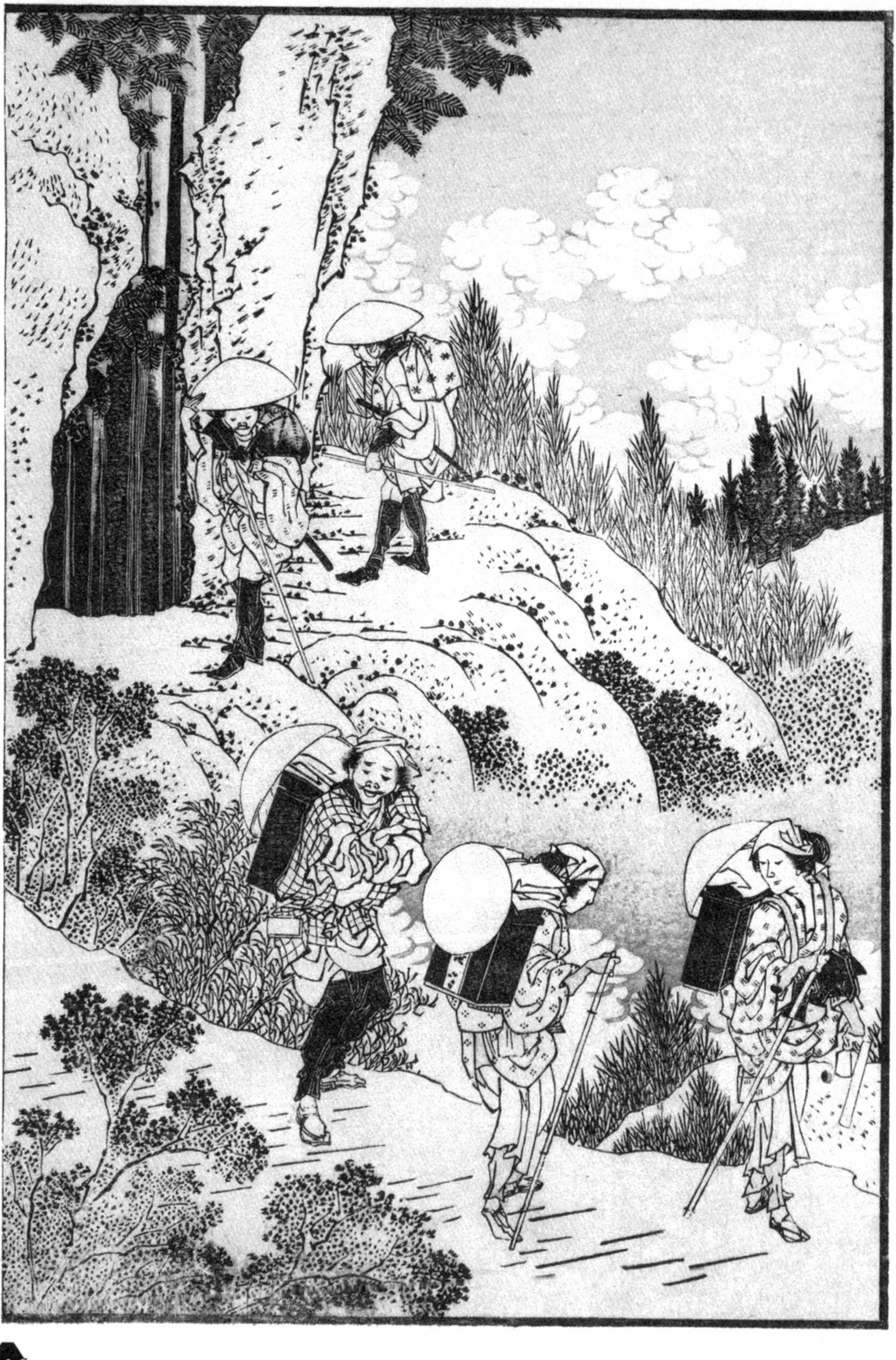

146 *Fuji in the Mountains of Taisekiji Temple*

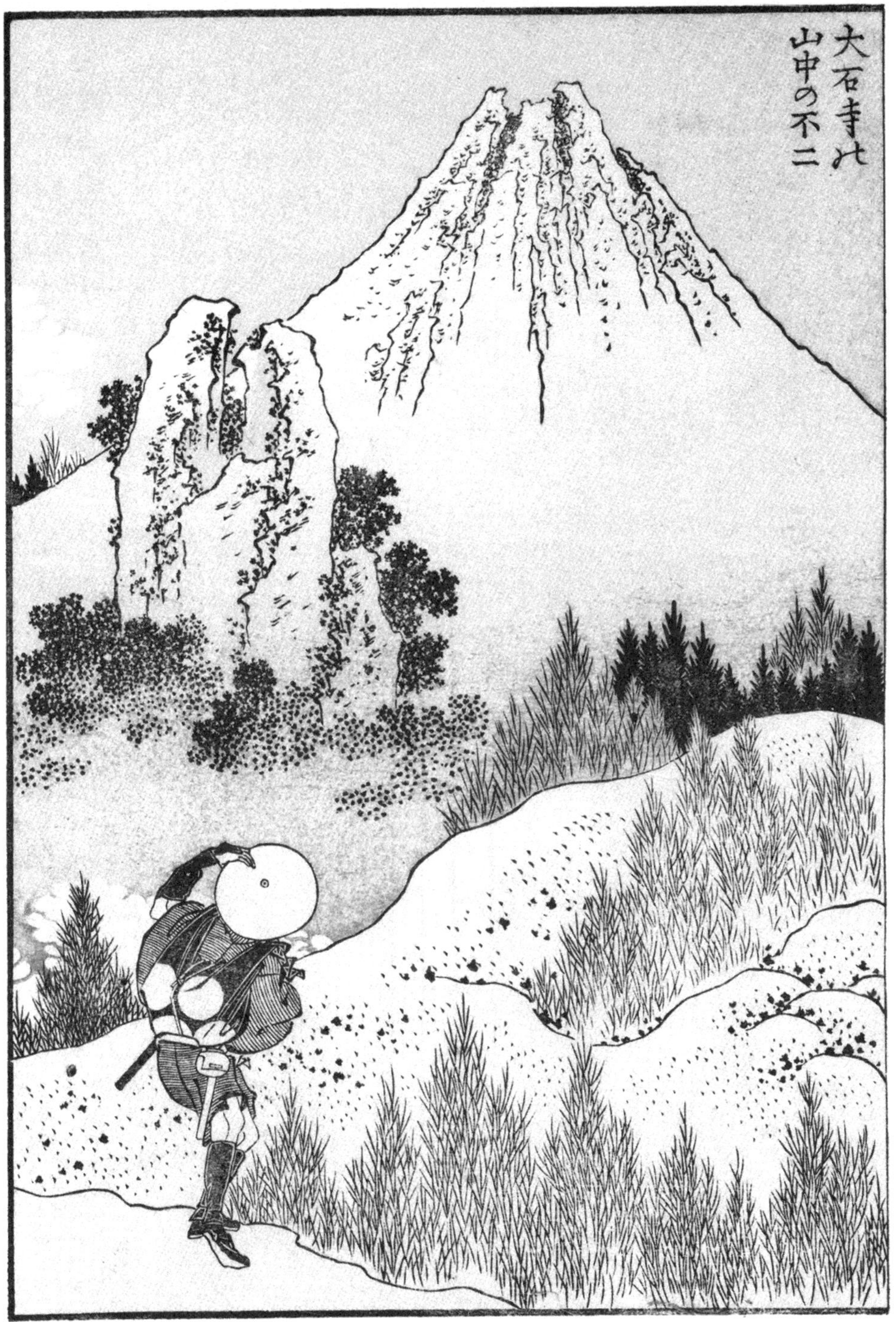
大石寺や
山中の不二

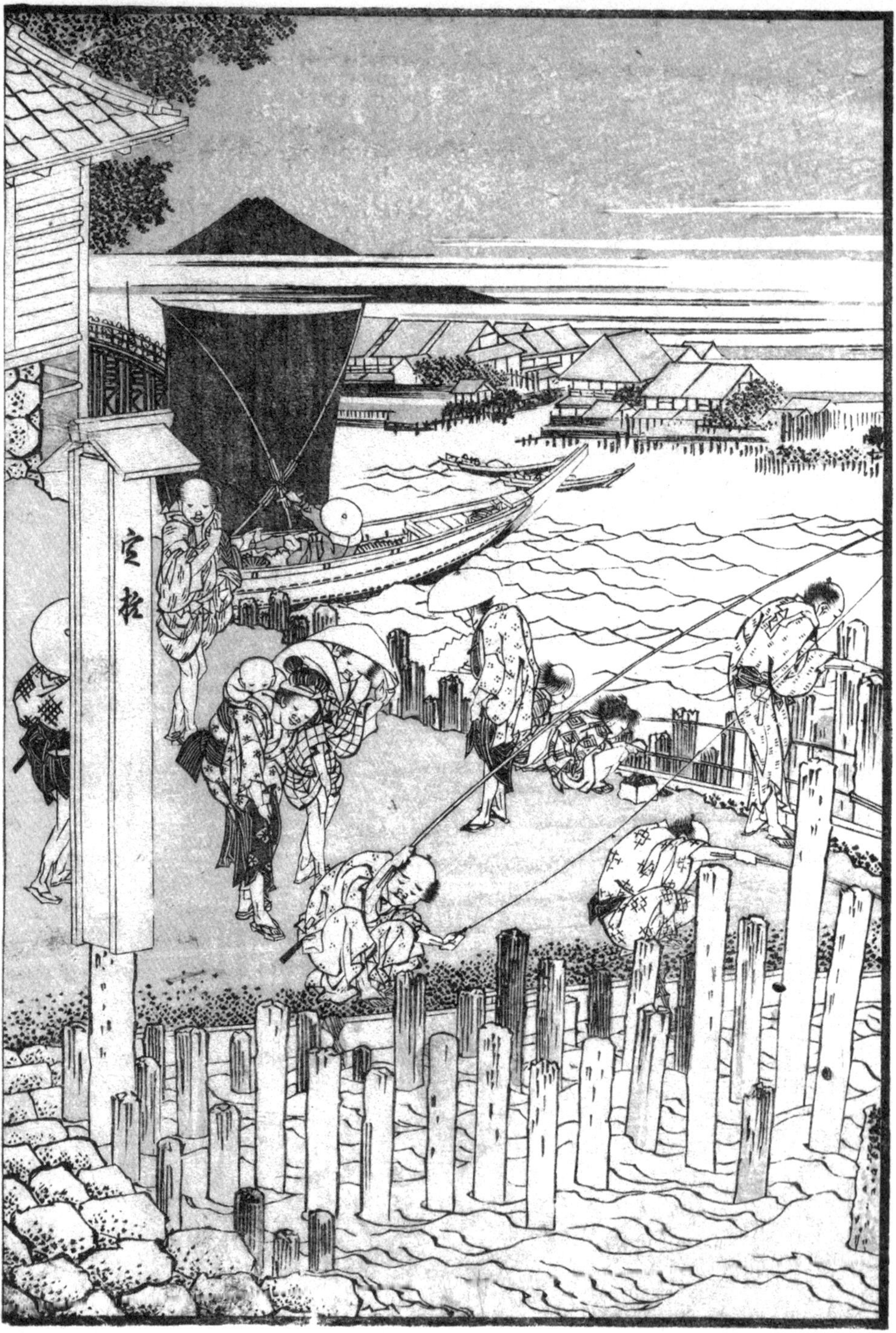

147 *Fuji in the Evening Sun at Shimadagahana*

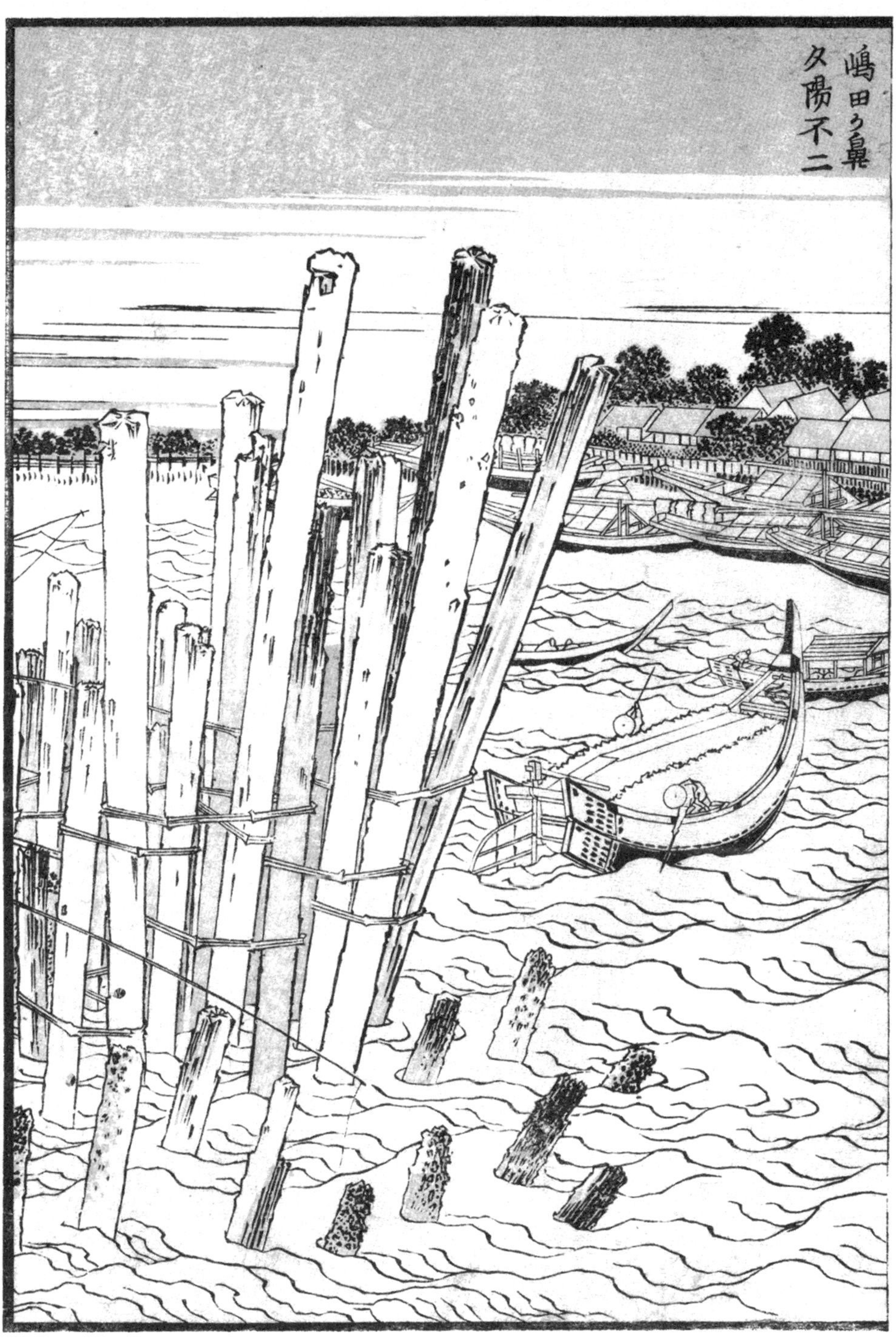

嶋田乃鼻
夕陽不二

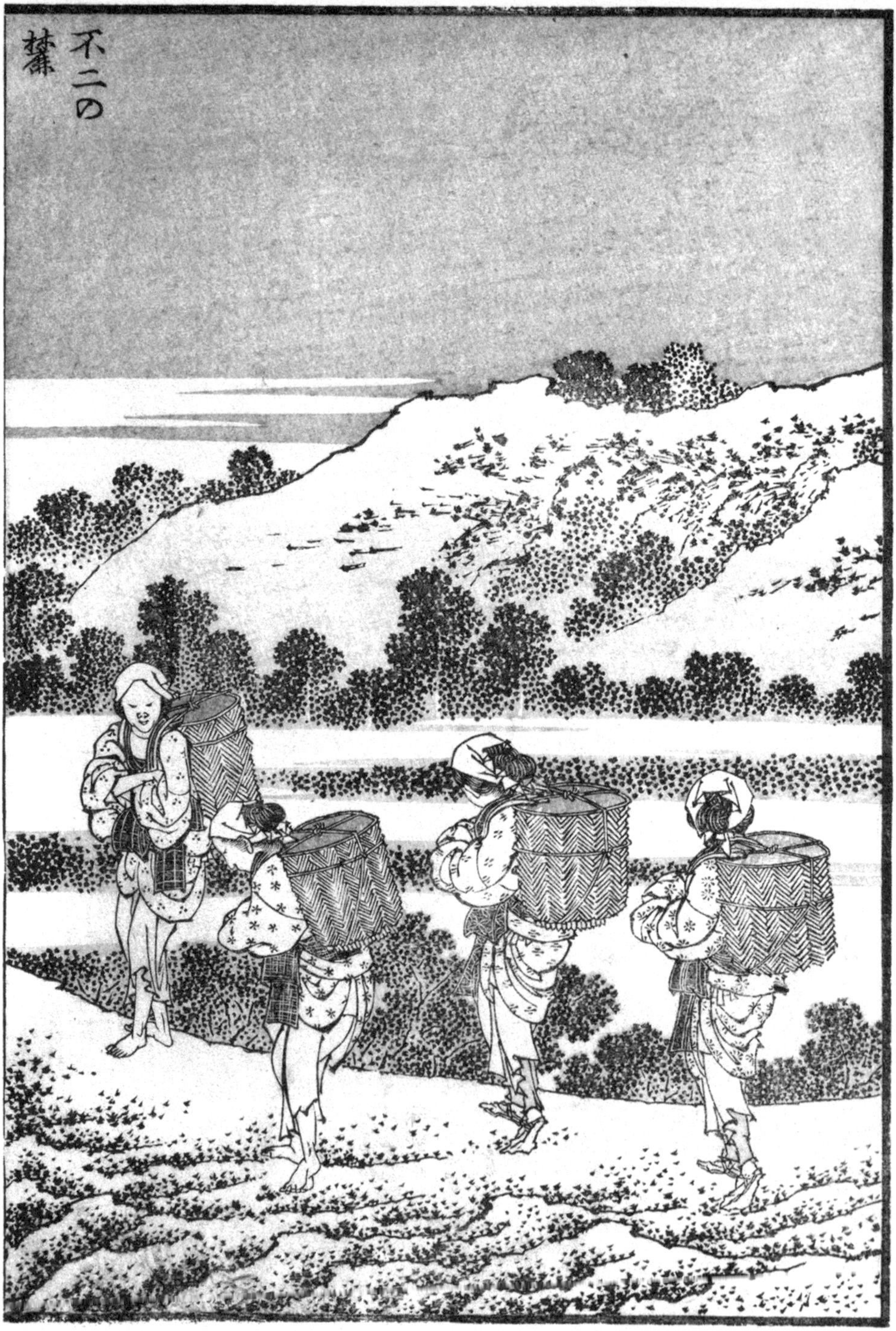

At the Foot of Fuji

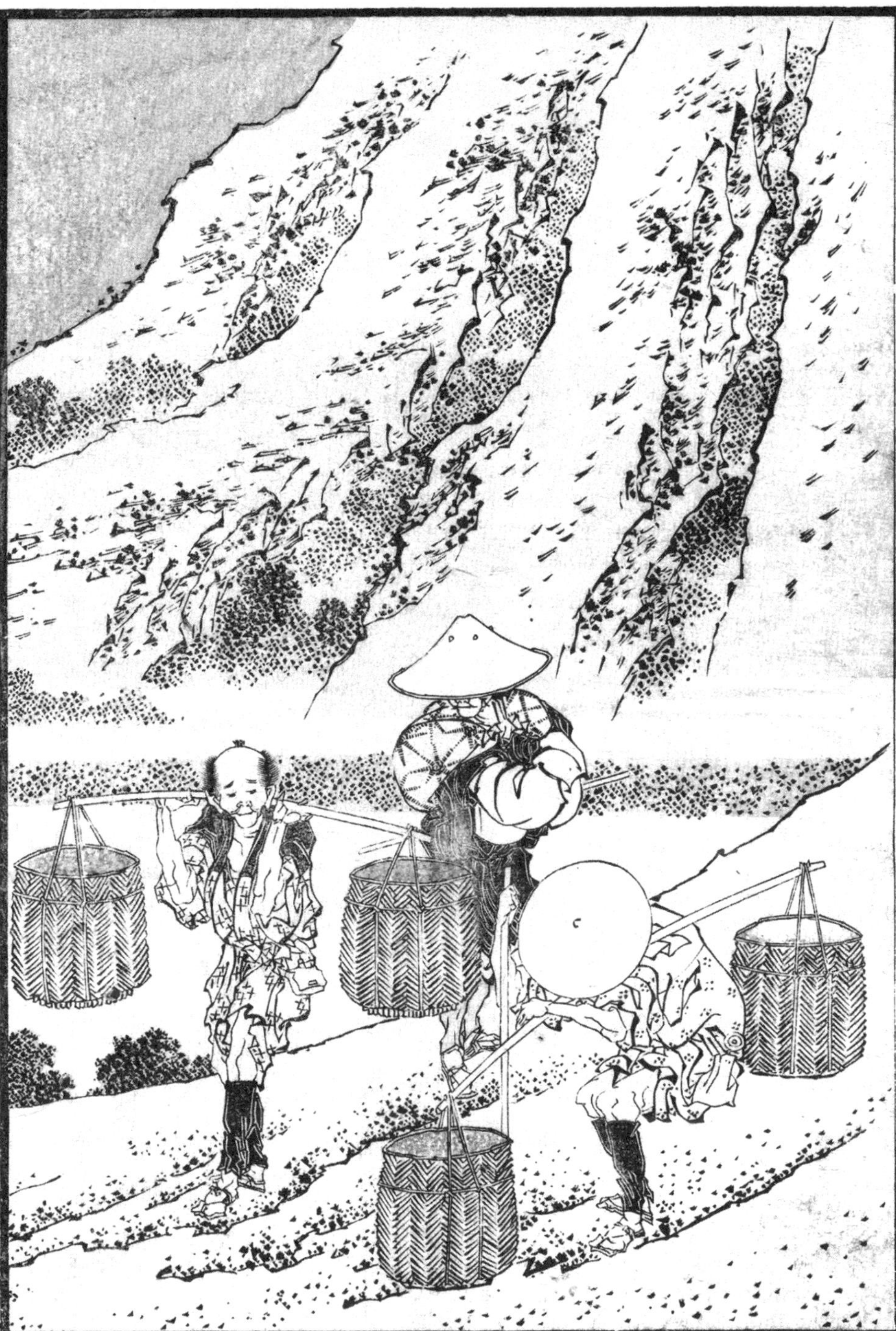

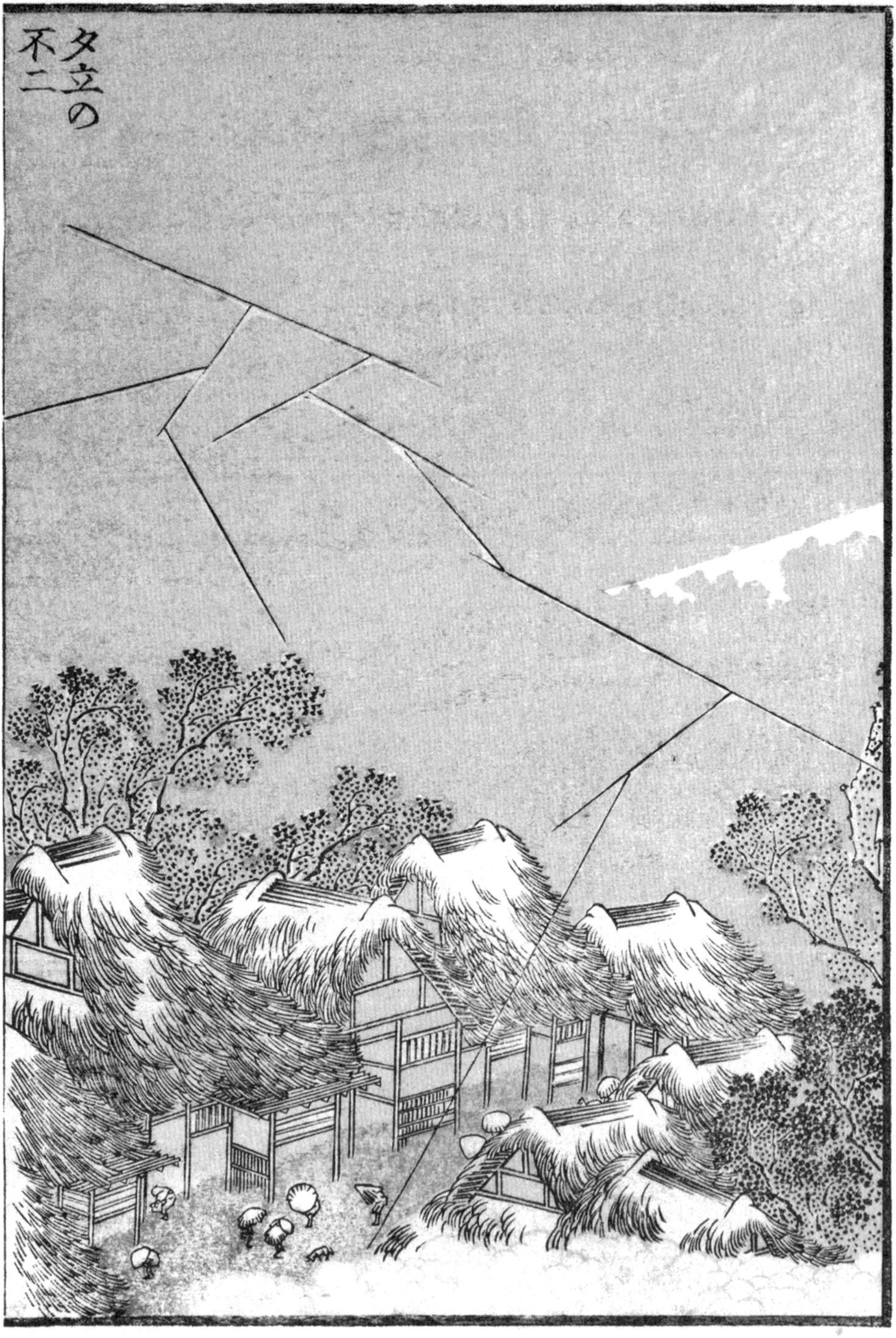

Fuji in a Thunderstorm

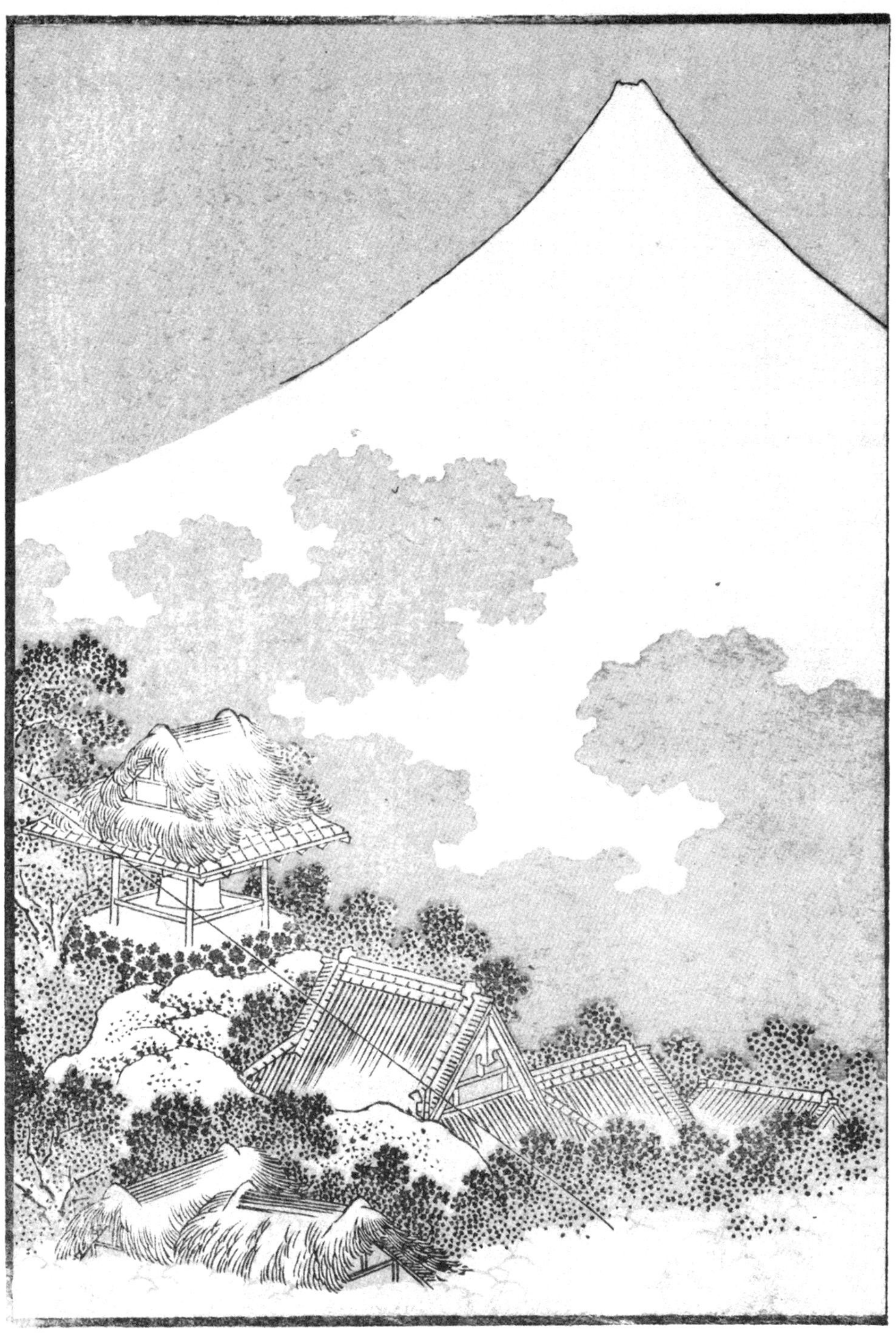

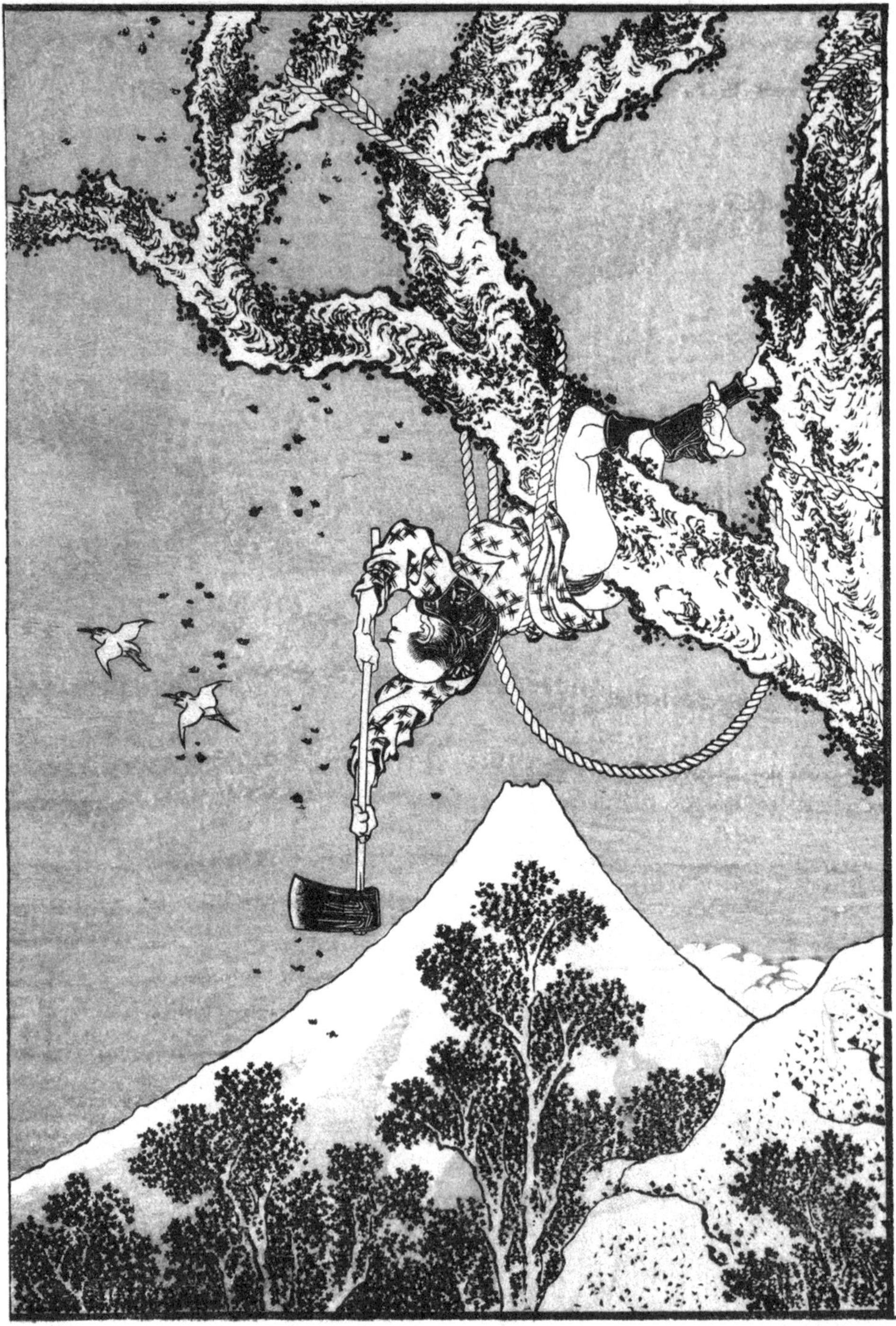

Fuji in the Tōtomi Mountains

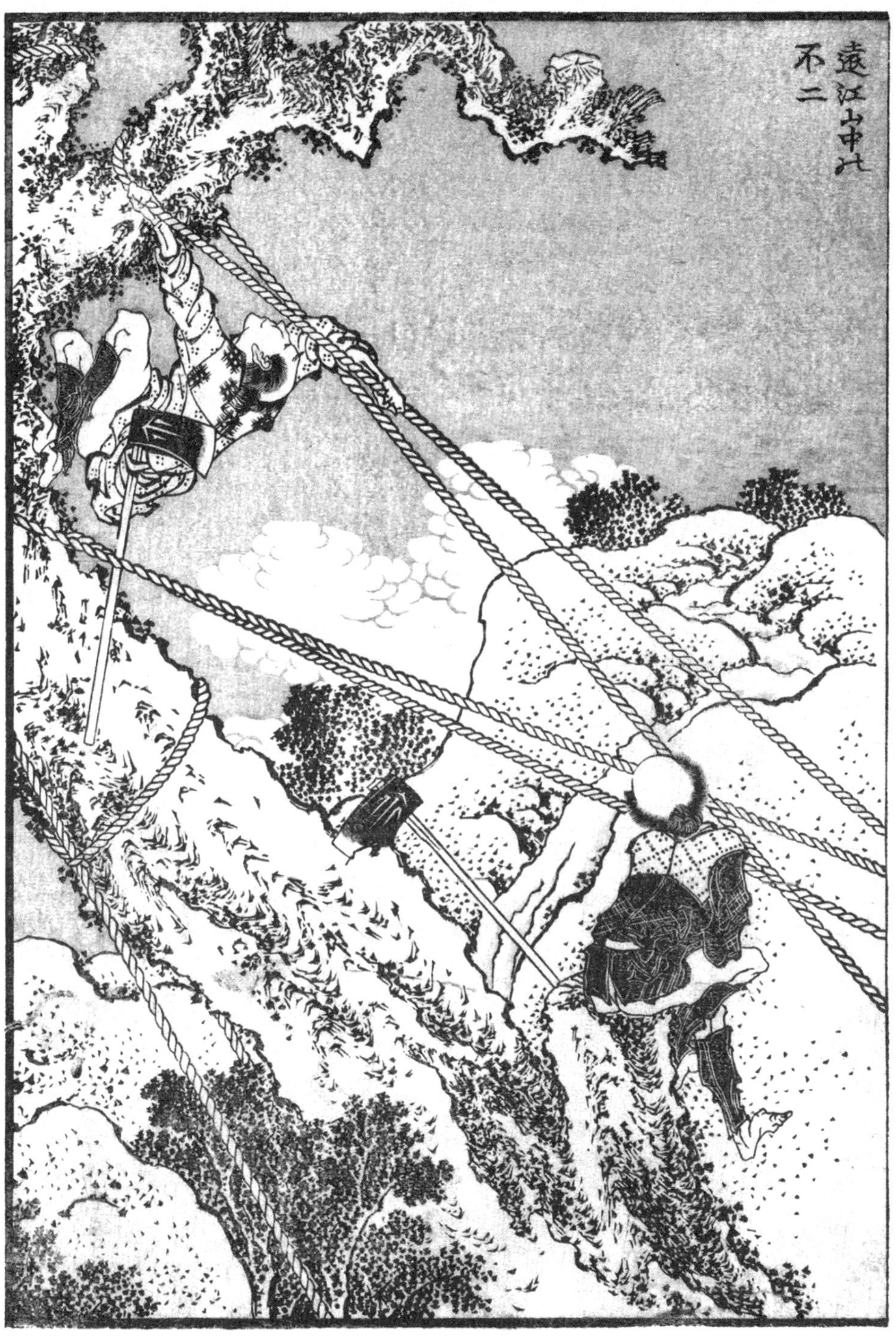

遠江山中ノ
不二

不二

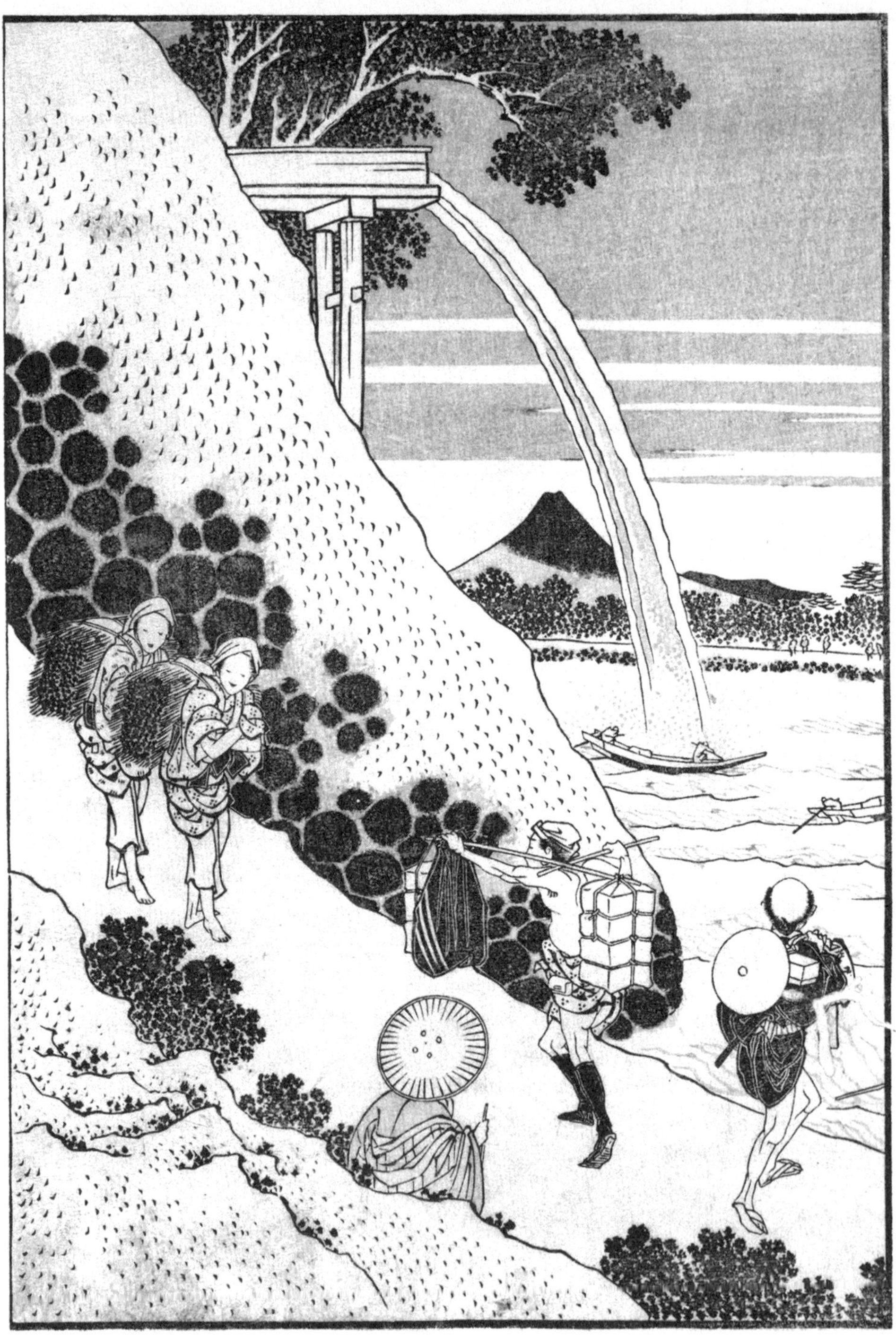

Fuji Under a Sluice

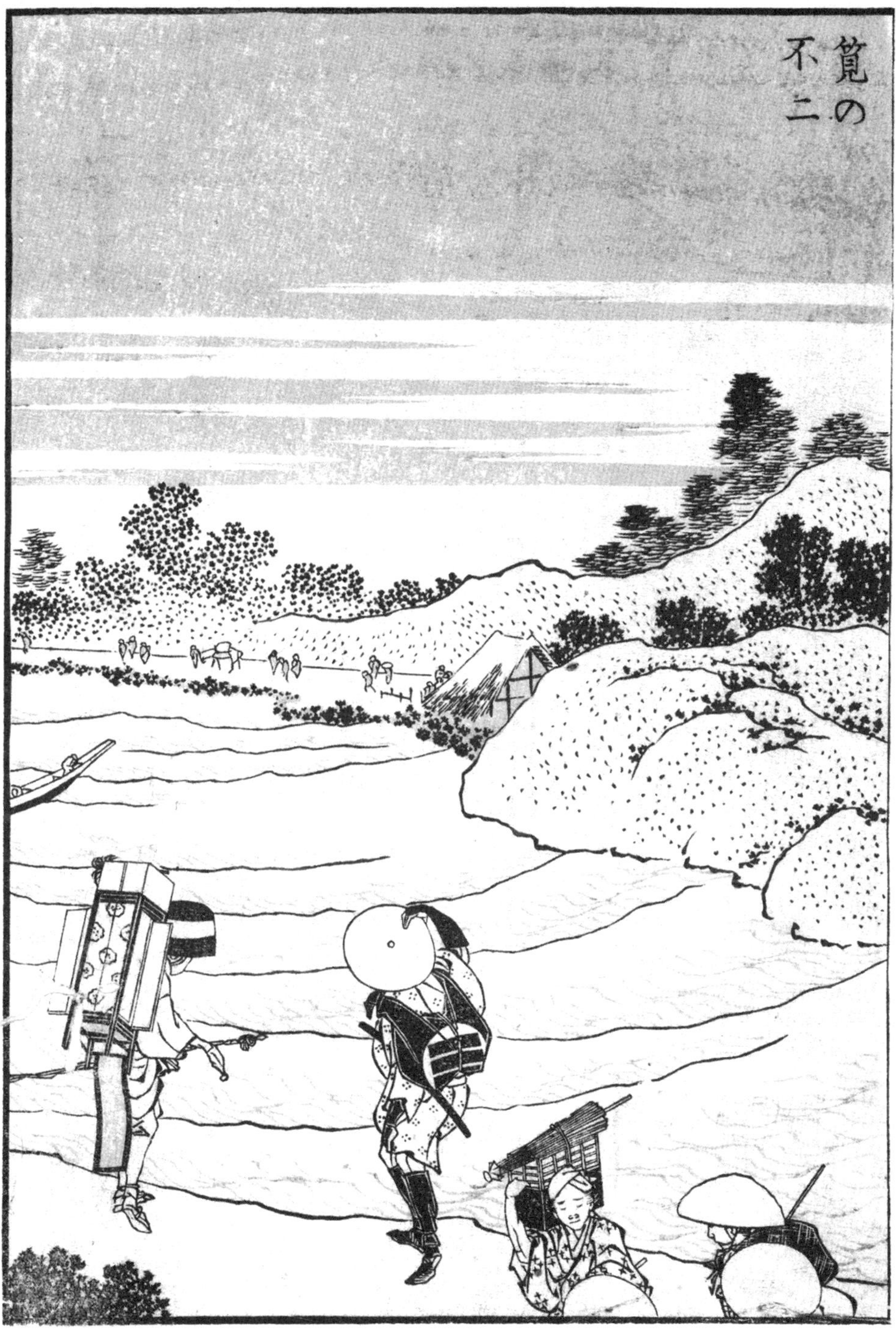
筧の
不二

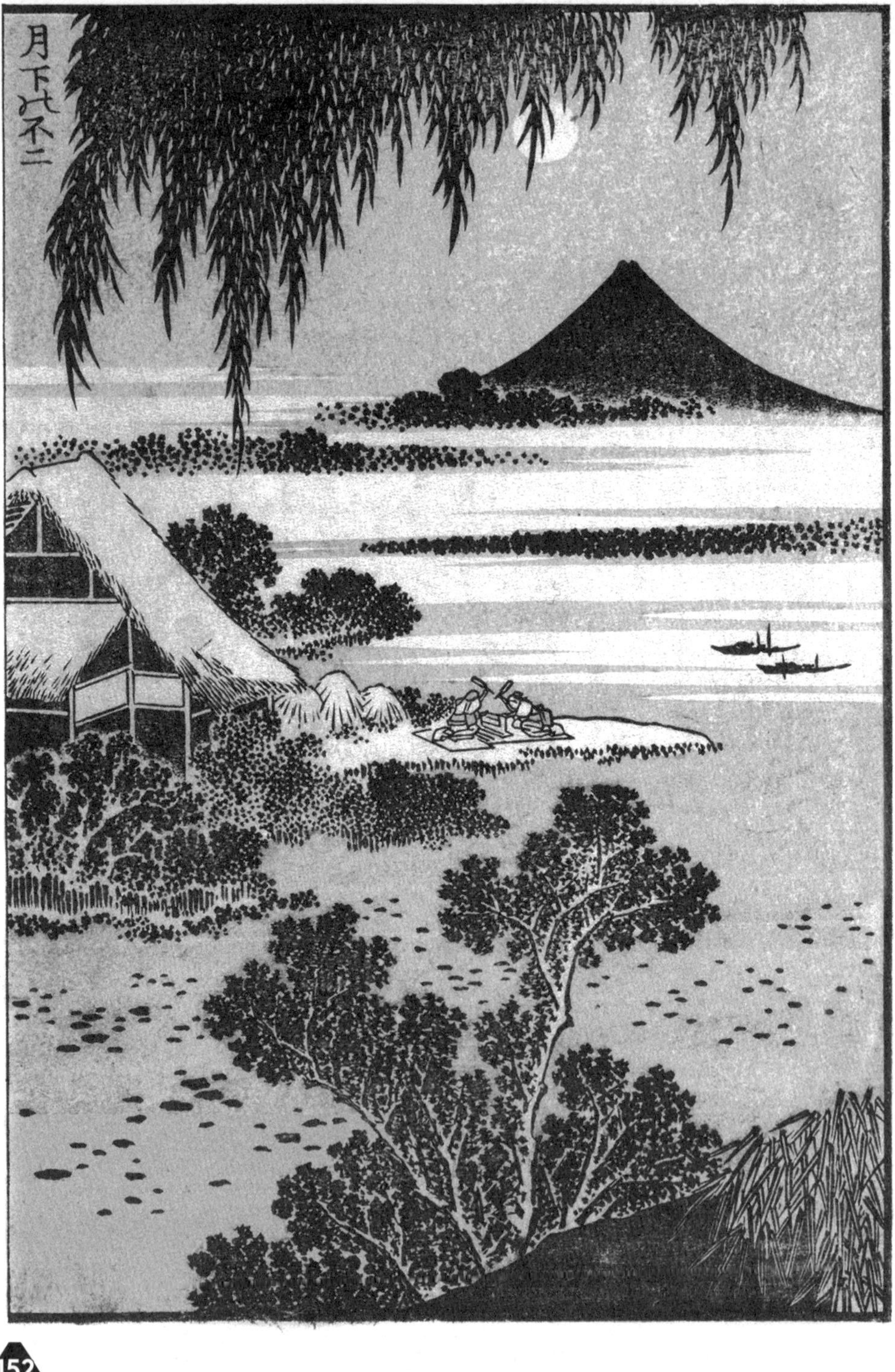

Fuji Under the Moon

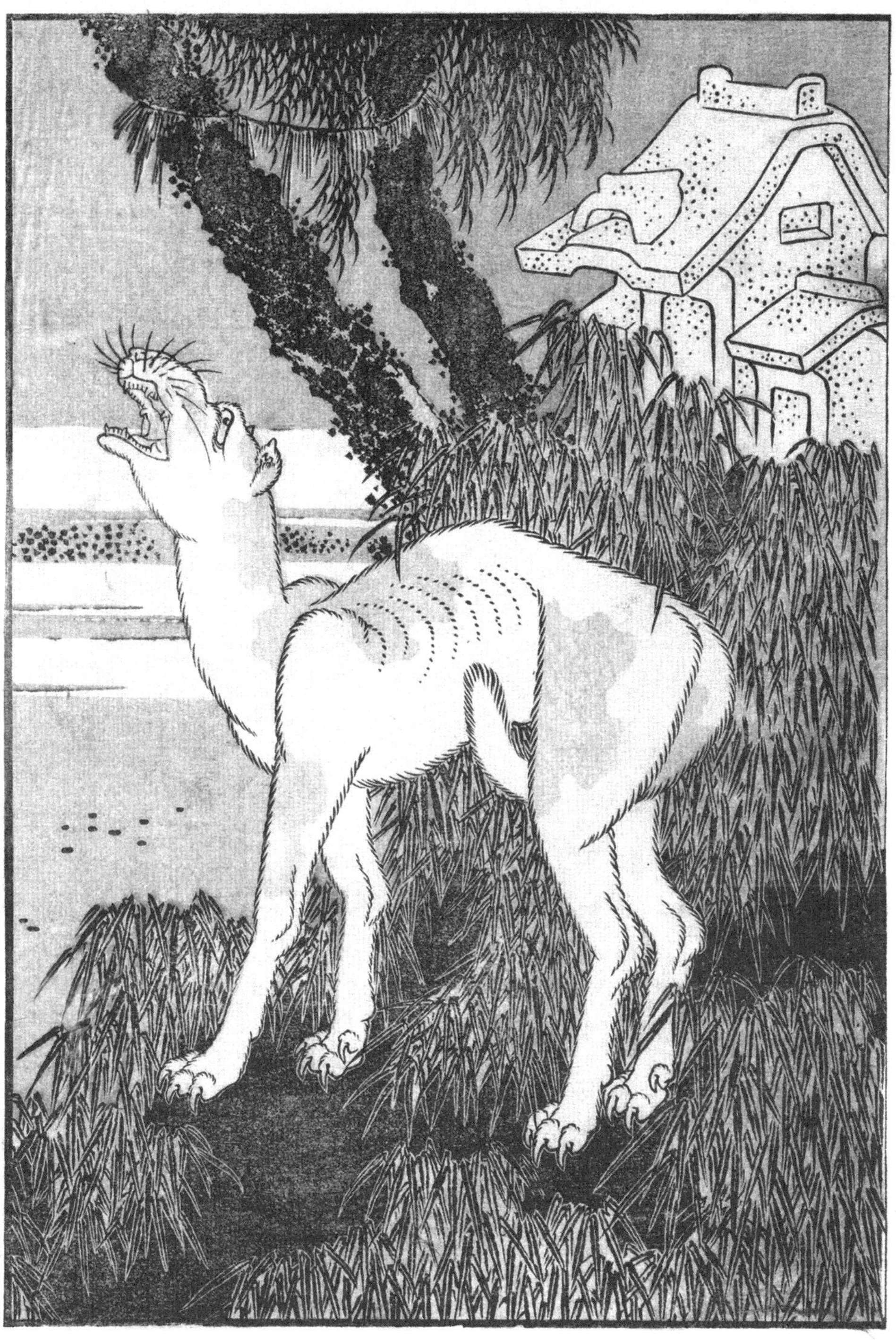

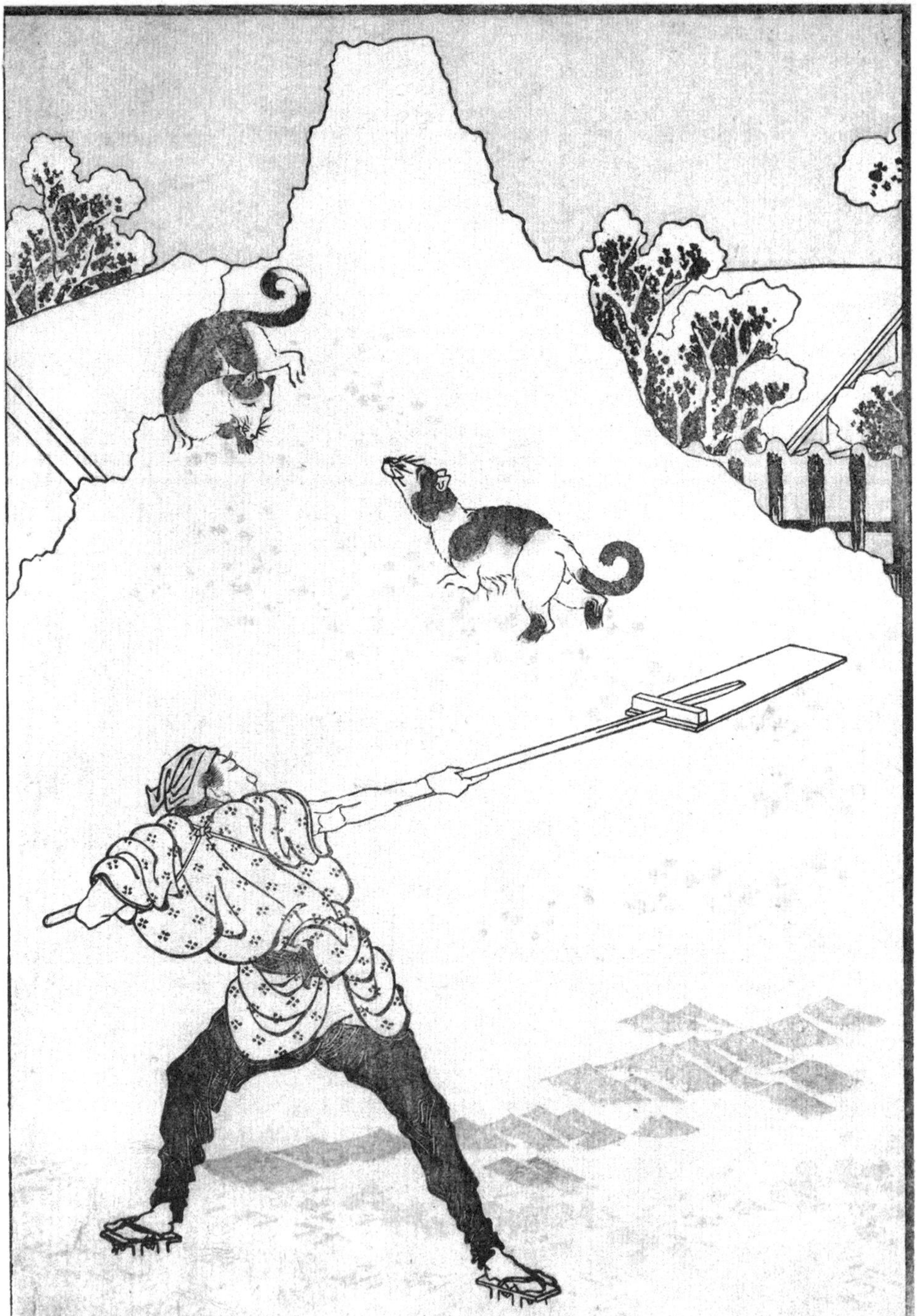

153

Fuji the Day After Snow

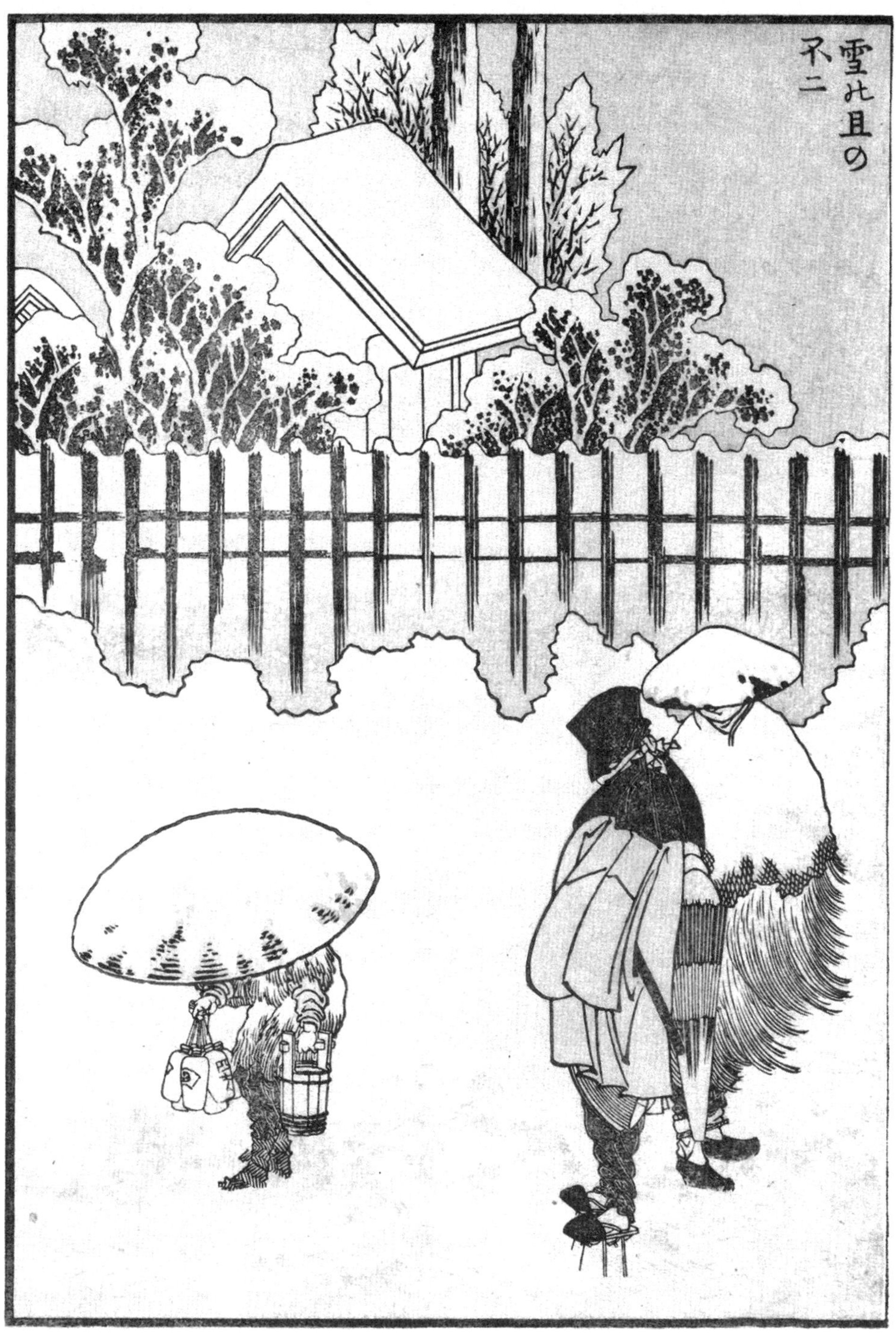

雪中の
不二

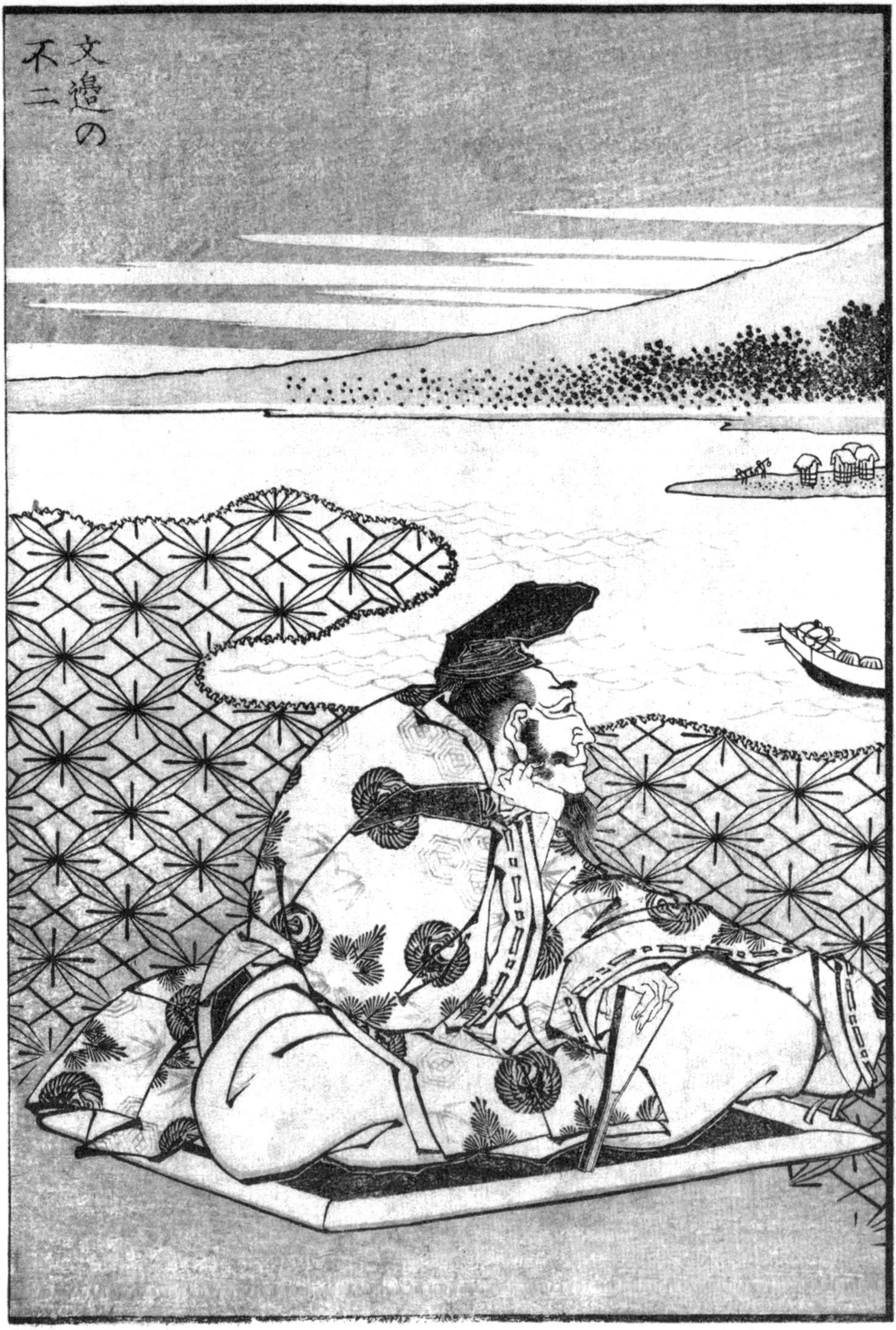

Fuji of Letters

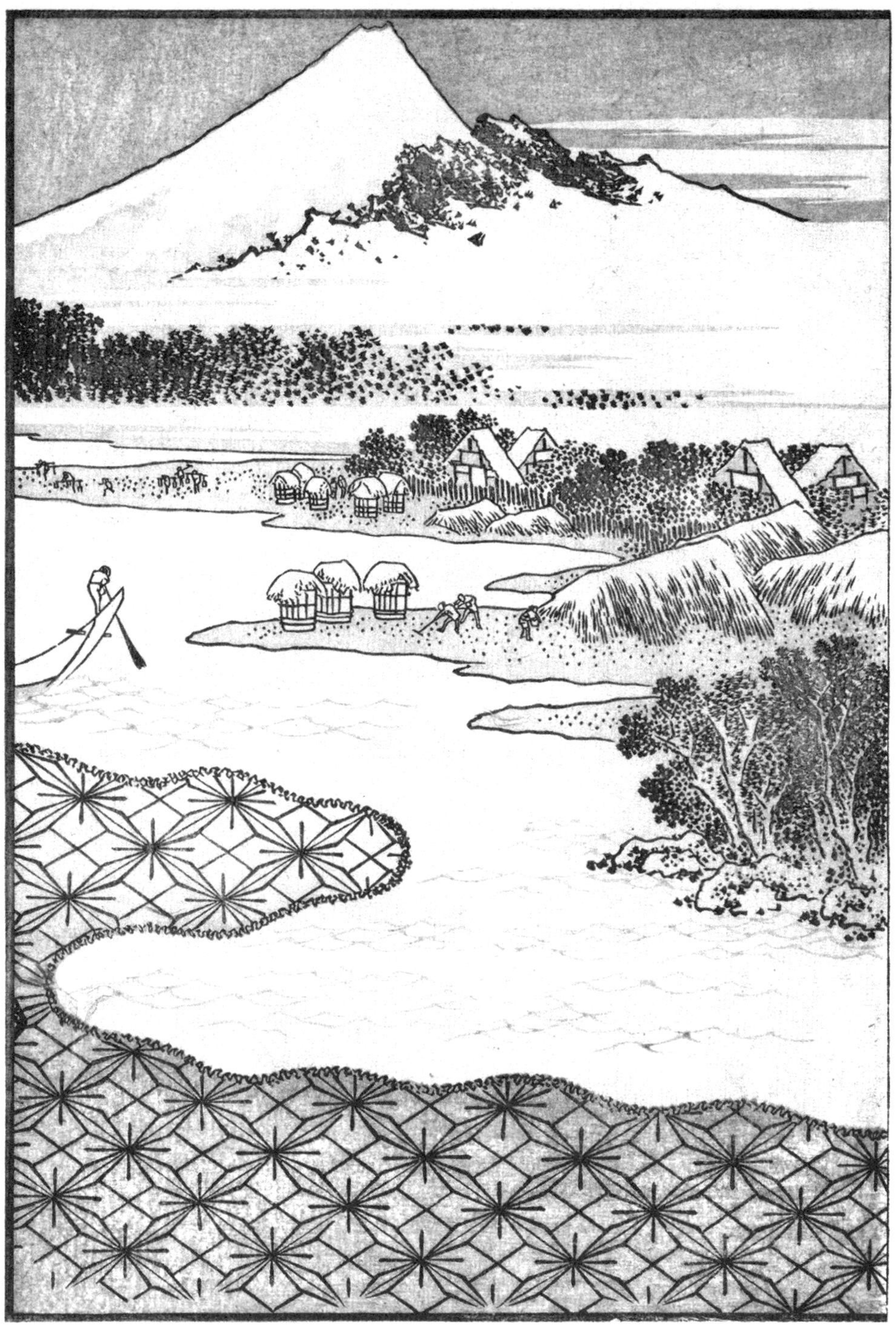

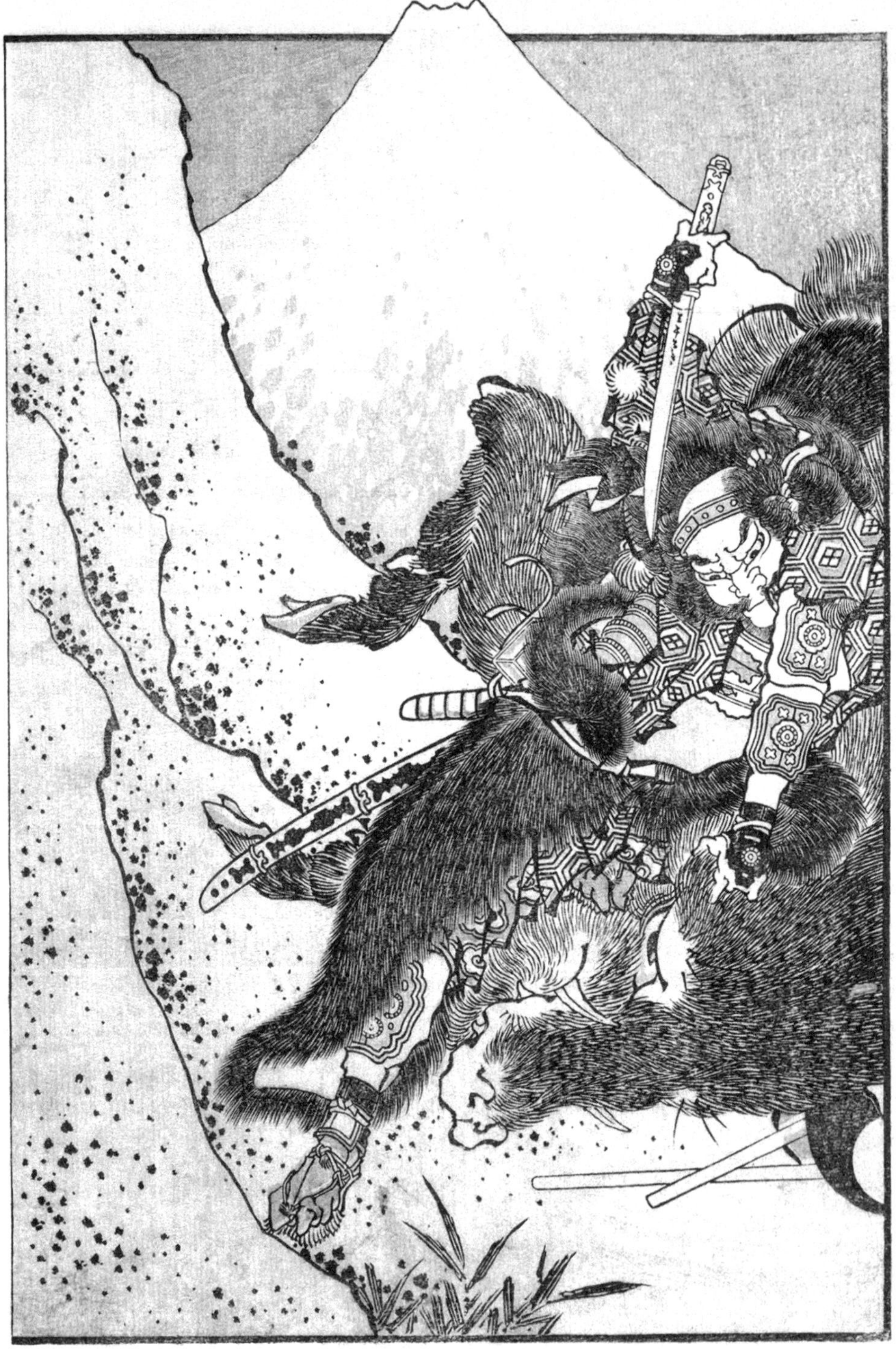

Nitta Hunting a Giant Boar on Mount Fuji

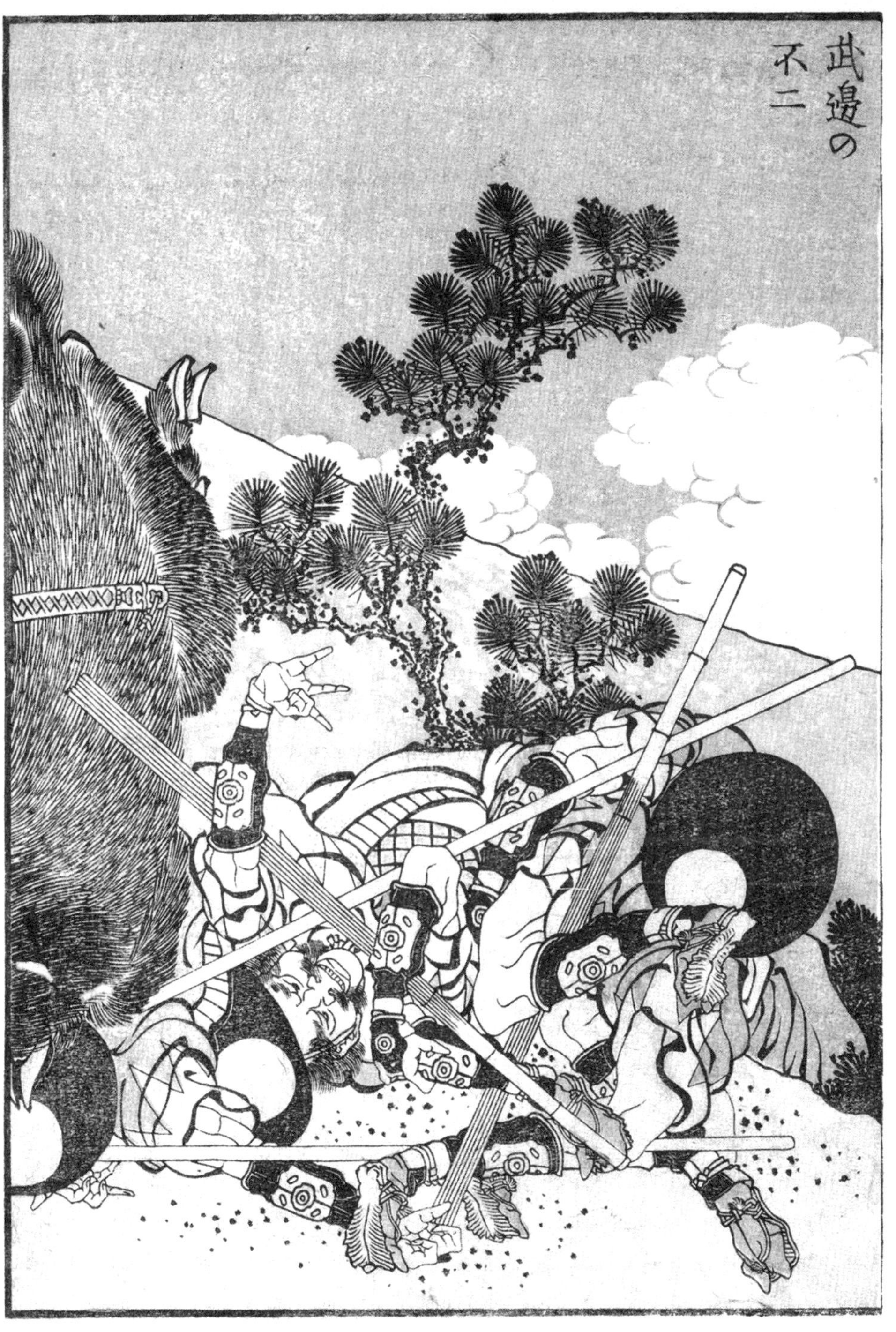

武邊の
不二

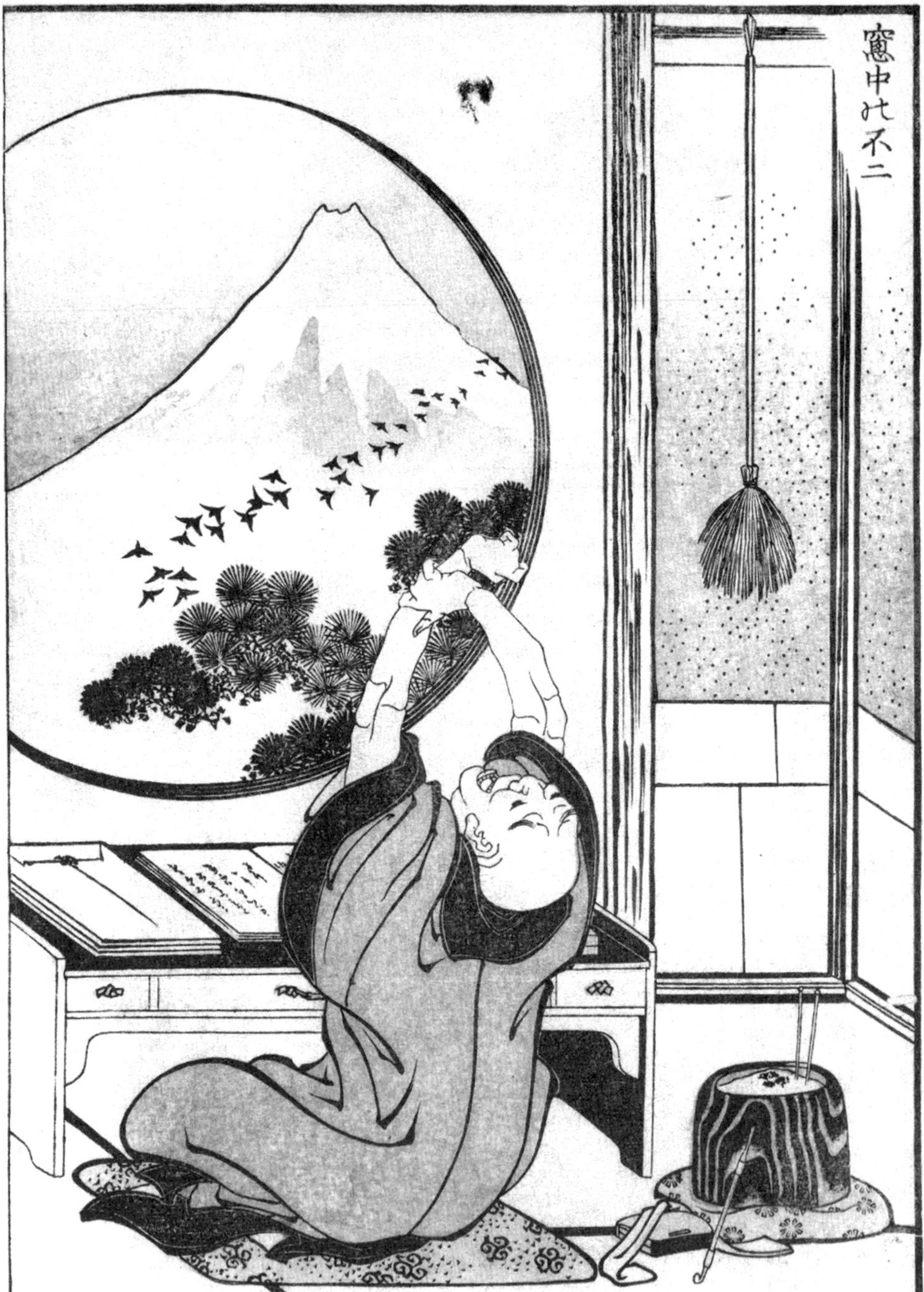

 Fuji in a Window

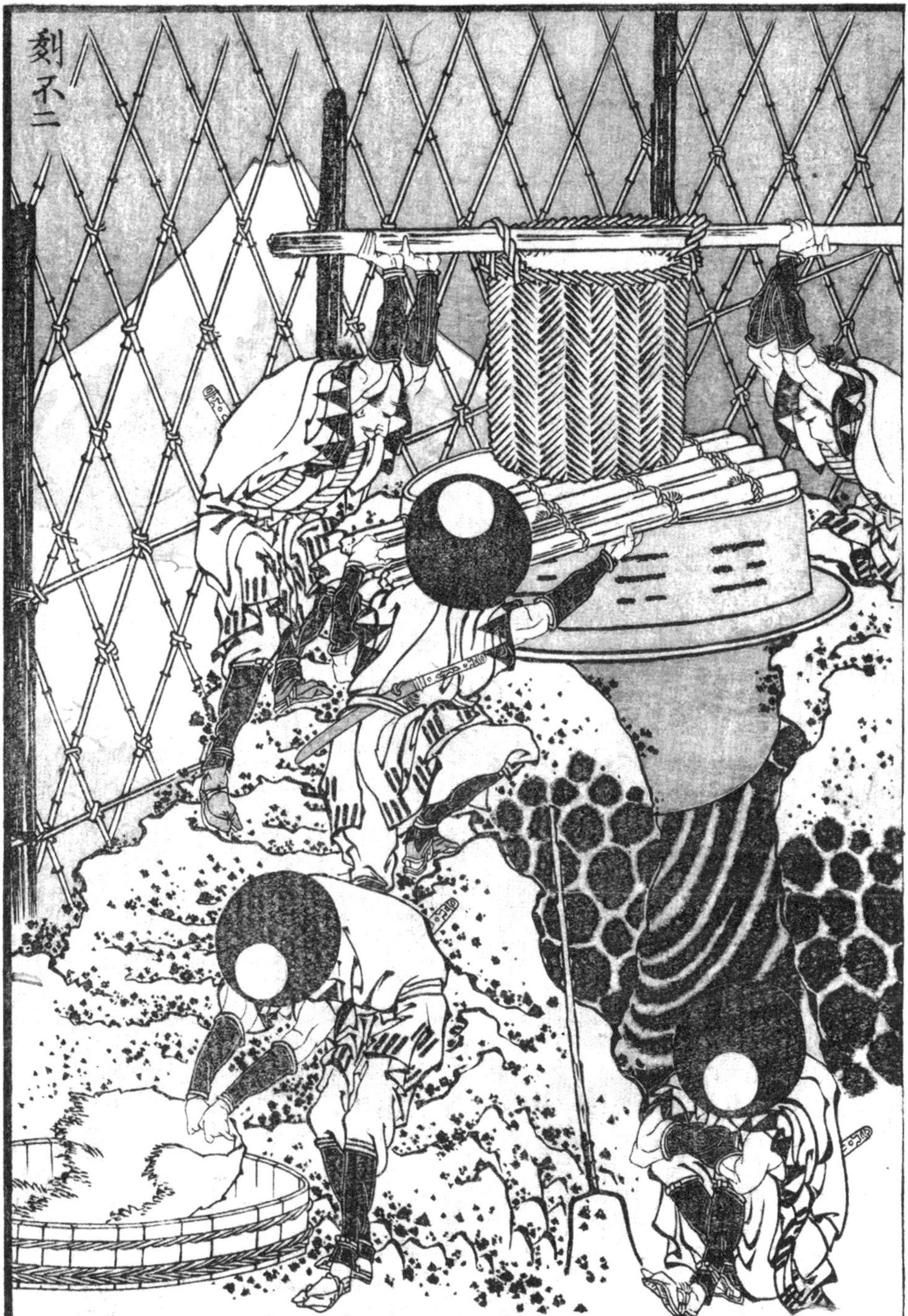

157

Fuji Carved

七十六齢　前北齋為一改　画狂老人卍筆

己六才より物の形状を写の癖ありて半百の此より数々画図を顕すといへども七十年前画く所は実に取るに足るものなし七十三才にして稍禽獣虫魚の骨格草木の出生を悟り得たり故に八十才にしては益々進み九十才にして猶其奥意を極め一百歳にして正に神妙ならん歟百有十歳にして一点一格にして生るがごとくならん願くは長壽の君子予が言の妄ならざるを見たまふべし

画狂老人卍述

江川留吉　〔五常亭〕

剞劂

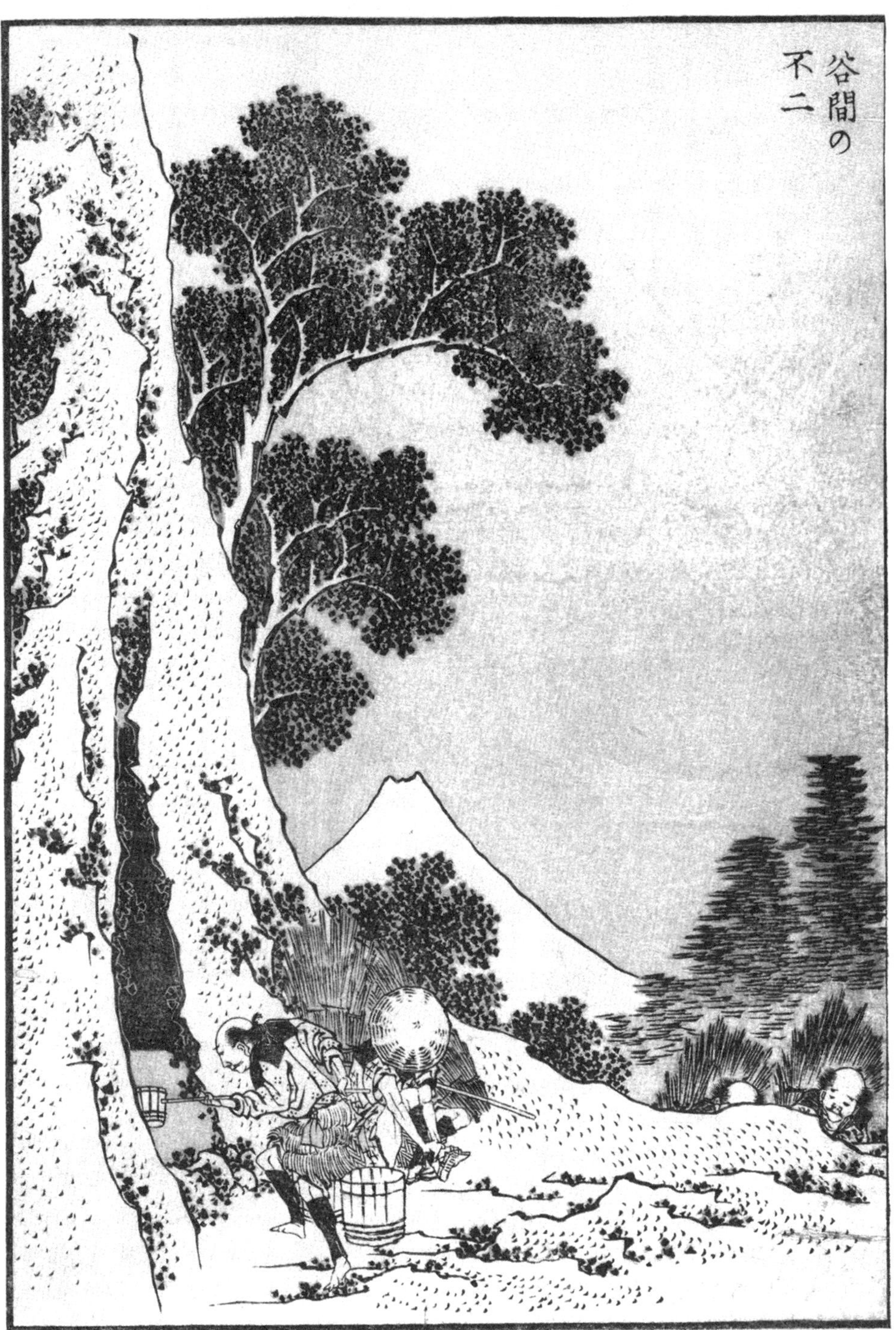

158 *Fuji in a Valley*

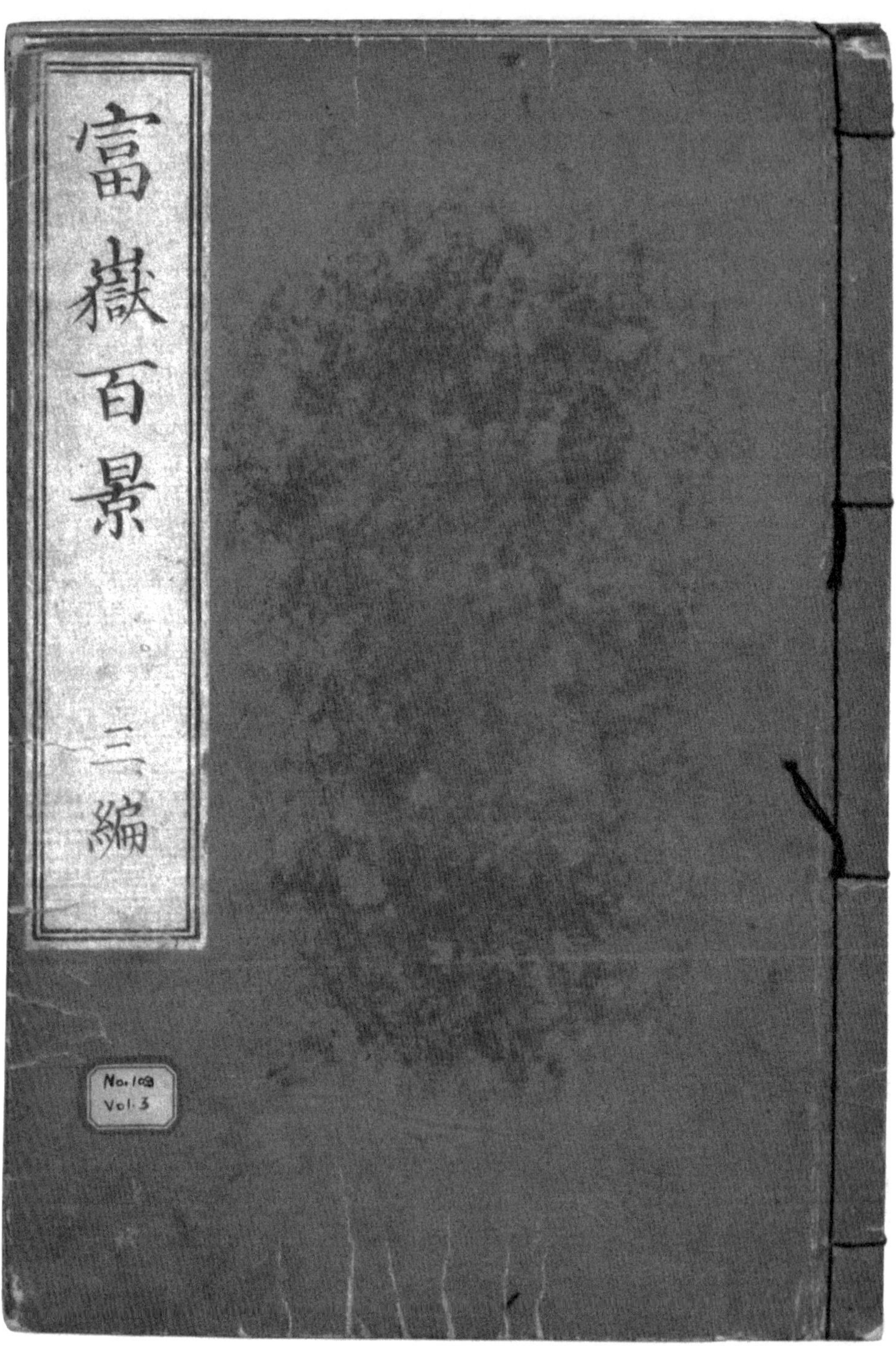

One Hundred Views of Mount Fuji, Volume 3: cover

漁家百景 近刻
圓方長短一百自在圖會 近刻

月下百景 同
百馬百牛 同

農家百景 同
百禽百獸 同

天保六乙未年春三月發行

尾州名古屋　永樂屋東四郎
江戸麹町四丁目　角丸屋甚助
金馬喰町二丁目　西村與八
全　西村祐藏

書林

君錫子の百富士を畫乃正がら

ふよう望北齋翁の富嶽百景

畫乃崎うる者なり翁雄健走

筆をにて一富峰をよく楷墨の

間は鼓舞す八面向皆寫し得て

きハめて訥絶するり聞翁の齢

今九十を踰て視聴なお少年

尾張東壁堂藏板畫譜畫手本目録

福善高畫譜　金氏畫譜　一筆畫譜　英勇畫譜　浮世畫譜　同武編　北齋畫譜　同中編　同下編

文鳳麐畫　蕙高廉畫　同二編　同三編　同四編　同五編　神車行燈　同武編　北齋女今川

武勇魁圖會　同二編　珖珠漫畫　北溪漫畫　北雲漫畫　北齋漫畫　繪本庭訓　同中編　同下編

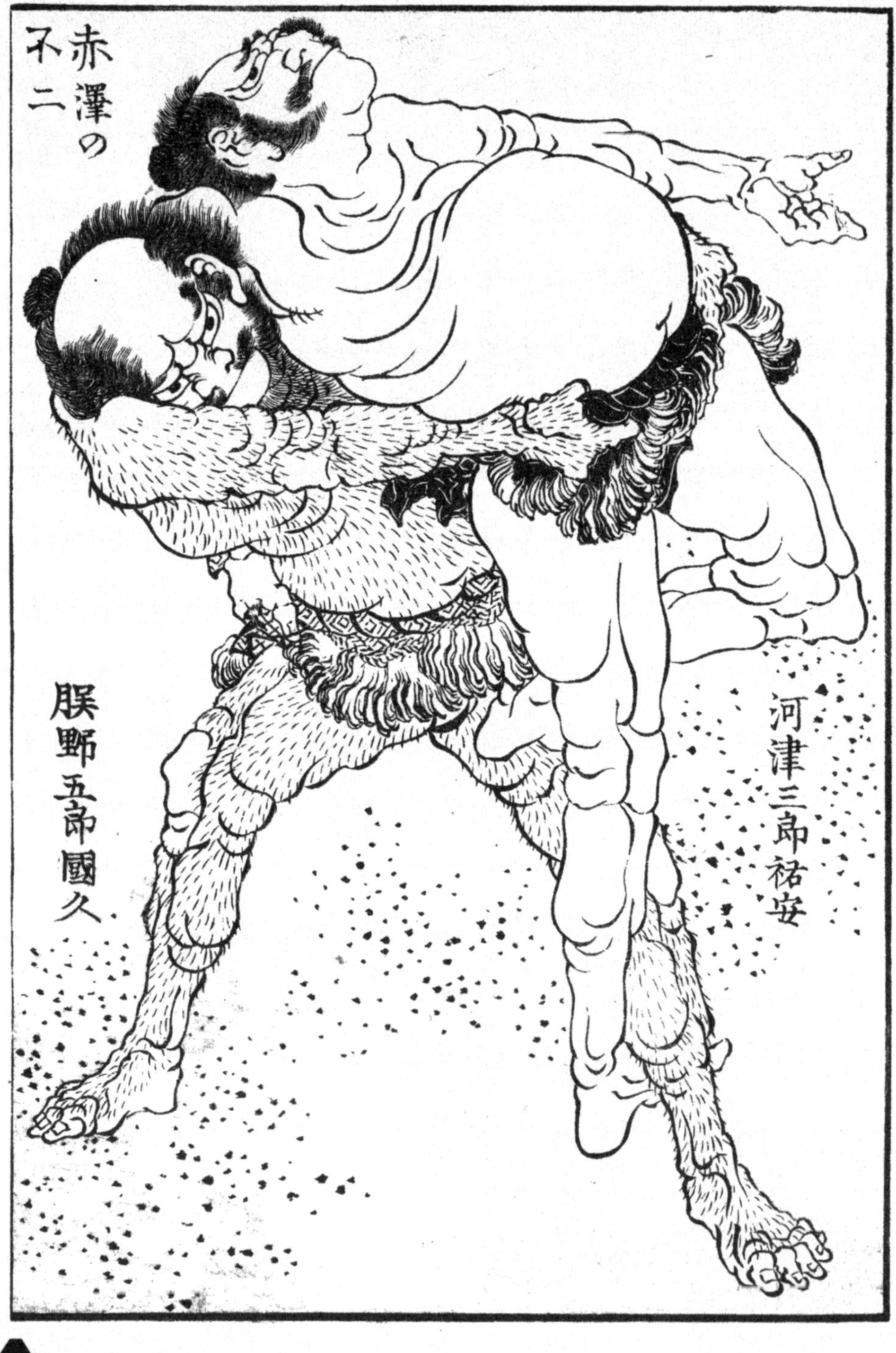

Fuji at Akazawa

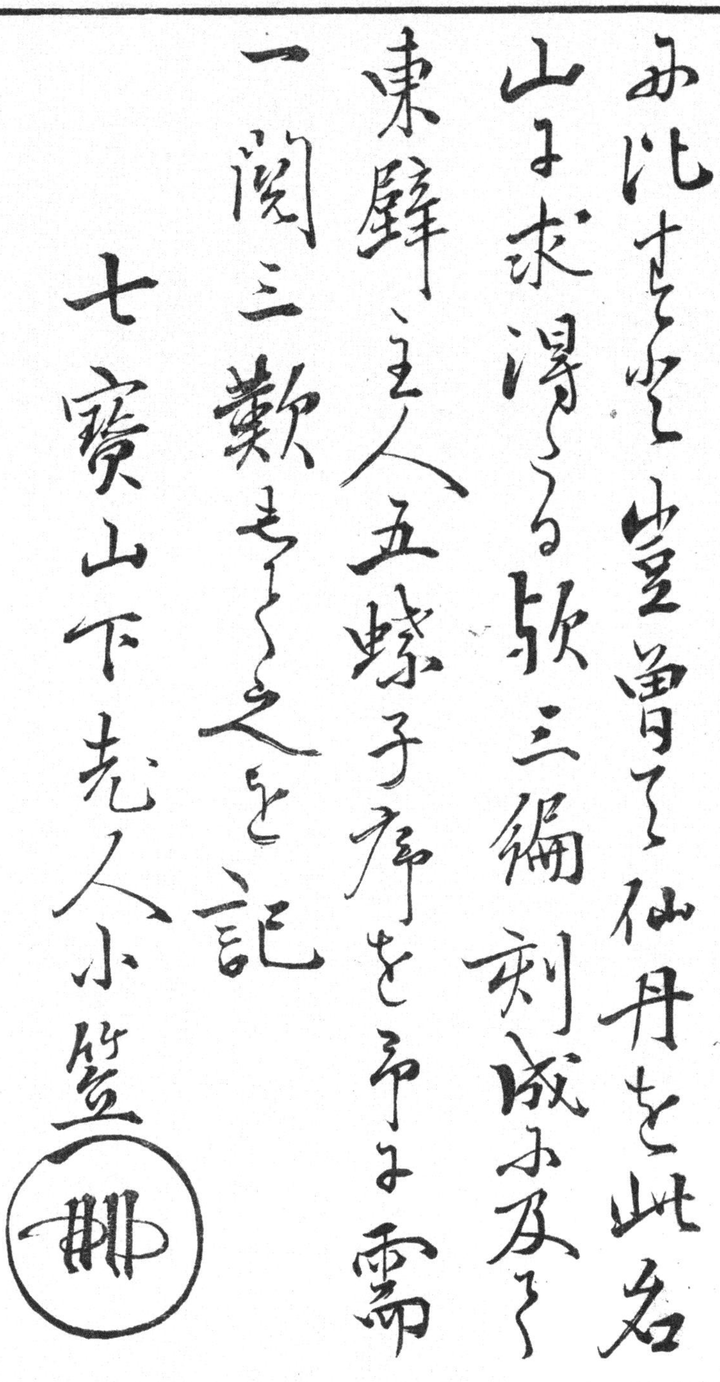

西北に空しく山豈曾て仙丹を此君
山を求め得る歟三編刻成小及ひ
東壁主人五蝶子序を示す需
一閲三歎もて之を記
七寳山下老人小笠

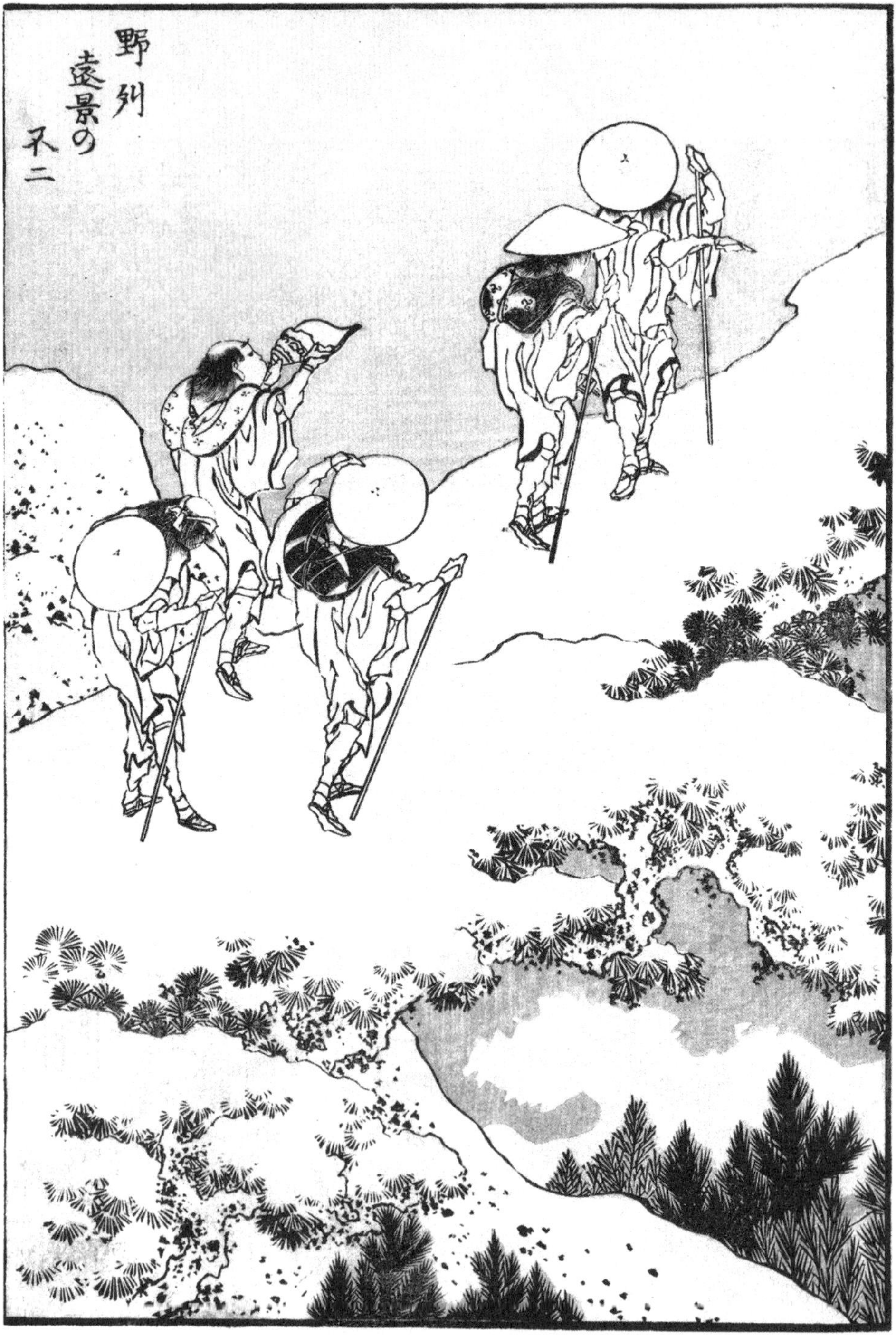

160 *Fuji in the Distance from Shimotsuke Province –*
Pilgrims Crossing the Pine Arch on Mount Nantai

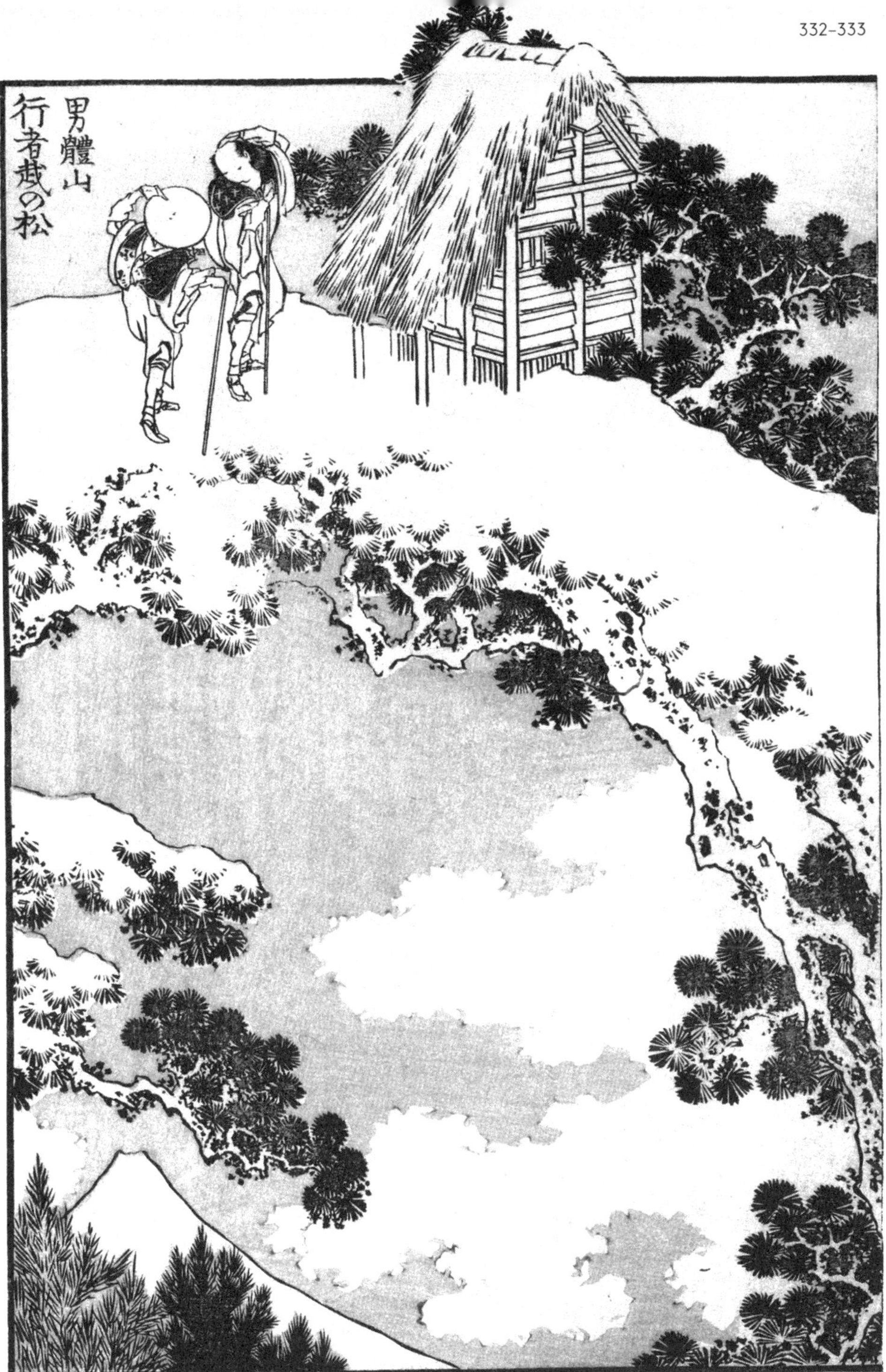
男體山
行者蔵の松
男體山
行者蔵の松

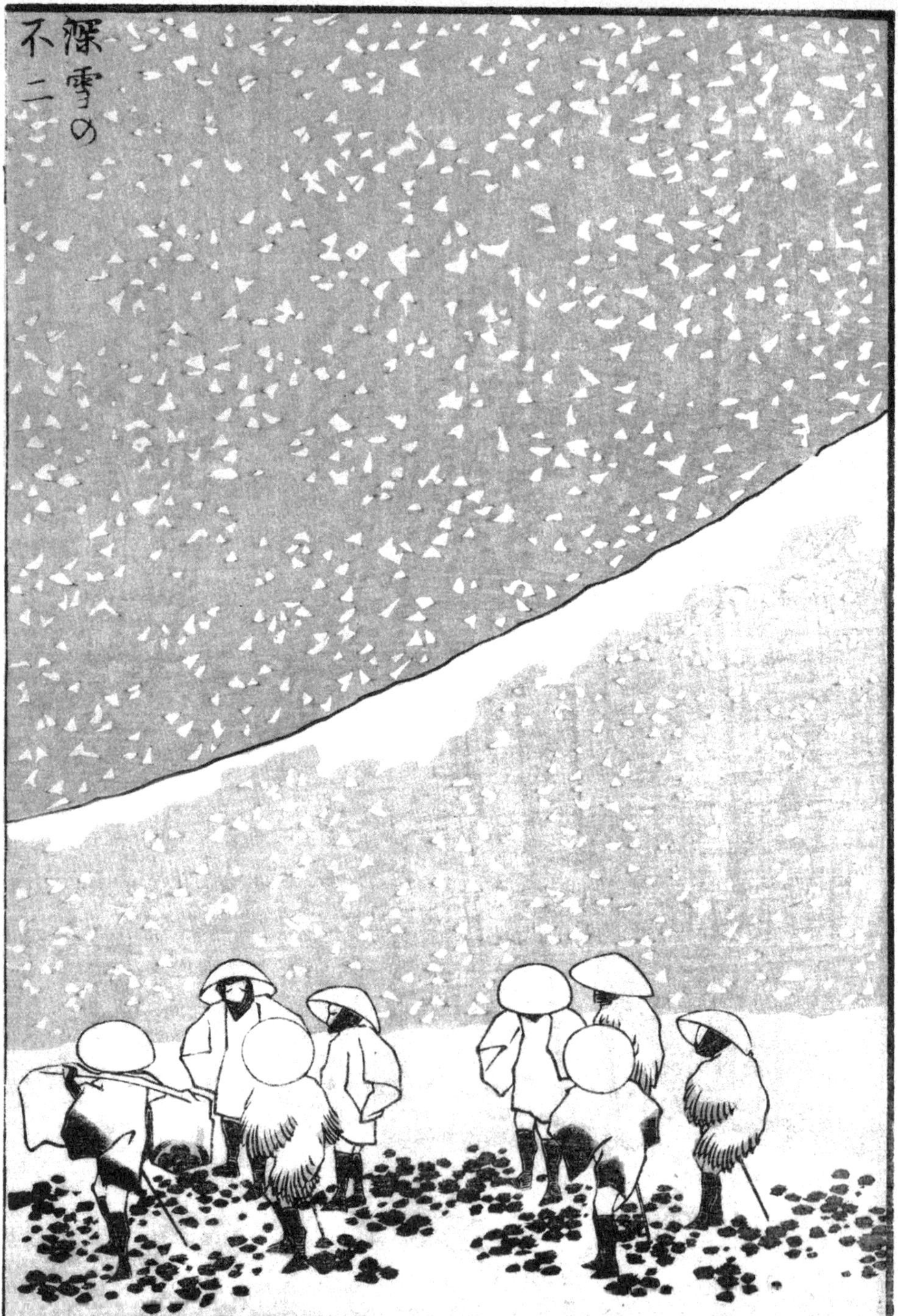

深雪の不二

Fuji in Deep Snow

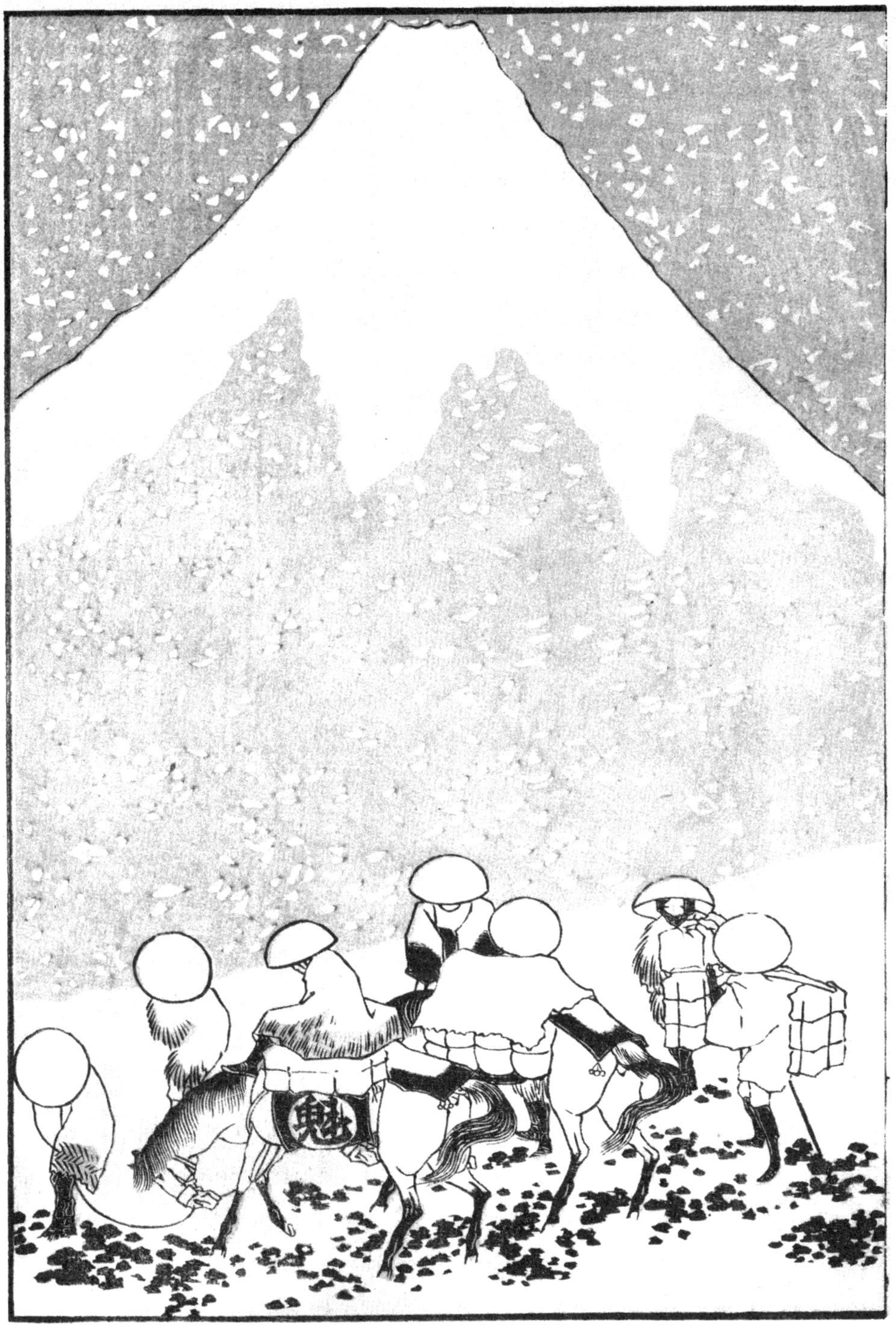

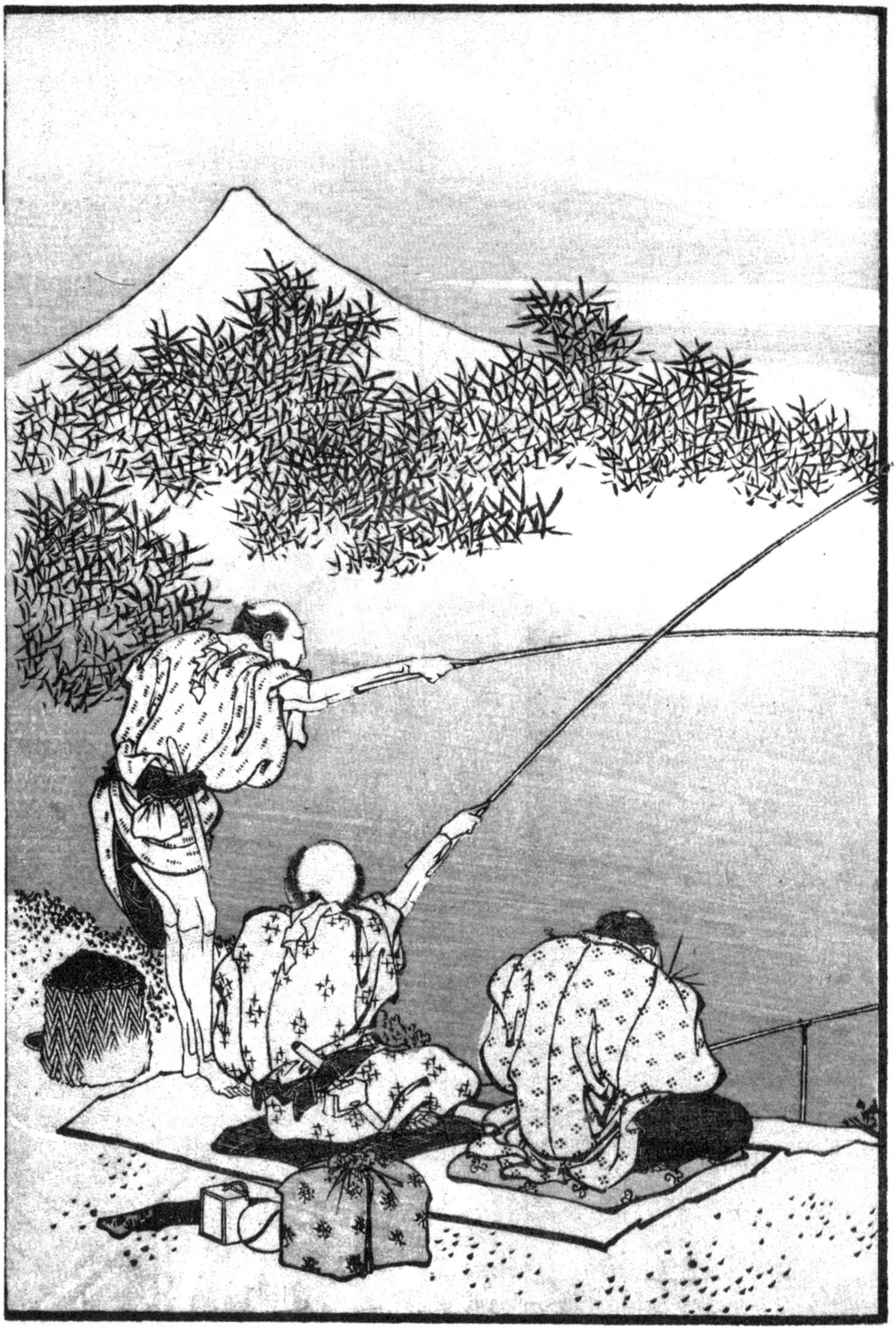

A Noble's Villa – Fuji from Sunamura

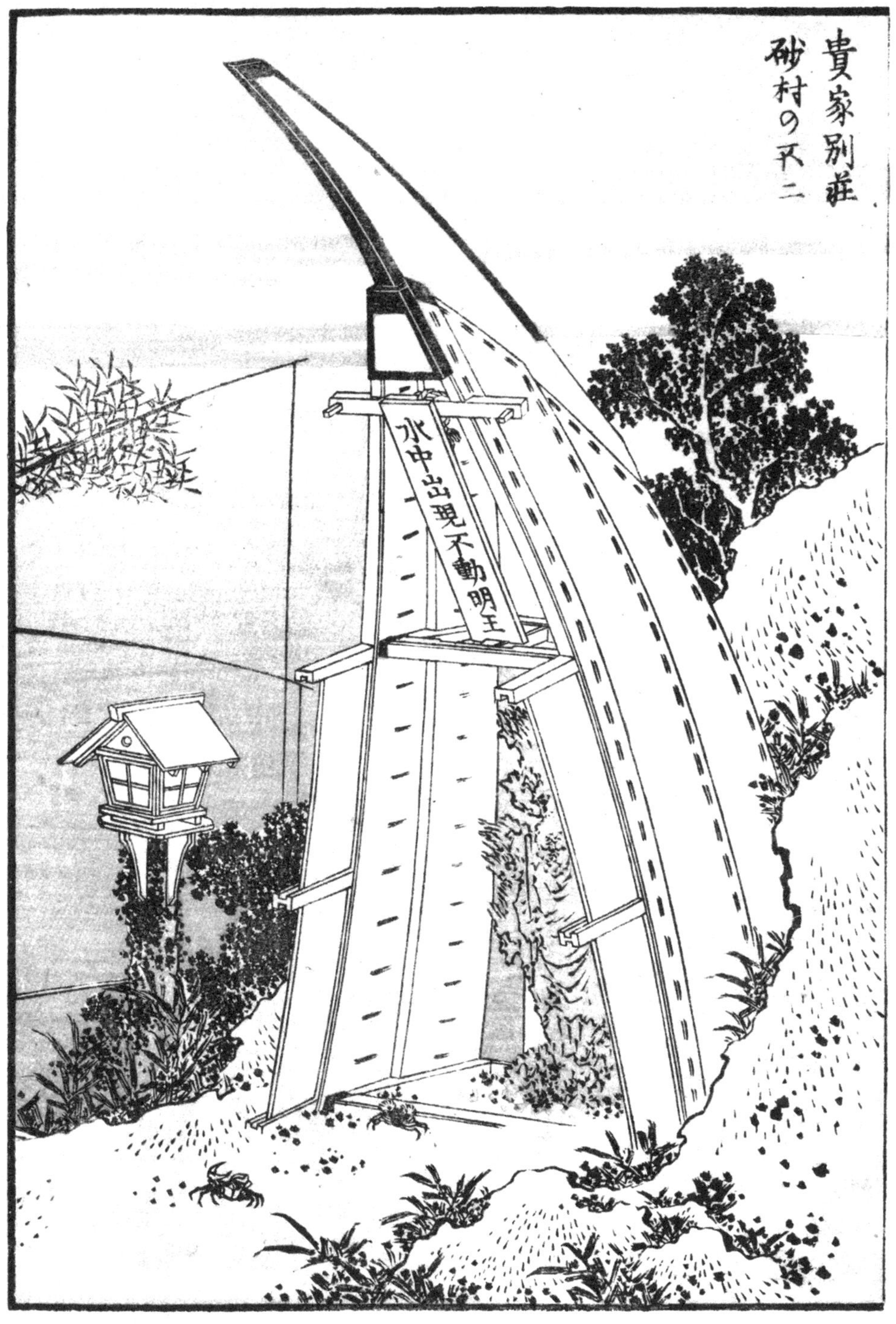
貴家別莊
砂村の又二
水中山現不動明王

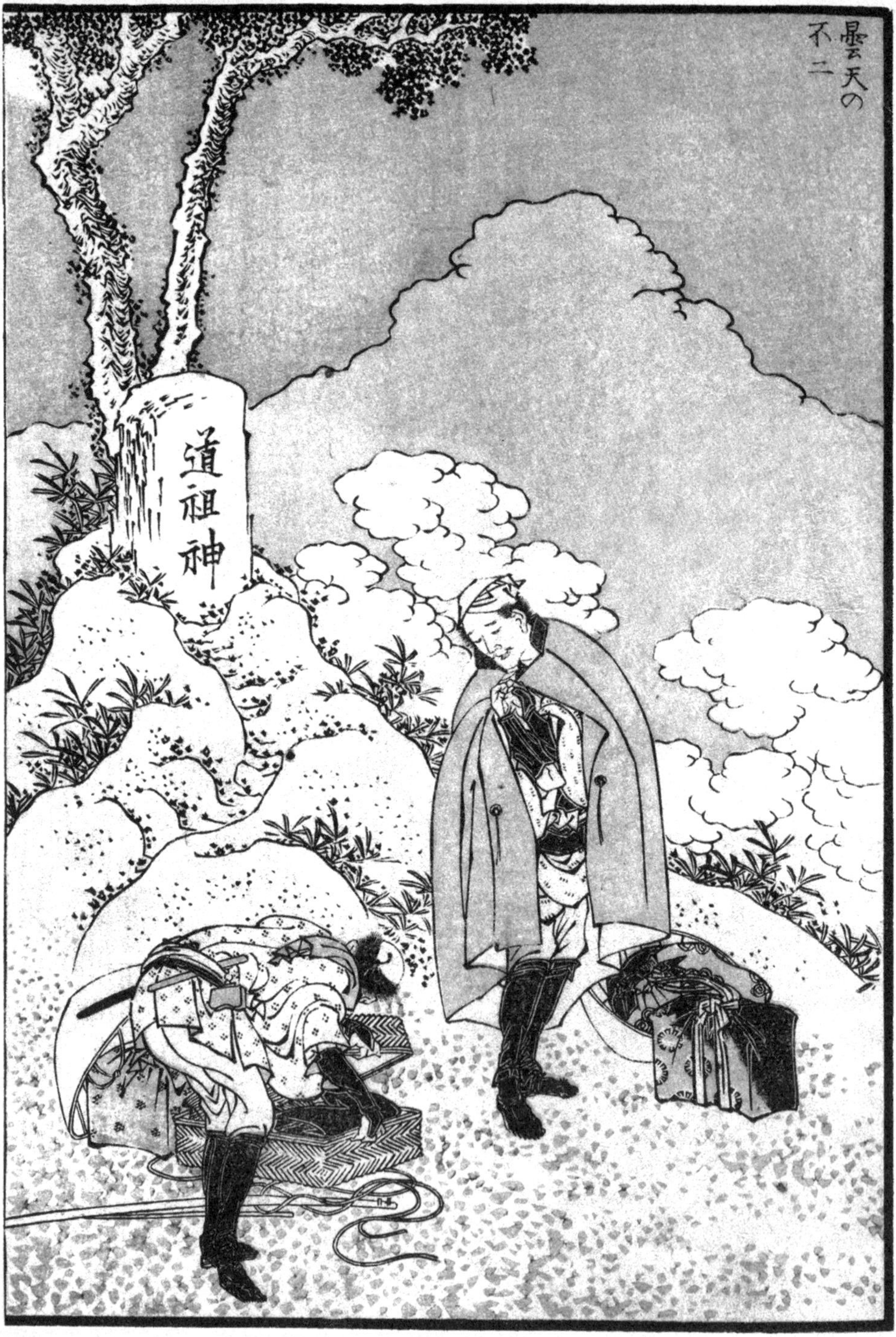

163　*Fuji Under Clouds*

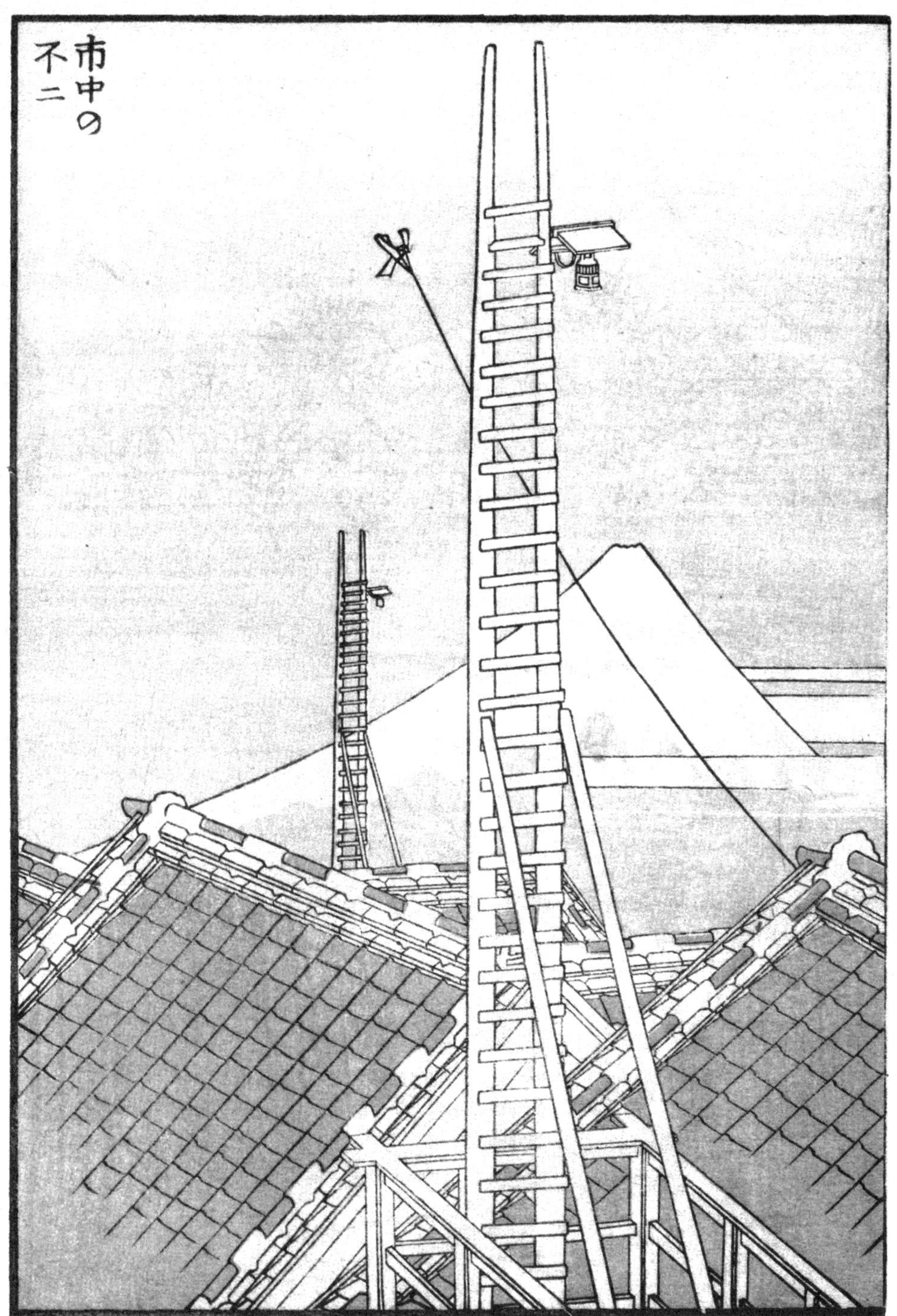

164

Fuji in the City

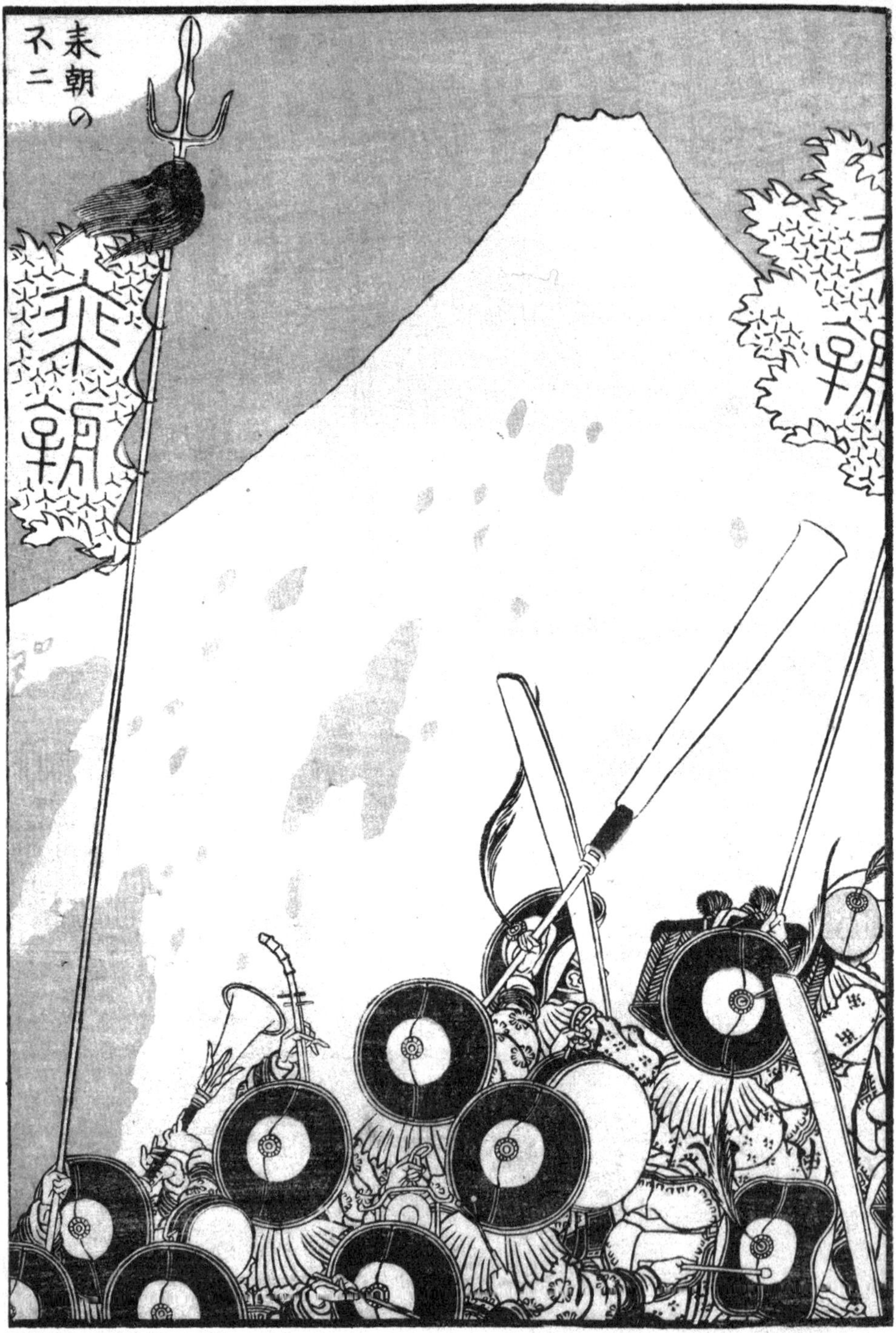

Fuji and Foreign Embassy

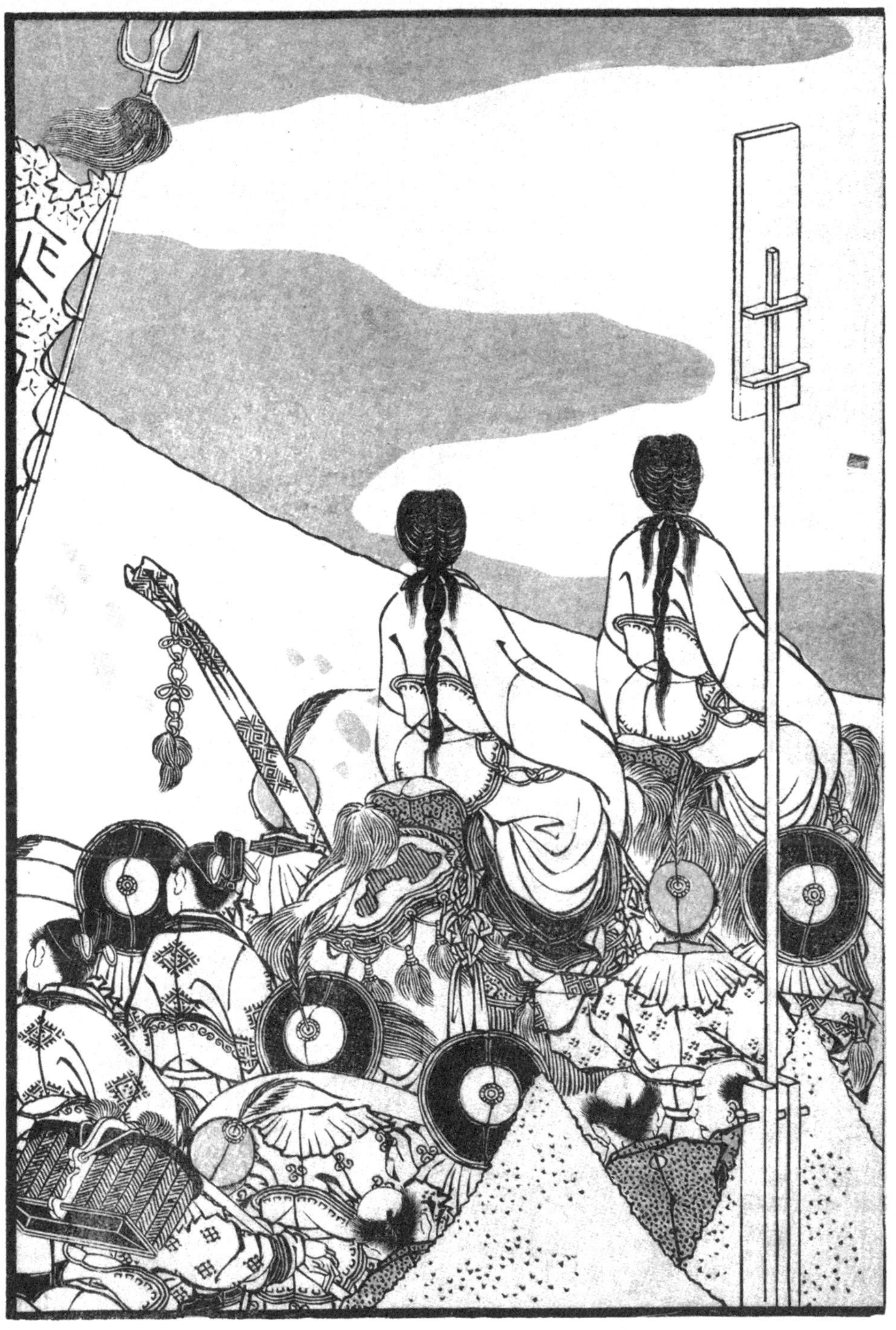

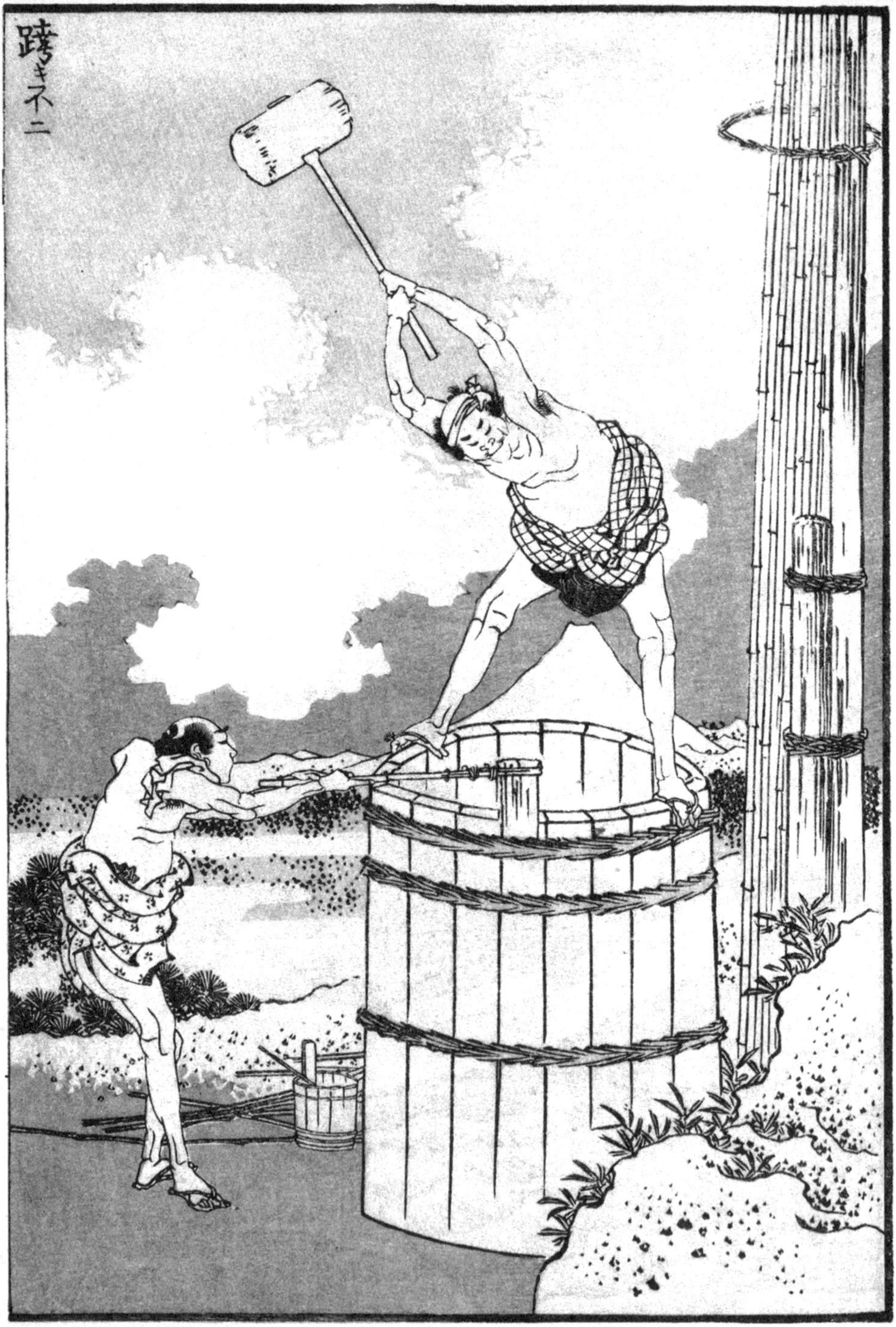

Fuji Straddled

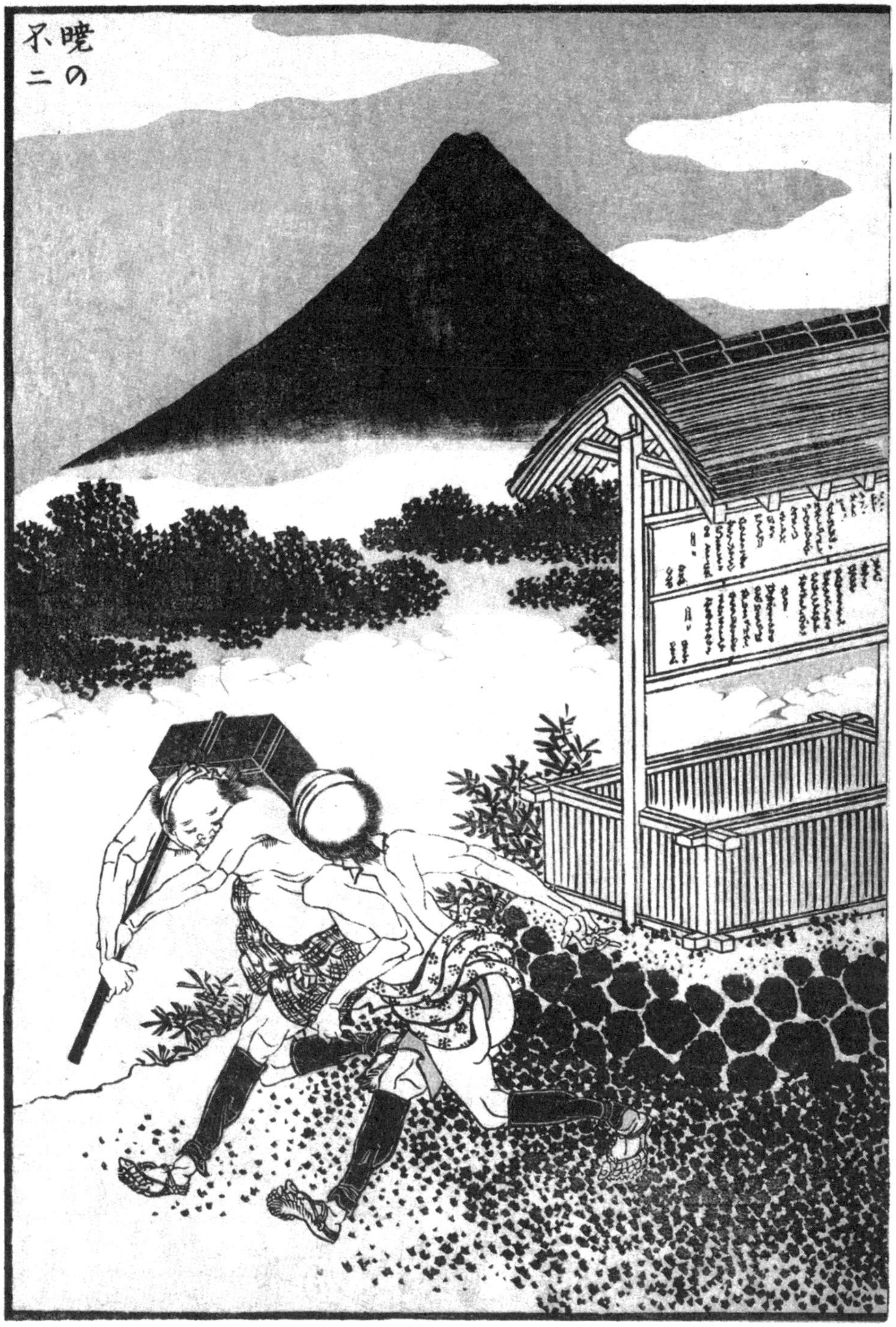

167 *Fuji at Daybreak*

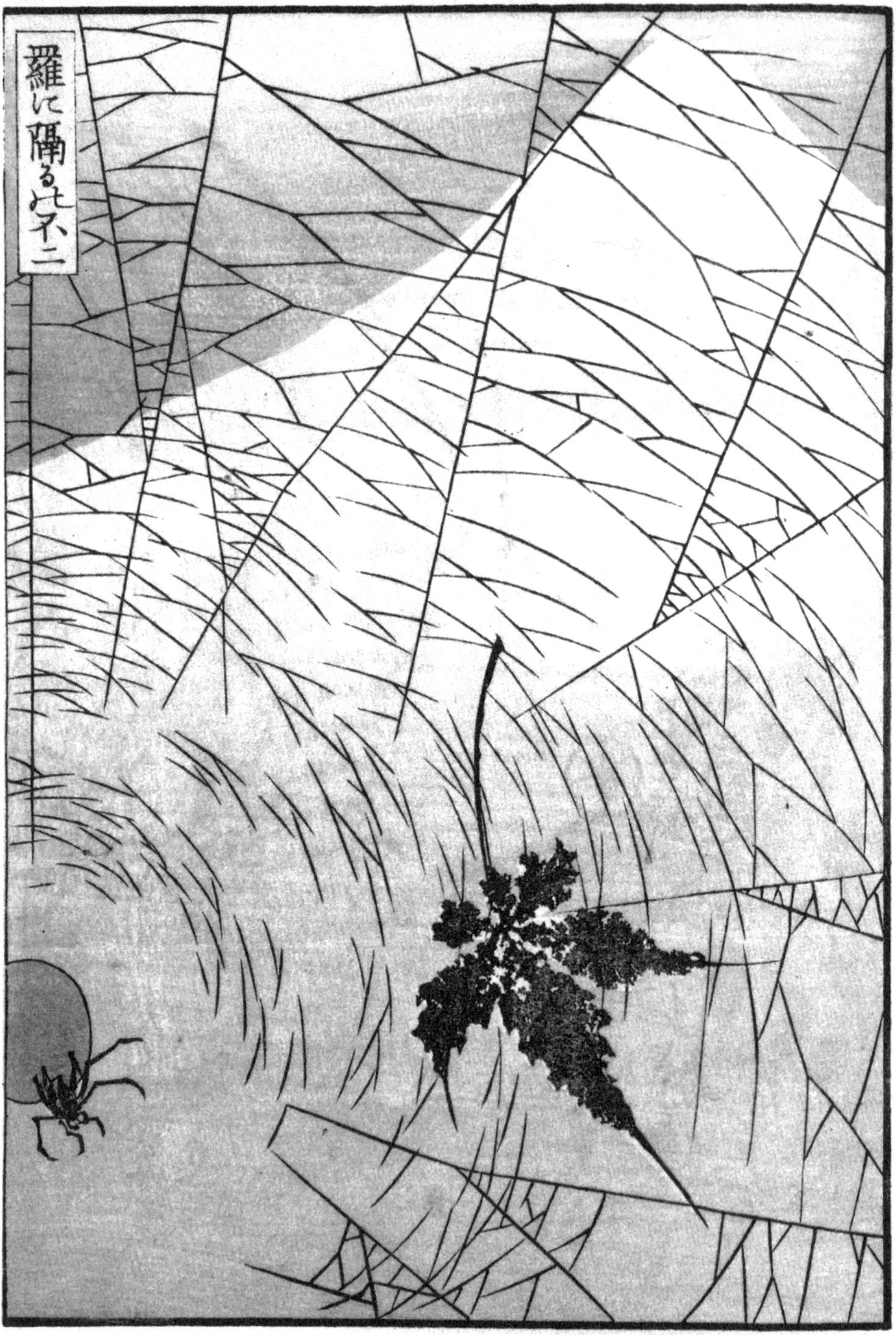

Fuji Through a Web

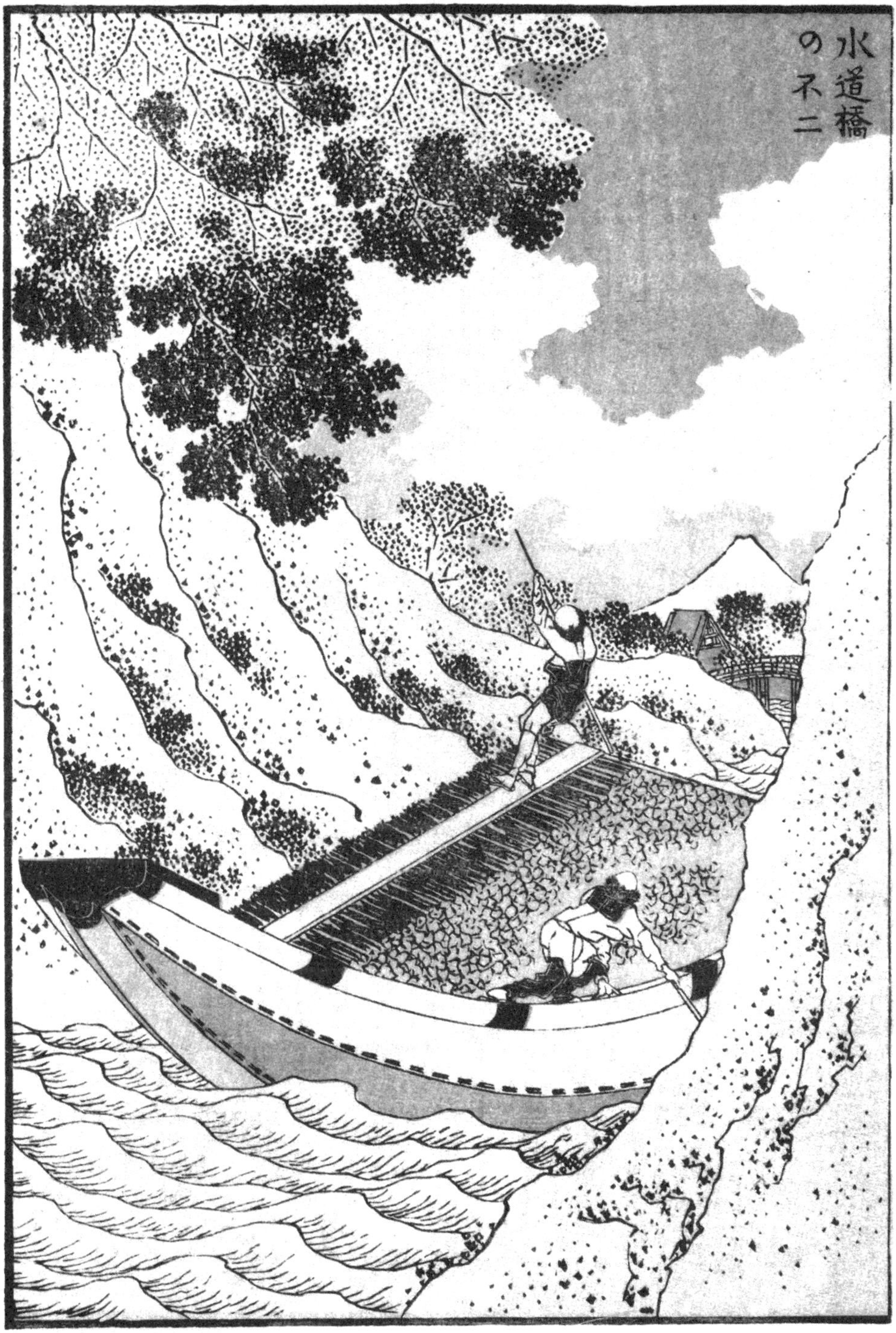

169   *Fuji from Suidōbashi*

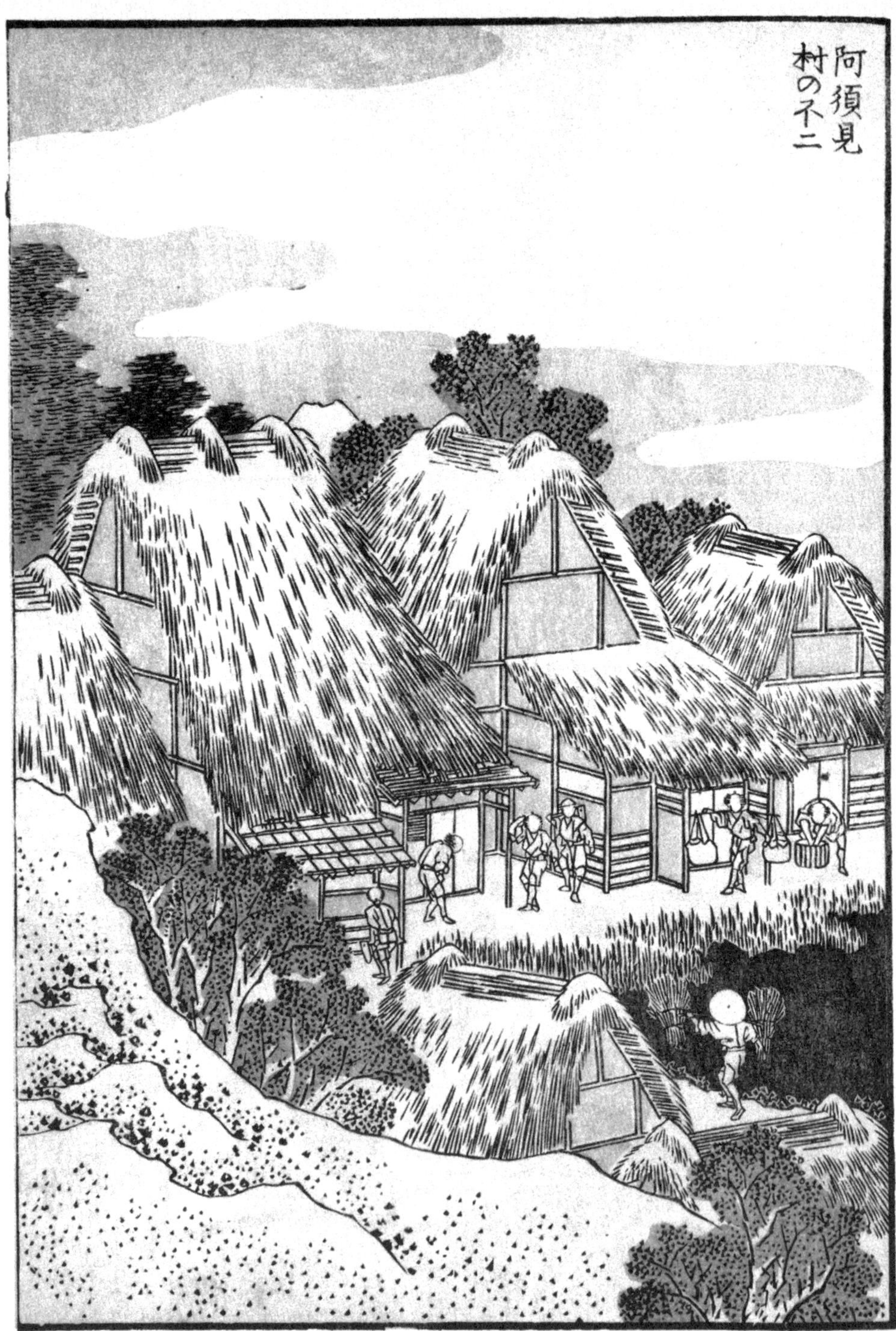

 Fuji in Asumi Village

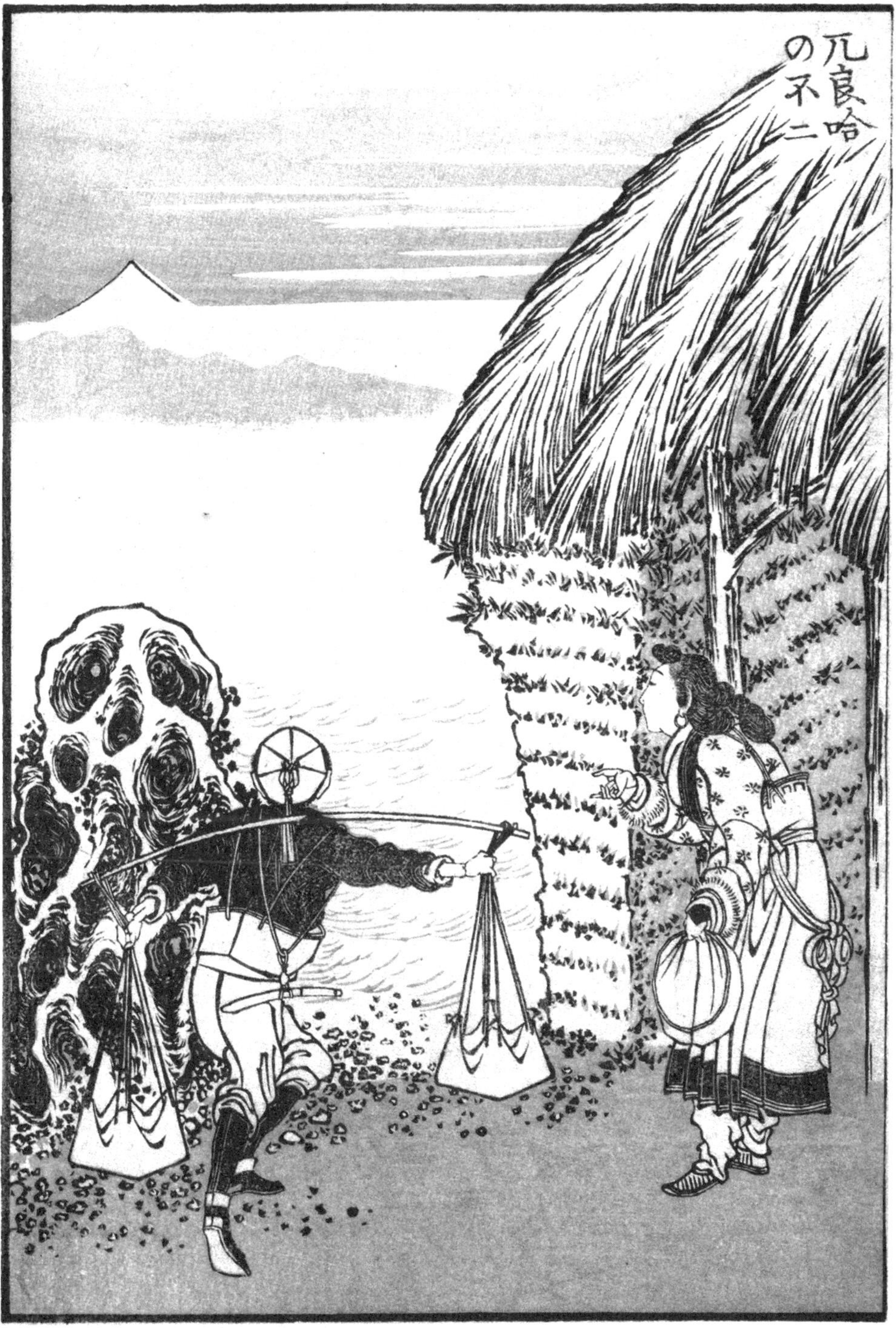

171 *Fuji from Orankai*

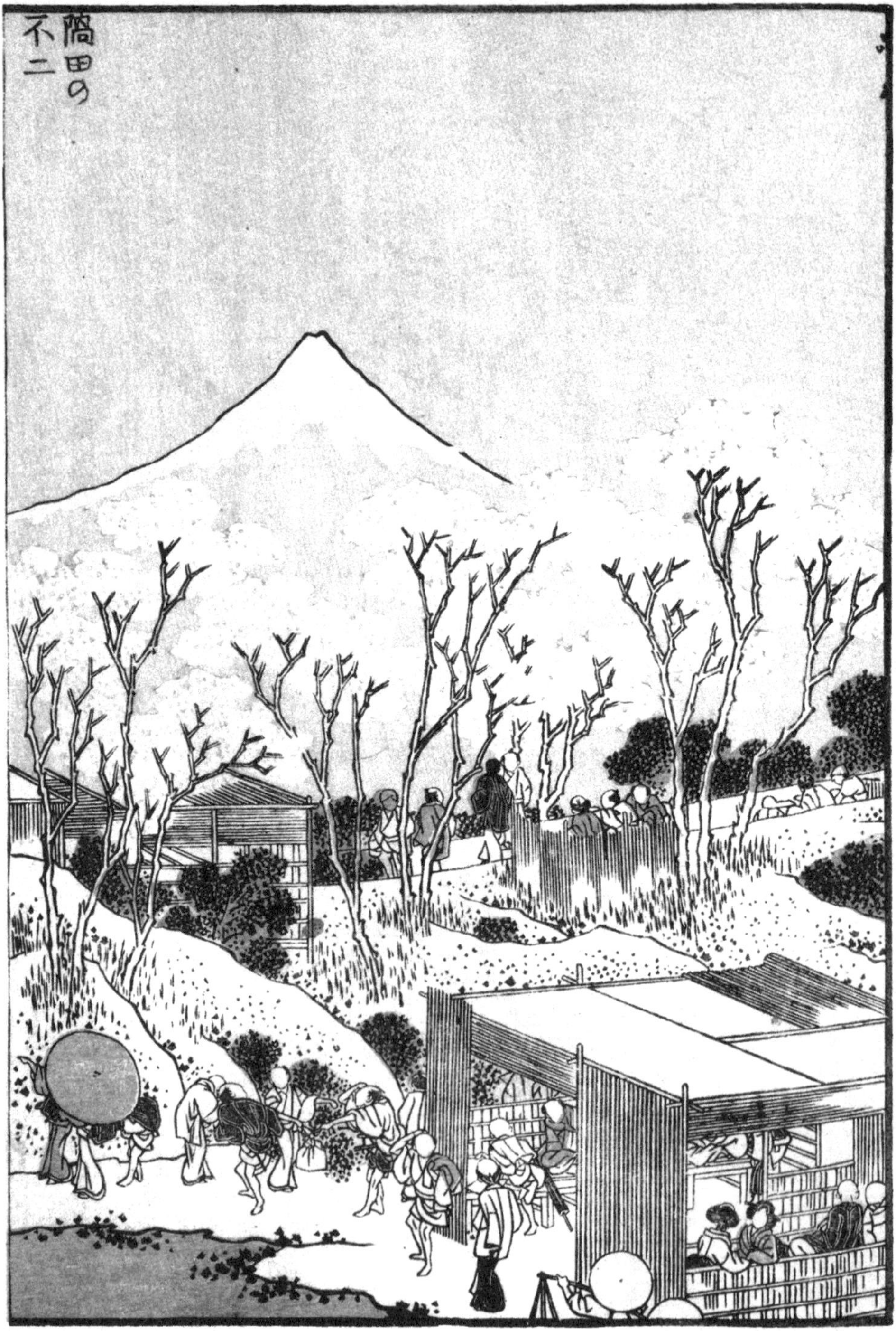

172　*Fuji from the Sumida River*

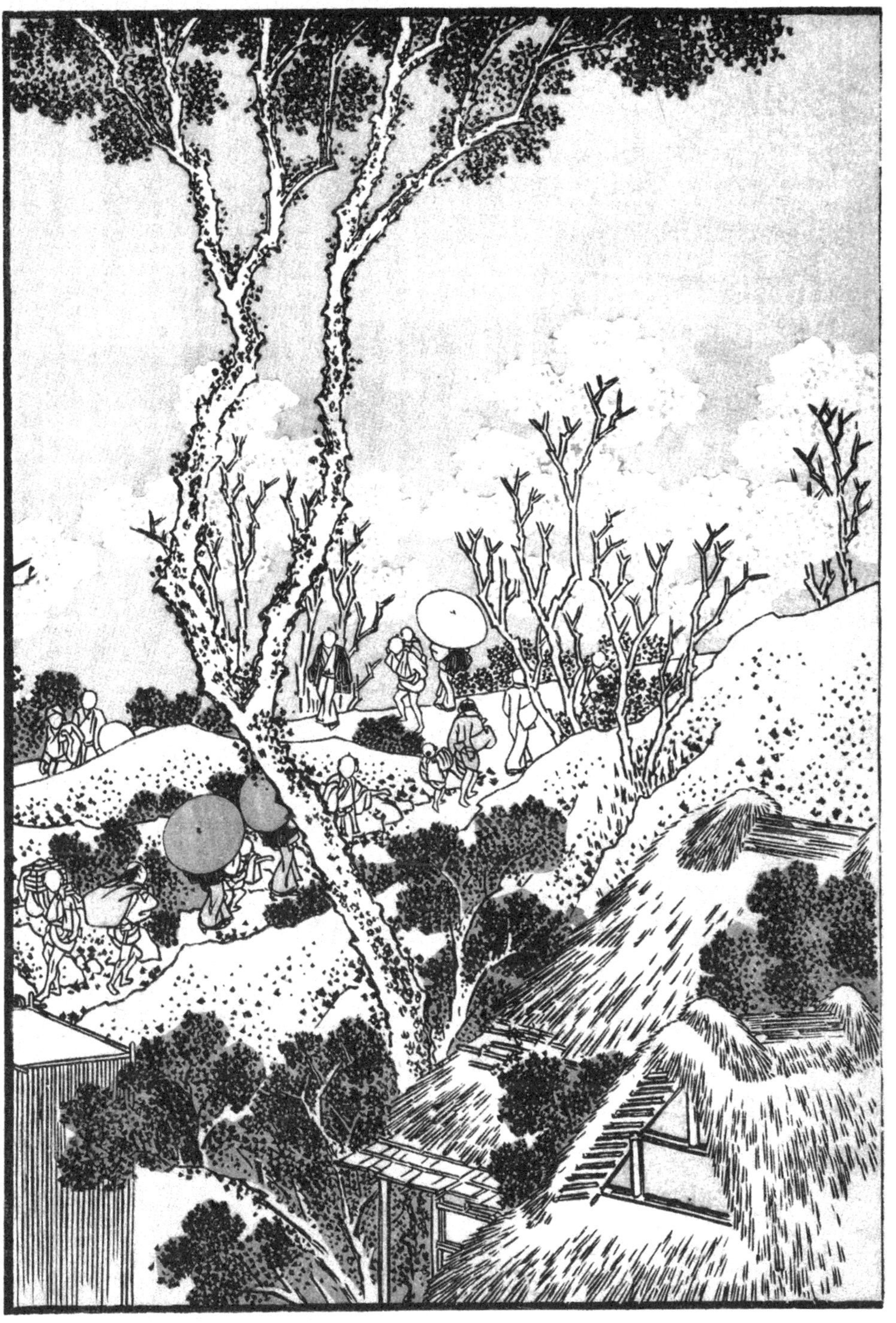

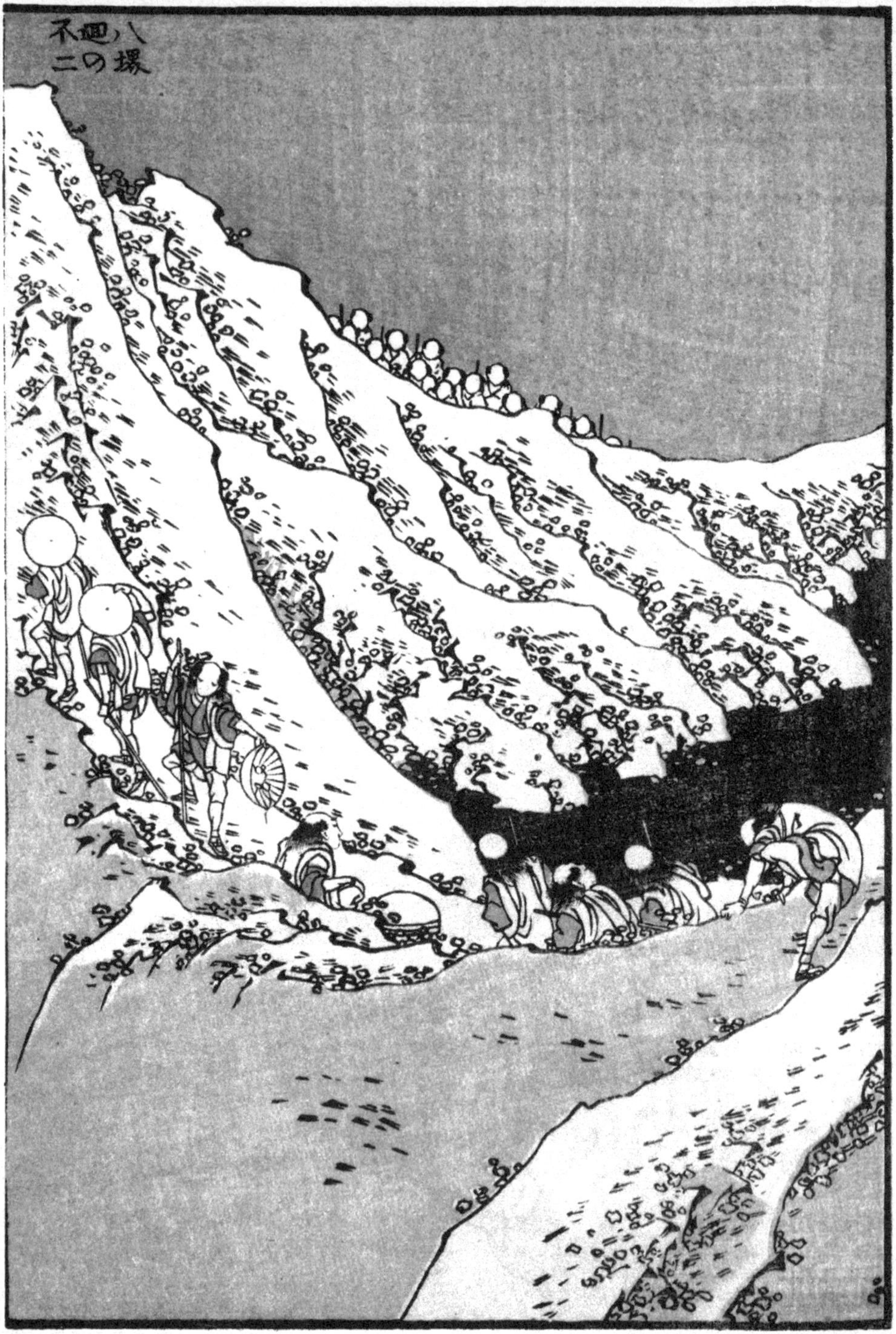

Circling the Crater of Fuji

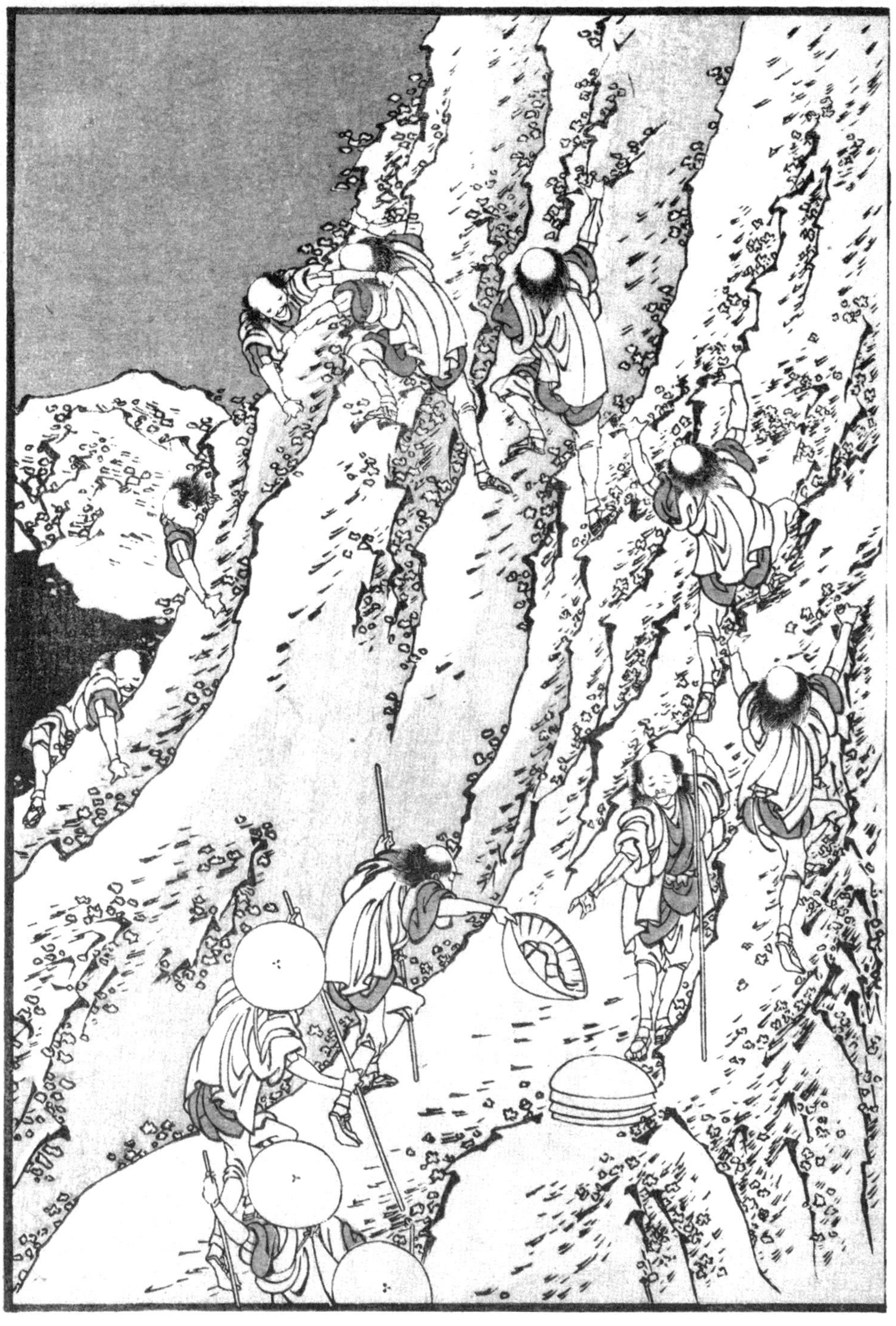

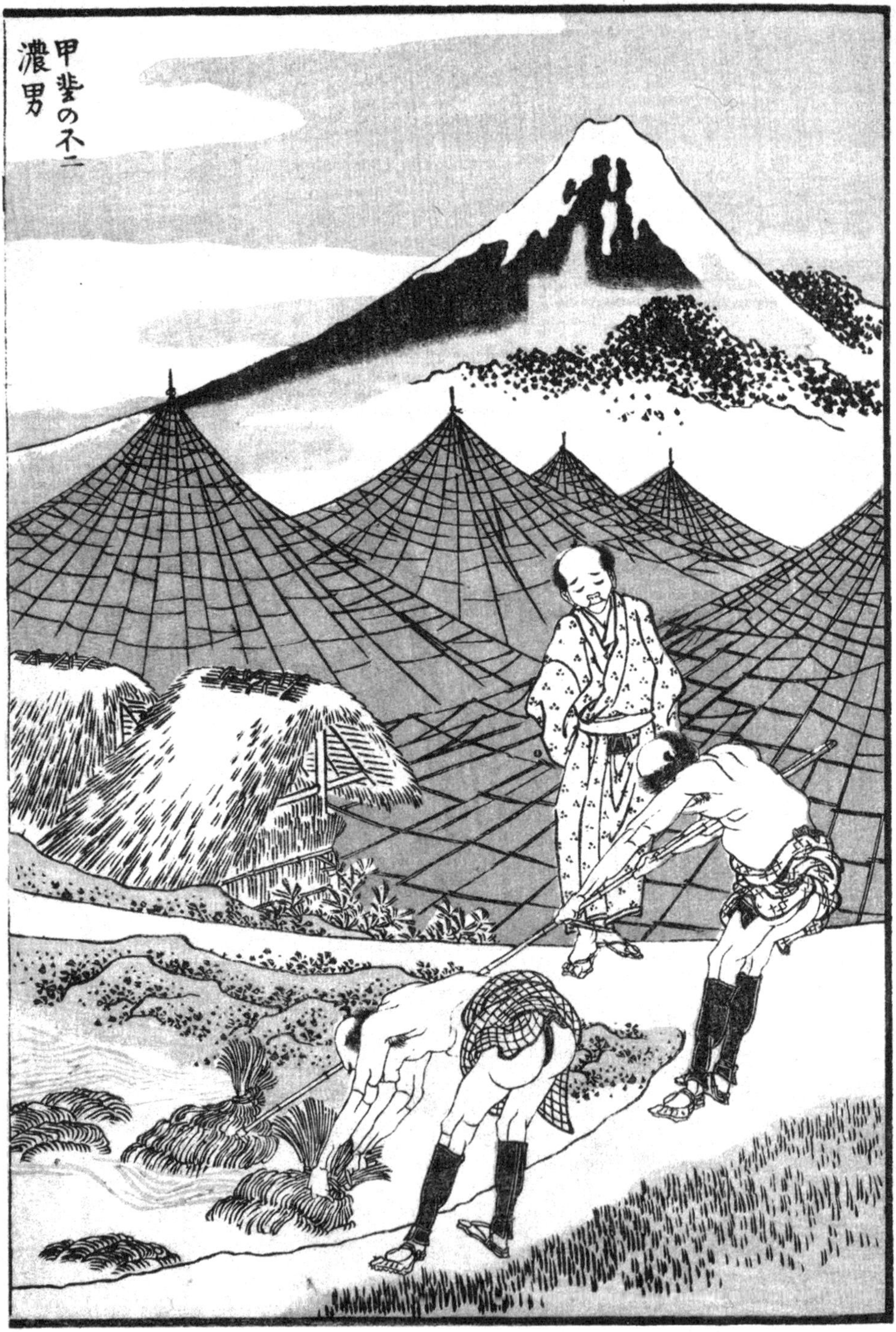

The Farmland of Fuji in Kai Province

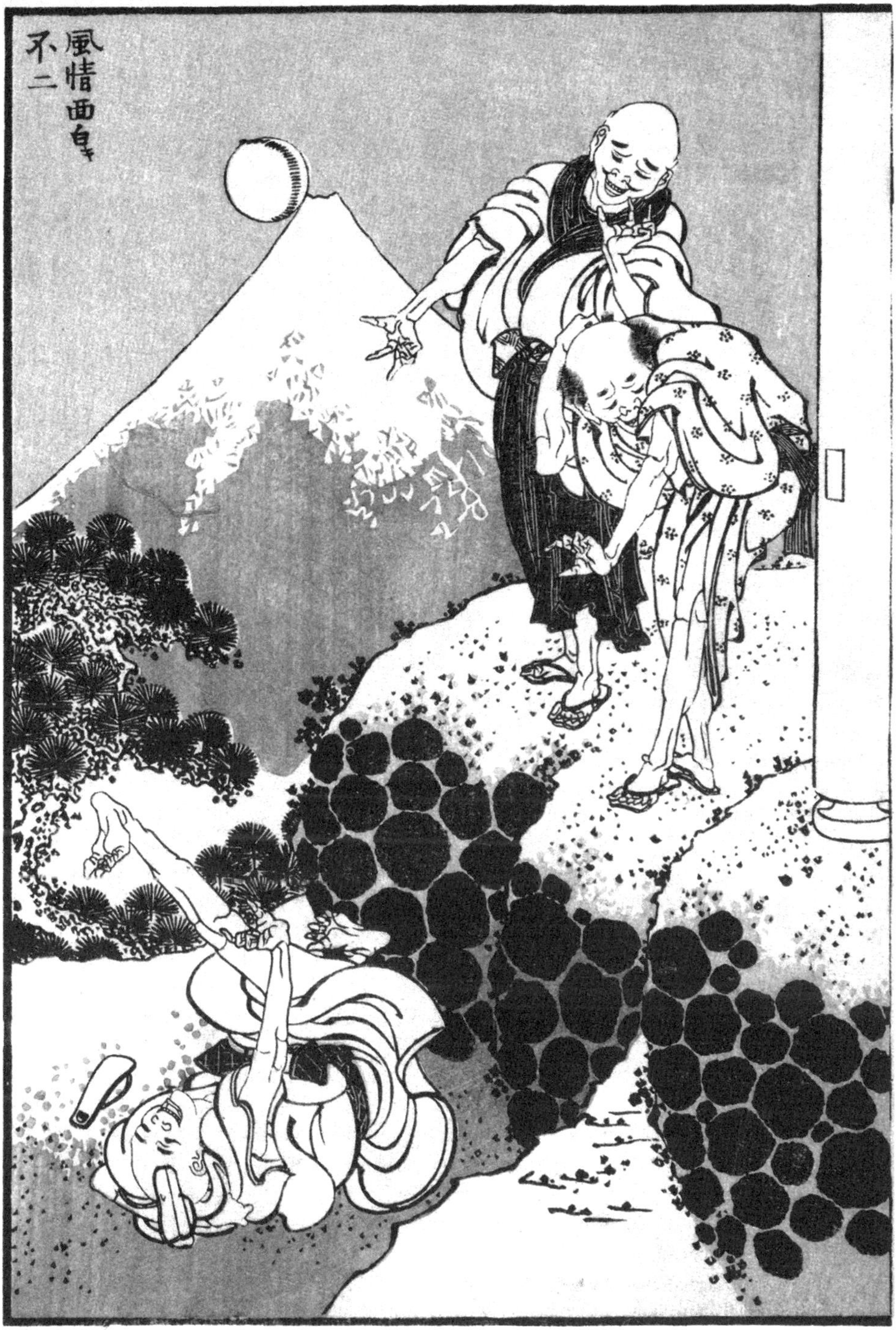

175 *Fuji of Elegant Delight*

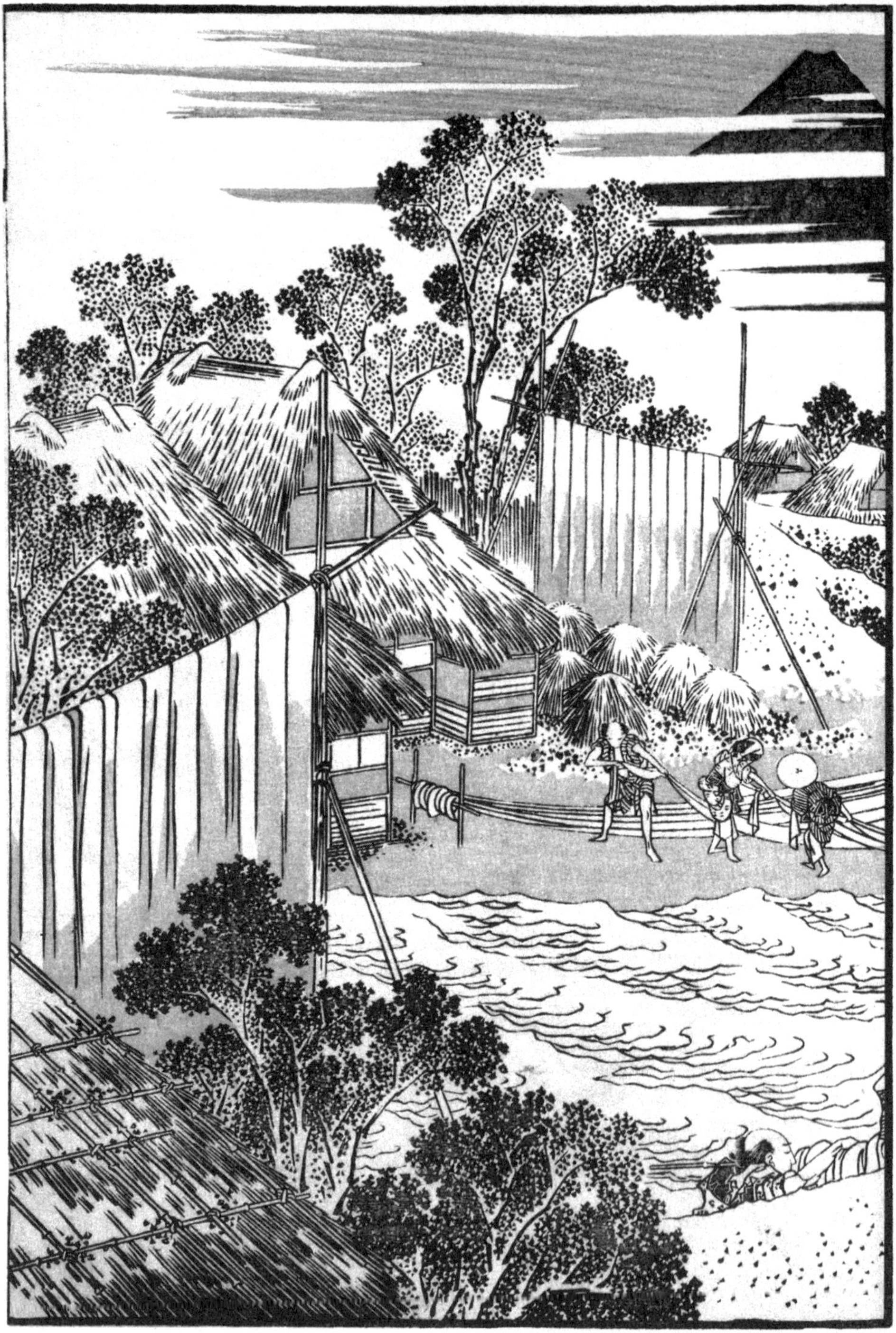

 Summer Fuji in Inage-ryō

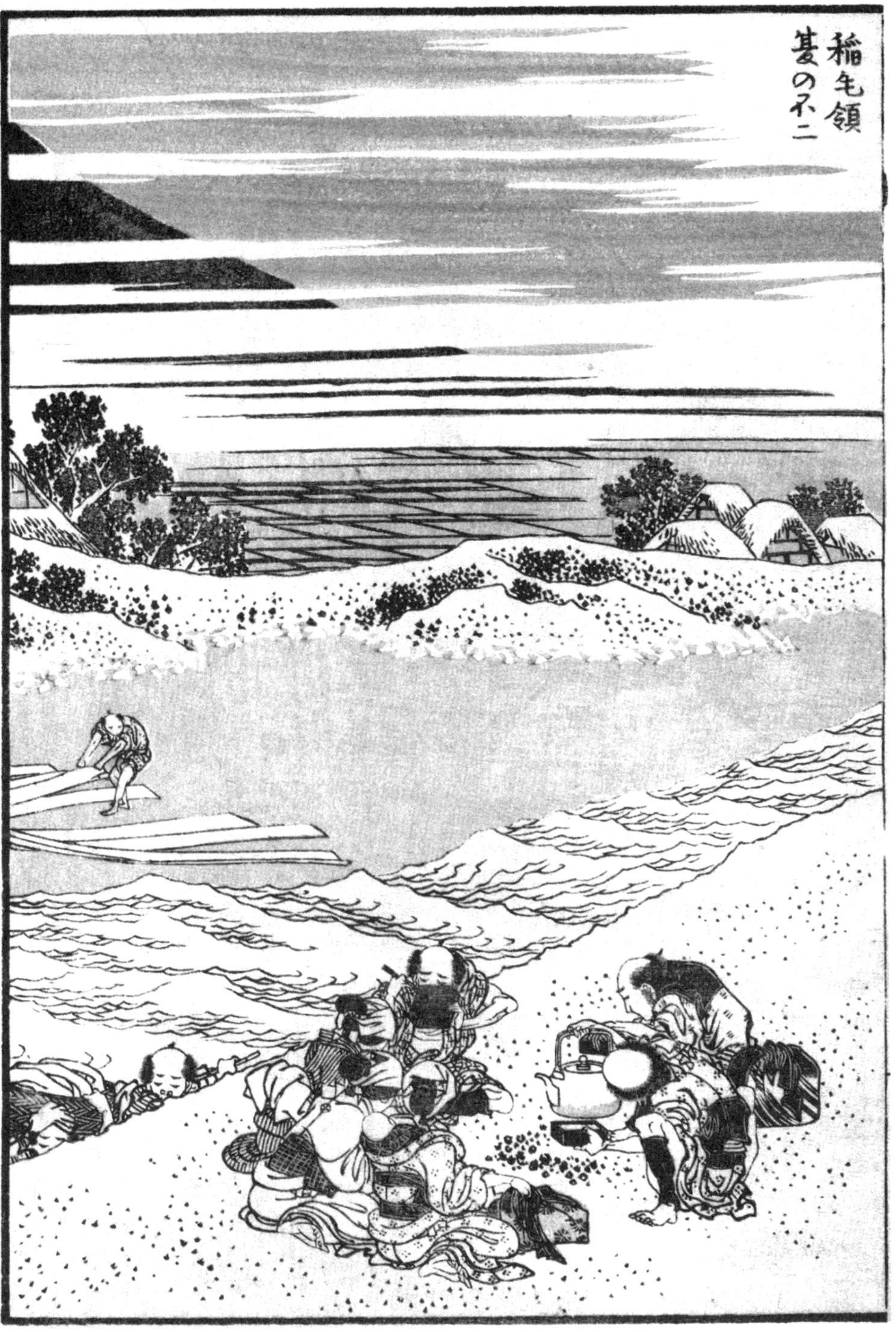
稲毛領
其の不二

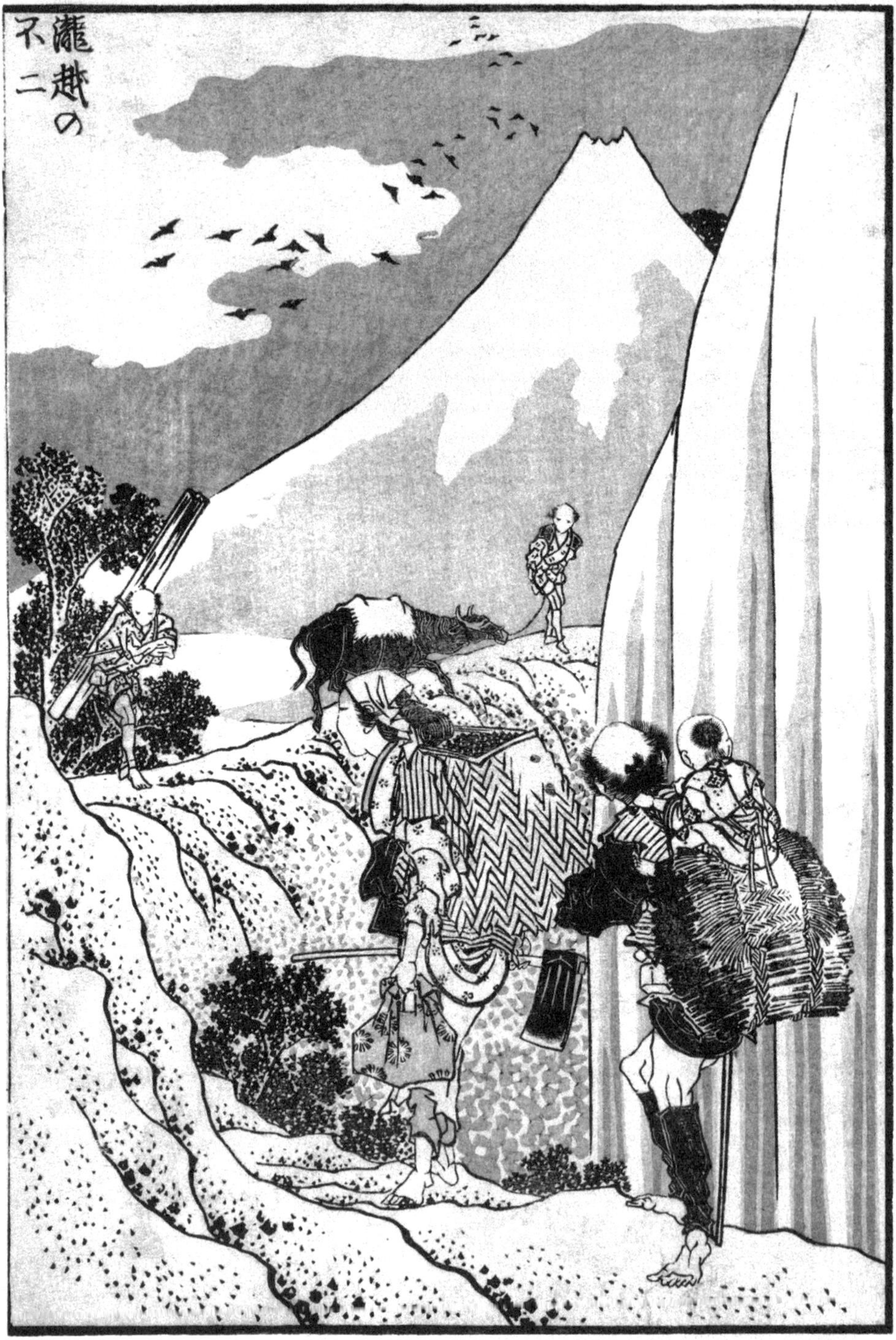

Fuji over a Waterfall

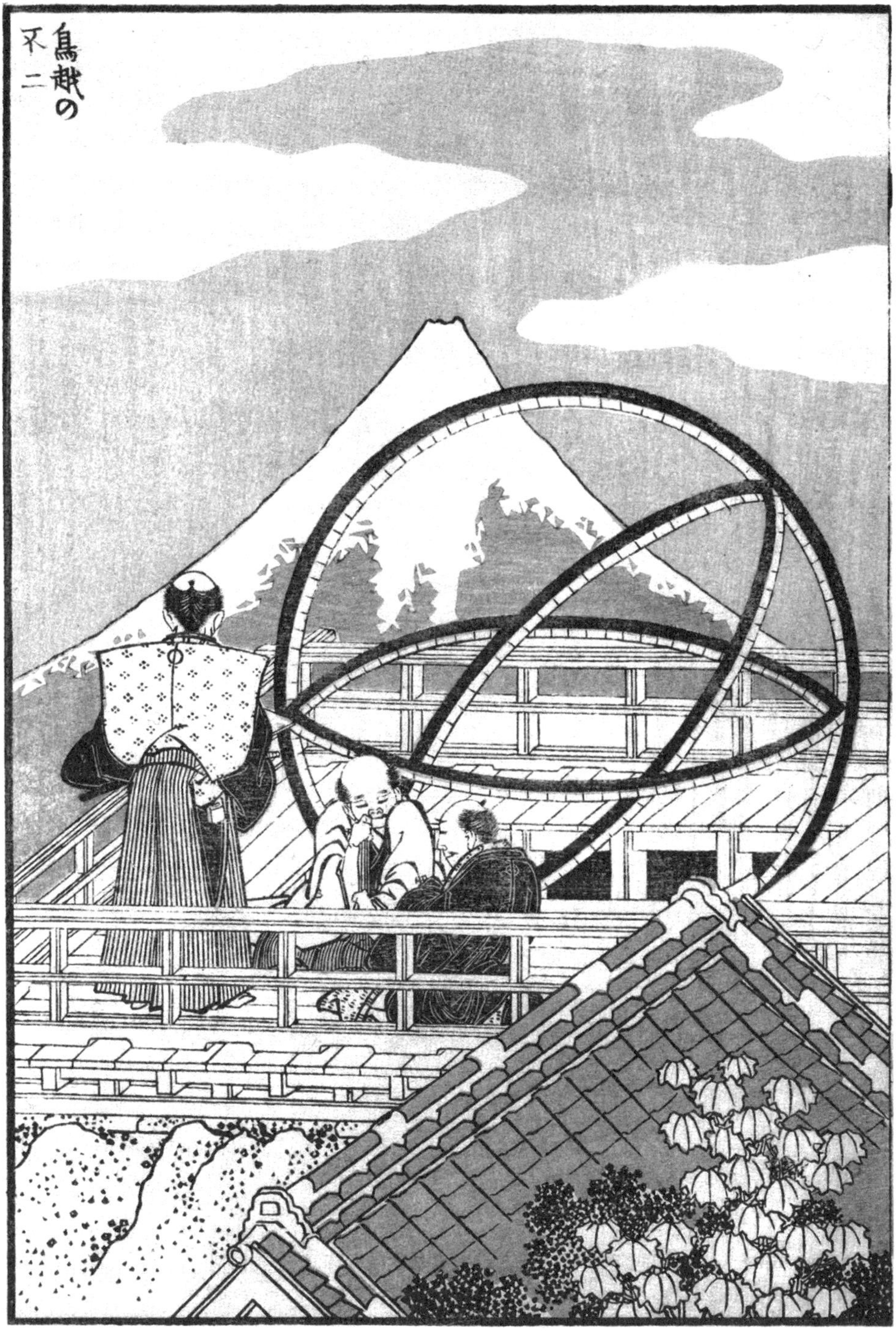

178 *Fuji at Torigoe*

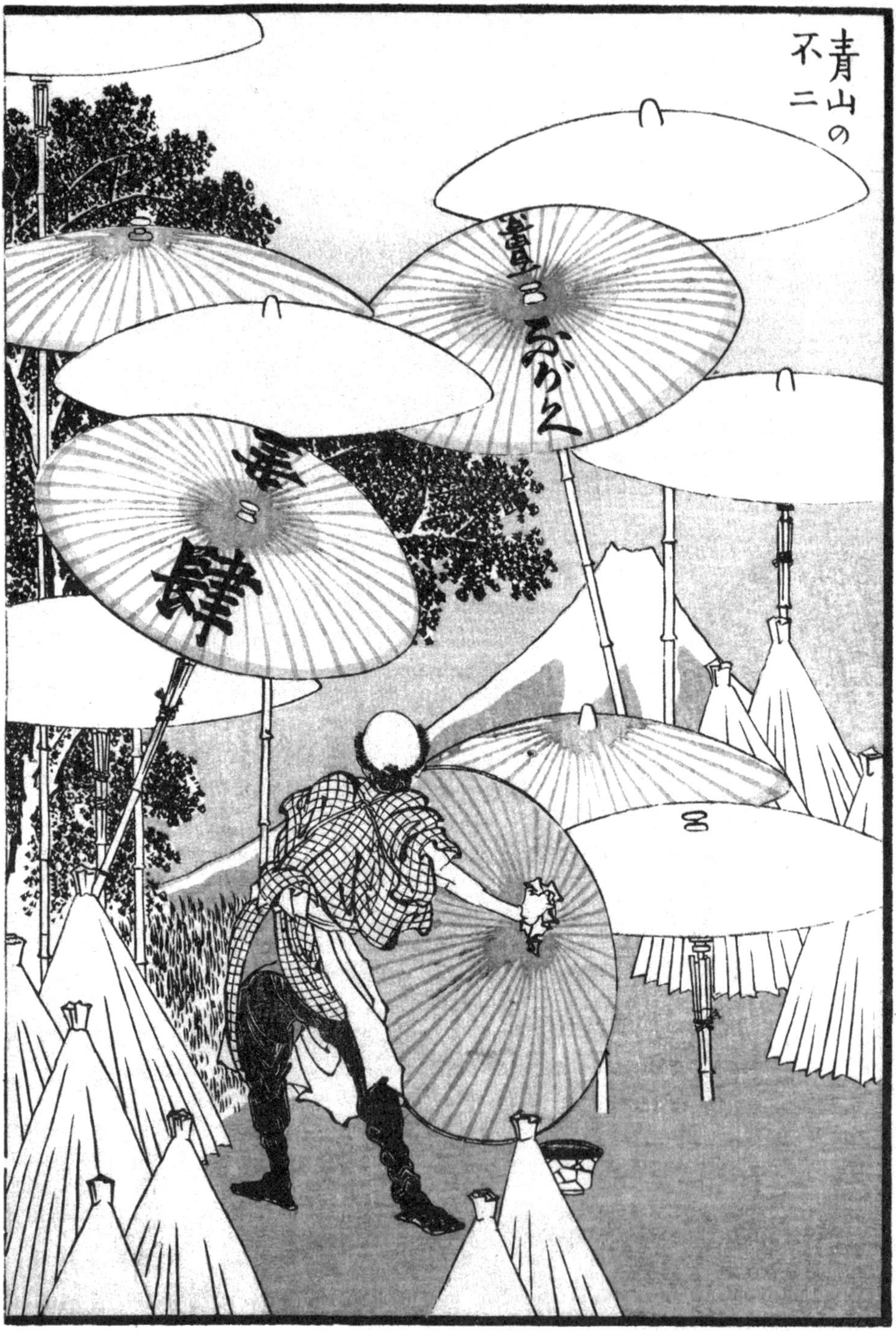

179 Fuji at Aoyama

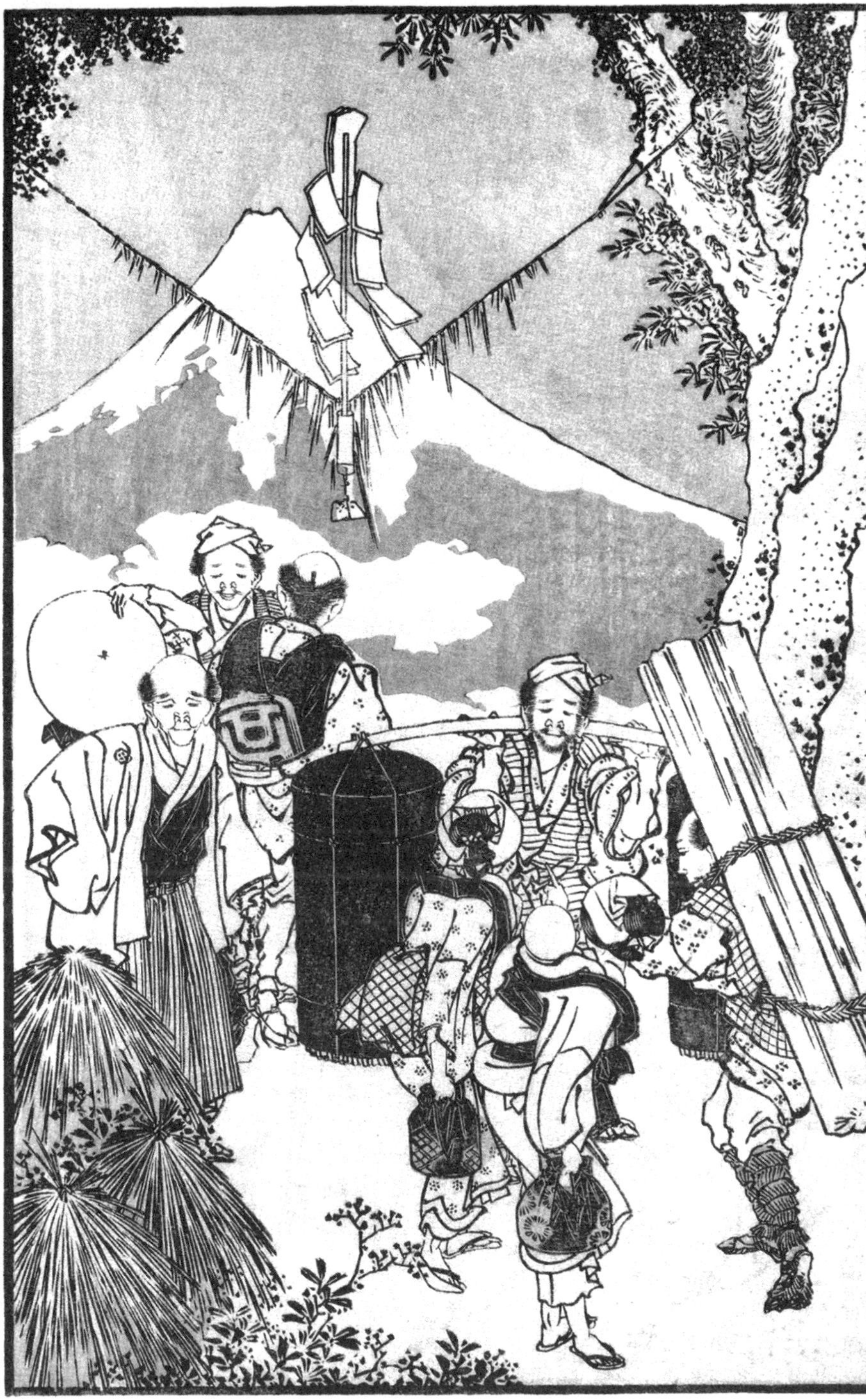

180

Fuji at a Village Boundary

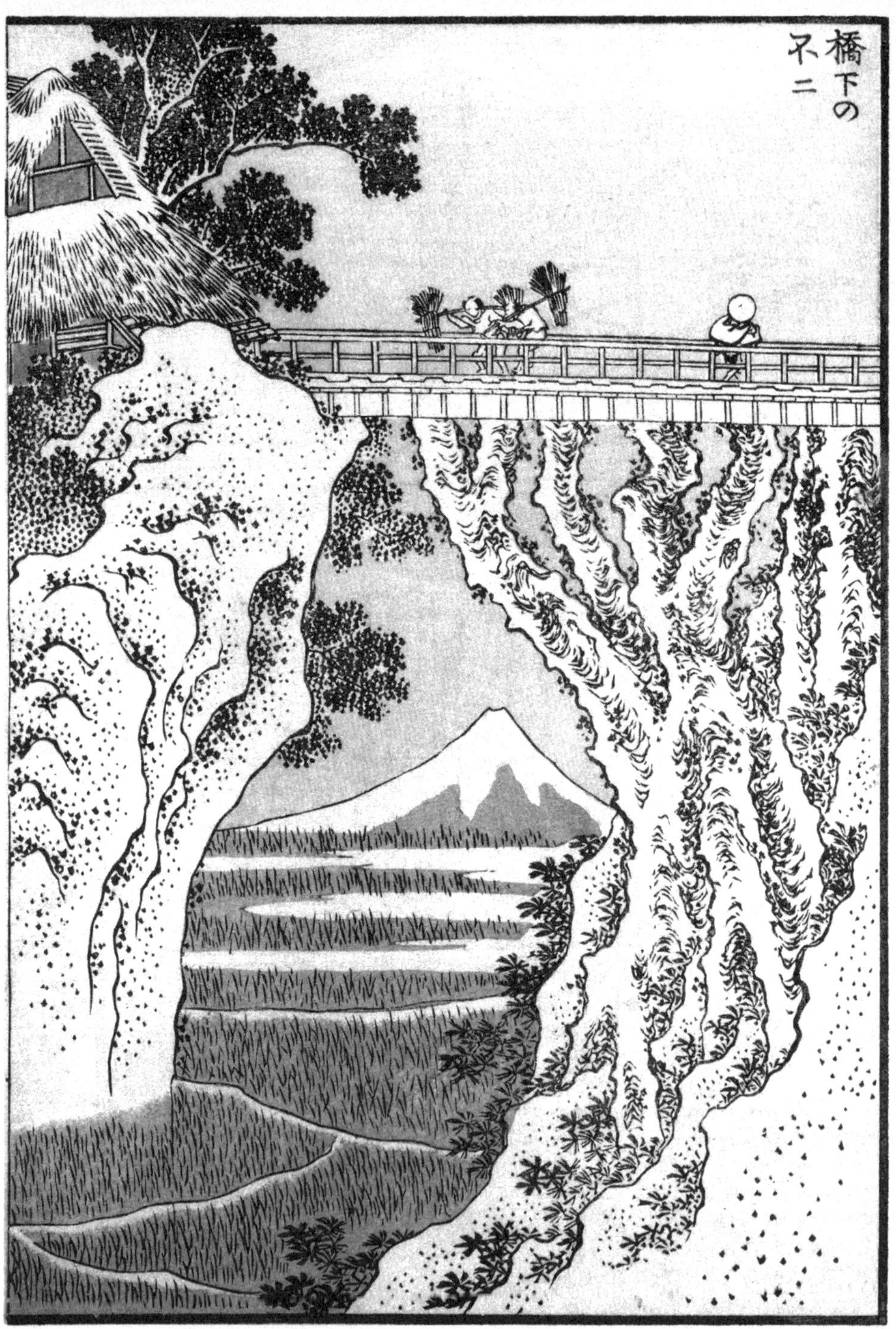

Fuji Under a Bridge

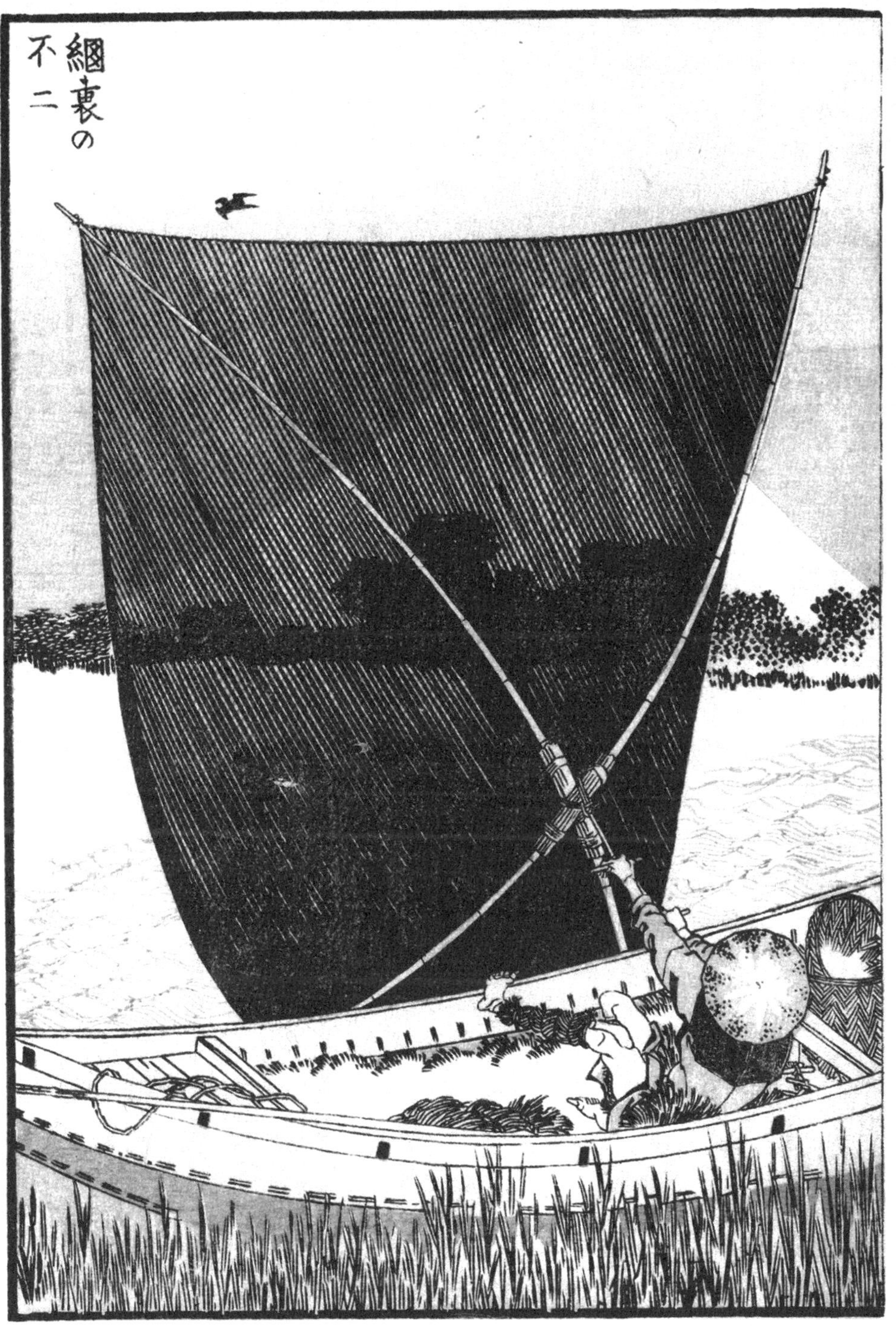

182   *Fuji Behind a Net*

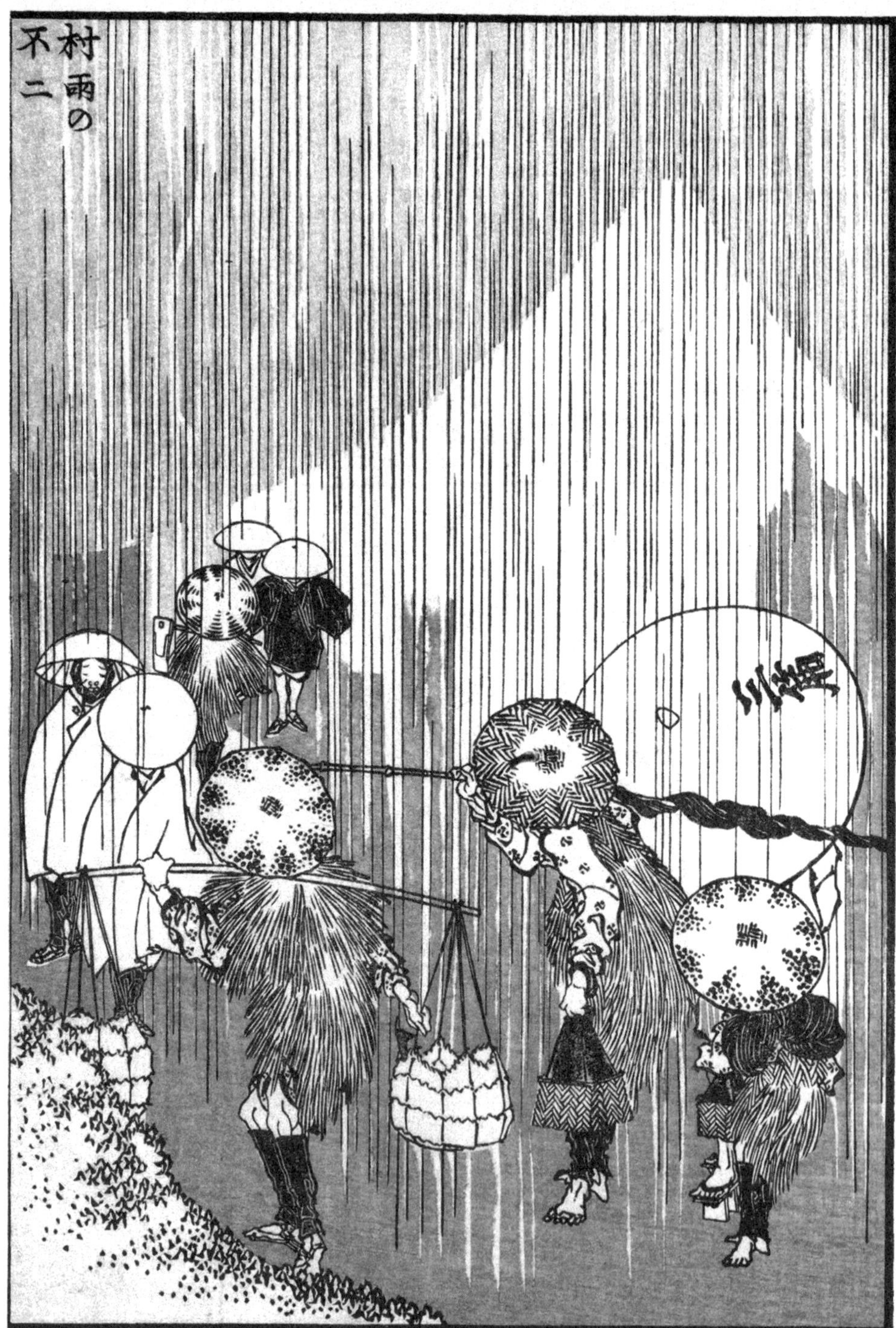

Fuji in a Downpour

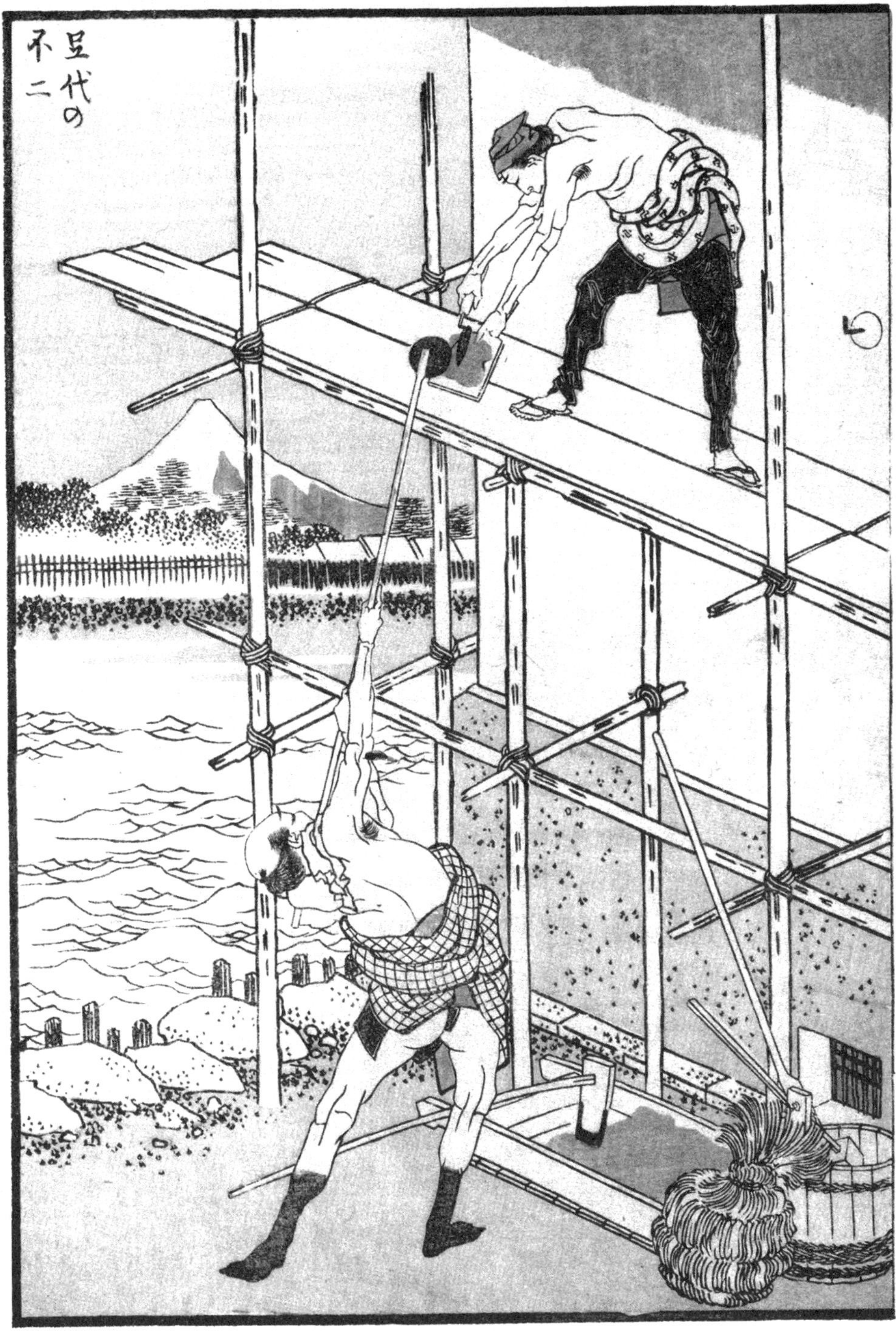

184   *Fuji with a Scaffold*

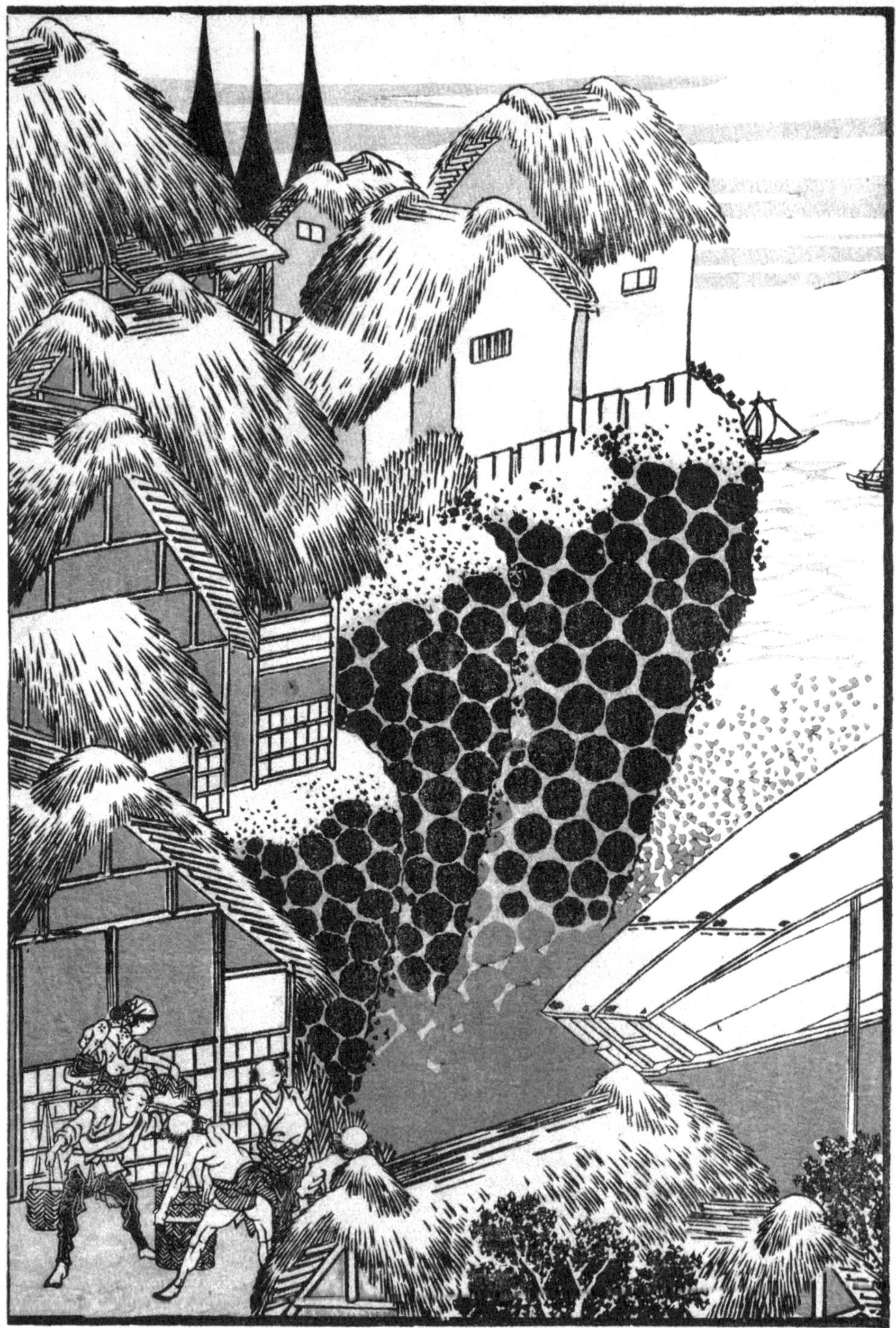

185 *Fuji with Smoke Signals*

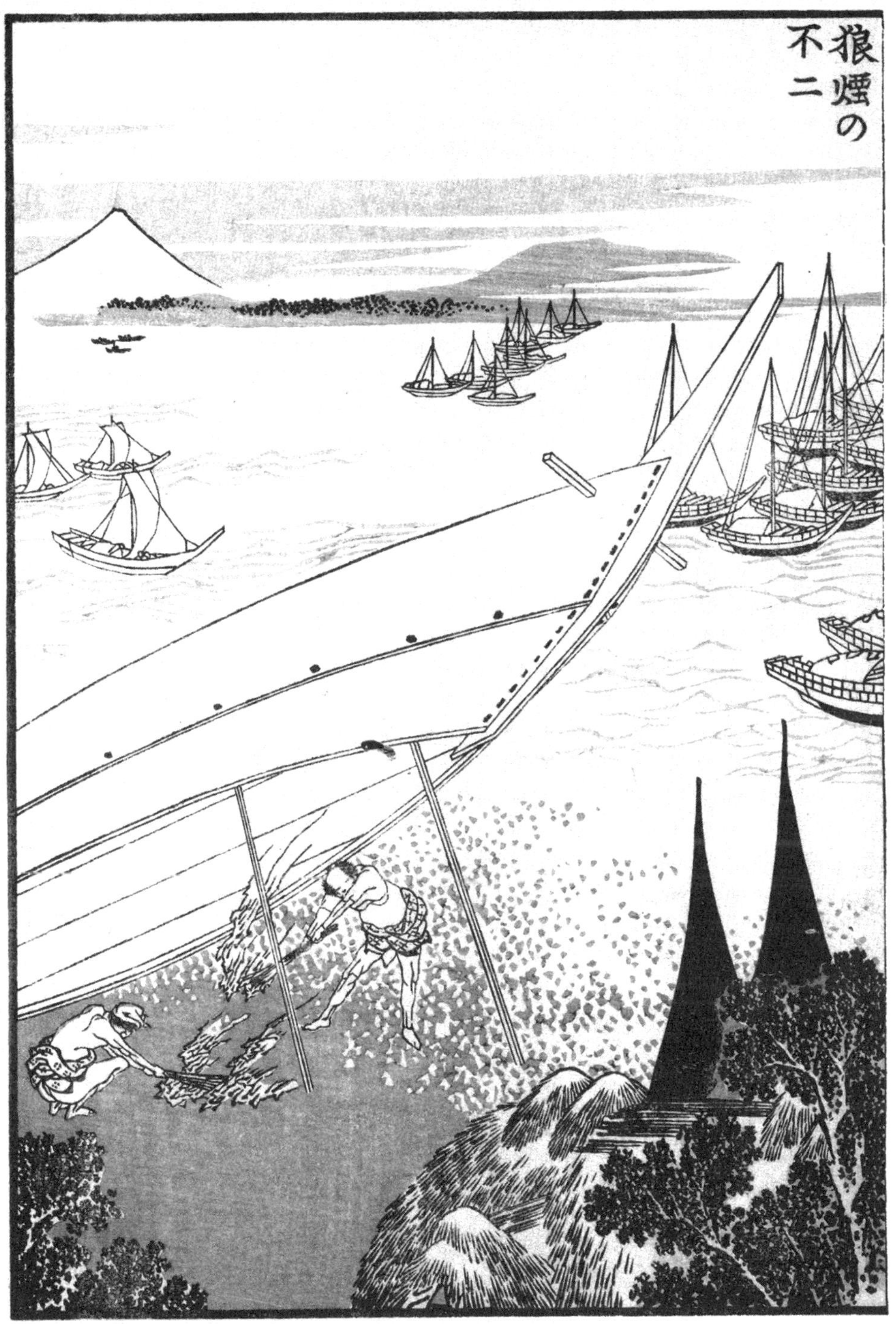

狼煙の
不二

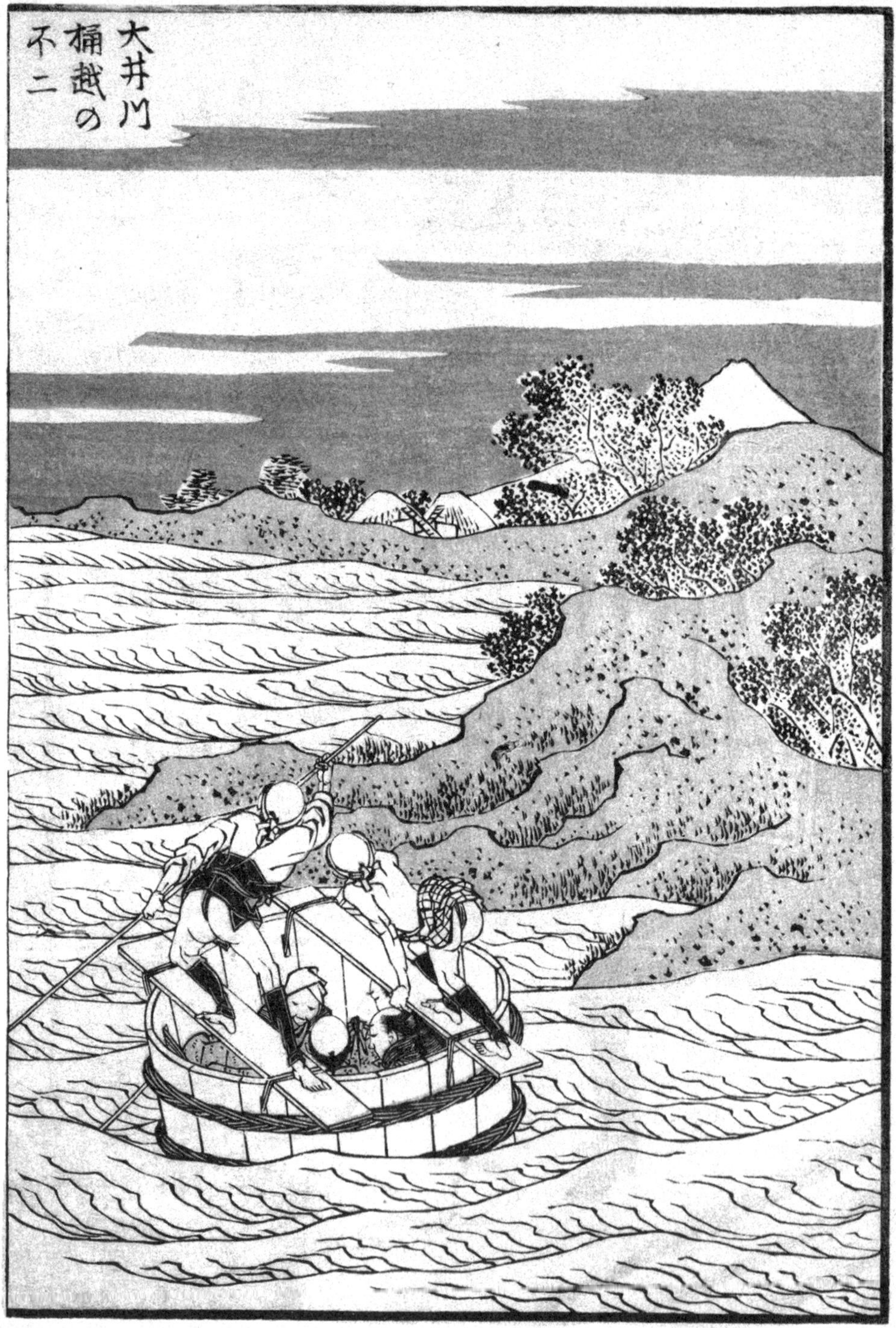

186 *Fuji from the Bucket Ferry on the Ōi River*

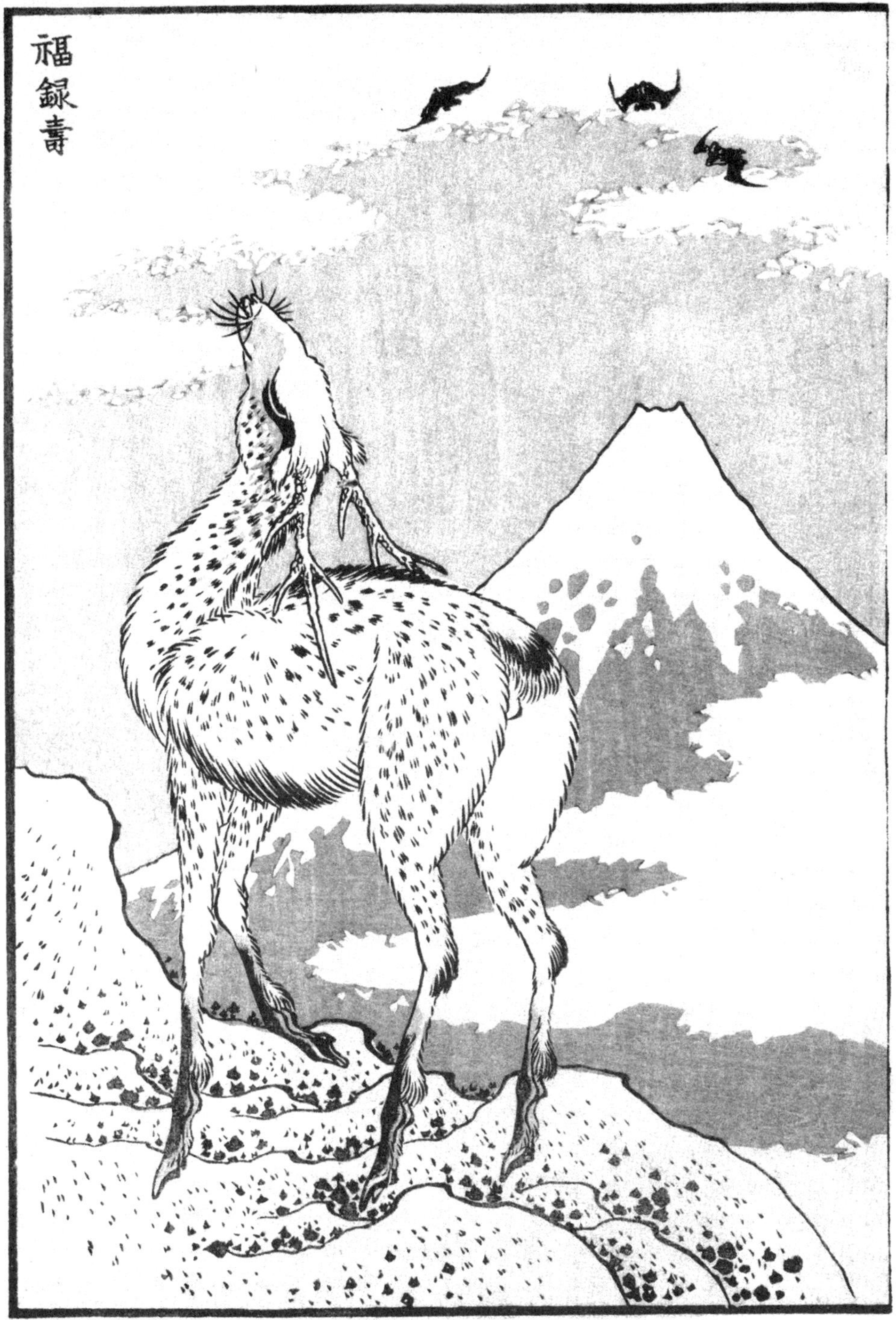

187 *Fukurokuju*

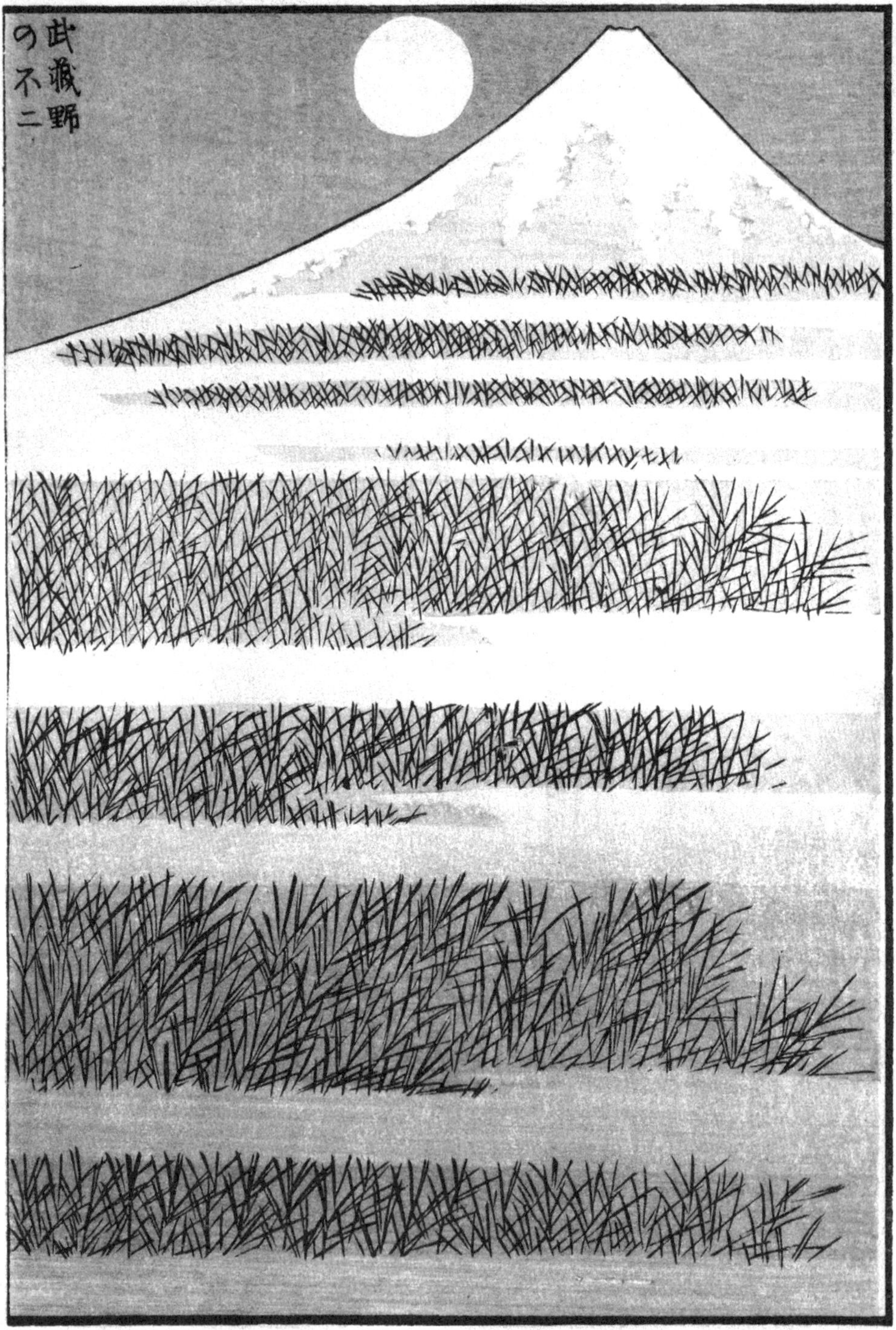

Fuji Seen from Musashino

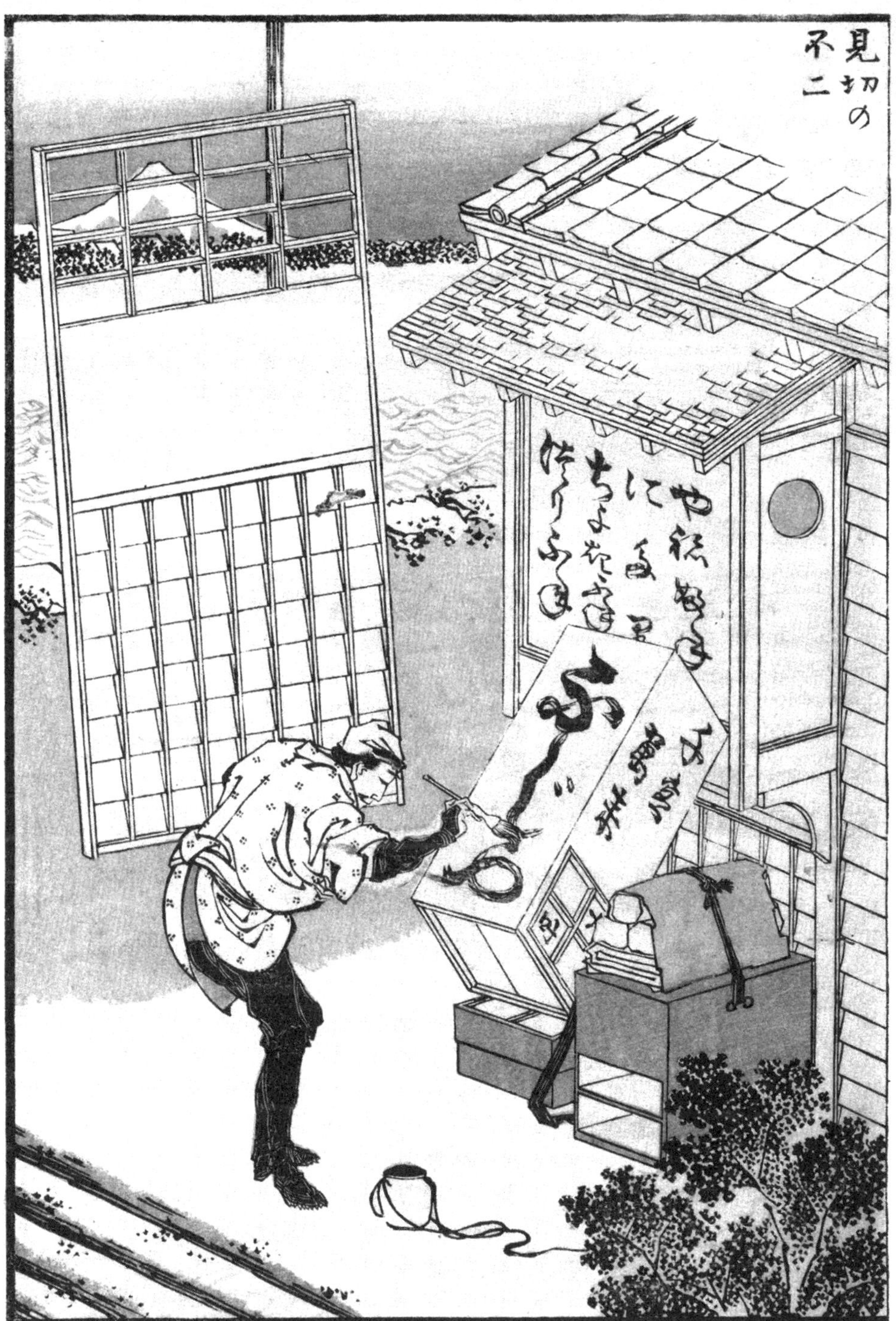

189

Fuji Through a Partition

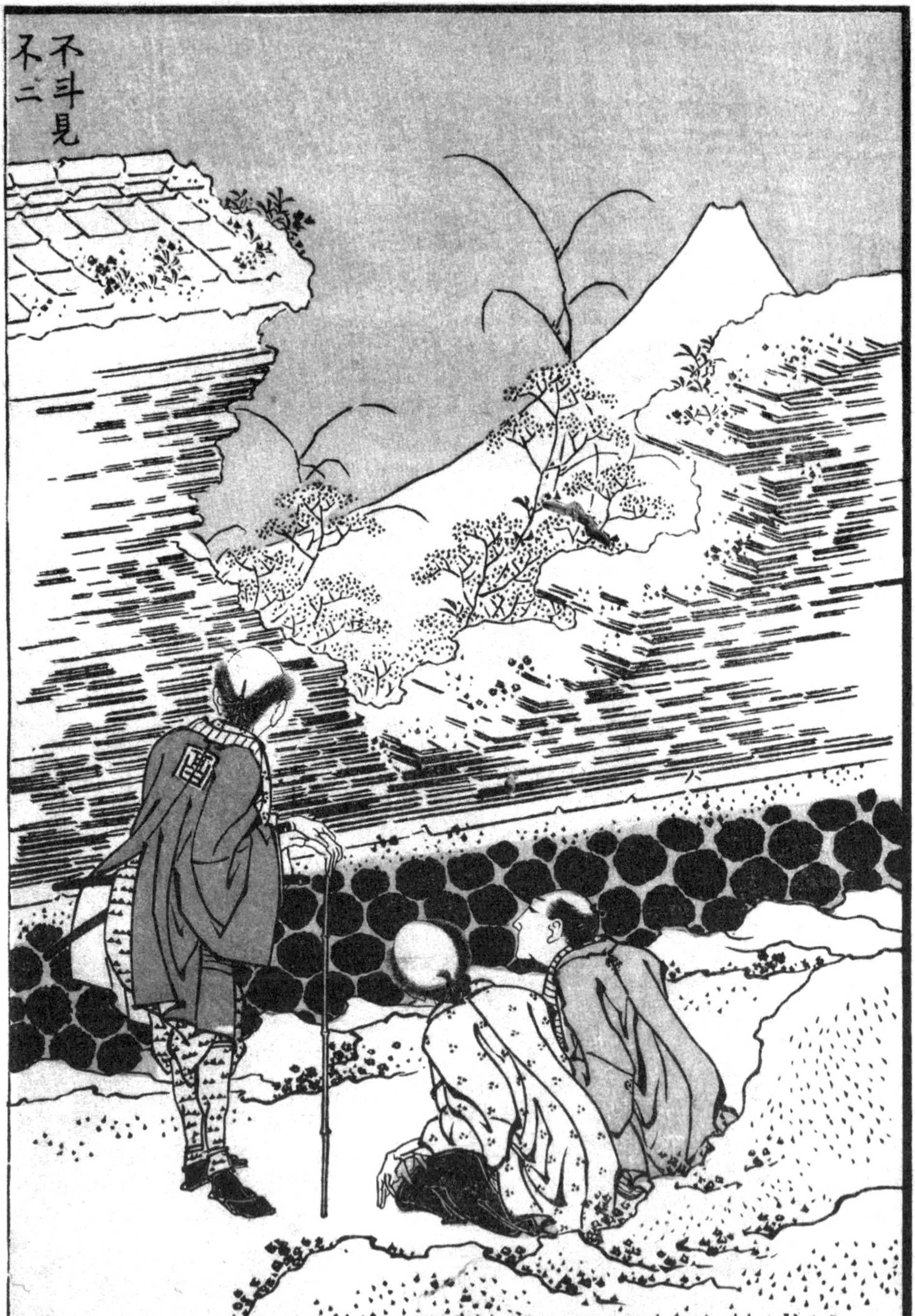

Surprise-View Fuji

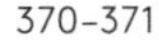

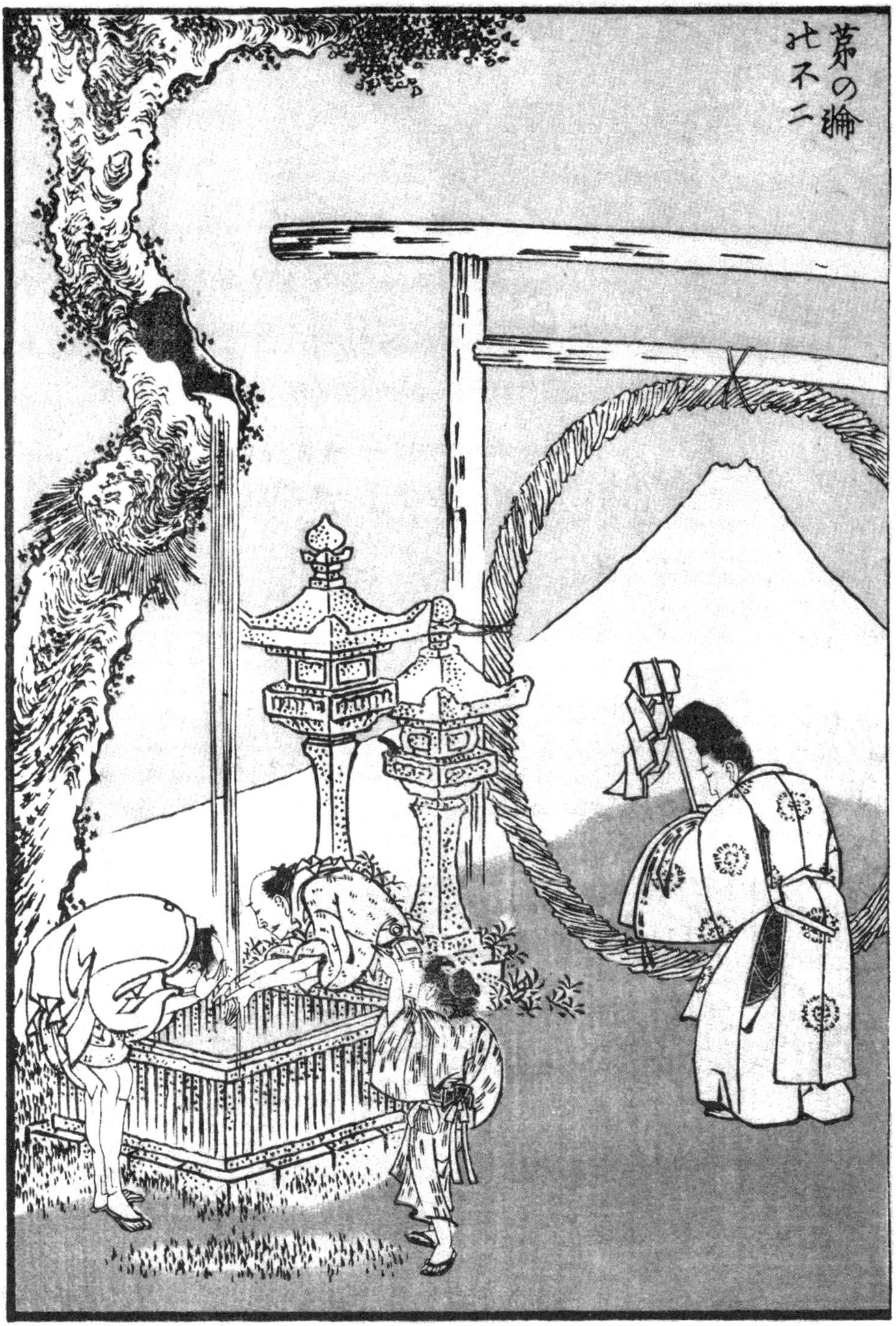

Fuji in a Grass Hoop

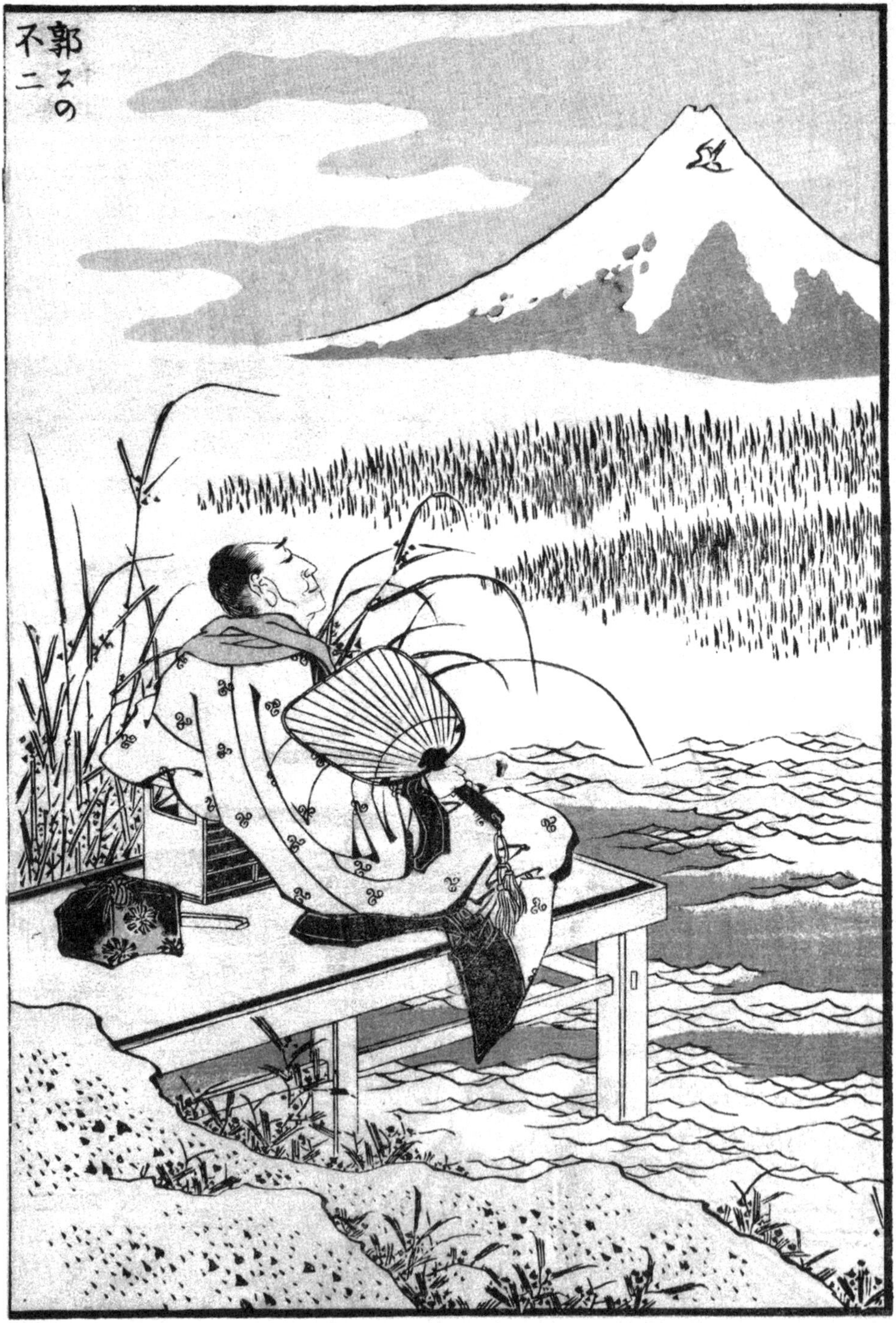

Fuji with a Cuckoo

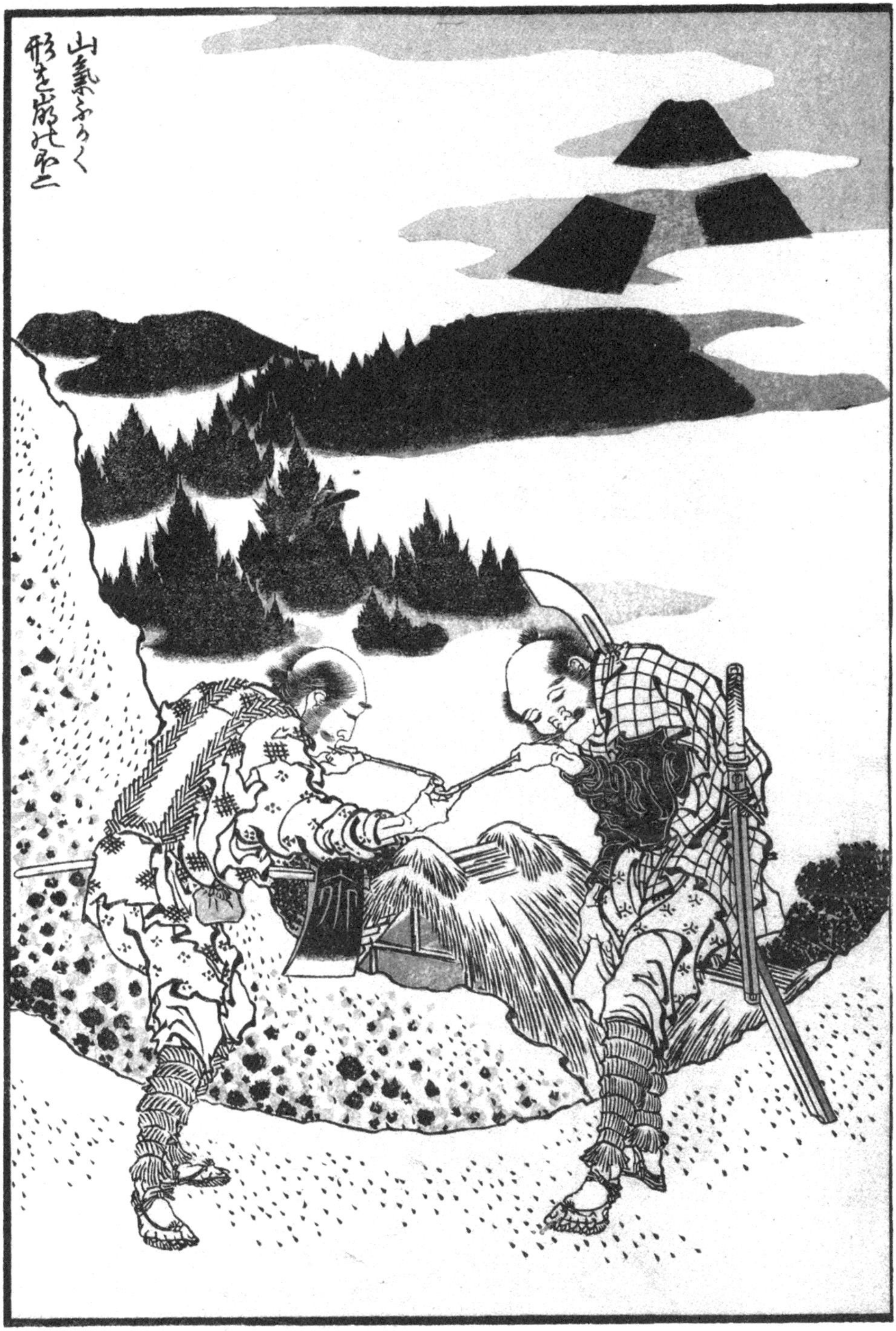

Fuji with Broken Form in Deep Mountain Mist

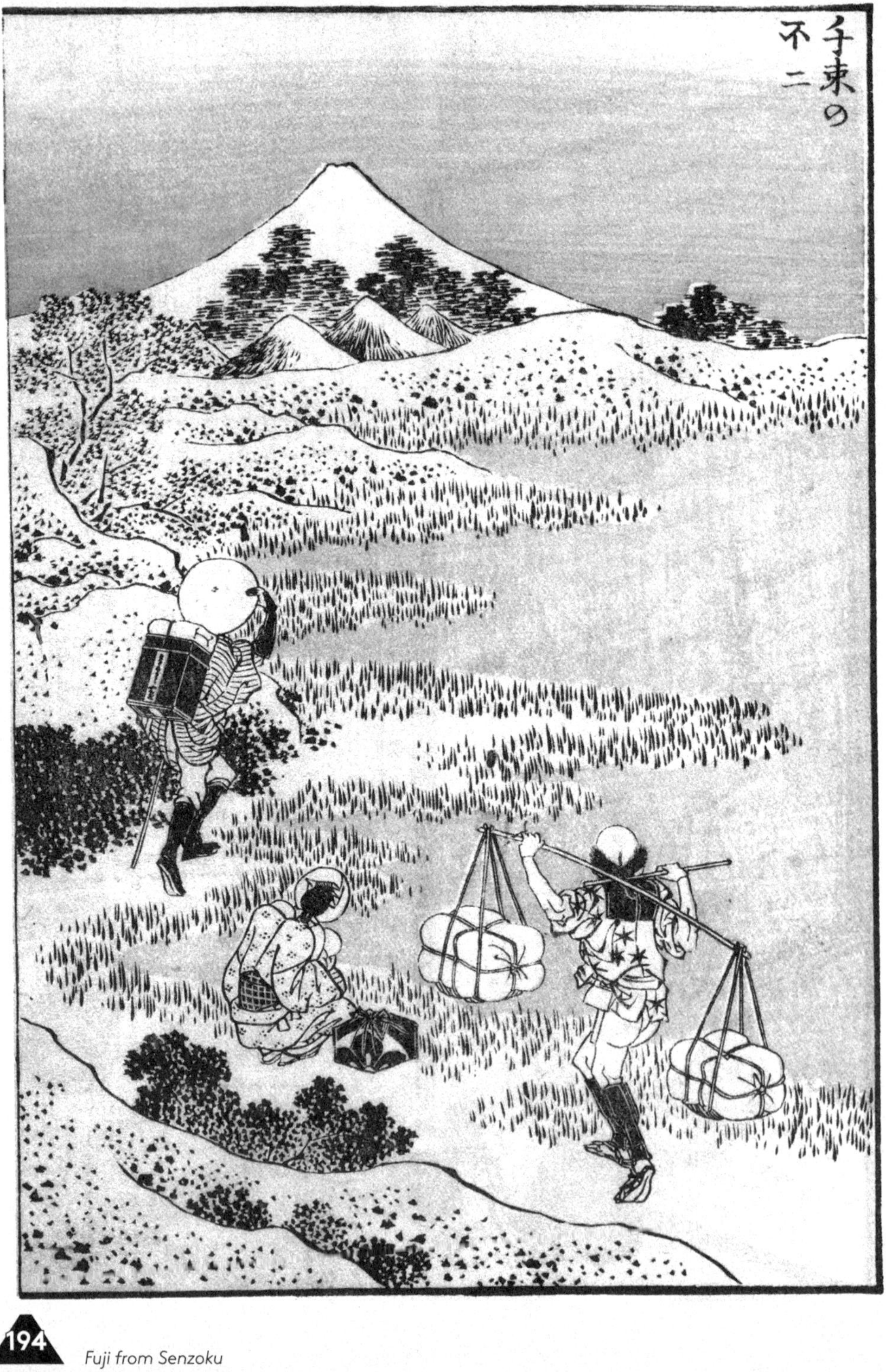

Fuji from Senzoku

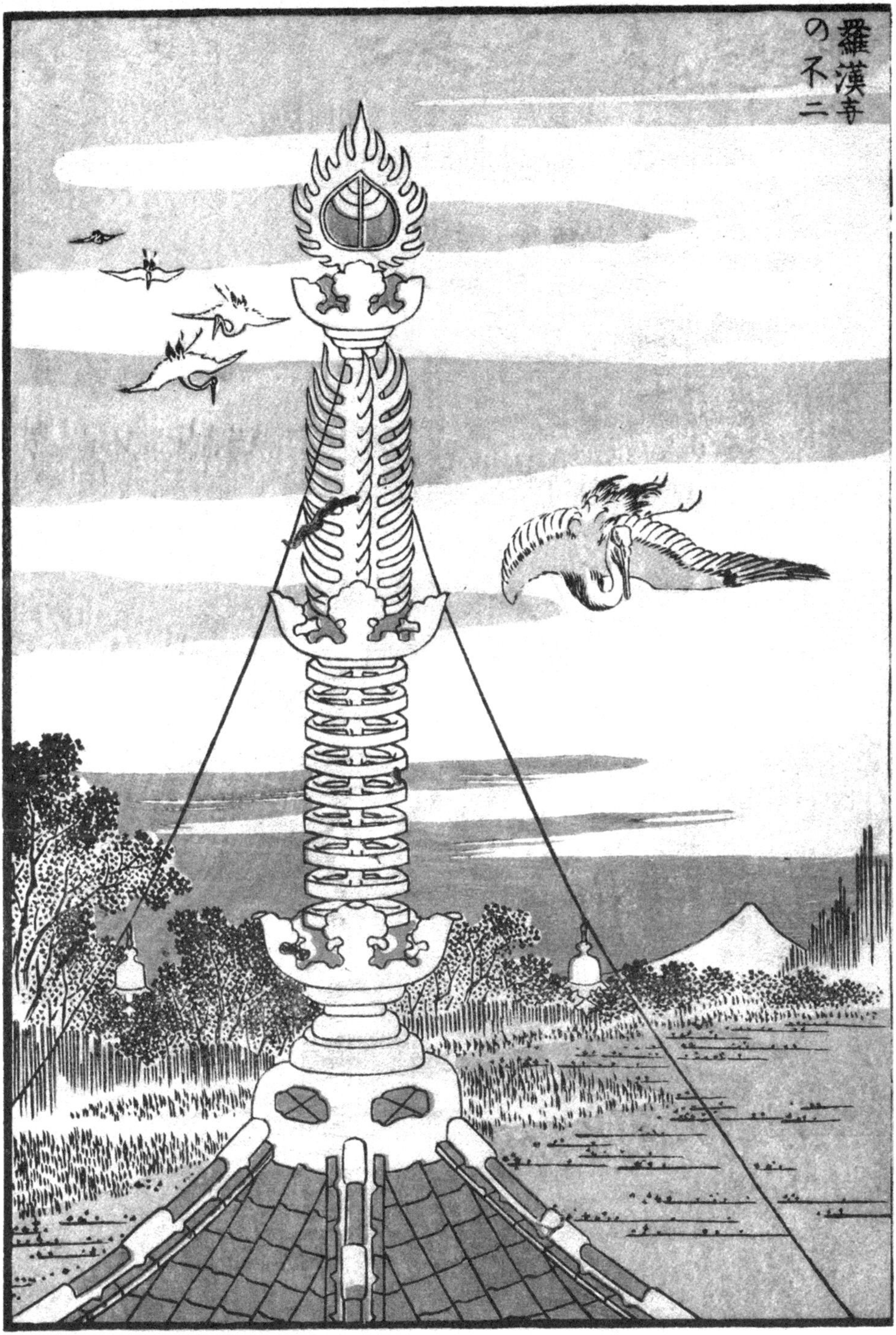

195   *Fuji from Rakanji Temple*

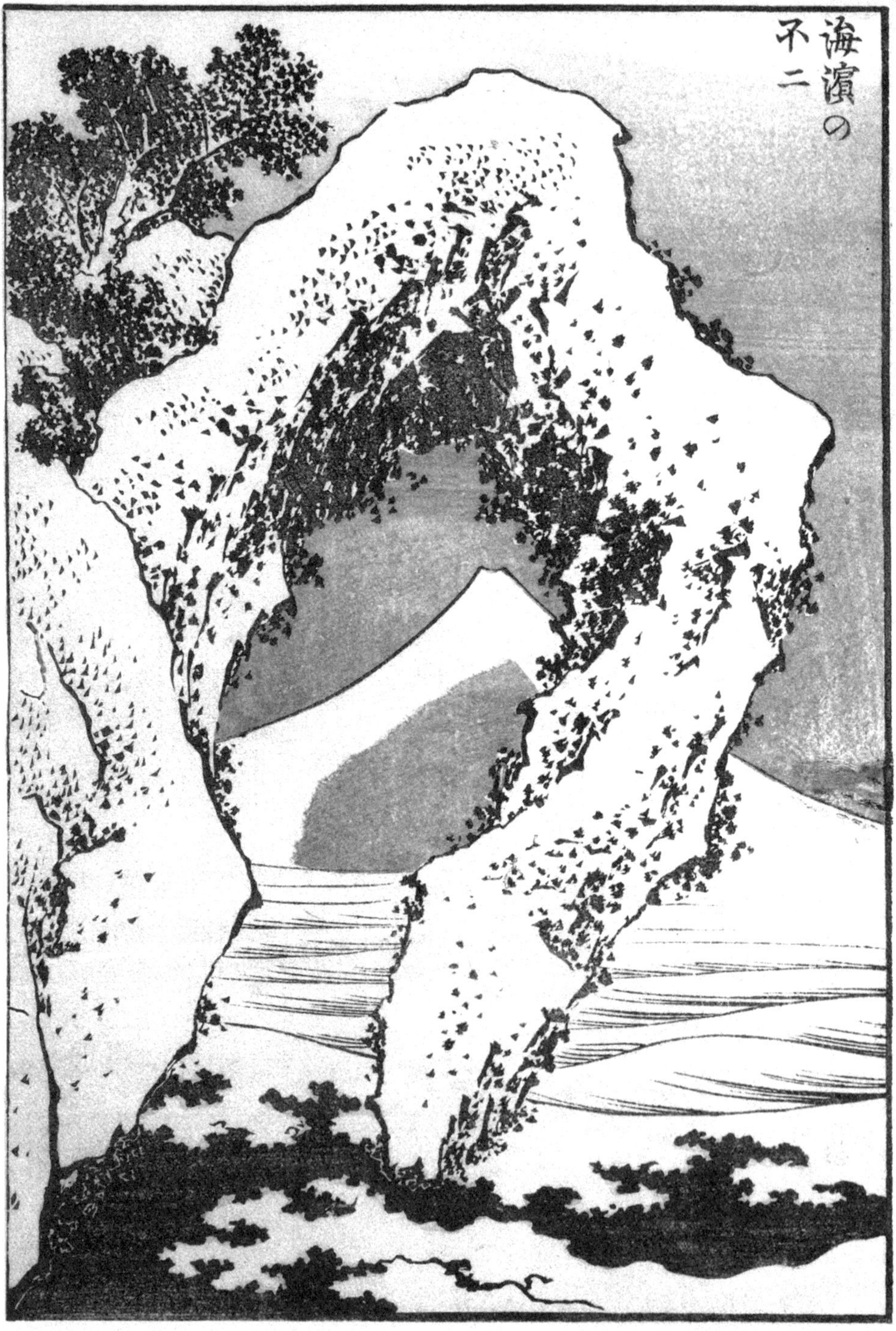

Fuji from the Seashore.

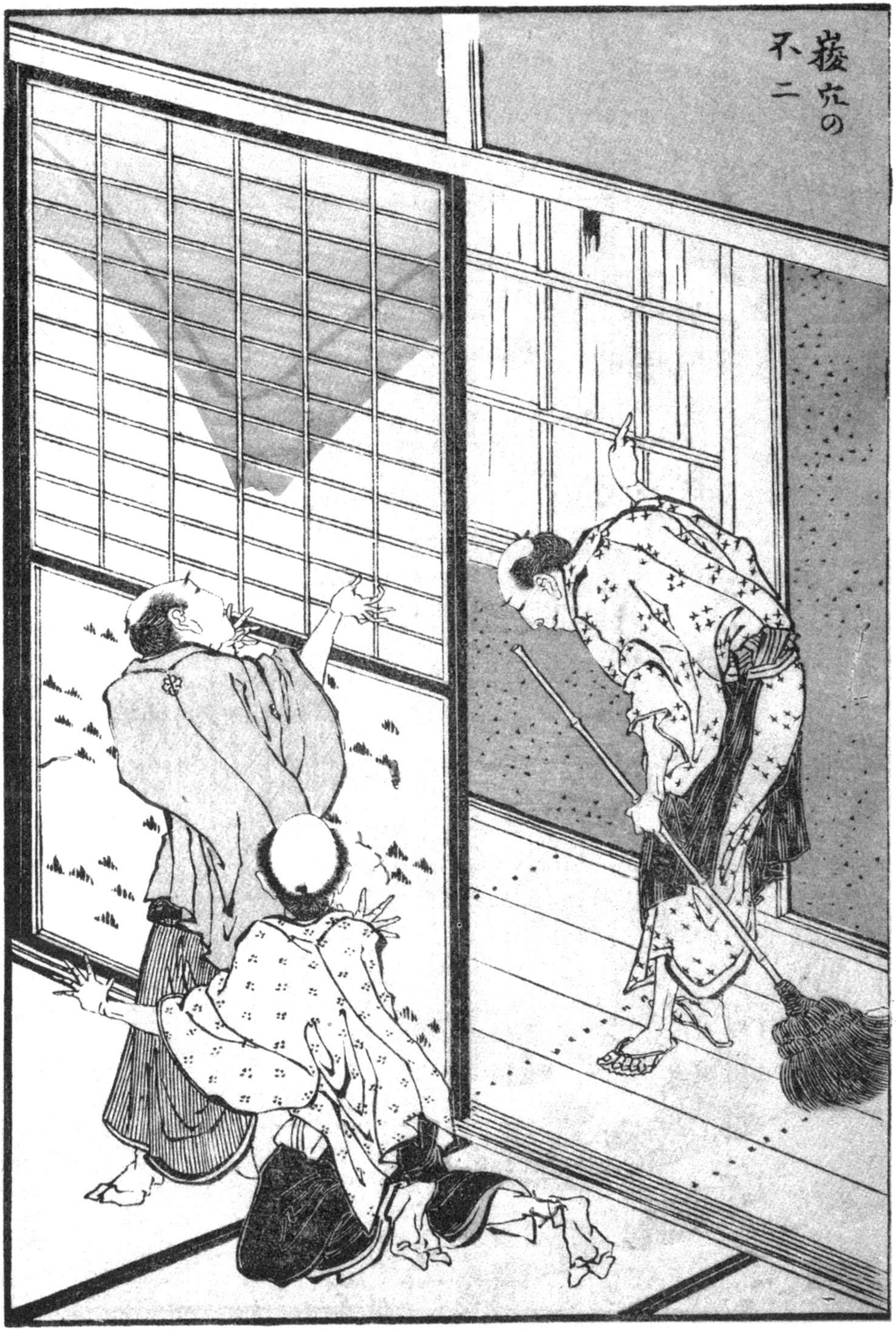

節穴の
不二

Fuji Through a Knothole

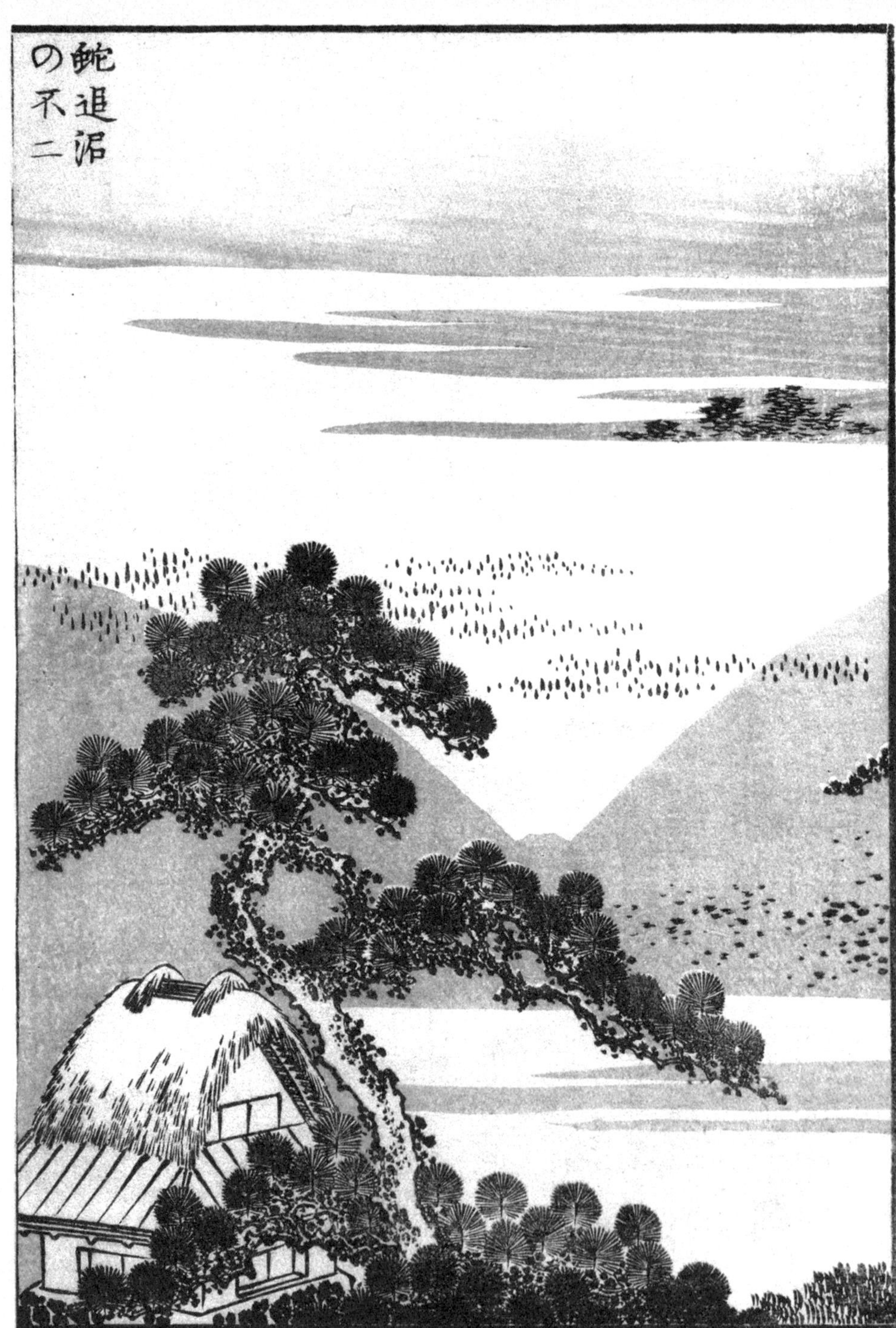

198 Fuji from Snake-Crossing Swamp

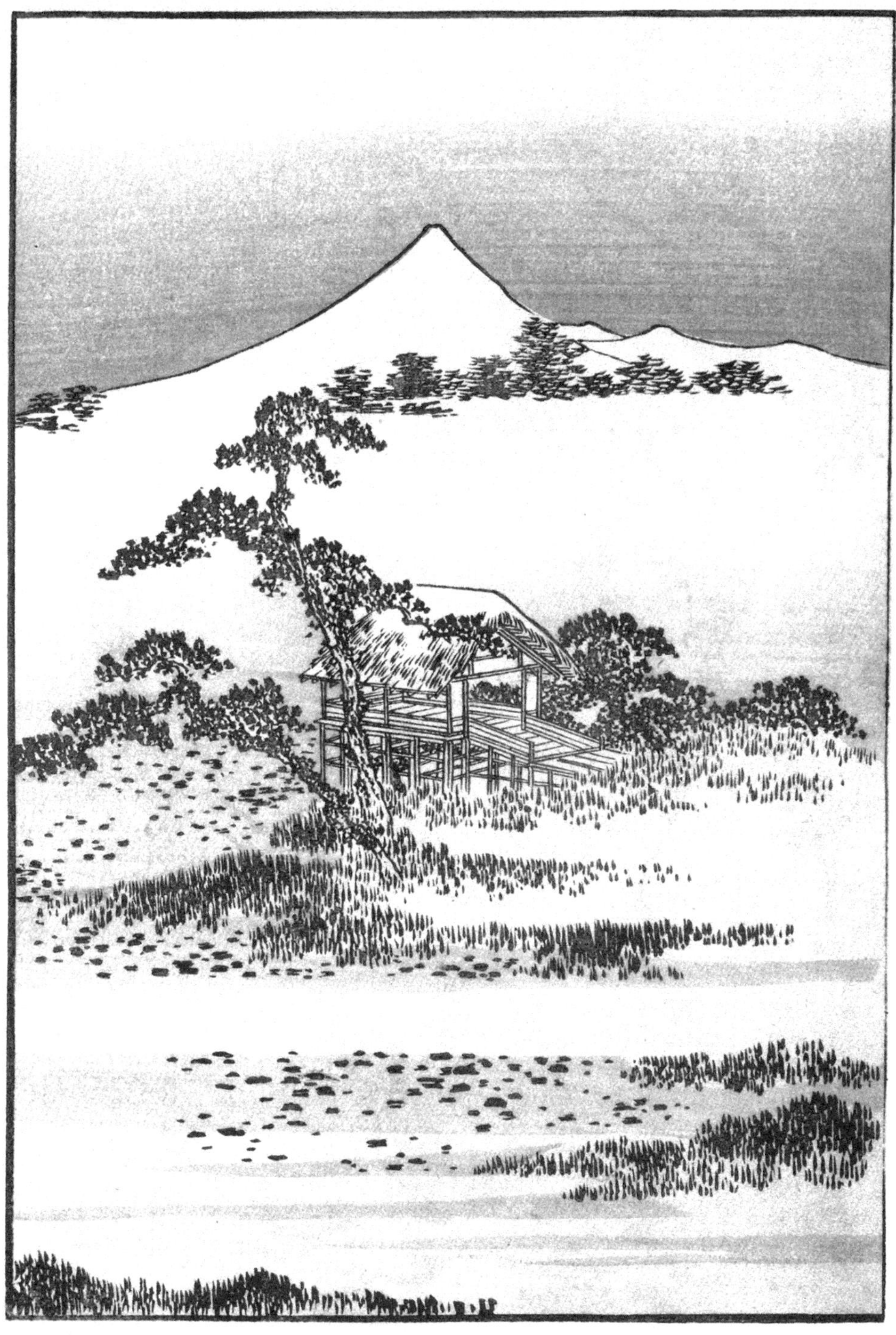

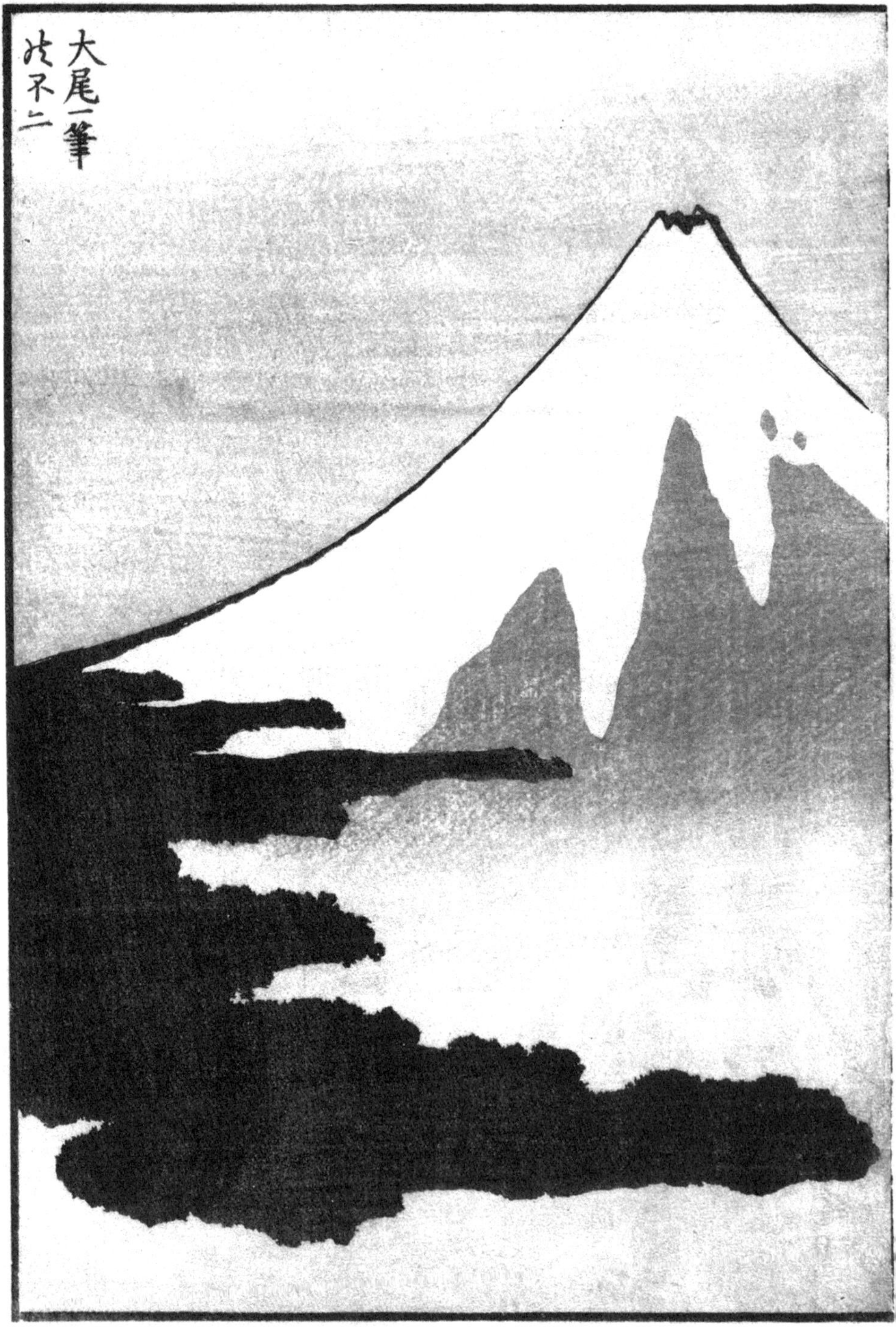

Fuji Concluded in One Stroke

Chapter 4

Fuji Forever

As he approached his final years, Hokusai moved away from *ukiyo-e* prints and focused instead on picture books, drawing manuals and brush paintings. His reasons for no longer producing *ukiyo-e* remains unclear. *Thirty-Six Views of Mount Fuji* had been a huge success, and he must have done well with *A Tour of Japanese Waterfalls* and other large full-colour prints. It is possible that Hokusai was simply being Hokusai.

One possible explanation may be the arrival of the young Utagawa Hiroshige (1797–1858), a master *ukiyo-e* artist whose reputation is equal to that of Hokusai. Shortly after the publication of *Thirty-Six Views of Mount Fuji*, Hiroshige published *Fifty-Three Stations on the Tōkaidō Road*, a hugely successful album that rivalled Hokusai's work. Hiroshige excelled in lyrical expression of feelings and faithful renditions of real scenery, and people were captivated by his style. Drawing realistic scenery had never been uppermost in Hokusai's mind. He was far more interested in clever compositions in which all the elements fitted into the frame, spectacular visual effects that surprised the viewer and, above all, enhancing the degree of perfection in the image. Rather than adjusting to the tastes of the masses, his own artistic ambitions probably won out, but the popularity of Hiroshige gradually came to dominate the world of *ukiyo-e*.

Another reason for Hokusai's move away from *ukiyo-e* might have been the fact that the epic series of full-colour woodblock prints he started working on in 1835 had come to a standstill. He had planned a series of one hundred pictures based on the idea of a nurse explaining the poems in *Hyakunin isshu*, a famed collection of one hundred poems by one hundred poets compiled in the 13th century, to her young charges. Had the series been completed, it may well have gone down in history as a masterpiece. However, the work stopped at twenty-seven colour prints. Since sixty-three preparatory drawings by Hokusai and one copy of the printer's proof still survive, it is assumed that Hokusai had completed all the drawings. The specific reasons for the setback are not known, but it is not difficult to guess how disappointing this must have been for Hokusai.

Although the theme for the series *One Hundred Poems Explained by the Nurse* comes from classic Japanese literature, when looking at *Poem by Yamabe no Akahito* [394–395], it is clear that the travellers on the road are from the contemporary Edo period. Few of Hokusai's images match the historical content of the poems or depict scenes from the Heian period or in a palace setting. Instead, they mostly feature ordinary townspeople. Rather than staying true to the original work or the significance of the poems, Hokusai chooses to depict realistic scenes that were more familiar to the people of Edo. Therefore, Hokusai's *One Hundred Poems* prints are based on his own original interpretations. However, this was all to no avail: the images were not popular, possibly because his interpretations were too far-fetched or difficult to understand. This is thought to be another reason why publication of the proposed book was cancelled. After this, Hokusai started to concentrate on brush paintings.

Going back in time to the early Tempō era (1830–1844), we find two brush paintings of Fuji: *Mount Fuji and Enoshima* [388–389] and *Country Scenes and Mount Fuji* [390–391]. Both paintings were created at around the time of *Thirty-Six Views of Mount Fuji*, but their scale is far larger than the colour woodblock prints. *Mount Fuji and Enoshima* is a *fusuma-e* – a painting for a sliding door panel – and *Country Scenes and Mount Fuji* is painted on a *byōbu* folding screen. Both works feature the colours that Hokusai favoured for his woodblock prints: dark blues, greens and browns. Showing men thatching the roof of a country house and women threshing rice in front of the house, *Country Scenes and Mount Fuji* is probably an autumn scene. The composition bears some similarities to *Thirty-Six Views of Mount Fuji*, including the way that the outline of Fuji is echoed by the lines of the thatched roof, and the way that the activities of ordinary people are depicted in the foreground of a view of Mount Fuji.

Hokusai started to add his age to his signature at around the time he turned eighty in 1839. In his afterword for *One Hundred Views of Mount Fuji*, he wrote: '…from the age of eighty-six, I shall make great progress while at the age of ninety I will do so even more. It is my greatest wish to reach one hundred, when my work would become truly marvellous. If I live to be one hundred and ten, every dot and every line would be as if coming to life.' It would seem that by adding his age to his signature, Hokusai was marking this path of continuous improvement, one picture at a time, towards the state of mind that he dreamed of achieving.

The hustle and bustle of Edo and the figures of hard-working labourers depicted in his *ukiyo-e* are not present in the brush paintings of this period. Instead, Hokusai often depicts Japanese or Chinese legends, religious subjects, natural objects, or fantastical subjects such as the phoenix, tiger, dragon or other sacred beasts. Far from seeking a quiet retirement in his final years, Hokusai worked passionately on developing new techniques and styles until the end of his life. This is particularly striking in his landscape images, in which we see the influences of Chinese painting, and the techniques of Ming dynasty literati painting and Qing dynasty landscape painting, especially in the way he draws lines and dots.

Images of Fuji from this period include *Boy Viewing Mount Fuji* [396–397], which depicts a boy seated on a tree trunk, playing the flute while looking towards the mountain, and the lyrical *River Landscape: Ferryboat and Mount Fuji* [398], which shows a ferryman crossing a calm river. The foreground, middle ground and background are arranged in a vertical format that resembles traditional landscape painting, with a tranquil Fuji appearing beyond the far edge of a quietly flowing river. Compared to the realistic views of Fuji depicted in *ukiyo-e*, the mountain in both paintings has the mysterious aura of a sacred place.

When Hokusai turned eighty-eight in 1847, he began to use a seal modelled on the Japanese character for one hundred. This is another indication of Hokusai's ambition to live a long life and to confront the 'divine state in my art'. As well as indicating a number, the term for 'one hundred' was also used to mean 'an extremely large number, everything, or eternity'. The *manji* (swastika) character that Hokusai appended to his artist name was likewise used as a universal symbol for longevity. Perhaps Hokusai was already looking towards a universal realm beyond Edo, Japan, and even beyond time, by transcending all specific schools, *ukiyo-e* artists, or existing frameworks for pictorial expression.

This book brings together more than two hundred pictures of Fuji, beginning in Hokusai's Sōri period and concluding with *Dragon Flying over Mount Fuji* [400]. In this image, Fuji has become an abstraction, a sublime shape covered in white snow and glowing with light. A dragon soars above the peak that was Hokusai's goal. As if guiding us towards further heights, the dark clouds surrounding the dragon rise into the heavens, lingering for a moment before drifting upwards. The lively motion of the dragon transcends the 'divine state in my art' and has the momentum to soar even higher.

Three months after finishing this painting, Hokusai was on his deathbed. Ninety years of devotion to art came to an end in the spring of 1849.

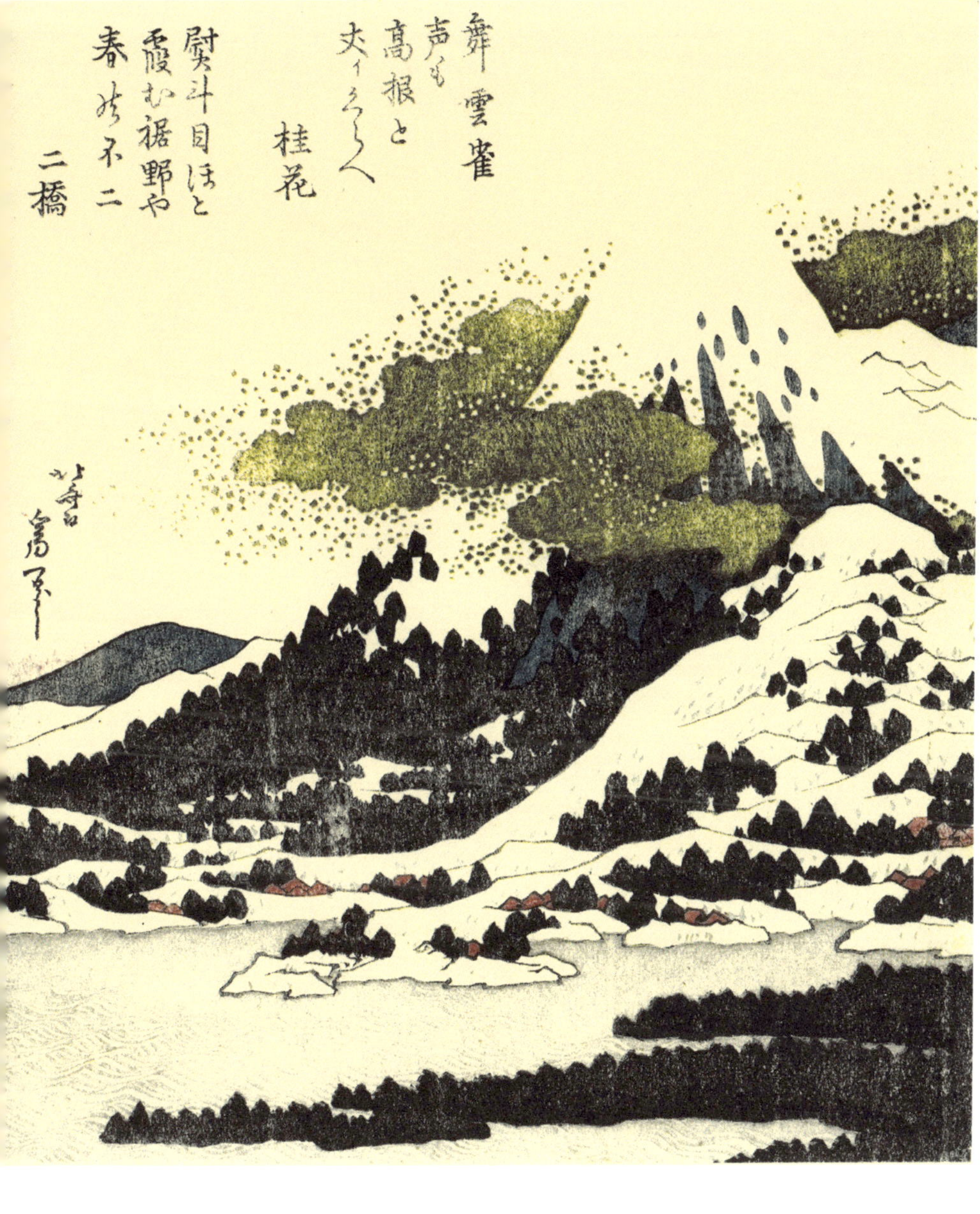

Untitled
kyōka surimono, signed Hokusai Aratame Iitsu hitsu

Early 1830s. Size unspecified. © The Trustees of the British Museum, 1937,0710,0.214

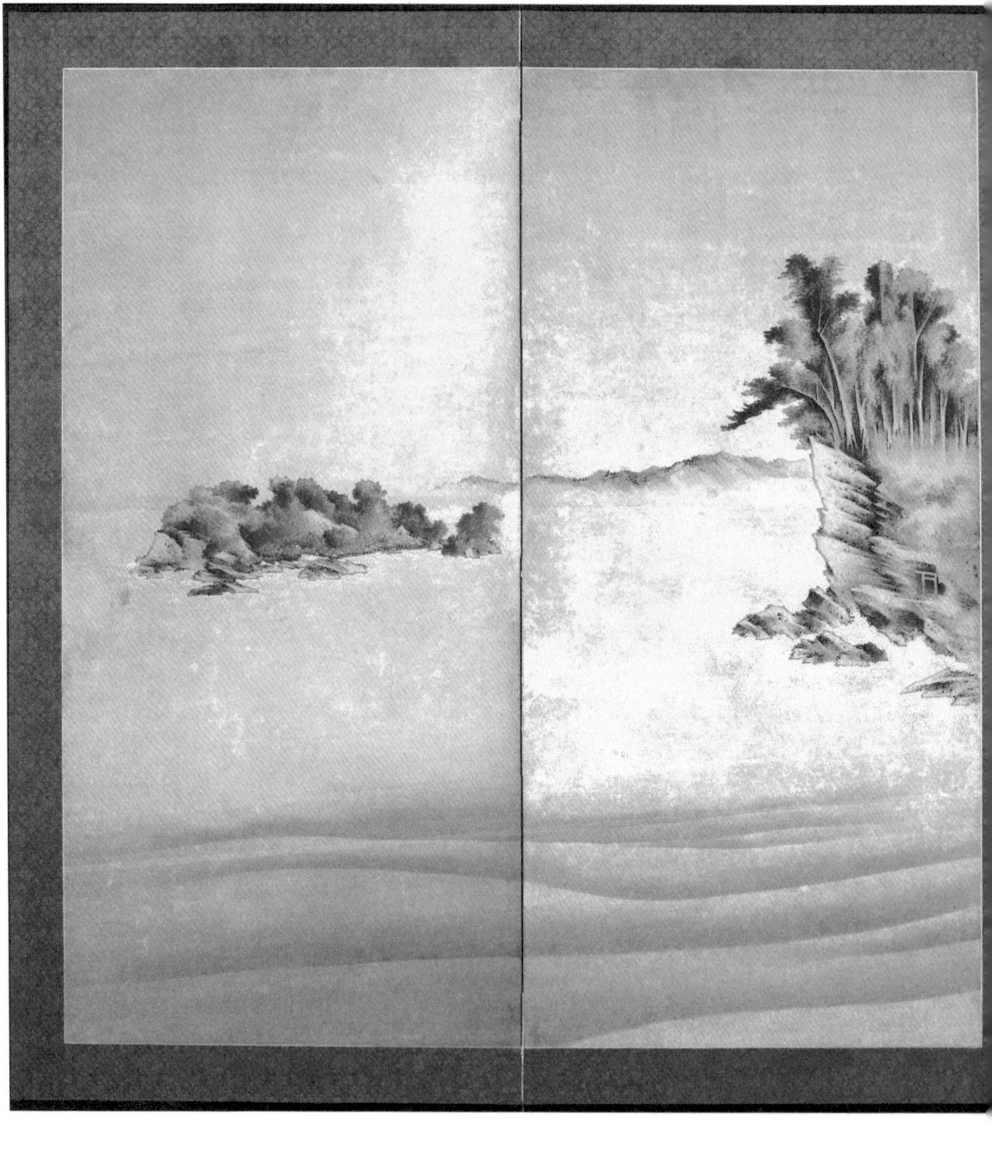

201 *Mount Fuji and Enoshima*
colour on paper, pair of two-panel folding screens, signed Katsushika Zen Hokusai Iitsu ga

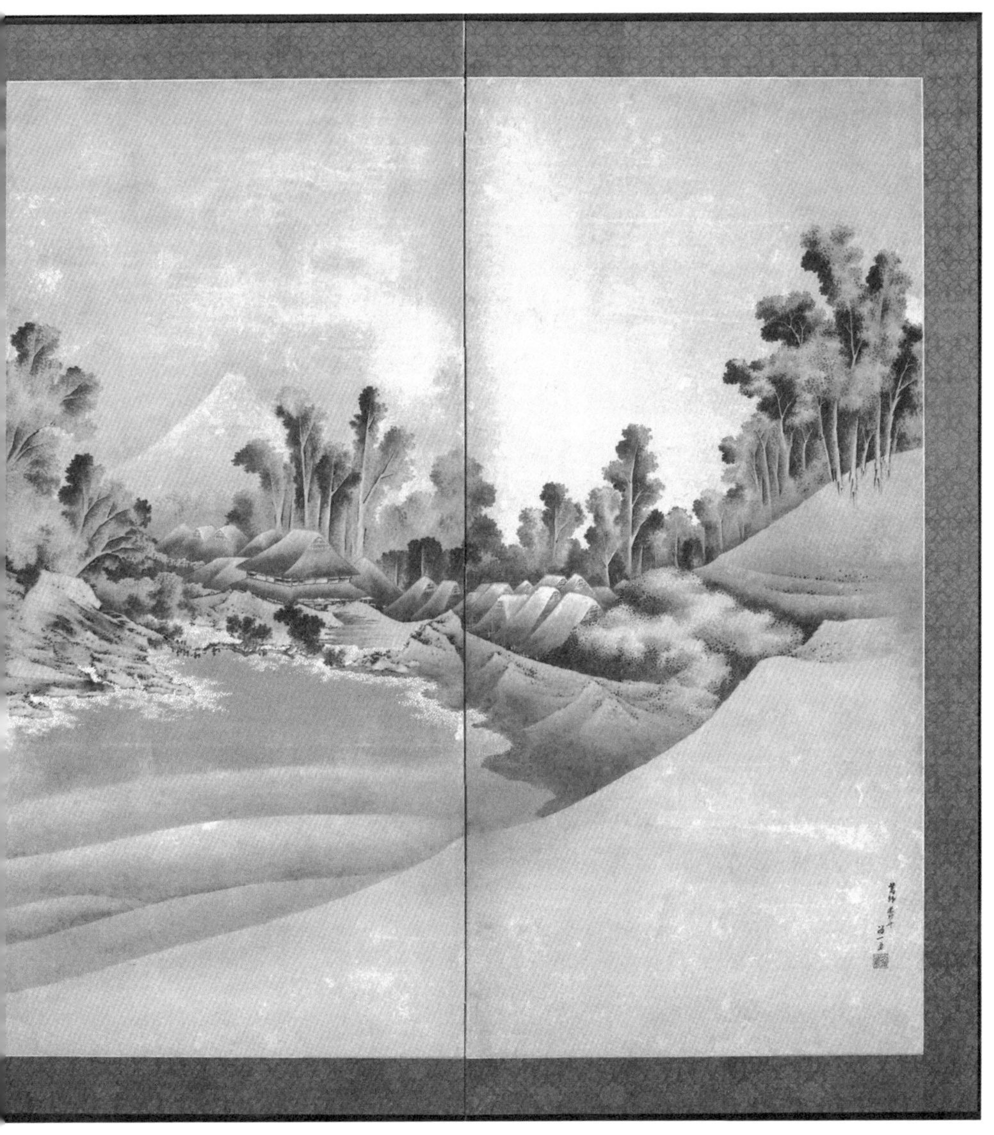

. 1825–31. 90.7 × 187.1 cm. National Museum of Asian Art, Smithsonian Institution,
reer Study Collection: Gift of Charles Lang Freer, F1904.175-176

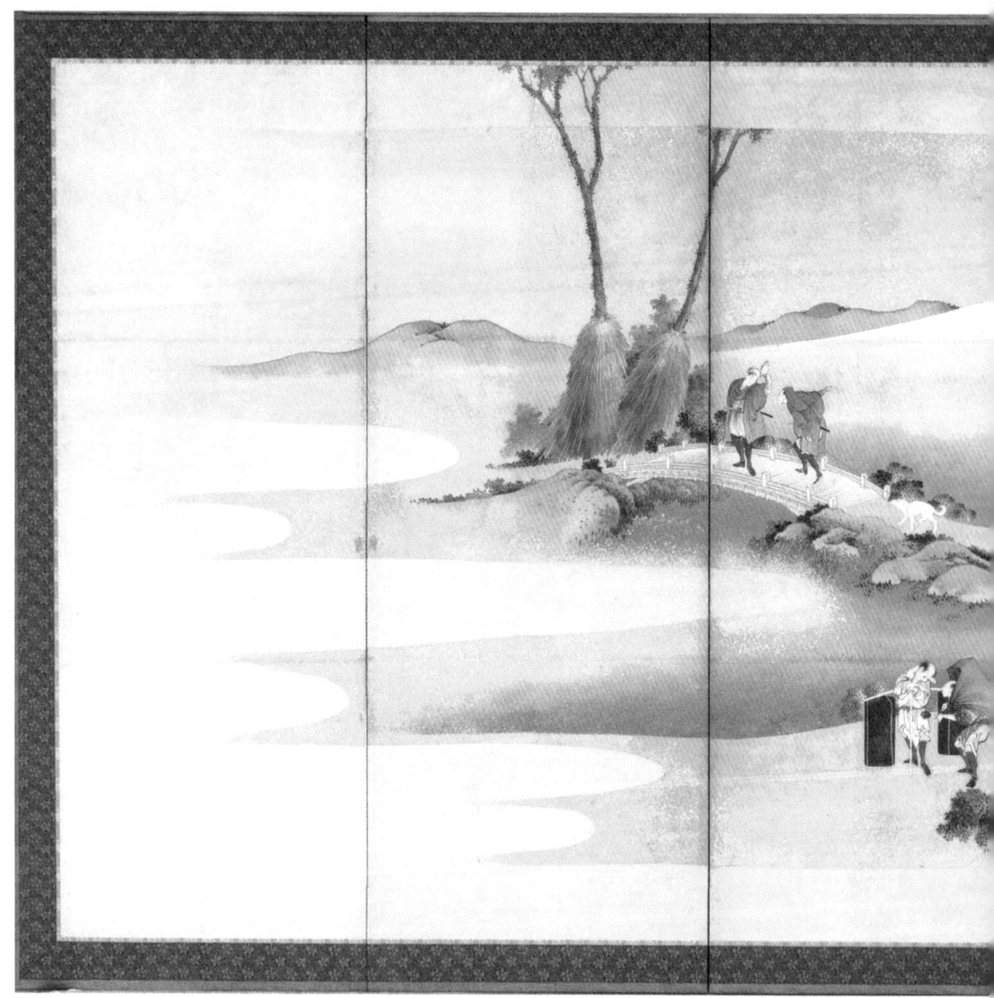

Country Scenes and Mount Fuji
colour on paper, one of a pair of six-panel folding screens (right side), signed Zen Hokusai Iitsu ga

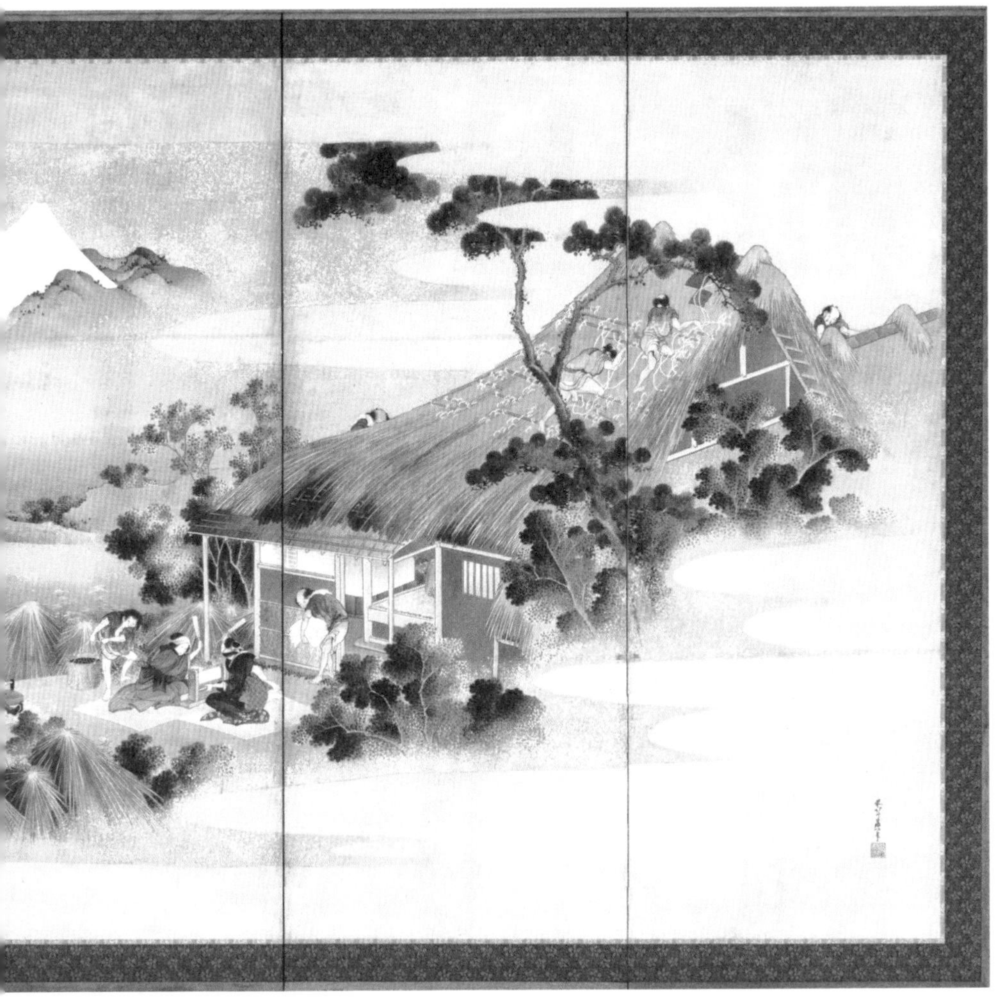

c. 1830–32. 169.1 × 369.8 cm (total). National Museum of Asian Art,
Smithsonian Institution, Freer Study Collection: Gift of Charles Lang Freer, F1902.48

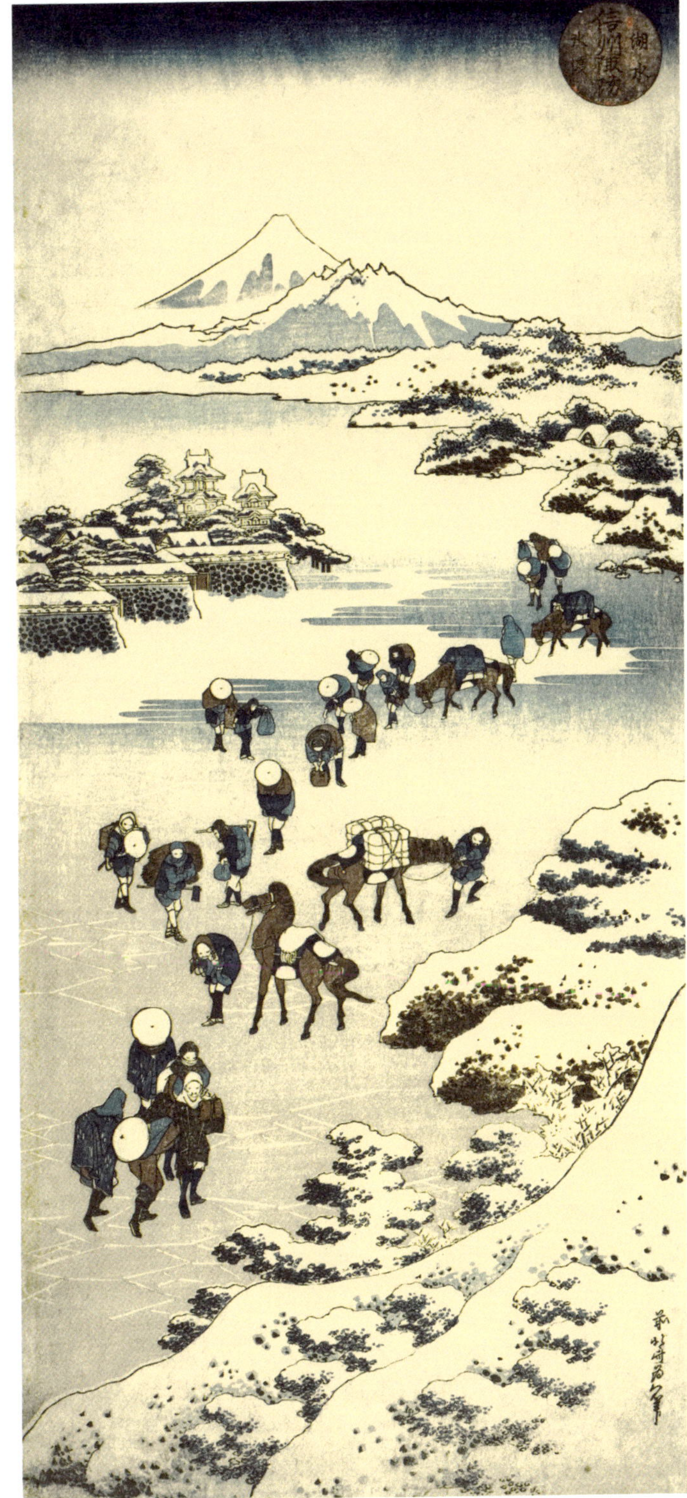

信州諏訪湖水氷渡

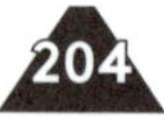

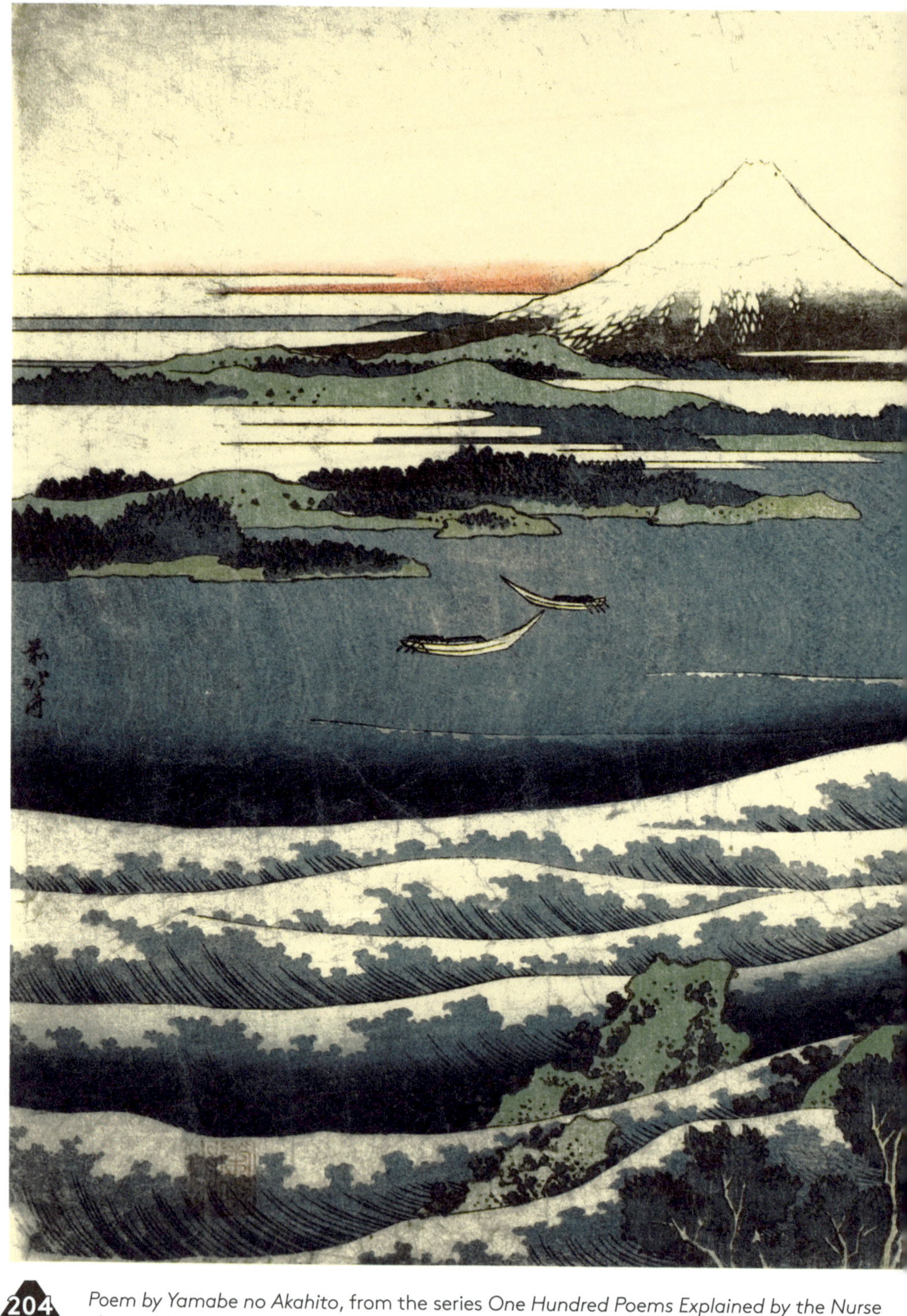

204 *Poem by Yamabe no Akahito*, from the series *One Hundred Poems Explained by the Nurse*
ōban nishiki-e, signed Zen Hokusai

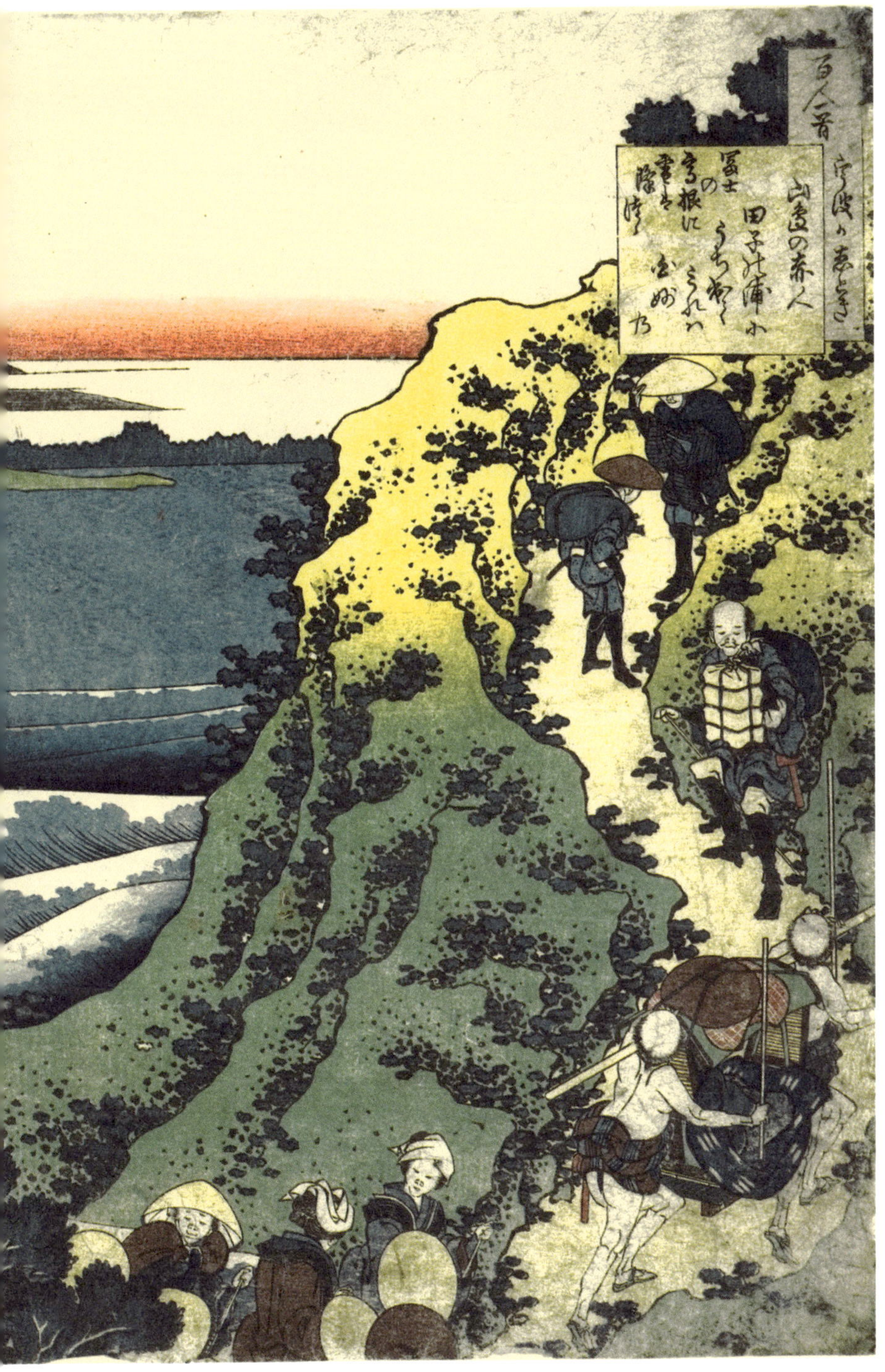

c. 1835–36. 25.2 × 37 cm. Bequest of Henry C. Schwab, The Art Institute of Chicago, 1943.830

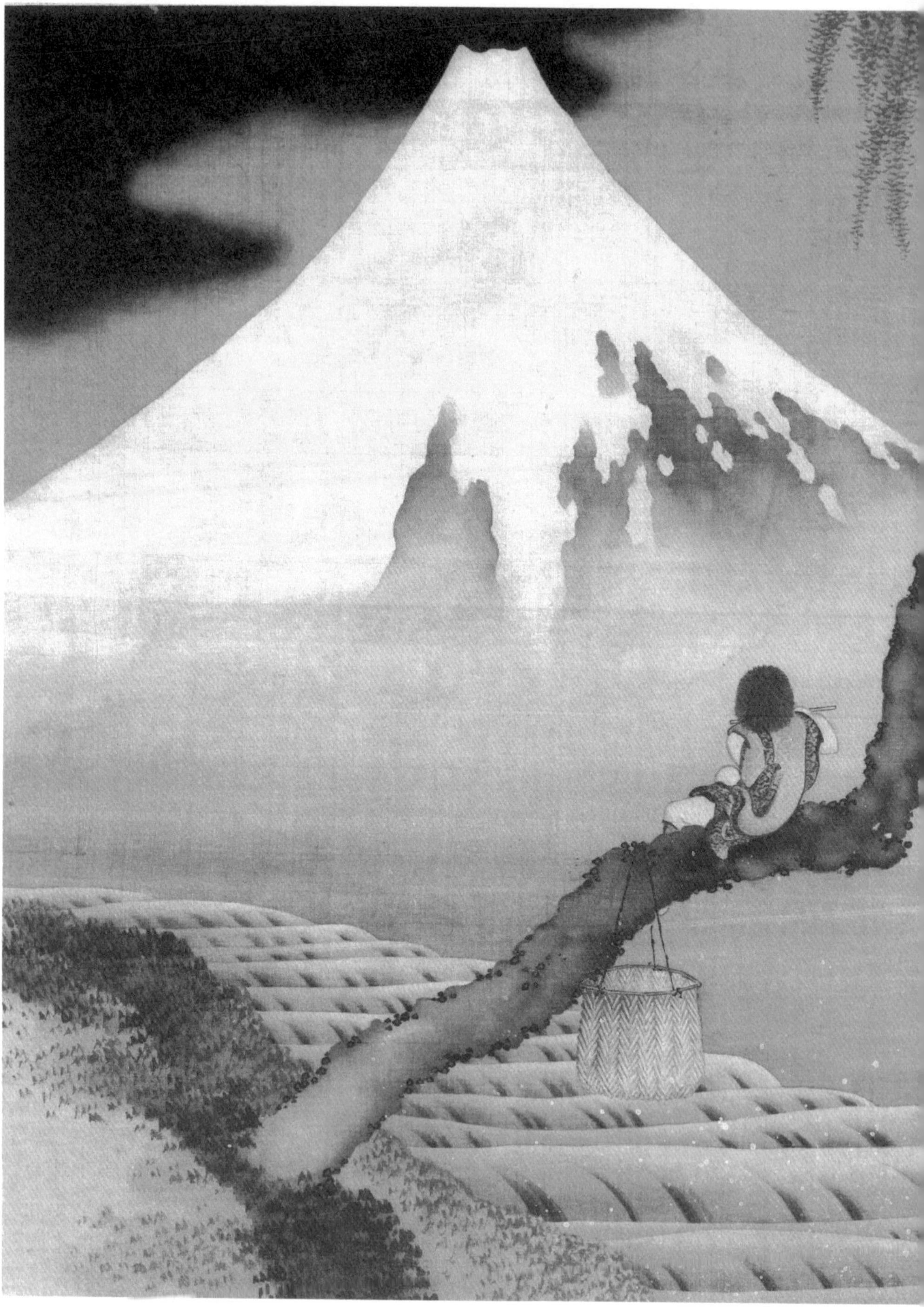

205 *Boy Viewing Mount Fuji*
colour on silk (*kakejiku*), signed Gakyō Rōjin Manji hitsu yowai hachijū

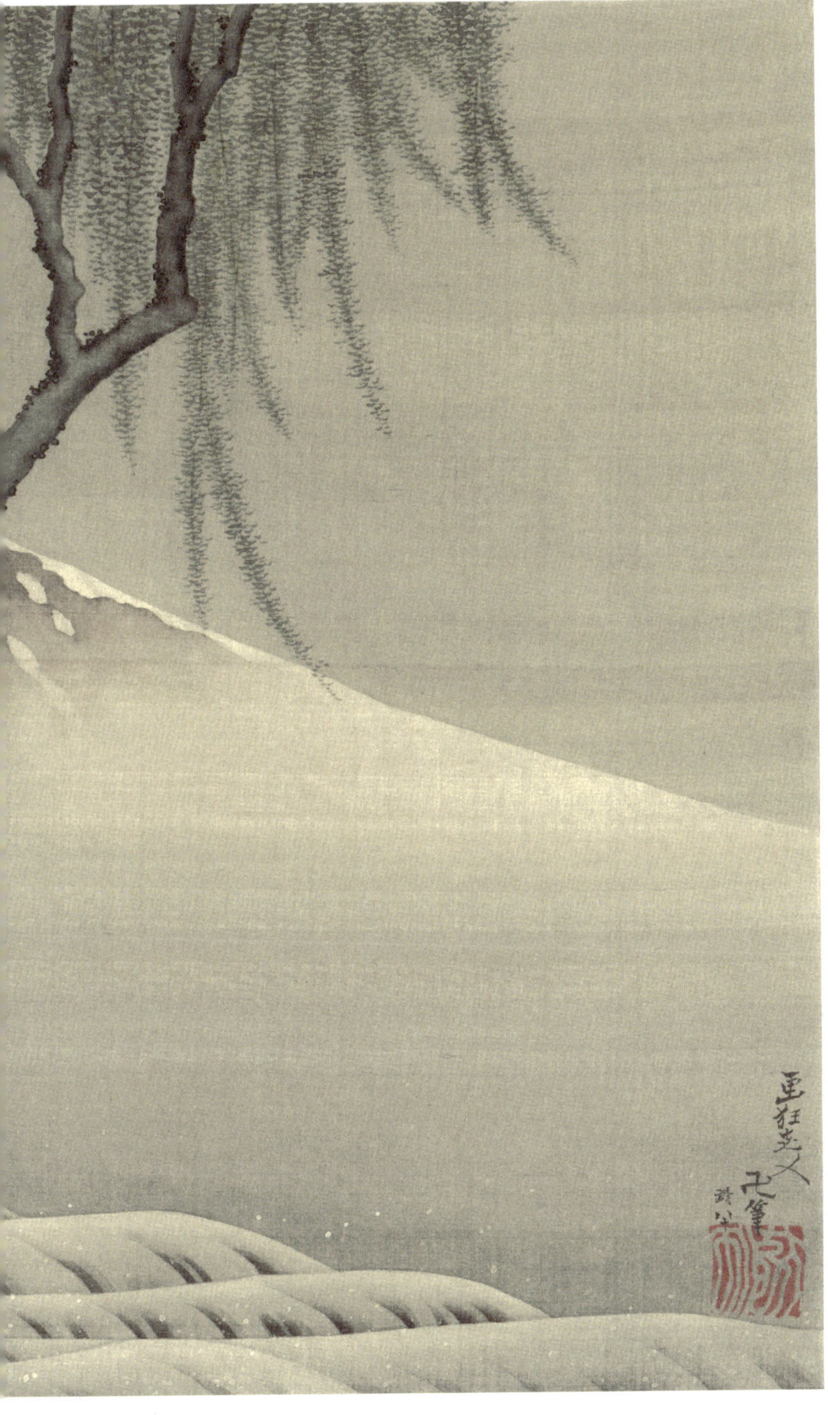

1839. 36.2 × 51.3 cm. National Museum of Asian Art, Smithsonian Institution,
Freer Study Collection: Gift of Charles Lang Freer, F1898.110

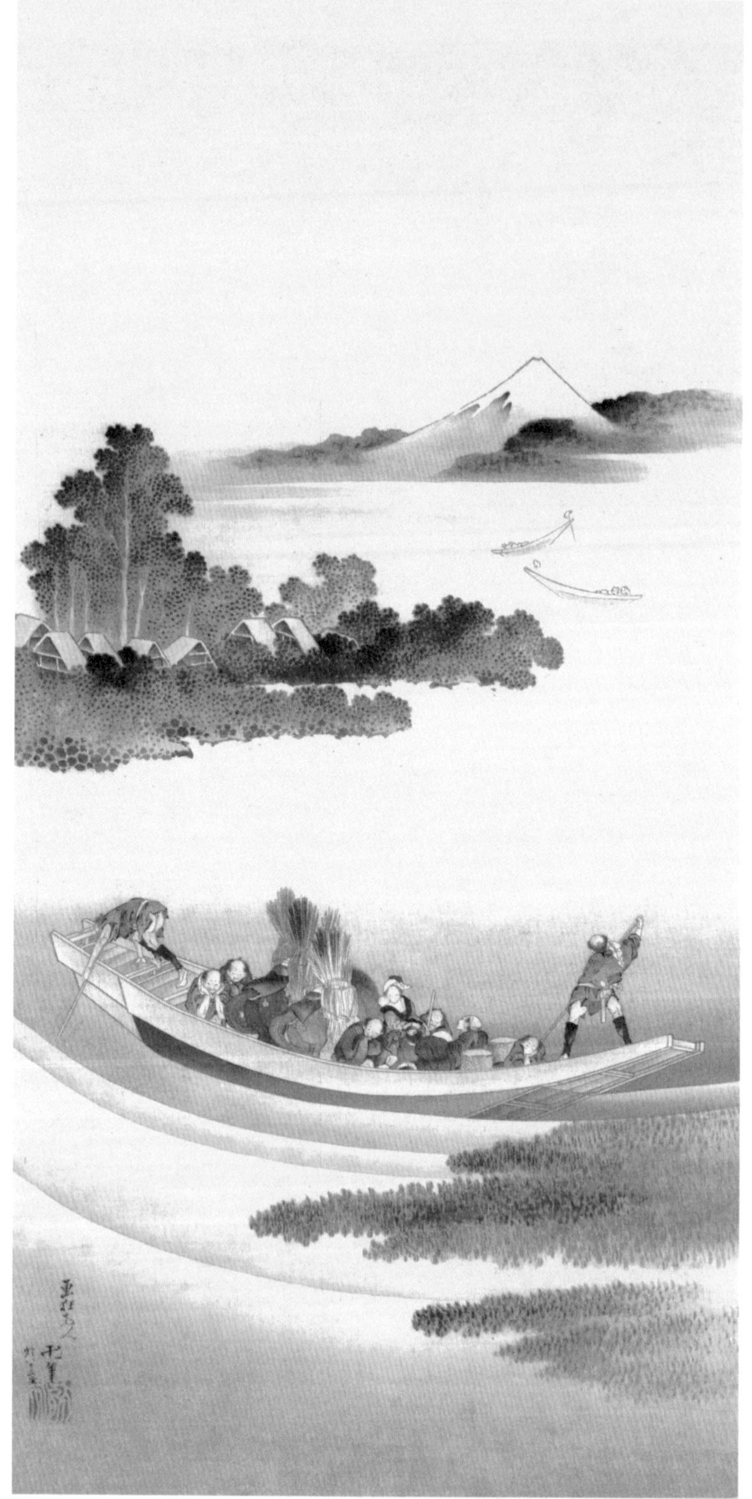

River Landscape: Ferryboat and Mount Fuji
colour on silk (*kakejiku*), signed Gakyō Rōjin Manji hitsu yowai hachijūsan

206

1842. 84.9 × 42.7 cm. National Museum of Asian Art, Smithsonian Institution, Freer Study Collection: Gift of Charles Lang Freer, F1903.109

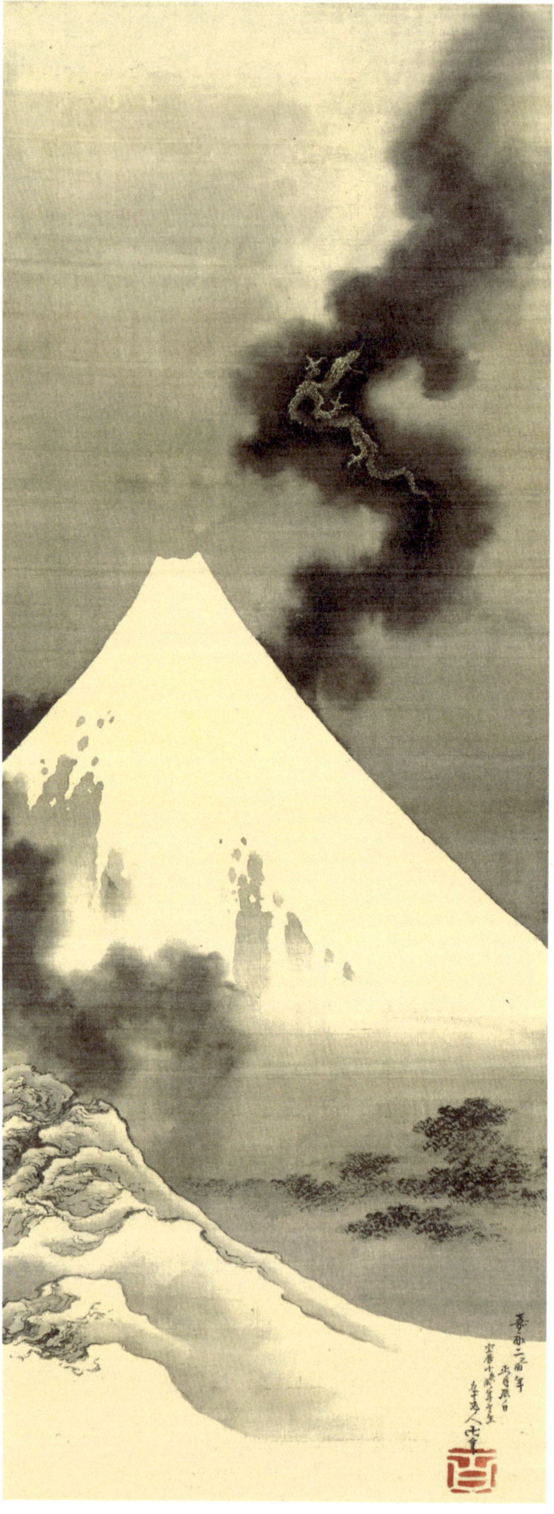

207

Dragon Flying over Mount Fuji
light colour on silk (*kakejiku*),
signed Kyūjū Rōjin Manji hitsu

1849. 95.8 × 36.2 cm.

Hokusai and the Laws of Perspective

Fuse Hideto

Hokusai and the Laws of Perspective

Fuse Hideto

Hundred Views of Mount Fuji, produced a few years later, has the appearance of a supplementary work, or a sketchbook of ideas about Fuji. Whereas *Thirty-Six Views of Mount Fuji* is painterly, there is much about *One Hundred Views of Mount Fuji* that is literary, or more precisely, based on natural history and the observation of natural phenomena.

I have chosen *Thirty-Six Views of Mount Fuji* as the sample for my analysis of Hokusai's images of Fuji, not the least because of the limited space available to me. My focus will be on composition, particularly the laws of perspective.

Leonardo da Vinci perfected the techniques of perspective drawing during the Renaissance, but his was a linear perspective or receding perspective. That is to say, objects in the foreground look larger and objects in the background look smaller. When the objects are organized and positioned according to how far away they appear, everything converges towards a single point. You could say that the composition is based on hidden lines. This is why receding perspective is also referred to as linear perspective.

The vanishing point is the single point where these lines converge. The technique is also known as the one-point perspective system. *Nihonbashi Bridge in Edo* [166–167] in *Thirty-Six Views of Mount Fuji* is an example of one-point perspective, in which the buildings on either side of the central river recede towards the back of the picture. Both the river and the buildings guide the eye to a single vanishing point. In other words, the picture is based on the techniques used in the traditional Western system of perspective.

However, there is more to perspective than lines leading to a single vanishing point, which is often what first comes to mind when we hear the term. There is atmospheric perspective, where distant objects appear shrouded in mist, and colour perspective, where red appears closer to the viewer than blue. Several types of perspective are combined in *Nihonbashi Bridge in Edo*. However, even if only one-point perspective is used, there is another issue that must not be overlooked: the height of the horizon line in the picture. The vanishing point overlaps with the horizon line, but the height of the horizon line can be positioned differently.

According to the laws of perspective, the position of the vanishing point (= the height of the horizon line) corresponds to the height of the vantage point from which the scene is viewed. Therefore, if you are looking towards the horizon from a position on the ground (literally, in the dirt and dust), the horizon line (= the vanishing point) will be at the bottom of the picture. But, if you are viewing the scene from a platform or the top of a high building, the horizon line will be at the top of the picture. If your eyeline is at an intermediate height and you are facing straight onto the scene, the horizon line will be in the centre of the picture. In other words, perspective also reveals the vantage point of the viewer.

How high is Hokusai's Fuji? By this, I mean the foot of the mountain and its position in the picture because the foot of the mountain is more or less at the height of the horizon. I have found that the horizon line in the pictures can be roughly classified into high, low, or intermediate positions. For example, the foot of Fuji is at the bottom of the picture in *A Mild Breeze on a Fine Day* [138–139] and *Shower Below the Summit* [140–141]. Here, Hokusai has not only drawn Fuji so large that it dominates the whole picture, but since the viewpoint is low, he also emphasizes the height of the mountain by creating the illusion of looking up. When Mount Fuji is placed in a high position in the picture, the viewpoint is also high, creating the sense of a bird's-eye view. When Fuji is positioned in the middle of the picture, the viewpoint is at horizon height.

When you focus on the position of (the foot of) the mountain and look at the variety of expressions in the pictures in *Thirty-Six Views of Mount Fuji*, the scenery acquires a sense of depth and the landscape seems to expand. I like to look at Hokusai's Fuji in this way and to experience the landscapes that stretch around the mountain. I even feel happy that I am 'here' in this world surrounded by its expanses, its depth and its profundity, and that I can personally experience Mount Fuji within a specific geographic space. Cézanne said that a sense of depth is vital to art; this depth is not only an emotional metaphor, but also a physical position. When you experience this feeling, you know that you are alive and that you exist in this world.

Since I specifically mentioned Cézanne, I would like to draw some comparisons between Hokusai and Cézanne. Both artists depicted mountains: Hokusai, of course, drew Mount Fuji and Cézanne painted Mont Sainte-Victoire. But it would be a waste to

Leonardo da Vinci, *Adoration of the Magi*,
perspective sketch, 1481, ink and paper,
Uffizi, Florence

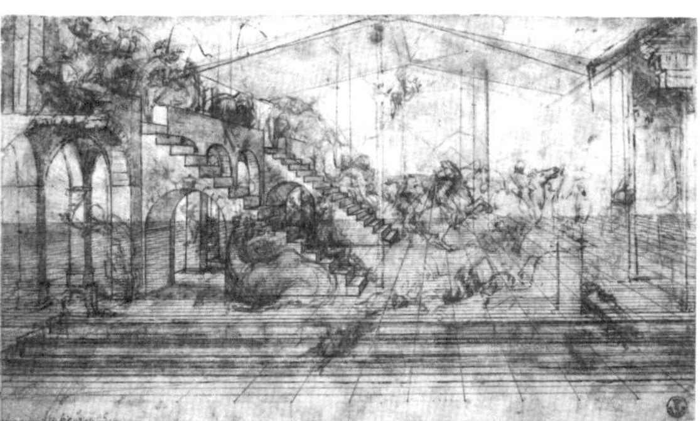

call them painters of mountains and to conclude the discussion by comparing their motifs. When pictures by these two artists are placed side by side, it is possible to discover more surprising ways of looking at art and more about the appeal of painting.

The point is perspective. As a painter, Cézanne transcended the linear perspective that dated back to the Renaissance and successfully created a new painting space. A painting by Cézanne could be viewed from multiple points in space, not only straight on, but also from the extreme left or right relative to the painting. Depending on the position of your viewpoint in relation to the picture, you may sometimes see profound depth in one place, but at other times, depth, presence and reality may appear somewhere else. It is fascinating to try out this way of looking at Cezanne's pictures on Hokusai's Fuji.

Let's look at one example: *The Surface of the Water at Misaka in Kai Province* [172–173]. The surface of the lake in the foreground contains an inverted reflection of Fuji. Ordinarily, a mirror image should be aligned and symmetrical, but, in this picture, the reflection is not aligned with the mountain. But let's see what happens if we look at the picture from the left side (i.e. diagonally, relative to the picture), in order to align Mount Fuji with the reflection in the surface of the lake. What do you think? Seen from this viewpoint, does it not immediately strike you that there is more depth to the arrangement of mountains and houses in the foreground? Hokusai was indeed not only working with linear perspective, but he was also developing a completely different way to render space and reproduce a sense of depth in art.

I will close here as I have reached the word limit, but looking at Hokusai's pictures of Fuji from the viewpoint of linear perspective alone is a hidden source of much pleasure.

So how many Mount Fujis are there? In Hokusai's works, there are as many different Fujis as there are images.

Paul Cezanne, *Mont Sainte-Victoire*, c. 1902–6, oil on canvas

The Metropolitan Museum of Art, New York, Walter H. and Leonore Annenberg Collection, Gift of Walter H. and Leonore Annenberg, 1994, Bequest of Walter H. Annenberg, 2002. #1994.420

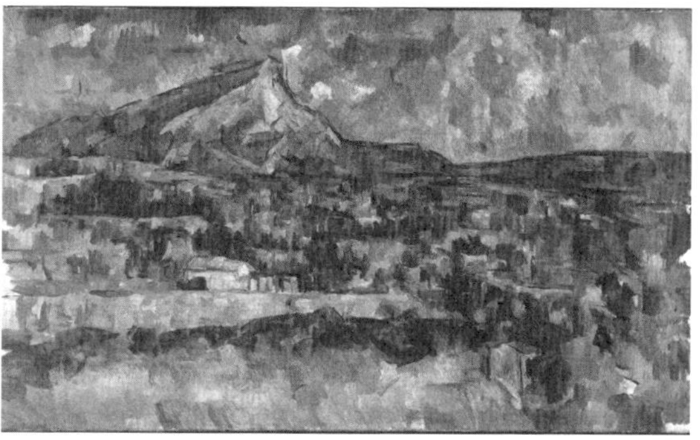

Chronology of Hokusai's Life

For convenience, each period is defined by the artist name that Hokusai used at that point in his career. In cases where it is uncertain when he changed names, or in transitional periods in which he used more than one name, we have noted the reference years as it is difficult to make clear distinctions. In the Sōri period, he used the name Sōri for about three years before taking the name Hokusai Tokimasa. However, the Tokimasa period has been merged with the Sōri period since the style is considered a continuation of the Sōri style. The same criteria apply to some of the other periods listed below.

As was the custom in the Edo period, ages are given according to the traditional system. Newborn babies were considered to be one year old, and a year was added to a person's age every New Year.

Works with an unknown year of production (or publication), or with an estimated long period of production are marked with a bullet point (•). Since production dates are not always clear for works made in the same year, the order in this chronology does not necessarily correspond to the order of production.

The information included in the Main Events column focuses on topics covered by this book. It is not a comprehensive history of Hokusai's career.

This chronology is based on sources listed in the bibliography on page 414.

	Western Dates	Japanese Dates	Age	Works	Main Events
Childhood	1760	Hōreki 10	1		Born at Honjo-Warigesui in Edo on 23 September. Given the name Tokitarō at birth, he is later named Tetsuzō.
	1765	Meiwa 2	6		Develops an interest in drawing around this time. Suzuki Harunobu starts to produce full-colour woodblock prints.
	1773	An'ei 2	14		Starts an apprenticeship with a block cutter around this time.
	1778	An'ei 7	19		Enters the studio of Katsukawa Shunshō.
Shunrō period	1779	An'ei 8	20		Starts to publish works under the name of Katsukawa Shunrō.
					In this period, Hokusai was learning to become an *ukiyo-e* artist and worked with many different motifs. He focused on creating portraits of actors, but also produced pictures of beautiful women, warriors, children, *ukiyo-e*, and prints, as well as illustrations for *kibyōshi* and *sharebon* stories.
	1794	Kansei 6	35		Abandons the Shunrō name and, inspired by the Tawaraya Sōtatsu school, takes the name Tawaraya Sōri.
Sōri period				• *Surimono* print: *Man and Woman Asleep Beside a Kotatsu Table*, p. 33	Produces *surimono* prints, *kyōka ehon*, and other types of work he hardly touched during his Shunrō period. Referred to as Sōri-style, his lyrical depictions of elegant women (*bijinga*) were particularly well received.
	1797	Kansei 9	38	*Kyōka ehon*: *Spring at Enoshima*, from the *Willow-Silk* album, pp. 34–35	
				Kyōka ehon: *The Mist of Sandara*, pp. 40–41	
	1798	Kansei 10	39		Passes the Sōri name to a student and takes the name Hokusai Tokimasa. Starts to work as an independent artist without an affiliation to any school.
	1799	Kansei 11	40	Woodblock print: *The Top of Mount Fuji*, pp. 42–43	Throughout Japan's Kyōwa era, Hokusai continues the style he established in his Sōri period, but he starts producing full-colour woodblock prints again and works on a variety of motifs. He also produces pictures of famous places that bear a resemblance to the subsequent *Thirty-Six Views of Mount Fuji*. It was a time when he experimented with many painting styles including the Chinese Nanpin School and Western-style landscape painting.
				• Woodblock print: *Enoshima*, pp. 36–37	
				• Woodblock print: *Untitled*, pp. 38–39	
				• *Surimono* print: *Ladies with Young Pine Trees and Mount Fuji*, pp. 44–45	
				• *Surimono* print: *Gathering Shellfish*, pp. 46–47	
				• *Kyōka surimono* print: *Untitled*, pp. 48–49	
	1802	Kyōwa 2	43	Colour *surimono* prints: *Fifty-Three Stations on the Tōkaidō Road*, pp. 64–67	Jippensha Ikku publishes *Travels on the Eastern Seaboard*.
				• Colour *surimono* print: *Evening Glow for Date no Yosaku and Seki no Koman* from the series *Eight Views of Tragic Lovers*, p. 68	

	Western Dates	Japanese Dates	Age	Works	Main Events
Hokusai period	1804	Kyōwa 4/ Bunka 1	45	*Kyōka ehon: Mountains upon Mountains*, pp. 50–51	Paints a portrait of the sage Daruma on an expanse of paper measuring 18 × 11 metres on the grounds of Gokokuji Temple in Edo Otowa on 13 April.
				Colour *surimono* print: *Hara* from *Fifty-Three Stations on the Tōkaidō Road*, p. 69	In the early Bunka period, a tremendously productive time, Hokusai teams up with the fiction writers Kyokutei Bakin and Ryūtei Tanehiko to work on *yomihon* book illustrations, in addition to creating *kyōka ehon* and *surimono* prints. He works on illustrations for nearly 200 books over this ten-year period.
				Soroimono print series: *Fifty-Three Stations on the Tōkaidō Road*, pp. 70–75	
				Surimono print: *Untitled*, pp. 54–55	
				• Woodblock print: *Mount Fuji Under High Bridge*, pp. 88–89	
				• *Surimono* print: *Mount Fuji*, pp. 56–57	
				• *Surimono* print: *Untitled*, pp. 58–59	
				• *Surimono* print: *Scene in May: The Boys' Festival*, pp. 60–61	
	1805	Bunka 2	46	*Surimono* print: *Untitled*, pp. 62–63	The first edition of *The Water Margin* with text by Kyokutei Bakin and illustrations by Hokusai is published. Hokusai starts using Katsushika Hokusai as his artist name.
				• *Kyōka ehon: Kamakura Village*, pp. 90–91	From the Kyōwa era to the early Bunka era, Hokusai produces several *soroimono* series on the theme of the *Fifty-Three Stations on the Tōkaidō Road*. He starts using more structural and creative techniques in his landscape images.
				• *Kyōka ehon: Panoramic Views along the Banks of the Sumida River*, pp. 52–53	
	1806	Bunka 3	47	Colour *surimono* print: *Fujisawa*, from *Fifty-Three Stations on the Tōkaidō Road*, pp. 76–77	
				Colour *surimono* print: *Fifty-Three Stations on the Tōkaidō Road*, pp. 78–79	
				Surimono print: *The Eastern Journey of the Celebrated Poet Ariwara no Narihira*, pp. 80–81	
				Colour *surimono* print: *The Storehouse of Loyal Retainers, a Primer*, pp. 84–85, 87	
				• *Surimono* print: *Parody of Narihira's Journey to the East*, pp. 82–83	
				• Brush painting: *Landscape: Clam-Gatherers on the Shore*, pp. 96–97	
	1807	Bunka 4	48		The first volume of *Strange Tales of the Bow Moon* is published with text by Kyokutei Bakin and illustrations by Katsushika Hokusai.

	Western Dates	Japanese Dates	Age	Works	Main Events
Taito period	1810	Bunka 7	51		*Foolish Ono's Nonsense Picture Dictionary*, his first drawing manual, is published.
				• Colour *surimono* print: *Eight Views of Edo*, pp. 92–95	
	1812	Bunka 9	53		Prepares about 300 preliminary drawings for *Hokusai Manga* during a stay at the home of Maki Bokusen, a student in Nagoya, in the autumn.
	1814	Bunka 11	55	*Mount Fuji in Winter*, from the drawing manual *Pictures After Nature*, pp. 104–105	The first volume of *Hokusai Manga* and a sequel to *Quick Lessons in Simplified Drawing* are published.
	1815	Bunka 12	56		Starts using the name Taito around this time.
	1817	Bunka 14	58	*Mishima Pass in Kai Province*, from the drawing manual *Hokusai Manga*, Vol. 7, pp. 106–107	In the Bunka–Bunsei eras, Hokusai concentrates on creating drawing manuals. As well as publishing further volumes of *Hokusai Manga*, he produces manuals specifically designed for beginners, and collections of designs for craftsmen to copy. He continues to work in this genre until the end of his life.
	1818	Bunka 15/ Bunsei 1	59	Colour *soroimono* print series: *The Famous Places on the Tōkaidō Road in One View*, pp. 98–99	
Iitsu period	1820	Bunsei 3	61	Drawing manual: *A Picture Album by Hokusai (Hokusai Gafu)* (monochrome print), p. 110	Starts using the name Iitsu around this time.
	1821	Bunsei 4	62	*Surimono* print series: *A Matching Game with Genroku Poem Shells*, pp. 100–101	In the early Tempō era, Hokusai creates many full-colour woodblock prints in addition to outstanding *surimono* prints. Over a four-year period, he focuses on several series of large colour woodblock prints including *Thirty-Six Views of Mount Fuji*, *A Tour of Japanese Waterfalls*, and *Wondrous Views of Famous Bridges in Various Provinces*.
	1822	Bunsei 5	63	*Surimono* print series: *A Set of Horses*, pp. 102–103	
	1823	Bunsei 6	64	Drawing manual: *Popular Designs for Combs and Tobacco Pipes*, pp. 108–109	
				• Brush painting: *Mount Fuji and Enoshima*, pp. 388–389	
				• Brush painting: *Country Scenes and Mount Fuji*, pp. 390–391	
	1831	Tempō 2	72	Colour *surimono* prints: *Thirty-Six Views of Mount Fuji*, pp. 116–207	
				• *Surimono* print: *Untitled*, p. 387	
				• Woodblock print: *Crossing the Frozen Lake Suwa in Shinano Province*, p. 393	
	1833	Tempō 4	74		Utagawa Hiroshige starts publishing *Fifty-Three Stations on the Tōkaidō Road*.

	Western Dates	Japanese Dates	Age	Works	Main Events
Gakyō Rōjin Manji period	1834	Tempō 5	75	Picture book: *One Hundred Views of Mount Fuji*, Volume 1, pp. 215–270	Hokusai starts using the name Gakyō Rōjin Manji around this time.
	1835	Tempō 6	76	Picture book: *One Hundred Views of Mount Fuji*, Volume 2, pp. 271–326	After stopping work on the print series *One Hundred Poems Explained by the Nurse*, Hokusai moves away from woodblock prints and concentrates on brush painting and printed books including drawing manuals and *yomihon*. The motifs no longer feature contemporary fashions and customs, like his *ukiyo-e* prints; instead, his subjects include Japanese or Chinese legends, religious themes, natural objects, and fantastical motifs such as the phoenix, tiger, dragon and other sacred beasts.
				• Colour *surimono* prints: *One Hundred Poems Explained by the Nurse*, pp. 394–395	
				• Picture book: *One Hundred Views of Mount Fuji*, Volume 3, pp. 327–380	
	1839	Tempō 10	80	Brush painting: *Boy Viewing Mount Fuji*, pp. 396–397	
	1842	Tempō 13	83	Brush painting, *River Landscape: Ferryboat and Mount Fuji*, p. 399	
	1849	Kaei 2	90	Brush painting: *Dragon Flying Over Mount Fuji*, p. 400	Hokusai dies on 18 April. This is how Iijima Kyoshin describes Hokusai on the verge of death in his *Biography of Hokusai*: 'Lying on his deathbed, Hokusai drew a deep breath and before he died haltingly murmured, "If Heaven granted me another ten years, or even five more years, then I could become a real painter."'

Glossary

aizuri-e: images printed predominantly in blue ink

bijinga: a genre of image depicting beautiful women

byōbu: folding screen made from multiple panels

chūban: print format measuring 29 × 22 cm

e-goyomi: picture calendar

edehon: drawing manual

ekaki uta: picture-drawing verses (instructions for drawing
in the form of verses)

fūkeiga: landscape painting

fusuma-e: painting on a sliding door panel

gachū-ga: a picture that appears within another picture

hanpon: any type of book printed from woodblocks

hanshibon: book format measuring 17 × 24 cm

kakejiku: hanging scroll

kibyōshi: illustrated popular fiction, taking its name from its yellow covers

kokkeibon: humorous novel

kyōka ehon: printed book of humorous verses

meisho-e: pictures of famous places

mitate-e: parody pictures

moji-e: 'visual pun' pictures in which characters from the
Japanese syllabary are incorporated into the image

nagaban: print format measuring 56 × 25 cm

nikuhitsu-ga: brush painting

nishiki-e: full-colour woodblock print on a single sheet

ōban: print format measuring 39 × 26.5 cm

omohan: the key block, used to print the outlines for a woodblock print

sharebon: genre of satirical literature about life in Edo's pleasure quarters

soroimono: prints published in a series with a shared title

sumizuri-e: images printed predominantly in black ink

surimono: high-quality woodblock print made on commission

tate-e: print in a vertical format

ukiyo-e: literally 'pictures of the floating world': a genre of art that
depicted the hedonistic life and culture of the city of Edo

yakusha-e: portraits of stage actors

yoko-e: print in a horizontal format

yomihon: woodblock-printed novel

Bibliography

Kobayashi Tadashi, *Fugaku sanjūrokkei*, 'Ukiyoe taikei 13', Tokyo: Shūeisha, 1975

Jack Ronald Hillier, *Hokusai: Paintings, Drawings, and Woodcuts*, Oxford: Phaidon, 1978

Suzuki Jūzō, *Fugaku hyakkei*, Iwasaki Bijutsusha, 1986

Peter Morse, *Hokusai: 100 Poets*, London: Cassell, 1989

Richard Lane, *Hokusai: Life and Work*, London: Barrie & Jenkins, 1989

Suzuki Jūzō, *Ehon to ukiyoe: Edo shuppan bunka no kōsatsu*, Tokyo: Bijutsu Shuppan-sha, 1980

Nagata Seiji, *Hokusai bijutsukan*, 5 vols. Tokyo: Shūeisha, 1990

Asano Shūgō and Yoshida Nobuyuki (eds.), *Ukiyo-e wo yomu 4: Hokusai*, Osaka: Asahi Shimbun, 1998

Iijima Kyoshin, *Katsushika Hokusai den*, revised by Suzuki Jūzō. 'Iwanami Bunko' series, Tokyo: Iwanami Shoten, 1999

Nagata Seiji, *Katsushika Hokusai*, 'Rekishi bunka raiburarī' series, Tokyo: Yoshikawa Kōbunkan, 2000

Ōkubo Junichi, *Senpenbanka ni egaku Hokusai no fugaku sanjūrokkei*, 'Āto serekushon' series, Tokyo: Shōgakukan, 2005

Nagata Seiji (ed.) *Motto shiritai Katsushika Hokusai–shōgai to sakuhin*, 'Āto bigināzu korekushon' series, Tokyo: Tokyo Bijutsu, 2005

Kobayashi Tadashi, *Hokusai no bijin*, 'Ukiyoe gyararī 2' series, Tokyo: Shōgakukan, 2005

Tsuji Nobuo, *Hokusai no kisō*, 'Ukiyoe gyararī 3', Tokyo: Shōgakukan, 2005

Hokusai, exhibition catalogue, Tokyo: National Museum, 2005

Ann Yonemura, Nagata Seiji, Kobayashi Tadashi, Asano Shūgō, Timothy Clark, Naito Masatoshi, *Hokusai*, Washington DC: Smithsonian/Freer Gallery of Art, 2006

Asano Shūgō (ed.), *Hokusai ketteiban*, 'Bessatsu taiyō' series, Tokyo: Heibonsha, 2010

Tanabe Masako, *Hokusai hyakunin isshū: uba ga etoki*, 'Nazotoki ukiyoe sōsho' series, Tokyo: Nigensha Publishing, 2011

Ōkubo Junichi, *Hokusai*, 'Iwanami Shinsho' series, Tokyo: Iwanami Shoten, 2012

Christine Guth, *Hokusai's Great Wave: Biography of a Global Icon.* Honolulu: University of Hawaii Press, 2015

Timothy Clark, Roger Keyes, *Hokusai: Beyond the Great Wave*, London: Thames & Hudson, 2017

Hokusai's Brush, Washington DC: Smithsonian/Freer Gallery of Art, 2018

Sarah E. Thompson, *Hokusai's Landscapes, The Complete Series*, Boston: Museum of Fine Arts, 2019

Acknowledgments

Many people provided support and assistance to make this publication happen. To them, I express my respect and gratitude. First, I would like to thank the museums, institutions, and libraries that agreed to provide illustrations and source materials. The book's foreword is by Frank Feltens, curator of Japanese art at the Smithsonian's National Museum of Asian Art. He has been a valued mentor since we first worked together on the publication *Hokusai's Brush* (2018), which was a guide to the world's largest collection of Hokusai's paintings, sketches, and drawings housed at the Smithsonian. The art critic Fuse Hideto contributed the book's final essay, in which he explores new directions of discourse on Hokusai, not only from the perspective of the visual arts, but also from anthropological and anatomical perspectives. The English translations by Lis-Britt Dalkarl were as precise as they were fluid in expression. The book's design is the work of Koinuma Keiichi and Sam Clark, who actualized the book's overarching concept. Thanks to the outstanding colour separation and printing plate preparation of Kumakura Katsumi, the printing director, and Itakura Toshiki of Yamada Photo Process, artwork that is over two hundred years old has been given freshness and vitality on the printed page. The team at Thames & Hudson and Ivan Vartanian of Goliga Books guided this book by providing generous understanding, continuous support, and clear advice.

Lastly, this book owes much to Uragami Mitsuru, one of the world's leading private collectors of Hokusai's work. He acts an ambassador for Hokusai and communicates the appeal of the artist's work to us today. About ten years ago, he provided access to his collection for the preparation of *Hokusai Manga* (Thames & Hudson, 2018). As editor, I cannot express how much I was inspired by his vast knowledge and the ways to enjoy Hokusai that he has shared with me. This book was also inspired by the thought-provoking ideas of the art directors Sobue Shin and Fujii Haruka, who worked with me on *The Complete Hokusai* exhibition in 2021.

It is my hope that the insights gleaned from many who have shared their knowledge have found expression in this book. There are others who I haven't mentioned by name that were integral to the making of this book. To them as well, I would like to extend my heartfelt gratitude.

Wada Kyoko

About the Authors

Frank Feltens

Frank Feltens is curator of Japanese art at the Smithsonian's National Museum of Asian Art. He holds a PhD in Japanese art history from Columbia University. Feltens is a specialist in Japanese painting of the early modern period and the late medieval period, and has published and lectured on a wide range of topics related to Japanese art. His recent books include *Hokusai's Brush* (Seigensha, 2018; Smithsonian Books, 2019) *Ogata Kōrin: Art in Early Modern Japan* (Yale, 2021), and, with Yukio Lippit, *Sesson Shūkei: A Zen Monk-Painter in Medieval Japan* (Hirmer, 2021). He has curated a number of exhibitions at the Smithsonian including *Hokusai: Mad about Painting* (2019–21) and *Mind Over Matter: Zen in Medieval Japan* (2022). Additionally, he is also a practitioner of the Japanese tea ceremony in the Urasenke tradition and has received the honorary tea name Sōchoku in 2017.

Fuse Hideto

Fuse Hideto is an art critic. After graduating from the Department of Art at Tokyo University of the Arts, he completed his PhD at the university's Graduate School of Arts where he specialized in the art of anatomy. Subsequently, he studied under Yōrō Takeshi at the Department of Anatomy, Tokyo University. He is currently professor at the Faculty of Fine Arts at Tokyo University of the Arts. Fuse published his first book, *Nō no naka no bijutsukan*, while still at graduate school. To date, he has published more than sixty books including *Da Vinci, Gohyakuichinenme no tabi* (Shueisha International), and *Gendai āto ha sugoi* (Poplar Publishing). He also lectures online at Dennō Academia.

Wada Kyoko

Wada Kyoko is a book editor who focuses on Japanese art, modern art, and photography in Japan and abroad. Publications edited by Wada include *Japanese Photobooks of the 1960s and '70s* by Kaneko Ryūichi and Ivan Vartanian (Aperture Foundation/Akaaka), *See/Saw: Connections Between Japanese Art Then and Now* (Chronicle Books/Heibonsha), *Flora Magnifica* and *Flower Art* by Azuma Makoto and Shiinoki Shunsuke (Thames & Hudson/Seigensha), *Hokusai Manga* Vols. 1–3 (Thames & Hudson/Seigensha), *Yōkai Manga* Vols. 1 and 2, *Hokusai no nikuhitsu*, and *Hokusai zukushi* (Seigensha).